VIEWS ACROSS THE BORDER

VIEWS ACROSS
THE BORDER

The United States and Mexico

Edited with an Introduction by
Stanley R. Ross

Published in Cooperation with
The Weatherhead Foundation

UNIVERSITY OF NEW MEXICO PRESS
Albuquerque

Main entry under title:

Views across the border.

    ''Papers . . . first presented at a conference in April 1975 in San Antonio.''
    Bibliography: p. 427
    Includes index.
    1. United States—Relations (general) with
Mexico—Congresses. 2. Mexico—Relations (general)
with the United States—Congresses. 3. United
States—Boundaries—Mexico—Congresses. 4. Mexico
—Boundaries—United States—Congresses.
5. Mexican Americans—Social Conditions—

© 1978 by The Weatherhead Foundation. All rights reserved.
Manufactured in the United States of America
Library of Congress Catalog Card Number 76-57533
International Standard Book Number 0-8263-0445-1
First Edition

CONTENTS

The Weatherhead Foundation wishes to reiterate its thanks to the chairman of the conference, Stanley R. Ross, and to all of the other participants for their work on this important subject.

We also express our special thanks to Janelle D. Specia who supervised the conference accommodations at the St. Anthony Hotel; to Martín Jankowski for his assistance to the chairman; to Hugh W. Treadwell, Director of the University of New Mexico Press, for his farsighted concern with border issues; to the editorial staff of the Press; and to Muriel A. Golden for the overall coordination of the conference and this publication.

FOREWORD

Americans have had limited experience with political borders and their effects. The two long unfortified international borders fixing the northern and southern limits of the continental United States have been lines of peaceful transit and commerce between the United States and Canada and the United States and Mexico for more than one hundred years. Passage from one state to another, land travel from New York to Oregon and points between, is not hampered by customs inspection. Neither the Immigration and Naturalization Service nor the individual states themselves interfere with the travel of Americans from one geographical area to another.

The forty-eight states of the continental United States are knit together in such a way as to invite movement of all sorts. Apart from such basic requirements as having a valid license for operating a vehicle, and federal regulations governing interstate commerce, Americans may move with great freedom within a vast area defined by the two international borders and by our coasts, washed by the Atlantic and Pacific oceans. (Coastal limits, of course, are borders of a kind and, as the oceans are increasingly considered natural resources open for exploitation, nations will contend and clash to the extent of their national claims of sovereignty. The recent "war of the cod" between Great Britain and Iceland is one example of a dispute over water borders.) Two results of this freedom are that Americans are a very mobile people, taking up old roots and putting down new ones frequently, and that the bulk of our population has been tilting westward for two hundred years and more.

Much of the continental United States was acquired by purchase rather than by conquest—the Louisiana Purchase and the Gadsden Purchase, and most of our treaties for national land, were reached without long discord or war. (Alaska, "Seward's folly," is not contiguous, nor are the Virgin Islands.) Even the Treaty of Guadalupe Hidalgo, signed after the Mexican War, may be interpreted as a kind of purchase. The United States paid Mexico $15 million and assumed the obligation of arbitrating all resultant land claims in the area. The treaties settling disputed lands between Maine and Canada and between Oregon and Canada were difficult to conclude, but they were not negotiated under the threat of warfare.

By contrast, borders have been flashpoints of contending interests and claims among political states in Europe and in Latin America. These areas are not the only ones where borders produce friction and have led to battle. The tangle of problems among Egypt, Israel, Jordan, Lebanon, Syria, and the Palestinians persists because there has been no satisfactory resolution of who is to get what territory legitimately and hold it without fear of future attacks.

Much of European history was determined by the issue of the drawing of borders. The purpose of many wars, fought out of complex motives, was to establish borders which were then set up as protective zones between hostile states. Agreements on the location of a border and rights of passage across it might break down, causing tension among principalities, empires, or dynasties. Armies would then be on the move; and after much fighting and bloodshed, diplomats would convene and redraw the European political map—its borders—in ways acceptable to the conquering states in order for a balance of power to exist.

The old Roman *limes,* or fortified boundary—a physical dividing line for military, commercial, political, and settlement purposes—was still operative in Europe during the French Revolution, the Napoleonic Empire, the Congress of Vienna, and, after World War I, at the Paris Peace Conference. Borders had to be delineated and maintained and when the agreed-upon system broke down, friction developed and led to the outbreak of war.

The point is not to oversimplify European, Latin American, or Middle Eastern history by overstating the instability of their borders. Rather, it is to make a distinction between what has happened with borders in Europe and what has not happened with them in North America. The United States has experienced some border friction from its beginnings—with Indians, Spaniards, English, Mexicans, and among ourselves. The Mason-Dixon line was a real border once (in the 1760s) and now is only a metaphor; the Kansas-Nebraska Territory had its border skirmishes, but it was no Schleswig-Holstein, Alsace-Lorraine, or Trieste. The War between the States was protracted on the battlefield and in its resolution, but it was fought, among other reasons, to keep the Union intact. The war with Mexico (for land that is now the American Southwest) was the closest experience Americans have had to a real European war—except perhaps the War of 1812. The Mexican War was a short war, however; no great numbers of soldiers were involved, and most Americans then welcomed the addition of the new territory to the ''westward course of empire.'' And the war was viewed and waged largely in domestic terms. The Wilmot Proviso (1846), although never passed by the Senate, aimed at purchasing the territory in dispute with Mexico and proposed that all newly acquired lands exclude slavery. The war was concluded in 1848 by the Treaty of Guadalupe Hidalgo that, among other things, established a boundary line between the two nations.

Why have borders in Europe so often become battlefields while on the American continent they have not? Some explanations are evident. The American lands were sparsely populated by an indigenous population that could not successfully resist the steady influx of immigrants from Europe and settlers from the East moving West. The European states after the French Revolution were more interested in maintaining a balance of power among themselves than in contesting the westward advance of the new United States on the American continent. Borders in North America have been dual or mutual, between two nations, while in Europe borders have been multiple, with one state usually confronting two or more nations.

Perhaps somewhat less obvious was the effect of the Northwest Ordinance of 1787, which set down the requirements for territories to enter the Union as new states on an equal footing with the older ones. American history, according to Frederick Jackson Turner and others, taught that the continental experience of occupying and settling lands west of the Appalachians was an incorporative process of a series of frontiers moving westward. And Americans have been so unconcerned with borders as an element of their history that even contemporary textbooks of American history do not include borders in their indices.

Frontiers overlapped and succeeded one another, in this view, almost as if the process were the revelation of an inevitable law of American history. The word "frontier" had a looser connotation than "border." Frontiers inherently moved, borders were militarily static or politically volatile; frontiers might be brawling and lawless, but they beckoned with romance, individualism, and the lure of land and wealth. A frontiersman was a restless soul, a real being transformed into enduring myth by Davy Crockett, James Fenimore Cooper, Bret Harte, Owen Wister, and Jack London, and countless "border" ballads. The American frontier was a moving line, a cutting edge for democracy and civilization, an invitation to greater opportunity. The European border, by comparison, has been a line of demarcation or buffer zone between potentially or actually aggressive states, guarded by outposts and garrisons, a place to be stopped and searched, a formidable obstacle to man's quest for freedom of movement—a throwback to the Roman *limes* (from which we get our English word "limit"). The American frontier beckoned, the European border repelled.

Today the United States does have two of the longest—unfortified—international borders of any nation in the world. It is true that they have not yet caused conflicts of the violence and intractability of borders in Europe.

For that, we and our Canadian and Mexican neighbors can be grateful. Now, for the first time, both borders portend more abrasive issues than those we have experienced in the past. There is irony in this at a time when the European community is seeking to overcome its history of border irritations and to achieve political and economic unity, thus lessening the significance of the border in the conduct of affairs among states.

The American attitude toward the United States-Mexican border has been both indifferent and complacent. We do not expect to have a war with Mexico; in fact, the prospect of warfare is so remote that it is not considered in the making of our foreign policy. Most Americans, and probably most Mexicans, are not aware of the changes that have occurred since World War II along this two-thousand-mile pencil-thin line on the map between the two countries.

American interest in this border has been sporadic. The Rough Riders— correctly known as the First Regiment of the U.S. Cavalry Volunteers— trained near it at the time of the Spanish-American War. Pancho Villa raided Columbus, New Mexico, and, in response, General Pershing led a punitive expedition into Mexico to search for him in 1916. The Zimmermann note from Germany to Mexico in 1917, promising the return of much of the American Southwest, its "lost territory," if Mexico sided with Germany against the United States in the World War, reflected the European attitude toward borders and border diplomacy. The violence of the Mexican Revolution (1910-20) focused attention on the flow of exiles, gunrunning, propaganda, and mercenary soldiers. By 1934, when Lázaro Cárdenas began his presidential term and the Revolution itself became institutionalized—and the modern Mexican state more firmly established—the border began to exist as borders do between two independent states, but still in an American and not a European context.

It was not until after World War II, when, with more people converging on the area, border issues became more numerous, that the United States started to view it on a more consistent basis. The implementation of the Bracero Program for the control of Mexican immigrant labor under contract in the United States is a case in point.

*   *   *   *   *

The issues examined in this book illustrate the complexity of the border between Mexico and the United States. The border, rather than being just a line on a map, is a region where two different civilizations face each other and overlap. It is an area growing in people and industry and in influence on both countries. We know many of the statistics about this growth but we do not yet know their meaning. We know that legal and illegal immigration (mostly from

Mexico into the United States) is an overriding matter and that goods valuing billions of dollars crisscross the border each year. Even with such an important aspect of the border, our tabulations are only approximate, our systems of control uneven in application. As a nation we have yet to make the border one of the basic ingredients in the formulation of foreign policy between Mexico and the United States.

The essays in the present volume address most of the border matters that have been examined before, but usually not in relation to each other. When the papers were first presented at a conference in April 1975, in San Antonio, one of our hopes was that a more integrated view of the border would emerge. The reader of this book may be able to take the information and interpretations offered in it and derive a more general understanding of *the* border's—and *a* border's—complexities.

Neither the conference nor the book can answer, or even explore, all of the questions that crop up along the edges of the United States-Mexican border. For example, we assume that the border exerts a cultural influence in the northern states of Mexico and in the American Southwest. This premise may be extended to say that the border is indeed a distinctive element of the sections of Mexico and the United States it transects. But, so far, our studies of ''border culture'' are partial and the conclusions tentative. More research and legwork will be needed before we can speak knowingly of the traits and consequences of a ''border culture.''

In this book, some aspects of the border are not dealt with in extensive detail, but still they are of basic concern before we can understand how the mechanics of the border operate. For example, what is the religious life of the people on the border and how do the churches care for their parishioners? Are there physical and mental health problems that borders in general, and this border in particular, cause in people who live astraddle them? How does the whole system of law enforcement really function, from top to bottom, from the local levels of the county sheriff up to the state and federal levels? How effective are border authorities in controlling the flow of narcotics and other material goods and the movement of money and people? What kind of educational system has developed and how will local school boards and state and federal authorities finally decide about the need and adequacy of bilingual training? What is the nature of entertainment, leisure, journalism, and recreation in the border zone? How does the border influence local forms of art and music and speech? Does the border belt have a characteristic physical environment, or must its length be broken into ecological districts—ecosystems—determined by water, sand, natural resources, mountains, economic development, and military installations? And, not finally, for our list of questions is lengthy, can we speak of the United States-Mexican border as one long distinctive unit of land and people, a cultural and economic zone that thrives with people and problems because of the boundary limit itself, or do we speak of it only figuratively and out of convenience? That is to say, must we ultimately deal with a series of border segments—one situation in Texas and Tamaulipas and Chihuahua, and another in California and Baja California—rather than conceptualize the border as having some particular unity?

In sponsoring the conference and assisting in the publication of this book, the Weatherhead Foundation wanted to bring United States-Mexican border matters to the attention of people in the border region and throughout both nations. The Foundation has had a Southwest program for some ten years and one of its main concerns has been the role of the border in northern Mexico and the American Southwest. As Americans we must learn more about borders and realize that, more often than not in history, borders have been trouble spots. While the American experience has been relatively free of border abrasiveness and Americans have the habit of ignoring borders and moving freely within a continental society, these conditions are not guarantees that our good luck will continue with Mexico or with Canada.

With such books as this, with the formulation of foreign policy based more realistically on the dynamics of borders, and with good fortune and good will on both sides, let us hope that North America's borders will never become barriers, but will be regions where different peoples can live side by side, creating new ways of life, and thereby enriching the cultures of the United States and Mexico.

Richard W. Weatherhead
President
The Weatherhead Foundation

March 1977
New York City

Bakersfield

CALIFORNIA

Santa Barbara

Los Angeles

San Diego

Tijuana

El Centro
Calexico

Mexicali

Ensenada

Colorado River

ARIZONA

Phoenix

Tucson

Columbus

Nogales

Douglas

Nogales

Agua Prieta

PACIFIC

OCEAN

GULF

BAJA

OF

CALIFORNIA

CALIFORNIA

SONORA

Hermosillo

CHIHUAHU

Guaymas

0   50   100   150   200 Miles
0   50   100   150   200 Kilometers

Principal Highways

La Paz

The Border States

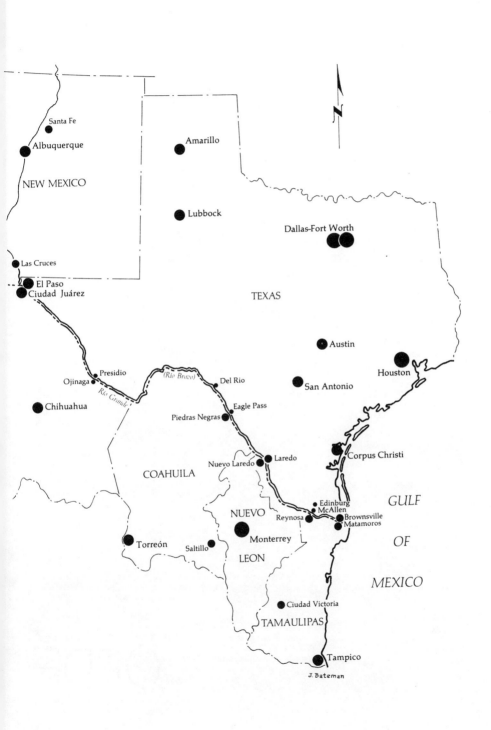

Santa Fe

Albuquerque

NEW MEXICO

Amarillo

Lubbock

Dallas-Fort Worth

Las Cruces

El Paso
Ciudad Juárez

TEXAS

Austin

Presidio
Ojinaga

(Río Bravo)

Del Rio

Houston

San Antonio

Chihuahua

Río Grande

Eagle Pass

Piedras Negras

Laredo

Corpus Christi

COAHUILA

Nuevo Laredo

GULF

Edinburg
McAllen

NUEVO

Reynosa

Brownsville
Matamoros

OF

Torreón

Saltillo

Monterrey

LEON

MEXICO

Ciudad Victoria

TAMAULIPAS

Tampico

J. Bateman

Introduction

With the signing of the Treaty of Guadalupe Hidalgo in 1848 by representatives of the governments of Mexico and the United States, formally ending the Mexican-American War, seventy-five thousand people of Mexican citizenry were given the choice of becoming citizens of the United States or returning to Mexico. Most elected to remain in the territory of their ancestors. Many believed that their land was only temporarily occupied.

To a large degree the modern boundary of Mexico and the United States is based on the Treaty of Guadalupe Hidalgo and on the Gadsden Purchase Treaty of 1853. Physically the border today consists, after rectification for river shifts, of 1,905 miles, including 1,230 miles of river (20 miles of the Colorado River and 1,210 miles of the Río Grande) and 675 miles of land (boundary between El Paso and the Pacific Ocean). Texas, New Mexico, Arizona, and California are the political entities on the United States side of the border while Tamaulipas, Nuevo León, Coahuila, Chihuahua, Sonora, and Baja California compose Mexico's tier of northern frontier states.

This is the official dividing line, but there is no insurmountable physical barrier—as is indicated by the estimated seven or eight thousand Mexican nationals who illegally enter the United States each day in search of work. There are, however, very important cultural and economic frontiers. And, as Ignacio Bernal explains in "The Cultural Roots of the Border: An Archaeologist's View," the border is built upon layers of older cultural worlds. This area, which both separates and joins two nations, is dynamic; it has an evolving life—an existence—of its own. It is also the cultural frontier with Latin America.

Too often, the problems of the border have been treated as purely local or regional matters which only occasionally are viewed as proper subjects of national policy, worthy of attention in Mexico City and Washington. Yet relations with our neighbor, Mexico, often have foreshadowed the delineation of broader policy, affecting other international relationships as well.

The border area and its inhabitants are complex, and although some of the material presented here may seem confusing or inconsistent, the contributors

1

do try to clarify the issues. Often seemingly contradictory conclusions drawn from the same materials result from the disparate viewpoints of the authors. They represent a balance of Mexican and United States (both Anglo- and Mexican-American) scholars and public officials, of established academicians and young scholars with diverse ideological orientations. Seven specific problems areas are discussed:

1. The Culture of the Border
2. The Politics of the Border
3. The Economics of the Border
4. The Migrants of the Border
5. Health Along the Border
6. The Individual and Social Psychology of the Border Population
7. The Ecology of the Border

But the result of this effort to clarify and define, I think, is a book that dynamically spells out the multidimensional nature of the border area and the people who inhabit it. Individually, the essays illustrate the authors' awareness of specific aspects of the border area and its people; as a totality, the essays are like shafts of light on a little-known mass—a mass in need of continual study and scholarship. I believe that the essays include data, information, and insights that represent breakthroughs in the understanding of the area. Mostly they point out the problems and the difficulties of coming up with solutions. In many cases solutions, such as coping with illegal entry of Mexicans into the United States, must come from government bodies. However, it is hoped that books like this will alert officials to the totality of the problems. This might complicate the decision-making process. But making decisions involving people usually should be a continuing process: people change, things change, problems change—decisions should mirror these changes.

Before discussing the seven specific problem areas on which the essays focus, it may be helpful to discuss briefly the whole matter of boundaries, frontiers, and borderlands—placing the Mexican-United States border region in the framework of knowledge about such areas in general.

From earlier times down through the classical and medieval periods in the Old World there were no "international boundaries," but rather separate zones, most commonly based on natural barriers—conspicuous, easily identified, and physically unmistakable by any potential intruder. It was with the emergence of the nation state that international boundaries—those between two national states—came into being. A boundary came to be defined as a limiting line, delimiting territorial jurisdiction, a territory vested with certain independence, or the limits of sovereignty. As such, it has been taken as a measure of a state's power. As Charles de Visscher defined it, "The firm configuration of its territory furnished the state with the recognized setting for the exercise of its sovereign powers."[1]

Territory has psychological importance for nations often quite out of proportion to its intrinsic—economic or strategic—value. Sentiments of national pride and honor are involved. Consequently, the boundaries of national territory are often sources of conflict. In the seventeenth and eighteenth centuries, the need for fixed boundaries was met with emphasis on natural features. Lord Curzon felt such boundaries were superior both because of greater clarity of definition and because of the strategic considerations of defense.

What is too easily lost from view is the fact that boundaries have significance chiefly in relation to human beings. And almost every definition offered includes recognition of contact as well as separation. In essence, boundaries are often zones of transition rather than sharply defined lines.

Part of the difficulty in discussing boundaries, frontiers, and borderlands has been the interchangeable use of the terms. While there is no universal agreement or practice, some general definitions have been widely accepted since the late nineteenth century.

Increasingly there developed agreement that the boundary line is linear, a limiting line. In contrast, the frontier is zonal, having width as well as length. Such regions or zones often precede the delimitation of a boundary.[2] John R. V. Prescott draws a further distinction: he prefers to employ the term "frontier" when referring to the zonal division between states, while introducing the term "borderlands" for that which "stretches inward from the boundary and merges imperceptibly with the state."[3]

Frontier zones may be viewed in a political, economic, social, cultural, linguistic, religious, and even ideological sense. They have been viewed as a place, a situation, and as a process. Since the zones antedate the delineation of a dividing boundary line, there frequently has been overlap rather than clear division. Historically, the political frontier between states was most likely to be found in a more isolated, less attractive, and less densely populated zone. The inhabitants of such zones tended to have a lower standard of living. If the two nations facing each other in a given frontier zone are significantly different but without real conflict potential, the zone may become a mere migratory region with a mixing of peoples and cultures but without genuine solidarity. Then, as Jorge Mañach has observed, the area not infrequently develops into a disordered zone of vice and adventure.[4]

Terminology also evolved to specify the area between the settled and the uninhabited—or relatively uninhabited—part of a single state. This is called a *settlement frontier*. Specialists tend to separate settlement frontiers into two types: the *historical frontier*—which marks the *de facto* limits of the state's political authority; and the expanding, *moving frontier,* which has been very much a part of North American history. The United States Census Bureau defined the frontier zone in 1890 as that beyond which there was a density of fewer than two persons per square mile.

Using these definitions, frontiers, boundaries, and borderlands developed generally in that order within the area joining the peoples of Mexico and the United States. The Mexican-United States border does evidence both some of the characteristics common to all or most borders as well as some unique features. Furthermore, the area has experienced frontiers as both the political and settlement types.

The Mexican-United States boundary is today regarded as a long-standing dividing line reasonably well located relative to the seats of power of the two nations. Omitting any seemingly unlikely Mexican irridentism or Mexican-American separatism, there remains little controversy about the boundary in a territorial sense. Among its features is the fact that transcontinental boundaries between single pairs of countries are found only in Central and North America and only in the latter are they of significant dimensions. Long, unfortified land boundaries exist between the United States and both Mexico and Canada. However, significant cultural contrast characterizes only the former if one ignores that part of the northern border dividing New England from French Canada.

Both the Mexicans and their northern neighbors have a rich frontier tradition. Going back to the Spanish Peninsula one finds the frontier experience involved in the eight-hundred-year reconquest of the area from Moslem control. The *Reconquista* was more than a military and political struggle: it was a recolonization of the Iberian peninsula and a frontier movement in the later American sense of the term.[5]

When the Spaniards came to New Spain, as they named colonial Mexico, the explorer, conqueror, and missionary spread out northward and southward chasing the chimera of "mysteries" and searching for new empires to conquer, new wealth to acquire, and new souls to save. The northern reaches would prove disappointing and hostile. Indeed the area was so remote that in 1776, the Spanish authorities carved out a defensive and administrative area described as the "Internal Provinces." With good reason Miguel León-Portilla wrote that "In Mexico the North has always been thought of as a physical and cultural frontier and also very frequently as a country in which, if indeed there may be wealth, development of human life is not easy.''[6]

Settlement may have been sparse, but a *norteño* culture emerged as presidios and missions, way stations and mining towns, ranches and estates were painfully established. There was concern about the aboriginal marauders and about the intrusion of other Europeans, including the Anglo Americans who were established on the Atlantic seaboard. Time and again there were proposals and even efforts to establish a buffer zone against the advancing energetic frontiersmen from the Anglo-Saxon world.

In his essay entitled ''The Significance of the Frontier in American History'' (1893), Frederick Jackson Turner first articulated the thesis that the long-term availability of a frontier of free land in what was to become the United States contributed decisively to its development. Turner felt that the westward movement was a unique experience that had helped shape American national character, institutions, and social dynamism. The frontier had ''Americanized'' men and institutions. Agreeing with Turner, Jorge Mañach attributes to the frontier an ''expansive, daring, pugnacious spirit of individual and autonomous effort. . . .''[7]

Inevitably and inexorably this Anglo-Saxon westward movement would penetrate and clash with the Spanish-Mexican frontier zone. The latter was no uninhabited wilderness, although it was sparsely settled and ineffectually held. Thus began the confrontation of two civilizations.

Ideally, having two nations with such disparate cultures as those of Mexico and the United States, there would be mutual interpenetration, with each culture complementing and enriching the other. However, what has tended to occur—and particularly in the frontier zones during the past thirty years—is a massive penetration of the American culture on the Mexican life-style.

The extensive communications media in the United States have been most responsible for this. American movies, radio, television, and newspapers disseminate in Mexico, as they do throughout a large part of the world, images of life styles and consumer habits more compatible with inhabitants north of the border. American tourism and, more recently, Mexican travel to the States, have tended to reinforce this imagery. Mexican movies, radio, television, and newspapers are also widely disseminated in the United States and play an important role in reinforcing Mexican cultural and language traits among Mexicans and Mexican Americans. Thus, media-induced cultural penetration is not entirely a one-way process. However, it is far from balanced, and those mindful of the need to maintain the integrity of Mexico's own culture despair over the ''cocacolization'' of the border areas. But the dominance of the United States economy is conducive to it; and the pervasiveness of its communications media guarantees it.

It was not always so. When the North Americans went beyond that region peopled only by aborigines, they found that they were latecomers. Instead of bringing civilization to the frontier, they were encountering an even older and more established civilization. But as Joe Frantz notes in his essay, "The Borderlands: Ideas on a Leafless Landscape," the fact that the culture confronting the North Americans was largely European did not give them pause. The culture was still alien to their Anglo-American experience. To fuse two or three cultures did not seem to occur to them either. "Rather, as a pragmatic people, they observed Hispanic culture being as alien as the aboriginal culture," Frantz says, "and must have reasoned, if indeed they thought at all, that the only way to handle an alien situation was to root it out. But of course, they were dealing with a people who were dug in deeply already, and who did not root out easily."

The earlier influence that Mexico's culture had on the northern American settlers often has been overlooked. Take the *ranchero* of Mexico. As Américo Paredes points out in his essay, "The Problem of Identity in a Changing Culture," he was rough-mannered and a superb horseman. Add the six-chambered revolver, which was distinctively Anglo-American, and you have the American cowboy of fiction and popular legend—the ideal figure of many an Anglo male. "The cowboy as a *macho* image was carried by the Texan," Paredes says, "along with other elements of the 'cattle culture,' to other areas of the border, as well as to other parts of the West. The idea of the cowboy as the American *macho* becomes so pervasive that it can influence the private and public life of Theodore Roosevelt. . . ."

On a more popular level, a strong case can be made for the influence of Mexican eating habits on the Anglo Americans living in the border regions. O. Henry humorously illustrates this in his poem "Tamales," in which Don José Calderón Santos Espirition Vicente Camillo Quintana de Ríos de Rosa y Ribera takes revenge on the Texans for having killed his grandfather by selling them greasy tamales:

> What boots it if we killed
> Only one greaser,
> Don José Calderón?
> This is your deep revenge,
> You have greased all of us,
> Greased a whole nation
> With your tamales. . . .

Part of the difficulty in determining the roots of the culture on the border, according to Carlos Monsiváis, is the propaganda machine of the Institutional Revolutionary Party (PRI). The main problem in defining Mexican culture along the border, he says in his essay, "The Culture of the Frontier: The Mexican Side," is in "separating the real culture from that fabricated by our country's political bureaucracy, a systematic demagoguery and sociopolitical coalition in which the liberal left prominently participates."

Whether the culture is real or imagined, its effect on modern-day problems besetting the border regions is pervasive and, as is fitting, it finds its way into all the essays in this book. The four essays devoted primarily to border culture place it within an overall framework of past and present border reality.

With some justification, the late Frank Tannenbaum, the eminent Latin Americanist, often described Mexico as the anvil of American foreign policy. For the governments of Mexico, the overriding political problems with the United States have been and are basically twofold: how to maintain an independent external policy and how to manage their own affairs in their own interest when contiguous to a superpower. As the apt phrase has put it, "Oh poor Mexico, so far from God and so close to the United States." Or, in epidemiological terms—which are most appropriate to difficult economic times—when Uncle Sam catches cold, Mexico sneezes.

In considering the present-day political interactions between these two nations, one always must keep in mind the outcome of the Mexican-American War (1846-48): Mexico lost one-half of its national territory and acquired a bitter heritage of fear, resentment, and distrust for its northern neighbor.

During the latter half of the nineteenth century there were many border problems. These involved movements of bandits and revolutionaries as well as of marauding Indians, none of whom showed much respect for the international boundary line. Furthermore, there has always been a contraband problem. During the American Civil War, cotton found its outlet to the south, while trading caravans in northern Mexico thrived as never before.

With the coming of the Mexican Revolution in the twentieth century, the border area became a logical jumping-off place for those opposing an incumbent regime, not to mention a haven for exiles. The protection of Americans and their interests, hazards of armed conflict in border towns, and the pursuit of revolutionary raiders led to several incursions into Mexican territory, the largest and best-known being the pursuit of Francisco Villa by Pershing's Punitive Expedition.

Today, though border problems are evident to those who live close to both sides of the line, they have received national attention too infrequently.

Furthermore, while a source of irritation, only occasionally have they threatened relations between the two countries. Indeed, while in the early decades of this century Mexican-United States relations were complicated by problems of recognition, claims, debts, and expropriation, in the period since World War II none of these problems has caused conflict. In fact, recent decades have been marked less by quarrels and threats and more by the solution of long-standing and annoying, minor yet symbolic, disputes. Periodic meetings have taken place at the border between both nations' chief executives and several agreements have been signed for undertaking joint projects.

In 1944, a treaty on boundary waters provided for the construction of dams and irrigation works on the Río Grande and other rivers. The middle of the Río Grande's deepest channel was made to serve as part of the international boundary and the resulting parcels of land cut off from each nation were exchanged. However, some 630 acres in the area of El Paso, known as the Chamizal, remained an irritant. An arbitral award in 1910, favoring Mexico, was rejected by the United States, and for half a century the unresolved matter served to complicate relations between the two nations. Finally, in 1963, President John Kennedy signed the Chamizal Treaty and directed that the matter be resolved consistent with the arbitral award.

Thus the last territorial boundary question between the two nations was resolved. Political considerations and emotions of national pride gave the issue an importance far beyond its intrinsic value. The agreement made possible other agreements: the settlement of the Pious Fund of the Californias,* involving Mexican payments for certain mission properties; arrangements on airline routes, radio and television channels; and cooperation in the control of diseases—such as joint programs to eradicate hoof and

---

*There is a long history of litigation surrounding the Pious Fund of the Californias which was established in the late seventeenth century to promote missionary work in California. After the Jesuits were expelled from the Spanish dominions in 1767, the Spanish government took over the fund, and then Mexico after its independence in 1821.

In 1842, the properties were sold and the resulting funds went to the national treasury but with the understanding that the Mexican government was obligated to provide annually 6 percent of the capital value of the fund to the missions. When California became part of the United States both the missions and the state wanted the Mexican payments to continue. Mexico did so, with interruptions, until recent times.

In the late sixties, negotiations resulted in an agreement whereby Mexico made annual payments until a lump sum settlement was achieved. The $720,000 proceeds were used by the United States hierarchy to support a seminary where priests were trained for careers in Mexico. When the seminary closed, the endowment was turned over to the Mexican hierarchy to employ for that purpose.

mouth disease *(aftosa),* control screwworm fly infestation, and more recently, a shared concern about the spread of Venezuelan equine encephalomyelitis.

In another area—regarding differing claims on the extent of territorial control over adjacent waters as well as fishing rights—the two nations have agreed to disagree about the extent of the territorial waters while compromising on fishing rights. Mexico has successively claimed three, nine, twelve, and, most recently, two hundred miles of territorial waters. The United States long held to the three-mile limit, but since World War II has asserted its claim to resources on the continental shelf to twelve miles. Recently the United States Senate passed a resolution favoring jurisdiction to two hundred miles. Mexican seizure of United States fishing craft underscores the international aspect of the problem.

In the Guadalupe Hidalgo Treaty of 1848 and the Gadsden Purchase of 1853, the only references to the boundary rivers (the Río Grande and the Colorado) were in terms of navigation. Today, concern tends to focus on the river waters for irrigation, for city water supply, and for seasonal control of the waters to avoid disastrous flooding.

For the past fifteen years a problem relating to the quality of river water distributed southward from dams to irrigation projects north of the border has troubled relations between Mexico and the United States. The salinity of the waters from the Colorado River has adversely affected Mexican crops in the Mexicali Valley, spoiled the land in the area, and brought into the open differences between the two governments' interpretations of the Water Treaty of 1944.

The problem arose because the Wellton-Mohawk Project, undertaken to bring water to the Imperial Valley in California, was pumping saline water back into the Colorado River. A 1972 hydraulic engineering survey showed that the Wellton-Mohawk water had a salinity of 4,000 parts per million, as contrasted with 1,300 parts per million for other Colorado River water.

Mexico argued that it had a right to receive usable water both under the specific agreements between the two countries and under generally accepted international law, which specifies that no action be taken that will diminish the value and usability of boundary water to another country.

In 1972, the leaders of the two nations agreed to seek a permanent, definitive, and just solution. Alternatives included elimination of the source of the problem, substitution of Imperial Dam quality water, or the desalinization of the Wellton-Mohawk drainage. Desalinization, although expensive, had the advantage of minimizing the loss of water, limitation of development, and environmental problems. Further, it promised invaluable experience as a pilot effort in desalinization.

Under an agreement reached in 1973, the United States is constructing the world's largest desalinization plant near Yuma, Arizona, about 175 miles east of San Diego. When the plant is in operation in the early 1980s, Mexico will be assured quality water to the Mexicali Valley.

It is very clear that the economic situations on both sides of the border, and the interaction between them, have far-reaching repercussions. Two key aspects of the economic frontier emerge from the imbalance of the economies which meet at the border: economic dependence and economic disparity.

The great gap between Mexico and the United States in their economic levels is critical for both countries. In 1970, the United States gross national product was $974 billion while Mexico's was $33 billion. The United States per capita national income that year was approximately $4,300, while the figure for Mexico was $550. A keen observer of border economic affairs, Fred H. Schmidt, has written that "neither the per capita gross national product nor the per capita income of any country in the world even comes near the *amount of the difference* in per capita income between the United States and Mexico."[8]

Often overlooked, however, is that this disparity migrates with the Mexican over into the northern side of the border. A United States Commerce Department study identified three Texas border metropolitan areas as the poorest in the United States in 1969: McAllen, with annual personal income per capita at $2,343; Laredo, $2,516; and Brownsville, $2,607. For the United States as a whole, it was $4,045.[9] Poverty is more than twice as prevalent among Mexican Americans as in the nation as a whole. Those of Mexican origin represent more than 70 percent of the unskilled and semiskilled labor in the border states. Whether one considers education, income, or type of labor, the Mexican Americans and the migrant Mexicans predominate at the lower end of the scale.

The poverty in the towns on the Mexican side of the border has been exacerbated by rapid population growth, as those living in rural areas have migrated *en masse* to the border communities. From 1950 to 1960 and from 1960 to 1970, the population of the Mexican border towns grew 6.3 percent and 4.1 percent respectively. In actual numbers, the population increased from 1.568 million in 1950 to 2.334 million in 1970.

The Mexican government has undertaken a much-publicized effort to stimulate economic growth in the frontier zones. One of the better-known programs, which has been pushed by the government since 1965, is that of the *maquiladora* plants—mostly manufacturing assembly plants that export 100 percent of their production. A majority of the plants import components from the United States, assemble them, and export them back to the United States.

Despite the *maquiladoras,* border manufacturing has had little effect on employment opportunities, according to Víctor Urquidi and Sofía Méndez Villarreal. In their essay, "Economic Importance of Mexico's Northern Border Region," they note that in 1970 this sector provided employment for 94,052 individuals, barely 15.6 percent of the area's economically active population. This figure includes the workers hired by the *maquiladora* plants. Only 25.8 percent of the Mexican border region population was employed in 1970.

Mexico's proximity to the world's largest industrial producer and the richest consumer of raw materials and agricultural products has resulted in the United States commanding almost a monopolizing control over Mexico's exports and imports. The nation's dependence on the United States for foreign trade reached a peak in 1942. In that war year, during which many foreign markets were closed to Mexico, that country sent the United States 91 percent of its total exports and obtained 87 percent of its imports from its northern neighbor. By the 1970s, despite the end of the war, the passage of three decades, and strenuous efforts to diversify Mexico's trading partners, the United States still accounted for 66 percent of Mexico's total foreign trade.

During recent decades, direct foreign investment has been rising until it now exceeds quantitatively prerevolutionary foreign investment. By 1970, the direct foreign investment was more than $2 billion, of which 85 percent belonged to United States firms. While this proportion is not large in relation to the total direct investment (both national and foreign)—it is variously estimated from 8 to 11 percent—some observers hasten to point out that the foreign investment is concentrated in the more dynamic sectors of the economy—manufacturing and tourism. For example, in 1970, 47 percent of the richest firms and 61 percent of those producing capital goods were foreign-owned, primarily by Americans. A high price is paid for the transfer of technology, involving charges for foreign-controlled patent rights and restrictions on their use.

The Echeverría administration sought to increase control over foreign corporations and increase technological transfer. However, like its much-proclaimed identification with the Third World and efforts to diversify trading patterns, there tended to be a significant gap between proclaimed intentions and reality. The oratory did create an unfavorable climate for investors—both domestic and foreign—and unchecked inflation and an accelerating unfavorable trade balance resulted in Mexico's first devaluation of the peso in more than two decades. The economic situation greeting Echeverría's successor, José López Portillo, in 1977 is worse than anticipated and dependence on the United States greater than ever.

There is a social aspect to the economics of the border that is deserving of some mention. The United States has established a number of military bases in the border zone and there has been a tendency for soldiers to obtain services in Mexico which the nominal Puritanism of their own country, at least until recent times, did not generally easily provide. It was with this in mind that Ovid Demaris entitled his flamboyant journalistic account of border prostitution *Poso del Mundo* ("Sink of the World") and categorized the border from Tijuana to Brownsville as a "sixteen hundred mile pleasure strip oriented to gringos with low libidinal thresholds."[10]

Between 1939 and 1973, nine million legal immigrants came to the United States from countries all over the world. During these same years, more than nine million illegal Mexicans were apprehended and deported from the United States. But those who were caught and returned to Mexico probably represented only 30 percent of the aliens who crossed the border illegally and remained undetected. It has been estimated that the number of resident illegal aliens ranges from 4.5 million to 8 million and more. To a great extent, what has drawn such numbers from Mexico is the economic disparity between the two countries. Even substandard wages and working conditions have lured millions across the border; compared to Mexican wages, those paid the illegal migrants in the United States are high. It is this differential that constitutes a powerful element in the push-pull forces attracting millions northward.

The push-pull factors have been operative despite the impressive political stability and economic development which has characterized Mexico in recent decades. The explanation lies not only in the relative attractiveness of opportunity north of the border, but also in the fact that improved conditions in Mexico have stirred rising expectations which are difficult to satisfy for the multiplying Mexican population—one of the most rapidly growing in the world.

The illegal migration of Mexican nationals in the border regions of the United States and beyond is unquestionably the most serious and all-pervasive problem affecting the relations between the two countries. It probably will remain so until the turn of the century.

Leonard F. Chapman, Jr., former Immigration and Naturalization Commissioner, warned that the "United States is being overrun by illegal aliens." Highly critical of the price being paid for the presence of the illegal aliens, he called for more adequate funding and effective control legislation:

They are occupying jobs that are needed by unemployed citizens. They are not paying their share of taxes, and often pay none at all. At the same time they are using public services, educating their children in our schools, and often collecting welfare and even unemployment payments.

Unless adequate resources and legislation are forthcoming immediately, the flood of illegal entries we are now experiencing will become a torrent.[11]

Not everyone would agree with Commissioner Chapman's opinion, but the charges are frequently heard. A Texas state representative, Dan Kubiak, complained that the sixty-one Texas school districts along the border were spending $40 million to educate Mexican alien children.[12] The Texas governor's office and the state's Department of Community Affairs sponsored a conference on juvenile delinquency—petty crimes, vandalism, and gang fights—involving juvenile aliens.

However, a survey of almost eight hundred illegal aliens (61 percent from Mexico) undertaken by the United States Department of Labor in late 1975 suggests that some of these allegations are exaggerated. Among those surveyed, 31.5 percent had filed United States income tax returns; 3.9 percent had collected some unemployment insurance; 1.3 percent had obtained food stamps; 0.5 percent had received welfare payments; and only 7.6 percent had children in American schools.[13]

Unquestionably, the presence of migrants, particularly the illegals, causes disruption of the normal labor market in the Southwest and increasingly in some northern cities. While not causally responsible, the migrants clearly have added to the dimensions of the problems of the border region in terms of health, unemployment and underemployment, education, and poverty. They help to explain the limited effect of public policies directed toward the abatement of such problems and the reduction of human suffering in the region.

Their illegal status makes the aliens particularly vulnerable to exploitation and mistreatment. As Tad Szulc sums up the aliens' predicament in his essay on the foreign policy aspects of the border, they are people who constantly must fear discovery and expulsion, living lives of the hunted. They suffer exploitation by employers who, if the "illegal" protests, will report him or her to the dreaded Immigration Service. They are deprived of social services and other such benefits of American society: "They must live as invisible people, unprotected by any United States laws. . . . They are humans deprived of any shred of dignity."

At the very time that mechanization and irrigation, not to mention some shifts in crops, are reducing the need for less expensive, seasonal hand labor, the influx of large numbers of migrants continues. While newspapers and politicians continue to equate the problem with the agribusiness farmer, Mexican workers increasingly are being attracted to such urban centers as Los Angeles, Chicago, and Detroit.

It is interesting how ambivalent are the attitudes toward this migration. The Mexican government has mixed reactions to the mass movement of workers to the United States. On the one hand, it is clearly a political and economic safety valve, not to mention the importance of migrant remittances as an offset to unfavorable international exchange balances. Mexico is reluctant to restrict its own nationals and is very much concerned about the mistreatment of the "undocumented Mexicans" in the United States. Similarly the United States government has been ambivalent; it has been slow to come to grips with the problem, reflecting the crosscurrents of political pressures from contradictory interest groups.

Farms, ranches, and urban businesses, all interested in cheap labor, have pressed for more liberal legislation and a less rigid enforcement policy toward illegal aliens. Labor groups, feeling the pinch of competition from illegal migrants (or even legal ones, for that matter) generally have favored a more restrictive policy with more effective enforcement.

Mexican Americans, competing with the illegal aliens, probably have suffered most. However, they have had little influence on the policies relating to illegal migration or to the "commuter" arrangement, whereby Mexican nationals are legally permitted to commute daily across the border to jobs in the United States. What influence Mexican Americans might have has been weakened by their own ambivalence and divided loyalties. They have strong kinship and cultural bonds with the Mexican workers, yet in their own self-interest, they find themselves opposing the influx of migrants, legal and illegal, because of the competition for jobs; they may even find themselves siding with immigration officials whom they would, traditionally, distrust.

Movement across the border is deeply rooted historically. Migration—legal and illegal—has been encouraged and discouraged depending on times and circumstances. Mexicans were welcomed as workers during the mining booms and railroad construction periods, protected and turned back during the Mexican Revolution. World War I raised the demand for Mexican labor, while the Great Depression brought repatriation of more than 300,000 Mexicans. World War II reversed the tide once more.

The Bracero Program, begun as a wartime emergency measure in 1944 for contract labor for railroads and agriculture, continued for many more years than planned and became a catalyst for Mexican migration, both legal and illegal. Legal movement of contract migrants and others was accompanied by an ever-increasing stream of illegals. In 1964, the United States Congress, under pressure from organized labor, failed to renew the International Agreement on Migrant Workers (1951). The Bracero Program was ended, thus contributing to a new wave of illegal migrants that has grown continuously ever since.

Change in the immigration laws of the United States has added to the problem. Except for Canada, nations of the Western Hemisphere had been exempted from the numerical limit placed on immigration according to a national origins quota system. In 1965, a numerical quota (110,000) for immigration from the Western Hemisphere was imposed for the first time. Furthermore, aliens from this area became ineligible for an adjustment of status. This meant that to become a permanent resident, a Western Hemisphere alien had to leave the country, obtain a visa from a United States consul, and was subject to Labor Department certification that resident qualified workers were not available nor would the employment of the alien adversely affect wages or working conditions.*

The United States government designated a special study group in 1972 composed of representatives of various federal agencies under the chairmanship of Roger C. Cramton of the Justice Department. This committee's report, dated January 15, 1973, was encouragingly entitled "A Program for Effective and Humane Action on Illegal Mexican Immigrants." The report's recommendations included:

— substantial strengthening of border surveillance personnel
— penalties for employers who knowingly employ illegal aliens
— effective interagency cooperation to locate deportable aliens and protect them from abuse
— economic and technical assistance to develop more employment opportunities on the Mexican side of the border
— legalization of the residence of illegal aliens who have resided in the United States for ten years.

Unfortunately, no broad action has been taken on these recommendations, although there have been some legislative proposals.

Study on both sides of the border and discussions at the highest levels are encouraging indications that this pressing problem is beginning to receive the

---

*In the fall of 1976, the law was modified to equalize treatment of immigrants from both hemispheres. The adjustment of status became available for Western Hemisphere aliens who also came under the preference system and per country numerical limitations.

attention it merits. However, this problem simply cannot be solved until the Mexican economy is capable of providing enough jobs for its citizens. Given the high birth rate in Mexico, and the projected economic growth rate, there is little likelihood that the wave of Mexican immigration can be halted in this century.

While illegal migration is unquestionably the most important problem affecting the relations between Mexico and the United States, it is not the only one. Several others also fall into the ''illegal'' classification.

Of binational concern is the problem posed by drug traffic, including the smuggling of amphetamines, marijuana, and the hard drugs (heroin and cocaine). In 1974, it was estimated that the marijuana traffic from Mexico amounted to three-quarters of a million pounds, with a street value of a half billion dollars—more than from Canada and the country's coasts combined. It is reported that private planes have brought in more than half of the Mexican marijuana.[14]

However, it is when one turns to the hard drugs that it becomes very apparent that the ''French connection'' has been replaced by the ''Mexican connection.'' The ''Mexican brown'' variety of heroin (so called because of its impurities; it is only 65 percent pure in contrast to the 90-percent-pure variety that formerly came from Europe) rose from 40 percent of the confiscated street heroin in 1972 to 63 percent in 1973, to 76 percent in 1974, and to 90 percent of all confiscated heroin in the first half of 1975.[15]

For some time, the United States has been pressing Mexican authorities for tougher action against heroin traffickers. More recently, Mexican national concerns have prompted a more energetic response from that nation. In late 1975, the Mexican government organized a broad campaign against narcotics. For the first time, herbicides are being used in marijuana and opium poppy fields. And early in 1976, the two governments announced plans to set up ''twin'' commissions to fight the drug flow across the Mexican-United States border. In June 1976, the Mexican government pledged to continue its program of eradicating opium poppy fields on a year-round basis.

While on the one hand the United States has pressed Mexico to help control and reduce the drug traffic, it has responded to public clamor about the treatment of some six hundred United States prisoners in Mexican jails— many of them on charges involving narcotics. In 1976, a treaty providing the basis for transfer of prisoners was signed by the two nations and ratified by the Mexican legislature. The United States Senate is expected to give its required consent. Cases would then be handled on an individual basis with legal challenges to the validity of the Mexican legal process, and to continued incarceration in the home country, unpredictable as to outcome. In early

1977, the issue continued as an irritant to Mexican-United States relations.

Recurring press reports have suggested ties between the illegal movement of drugs and arms. The Mexican government takes no official public cognizance of the allegations that narcotics are being used to pay for illegal arms, and a spokesman for the United States Department of State ridiculed the suggestion. Nevertheless, the reports persist.

In addition to the socially harmful illegal traffic in drugs and arms, Mexico is concerned about other contraband, particularly the smuggling of consumer goods, that is damaging to its economy. It is difficult to calculate the dimensions of this illegal movement of goods but, in 1971, the Mexican Secretary of the Treasury made some conservative estimates which put a value of 3,000 million pesos ($240 million) on contraband entering Mexico during the previous year. This figure equaled one-half of Mexico's legitimate trade deficit with the United States that year. Obviously, such illegal traffic in consumer goods is very disruptive of the Mexican economic process.

Poverty underlies and aggravates the health problems of the population on both sides of the Mexican-United States border. However, in the case of Mexico, poverty is not confined to the border towns. Despite impressive progress in recent decades, crippling poverty and the health problems accompanying it continue to be found in many parts of Mexico. In fact, the Mexican border zone is relatively well off compared to the rest of the republic, excepting the Federal District. In contrast the border region on the United States side is characterized by comparatively poor health conditions paralleling the economic poverty of the region.

Available infant mortality statistics appear to belie these generalizations. Infant mortality indices tend to reflect fairly reliably economic, social, and health development. While Mexico has recorded progress over the past three decades in this regard, the infant mortality rate remains high throughout Mexico. Although it appears to be slightly higher in the border states as a whole, Ricardo Loewe feels that this is probably attributable to better record keeping in the municipalities adjacent to the border, where medical attention at the time of delivery is more likely.

On the Texas side of the border, the 1970-72 infant mortality rate—defined as the number of deaths under one year of age per thousand live births in a calendar year—was often lowest in border communities. However, Charles Teller attributes this to unreliable record keeping.

Part of the problem in determining health care needs that might be unique to the border region is the heterogeneity of the people. They include rural peasants and urban Mexican nationals, first-generation immigrants and fourth-generation United States-born Chicanos, reservation and urban Indians, and Anglo Americans—the rich ranchers and industrialists, the middle class, and the very poor.

But this is no time to undertake rarefied research to see if one or several of these diverse ethnic and socioeconomic groups has health difficulties peculiar to itself. A high priority in the borderlands must be to increase the number of physicians, laboratory technicians, dentists, pharmacists, and nurses. The number of people per physician in the border states of Mexico varies from 1,171 to 1,771—in Mexico as a whole it is 1,500. While the ratio of physician to patient is lower on the Texas side of the border, this does not mean that the poor people use physicians. The poor in Texas, like poor people in most places, consider physicians a luxury—one they seldom can afford.

The Chicano, perhaps because he has been studied more extensively than other ethnic groups in Texas, is presented as having particular difficulty approaching health care personnel. "Many Chicanos feel particularly trapped in the middle and not fully respected by either side," Teller says, "although you often hear the comment that they are treated with more dignity by Mexican doctors than by Anglo ones."

Beside the need to improve the quantity and quality of the health care in the borderlands, a major factor that would reduce the mortality rate would be a decrease in the birth rate. The fertility rate on both sides of the border is inordinately high, compounding the health care needs of the region.

But the immediate answer to these health care needs in the borderlands is economic. As a representative for the United Farm Workers told a Senate subcommittee hearing on the effect of federal health care programs in the lower Río Grande Valley counties:

> I have continually stressed what the Texas branch of the union feels will contribute most to good health—fair wages. We do not want new programs which create complacency, tenure-oriented bureaucracies, and don't deliver. We want no new legislation unless it is designed and is passed to support the farm worker in his struggle to gain a fair wage. We do not want legislation which purports to help, but really traps the workers in a maze of restrictions which would vitiate the farm movement.[16]

In addition to the problems related to physical well-being, there also needs to be attention paid to problems of mental health and, more broadly, toward an understanding of the individual and social psychology of the border populations. Results of "Views of Life" questionnaires given to fourteen-year-old American and Mexican boys showed in general that the Americans tended toward patterns of "active self assertion," while their Mexican counterparts preferred "affiliative obedience." It would appear from this that there should be a natural attraction between the two, each satisfying the deep psychological compulsions of the other.

However, other tests, as related in the essays dealing with the psychology of those living in the borderlands, indicate differences between Mexicans and Anglo Americans that are less compatible. For example, Mexicans test as being more flexible in playing roles and in being more sensitive to emotional variations in relationships with others, while Americans tend to be more rigid and follow certain established patterns in their interactions. The consistent interaction pattern demonstrated by the American can easily lead the Mexican to feel that the American is cold, impersonal, and distant. On the other hand, the American reacts to the flexibility of the Mexican by thinking him superficial and, perhaps, somewhat hypocritical.

Wayne Holtzman lists a number of speculative conclusions about Mexicans in general drawn from various testings:

1. Mexicans, particularly women, tend to be "passive obedient."
2. Fewer Mexican fathers, particularly from the lower-class group, share activities with their sons.
3. Mexican children are given less responsibility in the home.
4. Mexican children are more likely to have their friends chosen by their parents.
5. Mexican mothers are more likely to admit to problems in child rearing and to express the attitude that child rearing is difficult.
6. Mexican mothers are less accepting and more controlling of their children.
7. Mexican mothers value independence in their children less than American mothers.
8. Curiosity, which implies looking into things on one's own, is less valued in children by Mexican mothers.

Although research data dealing with border health prove to be meager, numerous studies have been undertaken on the psychology of border populations. However, Rogelio Díaz-Guerrero, in his essay "Mexicans and Americans: Two Worlds, One Border . . . and One Observer," indicates a note of skepticism with the conclusions drawn by some of the tests. He points out that in tests of American and Mexican secondary and postsecondary students, the Americans come off as being much more optimistic about life in general than the Mexican students. The Mexican students seem to indicate that life is to be endured while the American students say overwhelmingly that life is to be enjoyed.

"In reality," Díaz-Guerrero says, "Mexicans certainly look as though they are enjoying life far more than Americans. Americans look as though they are just enduring it. Americans should think this over many times."

Mexicans tend to regard American concerns with ecology as the latest fad in a rich country seeking distraction from the real problems such as nutrition, housing, and public health. In his essay, "Ecology of the Border Region," J. Alberto Villasana Lyon says, "We Mexicans cannot get excited over ecological problems that are the by-product of industrial development." Mexico would like to have such problems.

But Mexico often is the recipient of those by-products without benefit of the industrial output. Air and, many times, water pollution, which originate north of the Mexican-United States border, do not request permission before entering the nation south of the border.

In terms of priority, however, Villasana indicates that Mexico's interest and response to ecological pollution problems will be in direct proportion to their effect on its economy. Mexico is very much interested in the quick reduction of the high salinity of northern waters, which adversely affects the crop production in Mexicali. Without food people will starve, so food naturally is a concern of high priority. Air pollution is of less concern; given the choice between preventing malnutrition and emphysema, Mexico will decide in favor of feeding people.

This study of the border between Mexico and the United States has presented a major area for research, aimed at the understanding of some fundamental problems which deeply affect the development of large regions of both countries and the nations as a whole. In providing a setting for the comparative study of social institutions and cultural values, it also presents a microcosm of the international relations between two nations, from which much can be learned.

The essays comprising this book, then, are intended to shed light on misunderstandings and misconceptions concerning the border and frontier zone that joins and separates Mexico and the United States. The thoughts expressed are working words, subject to revision, with the acquisition of additional information and changed circumstances. The ideas are not immutable but should serve to further discussion and inquiry.

At the official government level, many of the conflicts and confrontations described here have already been resolved. But on the human level, the problems and opportunities remain as numerous as the people who live and interact daily in the border region. Pervasive poverty on both sides of the border can compound any problem and undermine most opportunities, and although its physical burden cannot soon be removed, demonstrated good will, a gracious spirit of cooperation, and openness toward the needs and ideas of others can relieve some of the mental anguish of poverty.

It is the belief and hope of all who participated in the making of this book that it will stimulate further research, enhance the reader's understanding of border issues, and, in some measure, help to guide others to the solution of some of the problems affecting millions of lives not only in the borderlands but in Mexico and the United States generally.

The editor takes this opportunity to acknowledge the secretarial assistance provided by Geraldine D. Gagliano, assisted by Anna Hall, María García, and Sharee Aery, and the research assistance provided by Beecher Ellison, who prepared the bibliography under the editor's direction, and Carol Wood Garcés.

Stanley R. Ross
University of Texas at Austin

NOTES

1. Charles de Visscher, *Theory and Reality in Public International Law* (Princeton: Princeton University Press, 1957), p. 197.

2. Ratzel, Fawcett, Lapradelle, and Ancel as cited in John R. V. Prescott, *The Geography of Frontiers and Boundaries* (London: Hutchinson and Co., 1965), pp. 10, 15, 17, and 19. See also S. Whittemore Boggs, *International Boundaries: A Study of Boundary Functions and Problems* (New York: Columbia University Press, 1940), p. 22.

3. Prescott, *The Geography,* pp. 33-34.

4. Jorge Mañach, *Frontiers in the Americas: A Global Perspective,* trans. Philip H. Phenix (New York: Teachers College Press, 1975), p. 15.

5. Charles J. Bishko, "The Castilian as Plainsman: The Medieval Ranching Frontier in La Mancha and Extremadura," in Archibald E. Lewis and Thomas F. McGann, eds., *The New World Looks at Its History* (Austin: University of Texas Press, 1963), p. 45.

6. Miguel León-Portilla, "The Norteño Variety of Mexican Culture: An Ethnohistorical Approach," in Edward H. Spicer and Raymond H. Thompson, eds., *Plural Society in the Southwest* (Albuquerque: University of New Mexico Press, 1975), p. 77.

7. Mañach, *Frontiers in the Americas,* p. 13.

8. Fred H. Schmidt, "The Current Economic Conditions of the Mexican Americans" (Paper presented at the Conference on Economic and Educational Perspectives of the Mexican American, Aspen, Colo., August 1972), p. 5, as cited in Vernon M. Briggs, Jr., *The Mexico-United States Border: Public Policy and Chicano Economic Welfare,* Studies in Human Resource Development, no. 2 (Austin, Texas: Center for Human Resource Development and the Bureau of Business Research, 1974), p. 3.

9. "Poorest Area in America Begins to Fight Its Way Up," *U.S. News and World Report,* 7 October 1974, pp. 45-48.

10. Ovid Demaris, *Poso del Mundo: Inside the Mexican American Border from Tijuana to Matamoros* (Boston: Little, Brown & Co., 1970), p. 4.

11. Donald E. Mullen, "Illegal Aliens Stymie U.S. Immigration Office," *The News* (Mexico City), 12 January 1975, p.6.

12. Statement by Representative Dan Kubiak, *Austin American Statesman,* 24 December 1975.

13. *Austin Smerican Statesman,* 20 November 1975.

14. Dan Rosen, "High in the Sky," *New York Times Magazine,* 15 June 1975.

15. *The Daily Texan,* 28 October 1975.

16. U.S. Senate, *Health Services for Domestic Agricultural Workers,* Joint Hearing before the Subcommittee on Health and the Subcommittee on Migratory Labor (Washington, D.C.: Government Printing Office, 1972), p. 51.

PART I

The Culture of the Border

The Cultural Roots of the Border:
An Archaeologist's View

Ignacio Bernal

For some delightfully sibylline reason, it occurred to the editor of this volume to include an archaeologist. Like the sibyl, then, I must introduce some complications even if these refer to remote times.

The border zone with which we are concerned defines the exact political limits of two nations, Mexico and the United States. But another border is involved, a cultural one, which separates (although much less clearly) two cultures that grew out of different origins and histories.

Historians, sociologists, economists, and psychologists will speak about a dividing zone, which essentially derives from the Treaties of Onís (1819-32) and those following the War of 1847. They also consider the boundaries that marked the limits between the maximum expansion achieved by New Spain and those regions untouched by the Spanish Conquest. This is what is traditionally called history, although I refuse to accept the position that history begins only with the arrival of the Europeans.

But if we go back to the indigenous periods, we find yet another series of borders, not sharply defined it is true, but already existing, and which gradually changed during the pre-Cortesian past. The territorial divisions were so different, both geographically and in the cultural sense, that they converted the region we are examining into a nonborder, since this lay elsewhere and was slowly altered with the rhythm of various periods. I will not refer to the modern ramparts created by passports and customs offices but rather to various borders between cultures that were in different stages of development.

It is obvious that today's long boundary line between the United States and Mexico had no meaning in ancient times. In those days the borders between the various regions were different and separated contrasting cultures. Although showing certain similarities, they did not form a unit, nor did they share a common origin or a parallel history. In that period we find a civilization in one region; another area in the process of development, or underdeveloped as we say today; and two cultures that still retained a primitive background with only incipient agriculture and sedentary life. During long millennia these regions in various stages of development influenced each other in different ways.

There was civilization in Mesoamerica; a laborious culture in the United States Southwest. Areas of low culture were those of California in the west, and in the east the region from Soto la Marina northward, including the rest of Texas and Oklahoma and ending at the Bay of Galveston. Both the general area and the subdivisions among these three types of cultures were always arbitrary, and although various ways of grouping the peoples of this region have been proposed, I will use a simple scheme which perhaps is adequate for our purpose.

It seems unnecessary to mention the thousands of years that preceded the formation of the three cultural zones. During those millennia the Panamerican archaic period was developing; exact limits did not exist. It is only from the third millennium B.C., with the gradual growth of an economy based on agriculture and the remote origins of what would become Mesoamerican civilization, that we can point out, however tentatively, certain areas that were becoming differentiated and, therefore, creating borders.

Two thousand years later, toward the first century before Christ, the Mesoamerican border would move slightly north of the modern cities of Tepic and Morelia and extend toward the Gulf of Mexico, forming a northeastern wedge that crossed part of the Huasteca. South of this border lay Mesoamerica, and to the north that vast area the Spaniards would call vaguely "the Great Chichimeca."

Some nine centuries later, after the sensational period of Teotihuacán expansion and the true beginning of Mexican history, this border would remain surprisingly unchanged, save for extensions northward that reduced the Great Chichimeca and enlarged Mesoamerica. One extension reached the coastal region of the southern half of Sinaloa, while another included almost all the rest of Jalisco, large western sections of the states of Aguascalientes and Zacatecas, and even considerable land in Durango. To the east the border remained almost unchanged.

During the Toltec period, from the tenth century on, Mesoamerica broadened in the west, occupying all of Sinaloa as far as the Río del Fuerte, while in the Gulf of Mexico the northern border reached the Soto la Marina region. Nevertheless the Central Highlands' influence was apparently weaker than at the end of the Classic period. One can say, for the first time in native history, that Mesoamerica shared a border with the United States Southwest, since the Mesoamerican territory included southern Sonora. After the fall of Tula towards the year 1200 this border receded, when the Chichimecs increased their territory at the expense of Mesoamerica. All the noise and fury of the Mexica empire did not change this.

I have abridged the story drastically, but I hope I make clear that in the pre-Hispanic period, the border was not a political one like that separating our countries today. It was a cultural border, which of course was never the subject of treaties or of lines marked in a geography text. What it indicates is the difference between various cultural areas; one, as I said, was civilized, another in an advanced stage of culture, and others still quite primitive. Today we can recognize the existence or absence of various types of Mesoamerican traits in archaeological sites of the Great Chichimeca. Even this is variable, however, since these traits are often hidden beneath the local culture.

Outside Mesoamerica I would like now to try to define the limits of the high culture area, and also of the two most backward ones.

The region we call the United States Southwest was by far the most important extension of the high culture area. No matter how its cultures are grouped, archaeologically this area includes all the greater Colorado basin in the west, all the territory to the Pecos River in the east, then the land extending southward to the juncture of the Bravo and Conchos rivers, and reaching the Gulf of California at the mouth of the Fuerte River. Thus, in the United States it comprises the southern sections of Utah and Colorado, and all of New Mexico and Arizona (the "Four Corners"), and in Mexico a large part of Chihuahua and Sonora. The two Californias and Texas are clearly excluded.

The Southwest attained considerable eminence. It was an agricultural world, sedentary and pottery-producing. Its towns were fairly large and had a degree of planning and important architecture, although not to be compared with Mesoamerica. Mural painting was sometimes used. Commerce and ceremonialism were present although less elaborate than in Mesoamerica. Many of these features of high culture had Mesoamerican origins.

Concerning the areas of limited cultural development, the first one has been called Northeast Mexico-Texas. It was peopled by nomadic groups whose campsites were changed each season in order to follow the route for gathering nuts, cacti, roots, and other plant foods, and for hunting animals. Along the coast they obtained fish and other sea foods. They received nothing or very little from their neighbors in the southeastern United States, and it was not until shortly before the year 1000 that some Mesoamerican traits, such as ceramics, appeared in the area.

The other low culture area that is partly a Mexican borderland or frontier of New Spain is the west. But the two Californias and Nevada cannot be included in the same culture area, although they do share many features. They did not play an important role in ancient history and their contacts with the Southwest were fleeting. In certain subareas they also reflected a desert culture.

Outside the Southwest the Great Chichimeca was sparsely populated by nomadic or seminomadic groups, without the improvements that characterize Mesoamerica and the Southwest. The cultural differences between the divisions are tremendous. It must be emphasized that during most of its history Mesoamerica bordered precisely on the more backward peoples, and not the advanced ones of the Southwest. The term "Great Chichimeca" obviously refers more to ethnography than to data derived from archaeology. In view of the heterogeneous nature of the northern border of Mesoamerica, we can see that civilization had to contend with a great variety of neighbors.

It would be false to think of Mesoamerica as a monolithic state or a unified culture that encompassed all of its vast territory. It is evident that nuclear Mesoamerica was highly developed, and at the same time a series of marginal regions in the north and west were barely Mesoamerican and their degree of civilization varied considerably by area and period. Thus Sinaloa was always marginal, while Michoacán became fully Mesoamerican after the year 1000. These marginal areas—the marshlands—were not all the same either, nor did they attain the same degree of cultural evolution.

Ecology and geography must have been the basic causes of this variation, but I do not believe they were the only ones, since physically some marginal areas of Mesoamerica could well have developed into nuclear ones, and vice versa. The human factor was probably the most important one. Even with the powerful influence and development of the Olmecs, the geopolitical problem of Mesoamerica was defined and solved only after the time of Christ. This was due to the extraordinary success of Teotihuacán, which for the remainder of pre-Hispanic history marked the Central Highlands as the cultural axis, with the Mexico-Puebla valleys as its nucleus—a situation that also characterizes the present.

Even this nuclear Mesoamerica encompassed states and tribes that had great ceremonial complexity, and others that did not. Some regions were expanding, and some remained static: in other words, they resembled a whole mosaic of cultural, political, and economic conditions. Like the Great Chichimeca, it was an area formed of diverse parts. The logical consequence was the existence of a frontier area that had no precise boundaries, and the farther north this went, the less connection with civilization it had. This is especially clear in the east, not only in the Gulf Coast region but also in Coahuila and Texas.

The advancing and receding of the Mesoamerican border in the north apparently did not depend so much on conquest or massive interventions that we could call imperialistic, but rather on expansion of a different type, not by conquest but based on trade. It was the great merchants—whom the Mexica would call *pochtecas*—who were the principal means of bringing about the widespread diffusion that must have taken place in gradual stages. By this I mean that a merchant did not always travel personally, let us say from Tula to Casas Grandes, but his products or concepts spread from group to group, undergoing countless changes on the way, so that ideas and objects reached their final destination with features that were sometimes hard to recognize.

Interaction was taking place continuously during two millennia, with certain groups influencing others, and by many means causing the border to advance or regress. Using Kelley's metaphors,[1] we can say that the Mesoamerican often embarked on the Chichimec sea, and the Chichimecs frequently landed on Mesoamerican territory. This interaction was decisive for the cultural history of the two areas and produced a series of interesting intermediate situations that we hope some day to understand.

I have already said that this nonfrontier seems to be a fundamental factor for clarifying much of the past. Our interest lies in emphasizing that the vast dividing zone lay far south of the present border and did not separate two states but rather a civilized area from other areas in the north that were less, or not at all, civilized. Certain consequences that derive from this ancient situation still affect the life and culture of these two regions today.

After the voyages of Columbus and the later conquest of the southern area by Spain and of the territory in the north by other Europeans, the location of the present-day border region remained basically unchanged. The influence of what later would be the United States of America was not felt until much later. The Spanish influence, or rather that of New Spain, began in the sixteenth century. But basically these vast regions of northern Mexico and the southwestern United States were the colony of a colony, a ''Far West'' that was not altogether subjugated and where the Spanish establishments were like islands in a vast native sea of sedentary or nomadic peoples who followed almost pre-Columbian cultural patterns. New Spain violated those native culture areas beyond the borders of Mesoamerica, and from the viceregal capital tried to govern vast lands in the north that had never belonged to Mesoamerica.

Toward the end of the Colonial period, the Spanish government, influenced by José de Gálvez, tried to change this situation. They even went so far as to talk about creating a separate viceroyalty that would include the inner provinces. But Gálvez's ideas were never carried out except for brief episodes. Much has been said about political intrigue and viceregal ambition, but perhaps the main reason for failure was the tremendous difference between the real New Spain and its northern possessions. The process was to be repeated but in the opposite sense after the war with Texas and the Mexican-American war of 1847.

I will not dwell on this period since it is so well known, but I do want to point out that, until the beginning of the nineteenth century, New Spain bordered on groups that in general were not cohesive and had no well-defined borders. Later, a reduced part of Mexico bordered on the Republic of Texas, and after 1847, on the United States. It was then converted into the modern border we know today.

These and other events produced immense differences between central Mexico and its northern frontier region. I believe the same thing happened on the other side of the Río Bravo, known to the north as the Río Grande. Although for different reasons, we can find a parallel in the relationship between the Texas culture and that of New England, on the one hand, and central Mexico and its northern zone on the other. Although the cultural process is different, I mention it to show how complex the historical formation of the present border has been, in addition to the countless times its location has been changed.

The historical significance of the border region, which I have barely sketched in outline, is reflected in certain aspects of today's culture.

The obvious cultural differences that exist between northern Mexico and the rest of the nation—the part that was Mesoamerica—derive in large part from ancient conditions. The central Mexican represents the fusion of two worlds: the native and the Spanish one. This fusion shapes his personality, his way of life, and his future to such a degree that he cannot ignore the voice of either one without risking the loss of half his being. This is much less evident in northern Mexico.

If we should make a catalog of the innumerable native traits that have survived in the life of Mexico today, however altered they may be, I believe we would see that few of these appear in northern Mexico.

Culture there has aspects that refer to contemporary influence, but other more abstruse characteristics derive from the changing situation that I have tried to synthesize. We should note how different the Mexican-United States border is from one that is merely political, such as the one separating Mexico and Guatemala. In this case both nations had a common origin and a parallel history. Both were part of Mesoamerica and of the Spanish viceroyalty, and had a very similar period of independence. On the other hand, the indigenous influence in northern Mexico is infinitely less than in the rest of the country. Sometimes the difference lies in a complete absence of such native influence, when only certain traits have survived in ethnography, folklore, or crafts, but not in national life. In addition, the odd remnants of indigenous culture that survived in the north are curiously different from those that persisted farther south.

Examples from daily life in central Mexico call attention to some of its differences with the border region. What happens to the tortillas, tamales, atole, and the whole maize complex? Fruits and herbs for seasoning and many food preferences, the ways of preparing dishes or of combining ingredients, which often do not come from European cuisine but from the native one, are different in the north. Because its people did not practice agriculture, there is less use of corn and beans as staple foods. On the other hand, its consumption of meat is greater. The same is true of utensils such as the *metate,* the *comal,* lacquered bowls, *bules* or double gourds, and *equipales* or reed and leather chairs, all of which originated in Mesoamerica.

Linguistically there are great differences. We Mexicans use many words that come from Nahuatl. This is readily seen in the huge dictionary by Santamaría.[2] Along the border, Spanish is not mixed with Nahuatl but with English. Cervantes would be amazed if he were invited *"al 'lonche,' llegando en una 'troca,' y debiendo después pagar el 'bil.' "* Of course this may lead to a new international language, no matter how awful. But many of the changes in verbal conjugations that are considered typical of the Southwest also occur throughout Mexico; they indicate a rural type of speech. These include *"hablates,"* *"vivites,"* and is also true of metathesis as in *"pader."*

Near the border Mexicans seem to use less diminutives such as *"ahorita,"* *"al ratito,"* and *"lueguito,"* which, by decreasing the size of an object, make it sound more amiable. These come from the native world of courtesy which we inherit from Nahuatl, and the same is true of the "Please go ahead," and "This is your home." All this is completely foreign to the blunt directness of the Spaniard and typical of the bland politeness of the Mexican. It derives in part from the *"huehuetlatollis,"* or long ceremonial speeches that the Mexica loved so much.

Although growing out of the same historical background, but also for other complex reasons, I believe there are great differences in the markets, for example, and in the urban planning of towns where the typical ancient complex of church-palace-market-plaza formed a vital unit.

People from central Mexico consider the northerners less complicated than themselves, clearer and more direct, with simpler manners and less affability, but much more practical, enterprising, and efficient. This difference is due first of all to the fact that native influence did not exist in the north. The Spanish civilization was the same; what changed was the native one.

Like most borders, especially recent ones, there is considerable contrast between its modern cultures and the nuclear or aboriginal one. Here I do not refer to Indian differences but to European ones. Between New England and Texas, for instance, and between central Mexico and its northern frontier the differences are quite obvious. Since the pre-Columbian past scarcely played a role in the border areas and they are therefore mainly of European ancestry, are their present similarities due to that fact or to the interaction between both?

Some of my fellow essayists speak of *two* human groups: the United States and the Mexican. Is this what we really mean? Perhaps if we would discuss—apart from Indian ancestry or cultural influence—the border cultures of today, precisely as border cultures and not as small segments of larger nations, we would come closer to the truth.

NOTES

1. J. Charles Kelley, Basil C. Hedrick, and Carroll L. Riley, eds., *The Mesoamerican Southwest: Readings in Archaeology, Ethnohistory, and Ethnology* (Carbondale: Southern Illinois University Press, 1974), pp. 23-25.
2. Francisco J. Santamaría, *Diccionario de mejicanismos* (Mexico City: Ed. Porrúa, 1959).

2

The Borderlands:
Ideas on a Leafless Landscape

Joe B. Frantz

North Americans have a sometimes deserved reputation for being unthinking and insensitive. Accusations appear abroad, as characterized by the so-called Ugly American who means well but frequently blunders because he just does not understand. At home such charges emanate particularly from the field of civil rights, where the Anglo American has a history of ignoring certain rights of minorities, not through malice but simply because he has never thought about them.

The North American historian is just as guilty. He has built a whole school of frontier history around the writings of Frederick Jackson Turner, basically a careful and thinking man, but one who talked and wrote in such terms as the "cutting edge of civilization" and about the thin line that separated the westering civilization from the retreating wilderness. In these preachments the historian seldom if ever challenged the thesis that the wilderness was real by asking whether the moving frontier stopped at a line separating established cultures rather than one denoting a demarcation between civilization and wilderness.

Nor did the historian consider, much less expatiate on the fact, that the farther into his wilderness the North American traveled, the less wilderness, real or synthetic, did he face. In that vast area between the Virginia Piedmont and the cisalpine portion of the Rockies the frontiersman ran more and more into people—Europeans, who were the only ones he really recognized as people. True, they were scattered, as the French trappers were throughout the broad upper Mississippi and Ohio valleys. But the French were there nonetheless, adapting, and in their way civilizing, for a century or more before the Anglo-American frontiersman caught up with them.

But when the Anglo Americans moved out of the trees and onto the plains of the Southwest they truly lost all excuse for claiming themselves as a civilizing force. Here they ran into stabilized Indian pueblos, ongoing civilizations hundreds of years older than their own. Here they met the Spanish Mexicans, with a capital at Santa Fe that made their own later capitals in Philadelphia, New York, and Washington look upstart by comparison. And they found an organized mission system stretching from Los Adaes in western Louisiana to Misión San Antonio de Padua in upper California, as hard at work to bring the Indians into the folds of Christianity as any hot-eyed congregationalist from the newfangled Bay State of Massachusetts. The Southwest did not *have* to be civilized because it already had the accouterments of civilization—government, taxes, prisons, schools, churches, sin, and social strata.

So the idea of an edge separating civilization on the east from wilderness on the west just does not apply in the case of the Spanish Borderlands. The Borderlands were settled and civilized and stabilized long before New England and New York began to think of independence. Civilization did not lie on the eastern side of the moving frontier—civilization lay on both sides of that cutting edge, except that this thought never seemed to occur to the North Americans pushing westward nor to the chroniclers writing about the experience generations later.[1]

When the North Americans passed that part of the void peopled only by aborigines, they found then that they were latecomers and that instead of bringing civilization to the frontier, they were encountering civilization. The fact that the culture confronting them was European did not give them pause, for the culture was still alien to their Anglo-American life-style. To fuse two or three cultures did not seem to occur to them. Rather, as a pragmatic people, they observed the Hispanic culture as being as alien as the aboriginal culture, and must have reasoned, if indeed they thought at all, that the only way to handle an alien situation was to root it out. But, of course, they were dealing with a people who were dug in deeply already, and who did not root out easily. Thus began a conflict which has given so much vitality to the story of the Spanish Borderlands.

Just as the storied Robber Barons of latter nineteenth-century United States fame were not called by that name until Matthew Josephson's book appeared in the 1930s, so the people along the Borderlands did not use the term "Borderlands" until after 1921 when the *Yale Chronicles of America* series brought out Herbert Eugene Bolton's volume, *The Spanish Borderlands:*

A Chronicle of Old Florida and the Southwest.[2] In historical circles, then, the term is barely a half-century old, as is the argument of where the Borderlands exist, a viewpoint that varies with an author's or discussant's interest. For Bolton the Borderlands included all that area within the United States once held by Spain—from Florida to California. Today most historians have edged the eastern boundary ever westward, until now it is frequently restricted to the area from Texas to the Pacific.

Even when we take the more limited view, we can't be too precise about the geography of the Borderlands, for in the United States we are not even sure of the limits of the Southwest. To some, the Southwest includes only New Mexico, Arizona, and extreme southern California. Texas thinks of itself—of itself alone—as the Southwest. In athletic circles a Southwest Conference exists that includes the University of Arkansas. All of these southwestern areas lie west of the University of Michigan, which in its school song speaks of its teams as the "champions of the West," although it lies a good thousand miles east of Denver.

But since we have to limit somewhere, I place my boundaries for the Spanish Borderlands today from Texas to California, with an occasional bow toward Spanish Louisiana. My reasoning may be due more to territorial conditioning than to history, but to me the Borderlands must lie opposite the states of north Mexico, must be arid, must have a strong and identifiable Indian culture with a strong Hispanic overlay, and must be basically trackless and treeless except for defiant, contrary islands here and there. The culture is a range culture, the vistas have spaciousness, and the people show an amplitude of spirit that disappears when they pack more closely together.

The tragedy of the Borderlands is not that its people could not coalesce, but that one group seemingly had to be superimposed on the other. Historically the Indian, the original inhabitant of the Borderlands, seemed destined to lose, for he was running into two expansionist peoples. The northward civilizing push of the Spanish has not been sufficiently acclaimed, though we endow individuals like Francisco Vásquez de Coronado with a considerable niche in our national pantheon of heroic antecedents. But other Spaniards left the lush life in the Valley of Mexico and in the Bajío above it, and thrust themselves forward into a land disposed to yield nothing ungrudgingly. On today's fast highways the areas from Saltillo to Torreón and Piedras Negras, from Chihuahua to Juárez, from Guaymas to Nogales, or lately from La Paz to Tijuana are interminable and forbidding. What must they have been like or how much they must have affected the early Spaniard when he traversed that bleak landscape at a pace of thirty miles a day, knowing that for the past ten days he had walked from one windswept horizon to another and that after he camped at night he would awaken to see the same horizon another day's journey away, and that he would repeat this experience interminably, day after day after day. The three elements of life that men usually take for granted would seldom come from the land—no Elysian Fields of water and berries and fruits, just scant shelter, and only an occasional hide or field of rushes to shelter his body from the penetrating winter wind or the searing summer sun.

And yet they trod on, leaving a part of themselves as they passed through a barren land into another equally barren land, and they built Tucson and Santa Fe and Santa Barbara. And they introduced European cattle into the future United States. They grew grapes and made wine and planted gardens. In the winter they saved souls, only to see those blithe spirits disperse with the coming of spring and the flowering of meadows. They introduced law, systems of water rights, and a sense of organization, and they improvised to make local conditions fit rules disseminated from undiscerning places like Madrid and Mexico. They held fandangos, they danced and laughed and flirted and married and got drunk and suffered remorse and bred and, all things considered, they flourished.

They built a superstructure of Spanish heritage, overlaying the Indian culture that preceded them. Overlaying and absorbing, but not destroying. Basically they perceived the Indian as a human being, and echoing Bartolomé de las Casas, felt that all the people of the world were truly people. Although they might be paternal toward the Indian, nevertheless like good, stern parents they recognized that he was some kind of child of God and therefore worthy of a sort of contained freedom. But most of all, they took the land as they found it, and they adapted. They adapted in a way that holds lessons for us latter-day saints who have suddenly discovered environmental values. If we North Americans could have learned the lesson they had to teach us, we quite possibly could have avoided many mistakes that haunt us today and would not have to echo the late Noel Coward when he wrote, ''I have those twentieth century blues.''

One European term avoided on the Spanish Borderlands, or perhaps misused, is ''frontier'' or ''*frontera.*'' Europeans speak of the boundary that separates France from Germany or France from Iberia as a frontier. Such a boundary may be natural, as between France and Spain, or may be political, as between France and Germany. In the political instance, Alsace-Lorraine can move into Germany or into France with equal physical and comparable economic facility. But moving Catalonia or Aragón back and forth across the Pyrenees would unscramble the orderliness of life in either of those regions.

For these frontiers are not frontiers in the sense of empty spaces. They are frontiers filled with people, who in turn are filled with the passion of nationalism. But the frontier of the Spanish Borderlands is not a frontier between nations. The frontier of Chihuahua differs little from the frontier of New Mexico, while the mesquite and huisache in Coahuila, Nuevo León, and Tamaulipas look exactly like the mesquite and huisache along the Texas side of the Río Grande. On the Mexican side, Spanish is the official language, while on the Texas side there is spoken an informal language loosely described as Spanish. The same observation holds true for Sonora and Arizona, and for Baja California Norte and California. In short, the situation may be summed up as a matter of vantage point: the Sonoran desert extends into Arizona, or the Arizona desert extends into Sonora. The culture accompanying that desert is similar on either side. In Laredo and McAllen the *cantinas* dispense Dos X's and Carta Blanca almost as readily as if they were homemade, and hungry Texans probably eat more Mexican food, pseudo or real, per capita than do the Mexicans. In the European sense then, the frontier just does not exist along our borderlands.

So in Mexico they speak of the frontier as that area to the north in which population is sparse and civilization thins out. And in the United States they speak of the frontier in the words of Frederick Jackson Turner and Walter Prescott Webb—as the area to the west where the population is sparse and civilization again thins out. The concept of frontier is the same in either country, and neither natural boundaries, like the Río Grande, nor artificial boundaries, as laid down by purchase or conquest, can change the interpretation and the understanding of the word.

In the Mexican-United States sense then, no frontier exists between the two nations. Yet all along the two thousand miles a borderland persists. The trouble is that needs and opportunities do not stop short of a drawn line. If Phoenix needs water for irrigation and for its people, so does Hermosillo. The need is mutual, and in a broad sense the resource or danger is therefore mutual. Apaches fought without regard to the border, committing their depredations or defending their homelands, depending on the point of view, on either side. Mexicans south of the Río Grande crossed into Texas to recover strayed or stolen cattle, and were called bandits by the Texans. Tejanos crossed to that south side of the Río Grande into Mexico to round up their cattle that had strayed or were stolen and were labeled *bandidos* by the Mexicans. On either side of the border both groups fought for the same goals. And they viewed each other in precisely the same terms. Mexico carried on a massive inoculation campaign against *aftosa,* while United States technicians assisted because, if they didn't, the United States would soon feel the thrust of the dreaded hoof and mouth disease.

One hundred miles east of El Paso and Juárez, near where Guadalupe Peak lifts its sheer limestone wall nine thousand feet above the level plain, a vast deposit of salt lay for centuries under a chain of shallow lakes. The Mexicans, first on the scene, had paid no attention to the deposit, for their interests tended northwestward to the Tularosa or San Andrés *salinas*. But during the American Civil War, the Mexicans decided that the salt near Guadalupe might be superior. Despite the fact that the trip to the lakes included seventy waterless miles, men journeyed from the interior of Mexico to obtain salt for their families and neighbors. Americans, of both Anglo and Mexican extraction, followed the Mexicans into Chihuahua and Sonora, selling and trading salt.

Theirs was a good business, except that some North Americans, astute if not principled, reasoned that since the lakes sat on public lands, they could get control of them by obtaining state bounties or land scrip. From as far away as San Antonio, over six hundred miles, Samuel Maverick put together enough scrip to cover two sections of land. At this land grab, the Mexican viewpoint ranged somewhere between sadness and outrage. But those North Americans who had been left outside of Maverick's holding resolved to act—to form a so-called "salt ring" to take up the deposits missed by Maverick. Joining the ring was Father Antonio Borrajo, the parish priest of San Elizario, a churchman with great influence among the Mexicans along the border.

The ensuing story is a complex one that can be summed up quickly as the El Paso Salt War of 1877. All along the upper valley of the Río Grande, war broke out. The cry of "¡mátenlo! ¡mátenlo!"—"kill him! kill him!"—was heard frequently. Men were shot, Texas Rangers were called, and reputations were ruined. The madness came to an end only after a firing squad in San Elizario lined up certain offending North Americans, shot them, yelled for more *gringo* blood, and then listened as one of their own, Chico Barela, told his fellow Mexicans that if they persisted in the blood bath he "would turn his men loose on them."

When Barela spoke, men listened. Barela was from Ysleta, a man of no education who had a semiprivate army of Mexicans there. Generally quiet, with light skin, brown hair, and blue eyes, Barela on the surface was another peaceable border farmer, his serenity marred only by the fact that the betrothed of his daughter Pancha had been killed and the girl never married. Earlier, when the North Americans had tried to send a troop of fourteen men through Ysleta, Barela had stopped them with an improvised army of his own, and had told the *norteamericano* captain, "There is not a man among us who is not a resident of this country. This matter is none of your business." To prove his point, he and his men had driven off the Americans.

Now Barela escorted the hated Texas Rangers as far as Ysleta, which cooled the people around San Elizario but also brought out United States troops from three forts. The governor of Texas, Richard B. Hubbard, sent to Silver City, New Mexico, for thirty hired gunmen, who quickly put themselves under the command of Sheriff Charles Kerber of El Paso. Many of the Mexicans on the United States side fled in terror into Mexico, where as winter came on they perished both for want of food and from exposure to the cold in and around Zaragoza. The gang from New Mexico raped and robbed, and were finally dispersed; the soldiers began to quarrel among themselves, even to the point of murder, and gradually the war petered out.

Naturally, the Congress of the United States sent a delegation to El Paso for an official investigation. Witnesses were struck dumb, and soon the incident was forgotten by everyone except those who took part. But on either side of the border they did not forget, although, in the words of C. L. Sonnichsen, "No one was punished; no one was tried; no one was even arrested." One Texas Ranger, filing a minority report, held that the Mexicans were more numerous and better organized than had been admitted and urged the United States to demand that the Mexican government punish criminals and make reparations totaling $31,000. Both requests were ignored.

In the long view of history, the incident is unimportant except as another illustration that border friction can flare very easily and that, in such instances, pride of race will override official citizenship. It also proves, as its principal chronicler avers, that "men can die bravely in a bad cause "[3]

The Borderlands, then, like the European frontier, are a breeding ground for little tensions. Leander H. McNelly might lead his Texas Rangers on a charge into Mexico in defiance of all rules of border sanctity, thereby enraging Mexico's officialdom, terrifying the local citizens, and scandalizing the United States Secretary of War. And Pancho Villa might make raids into the Big Bend country and again into Columbus, New Mexico, killing more *norteamericanos* than the United States realized were there; and John J. Pershing might use northern Mexico as a punitive finishing school for his future duties with the American Expeditionary Force in France. But none of this border friction was ever allowed to erupt into a major war, only in skirmishes, some of them protracted and all of them more on the *opéra bouffe* level than vicious or tragic—more on the order of high jinks or effervescence engendered by an excess of *machismo*.

Exceptions, of course, are the struggle along the imprecise border separating the newly proclaimed independent Republic of Texas from Mexico and the offshoot a decade later known as the Mexican War. In some respects the Texas Revolution occurred in part because of a union of Texans with other Mexican liberal groups to force President Antonio López de Santa Anna to adhere to the democratic principles enunciated in the Mexican Constitution of 1824. The flag that flew over the Alamo was the Mexican flag of 1824 with those numerals plainly imprinted upon it.

But in its less admirable form the Texas Revolution also represented a conflict of cultures and a suspicion born of differing ethnicity and language. It also represented a part of the kinetic nationalism developing in the United States, which became enveloped in that evangelical neoreligious cloak known as Manifest Destiny. Texas was supposed to have been colonized by Anglo Americans as a buffer between Mexico and the United States with its taking ways. But the only people colonized in numbers were those same Anglo Americans who brought their Manifest Destiny state of mind with them. And so a slice of the Mexican pie approximately the size of France was lifted from Mexico and deposited as a temporary independent republic, still a diminished buffer of sorts, which shortly would disappear entirely to become a portion of the expanding United States.

The war with Mexico was not fought for principle, except as aggrandizement of the United States was a matter of principle. Probably the war was inevitable, for Mexico was still shaking down from its ten-year total immersion in the waters of revolution against Spain. Evidence exists that at first many conservative Mexicans welcomed the coming of United States troops, hoping that they would bring stability to a nation that existed, in the words of one Texas critic, in a state of "chronic revolutionizing." But the United States was not interested in Mexican stability, except as it prevented occasional incursions of Mexican raids into Texas. Instead, the United States was more concerned with stabilizing the border, even if such stabilization brought the "burden" of new territory. Although the United States purchased a region that ensured its greatness from coast to coast, the Borderland was moved only a few hundred miles or so south, or roughly from Santa Fe to El Paso, from Tucson to Nogales, or from Monterey to San Diego.

As for violence, it should be pointed out that modern research indicates a smaller incidence of crime along the Borderlands than in the more thickly settled areas. The statistics are not overpowering, either for the areas to the interior or for the Borderlands, for crime records generally were undependable. For instance, in 1880 San Francisco reported 8,694 saloons, while Boston—50 percent larger—had only 2,347. Leadville, Colorado, a comparative village, "calmly indicated an astonishing 100 houses of prostitution, or one for every 148 residents." According to the census, Boston hardly knew what a bordello looked like.[4] Now no one who knows the history of those cities would deny that San Francisco and Leadville were intemperate towns, insofar as vice and pleasure seeking were concerned. But no one who knows Boston and the thirst of its immigrant population would believe that the ratio of saloons to people would be only one-sixth of what it was in San Francisco or that the carnal needs of that same population would be virtually nonexistent. While Boston may have been the home of puritanism, no reason exists to believe that its people were pure.

And while Boston is under consideration, consider the fact that in colonial days "it had more than its share of seamen, dockworkers and unemployed laborers looking for excitement." The Boston scene provided a natural outlet for men to "let off steam under the cloak of patriotism. The Stamp Tax Riots, the Boston Massacre, the burning of the British revenue cutter *Gaspee,* and the Boston Tea Party, were all part of a carefully executed campaign of violent politics," according to one historian.[5]

On the other hand, the Borderlands had little such opportunity to mask its hates as patriotic, for the area was insufficiently populated for citizens' extralegal activities to have any organized effect on broad aims in either the United States or Mexico. Along the borderline men were necessarily individualists, not part of a movement. They shot to take; they knifed from fear; they brawled because they were drunk. They did not get caught up in national political movements, but kept their vendettas singular and direct rather than massive and adroitly political. If they were political, politics then was local, never national. An assassination or a burning in the Distrito Federal or the District of Columbia might have national or even international significance; the same activity in Cananea or Lordsburg was damned simply as an isolated act of viciousness. Over the generations *leaders* were shot in Washington, Buffalo, New York, and Mexico City, not to mention latter-day tragedies in Memphis, Los Angeles, and Dallas. Only men, never leaders, were shot along the border.

The simple fact is that violence in the Borderlands was more spectacular. Kill three men in a free-for-all in an eastern tavern and who notices? Stage a shootout at the O. K. Corral in Tombstone in which some generally worthless characters get killed, and Zane Grey, the most widely selling novelist of the American West, can write lurid accounts, as in *To the Last Man,* to be read by generations of youth and adults, Borderland housewives, and New York dentists. The moviemakers go on to recreate the sordid episode, and then film sequels and variations, thus converting Tombstone into a trap and a mecca for tens of thousands of sweltering tourists braving one-hundred-ten-degree heat to see where this heroic event happened. Tombstone, away off from anywhere, attracts more tourists than Faneuil Hall in Boston or Chapultepec Heights in Mexico. A tawdry gunbattle of no significance outdraws the patriotic sites of two fine nations.

Let us examine another aspect of this Borderland preoccupation with violence. With the *norteamericano*'s penchant for self-flagellation, he sees his countrymen's move against Mexico as a facet of his tendency toward racial arrogance. In one sense he is correct, but the difficulty is that we magnify such incidents and denounce the excess of the American against his Mexican neighbor as an unremitting, exclusive sort of hatred. In perspective, we must remember that beginning in the 1830s mob violence "became a feature of American life—not urban life, or southern life, or western life—but American life."[6] Thus we find mobs active throughout New England against Catholics and Abolitionists, harassing the Catholics and blacks in Philadelphia and Cincinnati, running Mormons out of rural Missouri and Illinois, and chasing Mexicans in Texas, gamblers in Vicksburg, landlords in New York, and prostitutes, foreigners, and any other nonestablishment people "wherever they found them."[7]

The disturbances occurred equally in urban and rural areas. Whatever the reasons, violence had become, as the Black activist Rap Brown would say a century and a quarter later, "as American as cherry pie." Thus, in May 1844, thousands of Protestants roamed the streets of Philadelphia for three days looking for Irish Catholics, priests, and nuns, killing thirteen, injuring fifty others, and destroying two churches. In Lawrence, Massachusetts, a mob of fifteen hundred burned the homes and churches of Irish workers. St. Louis suffered an election riot in 1854 that resulted in the death of ten men, while in Louisville, Kentucky, a mob marched through the gambling section of town, killing twenty men.[8] In Texas a little later, the "people," whatever that term means, shot Germans with Unionist sympathies as willfully as they would have shot runaway Blacks or Mexicans with unexplained possession of cattle. Only the fact that these incidents occurred in the Borderlands makes them different from what happened to the north and east.

All over the United States racial difficulties cropped up, the most notable occurring during the Civil War. When in July 1863, street gangs of Irish workers and others, fearful of being drafted into the Union Army, fought local police, United States troops rushed in from the Gettysburg campaign, and between times killed or wounded more than a thousand Negroes, just because they were seen as threatening white workers' jobs. The often sordid history of the decimation of the native Indian population is too well known to recount here, but in part is explainable, if not excusable, again because of the conflict of cultures and the white man's bigotry toward the red man. But since the white Protestant practiced the same sort of bigotry against the white Mormon, then we must be cautious in placing too great weight on a charge of racial arrogance. If the majority of Mexicans had been as white as the whitest sand, would Texans have moved against them because they were Catholic, spoke a different language, and followed a different governmental system? I suspect so. If the Mexican had been white and Protestant, the language alone would have been a barrier. Any variance from the Anglo American's norm would have frustrated him. And frustration, in the words of David Abrahamsen, "is the wet nurse of violence."

On the other hand, perhaps Mexicans should light candles on the altar of the Blessed Virgin in thanks for this arrogance on the part of the *norteamericanos*. At the time of the signing of the Treaty of Guadalupe Hidalgo in 1848, if the United States had behaved like the Prussian victors in the Franco-Prussian war of the 1870s or the Allied victors at Paris in 1919, the *norteamericanos* might have taken anywhere from half to all of modern Mexico. But if it had been adamant in its demands for the utmost territory, the United States would have been forced to absorb an alien culture, government, and religion. Leaders of the United States, understanding the problem that would ensue, feared that the assimilation of the Mexican into the Anglo-Saxon mores of the United States was impossible, or at the least, difficult. How much more judicious to take less land but acquire more serenity and orderliness! So the United States agreed instead to the cession of the sparsely settled Southwest, confident in its forevision that its whites would one day become the dominant group in that area. We didn't gobble up everything in sight, partly because we felt we couldn't digest such a giant bite.

The incredible outgrowth of all this *gringo* aggression is that, as Daniel Cosío Villegas has observed, these "events, painful and unjustifiable as they undoubtedly were, have left the Mexicans neither a desire for revenge, nor a feeling of enduring rancor." Instead, still quoting Don Daniel, the Mexican reacts with "feelings of distrust and skepticism"[9] whenever another United States politician proclaims that from this day forward the two countries are going to be the greatest of friends. Animosity reaches back for generations, even centuries, and stretches from Colorado River water rights along the Sonora-Arizona border across to the Gulf of Mexico, where Texan and Yucatecan fishermen sometimes grapple over shrimp beds.

No better example can be found than the Chamizal boundary dispute between Mexico and the United States over the six hundred acres between El Paso and Juárez lying between the bed of the Río Grande as surveyed in 1852 and the river's present channel. The dispute originated in the interpretation of the Treaty of Guadalupe Hidalgo, signed nearly 130 years ago. The Río Grande, of course, would not hold to channels, and the question of whether ownership of the Chamizal area shifted with channel changes became a continuing source of irritation between the two nations. In 1884, a treaty stated that the boundary "shall follow the center of the normal channel . . . notwithstanding any alterations in the banks or in the course of those rivers, provided that such alterations be effected by natural causes through slow and gradual erosion and deposit of alluvium, and not by the abandonment of any existing riverbed and the opening of a new one." In short, when changes in the course of a river are caused by a deposit of alluvium, the boundary changes with the river, but when changes are due to avulsion, the boundary remains with the old channel.

Nothing was settled really. Successive attempts to end the dispute through diplomacy were abortive. In 1910, an arbitration committee was named to decide "solely and exclusively as to whether the international title to the Chamizal Tract is in the United States of America or in Mexico." Without going into detail, after the arbitration commission divided the tract between the two countries, the United States refused to put the terms of the award into effect.[10] From 1911 forward the issue again irritated both sides, but particularly Mexico, which accused the United States of bad faith. Although many suggestions were broached, the United States continued to hold the Chamizal under its jurisdiction and that of the state of Texas. The only advantage was to the local taxpayer, whose delinquent taxes were not contested by either the state or federal government because his property lay in disputed territory. For all practical purposes the Chamizal became an integral part of the city of El Paso.

Then on January 14, 1963, the Chamizal dispute was formally settled with exchange of ratification of a treaty which followed the 1911 arbitration recommendation. In 1964, President Adolfo López Mateos and President Lyndon B. Johnson met on the border to end the dispute officially. In October 1967, Johnson met with Mexican President Gustavo Díaz Ordaz on the border to formally proclaim the settlement.

Although the Chamizal was a small dispute when viewed on the large canvas of international diplomacy, more than a century had been required to settle it. Now the only big unsettled border problem between the two nations concerns the salinity of the Colorado River, and one can agree with Cosío Villegas when he writes "With the exception of Canada, it is doubtful that the United States has had better [official relations] at any time with any other country, especially with any of its neighbors," than it has with Mexico.[11] Cosío Villegas continues:

And yet I believe that Mexico and the United States are so far from resolving their problems that, in truth, it can be said that the process of understanding has not yet even begun. The abundance of past issues, the persistence and magnitude of present ones, could ruin official relations or convert them into a meaningless farce. And not, of course, because the leaders of either country lack good will or even intelligence, but because the forces working against good relations are numerous and persistent, exceptionally vigorous, and to make matters worse, irrational in nature.[12]

While the historian's role is not to indulge in *cantina* conjecture, one can't help wondering what the history of the Borderlands would have been if in 1849 gold had been discovered at Sutter's Mill *in Mexico!* Or if all the copper in Arizona and Utah, the uranium in New Mexico, the California timber, lettuce, grapes, and climate and the silver in Nevada had been left under Mexican sovereignty. These resources—agricultural, mineral, and hydraulic—, some of which were extraordinary, gave the United States a balance and abundance which has helped to make it a power in the world. Mexico in turn has been fragmented by mountains and dried by desert, and its lush areas enervated by heat and humidity. It has had to rescue its mineral resources from foreign hands, and it has had to go outside its borders for markets. In many ways the two countries were about equal in the 1840s, but the United States wound up holding a winning lottery ticket which it could cash in for investment and aggrandizement.

Thus far not much has been said here in the traditional sense about the historiography of the Borderlands. The omission has been deliberate. Hubert Howe Bancroft wrote his six-volume history of Mexico between 1880 and 1888. Before that appeared William H. Prescott's *History of the Conquest of Mexico,* which is great primarily because it was early. Likewise, Bancroft's two volumes on *The North Mexican States and Texas* are, in the words of Eugene C. Barker, "the most satisfactory comprehensive history of Texas available."[13] Again, though Bancroft's works are dated, his fame endures in great part because of the collections of information which he assembled and the fact that he acted as a springboard for other students, both north and south of the Borderlands. Bancroft's Borderlands, insofar as the United States is concerned, dealt considerably more with California than with the area to the east.

As indefatigable as Bancroft himself was Herbert Eugene Bolton, previously mentioned as the popularizer of the phrase, "the Spanish Borderlands." When he wrote a book by that title, the subtitle delineated the region as *A Chronicle of Old Florida and the Southwest.* Probably one of Bolton's editors, perhaps Allen Johnson, editor of the *Chronicles of America* series, deserves the credit for having originated the term, but as in the story of the host of precursors of Robert Fulton's steamboat, Bolton "certainly was its great popularizer," and he inspired a small legion of students to study this area of American history. In many ways his articles in such journals as the

American Historical Review and his chapter, "Defensive Spanish Expansion and the Significance of the Spanish Borderlands," in the *Trans-Mississippi West* are as important as his books.

Bolton is also almost solely responsible for the discovery of Father Eusebio Francisco Kino, the so-called "Padre on Horseback," to whom Arizona and the North American cattle industry owe so much. Although Father Kino may have thought that California was a large island, he was ready to admit his mistake when he pursued the Gila and the Colorado to the head of the Gulf of California. *"California no es isla, sino peninsula,"* he wrote in triumph as he began to rectify previous American maps. Bolton wrote three books on this remarkable man, the last a full biography entitled *Rim of Christendom: A Biography of Eusebio Francisco Kino, Pacific Coast Pioneer,* reprinted as recently as 1960. In fact, it is notable that in the capitol building in Washington, D.C., where each state is permitted just two statues of individuals who are its principal heroes, two of the statues in the precious selection are of Spanish Borderland missionary-explorers: Kino for Arizona and Fray Junípero Serra of California.

Charles W. Hackett, a Bolton student who, after a lapse of time, took his mentor's place at the University of Texas, was another assiduous delver into early Borderland history. Although his work is notable for its completeness and adds considerable knowledge, it is short on interpretation.

On the Mexican side two of the principal interpreters of the Borderlands are Vito Alessio Robles and Daniel Cosío Villegas. Alessio Robles's two-volume *Coahuila y Texas* deserves the appellation of being a standard resource. His biography, *Francisco de Urdiñola y el norte de la Nueva España,* is valuable for understanding early relationships. Alessio Robles also edited the four volumes of Alexander von Humboldt's groundbreaking *Ensayo político sobre el Reino de Nuevo España,* which has been widely translated and extensively read a century and a half after publication. In a public career that extended over a half-century, Daniel Cosío Villegas published innumerable books, two of which are especially pertinent here: *Estados Unidos contra Porfirio Díaz* and *Extremos de América,* both now translated into English. Here is possibly Mexico's most incisive interpretive intellect at work, a multidisciplined man who represents the Emersonian ideal of a scholar—"a man thinking." He also founded and for several years edited *Historia Mexicana,* a high-quality professional journal whose contents at times bear on the problems discussed here.

Walter Prescott Webb was also intrigued by the Borderlands, but, as was his wont, perceived it in an institutionalized manner. As a young man he had absorbed an American populist viewpoint that for years left him narrowly unconscious of the culture and aspirations of the people on the far side of "his" border. Webb's was more a nineteenth-century view in which the United States was both right and inexorable. This is not to fault the man, for he merely reflected the same lack of concern and understanding toward other people that characterized most of his contemporaries. He arrived at most intellectual decisions late in life, and in his later years regularly said that he intended to rewrite *The Texas Rangers* and *The Great Plains* so as to give the Mexicans and the Indians a fairer portrait.

Webb had ridden along the border with the Texas Rangers, who in their turn believed that every Mexican was ipso facto bent on circumventing the laws of the United States. Undoubtedly, Webb viewed Mexicans through a Ranger lens and consequently the object of his sight was colored by his intimate association with this remarkable lawkeeping body. Webb saw Mexicans as bootleggers and smugglers, and felt that any Mexican on the United States side of the border who couldn't explain why he was there was probably up to no good. The fact that he neither spoke nor read Spanish must have hampered his efforts at understanding. Again, later in his life Webb often regretted that he had not learned Spanish because of the enrichment the knowledge would have given him on the subjects in which he was interested.

Webb saw the Borderland as a desert, short on water and overbearing in climate. He felt that border people magnified their triumphs *and* their defeats and that they exaggerated because they had so little to talk about. He liked their excesses, but as he often said of his fellow Texans, he wished they would show more intellectual concern and especially would learn silence.

But all of these opinions came in Webb's conversations with friends. After he published *The Great Plains* in 1931 and *The Texas Rangers* in 1935, he abandoned those more local concerns to chase after world frontiers. A man acutely aware of his shortcomings, he knew that in many ways he was a sort of southwestern parochial, but felt that he shared with Borderlands people an ability to bring more perspective to large problems while indulging in talk about local problems barely above the rank of gossip.

As to other Borderlands, he was intrigued by them only if they fit his thesis that the frontier had spawned a set of conditions whose validity was rapidly passing. Siberia with its thousands of miles, largely impenetrable, along the boundary lines of central and southern Asia, intrigued him, but mainly because it disputed his own theory that an open frontier brought boom conditions that in turn led to a sort of democracy and a tendency toward expansive capitalism. He felt that the experience of the Australian frontier most nearly duplicated the qualities of the American frontier, though Australia is an island entire of itself and shares no common borderland with other nations and cultures.

Likewise the South African frontier concerned him, and he felt that southwesterners on either side of the Mexican-United States Borderland would be at home in that region of the world and would face similar opportunities and rejections. He accepted the Canadian borderland, French or Anglo, as an extension of the United States's experience, and he felt that Argentina's south and west resembled the west of the United States, except that Argentina's grass was more lush. Finally, Brazil was an object of his concern, but since he read neither Portuguese nor Spanish, he couldn't study much beyond popular accounts of that forested subcontinent.

Journals such as the *Southwestern Historical Quarterly,* the *New Mexico Historical Review,* and *Hispanic American Historical Review* are also valuable. On the whole Mexican journals have focused less on the Borderlands than have those in the southwestern United States, and have done comparatively little with more modern studies.

Throughout this somewhat attenuated essay I have spent an inordinate amount of time analyzing in terms of people, but to me people comprise the special character of the Spanish Borderlands. The Anglo Americans who came to Texas found a reasonably sophisticated, organized government under a foreign power. The same thing happened to those men who walked the trail into Santa Fe or followed Max Moorhead's trail to Chihuahua. In a strong sense, cultures collided and something had to give. The Yankees made the Mexicans do the giving. As John Francis Bannon, another priest-historian of the Borderlands, writes, "The Borderlanders were foreigners, and the Anglo-American frontiersman was a particularly chauvinistic soul. More than that, the Borderlanders were, ethnically, a curious breed of men, in many instances the product of the racial intermingling with the native Americans, whom the Anglos disliked and distrusted and whom they never took the trouble to understand. It might have been no better for the Borderlanders had their blood line been pure Spanish."[14]

But the Borderlands were too remote and promised too little to attract the better classes of society, whether from New Spain or from the United States. A naturally quarrelsome and often acquisitive people, the Borderlanders were apprehensive about the Indians, Christianized or not. An Indian was an Indian, and not to be trusted. Since distrust breeds distrust, then suspicion on the Borderland ran rampant. Nor had the *gringo* Borderlanders been given time to adjust. They still built their houses as if they were being erected in Swampscott or Salem. Adobe houses to them, no matter how much more indigenous and more comfortable, were nothing but dried mud. They could not comprehend a country without trees and without water, nor did they understand the dietary differences. Truly the Anglo Americans entered the area too soon. They themselves needed more seasoning before encountering a *chile* culture, less callow innocence.

And yet the Spanish Borderlands made their imprint on these hostile, tentative latecomers. California and Texas architecture, place names, chains of missions, methods of mining and of raising livestock, and irrigation tactics were all borrowed from the Spanish and the Indian. Unfortunately, though, we cannot order amiability, and tensions prevailed. This is a pity, for on both sides the people were remarkable. They had gentled an irascible land, they had learned to live with a nature that usually took and seldom gave, and they lent a distinctive quality to a large region that has endured in its own special way despite all the Howard Johnsons and Holiday Inns. They left a mark upon the land far disproportionate to their numbers. That is all you can ask of any people.

NOTES

1. See John Francis Bannon, *The Spanish Borderlands Frontier 1513-1821* (Albuquerque: University of New Mexico Press, 1974), pp. 3-7.

2. (New Haven: Yale University Press, 1921). See also John Francis Bannon, ed., *Bolton and the Spanish Borderlands* (Norman: University of Oklahoma Press, 1964).

3. See Charles Leland Sonnichsen, *The El Paso Salt War, 1877* (El Paso, Texas: C. Hertzog, 1961).

4. Frank Richard Prassel, *The Western Peace Officer: A Legacy of Law and Order* (Norman: University of Oklahoma Press, 1972), pp. 7-8. See also Joe B. Frantz, "The Frontier Tradition: An Invitation to Violence," pp. 101-19, in Hugh Davis Graham and Ted Robert Gurr, eds., *Violence in America: Historical and Comparative Perspectives; A Report to the National Commission on the Causes and Prevention of Violence,* vol. 1 (Washington, D.C.: Government Printing Office, 1969).

5. W. Eugene Hollon, *Frontier Violence: Another Look* (New York: Oxford University Press, 1974), p. 10.

6. Leonard L. Richards, *Gentlemen of Property and Standing: Anti-Abolition Mobs in Jacksonian America* (New York: Oxford University Press, 1970), pp. 11-14.

7. Hollon, *Frontier Violence,* p. 25.

8. Ibid., pp. 25-26.

9. Daniel Cosío Villegas, *American Extremes* (Austin: University of Texas Press, 1964), pp. 29-30.

10. Walter Prescott Webb and H. Bailey Carroll, eds., *The Handbook of Texas* (Austin: The Texas State Historical Association, 1952), 1:328.

11. Cosío Villegas, *American Extremes,* p. 28.

12. Ibid., p. 29.

13. Quoted in Webb and Carroll, eds., *The Handbook of Texas,* 1:104-5.

14. Bannon, *The Spanish Borderlands,* p. 231.

3

The Culture of the Frontier:
The Mexican Side*

Carlos Monsiváis

A TIJUANA

1. Diluvio luminoso de colores
en la estridencia de tu sed nocturna . . .
Ciudad de sortilegio; sensual urna
que sublimó el Amor de los Amores.

La sencillez de tus agrestes flores disfrazas de falena taciturna,
desmadejando su caricia diurna
en un boato confín de miel y albores.

En el ámbar licor surgir pareces
con tus cítricas llegas—mil toronjas
que ofrendan sus jugosas morbideces.

Un frenesí sajón hurta tus lonjas
y ora por tus pecados feligreses
la perpetua plegaria de tus monjas.

TO TIJUANA

There's a luminous flood of colors in your shrill nocturnal thirst,
city of sorcery, the sensual urn where highest love became sublime.

You turn your simple wildflowers into taciturn evening moths, leaving
their day's caress to languish in the glitter touching honey and dawn.

---

*Translated from the Spanish by Miguel González-Gerth [Editor's Note].

In amber liquor you emerge, dotted with citruslike blisters, a thousand grapefruits offering juicy morbid flesh.

A Saxon madness plunders your storehouse while the steady prayer of your nuns begs forgiveness for parochial sins.

> From ''Triptych to Baja California''
> by Miguel de Anda Jacobson

EL PRONÓSTICO

2. Traigo un pronóstico muy sicodélico
    que la Península se quiere hundir,
    Dicen los científicos con mucho pánico
    que California se va a acabar.

    Yo creo que es mentira (¡pura piña!)
    no creo que sea verdad
    pero por si acaso, me voy a confesar.

    Si se hunde Tijuana ¡Qué felicidad!
    Si se hunde Tecate ¡Qué felicidad!
    Si se hunde Mexicali ¡Qué felicidad!
    Si se hunde El Rosarito ¡Qué felicidad!
    Si se hunde Ensenada ¡Que felicidad!
    Si se hunde La Paz ¡Qué felicidad!

    ¡Qué felicidad! ¡Qué felicidad! ¡Qué felicidad!
    ¡Qué felicidad! ¡Qué felicidad! ¡Qué felicidad!
    Al fin tendremos agua que nadie va a pagar.

THE FORECAST

Here's a very psychedelic forecast. The peninsula is going to sink.
The scientists are saying with alarm that the end of California is in sight.

I think it isn't, really (it's all hogwash!). I don't believe it's
true. But I'm going to confession, just in case.

How great! Oh wow! How great! How great! Oh wow! How great!
At last we'll have some water for which we don't have to pay.

Popular song in Baja California
Lyrics by Ramón Rincón
as sung by Los Ban's

3. La esencia histórica de Tijuana es el turismo.

Tijuana's history is no more than tourist trade.

Professor Rubén Vizcaíno
Baja California State Historian

Very little reference material or research exists on the topic of border culture. Consequently, in the preparation of this essay, I had to resort to sheer hypotheses, in many instances, the validity of which I am by no means certain. The main difficulty I have in defining Mexican culture along the border is in separating the real culture from that fabricated by our country's political bureaucracy (a systematic demagoguery and sociopolitical coalition in which the liberal left prominently participates). In recent years there has been a campaign of cultural nationalism intent on protecting the Mexican border region from imperialist infiltration. This Mexican cultural nationalism has had two periods of evident popular and massive force: the first during the years from 1915 to 1925 reaching its peak with José Vasconcelos's term as Secretary of Public Education. The second period came during the presidential administration of Lázaro Cárdenas (1934-40). More recently this cultural nationalism has lacked the active political support of the masses and the political credit and trust that economic nationalism or revolutionary impulse had given it.

When cultural nationalism is decreed, it becomes stereotyped. A curious example of privately originated popular forms is the *mariachi* as we know it today. It was created by Don Emilio [Azcárraga], the genius of Mexican mass media, after a visit to Los Angeles. He came to the conclusion that the sound of a musical aggregation could be improved a great deal by adding a trumpet and other instruments not employed by the traditional mariachi group and more frequently used in the United States.* The "Ballet Folklórico," at its best under the direction of Amalia Hernández, has been staged basically by American choreographers.

Along the border, therefore, the problem of identity surfaces only within the context of specific political and economic struggle, such as the controversy over the salinity of the Colorado River or the appropriate legislation regarding the American-owned assembly plants *(maquiladoras)* or that relative to the migrant workers. To be a Mexican once again has

---

*According to Carmen Sordo Sodi and Juan Garrido, Azcárraga did this in 1930 when he founded XEW. See Claes af Geijerstam, *Popular Music in Mexico* (Albuquerque: University of New Mexico Press, 1976), pp. 43 and 155, n. 16 and n. 17 [Editor's Note].

an urgent connotation, as in the case of the Chicanos, for whom ethnic identity is a class determinant. The migrant worker or *bracero* looks at his Mexican origin not as a banner of patriotism, but rather as the reason for his oppressed condition. What happens is that the government people responsible for disseminating official Mexican culture have not defined either explicitly or implicitly what constitutes the imperialist culture they wish to reject. The term has appeared vaguely just as something of it exists in the Institutional Revolutionary Party (PRI) doctrine, but lacking a definition, imperialist culture turns out to be an actual threat which centers on Mexican border life, mores, and language. The truth is, however, that such life, mores, and language cannot be reestablished as they might have been, owing to the constant movement and the extreme variety and transientness of migrants and their dialects.

The official conception of what border culture is could not be more idealistic and misleading. Such a process of concealment is quite similar to the one used throughout the country. The only difference is that it emphasizes the idea that culture is being protected by a people who, at the middle-class level, want nothing more than to be like their American models, and who, at the mass level, have no material resources or cultural organizations with which to achieve such a desirable ethnicity.

Two grave mistakes are often made: 1) pitting a mythical and ultimately harmless indigenousness against an economic plunder, and 2) not seeing that in the last few decades the Mexican masses progressively have been abandoning the old traditions in favor of the new ones created and stimulated by the popular industrial culture.

Now classical Mexican culture and tradition have been perused and admired and immobilized by the domestic and foreign tourist trade. Cultural nationalism, insofar as it refers to the masses on the border, has taken refuge in a picturesqueness created by the mass media. That does not mean that it is, therefore, less authentic or less vital due to its obvious commercial origin.

A perfect example of the stereotyped Mexican bully, part of that *machismo* so well-defined in Dr. Paredes's essay, is portrayed by the late Mexican actor, Alfonso Bedoya, in *The Treasure of Sierra Madre.* When he gets close to Humphrey Bogart and is about to kill him, Bedoya says, ''We have built too many streets.'' Another aspect is the impression made by border culture as seen from the perspective of Mexico City. The first impression is the same as it was in the case of Cantinflas. It is sort of an inverted impression. Cantinflas represented the *peladito,* the lumpenproletarian rendered harmless and entertaining.

The basic problem with Mexican culture along the border continues to be the problem of a dependent society in which an apparent cultural nationalism is accompanied by resignation to exploitation. The concept of ethnic identity so important to Chicanos has no such strength in Mexico because Mexican ethnicity is also the property of the power structure that has subordinated it to demagoguery and because no political body takes it upon itself to define Mexican ethnicity in a critical and meaningful way. In order to lay the groundwork for a critically and imaginatively vital border culture, economic independence and democratic processes will first have to be achieved. These are necessary to destroy in the people of the border region the sense of living in temporary communities at the service of the tourist trade, where they feel they are economically and socially inferior. There cannot be a free Mexican culture along the border without economic independence.

Mexican culture along the border is somewhat of an enigma. One is surprised to find that despite the proximity of the United States, there are in the border towns certain manifestations of a desire to remain Mexican in custom and behavior. Officially this desire is confined to defiant soapbox oratory. But there is in the average citizen a definite, though vaguely expressed resistance, not so much to foreign influence in cultural matters as to imperialism in politics and economics.

Confronted with these phenomena, the official representatives of culture (bureaucrats that only by mistake can reflect a defined cultural policy) repeat the old theses: "preservation of our temperament" *(idiosincracia),* "maintenance of our spiritual values" *(esencias),* "safeguarding of our traditions" *(raíces).* The governmental machine raises a flag of cultural independence emblazoned with nationalist and folkloric mottos aimed at capitalizing on immediate political objectives. Along a frontier which has been besieged, infested, devastated, and conquered by an imperialist economic complex, Mexican nationalism swells up patriotically, as it does on the festive September 16. Mexico periodically opposes her ideal or theoretical categories of national selfhood to an overwhelming presence with worldwide resonance to the myth of the American way of life (which represents the highest economic status). Which are our "spiritual values"? How do we define "our temperament"? What is the thrust of "our traditions"? All these things are supposed to have been handed down from time immemorial, as *eternal* norms in the life of a people. In simple terms and actual practice, "traditions," "temperament," and "spiritual values" are translated into the traditional cult of the hero, the Ballet Folklórico, the trappings which identify a type found in the movies and popular songs, the mythical and magical concept of history, and the insistence on the impossible "purity of language." All this means is that we have turned away from what history really is—the consequences of territorial loss, including the break with our colonial and independence-oriented past. The defeat of 1847 may have fostered nationalism in the border region, but it did not subsequently strengthen the area's economic ties with the metropolitan area in central Mexico. The tremendous defeat and the evident rapacity of imperialism have fed our cultural nationalism since the middle of the nineteenth century, culminating with the administration of General Lázaro Cárdenas. (José Vasconcelos's program as Secretary of Public Education, despite its cultural missions, scarcely had an effect on the border.) Lacking better forms of expression, Mexican cultural nationalism goes on repeating the same external symbols strengthened by others created by the Revolution.

Those external symbols tell us of historical conquests and the immutability of popular customs; they describe everyday life and the political and social achievements of a people. Thus cultural nationalism has functioned as a record, a catalog of properties, an acknowledgment of acquisitions (holidays, regional garb, poets, decisive battles, leaders and heroes, feats, and culinary styles). On the border, this inventory has scarcely been marred by foreign influence. It has remained basically the same as it was when it came from the metropolis, but it has been augmented by a marginal human type, existing precisely on the border, that earns priority—the cultural renegade *(descastado)*. This figure of the cultural renegade has come to symbolize betrayal. Whatever he is supposed to have abjured, and for whatever reason, the *descastado* is usually the subject of a heated "defense of one's nationality," something upheld more by faith than by proof.

There has never been (and given the Mexican power structure there *cannot* be) any public admission that the myths of national immutability (tradition, spiritual value, or temperament) can only arise and become real in a continuous democratic process which, when not forthcoming (when not encouraging critical awareness in the masses) leads to dissemination by the state of a glorious brand of nationalism. And herewith the contradiction: for the sake of nationalism the state turns its back on democracy. With nationalist authoritarianism, the state normally equates "independence" with insularity, with the guarantee of absolute power within limits. Hence the cry (which varies in vehemence, depending on changes in the national administration) for autonomous culture and ideology, free of debts and interrelations, neither leftist nor rightist, rejecting everything foreign in a constant show of uniqueness. National character as the exception or anomaly was never thus conceived elsewhere: national character as a once-only marvelous experience, hedged in by the envy and the desire to submit to foreign powers; all this usually disconnected from any real economic and political struggle.

Any attempt to define something as huge and complex as Mexican culture along the border stumbles on the government's decision never to place it in the right perspective. The idea is to build indiscriminately a mythological structure based on an illusory national process as a bulwark against foreign penetration. Everything foreign is chauvinistically denied or disregarded; in a world progressively subjected to the media, this is nothing less than suicidal. Again the contradiction: "denial or disregard of everything foreign" are only words emanating from bureaucratic rituals. The opposite is true—an attitude of idolatry, a desire to make a fetish out of the grandeur represented by modern technology and the "American way of life." This contradiction has an immediate effect: demagoguery remains exposed in the act of worshipping what it denied, having underestimated its strength and having dealt in generalities.

The failure of a policy directed against all that is foreign and the disaster of nationalist rhetoric are obvious. It does not, however, mean that we should not keep up a nationwide campaign of cultural recuperation and definition. To gain and make use of cultural independence is not to indulge in self-analysis. Of course, no culture can survive without the right amount of assimilated influence from its neighbors. "Purity" itself is a kind of self-destruction. Take, for example, those individuals whose passivity limits them to the words accepted by tradition, while popular speech renews itself and produces another language. But if there is no place in Mexican culture for "foreign influence" and "new ideas," in the social and economic life of the country, exploitation, looting, and the omnipresence of the transnational corporations certainly do exist.

We come upon the inevitable paradox embodied in a fervently nationalistic cultural policy of a dependent society. To explain the paradox we must first do away with the customary fears regarding the Mexican government (which make it an inflexibly obedient servant of imperialism) and consider the government's need for its own living space, where it can make and implement its own decisions. Second, we must acknowledge that the cultural apparatus imposed by the institutions that govern our social conduct provide the justification of the roles we play and set their relationship to other roles within our society. This cultural apparatus encourages conformity and submissive acceptance of the status quo, dictating norms for "self-realization" most in keeping with the reward-getting doctrine established by the "system." In this regard one might even think of culture as a sort of screen between the Mexican people and the world, enhancing a limited view of social change, political expression, and progress of the individual citizen. Thus, we restrict our demands for transformation merely to what is attainable within familiar contexts.

In dependent societies cultural institutions play a dual role: first, to justify the power wielded by a colonial class, by instilling at every social level its values and ideas, as if they reflect the natural order of things; second, to exert their authority in the interest of both the class they represent and the international imperialism to which they are subordinate. That is the reason why the ultimate goal of such institutions is to identify and to discriminate, that is, to unite and to alienate. This dichotomy is manifested as follows: on the one hand, we have a consumer-oriented culture; on the other, we have a society whose lower classes are exploited, prevented from making excessive and unattainable demands, and encouraged in a fatalistic attitude—the resigned acceptance of the status quo.

Along the border, this cultural apparatus employs a devastating logic. The notion is spread about that these are only "migrant towns," without roots or tradition, mere gathering places. If revenue is collected there, it is in the fulfillment of administrative duty. And yet, industrial growth (determined by the population explosion around Tijuana, Mexicali, and Juárez) and the corresponding social psychology remain under the sway of the tourist trade, as communities at the beck and call of the visitors. The emphasis on individualism and "self-realization" take on the coloration of economic success, identified with the culture to which the border Mexicans are willing everyday servants. Since to a great extent this Mexican culture along the border depends on the transient clientele of American tourists, it naturally gives way to unavoidable glorification of a consumer mentality.

The border as a populated area is not only exploited but overexploited. Places piously called "vice towns" are really places where intense economic and social exploitation takes place. The word "vice" is not restricted to a moral meaning; it also represents an economic reality. Consequently, we must abandon all self-righteous attitudes if we wish to know the reasons for the border situation. (The degradation of prostitutes, for example, is not a question of morals as much as it is of labor relations.) To pass moral judgment only on what goes on in either Juárez or Tijuana is to obscure the facts. The rest of the country is afflicted with the same problems (white slavery, alcoholism, and heavy drug usage). The difference lies in the degree of organization of vice and its economic power.

During the twenties, when the Mexican Revolution became institutional-ized, it seemed natural that certain border towns should exploit sexual plea-sure and various kinds of "vice." Let me turn to the use of anecdote as secret history about border culture. Where a trade school now stands in Tijuana, the Casino de Agua Caliente opened its doors back in 1926. It was owned by an American chain of casinos, famous for bathing facilities lined with tile imported from Italy and complete with Neptune's fountain. Its years of glory were the late twenties and early thirties, when General Abelardo Rodríguez (who owned the Cuernavaca Casino de la Selva) was president of the Republic. The Casino de Agua Caliente became second only to the Monte Carlo Casino in the whole world and its peak corresponded with the Hollywood heyday and, naturally, with Prohibition.

From Hollywood came the stars, the producers, the directors, the hopefuls—all would come. They stayed at the Casino, where there was a hotel. They parked their long automobiles in the carports, lived in bungalows, walked about in the gardens carefully landscaped with grass and abounding in palm trees, stepped on rich oriental rugs, and admired the variety of plants. Douglas Fairbanks came there. The as-yet-unknown Clark Gable strolled there. Lola Cansino, later known as Rita Hayworth, began by working there. Fortunes were lost and won there. Cliché. Many tragic suicides due to the stock market crash took place there. Cliché. A man there once gave the parking attendant first his car keys and then his car as a gift, after having won millions of dollars in one night. Movie cliché.

Tijuana became internationally famous thanks to Prohibition. If, according to Lázaro Cárdenas, the first aim of the Revolution had been to shut down the vice and exploitation centers, its moral thrust soon played out. Instead the inauguration of large gambling establishments, among other things, took place, such as Agua Caliente, El Tecolote, El Foreign Club of Tijuana, and others in Baja California. There were gaming tables available in several border towns and in many of the interior towns such as the Casino de la Selva (Cuernavaca) and a really magnificent club in San Bartolo Naucalpan outside Mexico City. All of these were authorized (and not merely partially utilized) by President Abelardo Rodríguez, who had been governor of the northern part of Baja California. In 1933 a satirical acrostic went around: "Fueron Ordenados Rateros Elegantes Iniciativa Gobierno Nacional// Calles Logró Unificar Bandidos" (Elegant thieves were ordered at the instigation of the National Government// Calles succeeded in unifying bandits). The Foreign Club became the supreme symbol of corruption.

In his autobiographical *Apuntes* of December 1934, President Lázaro Cárdenas includes among the serious problems he will have to face "the vice centers operated with authorization from federal and local public officials. . . . I will find great obstacles . . . to a program of moral development." And he continues:

> The spread of vice has given a powerful weapon to the enemies of the
> Revolution and has deserved scorching criticism from the revolutionary

sector now marshalled against the governments of the regime. General Calles was one of the first (1915) to launch a campaign of moralization. While governor of Sonora, he prohibited the manufacture and sale of alcoholic beverages and shut down all gambling establishments. As long as immorality is looked upon with complacency, there cannot be a government of the people. The interests often dug in through the misconduct of those entrusted with public office must be attacked most vigorously.

Pssst, pst, señor. *Ey,* americano, *you want a leetle, yes? Come here, I tell to you something special. One* minuto, *okay? You like girls, eh? I got this booteeful girl, very really terreefic girl. Her home is Hermosillo and got her myself just yesterday. Oh, very young, maybe twelve, but very big up here, yes?–big teets. Ay,* caramba, *is she hot stuff, and clean, real virgeen, and so booteeful, you won't believe it. So I tell you what, I make for you the real bargain. Twenty dollars and I take you there myself for nothing. Oh, if you want to give me little somethings for my time, well, that's okay. But everything first class, just like United States. We got blondes; you know, long-leg* americana *blondes. We got everything right here. You want nice little show? Two lesbians, real hot show–something you bet you never see before, believe me. These girls put on real terreefic show. That I guarantee you personally myself. No? Okay, how about man and girl? Two men and girl? Two girls and man? Wait, I got something you bet you never see before. How about girl and burro? Girl and two burros, fuck and suck, everything you like, all positions, real hot show. Homosexual show? Two good-looking guys, big muscles and strong, you know,* muy hombre: *really terreefic show, believe me. How about it? Ey, wait, I got to tell you about the best dirty movies in town, in booteeful colors, twenty-six positions, with real movie stars from Holleewood. No? Ey, what's the matter, meester? You just want to get drunk, or something? Ey, come back, I tell you about this great denteest, he fix teets with real gold. . . .*[1]

Cárdenas was the embodiment of revolutionary nationalist morality, one foundation of which has been showing the masses that the sacrifices expected of them are matched by governmental austerity and the restraining of private enrichment. As the thrust of revolutionary nationalism gradually became spent, the corruptive activities took over again, this time without the casinos. The border was seen in a different light, thanks to yellow journalism and rooted in refined contempt for underdeveloped countries. Those spreading this view exploited the tradition of American reporters shocked by Villa's or Zapata's cruelty. And now, they were "horrified" by the indescribable "sinfulness" prevalent in the border areas which regained dubious international popularity for thousands of American servicemen during the forties.

A prime example of how an image is built is Ovid Demaris's book *Poso del Mundo,* aimed at "exploring" life on the border. Strictly written to sell, the book is said to be a "shocking exposé of the sin cities along the Mexican-American border." But its real purpose can be easily detected: to present a Manichean thesis regarding the development of the border region and to blame the shameful situation on Mexican corruption and depravity. The red-light districts of Tijuana, Agua Prieta, Juárez, Matamoros, Acuña, Piedras Negras, and Reynosa are the traps where the Mexicans ("expert in the art of simulation") attract the tourists for purposes of crude prostitution, drug peddling, and smuggling. "Tijuana," says Demaris, "is the toughest, roughest, gaudiest, filthiest, loudest—the most larcenous, vicious, predacious—the wickedest bordertown of them all. . . . Good heaven, these kids have got to be a million miles from home to fuck those pigs."[2]

And so Demaris vindicates the tourist trade. His underlying message is the following: the hundreds or thousands of Americans who go out on the town and exchange greetings and watch the go-go girls and eat and look at cheap pre-Hispanic reproductions, silverwork, and sombreros and have their pictures taken leading donkeys groomed like goats and let their hair down in nightclubs and whorehouses are absolutely innocent. The fault is that of the way of life found along the Mexican border, with its base consisting of bribery and the manipulation of the drug traffic. All of this is seen from the perspective of an imperialist mentality, which jumps at the chance to point out the cultural defects of other countries. In regard to Mexico, such mentality looks upon widespread corruption (a corruption which even takes assistance from its American counterpart) as a hallmark or prime characteristic. And a corrupt country is inescapably a place for conquest. As might have been expected, Demaris emerges as a critical corrective for those who, with equal Manicheanism, had blamed the tourists for all the ills of a society.

And yet, Demaris points up a basic fact. The myths of prostitution and decadence in the affluent society are closely related to Mexican culture along the border. The Casino de Agua Caliente mythically represents the physical and psychological space where a certain power group carried on its ultimate fun and games. Accordingly, Tijuana came to stand for a place liberated from moral pressures, a sort of wanton utopia where oriental maharajas and fugitives from Prohibition organized a network of luxury, complacency, and stupefaction at their own wealth and their cult of emotions. There they strolled and talked in the Gold Room, admired the crystal chandeliers, played golf or went to the horse races or concentrated on playing poker and blackjack and roulette and shooting craps and trying their luck with the slot machines. Later they had to go to Havana when the agrarian reform and the oil expropriation came and the gambling houses were shut down. And George Raft at the Tropicana was the perfect image of that American and Old World migration as he had been at the Casino de Agua Caliente.

The debauchery myth, however, had been created. And along with it went the unwritten but never rejected agreement making the border a "free zone." There were, nevertheless, some interruptions. In 1970, the American government's "Operation Intercept" caused alarm, confusion, and economic panic. The pretext given for it was to stop the illegal entry of drugs, a depravity which was viewed as Mexico-based. In 1970, cartoonist Abel Quezada denounced Tijuana's vice and filth. Tijuana formed a vindication committee, which held meetings (one of them in a location on Avenida Revolución itself), collected one hundred thousand pesos, and printed public declarations which angrily rescued the city's dignity and rejected the outrage directed against it. That same year, thousands of school children in Juárez marched in a demonstration urging their parents to work against vice and its practices; in Tijuana a conference was organized to discuss steps to be taken against vice. Only fourteen persons attended. But the following information was made public: "There are twelve thousand prostitutes in Tijuana or, from the viewpoint of the town, twelve thousand goods for instantaneous consumption." These modes of protest proved weak and antiquated. There was no point in continuing to describe the border towns as "gutters" and "sewers." Social pragmatists, as soon as they became aware of the revenue, forgot about their wounded patriotism. The ultimate explanation is the same as before, namely, the tenuous relations that the border region has with the Mexican national economy determine the tenuous relations it has with the dominant culture in Mexico.

Today along the border, prostitution has diminished noticeably. With the withdrawal of American troops from Vietnam, sexual commerce has waned and family tourism is on the increase. Cabarets have lost ground (having moved to the outskirts) and there are more bars without floorshows. Now it seems that those who come looking for prostitution are Blacks, Filipinos, Chicanos, and Mexicans.

Prostitution, however, has left its mark. Along with the subculture of the success seekers (lectures on salesmanship, success motivation, sense of belonging, community-mindedness), another subculture flourishes, under the auspices of the prostitution industry. Its manifestation is the excess of beauty salons and hair stylists. This is the subculture of hairdressers and gigolos with their roadhouse and bawdy-house language. Moral judgment has been passed on this subculture with complete hypocrisy by the so-called respectable citizens. Border justice is meted out according to a double standard. It is not unusual for judges, mayors, and doctors to own the nightclubs and whorehouses as well as to benefit from related activities. Such an example has directly influenced the commercial aspect of popular culture. Economically and socially unable to assimilate American culture, while at the same time either ignorant of or negative toward Mexican traditions, border culture turns to mass culture in the form of picture magazine stories, comic strips, radio and television soap operas, "B" movies, and hero worship in sports and bullfighting.

There is great interest in the occult, such as black magic, yoga, astrology, and speculation about the presence on earth of beings from other planets. One can find such literature in the border bookstores next to basic pornography, textbooks, and mechanics' manuals. There are no visible signs of high culture. On the other hand, the subculture of prostitution is self-evident. Manifest are abject devotion to religious symbols, the need for instant bright futures, and naïveté and guilelessness as means of dealing with the world. Pornography in Tijuana or Ciudad Juárez does not evidence the distinctive signs which elsewhere in the country represent some accommodation to traditional morality. On the border, pornography is strictly a commercial element. Border morality is exempt from certain rigidities due to tolerance based on economic considerations, but it has continued to be based on respect for family, private property, and the State.

Subcultures mix and fuse. Along with the central culture (with its worship of heroes, Mexicanness, the Catholic religion, respect for national symbols, devotion for the typical, pride in the pre-Hispanic), there are to be found, at different levels, splinter and marginal elements: the occultist and yoga subculture, the oriental religions, the Hare Krishnas; the diverse and numerous Protestant denominations with their emphasis on productivity and the work ethic; the survival of romantic elements, the oratorial competitions, the abundance of theater groups without schools specializing in the dramatic art.

Mexican culture along the border is, therefore, a conglomeration. The traditional and the new, the metropolitan and the provincial, the rural and the foreign, are all mixed together often in social efforts to collect money in the very name of culture, searching for means to attain respectability.

How does culture along the border react to its counterpart which is known today as "Chicano" culture? And how does Mexican culture react to Chicano culture? Long after the legend of Joaquín Murrieta and the fear of Indian depredation had subsided, the character created by comedian "Tin Tan" was undoubtedly the first to represent a type associated with border culture. Tin Tan was born Germán Valdés in 1915 in Mexico City, but he grew up in that section of Juárez where they keep the fighting bulls. He went back to Mexico City in the mid forties to work in vaudeville. His gimmick was the *pachuco* character-type developed in Los Angeles, California. He made his movie debut in *Hotel de verano* and starred in *El hijo desobediente* (1945). His character portrayal (heralded by a song: "This is the *pachuco,* a most peculiar fellow. . . .") took off from the sartorial excess known as the "zootsuit." The *pachuco's* defiant dandyism was simultaneously an aesthetic outlook and an ethic, a stereotype that presaged the need of a counterculture, the resultant symbol of the Mexican Americans' first social clashes. Tin Tan borrowed that image, sweetened it, and adapted it for Mexican consumption.

But in Mexico, the *pachuco's* success was doomed to suffer from "mediatization." The zany character Tino Villanueva, for example, was taken by Mexicans as an innocuous preachment on *pochismo,* the imitation of American language and manners. And yet, Villanueva had been the victim of "juridical" persecution in the Sleepy Lagoon incident of 1942, the trial of a gang that gave way to a racist campaign against "Mexican juvenile delinquency," ending in 1944 with all the defendants acquitted. He had been subjected to police harassment and had taken part in the race riots of 1943 which occurred after American soldiers and marines had made a practice of stopping anyone wearing a zootsuit in midtown Los Angeles (ordering him to take off his "drapes" and beating him up). The *pachuco* in the Mexican-American ghetto reflected not mere eccentricity but a baroque search for identity, a desire to exist—precisely by means of conspicuous dress and speech—within a society that denied such existence (including cultural visibility and political participation). But for the Mexican people, the *pachuco* as embodied by Tin Tan and gigolo characters *(cinturitas)* in cabaret-style movies, was no more than a comic representation of a type intoxicated by the American way of life.

Even so, the character Tin Tan proved difficult to sponsor. Motion picture censorship, intent on preserving purity of custom and language, urged on even by language academicians, soon found fault with the *pachuco,* demanding that he tone down or change his speech, diminish his obvious cultural borrowing, and become just another urban comedian, free of what was precisely his significance. *Turidundá, dundá, dundá, dundá.* That very peculiar fellow, the *pachuco,* quickly disappeared from the precarious limits of recognition of distinctive cultural forms derived from a common source. When Tin Tan went from Humberto Gómez Landeros's musical farces *(El hijo desobediente; Músico, poeta y loco)* to Gilberto Martínez Solares's popular comedies *(El rey del barrio; El revoltoso)*, he shed his bilingualism, his huge watch chain and double-breasted jacket that came down below his knees, and became a character from the lower class of Mexico City.

Metropolitan Mexican citizens did not take seriously anything about Mexican culture along the border or about Chicano culture. The Mexican American of the 1940s barely made an impression on the Mexican, other than an impression of eccentricity and caricature. The fashion and dialect of border Mexicans left no mark, as they were used only for bad movies (such as Vicente Oroná's 1953 *Frontera Norte*) in which drug pushers and prostitutes were employed to try to create a sick movie atmosphere. One film that came close to being an exception was Alejandro Galindo's *Espaldas Mojadas* (1953), an unpretentious attempt to portray the misery of feeling uprooted among illiterate *bracero*-type migrant workers. Though the antiimperialism of *Espaldas Mojadas* was subdued, its exhibition was prohibited for several years by the censors. In this same context, the film *Salt of the Earth (La Sal de la tierra)*, which was made by an American, Herbert Biberman, is truly exceptional.

In the mid sixties, a comedian, Eulalio González, appeared in two movies, *El bracero del año* and *El pocho*. The character he played, "El Piporro," was definitely a product of mass culture in an industrial age. His dress included the proverbial Texas ten-gallon hat, frilly suede jacket, decorated cowboy boots, and a bandana around his neck. Sporting a big mustache, winking to the audience, and stomping when he danced, he was the stereotype of the border Mexican rancher—rough, quaint-talking and open-hearted. In *El pocho* (his best movie), he played the part of Joe García, "second-class citizen with a first-class girl friend," who marries an Anglo, collects compensation for property his parents owned in the Chamizal area, and is ready to enlighten and defend Mexican "greasers." Piporro, with his own brand of rebel yell as a sample of racial affirmation (accompanied by mariachis), is one of the few marks left by the border on Mexican popular culture.

In recent years, Mexican culture along the border has had some influence on juvenile speech. The youth movement known in Mexico as "La onda," a version of the hippie movement which began in 1966 and lasted until approximately 1972, derived its slang and its first knowledge of drug and rock culture from the rock groups in Tijuana and Juárez. Words like *"alivianarse," "tira," "afanarse," "role," "pasón," "rel," "simón"* and *"friqueo"* were undoubtedly taken from the border, whose culture became a source of marginality, either true or imagined, due in part to its potential for speech fabrication. Quite apart, the market represented by the Chicano moviegoer also has prompted the Mexican motion picture industry to produce a number of terrible films, such as *De sangre chicana,* in order to capitalize on the movement.

The border population grows amid alarming problems, such as poverty, unemployment, extremely high underemployment, poor housing and education, unsafe water and sewer systems. But these are problems it shares with the rest of the nation. Take education, for example, which runs the gamut from 20 percent illiterate to 1.8 percent well educated, the latter constituting the elite. With respect to housing, the eight million border Mexicans average six per house. Migrants abound: 50 percent of Tijuana's population and 34 percent of Mexicali's are migrant. Close to five hundred migrants arrive daily in Tijuana. They represent a "quest for gold"; in other words, they seek jobs in the United States. But they swell the population so that the town spreads out toward the hills in the typical disorder which is both the life and death of Mexican border towns. Their homes are mud huts or houses boasting either the "California" or "Provençal" architectural style that betrays so much misdirected imitation. Tijuana is simply there, accepts everything, its appearance reflecting the gossip that circulates about it. In the hills many *pollas* (wetbacks and other illegals) fall prey to unemployment, prostitution, or drugs.

The border population is the result of accumulation. From different parts of the country, from Sinaloa and Jalisco and Sonora and Nuevo León and Zacatecas and Durango, migrants come and undergo unification according to the rules of the game: the American practical approach to life, the ideal of citizenship as a form of business, and the belief in commerce as the builder of nationality. If the influence of the United States is universal, along the border it is overwhelming. It takes the form of myth, of modern production methods, of the social invisibility of poverty, of the socialization of technology. The border Mexican learns from his daily contact with American reality; he has come full circle, from a position of chauvinistic defiance to one of wallowing in "the Mexican's inferiority complex."

For the border Mexican, the American is not only a reality, he is a client. As such, his influence represents both an imposition and an intimate decision. Capitalist ideology and American status symbols become meaningful for the border Mexican. And yet he maintains an indigenous recess, kept alive and stimulated in genuine fashion, despite the artificiality of the contribution made to it by State promotion. It is related to Mexican folklore, worship of popular heroes of the movies, television and radio, enthusiasm for popular singers and ranchera music, and the native penchant for melodrama. The young listen to rock music but they also listen to Cornelio Reyna, Lucha Villa, Angélica María, Juan Gabriel, and the newest Spanish and Argentine singers. They are consumers of all the commercial garbage called *norteña* music, sung and sold by comedians like Eulalio González ("El Piporro").

Partly because of its keen receptiveness, an essential part of Mexican border culture has taken root in the industrial mass culture. The proportion of Mexico City homes with radio-television represent 29 percent compared with 35 percent in the border states and 46 percent in border municipalities. Nevertheless, border culture expands into a vacuum—into space where identity becomes rarefied and lost. Against the energy displayed by American cities (the speed of construction, a partially democratic system, the affluence which inflation and recession cannot yet damage significantly), the identity proclaimed by the Mexican border towns either evaporates or retreats to political speeches. National identity hence becomes another myth, with outcroppings of chauvinist expressions, local pride, and a passion for folklore. All this, of course, facilitates cultural infiltration.

A poverty culture has developed in the Mexican border slums. Its characteristics are decay, crime, and poverty. The individual's concept of identity, moral character, and world view are weak and disorganized. The churches usually do nothing but confirm the sense of marginality, helplessness, and dependence which, in most cases, derive from an objective reality.

Both the Catholic religion and Mexican folkways inspire renunciation and fatalism. Sometimes these give way to either self-confidence or group-confidence, depending on the opportunities that arise. Male chauvinism is prevalent, as it is in all Mexican culture, but perhaps intensified by a need for psychological compensation, considering the local limitations placed on the conventional male role. This acting-out behavior is, in general terms, what we call *machismo*.

Reward and future planning capabilities are meager. This is so because there are hardly any options. Psychological pathology is tolerated, a fact which can be functionally positive if we consider it in the light of the socioeconomic deprivation with which we are dealing. In effect, people suffering from certain modes of abnormal behavior can adapt easily, while in other communities they are usually put away under conditions similar to those of criminals. There is no sense of history. The majority view is provincially and locally oriented. The common values are: education as a tool, material welfare as a desirable goal, and self-sufficiency as an appropriate means. There is no local social structure beyond the family.

Those who live in a poverty culture, as migrants usually do, are aware of middle-class values, talk about them, and even defend some of them as their own. But as a whole, they do not live by them. They agree on certain special values, such as the desirability of conventional family life, which is not always attainable, and on the fact that world society essentially discriminates against the poor. Along the border, where exploitation is widespread and squalor hardly has been eased by industrial development, these fixed notions find ample support. For example, job insecurity is constant and labor and sexual abuse are oppressive for women workers in the American-owned assembly plants, or *maquiladoras*. There are five hundred such factories. Many of these women are subjected to a sort of slavery that turns them into objects and frightens them into submission before the physical and sexual desires of their employers. On the other hand, it might be argued that many girls who work in such plants have been trained as skilled laborers and have thus escaped the fate of prostitution.

The rapid growth in population and industry of the Mexican border towns has dispelled many old prejudices and commonplaces. Though one might view the tourist scene as evil and marginal, it does in fact play a central part in the community, serving as a prerequisite for its economic and cultural development. Thus Mexican culture along the border comes to represent, in general terms, a loss of identity (identity here meaning a political and cultural force), the dubious mixture of two national life-styles (each at its worst), the deification of technology, and a craze for the new.

Mass media impact is almost total. Oscar Lewis has shown that the urban poor do not want to identify with proletarian workers but rather with a future as consumers, their class consciousness attenuated by the vigor exerted by what might be called "consumer awareness." The result is a basically acquisitive and competitive orientation that makes for a vertical rather than a horizontal classification. The large number of American television channels and radio stations broadcasting their mythology of rugged individualism and personal achievement help to solidify the Mexican border's internal hegemony. The influence of radio programs is actually ambivalent. On one hand, there is commercial advertising interspersed with *bolero* music representing the sentimental side of culture, and *norteña* music representing the industrial folklore aspects. On the other hand, there is rock music as a transcultural innovation from the United States.

NOTES

1. Ovid Demaris, *Poso del Mundo: Inside the Mexican American Border from Tijuana to Matamoros* (Boston: Little, Brown & Co., 1970), pp. 1-2.
2. Ibid., p. 18.

4

The Problem of Identity in a Changing Culture: Popular Expressions of Culture Conflict Along the Lower Rio Grande Border

Américo Paredes

Conflict—cultural, economic, and physical—has been a way of life along the border between Mexico and the United States, and it is in the so-called Nueces-Río Grande strip where its patterns were first established. Problems of identity also are common to border dwellers, and these problems were first confronted by people of Mexican culture as a result of the Texas revolution. For these reasons, the Lower Río Grande area also can claim to be the source of the more typical elements of what we call the culture of the border.

The *Handbook of Middle American Indians* divides northern Mexico into four culture areas: (1) Baja California; (2) the northwest area—Sonora and south along the Pacific coast to Nayarit; (3) the north central area—Chihuahua, Durango, and some parts of Coahuila; and (4) the northeast area—Tamaulipas, most of Nuevo León and the lower-border areas of Coahuila, ending a few miles upriver from Ciudad Acuña and Del Río.[1]

The culture of the border is not only historically dynamic but has its regional variations as well. Because it is difficult to generalize on so vast an area, this essay focuses on one region, the northeast. It sometimes is referred to as the Lower Río Grande Border or simply, the Lower Border.[2] In a strictly chronological sense, this region may claim priority over the other areas. If we view a border not simply as a line on a map but, more fundamentally, as a sensitized area where two cultures or two political systems come face to face,

68

then the first "border" between English-speaking people from the United States and people of Mexican culture was in the eastern part of what is now the state of Texas. And this border developed even before such political entities as the Republic of Mexico and the Republic of Texas came into being. Its location shifted as the relentless drive south and west by Nolan, Magee, and their successors pushed a hotly contested borderline first to the Nueces and later to the Río Grande.

Certain folkloric themes and patterns spread from the Nueces-Río Grande area to other parts of the border as cultural conflict spread. That a distinctive border culture spread from the Nueces-Río Grande area to other border regions (as well as to other areas of the West) is a thesis explored by Professor Walter Prescott Webb in *The Great Plains*. In the chapter "The Cattle Kingdom," Webb sees his "kingdom" as developing a peculiar "civilization."[3] This "cattle culture" was the result of a union of northern Mexican ranchero culture, including techniques of raising cattle and horses, with new technological improvements brought in by Anglo Americans, especially such things as revolvers, barbed wire, and lawyers versed in the intricacies of land titles.

Much has been written about the blending of cultures in the southwestern United States, though less has been said about the impact of United States culture on northern Mexico. The number of books written about the influence of Mexican (or Spanish) architecture in the southwestern United States, if placed one beside another, would fill an extremely long bookshelf. Even more has been said and written about Mexican foods in the United States, an interest also manifest in the number of "Mexican" restaurants in almost any American town or city, patronized for the most part by WASP Americans. The ultimate in Mexican food in the Southwest and other areas are the quick-service chains that now sell tacos the way other chains sell hamburgers and hot dogs.

"Mexican food" is of course defined as tamales, tacos, enchiladas, chalupas, nachos, tostadas, frijoles refritos, and delicacies of that sort. What is rarely noted is that for the border Mexican of the past couple of centuries these foods have been almost as exotic as they are to the WASP American. One of the popular etymologies given for "greaser," an epithet applied by Anglo Americans to Mexicans, is that the term arose when the Anglos first encountered Mexicans in the Nueces-Río Grande area and were struck by the greasiness of Mexican food. O. Henry has enshrined this stereotype in his poem "Tamales," according to which "Don José Calderón Santos Espirition Vicente Camillo Quintana de Ríos de Rosa y Ribera" takes revenge on the Texans for having killed his grandfather at San Jacinto by selling greasy tamales to Anglos:

> What boots it if we killed
> Only one greaser,
> Don José Calderón?
> This is your deep revenge,
> You have greased all of us,
> Greased a whole nation
> With your Tamales . . .[4]

The author of "The Little Adobe Casa," a parody of "The Little Sod Shanty on My Claim," has a much better idea of the border Mexican's fare, perhaps based on more direct experience than O. Henry's. The singer lives in Mexico, where "the Greaser roams about the place all day." Still, he keeps hoping that some "dark eyed mujer" will consent to be his wife. Meanwhile,

> My bill of fare is always just the same
> Frijoles and tortillas
> Stirred up in chili sauce
> In my little adobe casa on the plains.[5]

Frijoles, chiles, and tortillas were the standard fare along the border, as everywhere else in Mexico, except that the tortillas were more likely to be made of flour than of *nixtamal* [cooked maize], while the frijoles were never refried but boiled and mashed into a soupy stew—*caldudos*. Tamales were eaten once a year, at Christmas after the yearly hog was killed; and a taco was any snack made of a rolled tortilla with some kind of filling. For a more varied daily menu there might be rice with chicken or dried shrimp, beef either fresh or dried, as well as almost any other part of the steer. And for a real treat there was *cabrito* [goatmeat].

Bigfoot (El Patón) Wallace, who was captured by Mexican troops after the Mier Expedition, used his alleged sufferings in captivity as an excuse for the barbarities he committed against Mexican civilians when he was a member of Hays's Rangers during the Mexican War. One of the examples of his mistreatment at Mexican hands is mentioned in John Duval's romanticized biography of Wallace. Wallace complained that after being captured, and during the time he spent along the Río Grande, all he ever was given to eat were beans, tortillas, and roast goatmeat.[6] Nowadays, many of Wallace's fellow countrymen journey all the way from central Texas to "in" eating spots on the Río Grande, to satisfy their craving for beans, tortillas, and roast goatmeat. But perhaps Bigfoot found border Mexican food too greaseless for his taste; he probably missed his sidemeat and the rich gravies he was accustomed to sopping his biscuits in.

A better case for the blending of Anglo-American culture with that of the northern Mexican ranchero may be made in respect to the more practical elements of the "cattle culture." Cattle and horses, as well as land, were Mexican to begin with; and when the Anglo took them over he also adopted many of the techniques developed by the ranchero for the handling of stock. The vocabulary related to the occupation of the vaquero also became part of the blend. These things also have merited the attention of scholars and popular writers alike, especially those interested in the process whereby the rough Mexican ranchero was transformed into the highly romanticized American cowboy. All these subjects, from food and architecture to the birth of the cowboy, have attracted interest mainly from the viewpoint of their impact on the culture of the United States. My own interest in the cowboy has been a bit more intercultural, I beliver, and it has focused on the manner in which an ideal pattern of male behavior has been developed interculturally along the border, subsequently to influence the male self-image first in the United States and later in Mexico. I refer to the familiar figure of popular fiction and popular song—the mounted man with his pistol in hand.[7] Take the Mexican ranchero, a man on horseback par excellence, add the six-chambered revolver, and you have the American cowboy of fiction and popular legend—the ideal figure of many an Anglo male. The cowboy as a *macho* image was carried by the Texan, along with other elements of the "cattle culture," to other areas of the border, as well as to other parts of the West. The idea of the cowboy as the American *macho* becomes so pervasive that it can influence the private and public life of Theodore Roosevelt, as well as the scholarly writings of historians like Walter Prescott Webb. Finally—aided in the last stages of the process by such books as Webb's *The Texas Rangers*—the cowboy has his apotheosis in Hollywood. The impact on a people of an idea or an ideal may be gauged by its influence on the folksongs of that people. Thus, it is worth noting that by 1910 the work of John A. Lomax, the great collector of North American folksongs, was beginning to make Americans see the cowboy as the national image and find the essence of the North American spirit in the cowboy, as expressed in the cowboy's songs. At that time the Mexican Revolution was just getting under way, and it would be almost a generation before romantic nationalists in Mexico would discover the essence of *mexicanismo* in the *corridos* of the Revolution.

The cowboy had influenced the border Mexican long before, and in a very direct way, because "cowboy" began as the name of the Anglo cattle thieves who raided the Nueces-Río Grande area in the late 1830s, and who, revolver in hand, began the dispossession of the Mexican on the north bank of the Río Grande. Understandably, the border Mexican developed a fascination for the revolver as a very direct symbol of power; he had learned the power of the pistol the hard way. Mexicans lent the image of the vaquero to their neighbors to the north, and the image returned to Mexico wearing a six-shooter and a

Stetson hat. The cowboy *macho* image influenced the Revolution, in men such as Roberto Fierro; but it was after the Revolution that the cycle was completed, with the singing *charros* of the Mexican movies. And it was at about this same time that anthropologists and psychoanalysts discovered *machismo* in Mexico and labeled it as a peculiarly Mexican way of behavior.

But life along the border was not always a matter of conflicting cultures; there was often cooperation of a sort, between ordinary people of both cultures, since life had to be lived as an everyday affair. People most often cooperated in circumventing the excessive regulation of ordinary intercourse across the border. In other words, they regularly were engaged in smuggling. Smuggling, of course, has been a common activity wherever Mexicans and North Americans have come in contact; and this goes back to times long before Mexico's independence, when Yankee vessels used to make periodic smuggling visits to the more out-of-the-way Mexican ports. The famous Santa Fe Trail, begun about 1820 between Santa Fe and Independence, Missouri, may be considered one of the largest and most publicized smuggling operations in history. But even earlier, smuggling had been fairly general from the United States into Texas. The fact that the United States had consumer goods to sell and that Mexicans wanted to buy made smuggling inevitable, and many otherwise respected figures in the early history of the Southwest seem to have indulged in the practice. Smuggling could even be seen in those early days as a kind of libertarian practice, a protest against the harsh customs laws of the colonial times that throttled Mexico's economy. So, smuggling was not peculiar to the Nueces-Río Grande area, while the romanticizing of the smuggler as a leader in social protest was not limited even to the border areas as a whole. One has only to remember Luis Inclán's *Astucia,* where tobacco smugglers in interior Mexico are idealized as social reformers of the gun and hangman's noose. (It is worth mentioning, however, that Inclán's hero sends to the United States for *pistolas giratorias* to accomplish his pre-Porfirio Díaz version of iron-fisted law and order.)

Borders, however, offer special conditions not only for smuggling but for the idealization of the smuggler. This sounds pretty obvious, since, after all, political boundaries are the obvious places where customs and immigration regulations are enforced. But we must consider not only the existence of such political boundaries but the circumstances of their creation. In this respect, the Lower Río Grande Border was especially suited for smuggling operations.

To appreciate this fact, one has only to consider the history of the Lower Río Grande. This area—presently Tamaulipas and the southern part of Texas—was originally the province of Nuevo Santander. Nuevo Santander differed from the other three northernmost provinces of New Spain—New Mexico, Texas, and California—in an important way. It was not the last to be founded, its settlement having preceded that of California by some twenty years. But it was the least isolated of the frontier provinces. Great expanses of territory separated the settlements in New Mexico and California from the concentrations of Mexican population to the south. The same was true of the colony of Texas until 1749. It was in that year that Escandón began the settlement of Nuevo Santander, and one of the aims of settlement was precisely to fill the gap between the Texas colony and such established population centers to the south as Tampico and Monterrey.

So from their very first days of settlement, the colonists of Nuevo Santander lived an in-between existence. This sense of being caught in the middle was greatly intensified after 1835. As citizens of Mexico, the former *neosantan-derinos*—now *tamaulipecos*—faced an alien and hostile people to the north. As *federalistas,* they also had to contend with an equally hostile *centralista* government to the south. For the people of the Lower Río Grande, the period from the mid 1830s to the mid 1840s was marked by cattle-stealing raids by Texas ''cowboys'' from north of the Nueces and incursions of Mexican armies from the south. It would be difficult to find parallels to this situation in the other frontier provinces; however, the bitter hatreds that developed in the Nueces-Río Grande area during that bloody decade were soon diffused to other areas of the Southwest, along with other elements of the ''cattle culture.''

The Treaty of Guadalupe Hidalgo settled the conflict over territory between Mexico and the United States, officially at least. It also created a Mexican-American minority in the United States, as has often been noted. But it did not immediately create a border situation all along the international line. The *nuevomejicano* in Santa Fe, the *californio* in Los Angeles, and the *tejano* in San Antonio were swallowed whole into the North American political body. The new border—an imaginary and ill-defined line—was many miles to the south of them, in the uninhabited areas that already had separated them from the rest of Mexico before the war with the United States. The immediate change in customs demanded of *tejanos, californios,* and *nuevomejicanos* was from that of regional subcultures of Mexico to occupied territories within the United States.

Such was not the case with the people of the Lower Río Grande. A very well-defined geographic feature—the Río Grande itself—became the international line. And it was a line that cut right through the middle of what had once been Nuevo Santander. The river, once a focus of regional life, became a symbol of separation. The kind of borderline that separates ethnically related peoples is common enough in some parts of Europe; but in the earliest stages of the border between Mexico and the United States, it was typical only of the Lower Río Grande, with some exceptions such as the El Paso area. Here a pattern was set that would later become typical of the whole border between

Mexico and the United States. Irredentist movements were shared with other occupied areas such as New Mexico, though the Cortina and Pizaña uprisings of 1859 and 1915 respectively were strongly influenced by the proximity of the international boundary. More to our point was the general flouting of customs and immigration laws, not so much as a form of social or ethnic protest but as part of the way of life.

When the Río Grande became a border, friends and relatives who had been near neighbors—within shouting distance across a few hundred feet of water—now were legally in different countries. If they wanted to visit each other, the law required that they travel many miles up or down stream, to the nearest official crossing place, instead of swimming or boating directly across as they used to do before. It goes without saying that they paid little attention to the requirements of the law. When they went visiting, they crossed at the most convenient spot on the river; and, as is ancient custom when one goes visiting loved ones, they took gifts with them: farm products from Mexico to Texas, textiles and other manufactured goods from Texas to Mexico. Legally, of course, this was smuggling, differing from contraband for profit in volume only. Such a pattern is familiar to anyone who knows the border, for it still operates, not only along the Lower Río Grande now but all along the boundary line between Mexico and the United States.

Unofficial crossings also disregarded immigration laws. Children born on one side of the river would be baptized on the other side, and thus appear on church registers as citizens of the other country. This bothered no one since people on both sides of the river thought of themselves as *mexicanos,* but United States officials were concerned about it. People would come across to visit relatives and stay long periods of time, and perhaps move inland in search of work. After 1890, the movement in search of work was preponderantly from Mexico deep into Texas and beyond. The ease with which the river could be crossed and the hospitality of relatives and friends on either side also was a boon to men who got in trouble with the law. It was not necessary to flee over trackless wastes, with the law hot on one's trail. All it took was a few moments in the water, and one was out of reach of his pursuers and in the hands of friends. If illegal crossings in search of work were mainly in a northerly direction, crossings to escape the law were for the most part from north to south. By far, not all the Mexicans fleeing American law were criminals in an ordinary sense. Many were victims of cultural conflict, men who had reacted violently to assaults on their human dignity or their economic rights.

Resulting from the partition of the Lower Río Grande communities was a set of folk attitudes that would in time become general along the United States-Mexican border. There was a generally favorable disposition toward the individual who disregarded customs and immigration laws, especially the laws of the United States. The professional smuggler was not a figure of reproach, whether he was engaged in smuggling American woven goods into Mexico or Mexican tequila into Texas. In folklore there was a tendency to idealize the smuggler, especially the *tequilero,* as a variant of the hero of cultural conflict. The smuggler, the illegal alien looking for work, and the border-conflict hero became identified with each other in the popular mind. They came into conflict with the same American laws and sometimes with the same individual officers of the law, who were all looked upon as *rinches*—a border-Spanish rendering of "ranger." Men who were Texas Rangers, for example, during the revenge killings of Mexicans after the Pizaña uprising of 1915* later were border patrolmen who engaged in gunbattles with *tequileros.* So stereotyped did the figure of the *rinche* become that Lower Río Grande Border versions of "La persecución de Villa" identify Pershing's soldiers as *rinches.*

A *corrido* tradition of intercultural conflict developed along the Río Grande, in which the hero defends his rights and those of other Mexicans against the *rinches.* The first hero of these *corridos* is Juan Nepomuceno Cortina, who is celebrated in an 1859 *corrido* precisely because he helps a fellow Mexican.

> Ese general Cortina
> es libre y muy soberano,
> han subido sus honores
> porque salvó a un mexicano.

> That general Cortina is quite sovereign and free;
> The honor due him is greater, for he saved a Mexican's life.

Other major *corrido* heroes are Gregorio Cortez (1901), who kills two Texas sheriffs after one of them shoots his brother; Jacinto Treviño (1911), who kills several Americans to avenge his brother's death; Rito García (1885), who shoots several officers who invade his home without a warrant; and Aniceto Pizaña and his *sediciosos* (1915). Some *corrido* heroes escape across the border into Mexico; others, like Gregorio Cortez and Rito García, are betrayed and captured. They go to prison but they have stood up for what is right. As the "Corrido de Rito García" says,

> . . . me voy a la penitencia
> por defender mi derecho.

---

*The uprising occurred on the Lower Río Grande Border and involved a group of Texas-Mexican rancheros attempting to create a Spanish-speaking republic in South Texas. Pizaña endeavored to appeal to other United States minority groups [Editor's Note].

> I am going to the penitentiary because
> I defended my rights.

The men who smuggled tequila into the United States during the twenties and early thirties were no apostles of civil rights, nor did the border people think of them as such. But in his activities, the *tequilero* risked his life against the old enemy, the *rinche*. And, as has been noted, smuggling had long been part of the border way of life. Still sung today is "El corrido de Mariano Reséndez" about a prominent smuggler of textiles into Mexico, circa 1900. So highly respected were Reséndez and his activities that he was known as "El Contrabandista." Reséndez, of course, violated Mexican laws; and his battles were with Mexican customs officers. The *tequilero* and his activities, however, took on an intercultural dimension; and they became a kind of coda to the *corridos* of border conflict.

The heavy-handed and often brutal manner that Anglo lawmen have used in their dealings with border Mexicans helped make almost any man outside the law a sympathetic figure, with the *rinche* or Texas Ranger as the symbol of police brutality. That these symbols still are alive may be seen in the recent Fred Carrasco affair. The border Mexican's tolerance of smuggling does not seem to extend to traffic in drugs. The few *corridos* that have been current on the subject, such as "Carga blanca," take a negative view of the dope peddler. Yet Carrasco's death in 1976 at the Huntsville (Texas) prison, along with two women hostages, inspired close to a dozen *corridos* with echoes of the old style. The sensational character of Carrasco's death cannot be discounted, but note should also be taken of the unproved though widely circulated charges that Carrasco was "executed" by a Texas Ranger, who allegedly shot him through the head at close range where Carrasco lay wounded. This is a scenario familiar to many a piece of folk literature about cultural conflict—*corridos* and prose narratives—the *rinche* finishing off the wounded Mexican with a bullet through the head. It is interesting to compare the following stanzas, the first from one of the Carrasco *corridos* and the other two from a *tequilero* ballad of the thirties.

> El capitán de los rinches
> fue el primero que cayó
> pero el chaleco de malla
> las balas no traspasó.

> The captain of the Rangers was the first one to fall,
> But the armored vest he was wearing did not let the bullets through.

*   *   *

> En fin de tanto invitarle

> Leandro los acompañó;
> en las lomas de Almiramba
> fue el primero que cayó.

> They kept asking him to go, until Leandro went with them;
> In the hills of Almiramba, he was the first one to fall.

> El capitán de los rinches
> a Silvano se acercó,
> y en unos cuantos segundos
> Silvano García murió.

> The captain of the Rangers came up close to Silvano;
> And in a few seconds Silvano García was dead.

Similar attitudes are expressed on the Sonora-Arizona border, for example, when the hard-case hero of "El corrido de Cananea" is made to say,

> Me agarraron los cherifes
> al estilo americano,
> como al hombre de delito,
> todos con pistola en mano.

> The sheriffs caught me, in the American style,
> As they would a wanted man, all of them pistol in hand.

The partition of Nuevo Santander was also to have political effects, arising from the strong feeling among the Lower Río Grande people that the land on both sides of the river was equally theirs. This involved feelings on a very local and personal level, rather than the rhetoric of national politics, and is an attitude occasionally exhibited by some old Río Grande people to this day. Driving north along one of today's highways toward San Antonio, Austin, or Houston, they are likely to say as the highway crosses the Nueces, "We are now entering Texas." Said in jest, of course, but the jest has its point. Unlike Mexicans in California, New Mexico, and the old colony of Texas, the Río Grande people experienced the dismemberment of Mexico in a very immediate way. So the attitude developed, early and naturally, that a border Mexican was *en su tierra* in Texas even if he had been born in Tamaulipas. Such feelings, of course, were the basis for the revolts of Cortina and Pizaña. They reinforced the borderer's disregard of political and social boundaries. And they lead in a direct line to the Chicano movement and its mythic concept of Aztlán. For the Chicano does not base his claim to the Southwest on royal land grants or on a lineage that goes back to the Spanish conquistadores. On the contrary, he is more likely to be the child or grandchild of immigrants. He bases his claim to Aztlán on his Mexican culture and his mestizo heritage.

Conversely, the Texas-born Mexican continued to think of Mexico as "our land" also. That this at times led to problems of identity is seen in the folksongs of the border. In 1885, for example, Rito García protests illegal police entry into his home by shooting a few officers of Cameron County, Texas. He makes it across the river and feels safe, unaware that Porfirio Díaz has an extradition agreement with the United States. Arrested and returned to Texas, according to the *corrido,* he expresses amazement,

> Yo nunca hubiera creído
> que mi país tirano fuera,
> que Mainero me entregara
> a la nación extranjera.

> I never would have thought that my country would be so unjust,
> That Mainero would hand me over to a foreign nation.

And he adds bitterly,

> Mexicanos, no hay que fiar
> en nuestra propia nación,
> nunca vayan a buscar
> a México protección.

> Mexicans, we can put no trust in our own nation;
> Never go to Mexico asking for protection.

But the *mexicanos* to whom he gives this advice are Texas Mexicans.

An even more interesting case dates back to 1867, the year Maximilian surrendered at Querétaro. A few days before this event, on May 5, Mexicans celebrated another event just as historic, the fifth anniversary of the defeat of the French at Puebla by Mexican troops under Ignacio Zaragoza. The little town of San Ignacio, on the Texas side of the river, celebrated the Cinco de Mayo with a big festival at which a local *guitarrero* sang two of his songs, especially composed for the occasion. One was "A Zaragoza," in praise of the victor over the French at Puebla; the other was "A Grant," in praise of Ulysses S. Grant, the victor over the Confederacy. The same set of symbols—flag, honor, country—are used in both songs.[8]

The simplest forms of verbal folk expression are names; they are also the first level of expression of stereotypes developed as a result of intergroup relations. When we name things, we give them a life of their own; we isolate them from the rest of our experience. By naming ourselves, we affirm our own identity; we define it by separating ourselves from others, to whom we give names different from our own. By naming others we also identify them, and thus make them easier to cope with. It has been a widely held belief throughout human history that one can acquire power over others—mortals and immortals alike—by knowing their names.

The names Mexicans and Americans have called each other along the border are a rich source of information about the history of their attitudes. We invent names—usually derogatory—for other ethnic groups by reference to the stereotypic image we have of the particular outgroup. Some names make reference to physical appearance, language, diet, or customs—the most obvious ingredients in the development of ethnic stereotypes. Others may be the names of occupations or social classes identified with the outgroup. Still others are personal names that evoke for the ingroup a fully realized image of the stereotype they attribute to the outgroup. Finally, some derogatory ethnic labels may be corruptions of the accepted, nonderogatory name for the group in question. And occasionally we have a situation in which a name coined for one outgroup is transferred to another group that demands more of the ingroup's attention.

American English has always been rich in derogatory labels for various ethnic groups. In *The American Thesaurus of Slang,* Berrey and Van den Bark list as many as 150 derogatory terms for the American Negro alone.[9] We would expect border English to be generously endowed with names for the Mexican, and we are not disappointed. The most common has been "greaser," which focuses on an aspect of physical appearance, the color and appearance of the skin—and perhaps of the hair. Along with its derivatives— "greaseball," "goo-goo," and "gook"—it once had a much wider ethnic range in American English.[10] In recent times, however, "gook" has been restricted to Orientals, while "greaser" long ago became the identifying epithet for the Mexican, to whom the term has been applied at least since 1836.[11] The Mexican's trouble with the long and short versions of the English "i" qualify him as a spic. "Spic," however, and its derivatives—"spig" and "spigotty"—are not used exclusively for the Mexican but may be applied to any speaker of Spanish, Portuguese, or Italian. The Mexican diet has been a much richer source of derogatory names, among them—"pepper belly," "taco choker," "frijole guzzler," "chili picker," and (of a woman) "hot tamale." Aside from diet, no other aspect of Mexican culture seems to have caught the fancy of the Anglo coiner of derogatory terms for Mexicans.

More fruitful sources have been names used by Mexicans to denote class or occupational distinctions among themselves, such designations being turned into derogatory terms for all Mexicans, or at least all those Mexicans the Anglo speaker disapproves of. Chief of these are *peón, pelado, mojado* or its English equivalent "wetback," *bracero,* and most recently *pachuco.* Various corruptions of "Mexican" also have been used as derogatory terms. Aside from the clipped form "Mex," the most common are "Meskin" (originally a nonderogatory, dialectal form of "Mexican") and its derivatives, "skin," "skindiver," and "diver." A special twist in the insulting use of national or ethnic names—one that seems peculiarly North American—is the application of the outgroup's ethnic designation to another member of one's ingroup. Southern whites, it is well known, have long insulted other Southern whites by calling them "niggers." Similarly, border Anglos have insulted each other by use of the epithet "Mexican." On occasion, one Anglo might insult another simply by calling him *"señor,"* the implication being that the person so addressed was a Mexican. Not surprisingly, the Anglo came to consider "Mexican" an insulting term when applied to Mexicans as well. The use of "Spanish" as a euphemism for "Mexican" is old on the border. As Bigfoot Wallace said of the surgeon who treated him kindly while he was a prisoner in Perote in the early 1840s, "He was a Castilian, or Spaniard, by birth, and not a Mexican, which may account satisfactorily in a great measure for the fact that he was not a bigoted tyrant in disposition. At any rate I hope he may live a thousand years. . . ."[12]

"Latin" is another current euphemism for the Mexican, but it seems to be fairly recent, having gained currency only in the 1920s, with the founding of the League of United Latin American Citizens. I am not aware of any names that were originally used by Anglos specifically for some other ethnic group and that were later transferred in toto to the Mexican. Mexicans occasionally have been called "niggers," but this seems to be merely an extension of the custom of using "nigger" as a form of insult.[13] The names mentioned reveal a stereotypic view of the Mexican that may be encapsulated in a proper name. Two names are especially favored in this respect. "Pedro"—usually pronounced with a long "e" as "Paydro"—evokes the fat, stupid, but basically harmless peon. "Pancho" suggests the bandit stereotype, the Mexican with the long mustaches and the cartridge belts crossed over his chest.

There is still another form of ethnic insult of long standing in American English, though it has not been especially notable in border culture—what Ed Cray has called the derisive ethnic adjective.[14] Some of these are very old, such as "Dutch widow" for a prostitute and "Dutch courage" for drunken belligerence. Collecting in Los Angeles, Cray lists a number of phrases using "Mexican" as a derisive adjective: Mexican car wash (leaving your car out in the rain), Mexican credit card (a piece of hose to siphon gasoline out of other people's cars), Mexican overdrive (driving downhill in neutral), Mexican promotion (an increase in rank without a raise in pay), and Mexican two-step (dysentery). These phrases, however, are wandering and adaptable forms that, like some jokes, may be fitted to many situations. One also hears of Jewish overdrive, Jewish car wash, Oklahoma credit card (in Texas, of course), and Irish promotion. Not even Mexican two-step (better known by its victims as the *"turista"* or *"*Montezuma's revenge*"*) can claim the honor of original coinage. In some parts of the South, dysentery has been known as the Kentucky or the Tennessee two-step. However, the tendency to use "Mexican" as an adjective to denote a make-shift job or product is an old one on the Río Grande border. Cray also reports it among Anglos in Los Angeles.[15]

In *The American Language* H. L. Mencken observes that as far as terms of opprobrium go "the American language boasts a large stock, chiefly directed at aliens."[16] Mencken's observation is entirely correct, but he goes on to remark that in the exchange of insults the United States gets off very lightly, "for only the Spanish-speaking nations appear to have any opprobrious names for Americans, and these are few in number." He cites but two, *yanqui blofero* and *gringo.*[17] Mencken is too quick to claim superiority in the art of the insult, for Spanish-speaking people have done much better than he suggests. Along the border I would estimate that there are between forty and fifty names used by Mexicans for the Anglo, about the same number that Anglos have used for the Mexican. Names for the Anglo, however, show a different distribution in the categories cited above. In devising names based on the Anglo's physical appearance, the Mexican has noted not only the Anglo's skin color but also the color of his hair and eyes, as well as the size of his feet, which are seen not only as huge but also as having a very bad smell. A few examples are *blancanieves, canoso, colorado, cara 'e pan crudo, cucaracho, cristalino, ojos de gato, güero,* and *patón.* Etymologically, *gringo* belongs to the names originating from the outgroup's difficulties with an ingroup's language, since *gringo* has a long history among Spanish-speaking peoples as a derogatory term for the non-Spanish-speaking foreigner. Few border Mexicans, though, are aware of the origins of *gringo,* and there are many who believe the U.S.-originated legend that the word was coined by Mexicans during the American occupation of Mexico City in 1846. But *gademe* certainly is a local invention, going back to the 1840s, and based on the Anglo's alleged custom of uttering a "goddam" with every sentence he spoke. *Sanavabiche* is often used in a similar manner, though at times it is difficult to determine whether the speaker is merely using the American expletive, "son-of-a-bitch." But much is made about *San Avabiche* as an American saint, leading to the phrase, *Hijo de un santo de los americanos.* Names referring to the Anglo's diet are few indeed. The most common one has been *repollero,* deriding the Anglo's taste for boiled cabbage, though at times I have heard *repollero* as a term for the Anglo truck farmer. The American taste for ham plays a big part in border folklore, and now and then one hears the term *gringo jamonero.* It is more common, however, for Americans to be derided as ham-eaters in prose narratives or in ballads such as "El corrido de Jacinto Treviño," in which the hero derides a bunch of *rinches* who are besieging him in a Brownsville saloon,

> Éntrenle, rinches cobardes,
> validos de la ocasión,
> no van a comer pan blanco
> con tajadas de jamón.

> Come on, you cowardly Rangers, who like to take unfair advantage,
> This is not like eating white bread with slices of ham.

In border versions of "La persecución de Villa" Pershing's troops are derided in much the same way,

> Cuando llegaron a México estos gringos
> buscaban pan y galletas con jamón,
> y la raza, que estaba muy enojada,
> lo que les dieron fueron balas de cañón.

> When these gringos arrived in Mexico,
> They were looking for bread and for crackers and ham;
> But the people, who were very angry,
> Gave them nothing but cannon balls.

Still another Anglo habit, tobacco chewing, has resulted in *mascatabaco.* No names that I know of have been coined on the border in reference to Anglo class or occupation designations, though some have been borrowed from other areas. Poor whites in central Texas were known among other Anglos as "cedar-choppers," a term the Texas Mexican renders as *postero* (fence-post maker) and which may be applied to any Anglo American. Border Mexicans also use *turista* for any Anglo they do not like, in ironic reference to the stereotyped American tourist of interior Mexico. The Mexican has no derogatory names at all based on official designations for the English-speaking citizen of the United States. They do use *míster* as the Anglo uses *señor,* to suggest ethnic origins in a contemptuous sort of way, as in the phrase *el míster ese. Los primos* might also fit in this category. Aside from the connotations of "stupid" in the term, *primos* is explained as meaning *hijos del Tío Sam.* Neither *americano* and *anglosajón* nor the clipped forms *anglo* and *sajón* carry the derogatory connotations that "Mexican" and "Mex" carry for the Anglo. *Anglo* is the most neutral of the two clipped forms. If a border Mexican is comparing Mexicans and North Americans to the detriment of the latter, he is more likely to use *sajón*. The border Mexican uses no English proper names to evoke the stereotype of the Anglo, as the Anglo does with "Pedro" and "Pancho." Nor does he use any of the names for the Anglo as derogatory adjectives.

The border Mexican is unique perhaps in the number of derogatory ethnic names he has transferred to the North American from other referent groups. Leaving *gringo* aside, which underwent a restriction of meaning, as did "greaser" in English, we have *birote, bolillo, gabacho, godo, güero,* and possibly *patón. Gabacho* is an old derogatory term for the Frenchman that began to be used for the Anglo during the 1930s among the urban Mexican Americans of Los Angeles, El Paso, Laredo, and San Antonio. As late as 1959, none of my colleagues in Mexico City had recorded the term in this sense. But in the early 1960s, *gabacho* was reported among the students at UNAM as a term for the North American. According to some informants from East Chicago, Indiana, *gabacho* (meaning American) had been taken to the Bajío area in the 1950s by returning migrant workers. *Güero* is a very common term for American on the border, though its use as an ethnic label is not recorded in the dictionaries I have seen. In his *Diccionario de Mejicanismos,* however, Santamaría gives us this stanza from a song dating from the French occupation. It is found under "Mariachi."

> Dicen que por el Naguanchi
> no puede pasar ni un güero
> porque le arrancan el cuero
> pa' la caja del mariachi.[18]

> They say that around Naguanchi not a single *güero* can pass,
> Because they will take his hide for the drum in the mariachi.

The reference is, of course, to the French invaders. *Bolillo* and its variant *birote,* both used for the Anglo on the border, are difficult to explain except in relation to the French troops of the same period. Anglos are associated in the border Mexican's mind with ham, not with French bread. I have to date found no written evidence of the direct use of *bolillo* for Frenchman, but there is evidence that the *juaristas* taunted the French and their allies with mocking references to French bread. In an article about folklore from northeastern Mexico during the French occupation, Manuel Neira Barragán says that the *norteños* sang a version of "Las Torres de Puebla" in which the victorious Mexican soldiers taunt the retreating French at the close of the battle of the Cinco de Mayo:

> ¿Qu'es de las piezas de pan?
> Aguárdenlas que ahí les van. Pam![19]
>
> Where are the loaves of bread?
> Get ready, for here they go. Bang!

Another song, quoted by Vicente Mendoza, shows the Mexican women who associated with the French in a desolate state after the fall of Querétaro and the capture of Maximilian:

> ¡Pobrecitas afrancesadas
> que piden piezas de pan!
> Apárenlas, que allá van.[20]
>
> Poor Frenchified girls, who keep asking for loaves of bread!
> Get ready, for here they go.

Godo, another border term for the Anglo, is widely known in Spanish America as a derogatory term for the Spaniard, though it seems to be rare in modern Mexico, since Santamaría does not list it in his *Diccionario de Mejicanismos. Patón,* according to Santamaría's *Diccionario General de Americanismos,* is applied to the Spaniard in Cuba. Again, Santamaría fails to list the term in *Mejicanismos,* though it has been used for the North American on the border since the early 1840s. In sum, we have at least four and perhaps six derogatory terms, once applied to Frenchmen and Spaniards, that have been transferred to the North or Anglo American.

In recent years anthropologists, sociologists, and even cultural geographers have been interested in the Mexican American's self-image as it is expressed in the names he uses in reference to himself. The results of such studies have been less than satisfactory, mainly because two important variables have either been ignored or not given their due weight. One of these variables is the Mexican American's bilingual/bicultural makeup, which allows (or forces) him to occupy somewhat different viewpoints at different times, depending on the language he happens to be using as an instrument to calibrate his experience. The other is the influence exerted on the Mexican American's (and even the Mexican's) self-awareness by the derogatory ethnic labels discussed above. In Spanish, border Mexicans* use terms like *mexicano, raza,* and *chicano* in reference to themselves, these being ingroup terms for the most part, to be used only among other *mexicanos.* In his more jocular moments the border Mexican is likely to refer to himself by such labels as *chicaspatas* or

---

*The term "Mexican" is used throughout this essay in a cultural rather than in a political or biological sense [Editor's Note].

ganado cebú, the mirror opposites of *patón* and *ganado Hereford.* When speaking in English, he may refer to himself as Latin, Spanish, or perhaps Mexican American. Only rarely will he call himself a Mexican, in English, especially if he is talking to an Anglo.

As has been noted, the border Mexican uses no derogatory adjectives based on names for the Anglo. He does, however, use "Mexican" as an adjective in some contexts resembling Anglo derisive adjectives such as "Mexican car wash." In most cases, though, "Mexican" is used to suggest a kind of simplicity and ingenuity that more than makes up for lack of complex technology. A *molcajete* [kitchen mortar used to grind spices] becomes a "Mexican blender," and a tortilla a "Mexican fork"; chile peppers are "Mexican vitamins," tacos are "Mexican hamburgers," and mezcal is "Mexican penicillin," a play on the old saying, *Para todo mal, mezcal.* These are employed equally well in English and Spanish, though usually only among other Mexicans. *A la mexicana,* always in Spanish, means doing something with wit and ingenuity rather than with much equipment and expense. All these denote a kind of ironic pride in identifying oneself as a Mexican. But when a border Mexican rolls down his car windows so he can enjoy his "Mexican air conditioning," he has moved very close to the Anglo's point of view. Again, a border Mexican foreman may correct another Mexican working for him, telling him, *"¡No seas . . . mexicano!"* instead of saying, *"No seas pendejo."* This is most common on the Texas side of the border, it is true, but it is not unheard of on the opposite side of the river. It is worth remembering that the saying that "P.M." in Mexico means not "post meridian" but *puntalidad mexicana* is common in the northern Mexican states and much further south as well.

There is no doubt that the border Mexican is ambivalent about the terms "Mexican" and *mexicano,* and there is little doubt also that the Anglo's use of "Mexican" as an insulting term has much to do with the Mexican's ambivalence. It is little wonder, then, that when English-speaking anthropologists ask unsuspecting *mexicanos* what they call themselves, the informants will answer "Spanish," "Latin," *raza,* Chicano, or what have you—anything but "Mexican."

If we compare the derogatory names that Anglos and Mexicans have given each other in close to a century and a half of border existence, we will agree that both have been equally inventive in insulting each other. But if we look at the names discussed above in relation to all other ethnic groups known by each culture, we will note significant differences. Berrey and Van den Bark list the following numbers of derogatory ethnic names for different groups in the United States: Negro, 150; Jew, 50; Irishman, 43; Frenchman, 25; German, 24; Italian, 13. These figures are far from complete, when we note that for the Mexican Berrey and Van den Bark list only 14 names. The Mexican, on the other hand, does not seem to have extended his inventiveness to other ethnic groups besides the American. He has a couple of names each for the Spaniard and the Chinese and half a dozen or so for the Negro (mostly taken from English), and that is all. Furthermore, some of the insulting names the Mexican formerly used for Frenchmen and Spaniards have been transferred to the American. This seems to be the result of a factor we might call ethnic visibility—the physical, cultural, economic, or political qualities of a group that draw the attention of others, either in a positive way or as an irritant. From Berrey and Van den Bark's list, it is obvious that the Negro is the most visible minority in the United States. In the Southwest the Mexican may claim honors for high visibility, but he is just one of many minorities that affect the WASP majority with feelings of tension and unease. For the Mexican, however, the Anglo fills the horizon, almost to the total exclusion of other ethnic groups—capable of excruciating visibility and high irritant power.

There are several other things worth noting about the names we have used in neighborly interchange along the border. One involves the matter of culture flow. It is the usual consensus that culture moves like water, from the high places to the low. This is not always true, and no better examples of an opposite view can be found than in the history of Spanish literature, where folk forms and themes were a major source for the literature of the Golden Age. In Mexico, also, scholars have usually believed that the folklore of the frontier regions is made up of local versions of items imported from interior Mexico. In other works I have attempted to show that this may not be entirely true of the *corrido*.[21] A similar case, I believe, may be made about Mexican folklore concerning the United States, especially in regard to names. It is a thesis that cannot be developed at length in this essay, but perhaps some short examples may gain it a hearing. During 1847 and 1848, American troops occupied Mexico City and other areas of interior Mexico. There was, of course, a great deal of popular feeling against the invaders, which was expressed in songs, *pasquines,* and *décimas.* I have delved into the records of the period to the best of my ability, and nowhere have I been able to find any other name used for the Americans but *yanqui.* On the Río Grande, however, names like *gringo, patón,* and *gademe* were being used for the Anglo by 1842. Almost a century later, in the 1930s, *gabacho* gains currency along the border as a derogatory name for the American; but it is not until the 1960s that it is reported in Mexico City. Perhaps some Mexicanist with more resources than mine will come up with contrary evidence to overturn this thesis; but on the basis of available data it seems that the derogatory names for the American gained currency on the border before they moved south into interior Mexico.

In "The Esoteric-Exoteric Factor in Folklore," William Hugh Jansen makes the point that our awareness of other groups besides our own is intimately related to our consciousness of ourselves as a group.[22] It would appear, then, that it is on the border that a Mexican national consciousness first manifests itself on the popular level. Intrusion by a foreign, greatly different people minimized differences among border Mexican subgroups. The necessity to identify and label the outsiders inevitably led to a need to establish one's identity, to ask the question of emerging national consciousness, "Who are we?"

But the appearance of an awakening sense of identity was coupled with a challenge to that same identity. Another thing we may note about the study of border ethnic names is the impact that the Anglo's insulting terms for the Mexican has had on the Mexican's ego, so strong an impact that it has affected the Mexican's terms of self-reference. The Mexican American is proud to call himself a *mexicano,* but he is often ashamed to be known as a Mexican. *A la mexicana* may have connotations of ethnic pride, but *¡No seas mexicano!* may be used as a half-insult even by some people on the Mexican side of the border.

It is questionable whether an identity crisis occurs with the border Anglo; at least the folklore does not seem to show it. One may observe identity problems among some individuals but rarely among groups. This obviously is due to the aggressive role of the Anglo culture in the border situation. The Anglo has taken liberally from the Mexican in creating his own version of a border culture, but such borrowings have not always been acknowledged. Even when borrowings are recognized, they are not seen as threats to the culture of the United States. They are cheerfully stirred into the great mix that is North American culture, whether one sees that culture as a pot of stew or as a bowl of tossed salad. The Mexican, on the other hand, has always been on the defensive in the border situation, afraid of being swallowed whole. He does not have to be sophisticated or an intellectual to realize the risk to his way of life that culture contact entails. The folklore shows his preoccupation about remaining "Mexican" even when he is becoming most Americanized. Still, the Anglo does show clear signs of tension and unease in his relationship with the Mexican.

Each group seems to have a double-faceted view of the other; we might say that one aspect expresses active hostility while the other one expresses animadversion of a latent sort. The Anglo's actively hostile stereotype of the Mexican is well known: he is dirty and greasy; he is treacherous, cruel, and cowardly; thievery is his second nature; furthermore, the Mexican American has always recognized the Anglo Texan as his superior. The Mexican American's actively hostile stereotype of the Anglo is not so very different: the Anglo is cruel and treacherous if he can get you in his power, but he is easy to outwit because he is so big and stupid; his victories over the Mexican are made possible by superior numbers and superior weapons; man for man, however, the Anglo is too fat and soft, too used to easy living to measure up to the Mexican. The less actively hostile stereotype of the Anglo shows him as good-hearted but boorish; he is very rich, having made his money by cheating other people—for example, cheating the Mexicans out of Texas; he is cagey and clannish, but he is so greedy and gullible that he can be tricked out of his money or even out of his wife by appealing to his cupidity; in general, he is not really a bad fellow, even though he speaks funny Spanish and allows himself to be ruled by his women. The corresponding stereotype of the Mexican shows him as a colorful but impractical character who speaks funny English; if old, he is a kind of Uncle Remus, full of antiquated and useless wisdom; if young, he loves flowers, music, and a good time, but it is hard to get a good day's work out of him.

There is an interesting difference in the Mexican and Anglo stereotypes of each other as they appear in border folklore and in related popular literature. The Anglo in border Mexican folklore is usually faceless and nameless, an idea or a feeling rather than a man. When he is singled out in a ballad or prose narrative, he represents a broad type: the Major Sheriff or the Chief of the Rangers in the *corridos,* the gullible tourist, or merely the stupid American who is tricked out of his money or his wife by the Mexican in the jokes. The Mexican, on the other hand, is rarely mentioned in the English-language folksongs of the border country. He plays a bigger role in the Anglo American legendary anecdote, especially in tales of buried treasure and in miscellaneous stories with a border-country setting. In tales such as these, the Mexican is never the major character but the companion, servant, or guide of an Anglo American. Nonetheless, the Mexican of the Anglo-American legendary anecdote seems to be much more of an individual than is the Anglo American of border Mexican folklore. He is Juan, the goatherd with a sense of humor and a flair for telling a good story; Jesús, the drunken but faithful servant; Alberto, the wise old vaquero—still stereotypes, apparently, but with more personality than the generic *cherife mayor* of the *corridos* or the *gringo pendejo* of the Mexican jokes.

Even in the most recent types of folklore, this difference in stereotyping appears. Young Anglos have combined the contemporary mock riddle with the well-known American institution of Colonel Sanders's Kentucky Fried Chicken and the "Mexican greaser" stereotype, to produce the following:

Q. What is brown, greasy, and sells fried chicken?
A. Colonel Sánchez.

Young border Mexican Americans, on the other hand, have taken two proverbs that go back to the Mexican colonial period: *Indio con puro, ateo seguro* and *No tiene la culpa el indio sino quien lo hizo compadre.* (An Indian smoking a cigar is certain to be an atheist. *And* The Indian is not at fault but rather he who trusts him.) To these they have added two real but nameless types in their experience: the Anglo politician who is very friendly and speaks Spanish to them only when he is running for office, and the cigar-smoking Texas Mexican political boss who sells out to the Anglo. The result is a proverb in the traditional style:

> No te fíes del mexicano que fuma puro,
> ni del gringo que te dice, "compadre."

> Never trust a Mexican who smokes a cigar,
> or a gringo who calls you "compadre."

We noted the American habit of using proper names as derogatory ethnic labels, not only Pedro and Pancho for the Mexican or Mexican American but Fritz for the German, Pat for the Irishman, Pierre for the Frenchman, Ivan for the Russian, Giuseppe for the Italian. There is a slightly literary air involved in this kind of ethnic naming, if seen from this broader perspective. And perhaps the difference is there—that the Mexican stereotype of the Anglo appears in songs and narratives belonging to a truly folk tradition (artistic but unreflecting expressions of a whole people), while the Anglo anecdotes about the Mexican most often betray the reflective eye of the conscious artist, or would-be artist. They are on the edge of that literature of the Southwest that J. Frank Dobie labored to bring into being, mostly by means of folklike sketches dealing with "colorful" Mexican characters. On the other hand, except for names and ethnic jokes of a fairly general kind, Anglo folklore almost ignores the Mexican. One might say that he has been observed by the Anglo, while the Anglo has been experienced by the Mexican.

So far we have dealt with generalizations about males made by other males. The stereotypes of Anglo and Mexican women also show some similarities. In both cases, the woman belonging to the opposing ethnic group is seen as both desirable and easy of access, but not worth marrying; however, the details fleshing out the pattern are different. In a way, the Anglo stereotype idealizes the Mexican woman. She is exotic, romantic, desirable; full of vivacity and sexual know-how. But, alas, she is "Mexican," and marriage to her involves falling into the sin of miscegenation. As an old cowboy ditty put it:

> But she was Mex and I was white,
> And so it could not be.

On the other hand, the Mexican stereotype of the Anglo woman portrays her as visually striking, all pink flesh and yellow hair, but not particularly satisfying in a sexual way; furthermore, she is shameless and dominates her husband.

It should be emphasized that these stereotypes, though often expressed in the performance of folk literature, do not necessarily jibe with observed behavior, either now or in the past. For example, Anglos did marry border Mexican women from the very earliest days, though when such marriages are mentioned in Anglo anecdote and song the women are called Spanish rather than Mexican. At the present time, moreover, one may hear from border Mexican informants about the shamelessness of Anglo girls, who date and wear revealing clothes, but the observer may also note that the informant's teenage daughters are wearing skimpy clothing, going out on dates, and acting very much like Anglos.

In the latter case we seem to have an example of culture lag, while in the former it is a matter of prejudice toward people with darker skins. At all events, the Anglo view of the Mexican woman seems to be less unfavorable than the Mexican view of the Anglo woman. In the Anglo stereotype, the Mexican woman has definite personal qualities as a woman, at least, though not necessarily as an individual. Such things as vivacity, a quick temper, faithfulness, jealousy, compassion, bravery, or even the ability to play the guitar add something to the stereotype. It is only the question of race that makes the Mexican woman an undesirable mate for the Anglo. The Mexican stereotype of the Anglo female, however, is based on a few very physical qualities; they are fair of skin and buxom of figure: *"gordas y bien coloradas"* as "El corrido de los ambiciosos patones" says. But the Mexican claims to have no real sexual interest in these red-faced, well-fed women, who, he avers, are insipid lovers. Their conquest is merely a way of injuring the Anglo man, like tricking him out of his money or using him homosexually. One must keep in mind that in reality unions of Mexican men to Anglo women were extremely rare on the border until recent years, while instances of Anglo men marrying Mexican women go back to the very first years of contact between the two peoples.

The border Mexican rarely gets to put his prejudices into action, if one discounts the rumors that circulated after La Raza Unida gained political control of Crystal City. Jokesters were passing the word around that Anglos were no longer being served at Crystal City's better restaurants and bars. But even these jokes make the point that the Mexican folklore about the Anglo is mainly compensatory, while the Anglo can on occasion put his own prejudices into action. In 1942 and 1943, young Mexican Americans of Los Angeles were subjected to beatings and other persecutions by police and military personnel during the so-called *pachuco* riots. The police justified their treatment of young Mexicans on biological grounds. Captain E. Duran Ayres of the Los Angeles police, in an official report, claimed that the Mexican will not use his fists, or even his feet, in a fight with a Caucasian, since the Mexican

> considers all that to be a sign of weakness, and all he knows and feels is a desire to use a knife or some lethal weapon. In other words, his desire is to kill, or at least let blood. That is why it is difficult for the Anglo-Saxon to understand the psychology of the Indian or even the Latin. . . . When there is added to this inborn characteristic that has come down through the ages, the use of liquor, then we certainly have crimes of violence.[23]

Carey McWilliams, who quotes Ayres in *North from Mexico,* emphasizes Ayres's view that the Mexican has an inborn blood-lust, the result of his ancestry, which leads him naturally to crime. McWilliams mockingly refers to Ayres as an "anthropologist."

Captain Ayres, however, is not the only amateur anthropologist who has had harsh words for the young Chicanos of Los Angeles. Having visited Los Angeles about the time of the "*pachuco* riots," Octavio Paz has some interesting things to say in *The Labyrinth of Solitude.* For Paz, the *pachuco* is "an impassive and sinister clown whose purpose is to cause terror instead of laughter." He is at once a sadist and a masochist. He seeks to become a criminal so he may bask in notoriety; he provokes Anglo society into taking action against him until retribution finally bursts over his head in a saloon fight, a raid, or a riot, from which all that the pachuco derives is "painful self-satisfaction."[24] If we are capable of imagining Captain Ayres reading *The Labyrinth of Solitude,* we may be able to picture his enthusiasm.

Ayres would have been even more enthusiastic about Paz had he been present in Batts Hall at the University of Texas, Austin, one night in 1969, when Octavio Paz delivered the Hackett Memorial Lecture of that year, "Mexico: The Last Decade." The bloody events of Tlatelolco the year before were still fresh in everyone's mind, and Paz's indignation was more than justified. That much would have troubled our hypothetical visitor, Captain Ayres, who might not have seen much difference between the beating and shooting of young Mexicans in Los Angeles and the same thing in Mexico City. But Ayres would have felt at home when the speaker assigned the blame for the massacre. It was not a case of overreaction by a group of armed men who took a brutally literal interpretation of their mission to preserve law and order. Mexican biology was to blame. Paz found the massacre to have "correspondences with the Mexican past, especially with the Aztec world, [which was] fascinating, overpowering, and repelling."[25] Behind the masked figure of the *tapado** was the masked figure of the Aztec priest, holding a bloody obsidian knife on high.

Captain Ayres was not in the audience, but hundreds of young Anglo students were; they formed the major part of the audience, in fact. I remember trying to study their faces for a clue to their thoughts. Many of them were products of the border culture of conflict we have been discussing. Their grandparents, and perhaps their parents, had grown up convinced that Mexicans were cruel and bloodthirsty because of their history and their "blood." Caught in the liberalism of the sixties, these students had come to label the attitudes of their ancestors as racism. And here they were now, listening while a prominent Mexican intellectual confirmed their discarded prejudices.

If I have given some space to Paz and his fondness for masked figures, it has not been out of mere captiousness but in the hope of making a point. It is worth noting that even intellectuals may indulge in self-derogatory stereotypes, all for the sake of art, of course. But the anonymous Mexican American who creates still another self-derogatory joke is an artist, too. I doubt that anyone of us would want to charge Paz with racism. He does get carried away now and then by his fascination with the bloodier aspects of the pre-Columbian cultures. A kind of inverted *indigenismo,* one might call it—the reverse of some contemporary revisionists, who would have us believe that the Aztecs never indulged in human sacrifice at all.

Paz's insensitivity to the problems and the potentialities of the young Los Angeles Mexicans is rooted in other causes. He speaks to us not with the voice of the future but with that of the past. His view of the *pachuco* is the same jaundiced view taken of the *pocho* by the Mexican intellectuals of the Revolutionary period. Paz's real complaint is that the *pachuco* does not act the way Paz thinks Mexicans should act.

Pocholandia, as we all know, is supposed to begin in the northern Mexican states, extending northward into the southwestern United States. It is synonymous with the "border culture" that occupies our attention here. And it has not been viewed any more sympathetically from the south than it has

---

*The unrevealed presidential candidate [Editor's Note].

from the north. The *pocho-pachuco,* with apologies to Octavio Paz, is not so much a creature hiding behind a mask as a poor soul wedged between the pyramid and the skyscraper.

But perhaps things are changing. Reading Mexican periodicals and listening to Mexican radio and television, one gets the impression that in a cultural sense the border has shifted south a bit, to a point somewhere below Mexico City, let us say. And that may be why the younger Mexican intellectuals are more sympathetic toward the *pocho-chicano* than their elders were; they are much more aware of our problems. Because in this, Octavio Paz did not miss the mark. He was wrong in assuming that the Mexican American had lost all his heritage. But he was right in noting that the *pocho,* living between two cultures, existed in a state of permanent crisis; and that the *pocho's* search for identity was a state shared by all Mexicans, and perhaps by all the world. If there was truth to such a view in the 1950s, it may be truer today, when the character of life has made borders less meaningful than they once were.

NOTES

1. Robert Wauchope, ed., *Handbook of Middle American Indians* (Austin: University of Texas Press, 1972), vol. 12, *Guide to Ethnohistorical Sources,* Part One, ed., Howard F. Cline (1972), p. 167. Adapted from R. C. West and J. P. Angelli, *Middle America: Its Lands and Peoples* (Englewood Cliffs, N.J.: Prentice-Hall, Inc. 1966).

2. See especially Américo Paredes, *With His Pistol in His Hand* (Austin: University of Texas Press, 1958) and idem, *A Texas-Mexican Cancionero* (Urbana: University of Illinois Press, 1975).

3. Walter Prescott Webb, *The Great Plains* (Boston: Ginn & Company, 1931), pp. 205-69.

4. O. Henry, *Rolling Stones* (New York: Doubleday, Page and Co., 1912), p. 258.

5. N. Howard ("Jack") Thorp, *Songs of the Cowboys* (1908; facsimile edition with variants, commentary, notes, and lexicon by Austin E. and Alta S. Fife, New York: Clarkson N. Potter, Inc., 1966), pp. 87-90.

6. John C. Duval, *The Adventures of Big-Foot Wallace* (Macon, Ga.: J. W. Burke, 1871); facsimile edition (Austin: University of Texas Press, 1947), pp. 171, 172, 197, 180, et passim.

7. Américo Paredes, "Estado Unidos, México y el machismo," *Journal of Inter-American Studies* 9(1967):65-84.

8. For a fuller treatment of these two songs see Américo Paredes, "Folklore e historia: Dos cantares de la frontera del norte," in *25 Estudios de Folklore,* Instituto de Investigaciones Estéticas (Mexico City: UNAM) 1971, pp. 209-22.

9. Lester V. Berrey and Melvin Van den Bark, *The American Thesaurus of Slang,* 2d ed. (New York: Thomas Y. Crowell Co., Inc., 1956).

10. H. L. Mencken, *The American Language,* supplement I (New York: Alfred A. Knopf, 1948), pp. 609-10.

11. In *Letters from the Frontiers* (Philadelphia: J. B. Lippincott and Co., 1868), G. A. McCall refers to northern Mexico as "Greaserdom."

12. Duval, *The Adventures of Big-Foot Wallace,* p. 225.

13. Ibid., p. 216.

14. Ed Cray, "Ethnic and Place Names as Derisive Adjectives," *Western Folklore* 21 (1962): 27-34.

15. Ibid., p. 28.

16. Mencken, *The American Language,* p. 595.

17. Ibid., p. 638.

18. Francisco J. Santamaría, *Diccionario de mejicanismos* (Mexico City: Ed. Porrúa, 1959), p. 697.

19. Angel Basols Batalla, et al., *Temas y figuras de la intervención* (Mexico City: Primero Congreso Nacional de Historia para el Estudio de la Guerra de Intervención, 1963), p. 71.

20. Ibid., p. 30.

21. "The Mexican *Corrido:* Its Rise and Fall," in *Madstones and Twisters,* Mody C. Boatright, ed., Publications of the Texas Folklore Society no. 28 (Dallas, 1958), pp. 91-105; Américo Paredes, *With His Pistol in His Hand,* pp. 129-50.

22. William Hugh Jansen, "The Esoteric-Exoteric Factor in Folklore," *Fabula: Journal of Folktale Studies* 2 (1959): 205-11; reprinted in Alan Dundes, *The Study of Folklore* (Englewood Cliffs, N.J.: Prentice-Hall, Inc., 1965), pp. 43-51.

23. Carey McWilliams, *North from Mexico* (New York: J. B. Lippincott Co., 1949), p. 234.

24. Octavio Paz, *The Labyrinth of Solitude,* trans. Lysander Kemp (New York: Grove Press, Inc., 1961), p. 16.

25. Octavio Paz, *México: La última década* (Austin: University of Texas Press, 1969), pp. 10-11.

PART II

The Politics of the Border

5

Regional Political Processes and Mexican Politics on the Border*

Antonio Ugalde

Two aspects of the Mexican political system related to the northern border require exploration: the political attitudes of the population of the border states and the policies of the central government toward the border. The highly centralized nature of the Mexican political system makes it unnecessary to look at each northern state's policies toward the solution of its social and economic problems. These matters are decided in Mexico City; the states have little or no autonomy.[1] At the same time we would like to determine whether or not the proximity of the United States exercises some influence on the political behavior of the inhabitants of the northern states.

Politics in the Border States

A study of the political process and behavior in the border states and their municipalities necessarily includes the same topics as those of any other state: conflict resolution, recruitment of elites, types of leadership, political behavior of the population, and political parties. From this point of view there is no difference between a study of Jalisco and one of Baja California. But there is something that makes the border region particularly interesting—what may be considered an additional independent variable: its proximity to the

---

*Translated from the Spanish by Miguel González-Gerth [Editor's Note].

United States. There is an important difference between the concept of an international border and proximity to the United States. When the political systems in the southern states of Chiapas, Quintana Roo, Campeche, and Tabasco are studied, their international borders generally have not been regarded as independent variables. The special attention paid to the proximity of the United States is due, without a doubt, to the historical development of the border region as well as to the extraordinary power and wealth of the United States.

When other disciplines have focused on the United States-Mexican border, they have tended to emphasize the two countries' mutual influences. Both American and Mexican economists, for example, agree on one thing: the interdependence of the border economies from Tijuana to Matamoros; in fact, the term "twin cities" is used to refer to such interdependence.[2] Cultural anthropologists, when speaking about the culture of the American Southwest and northern Mexico, recognize reciprocal influences in the two regions and define the resulting border culture as a "symbiosis."[3] Population researchers, geographers, and historians also have concluded that along the border there are influences exerted by the north on the south and by the south on the north.[4] This is not the case, however, when it comes to political sociology. It has been taken for granted that the positive influence is always exerted by the north on the south—to Americans it would be inconceivable and certainly undesirable for the Mexican political system to exert an influence on their democracy. Consequently, it is their belief that the influence exerted by the United States on Mexican politics is always benign, as any negative elements that might exist magically remain north of the border. Political corruption, violence, Tammany Hall bossism, and so forth are, therefore, not exportable. In brief, Mexico can only benefit politically from its geographical proximity to the United States, but a reciprocal operation is impossible. William D'Antonio and William Form, in a comparative study of Juárez and El Paso, comment as follows:

> Early in the research several Juárez leaders commented that, in evaluating their city's growth they more and more tended to compare themselves with El Paso rather than with Chihuahua City, the capital city of their state. This led us to speculate whether the American pattern of business and government relations might have an impact on C. Juárez. This might be expected if there were a great deal of contact between leaders of the two communities. Conceivably, the businessmen or the political leaders of the American city could serve as models to be imitated or avoided, depending on the values of the leaders and their evaluations of the American scene.[5]

Later in their study, D'Antonio and Form reach the conclusion that industrial leaders in Juárez do indeed regard their American counterparts highly:

> The El Paso influentials did not look to Mexico for new values, social contact, new ideas or intellectual challenge. . . . To the Mexican influentials, especially the businessmen, the border represented more than economic opportunity. Although they profited from the tourist trade, they also looked to the United States as a source of values, ideas, and ideals.[6]

American political scientists have been plagued by the idea that political development requires at least two political parties,[7] and it has been thought that the existence of a stronger opposition party in some Mexican border states is a consequence of the geographical proximity of the United States.

Thus, it is important that we examine those factors that might exert an influence on the political behavior in the Mexican border states and municipalities. Without claiming to be exhaustive, some of the factors could be:

1. The large number of Mexican nationals who work regularly and/or occasionally in the United States. Among these are the "green card holders," those holding seventy-two-hour passes, and the wetbacks or illegal migrants. The number of Mexican workers who cross the border daily or occasionally is relatively large,[8] and the time they spend at their jobs in the United States exposes these workers to both positive and negative aspects of the American political system.

2. The large number of Mexican nationals, around forty-four thousand, who work for American-owned cheap-labor assembly plants *(maquiladoras),* as a result of the border industrialization program.[9] The number has increased rapidly in the last few years, but the effects of the present economic crisis on the future are unclear. These workers observe the American companies' modes of authority, conflict resolution systems, and decision-making processes, which reflect the political culture of the United States.

3. The large number of tourists from both countries in the Mexican border states. Through the contact between American tourists and Mexican nationals, aspects of the American political system might be transmitted.[10]

4. Family ties that bind an indefinite yet admittedly large number of people on both sides of the border. Visits among these people also might result in the transmission of political awareness and political-cultural values from the United States.

5. The mass communications media that can easily cross the border and

reveal American political reality to radio listeners, televiewers, and readers.[11]

6. Last, the formal and informal relations between the border elites. Political, labor, religious, intellectual, and business leaders get together more or less regularly to study and discuss problems of mutual interest. It is possible that at these meetings some political-cultural norms and values can be transmitted to the Mexican leadership from their American counterparts.

Making use of the limited information available, the merits of the six foregoing possible influential factors will be discussed. The first is based on the indisputable presence in the United States of hundreds of thousands of Mexican laborers. Nevertheless, the conclusion reached regarding the possible influence on their political attitudes and values has not yet been documented. Something to be kept in mind is that a large number of the Mexican workers in the United States, perhaps the majority, come from the socioeconomically lower classes. Those who cross the border without papers, for example, hardly speak English, are almost illiterate, and, because of their illegality, are automatically ostracized from American society. Also it appears that their visits to the United States are usually very brief.

A study made of a poor neighborhood in Juárez suggests that as few as 6 percent of its inhabitants pick the United States as their favorite place to live. The study concludes that those living in the neighborhood look upon their work in the United States as a good opportunity to earn a lot of money in a short time or when they find themselves in dire need:

> These suggestions are supported by the relatively short periods of residency in the United States. Taking the total amount of time spent in the United States by those who worked there, 58 percent spent four months or less across the border, and 70 percent, less than six months, 80 percent spent less than twelve months, and only 20 percent spent one year or more, which is not a lengthy residence considering the many times they crossed the border.[12]

In that study of Juárez there is something even more significant. Only 1 percent of those who had come to Juárez from other areas (92 percent of those polled) stated that their reason for coming was the proximity to the United States.[13] So we are led to conclude that crossing the border is something sporadically done, in cases of dire economic necessity and with the intention of returning to Mexico as quickly as possible. Finally, it also must be kept in mind that many illegal entrants and workers holding seventy-two-hour passes do not reside permanently in border communities. They come from other Mexican states to the border in search of temporary work in the United States, after which they return home. In other words, the possible influence felt during their stay in the United States would be transmitted also to those other states of Mexico and not merely to the border states.

All the foregoing arguments lead to the conclusion that, first, if there is an influence it is slighter than might have been presumed, considering the brief stay in the United States and the social marginality of the Mexican workers, and, second, the fact that such an influence would extend into the interior of Mexico. In the final analysis, more research is required before we can either accept or reject the hypothesis.

The border industrialization program began in 1966, hence it is difficult to estimate to what degree the workers in those industries, mostly women, are being influenced by the American organizations' power structure, and what effects that could have on the workers' political behavior. Some of these industries have not permitted the workers to join the moderate labor unions (like CROC, CTM, and CROM) and have managed to establish subservient company-type unions. These American-owned enterprises, which operate under the pressure of competition from the Far East, are usually not very stable, and the methods of organization and operation are quite different from those of American companies. It could be suggested that if they do have some effect on the political thinking of the Mexican workers it is likely to be negative.

United States border tourism is attracted to the trade that takes place in well-established sections of towns like Avenida Revolución in Tijuana, the harbor and Calle Ruiz in Ensenada, and the PRONAF*Center in Juárez.[14] Mexican tourists in the United States go primarily to the supermarkets and shopping centers. Contact between tourists and natives is limited to simple commercial transactions. It is difficult to see in such contact, no matter how frequent, a source of influence on political attitudes. Up to now there is no study which could support such a possibility.

An important subject, which has not yet been studied, has to do with family relations among residents on both sides. All we know is that many Mexican Americans have relatives living in the Mexican border communities, with whom they exchange frequent visits. The lack of information about this social phenomenon is revealed by a footnote in D'Antonio and Form's comparative study of Juárez and El Paso: "Almost half of the population of El Paso was of Spanish-name background. Most of these people had friends whom they visited regularly."[15] Similarly, from a survey taken in Tecate,

---

*Programa Nacional Fronterizo (National Borderlands Program).

Baja California, John Price states that most Tecate residents cross the border often to shop (57 percent) and to visit relatives or friends (15 percent).[16] In his study of Tijuana, he comments ". . . there are thousands of significant kinship links between people in Tijuana and their relatives in Southern California. These are cemented by a great amount of visiting back and forth."[17]

Considering the strength of family ties and the important part they play in the socialization process, we can assume that frequent contact among relatives living on both sides of the border serves as important means of communication and exchange of political experience. But we must wait for more detailed studies of family relations across the border to know their real significance. We must not forget that Mexican Americans have been systematically excluded from American political life and, therefore, their view of the political process may be negative.[18]

There is no study on the impact of mass communications media on the border. The receptive capacity in the Mexican border states is high, as shown in Table 1.[19] When trying to estimate the influence of American broadcasting on the Mexican border towns, the large number of radios and television sets can be misleading because of the language barrier. American newspapers crossing the border are probably few. In Ensenada, for example, it was found that there were only a few dozen English-language newspapers for sale. The influence of the English language on the Mexican border population often has been exaggerated. *Pachuco* is spoken on the American side of the border, while on the Mexican side a few anglicisms have become accepted, such as *washateria, yonkería, lonchería,* and *troca,* some of which are used throughout Mexico. The influence of Spanish on border English is undoubtedly greater. Hence, it can be suggested that American mass communications media exert little influence on the political behavior of the Mexican border population.

The most detailed study of the relations among business and political elites is that of D'Antonio and Form. It shows that the nature of the contact among these elite groups is varied and complex. Businessmen and merchants meet frequently through civic organizations such as the Chamber of Commerce, the Rotary Club, and the Lions Club.[20] Of the thirty-seven businessmen interviewed in Juárez, four out of every five had contacts in El Paso. Similarly, relations among politicians on both sides of the border are firmer and develop through official bodies such as the United States-Mexico Commission for Border Development and Friendship, the Comisión de las Californias, the Border Cities Conferences, and at holiday ceremonies such as those commemorating July 4, September 16, and Pan American Day.[21] Juárez merchants tend to like and adopt American practices, but politicians cannot do this; the political structure and the national spirit are different in the two countries. "The businessmen evaluated general business-government relations in the United States as much superior to the Mexican . . . especially with respect to governmental regulation and ownership. . . . Expectedly, the Juárez politicos perceived the situation differently."[22] Very little is known of the relations among other elites. Our study of the labor movement in Ensenada shows that there is no effective influence from American labor leaders and that the workers in Ensenada look upon the American labor experience as irrelevant while regarding Mexican national leaders as models.[23] It would appear, then, that any influence among border elites is debatable, except where it concerns businessmen and merchants.

TABLE 1
Percentages of Televisions and Radios in the Home
Throughout the Border States
(1970)

	Radio	Television	Radio and Television
1. Baja California	30	5	57
2. Coahuila	63	1	24
3. Chihuahua	50	2	31
4. Nuevo León	41	3	45
5. Sonora	55	2	27
6. Tamaulipas	52	2	30

Source: Estados Unidos Mexicanos, Secretaría de Industria y Comercio, Dirección General de Estadística, *IX Censo General de Población. 1970 (con datos sobre la vivienda)* 23 de enero de 1970. Resumen de las Principales Características por Entidad Federativa, México, D.F. Noviembre de 1970.

The field work done to date in this area is not sufficient to prove that proximity to the United States must be considered an independent variable in the political behavior of the Mexican border population.

Another way of approaching our subject is to compare what we know of political behavior in the border states with that in other Mexican states. Quantitative electoral data would be particularly useful, but the Mexican government is known to be reluctant about making them accessible for study. Even data that should be common knowledge are kept secret, such as district election results. By way of hypothesis it could be said that if the opposition party gets more votes along the border, it might be due to the influence of the

American bipartisan system. It can also be said that if electoral absenteeism is lower in the border states, it could be due to the United States's example (though it must be kept in mind that voter participation in the United States is not very high). A greater organizational capacity among the Mexican border population, as shown by a larger number of labor unions, farm cooperatives, employer associations, and civic organizations also might be due to the American example.

Fortunately, Barry Ames has gathered data that are very useful for our study. The two dependent variables he used are voter turnout (ratio of votes to eligible voters) and the total number of votes compared to the Institutional Revolutionary Party's (PRI) share of the total vote.[24] The independent variables here are: urbanization; history of the states' separatist tendencies; proximity to the United States; the structure of the opposition, as measured by the number of parties; the percentage of the population affiliated with the PRI; government benefits to the communities, as measured by the number of water sanitation programs; and voter turnout as an independent variable where the second dependent variable is the number of PRI votes. Through a multiple standardized regression, Ames has measured quantitatively the influence of each independent variable on the six elections held between 1952 and 1967, three presidential and three congressional (the election results have been tallied by adding up the totals of the six elections).

As shown in Table 2, proximity to the United States, of all the independent variables, provides the weakest explanation in trying to account for the number of votes cast for the PRI. In other words, the existence of a relatively strong opposition party, such as the National Action Party (PAN) is not a consequence of proximity to the United States but of urbanization. A similar commentary may be made regarding the other dependent variable; voter turnout is due to the degree of urbanization and not to proximity to the United States.

Another means of assessing the effect that proximity to the United States has had on Mexican border communities is to observe the similarities and differences between these and other Mexican regions regarding other aspects of their local political systems. For example, organizational capacity in thirty-one communities (some of them border cities) is the subject of an interesting analysis performed by Susan and John Purcell.[25] From their data it is evident that border location does not result in high organizational capacity. William Tucker has compared the political process in three communities, two of them in the Mexican interior (Jalapa and Celaya) and the other on the border (Ensenada).[26] The similarity of these three local political systems is very clear. There is also much in common between the political behavior in the poor neighborhoods studied by Wayne Cornelius in the Federal District[27] and the one we studied in Juárez. Last, there is Price's very relevant study of politics in Tecate: "Tecate's border location was found to have no direct impact on Tecate's politics, although indirect influences from the United States in the form of economic and social ties were important."[28]

TABLE 2
Standardized Multiple Regression Coefficients Associated
with Turnout and Direction of Vote

Independent Variables	Dependent Variables	
	Turnout	*Direction of Vote*
Urbanization	-.055	-.579**
Historical Nonintegration	.320**	-.238**
Presence on U.S. Border	-.113	.045
Structure of the Opposition	-.305*	-.418**
Affiliated Members	.161	-.174
Benefits	-.085	-.080
Turnout	—	.276**
Multiple Correlation		
Coefficient	.531	.880
Coefficient of Determination	.282	.774

*Significant at the .10 level.
**Significant at the .05 level.

The foregoing evidence suggests that to date no study of the political systems in the Mexican border states and municipalities has shown either a positive or a negative influence on the political process and behavior in that region as a result of proximity to the United States. On the contrary, available community studies and quantitative analyses tend to show that local political systems along the border are similar to those in other Mexican regions, or more specifically, that "proximity to the United States" should not be considered to be an independent variable.

The Central Government's Policy Toward the Border

The centralized nature of the Mexican political system implies that decisions made in Mexico City for other regions are not necessarily aimed at solving local or regional problems. In some instances they benefit Mexico City itself or a few influential elites with local economic and/or political interests. In the case of the border states, and due to the interests of the United States along the border and in Mexico in general, the decisions made by the holders of power in the national capital also could be motivated by international considerations. Consequently, we need to look into the national and international decision-making processes and criteria.

The Mexican Revolution gave rise to a new sense of country and national unity. The end of the violence had scarcely permitted the institutionalization of revolutionary goals when the Great Depression extended into Mexico. Hardest hit were the border states, which had been politically and economically isolated. American incursions had kept alive the memory of the Guadalupe Hidalgo Treaty and the loss of vast territories that it represented. The possibility of another such national tragedy, as a result of direct American intervention or of separatist movements, encouraged the creation of a free-trade zone during the brief administration of Abelardo Rodríguez, who had been governor of Baja California and was familiar with the border region. Since that time the border states have enjoyed economic privileges, while at the same time they have undergone an economic and demographic development without precedent in all of Mexico. President Cárdenas enlarged the free-trade zone and continued adding to northern agricultural industries by incorporating large formerly arid areas for cotton and cattle raising.

The privileges of the free-trade zone were to have ended in 1956. Instead they were extended until 1966 and then again with some restrictions which, however, were offset by new privileges. Thus began the "Programa Nacional Fronterizo" and the border industrialization program midway through the sixties.[29] Understanding the reasons for the extension of these privileges may illuminate the decision-making process.

As has been stated, several important problems shared by the United States and Mexico have to do with the border. The fact that during the last few years many meetings of the presidents of the two nations have taken place along the border is more than symbolic. As Clark Reynolds summarized it, for the United States the main problems with Mexico are related to drug traffic, illegal migration, the United States industries along the border in Mexico, payment of royalties for United States technical patents, and policy changes that affect United States investments in Mexico.[30] It is evident that many of these problems revolve around the existence of a long boundary between the two countries.

And for Mexico, too, many of its problems with the United States are generated by the border situation. A few examples have been: water control and salinization, especially on the Colorado River; regulation of American broadcasting and telecasting involving retransmission from the Mexican border region; the "green card holders" problem; the wetbacks (deportation procedures and discrimination); border smuggling in either direction; consequences of American unilateral action against drug smuggling; the border states' balance of payments; and American fishing rights in Mexican territorial waters.[31]

In order to understand how border problems are resolved, we must first understand the principles behind Mexican foreign policy. Needless to say, given the power and wealth of the United States it is impossible for Mexico to negotiate on an equal basis. Lawrence Koslow has studied the content of Adolfo López Mateos's first five presidential messages and interviewed ten high government officials responsible for the formulation of foreign policy.[32] Table 3 shows the quantitative results of his study and interviews, which reveal the existence of two important principles behind the formulation of Mexican foreign policy: 1) the principle of nonintervention in the internal affairs of other nations; and 2) the principle of national self-determination (actually a corollary of the first). It should be noted that national sovereignty is not held in such high regard as either of the principles named above. Consequently, the Mexican government is free to recognize an economic dependence on the United States which, as we will see, is exactly the case.

It is impossible within the limits of this study to analyze the complex decision-making system used by the Mexican federal government with regard to its domestic policies. Much has been written on the subject, but I know of no work of synthesis wherein the principles for such domestic policy decisions are defined.[33] Thus, I shall limit myself to pointing out the principles which, in my opinion, guide these policies, even though at times they will not match what is stated publicly by the highest government officials (I refer to the obvious lack of consistency frequently found between word and deed). One of the most important principles is perhaps the maintenance of political "stability" by means of an authoritarian and centralized system. For Cockcroft and Anderson, the Mexican experience is an outstanding example of cooptation, in which the necessary political stability is obtained for the purpose of economic development.[34] The price for such stability is paid with favors and jobs, resulting in bureaucratic inbreeding and the creation of not a few quickly amassed small fortunes. A second principle is to maintain a high rate of economic growth (perhaps 6 percent annually), even if in the short run it maintains and/or increases the differences in relative income among the different social groups and geographical areas of the country.[35] The idea is that eventually, in the very distant future, everyone will benefit from the

economic growth. A third principle is the creation of jobs in which to employ
a rapidly growing number of people entering the ranks of the labor force, thus
trying to lower the alarming rate of unemployment.[36]

TABLE 3
Mexican Foreign Policy Criteria

	1	2	3	4
Nonintervention	4	4	2	0
Self-determination	3	5	1	0
Mutual Respect for all Nations	2	0	2	0
Egalitarianism	1	0	2	2
National Sovereignty	0	0	2	1
International Cooperation	0	0	0	1
Peaceful Settlement of International Problems	0	0	0	1

Question: There are many principles that guide Mexico's foreign policy. In your opinion as one
who occupies a high position in foreign policy decision making, which is the basic
principle on which you have based and will base your decisions? Which is the second
most important? Which is third? Which is fourth?

Before discussing the effects of policy decisions based on these principles,
it would be wise to consider the sources of wealth in the border region. Most
economic studies of this area show that its development is due to its proximity
to the United States. A typical example is Watry's statement that Tijuana's
economy "depends almost solely upon American tourism" and Mexicali's
"has been considerably aided by being located next to the American agricultural center in the Imperial Valley. Americans have supplied technology,
credit, machinery. . . ."[37] I prefer to put the emphasis as follows: the tourist
trade, the free commercial zone, and the thousands of Mexicans who work in
the United States have encouraged and accelerated the economic development
of the region. It must be kept in mind, however, that government irrigation
projects put large dry areas into profitable cultivation from Mexicali to
Matamoros. There is, in other words, an important source of wealth which is
independent of the United States. I would also argue that other sources of
wealth, such as the tourist trade, though related to the United States, do not
imply economic independence.

My hypothesis, resulting from the simultaneous interpretation of Mexican
domestic and foreign policies, may be stated thus: the Mexican government
has been willing to take advantage of the proximity and wealth of the United
States in order to solve part of its own national unemployment problem and, at
the same time, find the income necessary to maintain its political "stability."
Since the Second World War, the privileges enjoyed by the border states have

been given not so much to promote development and help solve local
problems but rather to satisfy the political and economic interests of the
country's power structure located in Mexico City.

Let us begin by looking at how sources of labor are created. We are all
familiar with the rapid population growth in the border states. As a way
station for waves of migrants bound for the United States, it can be assumed
that many either never left the Mexican side of the border or later returned to
it. Although there are no quantitative data on the origin of either legal or
illegal Mexican aliens in the United States, it is known that they have come,
and continue to come, from all the states in the Mexican federation. The
benefit of Mexican labor to the United States is, therefore, not the result of a
problem restricted to the Mexican side of the border but rather the result of a
problem throughout Mexico.

There is a lack of reliable information regarding the level of unemployment
in the various regions. What little evidence there is, however, suggests that
until very recently it was not higher in the border states than in the rest of the
country; in fact, it was precisely the opposite. In one of Juárez's poorest
neighborhoods, for example, it was established that the level of unemployment reached 26 percent of the economically active population and that 44
percent had only temporary jobs. Such percentages are undoubtedly shocking,
yet no more so than those reflecting the situation throughout the rest of the
country. Flores estimates that between 30 and 40 percent of the country's
economically active population is either unemployed or underemployed.[38] In
that same Juárez neighborhood, it was discovered that most adult migrants (84
percent) arrived there unemployed but soon found some kind of work, at least
temporary or part-time (see Table 4).[39] It was precisely for this reason—the
opportunity of finding work—that they had left their native regions and had
migrated to Juárez. It runs against all theories of migration that the cities
which attract migrants have a high unemployment level.[40]

This, of course, does not mean that at some future date the border towns
cannot suffer from unemployment; such possibilities exist in all cities that are
part of any economy based on capitalist principles. Heavy federal government
investments made along the border are not meant to help solve the local
unemployment but to promote new sources of employment which will attract
the unemployed from other parts of the nation. These investments quite
possibly may increase the differences in wealth among the various states of
the Mexican federation, but, as I have already pointed out, the distribution of
wealth is not a guiding principle of the government's domestic policy.

It is my belief that the border industrialization program is not intended to
solve the problem of unemployment that exists there. It may not even be

TABLE 4
Adult Migrants Seeking Jobs After Arrival in Ciudad Juárez

Time Unemployed	% (n-86)
Had Job on Arrival	16
One Month or Less	42
Two Months	9
Three Months and More	32
	99

meant to encourage the employment of possible migrants from other areas of the border.[41] If such employment had been intended by the Mexican government, it could have set up free ports in other parts of the country, as has happened in Panama, the Dominican Republic, and in many Asian countries. To be sure, the recent employment made possible by the American-owned cheap-labor assembly plants along the border are financially welcomed by Mexicans who did not already hold jobs. But it must be kept in mind that most of those workers are women and that in Mexico, where the family is a "traditional" institution, women are not considered part of the economically active population. It would seem more logical, therefore, to explain the border industrialization program in terms of the policies previously outlined. The program is the response to two pressures exerted simultaneously:

(A) On the one hand, pressure came from the powerful groups in the United States for whom the rise in the cost of Asian labor, the geographical proximity of the border, and the conditions of the Mexican worker became conducive to investment in the region. Observers of United States politics will not be surprised by the success the lobbyists of certain industries have had in the establishment of the free-trade zone along the border. The Mexican government has had to meet certain demands imposed by the giant to the north in order to attain reciprocity in diplomatic negotiations. Maintaining the status quo regarding green card holders (perhaps as numerous as the workers in the cheap-labor plants but earning much higher wages), allowing a situation to exist whereby thousands of wetbacks continue to cross over into the United States and find temporary employment, achieving the return to Mexico of the Chamizal territory, and the discontinuation of "Operation Intercept," all deal with employment in one way or another. But, the border states for many years have enjoyed a privileged situation and the new industries did not represent an innovation in policy.

(B) On the other hand, the privilege accorded the border region can partially be explained by the fact that there are powerful groups in Mexico which clearly find this advantageous. Despite restrictions imposed with each extension of a free trade zone, this privilege has continually been granted. The original need to integrate the region with the national economy lasted until World War II, but extensions were granted for three reasons: 1) Pressure was applied by organizations in the border towns (chambers of commerce, employers' associations, and workers' federations).[42] 2) Pressure came from a few, but extremely powerful, people with enormous vested interests in the border, such as the late Abelardo Rodríguez and now Miguel Alemán (both former presidents). It is said that Lic. Alemán has interest in extensive real estate for future development throughout Baja California. Further field work along the border region will reveal the names of the few other powerful individuals. 3) The federal government's own determination to receive the maximum income from its public investment has also been a factor. There is no way to justify public investment programs such as PRONAF once the economic development of the border region has equaled and surpassed that of other regions.[43]

It can even be suggested that the federal government has obtained more economic resources—from the free-trade zones—than it has invested. There is at present no detailed study of the ratio between investment cost and revenue from taxes and franchises. Existing studies of communities along the border, however, suggest that the region's development has resulted in a very comfortable balance at the national treasury. Thus, in Matamoros as far back as 1953 it was believed that the federal government had collected 421 million pesos in export duties on cotton during a very short period. An editorial in a local newspaper remarked that the federal government ''has collected in the area of Matamoros in these two and a half years enough money to beautify Acapulco and Veracruz, to build the Panamerican highway, or to build the port of Tuxpan, but it has not benefited our agricultural region, one of the most important and most neglected by the federal government in the whole country.''[44]

My study in Ensenada suggests also that the federal government derives more than it invests in the municipality. Significantly, the Treasury Department office in Ensenada keeps tax revenue data secret.[45] The Junta Federal de Mejoras Materiales (a federally organized improvements program) receives 3 percent of the customs revenue but zealously guards its books and has not been allowed to establish a local permanent fund over the years. So, if the federal government had been solely interested in developing regional economy, it seems that it would have set up agencies that it would have

endowed at least with monies obtained from the local economy. That was
ostensibly the original purpose of the Junta Federal de Mejoras Materiales and
of the juntas of Mejoramiento Moral, Cívico, and Material, all of which
quickly became tools for dispensing monetary gifts and special considerations
resulting in the enrichment of their officers.[46] Similarly, many of the
PRONAF programs were not intended to solve local problems. Several groups
in Ensenada wrote the president complaining about the "destructive" work of
PRONAF.[47] Perhaps the most incisive commentary on the federal investments
along the border came from a school principal and was published in a local
magazine:

> Other absurd public works are those whose cost has been underesti-
> mated. I assume that is what happened here in Ensenada with the work
> at Punta Estero. After investing more than forty million pesos it appears
> that PRONAF is going to stop construction. . . . With that money the
> urbanization problems of Ensenada could have been easily solved. . . .
> It is incredible that the tremendously expensive water and sewage works
> are left up to a municipality which, as everyone knows, lives in poverty.
> . . . The federal government always launches the construction of gran-
> diose projects, such as the new customs-house, Punta Estero, the seaside
> boulevard, and ignores the most urgently needed work. . . . It is more
> important to plan on paving streets and providing water and electricity.
> Plain common sense tells us that if we want to attract tourists we must
> not expect them to tread on human dung because the town has no sewer
> system. . . . Let us first set down our priorities in a rational manner.[48]

Much of the infrastructure along the border, then, is explained by the
federal government's determination to invest in those areas that can produce
the greatest income. The surplus is used to maintain the political "stability"
of the nation by creating new federal agencies whose officers are yes-men
ready to receive considerable remuneration.

In sum, it would be naïve to think that decisions made by the federal
government regarding the border reflect a desire to solve local problems.
Their purposes are to alleviate the country's unemployment, to negotiate
diplomatic understandings, to indulge powerful business interests on both
sides of the border, and to obtain the funds necessary to pay the price of the
country's political "stability."

NOTES

1. For a summary of many studies on the Mexican political system see Carolyn Needleman and Martin Needleman, "Who Rules México? A Critique of Some Current Views on the Mexican Political Process," *The Journal of Politics* 31 (1969): 1011-34.

2. C. Daniel Dillman, "The Functions of Brownsville, Texas and Matamoros, Tamaulipas: Twin Cities in the Lower Rio Grande" (Ph.D. diss., University of Michigan, 1968).

3. John A. Price *(Tijuana: Urbanization in a Border Culture?* [Notre Dame, Ind.: University of Notre Dame Press, 1973]) has discussed in detail the concept of symbiosis which, in our opinion, is of little utility. Whatever acculturation might be taking place in both sides of the border is not necessarily unidimensional. Price's biases can be detected when he says: "While cultural adaptation is a two-way street in this case, with Mexican culture and society having an impact on America, the fact that America is the economically dominant partner predisposes that Mexican culture will change more than American culture and that Mexicans will generally be forced into socially subordinate roles vis-à-vis Americans. There are some advantages to the Tijuanese in this process" (p. 174).

4. Bibliographical summaries of several disciplines can be found in the following sources: Ellwin R. Stoddard, "The Current Status of U.S.-Mexico Borderland Studies: Sociology and Cultural Anthropology," mimeographed (Paper presented at the Rocky Mountain Social Science Association, El Paso, Texas, April 1974); Charles R. Gildersleeve, "The Status of the Mexico-United States Border Studies in Geography," mimeographed (Paper presented at the Rocky Mountain Social Science Meeting, El Paso, Texas, April 1974); and Oscar J. Martínez, "The Growth and Development of Mexico's Northern Border Region: A Bibliographical Essay," mimeographed (Paper presented at the Rocky Mountain Social Science Association, El Paso, Texas, April 1974), for history.

5. William V. D'Antonio and William H. Form, *Influentials in Two Border Cities: A Study in Community Decision-Making* (Notre Dame, Ind.: University of Notre Dame Press, 1965), p. 16. The study ends with the following sentence: "One can only ponder the long-range consequences for C. Juárez of being on the border next to a United States city in which democracy, if still far short of achieving its promises for the great majority of the people, is nevertheless relatively well-equipped to tackle its problems" (p. 248).

6. Ibid., p. 218.

7. See for example, Raymond Vernon, *The Dilemma of Mexico's Development* (Cambridge, Mass.: Harvard University Press, 1963), pp. 190-93, in which the advantages and disadvantages of a multiparty system for Mexico are discussed.

8. An interesting study in which the number of green card holders is discussed is Vernon M. Briggs, Jr., "The Mexico-United States Border: An Assessment of the Policies of the United States upon the Economic Welfare of the Chicano Population," mimeographed (Paper presented at the Conference on Economic Relations between Mexico and the United States, Austin, Texas, April 1973). See also David S. North, *The Border-Crossers: People Who Live in Mexico and Work in the U.S.* (Washington, D.C.: Trans-Century Corporation, 1970).

9. The origins and development of the Industrial Border Program are well described in Donald W. Baerresen, *The Border Industrialization Program of Mexico* (Lexington, Mass.: D. C. Heath & Co., 1971). See also Susan Carey Fouts, "Mexican Border Industrialization: An Analogy and a Comment," mimeographed (Paper presented at the Conference on Economic Relations between Mexico and the United States, Austin, Texas, April 1973) and Liborio Villalobos Calderón, "La Industria Maquiladora Extranjera en México: Mal Necesario de una Sociedad Subdesarrollada," mimeographed (Paper presented at the Conference on Economic Relations between Mexico and the United States, Austin, Texas, April 1973).

10. Some social aspects of the tourism in Baja California are discussed by Price, *Tijuana*. The Programa Nacional Fronterizo (PRONAF) has published several monographs of Mexican border cities which include data on tourism.

11. International treaties regulate radio and TV broadcasting along the border, see Karl M. Schmitt, *Mexico and the United States, 1921-1973: Conflict and Coexistence* (New York: John Wiley & Sons, 1974), pp. 208ff. It should also be remembered that the United States press is probably read more widely in Mexico City than along the border.

12. Antonio Ugalde, et al., *The Urbanization Process of a Poor Mexican Neighborhood* (Austin: Institute of Latin American Studies, The University of Texas, 1974), p. 21.

13. Ibid., p. 20.

14. Programa Nacional Fronterizo, *Proyecto de un nuevo centro comercial en Matamoros, Tamaulipas: Análisis económico* (Mexico City, 1963), p. 13. See also Dillman, "The Functions of Brownsville, Texas and Matamoros, Tamaulipas"; Peter J. Watry, Jr. "The Economic Development of Baja California" (Ph.D. diss., University of Missouri, Columbia, 1970).

15. D'Antonio and Form, *Influentials*, p. 51.

16. Price, *Tijuana*, p. 138.

17. Ibid., p. 178.

18. Studies of political socialization of Chicano children suggest that their affective orientations toward the political system are not as positive as those of the Anglo children. See F. Chris García, *The Political Socialization of Chicano Children* (New York: Praeger Publishers, 1973), and Armando Gutiérrez, "The Socialization of Militancy: Chicanos in a South Texas Town" (Ph.D. diss., University of Texas, Austin, 1974).

19. Estados Unidos Mexicanos, Secretaría de Industria y Comercio, Dirección General de Estadística, *IX Censo General de Población. 1970 (con datos sobre la vivienda)* 23 de enero de 1970 (Mexico City).

20. Strictly speaking, the Mexican Chambers of Commerce, of Industry, etc., are not voluntary organizations. By law all businesses of certain size have to be registered and pay dues. However, the organization and functioning of the Chambers is similar to that of voluntary organizations.

21. The United States-Mexico Commission for Border Development and Friendship was established in 1966 and ceased to function in 1969. For more information about this and other commissions see Price, *Tijuana*, pp. 175ff., and Schmitt, *Mexico*, pp. 193-256.

22. D'Antonio and Form, *Influentials*, pp. 98-99.

23. Antonio Ugalde, *Power and Conflict in a Mexican Community: A Study of Political Integration* (Albuquerque: University of New Mexico Press, 1970), ch. 2.

24. Barry Ames, "Bases of Support for Mexico's Dominant Party," *The American Political Science Review* 64 (1970):153-67. Ames is particularly cautious in his analysis: "Since the border states are highly urbanized, it might be thought that the effects of the presence of the U.S. Border are masked by the more powerful variable of urbanization. However, an analysis of residuals (produced from a regression without this variable) shows that four of the six states on the U. S. border have higher actual PRI votes than would be predicted by their level of urbanization. Thus, although the demonstration effect of the United States may carry over into the border cities, it does not significantly affect the total vote of the state" (p. 165).

25. Susan Kaufman Purcell and John F. H. Purcell, "Community Power and Benefits from the Nation: The Case of Mexico," *Latin American Urban Research* 3 (1973): 49-78.

26. William P. Tucker, "Mexican Middle-Sized Cities: A Consideration of Studies of Three Cities," mimeographed (Paper presented at the Rocky Mountain Conference on Latin American Studies, Boulder, Colorado, 1972.

27. Wayne A. Cornelius, "Urbanization as an Agent in Latin American Political Instability: The Case of Mexico," *American Political Science Review* 63(1969):833-67, and "Political Learning Among the Migrant Poor: The Impact of Residential Context," *Sage Professional Papers in Comparative Politics, No. 01-037* (Beverly Hills, Calif.: Sage Publications, 1973).

28. Price, *Tijuana*, p. 139.

29. The National Border Program (PRONAF) includes the Mexico-Guatemala and Mexico-British Honduras borders, but its activities have been almost negligible in these areas.

30. Clark Reynolds, "Do Good Fences Make Good Neighbors? Recent and Prospective United States-Mexican Relations," mimeographed (Paper presented at the Conference on Economic Relations between Mexico and the United States, Austin, Texas, April 1973).

31. Schmitt, *Mexico* pp. 193ff.

32. Lawrence E. Koslow, "Mexican Foreign Policy Decision-Making: The Mutual Adjustment of Needs and Independence." (Ph.D. diss., University of California, Riverside, 1969), pp. 74ff.

33. An important book is Roger D. Hansen's *The Politics of Mexican Development* (Baltimore: The Johns Hopkins University Press, 1971). See also *El Perfil de México en 1980,* 2 vols. (Mexico City: Siglo XXI Editores, 1972) and Francisco González Pineda y Antonio Delhumeau, *Los Mexicanos frente al poder* (Mexico City: Instituto Mexicano de Estudios Políticos, 1973).

34. Bo Anderson and James D. Cockcroft, "Control and Co-optation in Mexican Politics," *International Journal of Comparative Sociology* 7 (1966): 11-28.

35. See, for example, the comment by David Barkin: "The government also contributes to this concentration, in spite of repeated declarations that one of its goals is to 'mitigate and correct imbalances in regional development.' Although the President declared, in 1970, that 'this objective received special attention in the annual financing of investment programs' the regional concentration of public investment was greater in the 1964-1970 period than during the previous administration. . . . The same is true for almost any aspect of economic, social and political life in which the government is involved. It goes without saying that these regional disparities are only indirect indicators of the unequal distribution of income mentioned above." ("Mexico's Albatross: The United States Economy" [Paper presented at the Conference on Economic Relations between Mexico and the United States, Austin, Texas, April 1973]). A historical study of regional disparities is John E. Leimone's "Patterns of Long Run Interregional Economic Growth and Development in Mexico, 1895-1960" (Ph.D. diss., Vanderbilt University, Nashville, Tenn., 1971): "The present study has provided evidence that during the period 1895-1960 interregional disparities in levels of per capita product in Mexico have tended to increase. This trend in interregional inequality was associated with . . . levels of public and private investment, especially in important aspects of economic infrastructure and transportation, electric generating capacity, and education" (p. 233). Leimone adds that there are no indications of future change. That the wealthy are getting wealthier and the poor poorer has been well-documented in Alonso Aguilar and Fernando Carmona, *México: Riqueza y miseria* (Mexico City: Ed. Nuestro Tiempo, 1967), and Ifigenia M. de Navarrete, "La Distribución del ingreso en México: Tendencias y perspectivas," in *El Perfil de México en 1980,* 1:16-72.

36. The national censuses have always underreported unemployment. Even studies which have looked at the unemployment situation have presented very limited data on the topic. See, for example, Gloria González Salazar, *Subocupación y estructura de clases sociales en México,* (Mexico City: Universidad Nacional Autónoma de México, 1972).

37. Watry, Jr., "The Economic Development of Baja California," p. 2.

38. Edmundo Flores, *Vieja Revolución, nuevos problemas* (Mexico City: Joaquín Mortiz, 1970).

39. Ugalde, *The Urbanization Process,* p. 23.

40. The results of our research in Juárez are very similar to those of Wayne A. Cornelius, *Politics and the Migrant Poor in Mexico City* (Stanford: Stanford University Press, 1975).

41. We are in disagreement with Vernon M. Briggs, "The Mexico-United States Border": "Ostensibly, the reason for the need for such a program [the border industrialization program] was the high unemployment in the northern states of Mexico due to the termination of the bracero program in December 1964" (p. 18).

42. Ugalde, *Power and Conflict,* chs. 2 and 3.

43. In spite of the many reports prepared by PRONAF, political considerations were a main factor in the investment of resources. Frequently, the investments were completely unrelated to the pressing social problems of the population.

44. Dillman, "The Functions of Brownsville, Texas and Matamoros, Tamaulipas," p. 211.

45. Ugalde, *Power and Conflict,* p. 123.

46. W. S. Tuohy, "Institutionalized Revolution in a Mexican City: Political Decision-Making in Jalapa" (Ph.D. diss., Stanford University, Stanford, 1967).

47. Ugalde, *Power and Conflict,* p. 128.

48. Juan Manuel Cullingford, "Debe cuidarse más la inversión oficial," *Huella* (Tijuana), 4 March 1967.

6

The Politics of the Texas Border:
An Historical Overview and
Some Contemporary Directions

Armando Gutiérrez

Introduction

The border between Mexico and the United States offers the researcher a unique chance to consider, on a micro-level, the relations between two countries. Several scholars specializing in this area have argued that the border is often the "testing ground" for policies that either government eventually hopes to implement on a broader level with other countries.[1] On a comparable micro-level, the American border businessman is concerned that the proximity and easy access to Mexico might encourage disruptive behavior, making protection desirable and necessary. This, combined with the massive migrations of Mexican nationals into the United States, providing a cheap reserve labor supply, make the area extremely interesting and inviting to the scholar.

The border has a long history as a "hot spot" for revolutionary activity. From the revolts of Juan Cortina and Chico Cano in the mid 1800s to the "Plan de San Diego" in 1915 and the socialist labor activities in the 1920s, the area has been a continual scene of controversy.[2] More than once Americans suggested that Mexico desired to foster a revolutionary spirit along the border in order to facilitate its eventual reincorporation of the Southwest. During the First World War, it was alleged that Germany encouraged Mexico to precipitate subversive actions along the United States side of the border with a view to weakening American domination in the area and affecting the balance of power more broadly. While these allegations have not been proven, there is no question that Germany, as evidenced by the Zimmermann note, intended to seek an alliance with Mexico in the event of United States entry into the war. The recapture of territory lost to the United States was to be the inducement for Mexican participation.[3] It amounted to one more element making the border a scene of continual economic, political, and social struggle. The legacy of these conflicts has yet to die.

Looking at the Texas-Mexican border, one finds that it is not a uniform area in virtually any sense. Only the fact that the Río Grande bisects it provides a common denominator to this area of nearly one thousand miles from Brownsville on the Gulf Coast to El Paso at the far west tip of Texas. The topography varies from the rich Río Grande Valley and the year-round fertility of the Winter-Garden area to the rugged mountains of the Big Bend region and the arid desert surrounding El Paso. Economically, the areas vary from the heavy dependence on agriculture in the Río Grande Valley, where Hidalgo County annually receives $85 million in agribusiness income, to the heavy ranching areas in Hudspeth and Presidio counties.

For a discussion of politics, however, the overwhelmingly important fact is the situation of the border as regards its Chicano population. Only two counties, sparsely populated Brewster and Terrell, have less than a majority of Chicanos within their boundaries. From the 56.6 percent in Val Verde to 97.8 percent in Starr, the area is at least numerically dominated by Chicanos.

The tumultuous political history of the Texas border area hints at its significance, and the present-day stirrings of the Chicano people, with the concomitant emphasis on their Mexican heritage, declare the area a potentially explosive one.

The purpose of this essay is to list, in an orderly fashion, the circumstances which give rise to political activity and to analyze the factors that may contribute to or mitigate against the success of such activity. The variety of social, economic, and political characteristics mark the region. These are examined here as they might affect the political views of the people in the area. Then they are viewed as they appear to be purely class or ethnic phenomena.

Next, this essay considers the politics of the border historically. In so doing I attempted to achieve some feel for the way in which Chicanos and Anglos have interacted over a long period of time. This view takes into account not only voting patterns but also the history of some ''machines'' within the region.

The present-day context of politics in the border region is then examined. This section deals particularly with the voting patterns during the three most recent gubernatorial elections. These elections were chosen because they marked the coming of a possible new age in Chicano politics. Before 1972, Chicanos approaching the polls had the choice between a conservative Anglo Democrat and a more conservative Anglo Republican. Perhaps the most surprising fact is that Chicanos voted at all. By 1972, however, with the development of the Raza Unida Party, the choice was expanded to include a young, dynamic Chicano, Ramsey Muniz, who promised far-reaching changes if elected. The voting patterns before and after the inception of the Raza Unida Party thus should prove to be most interesting and helpful in trying to draw some hypotheses regarding the direction of Chicano politics, and, by extension, of border politics.

In conclusion, this essay discusses the findings and the possible directions which border politics may take in the future. As such, alternatives ranging from violence to apathy are considered with an eye to developing an understanding of the dynamics which have made and continue to make the border such a fascinating place to study.

A Brief Look at Texas Border Conditions

The Río Grande Valley, of course, is famous for its rich agricultural lands and temperate climate but El Paso, at the other end of the border, is in a dry region that leaves one wondering how such a large city ever developed amidst such forbidding surroundings. Accordingly, the populations of the various counties making up the border differ to a great extent.

The most populous county is El Paso. The 360,000 inhabitants of this relatively small county reside largely in the city of El Paso, with only some 40,000 outside the city limits. At the opposite end of the spectrum, and almost midway along the border, is Terrell County. Over twice as large as El Paso County, it only has some 1,940 inhabitants, and nearly two-thirds of these live in the county seat of Sanderson. Table 1 presents these as well as several other characteristics for the counties comprising the area under study.

Not quite as varied as the geography and the populations of the area is the distribution of the Chicano population. While varying by over 50 percent, there are only two counties, Brewster and Terrell in the Big Bend area, in which Chicanos do not constitute a numerical majority. On the other hand, no county below Kinney has less than a 70-percent majority of Chicanos. Taken as a whole, the Chicano border population totals close to 600,000 as compared with slightly more than 240,000 Anglos.[4] The potential strength of the Chicano population hardly needs to be stated (Table 1.)

TABLE 1
Texas Border Counties: Population

County	Total Population (1970)	% Anglo	% Chicano
El Paso	359,291	40.0	56.8
Hudspeth	2,392	38.5	60.4
Presidio	4,842	24.4	75.2
Brewster	7,780	51.6	47.7
Terrell	1,940	56.9	42.9
Val Verde	27,471	40.6	56.6
Kinney	2,006	21.1	72.1
Maverick	18,093	9.5	90.3
Webb	72,859	12.6	85.6
Zapata	4,352	8.2	91.5
Starr	17,707	1.6	97.8
Hidalgo	181,535	20.1	79.1
Cameron	140,368	22.7	76.2

Source: *The Chicano Almanac,* Texas Institute for Educational Development (1973).

As we begin considering the conditions under which the people of the border live, it soon becomes apparent that the numerical dominance of the Chicano people is not translated into any socioeconomic category. Indeed, the conditions of Chicanos are strikingly depressed.

In no instance do Chicanos maintain an edge over Anglos in median level of family income. The highest level attained by Chicanos in this category is in El Paso where the level is $6,495 per year, the only county where Chicanos achieve a median level of family income of over $5,000 per year. In Kinney County, on the other hand, the median family income level is just over $3,000. It is eminently clear from these figures that, although virtually all of the counties on the border are relatively poor, Chicanos form a distinctly impoverished group.

When we turn our attention to the percentage of families that fall below the poverty level, we once again are struck by the depressed standard of living of the Chicano people. In all but one county, El Paso, nearly 40 percent or more of Chicanos fall below the poverty level.

Using a slightly different statistic, that of incidence of poverty, which takes into account several poverty-related variables, the contrast between Anglo and Chicano becomes startlingly apparent.[5] In all but one county, El Paso, the incidence of poverty among Chicanos is upwards of 37 percent. In seven of the counties over 50 percent of the Chicano population exist in a state of poverty. Perhaps the critical point here is the clear contrast between white and brown. The potential political ramifications of the contrast are almost too obvious to mention (Tables 2 and 3).

TABLE 2
Texas Border Counties: Income Levels

County	Median Family Income		Median Per/Capita Income		% Families Below Poverty Level	
	Anglo	*Chicano*	*Anglo*	*Chicano*	*Anglo*	*Chicano*
El Paso	$7,824*	$6,495	$1,799	$1,166	7.7	25.8
Hudspeth	5,313	4,127	993	710	9.8	42.1
Presidio	4,161	3,367	995	788	13.4	52.6
Brewster	5,642	4,734	1,215	808	16.6	39.4
Terrell	6,602	3,718	1,212	911	11.7	44.0
Val Verde	6,498	4,859	1,519	756	8.5	39.7
Kinney	3,905	3,088	875	680	12.8	63.8
Maverick	4,509	3,906	809	687	1.2	51.2
Webb	4,975	4,445	904	742	11.4	43.5
Zapata	NA	NA	NA	NA	NA	57.7
Starr	3,592	3,591	687	672	23.8	52.0
Hidalgo	4,780	3,957	836	621	13.6	52.8
Cameron	5,075	4,073	885	619	14.0	49.6

Source: *The Chicano Almanac,* Texas Institute for Educational Development, (1973).

* In reading the statistics for Anglos on Median Family Income, and Median Per/Capita Income it must be kept in mind that these are actually *total* figures. That is, they include Anglos *and* Chicanos. This obviously deflates the Anglo figures considerably. It is most difficult to extract separate Anglo figures, particularly when they are medians. That this fact makes a large difference can be seen by looking at the figures for Percent Families Below Poverty Level, which were computed. For example, Hudspeth County Anglos went from 28.1 percent to 9.8 percent below poverty level. Similar figures for Maverick County were 44.2 percent before and 1.2 percent after extraction. This is also the case for the figures in Table 4.

TABLE 3
Texas Border Counties: Poverty

County	Incidence of Poverty	Incidence of Poverty
	Anglos	*Chicanos*
El Paso	10.1	28.7
Hudspeth	20.7	41.5
Presidio	24.3	59.2
Brewster	26.1	42.6
Terrell	14.1	37.4
Val Verde	11.9	42.3
Kinney	11.7	75.5
Maverick	*	56.5
Webb	14.7	49.2
Zapata	*	67.8
Starr	*	56.9
Hidalgo	21.4	57.1
Cameron	17.3	54.6

*Sample size was not sufficiently large to avoid disclosure of information on specific individuals.

Source: *Poverty in Texas 1973,* Report by the Office of Economic Opportunity, Texas Department of Community Affairs (May 1974).

An area which has probably received the most attention in and out of government over the years is that of education. Virtually no one argues against the usefulness of education, and it is seen, more than any other factor, as the answer to the problems of poverty. Although there is a good deal of evidence that education can do only so much in relieving economic inequities and that racial prejudices will continue to affect the status of Chicanos, within and without the community, there still persists an emphasis on education as the panacea for Chicano problems.[6] Consequently, educational inequities often may be perceived as more important than economic ones. The economic pattern is paralleled by the educational disparities between the two ethnic groups.

In no county is the Chicano median level of school completed above junior high school. From a high of 8.1 years in El Paso County to a low of 4.2 years in Presidio, the Chicano lags well behind the Anglo in educational attainment. Neither male nor female Chicanos have been able to match their Anglo counterparts in going through the school systems of south Texas.

Perhaps the most important implication of this educational deficiency is the rationalization it allows for Chicanos' depressed economic conditions. That is, Chicanos are perceived (and perhaps even perceive themselves) as being poor because of their low educational status. The thrust of political activity, given this perception, will likely be directed at the school systems. To affect significantly the educational levels of entire population groups would require many years of activity. Political activity challenging the status quo may thus be deflected for years. This, of course, is precisely what has occurred with the Chicano people. For the past quarter of a century, most Chicano groups have emphasized educational attainment among their principal goals (Table 4).[7]

But this analysis of the political implications of the schools is incomplete. An alternative explanation asserts that the schools are a critical tool in developing a child's self-esteem and identity. A strong positive sense of self- and of group-identity, in turn, are crucial contributors to political activity and to a critical view of the social and political system.[8] The determinant of the direction that a child's perceptions take as he or she moves through the school system, of course, is largely due to the content of the school's messages. Control of the school system thus becomes the more important variable in determining the potential effects of the schools. In the end, then, although both groups may point to the schools as the solution to the Chicanos' depressed conditions, it may well be for completely different reasons.

Turning our attention to housing characteristics, we find a corroboration of our earlier findings. As the report on *Poverty in Texas 1973* indicated in its conclusions, ". . . the poor Mexican-Americans also lived for the most part

TABLE 4
Texas Border Counties: Education

County	Median School Years Completed			
	Total Population		*Chicanos*	
	M	F	M	F
El Paso	12.2	11.5	8.1	8.1
Hudspeth	9.5	10.2	5.2	5.1
Presidio	6.9	6.6	5.0	4.2
Brewster	12.0	11.7	6.5	7.1
Terrell	10.3	10.9	6.4	5.4
Val Verde	11.1	10.2	6.6	6.1
Kinney	7.8	6.3	4.5	4.4
Maverick	6.6	6.3	5.8	5.9
Webb	8.1	7.1	7.0	6.5
Zapata	6.2	5.7	5.3	5.0
Starr	5.9	5.9	5.7	6.0
Hidalgo	7.6	7.0	5.2	4.9
Cameron	8.7	8.4	6.0	5.7

Source: *The Chicano Almanac,* Texas Institute for Educational Development (1973).

in bad housing and some 30 percent lacked adequate plumbing facilities.''[9] The sobering part of these statistics, however, is that these conclusions were drawn for the state as a whole. The border region is recognized as a particularly poor area. Thus, we can safely assume that conditions undoubtedly are even worse for the Chicano who resides along the border.

Summarizing our findings regarding these selected socioeconomic characteristics, it is clear that the Chicano population residing in the border counties suffers as a group from depressed conditions and has been little served by governmental programs meant to alleviate these conditions. Moreover, the contrast between the Chicano and Anglo populations in relation to these conditions ranges from irritating to appalling. Chicano responses to these inequities, at this point, can only be hypothesized.

A Brief Political History of the Border

The border has seen virtually every imaginable style of political behavior. From lynchings and riots to political machines and voting, the border has not been devoid of activity.

One of the first incidents of political conflict along the border after the signing of the Treaty of Guadalupe Hidalgo involved Juan ''Cheno'' Cortina.

Championing the cause of the Mexicans on the United States side of the border, Cortina, a resident of Tamaulipas, sought to alleviate the unequal treatment to which they were subjected. His struggles with United States and Texas border authorities began in 1859 and did not end until 1875. Despite the fact that he was treated by the American press as a common bandit, the Mexican Americans on the border viewed him as a hero.[10]

A variety of similar struggles followed Cortina's wars. As McWilliams states in his account of Mexican-American history, ''From 1871 to 1875 the whole border was aflame with a type of lawlessness and violence even worse than open warfare.''[11] Shortly thereafter the Salt War broke out in El Paso. This short-lived conflict was followed by a period of relative peace until the early 1900s, when new outbreaks of violence signaled another era of discontent along the border. McWilliams, in discussing this period, says, ''From 1908 to 1925, the whole border was aflame, once again. . . .''[12]

Symptomatic of the period was the so-called Plan of San Diego. The uprising also has been identified with one of its leaders, Pizaña. The abortive effort to retake the Southwest promulgated a plan which contained an analysis of the oppression of poor people in the United States and called for an uprising not only by the Mexican Americans, but also by Blacks, Native Americans, and Oriental Americans, all of whom, it was argued, were the victims of ''Yankee'' racism and oppression. Although the actual clashes were scattered and never seriously challenged United States domination, the Plan articulated a resentment that had existed since the American annexation of the Southwest and that has persisted down to the present. Moreover, the view that Mexican Americans were only one of a number of groups suffering from Anglo domination was to resurface from time to time until the present, when it has become much more widely held.[13]

The end of the struggles associated with the Plan de San Diego marked the beginning of an era which was particularly concerned with labor problems. Labor activity, particularly in El Paso and in Laredo, was quite pronounced during the years that followed.[14] Similarly, several agricultural workers' strikes occurred during this period. This activity was especially evident in the Río Grande Valley.[15]

Concurrent with such events, there was a steady increase in the number of political machines emerging in the border region. In Laredo the famous machine of the Martin family was developing—a machine that has continued to the present. Similarly, in Starr County the famous Guerra-González machine has controlled politics for the last three-quarters of a century. Comparable situations have existed in virtually every county in the border region at one time or another.[16]

Border Politics Today:
The Beginnings of Change?

In recent years the border has felt the effects of some important new forces. The power of traditional machines and influential establishment types has begun to be challenged by the fledgling Raza Unida Party. Although the challenge is still in its beginning stages, a look at the last three gubernatorial races gives some hint of the potential effects of a third-party movement on the politics of the border.

It has been noted that the border has long been a stronghold of the Democratic Party. Never before has the party felt any challenge to its dominance of this region. Even in those instances where local machines have been challenged, such as in Starr County, the new groups never have sought to break the ties to the Democrats. Thus, local conflict has not affected voter turnout for the Democratic Party.

The 1970 race for the governor's chair gives an indication of the traditional strength of the Democrats on the border. Only in three counties, El Paso, Hidalgo, and Cameron (the most populous of the border counties) did the Democratic Party receive less than 60 percent of the vote. In no county was there any semblance of a threat to that party's dominance. In addition, voter turnout was generally around 50 percent. Statewide, the Democratic Party candidate Preston Smith received 53.57 percent, almost the exact percentage of registered voters who went to the polls.[17] Clearly, for the Democrats the border is an inordinately strong area. In no county in this region did Smith receive less than his statewide percentages. Indeed, most of his vote totals in these counties were well above the state averages (Table 5).

By the time of the general elections in November 1972, the Raza Unida Party had grown from its inauspicious birth in Crystal City, Texas, to a loosely knit statewide organization. In virtually no area of the state was there a well-defined organizational structure from which the party's gubernatorial candidate, Ramsey Muniz, could draw money and workers. His was basically a door-to-door, hit-and-run campaign. Few political observers gave Muniz a chance of gaining anything close to the 2 percent required to insure the party's survival.[18] While he was expected to manage perhaps five to ten percent of the border Chicano vote, no significant challenge was thought to be imminent.

As Table 9 vividly demonstrates, the impact of Muniz's candidacy was far from insignificant. Ranging from a low of 6.86 percent in sparsely populated Hudspeth County, to a high of over 37 percent in Maverick, the party astonished all observers with its showing. Moreover, the 6.3 percent showing of Muniz in the state nearly threw the election to the Republican candidate,

TABLE 5
Texas Border Counties: Voting Statistics
(1970)

County	1970 Population	1970 Registered	Democratic Vote %	Turnout %
El Paso	359,291	95,132	54.77	52.42
Hudspeth	2,392	900	73.74	66.00
Presidio	4,842	2,222	77.72	65.26
Brewster	7,780	2,878	62.83	60.95
Terrell	1,940	796	60.29	51.26
Val Verde	27,471	8,279	68.87	49.44
Kinney	2,006	984	78.06	60.67
Maverick	18,093	4,923	73.81	36.85
Webb	72,859	21,445	75.34	43.03
Zapata	4,352	2,284	65.52	49.78
Starr	17,707	8,272	60.25	66.42
Hidalgo	181,535	62,207	57.68	47.81
Cameron	140,368	48,040	53.36	45.85

Source: *Texas Precinct Votes '70,* V. Lance Tarrance, Jr. (ed.), Austin and London: The University of Texas Press, 1972.

Henry Grover, who lost the election by some 100,000 votes. Ramsey Muniz received just over 214,000 votes.

Of particular importance is the percentage loss which the Democrats suffered between 1970 and 1972. They lost ground in all but two counties between the two elections. In eight of the counties the loss was over 10 percent. Given the fact that in most of the counties the number of registered voters changed very little from 1970 to 1972, it can be inferred that the Raza Unida Party drew a good deal of its support away from the Democrats. This point cannot be pushed too far, however, as the party's workers did seek to mobilize new voters. It is, of course, impossible to know how many of the 214,072 votes were from new voters.

An additional point involves the situation of the Republican Party on the border. One might suspect that the Democratic Party loss might be attributable to Republican Party gains, particularly on the coattails of Richard Nixon. Table 6, however, demonstrates that such was not the case. Indeed, in every border county the percentage of the votes received by the Republican candidate for governor declined between the election of 1970 and that of 1972. Clearly, then, it is the emergence of the Raza Unida Party that explains the dramatic change in voting patterns on the border. It appears that a good portion of the support of the Democratic Party on the border was unenthusiastic and involved the classic "lesser of two evils" choice. In addition, the apparent lack of perceived threat from Muniz's candidacy caused the local Democratic machinery to be lulled into inaction again; the Democrats began the campaign early with a full-scale mobilization of the Mexican-American ''leaders'' within the Democratic Party. Unlike the 1972 elections in which Ramsey Muniz was ignored and almost never mentioned, in 1974 the Democratic candidate, incumbent Dolph Briscoe, had prominent,

TABLE 6
Texas Border Counties: Voting Statistics
(1970-74)

County	1970 Republican %	1972 Republican %	1974 Republican %
El Paso	45.23	40.00	32.46
Hudspeth	26.26	24.23	15.36
Presidio	22.28	21.01	12.28
Brewster	37.17	28.00	25.94
Terrell	39.71	19.47	16.76
Val Verde	31.13	21.51	12.21
Kinney	21.94	11.76	8.08
Maverick	26.19	19.52	10.54
Webb	24.66	13.09	7.64
Zapata	34.48	13.80	6.51
Starr	39.75	18.95	2.52
Hidalgo	42.32	28.83	26.50
Cameron	43.64	40.00	28.49

Source: Records from the Office of the Secretary of State, Election Division.

TABLE 7
Texas Border Counties: Reigistered Voters
(1970-74)

County	1970[a]	1972[b]	1974[c]
El Paso	95,132	98,539	139,921
Hudspeth	900	917	1,171
Presidio	2,222	1,854	2,475
Brewster	2,878	2,743	3,530
Terrell	796	911	1,021
Val Verde	8,279	7,079	10,570
Kinney	984	839	1,185
Maverick	4,923	3,720	6,497
Webb	21,445	20,467	26,627
Zapata	2,284	2,167	2,863
Starr	8,272	8,289	9,871
Hidalgo	62,207	62,811	78,153
Cameron	48,040	36,696	61,149

Sources: [a]*Texas Precinct Votes '70*.
[b]*The Chicano Almanac*.
[c]Records from the Office of the Secretary of State, Election Division.

middle-class Mexican Americans engage in a frontal attack on the Raza Unida Party. Efforts to identify the party as a "militant," "radical" organization which threatened to set back the "advances" the Mexican-American people had achieved in recent years (even though all recent statistical information failed to confirm such "advances") were launched throughout the state. In particular, Briscoe threatened to shut off funds to some of the pet programs of such traditional organizations as GI Forum and LULAC (Tables 7 through 11).[19]

TABLE 8
Texas Border Counties: Voting Statistics
(1974)

County	Democrat %	Republican %	Raza Unida Party %
El Paso	56.00	32.46	11.54
Hudspeth	81.00	15.36	3.60
Presidio	76.42	12.28	11.29
Brewster	60.87	25.94	13.17
Terrell	72.51	16.76	10.72
Val Verde	76.41	12.21	11.36
Kinney	85.47	8.08	6.43
Maverick	64.26	10.54	25.19
Webb	60.20	7.64	32.15
Zapata	69.68	6.51	23.79
Starr	85.93	2.52	11.54
Hidalgo	50.70	26.50	22.78
Cameron	56.84	28.49	14.65

Source: Records from the Office of the Secretary of State, Election Division.

TABLE 9
Texas Border Counties: Raza Unida Party Voting Percentages

County	1972	1974	Loss/Gain
El Paso	16.10	11.54	− 4.56
Hudspeth	6.86	3.60	− 3.26
Presidio	18.25	11.29	− 6.96
Brewster	28.01	13.17	−13.17
Terrell	15.01	10.72	− 4.29
Val Verde	24.47	11.36	−13.11
Kinney	12.08	6.43	− 5.65
Maverick	37.23	25.19	−12.04
Webb	27.62	32.15	+ 4.53
Zapata	28.71	23.79	− 4.92
Starr	18.04	11.54	− 6.50
Hidalgo	28.69	22.78	− 5.91
Cameron	15.00	14.65	− 0.35

Source: Records from the Office of the Secretary of State, Election Division.

TABLE 10
Texas Border Counties: Democratic Party Voting Percentages

County	1972	1974	Loss/Gain
El Paso	44.00	56.00	+12.00
Hudspeth	68.47	81.00	+12.53
Presidio	60.74	76.42	+15.68
Brewster	43.00	60.87	+17.87
Terrell	65.52	72.51	+ 6.99
Val Verde	53.76	76.41	+22.65
Kinney	75.83	85.47	+ 9.64
Maverick	42.90	64.26	+21.36
Webb	59.12	60.20	+ 1.08
Zapata	57.42	69.68	+12.26
Starr	62.85	85.93	+23.08
Hidalgo	40.41	50.70	+10.29
Cameron	44.00	56.84	+12.84

Source: Records from the Office of the Secretary of State, Election Division.

TABLE 11
Texas Border Counties: Democratic Votes

County	1970	1972	1974
El Paso	27,315	34,602	24,217
Hudspeth	438	446	696
Presidio	1,127	882	846
Brewster	1,102	1,081	610
Terrell	246	324	372
Val Verde	2,819	3,216	2,683
Kinney	466	477	465
Maverick	1,339	1,330	926
Webb	6,952	8,143	4,174
Zapata	745	774	855
Starr	3,310	2,267	3,201
Hidalgo	17,154	16,440	8,787
Cameron	12,415	14,354	9,396

Source: Records from the Office of the Secretary of State, Election Division.

The effectiveness of these efforts is evident from the results of the 1974 governor's race. In all but one border county, Ramsey Muniz received a smaller percentage of the vote than in 1972. The loss ranged from 0.35 percent in Cameron County to 13.17 percent in Brewster County. Moreover, given the fact that the Republicans also lost ground from 1972 to 1974, it is clear that the gains were made exclusively by the Democrats. They were able to recoup the losses that had befallen them in the previous election. Indeed, not only were they able in most cases to regain their previous proportional standing but also to add to this advantage. Table 12 appears to verify the substantial gains made by the Democrats in 1974.

Looking a bit deeper at the results in 1974, however, gives us a picture that is not as clear as it first appears. Shifting from the proportion of votes received

TABLE 12
Texas Border Counties: Raza Unida Party Votes

County	1972	1974
El Paso	12,703	4,991
Hudspeth	46	31
Presidio	265	125
Brewster	697	132
Terrell	74	55
Val Verde	1,464	399
Kinney	76	35
Maverick	1,156	363
Webb	3,855	2,229
Zapata	387	292
Starr	666	430
Hidalgo	11,656	3,918
Cameron	4,774	2,423

Source: Records from the Office of the Secretary of State, Election Division.

by the Democratic candidate to the actual number of votes received, indicates that in only a few cases were there gains made in the *number* of people voting Democratic. Thus, in Hidalgo County, for example, although Briscoe increased his proportion from 1972 to 1974 by over 10 percent, the number of votes he received was very nearly half that received the previous election. A similar pattern holds for several of the other counties. In the end, then, it is evident that virtually all of the candidates in 1974 *lost* votes. Some obviously lost substantially more than others.

Conclusion

Just as the political history of the Texas-Mexican border has been highly volatile with activity ranging from peaceful voter drives to outright racial violence, so the present-day border is a highly complex area that defies easy and rigid categorization. The picture drawn by this paper gives testimony to the value of studying the border as a social, economic, and political unit.

From the signing of the Treaty of Guadalupe Hidalgo in 1848 to the present, the border has seen constant conflict among a variety of groups. Oftentimes this struggle was clearly divided into one between Anglos and

Mexican Americans. At other times it took on the design of class warfare. But the turmoil was constant and cost the lives of countless victims, often people only tangentially involved in the conflicts.

Amid the explosive violence that pervaded the Texas-Mexican border, there occurred the development of strong political machines. These machines sought to control politics through the dispensation of rewards to their supporters and sanctions on their opposition. In the less-than-diversified economy of most sections of the border, the growth and perpetuation of these machines was an almost natural occurrence. In several cases the machines have managed to transfer power through the generations and thus today continue to control the economic, social, and political life of the areas.

In spite of all the violence and turmoil of border history, one fact stands out when considering the recent political experience of the border—the dominance of the Democratic Party. Even when local machines have encountered serious opposition to their control of a particular county, the challengers have seldom sought to change the voting patterns for statewide and national offices.

The dominance of one political party would not be so intriguing were it not for the realization that, economically, the entire border region has been (and continues to be today) a highly stratified society with a small elite dominating virtually every aspect of life. The poverty which the large majority of Chicanos live in would seem to demand change. It is important that this poverty has been prevalent for some time, and, in spite of the continuous stream of Democratic Party politicians promising to alleviate these conditions, little has changed regarding the distribution of wealth and services. Yet the dominance of the Democrats has continued. Given these conditions it would seem logical to conclude that a political party based on premises different from those of two existing parties, and, particularly one appealing most specifically to Chicanos, would be a quick success in this region. The results of such an undertaking are, as yet, inconclusive.

Clearly, the elections of 1972 seemed to suggest that a third party could seriously challenge not only the local machine dominance but also that of the statewide Democratic Party. But just as one is about to come to this conclusion, the 1974 elections appear to disprove it. What implications can we draw for the future of border politics from the data presented here?

1. The delivery of votes for the Democratic Party in the border counties is a highly efficient operation. Even in those areas where "machines" are not in control of local politics, there appears to exist a very experienced organization which sees that a minimum number of voters goes to the polls. The greater or lesser extent of voter turnout is related to the perceived threat of the

opposition. The organization's sole concern is to mobilize people who can be counted upon to vote a straight Democratic ticket. Insurance is obtained through control of the polls. The election judges, clerks, and poll watchers are hand-picked by the machine, usually having served in those positions for a good number of years. The importance of these positions is intensified in an area where illiteracy is high and the voter will often ask for help from the judge. The difficulty of breaking through these technical barriers is usually enough to preclude serious challenges to the dominant party.

2. What the above implies is that the party in power has access to resources, both monetary and otherwise, so as virtually to insure its continued domination. Add to this the reliance of the statewide Democratic Party on similar ''machines'' throughout the state, and one begins to understand the difficulty in bringing about change. In 1972 the Raza Unida Party candidate was not taken seriously by the Democratic nominee for governor. Thus, little effort was made to mobilize traditional support in the border communities. The result almost gave the election to the Republican candidate. In 1974, not only was money mobilized, but also the local Mexican-American members of the machines engaged in a furious campaign against the Raza Unida Party. This campaign involved the discrediting of the party as well as the gearing of the voting machinery so as to insure that the maximum number of ''unsure'' voters was steered to vote the easiest way possible—a straight Democratic ticket. In fact, virtually all the advertising done by the Democrats stressed the need to vote ''straight Democrat.'' The only response the Raza Unida Party could make was to try to reach people individually in their homes—a highly inefficient and time-consuming task.

3. Most important, the findings underscore the extreme difficulty involved in attempting to mobilize people to a new idea. Disregarding the imbalance of resources available to the different groups, the sociopsychological barriers involved are substantial. The first such barrier is the history of the situation. On the one hand are the many who have voted Democratic for so long that no other alternative is ever even considered. On the other hand are those who have traditionally not voted, either because of legal or extralegal obstacles (the poll tax, job intimidation) or simply because they perceive that they receive nothing in return for voting. Both situations require considerable effort to change, with no assurance that the individual will receive any or all of the intended message. At the same time, of course, one must realize that the ''other side'' is not likely to sit idly by while the changes are being wrought. Second, no two individuals will understand and internalize the justifications one gives for changing past patterns of behavior at precisely the same rate. Thus, one is compelled to deal in as individual a manner as possible. This is, naturally, a most inefficient and time-consuming process

involving an extremely large number of people. The implication of this is that change, particularly the kind that requires people to expend resources in order to achieve it, is a slow process.

The sheer mechanics of the operation are staggering. In a relatively small town such as Eagle Pass, with some fifteen thousand inhabitants and six thousand registered voters, fifty people working during the evening hours and on weekends will require at least a month or two to visit the homes of each potential supporter. Besides, it is highly unlikely that people will be converted, either to vote when they haven't been doing so or to change political parties[20] on the basis of a single visit. Changing an individual's philosophy about the political system does not normally come easily, particularly when the opposition is counteracting each move one makes. This refers not only to the Democrat or Republican that Raza Unida seeks to convert, but also, and perhaps even more so, to the nonvoter. Anywhere from 50 to 75 percent of potentially eligible Chicanos do not normally vote. This includes both those who have been registered but do not go to the polls and the nonregistered. It would seem possible enough to mobilize this most important group of potential supporters, but the reasons for not voting are likely to run quite deep. Rather than the apathy so often attributed to them, it is at least as likely that this group has concluded, consciously or otherwise, that voting does not do them any good. Even though there may be ambiguity as to exactly why support of a candidate or party is not translated into tangible goods, the realization is nonetheless enough to create a strong sense of alienation. It should be added that such alienation is not an unrealistic appraisal of the plight of Chicanos on the border. For their faithful support of the Democratic Party they have received the conditions stated at the outset of this chapter.

The point to be remembered about this alienation, however, is that in most cases it is apparently not party-specific. That is, it seems to be directed at the political process in general, rather than at a specific political group. This should not be surprising, for many times these people have been approached, by Chicanos and Anglos alike, with promises of the benefits to be gained by support. So it is not the case that Raza Unida Party workers are the first to approach them with promises of a better tomorrow. While it is true that this group has in many cases not been approached for some time, the memory seems to be vivid and long-lasting.

4. What this discussion implies is that raising the consciousness of people is a difficult process. Basically, one is confronted by three options in achieving that goal. On the one hand, there is the strategy discussed previously, of meeting and talking with people individually or in groups with the purpose of challenging the existing power distribution, thus compelling them to act. This strategy is, of course, wrought with a multitude of

handicaps, not the least of which is that even the party faithful, those willing
to engage in such work, also vary in their understanding and ability to transmit
the philosophy of the party. Some belong because it is in vogue, some because
friends or relatives belong, others because they perceive it as a safe haven
from the Anglo, and so on.

On the other hand, there is the strategy best proposed by Saul Alinsky. His
argument was basically to get people involved and *acting,* through whatever
means necessary, and to let the consciousness-raising take care of itself
later.[21] This strategy's effectiveness is best exemplifed not on the border itself
but in nearby Zavala County where the activity spurred by a school walkout
resulted in the creation of a Chicano consciousness probably unparalleled in
Texas.[22] The difficulty with such a strategy is, of course, that one cannot
usually manufacture an incident and the intensity and direction of the
subsequent activity are often unmanageable, if not unpredictable.[23] In
addition, as the 1974 returns indicate, one-time support for a party does not
insure future support. Thus, many who voted for the Raza Unida in 1972
failed to return to the polls in 1974.

A third option seeks to incorporate a little of the other two around an
ongoing organizational structure. The creation of a local party structure allows
the day-to-day kind of activity in between, as well as immediately prior to,
elections. An important consideration is that such a structure assures that if
and when an incident occurs, there will be an organization ready to attempt to
orchestrate the activity in such a way as to achieve the ultimate end.
Moreover, such an organization also can involve itself in service activities.
Providing food and clothing through the establishment of cooperatives, legal
and medical services, sponsoring cultural and educational activities, all give
the organization the legitimacy and credibility within the community that may
help overcome the skepticism toward political groups. The best example of
this kind of organization in action is in Webb County. Although in action for a
relatively short period of time in the county, the organization was able to
counteract the trend of the rest of the region and *gain* percentage support for
Ramsey Muniz. This, in spite of the fact that Laredo, with over 90 percent of
the county's population, has been a tightly controlled, machine-dominated
city for the last half century.

In the final analysis it appears that the border region is potentially as
explosive today as in the past. True, this explosiveness will not be likely to
manifest itself in the violence of the past, although that possibility is not out of
the question. But the potential for fundamental and highly significant change
is clearly existent in every border county. The 1972 elections made it clear
that such potential was alive, even if dormant. The 1974 elections

demonstrated that the local powers together with the statewide Democratic Party are not going to surrender control without a substantial and powerful struggle.

But the most intriguing, and as yet unanswerable, question involves the nonvoter. As was demonstrated, this group comprises at least half, and possibly as much as three-fourths of the potentially eligible electorate along the border. This can be seen particularly when we consider the generally large increase in the number of registered voters between 1972 and 1974 with the relaxation of registration requirements. Yet, in spite of this large increase, turnout was lower than ever. Evidently, getting people registered to vote has little to do with getting them to the polls on election day.

Essentially, one is talking about a majority of Chicanos who are disenfranchised. This exclusion is nonetheless substantial despite the fact that formal, legal obstacles have largely been removed. A long history of neglect has shaped a psychology that is not erased by the simple reform or removal of laws.

In essence, then, this group is "up for grabs." There is no reason to believe that its members lean one way or another. To mobilize the group is an obviously difficult task. But the reward is likely to be either a strengthening of the Democratic Party control of the area if they are mobilized to that party's side, or, if the Raza Unida Party is able to pull them in its direction, a new competitiveness that border politics has not seen for decades.[24]

Finally, examining the border in the much broader context of relations between the United States and Mexico, a change in the politics of the border as exemplified in the rise of the Raza Unida Party could usher in a new era in relations between the two countries. Rather than the generally one-sided policy that has seen Mexico with virtually no bargaining power and often the victim of United States foreign policy experimentation, such as in Operation Intercept, we might envision a local border political structure much less inclined to cooperate with the federal government in such schemes. In other important areas of commerce and transportation, we might see a similar situation in which powerful economic interests on either side of the border will no longer be given the preferential treatment of the past.

What the preceding discussion portends, then, is an explosiveness with ramifications potentially far beyond the border itself. The shock waves of fundamental change in the politics now prevalent on the border could be felt long distances from this thirteen-county area. Conversely, the change may be only temporary in the lives of the nearly one million inhabitants of this region. Whatever the results, the border promises to be as interesting to study tomorrow as it has been today and in the past.

136   *Armando Gutiérrez*

NOTES

1. Edward Jay Epstein, "The Incredible War Against the Poppies," *Esquire,* December 1974, p. 148ff. Dr. Jorge Bustamante has also espoused this idea to the author on several occasions.

2. Rodolfo Acuña, *Occupied America: The Chicano's Struggle Toward Liberation* (San Francisco: Canfield Press, 1972); Carey McWilliams, *North From Mexico* (New York: Greenwood Press, 1968); Emilio Zamora, "Chicano Labor History in Texas, 1900-1920," (undated manuscript).

3. Ibid.

4. In actuality, the number of Chicanos is probably a good deal greater than census figures indicate. See a recent report by the U.S. Commission on Civil Rights, *Counting the Forgotten: The 1970 Census Count of Persons of Spanish Speaking Background in the United States* (Washington D.C.: Government Printing Office, April 1974). I am greatly indebted to Ms. Evey Chapa for making me aware of this document, as well as a number of other sources used in this work.

5. Office of Economic Opportunity, *Poverty in Texas 1973* (Texas Department of Community Affairs, May 1974).

6. Dudley L. Poston and David Alvírez, "On the Cost of Being a Mexican American Worker," *Social Science Quarterly* 53 (1973): 697-709.

7. Acuña, *Occupied America,* pp. 223-24.

8. Armando Gutiérrez and Herbert Hirsch, "The Militant Challenge to the American Ethos: 'Chicanos' and 'Mexican Americans,' " *Social Science Quarterly* 53 (1973): 830-45.

9. *Poverty in Texas 1973,* p. 187.

10. Acuña, *Occupied America,* pp. 46-50.

11. McWilliams, *North From Mexico,* p. 108.

12. Ibid., p. 111.

13. Although little research has been done on the "Plan de San Diego," a few documents (including a translation of the constitution of the group) are available. The author is presently engaged in research on this topic.

14. Emilio Zamora, "Chicano Labor History."

15. Acuña, *Occupied America,* ch. 7.

16. For a discussion of these machines' effects on voting, see Clifton McCleskey, *The Government and Politics of Texas* (Boston: Little, Brown & Co., 1969), pp. 101-2. For a discussion of machine politics in South Texas during the early part of the twentieth century, see O. D. Weeks, "The Texas-Mexican and the Politics of South Texas," *American Political Science Review* 24 (1930): 606-27.

17. V. Lance Tarrance, Jr., ed., *Texas Precinct Votes '70* (Austin: University of Texas Press, 1972).

18. State law in 1972 said that in order to be a "major party" in Texas, the party's gubernatorial candidate must receive at least 2 percent of the total votes in that race. A "major party" can hold its own state-financed primaries and is automatically on the succeeding ballot. In 1973, the percentage was increased to 20 percent.

19. Such programs as SER, Manpower Training, and Jobs for Progress were projects which these groups had initiated and which were threatened with an exhaustion of funds. Briscoe met personally with leaders from these groups and promised to release some $2.5 million for these programs if he were reelected. This information was obtained from several Mexican Americans who met with the governor just prior to the election.

20. Political scientists have recognized for some time the strength of party identification. See Angus Campbell, et al., *The American Voter* (New York: John Wiley & Sons, Inc., 1960).

21. Saul Alinsky, *Rules for Radicals* (New York: Vintage Books, 1972), pp. 3-23.

22. Gutiérrez and Hirsch, "The Militant Challenge," pp. 830-45.

23. Kenneth Dolbeare and Murray Edelman, *American Politics* (Lexington, Mass.: D. C. Heath & Co., 1971), see especially ch. 19.

24. While some might argue that it is unrealistic to expect anything more than roughly 50 percent of eligible voters to turn out consistently, evidence from the one county where the Raza Unida Party has become the dominant force indicates that such is not the case. Zavala County, since the Raza Unida rise to prominence, consistently draws between 70 and 90 percent turnout from Chicanos.

PART III

The Economics of the Border

7

Economic Importance of Mexico's Northern Border Region[1]

Víctor Urquidi and
Sofía Méndez Villarreal

Mexico's northern border region is made up of thirty-five municipalities[2] located in the states of Baja California Norte, Sonora, Chihuahua, Coahuila, Nuevo León, and Tamaulipas.

According to the 1970 census, the total population of the border states* was 7,976,188, representing 17 percent of the national population. The population of the border municipalities* reached 2,334,553 in 1970, representing 29.3 percent of the border states' population, as well as 5 percent of the total population (Table 1). Today the estimated population of the border municipalities exceeds 2.7 million.

The growth rate of the border municipalities is even more significant. Between 1950 and 1960 the average increase in population among these municipalities was 6.3 percent. Particularly high were Tijuana with 9.8 percent, Mexicali with 8.5 percent, Juárez with 7.8 percent, and Ensenada with 7.6 percent. Between 1960 and 1970 the population increase of the border municipalities fell to 4.1 percent, but Tijuana and Ensenada remained high, with 7.5 and 5.9 percent respectively (Table 2). Between 1960 and 1970 the yearly increase in the border states was 3.7 percent while nationally it was 3.4 percent.

---

*"Border states" refers to the Mexican states bordering the United States; "border municipalities" refers to those subjurisdictions actually bordering the United States [Editor's Note].

Over three-fourths (75.6 percent) of the border region's population is concentrated in seven of the thirty-five municipalities. In each of these—Juárez, Mexicali, Tijuana, Ensenada, Matamoros, Nuevo Laredo and Reynosa—the population exceeded 100,000 in 1970. The population of the three largest municipalities (Juárez 424,135; Mexicali 396,324; Tijuana 340,583) accounted for 50 percent of the total border population (Table 2). The greatest problems found in the border region are naturally localized in these urban areas.

TABLE 1
Population by States and Municipalities of the Border Region
(1970)

Border States	Population of State (1)	Population of Border Municipalities (2)	% 2/1
Total	7,976,188	2,334,553	29.3
Baja California Norte	870,921	870,421	100.0
Baja California Sur	128,019	—	—
Sonora	1,098,720	215,136	19.6
Chihuahua	1,612,525	483,582	30.0
Coahuila	1,114,956	100,846	9.0
Nuevo León	1,694,689	370	—
Tamaulipas	1,456,858	664,198	45.6

Source: *IX Censo General de Población, 1970.* Dirección General de Estadística, SIC.

TABLE 2
Population of Border Municipalities
Originating from a Different State
(1970)

Municipalities	Population Total (1)	Population Originating from a Different State (2)	% 2/1
Total	2,334,553	683,684	29.3
Juárez	424,135	97,133	22.9
Mexicali	396,324	135,574	34.2
Tijuana	340,583	161,751	47.5
Ensenada	115,423	41,218	35.7
Matamoros	186,146	39,239	21.1
Nuevo Laredo	151,253	50,264	33.2
Reynosa	150,786	46,663	31.0
Other	569,903	111,842	19.6

Source: *Censo General de Población, 1970.* Dirección General de Estadística, SIC.

While the birth rate in Mexico fell from 45.2 to 43.4 per thousand between 1950 and 1970, in the border communities the change was from 45.6 per thousand in 1950 to 43.6 per thousand in 1970. On the other hand, the mortality rate in the border communities is lower than the national average. Between 1950 and 1970 it fell from 12.4 to 7.2 per thousand, while the national average fell from 16.2 to 9.9 per thousand. The same is true of the infant mortality rate.

Migration is an important factor in the population increase. In 1970, 29.3 percent of the population in the border municipalities had come there from other communities. Such migration on the national level reached only 15.3 percent. Tijuana, Mexicali, and Juárez attract the greater migration because, being the largest cities, they seem likely to offer better employment opportunities. According to the 1970 census, 161,751 migrants made up 47 percent of Tijuana's population, 135,574 made up 34 percent of Mexicali's, and 97,133 made up 23 percent of Juárez's (Table 2).

Population Economically Active (PEA)

In 1969, the percentage of PEA engaged in services and trade in the border municipalities (46 percent) was higher than the national average (32 percent). In mining and manufacturing (17 percent) it was slightly lower than the national average (18 percent), and in agriculture (23 percent) it was much lower than the national average (39 percent) (Table 3).

Wage-earning through services and trade is remarkably high in the border municipalities, and it accounts for a large part of the regional economy. While in 1970, these areas of activity at the national level claimed 23 percent and 9 percent respectively of PEA, in the border states they claimed 27 percent and 12 percent, and in the border municipalities 32 percent and 14 percent respectively. In three of these municipalities (Juárez, Tijuana, and Nuevo Laredo) barely 10 percent of PEA engaged in industry, while 36 percent in Tijuana and 39 percent in Juárez and Nuevo Laredo engaged in services.

The increase between 1950 and 1970 in PEA engaged in trade and services in the border communities (from 25 percent to 46 percent) is remarkably larger than that at the national level (from 21 percent to 32 percent). On the other hand, the percentage of PEA engaged in infustry in the border communities has fallen substantially, from 50 percent in 1950 to 29 percent in 1970, as compared with the national decrease in this category from 58 percent to 39 percent.

TABLE 3
Economically Active Population by Field of Activity
(1969)

	Mexican Nation	%	Border States	%	Border Munici-palities	%
Population Total	48,225,238	—	7,976,188	—	2,334,553	—
PEA	12,955,057	100.0	2,120,305	100.0	602,700	100.00
Gross Rate of Activity	26.9	—	26.6	—	25.8	—
Agriculture, Live-stock, Forestry, Hunting and Fishing	5,103,519	39.4	619,605	29.2	139,826	23.2
Mining and Manufacturing	2,349,249	18.1	418,089	19.7	104,869	17.4
Construction	571,006	4.4	123,398	5.8	37,970	6.3
Electricity	53,286	0.4	9,043	0.4	2,410	0.4
Trade	1,196,878	9.2	246,756	11.7	84,981	14.1
Services	2,933,595	22.7	580,485	27.4	190,453	31.6
Insufficiently Specified	747,525	5.8	122,929	5.8	42,189	7.0

Source: *IX Censo General de Población, 1970*. Dirección General de Estadística, SIC.

Agriculture and Livestock

The amount of arable land in the border municipalities is small. Data gathered in 1970 show that, according to the records, of 32.4 million acres only 7.6 percent or 2.5 million acres are arable land, whereas of the 357.3 million acres in the whole country 19 percent are arable.

In the border municipalities and border states, lands suitable for pasturage cover 63 percent and 65 percent of the territory, while the corresponding figure is 48 percent for the national territory (Table 4). The prevalence of grazing land over arable land suggests the higher potential for the raising of livestock in the border region, though naturally the possibilities of increasing such production also depend on the availability of other stock supplies.

Agriculture in northern Mexico is highly technical, enjoys more irrigation, and has easier access to supplies. It has been estimated that while the country as a whole has at its disposal one tractor for every 588.8 acres of cultivation, in the border states there is a tractor for every 252.4 acres, and in the border municipalities there is a tractor for every 138.8 acres. Similarly, the use of improved stock supplies, such as seed, fertilizer, and insecticide, is fairly general in the border region. As a result, of course, there is higher yield per unit worked, and the productivity indexes are higher than the national average in the cultivation of cotton, sorghum, wheat, alfalfa, and corn, which represent about 90 percent of the border region's total agricultural production. Despite the superior technology, agriculture in this region has been deteriorating since the mid sixties. While the value at steady prices of the national production of the five products cited went up between 1960 and 1970 at an average annual rate of 5.1 percent and in the border states at an average annual rate of 3.4 percent, in the border municipalities this value went down at an average annual rate of 2.6 percent (Table 5).

Consequently, the share of borderlands agricultural production decreased at the state level from 31 percent in 1960 to 17 percent in 1970. And yet certain agricultural products continue to have a positive economic importance. About 25 percent of the cotton grown in Mexico comes from the border municipalities, as well as 20 percent of the sorghum harvest (almost

TABLE 4
Classification of Recorded Lands
(1970)
(thousands of hectares)*

	National Total	%	Border States	%	Border Municipalities	%
Total	144,637	100.0	61,938	100.0	13,136	100.0
Cultivation	27,469	19.0	5,168	8.3	1,005	7.6
Native Grasses	69,789	48.2	40,386	65.2	8,318	63.3
Forests	18,478	12.8	6,417	10.4	469	3.6
Barren Lands	8,413	0.7	2,927	4.7	503	3.8
Other	20,488	14.3	7,040	11.4	2,841	21.7

Source: *Censo Agrícola-Ganadero y Ejidal, 1970.* Dirección General de Estadística, SIC.
       *1 hectare = 2.47 acres.

TABLE 5
Value of Principal Crops in Border Municipalities
(thousands of pesos in 1960)

Crops	1960	1970	Rate of annual growth
Cotton	703,987	218,100	-12.4
Sorghum	—	190,570	
Wheat	82,520	154,745	6.5
Alfalfa	28,624	49,520	5.6
Corn	44,760	46,747	0.4
Total Border Municipalities	859,891	659,682	-2.6
Total Border States	2,776,259	3,889,644	3.4
Total National	7,591,332	12,496,673	5.1

Source: Secretaría de Agricultura y Ganadería. Dirección General de Economía Agrícola.

two-thirds from irrigated lands), 29 percent of the alfalfa harvest (mostly around Mexicali, Ensenada, and Juárez), and 10 percent of the wheat harvest (mostly around Mexicali and San Luis Río Colorado). In contrast, only 3 percent of the corn grown in Mexico comes from the border municipalities, and then mostly from Río Bravo, Reynosa, and Matamoros.

The border municipalities' contribution to the national production of livestock has remained at approximately 3 percent. Cattle, goats, hogs, and poultry predominate. While national livestock production at current prices increased at a 7.3 percent average between 1969 and 1971, in the border region it increased at only 4.4 percent per year. This has resulted in shortages of livestock products in the region, which have required the importation of American goods to meet the demand.

Industries

These include mining and manufacturing. Baja California and Sonora are the two border states whose municipalities, touching the American frontier, have developed mining industries. With respect to Baja California the situation can be explained by the fact that all four of its municipal subdivisions are considered to border the United States. Mining in this state, however, is not particularly important. Sonora is a different matter. Mining for copper in the vicinity of Cananea close to the border accounts for 90 percent of the mining in that state. The opposite is true of Chihuahua, where scarcely .02 percent of its mining is done in the border municipalities. This means that the minerals used in Juárez's smelting and manufacturing plants do not come from Chihuahua border municipalities (Table 6).

In 1972, the border municipalities accounted for 11.2 percent of the total

TABLE 6
Percent of Border Municipalities' Contribution to State
Industrial Production
(1970)

Municipalities	Industries	
	Mining	*Manufacturing*
Baja California	100.0	100.0
Coahuila	12.9	4.5
Chihuahua	0.02	16.7
Sonora	90.0	13.5
Tamaulipas	27.2	41.4

Source: *Censo Industrial, 1970.* Dirección General de Estadística, SIC.

mineral production in the country. If, however, metals are excluded, the figure is reduced to 1 percent. According to data supplied by the Council for Non-Renewable Natural Resources, in 1972 the border municipalities produced 52 percent of the nation's copper, 9 percent of the fluorspar, 7 percent of the lead, and 5 percent of the gold.

In manufacturing there is a predominance of light industries that produce consumer goods. Their contribution to regional manufacturing was slightly over 60 percent, which is remarkably higher than the national average of 27 percent.

In the manufacturing industry of the border municipalities, food and drink are prominent at 35 percent and 15 percent respectively. These include bakeries, tortilla factories, meat, fish, fruit and vegetable canneries, wheat mills, and dairy processing plants. Next to these in importance are machine and electric equipment factories, which in 1970 accounted for 9.2 percent of the area's total manufacture. It is in this category that the *maquiladora* plants (see note 4), whose development has been encouraged since 1965, have had the greatest impact. Other industries of lesser importance involve the building and assembling of transport equipment, which account for 5 percent of the regional production, and the manufacture of chemicals and chemical products, which accounts for 4.5 percent.

Manufacturing in the border municipalities accounted for only 2.8 percent of the 1970 national manufacture. But the concentration of manufacturing industry in this area is remarkable. As much as 90 percent is based in the urban centers with the largest populations, namely Mexicali, Tijuana, Juárez, Ensenada, Nuevo Laredo, Tecate, Piedras Negras, Nogales, and Reynosa. Baja California alone accounts for 60 percent of the area's manufacturing. The probable reasons for this are the preferential treatment for years given Baja California by way of federal subsidies and exemptions and the establishment of free-trade zones, the growth in population with relatively high income, and its proximity to California, one of the richest American states.

Border manufacturing has had little effect on employment opportunities. In 1970 this sector provided employment for 94,052 individuals, barely 15.6 percent of the area's PEA. And it must be borne in mind that this figure includes the workers hired by the *maquiladora* plants.

Maquiladora Plants[4]

In 1965, a border industrialization program was initiated to encourage the establishment of plants for assembling, processing, and exporting American products. The idea was to establish these plants in industrial parks under the supervision and management of the National Borderlands Program (PRONAF) begun in 1962.

In March 1971, the program underwent important changes. Areas twenty-five miles long in the coastal regions became eligible for the establishment of these plants and they, in turn, became eligible for duty-free importation of any raw material, machinery, parts, and tools needed for manufacturing, assembling, and exporting their products in unlimited quantities. In October 1972, the legislation governing the program underwent further changes, more precisely defining the term *"maquiladora"* and extending the area where these plants might be established to anywhere in the national territory, with the exception of already highly industrialized districts.

The effect of these plants on the border economy can be gauged by their impact on employment, capital investment, and income received. The multiplication of the plants generally has had an important impact on the industrial structure of the border areas. The number of these plants has increased from only 20 in 1966 to 120 in 1970 and 476 in 1974.

Employment in the *maquiladora* plants reached 20,327 in 1970, representing 21.5 percent of the workers employed in border manufacturing. Machinery and other equipment in these plants was valued at 149 million pesos that same year, representing 5.3 percent of gross capital in all border manufacturing. Income received from this particular type of industry accounted for 27 percent of the total reached in border manufacturing by 1970, representing a higher increment than that of either employment or investment (Table 7).

Since 1970 there has been a remarkable increase in the number of *maquiladora* plants. Between 1970 and 1974 the number of these plants increased by 288 percent. The number of workers employed by them jumped from the 1970 total of 20,327 to 53,680 in early 1974, or 164 percent.[5] Other increases were: expenditures for wages and salaries, 194 percent; replacement value of machinery and other equipment, 424 percent. Income received from this industry rose from 676 million pesos in 1970 to 2,400 million pesos in 1974, or 256 percent (Tables 7 and 8). Gross receipts from the export of products manufactured at these plants amounted to $278 million in 1973 and $443 million in 1974, representing 5.8 percent and 7.1 percent of the total income in the balance of payments for the cited years.[6]

That the *maquiladora* industry is contributing to change the economic makeup of the border region is unquestionable. By March 1975, a third of income and employment in the area was due to that industry. Its impact has been most obvious in the less industrialized areas. In the border municipalities that lie in the state of Tamaulipas, for example, these plants provide over half of the blue-collar employment and payroll. In Juárez the corresponding figures are 30 percent of employment and 46 percent of wages paid. In Coahuila half of the industrial work force is employed in these plants, which account for 31 percent of the blue-collar payroll. In Baja California, on the other hand, where there already was more highly developed industrialization, these plants account for less than 25 percent of the blue-collar employment and payroll.

0   Final processing of electric and electronic products on the one hand, and of footwear and clothing on the other, account for 70 percent of these plants, 81 percent of their employment, 80 percent of their payroll expenses, and 77 percent of their income (Tables 7 and 8). It is, furthermore, a concentrated industry. According to 1970 figures, 71 percent of these plants with 68 percent of the workers so employed, and with 65 percent of the wages and salaries paid by industry along the whole border, were located in Baja California and Tamaulipas.

Border Trade

Border trade[7] traditionally has been favorable to Mexico. And yet in recent years the rate of increase in outlay has shown a tendency to be higher than in income. Between 1965 and 1972 the credit balance from border trade increased at a lower rate than did income (Table 9).

Until 1965, income had increased at a rate slightly higher than outlay. Between 1965 and 1972, the rate of income growth rose to 11.4 percent while the rate of outlay reached 12.4 percent. Up to now the rise in the rate of increase in the balance of payments has not been very significant. The credit balance of $392.1 million achieved in 1972 (the difference between an income of $1,061.1 million and an outlay of $669.0 million) represented an average annual increase of 9.8 percent over the balance of $204.3 million achieved in 1965. In 1973 and 1974, the balances in favor of Mexico were of $513 million and $554 million respectively.[8]

The varying rates in the increase of income and outlay are reflected in what we call the "retention coefficient" of foreign trade receipts.[9] Between 1950 and 1960, the yearly average of this coefficient was 38.4 percent. Between 1961 and 1965 it rose to 40.1 percent. But between 1965 and 1972, it dropped to 36.6 percent. The higher retention coefficients belong to the years prior to 1967, while between 1968 and 1972, the retention coefficient remained below 37 percent. The decrease in the proportion of dollars retained has had an apparent direct relation to the tourist trade along the border. In both 1973 and 1974, the retention coefficients have risen once again, based on preliminary estimates supplied by the Bank of Mexico, to 42.5 percent and 39.5 percent respectively.

Though the number of Mexican visitors crossing the border is normally

TABLE 7
Principal Characteristics of *Maquiladora* Plants by Type of Activity
(1970)

Kind of Manufacture	Number of Plants	Personnel Employed	Wages and Salaries	Value of Machinery and Equip. (millions of pesos)	Value Added
Total	120	20,327	325.5	148.7	675.8
Electric and					
Electronic	54	12,361	200.7	102.7	366.6
Textile	15	1,693	26.9	7.8	46.7
Food Products	5	610	5.6	.7	15.5
Lumber	7	415	8.7	7.4	52.4
Sporting Goods					
and Toys	4	2,914	47.7	7.4	36.0
Other	35	2,334	35.9	22.7	158.6

Source: Dirección General de Industrias, SIC.

TABLE 8
Principal Characteristics of *Maquiladora* Plants by Type of Activity
(January 31, 1974)

Kind of Manufacture	Number of Plants	Personnel Employed	Wages and Salaries	Value of Machinery and Equip. (millions of pesos)	Value Added
Total	466	53,680	956.0	780.3	2,408.2
Electric and					
Electronic	186	29,698	497.43	369.4	1,196.4
Textiles	97	9,363	195.4	56.5	381.0
Food Products	11	1,618	23.3	11.9	68.7
Lumber	20	957	22.7	19.4	88.7
Sporting Goods					
and Toys	11	3,497	56.2	20.2	54.1
Other	141	8,547	160.9	302.8	619.3

Source: Dirección General de Industrias, SIC.

larger than that of American visitors to Mexico, the latter country always has achieved a credit balance from border trade because the Mexican border visitor spends a daily average of seven dollars while the American visitor spends sixteen dollars. Recently, however, there has been a tendency toward a relative increase in money that Mexican visitors spend as well as in their number, which has caused a drop of the retention coefficient. Between 1965 and 1971, for example, the average spending of Mexican visitors rose by 8.7

percent annually, while that of the foreign visitors rose by only 7.5 percent. At the same time the number of Mexican border visitors increased by 4.3 percent annually, while the number of foreign visitors increased only 3.8 percent. During 1973 and 1974, according to preliminary data, gross receipts rose an average 15 percent per year while expenditures increased an average 13.1 percent per year. During 1974 alone expenditures jumped to 22 percent, which confirms the tendency mentioned.

TABLE 9
Border Trade
(millions of dollars)

Years	Income (1)	Outlay (2)	Balance (3)	Retention Coefficient (3/1)
1950	121.9	76.5	45.5	37.2
1955	261.7	151.2	110.5	42.2
1960	366.0	221.0	145.0	39.6
1965	499.5	295.2	204.3	40.9
1972	1,061.1	669.0	392.1	36.9
1973p.	1,208.1	695.0	513.0	42.5
1974p.	1,404.0	850.0	554.0	39.5

Rates of Growth

Years	Income	Outlay	Balance	Average Retention Coefficient
1950-1960	11.7	11.2	12.3	38.4
1960-1965	6.4	6.0	7.1	40.1
1965-1972	11.4	12.4	9.8	36.6
1973	13.8	3.9	31.1	42.5
1974	16.2	22.3	8.0	39.5

p. — preliminary
Source: Banco de México, S.A.

Some Socioeconomic Problems

The principal border cities have shown spectacular rates of population growth. Even though this rate has diminished in recent years, they continue to be higher than the national average. This fact indicates a tendency toward heavy internal (or domestic) migration.

Internal (or Domestic) Migration

The large number of migrants is due, on the one hand, to the possibilities, both real and imagined, of greater job opportunity and higher wages in the border towns and, on the other, to the dashed hopes of crossing "to the other side." It is unlikely that the abundance of labor in search of good wages will diminish. As a result of this process, slums have developed around the major border cities, posing their main social problem. It has been estimated that at the present time only 40 percent of the border population enjoys urban utilities.

According to projections made by the Center for Economic and Demographic Studies of El Colegio de México, the principal cities of the border area will reach the following populations by 1990: Juárez, 1,116,000; Tijuana, 965,000; Mexicali, 841,000; Nuevo Laredo, 490,000; Matamoros, 464,000; Reynosa, 404,000; and Ensenada, 229,000. These figures suggest how important the border cities are as an attracting force. Except for the Mexican metropolis, the border area has drawn the most immigrants from other parts of the country.

This migration, however, is not a recent process, as shown by the fact that, in 1970, 53 percent of the migrants to the border municipalities had been living there for over eleven years. Men have been numerically predominant, in contrast with the kind of migration to other Mexican urban areas. The ages of migrants throughout the country are the same, however, between ten and twenty-nine years old.

The vast majority of the migrant population along the border comes from the rural areas of the following states: Jalisco (15.6 percent); Durango (9.0 percent); Zacatecas (7.8 percent); Nuevo León (7.5 percent); and Sinaloa (7.3 percent). It is not to be expected that the birthrate among these groups will drop in the short run, which is an added factor helping to maintain or, if mortality continues to decline, even increase the natural growth of the border population.

Housing

Population growth and rapid migration have lightened the problems of housing, education, and unemployment in the border region. In 1970 the number of dwellings in the border states was 1,394,397, averaging 5.7 persons per dwelling, compared with the national average of 5.8. In the border municipalities, where the population is predominantly urban, the average is 5.5 per dwelling.

Though housing conditions along the border are not satisfactory, on the average they seem somewhat better than nationally. While one-room dwellings throughout the country constitute 40 percent of all housing, in the border municipalities they represent only 29 percent. The same is true of other features such as running water. Only 61 percent of dwellings throughout the country have such a convenience, compared with 72 percent of those in the border municipalities. Only 56 percent at the national level have gas, electricity, or kerosene for cooking, compared with 85 percent in the border communities. Radio and television in the home stand at barely 29 percent throughout the nation, compared with 46 percent along the border. Indoor plumbing stands at 42 percent nationally, compared with 50 percent in the border municipalities. The higher averages attained by the border region might reflect their higher degree of urbanization.

Education

Available data for 1970 show that among the border population over fifteen years of age 20 percent had no schooling whatever and 39 percent had not finished elementary school. These percentages are comparable to those found on a national basis. The border municipalities have a higher average population (34 percent) that completed elementary school than the national average (23 percent). The percentages of population with a secondary school education and with professional degrees are low in both cases: 4.3 percent and 1.9 percent in the border region and 4.0 percent and 2.2 percent in the country as a whole. It should be borne in mind, however, that these figures refer to a combination of urban and rural populations in the national averages and to essentially urban centers only in the border averages.

Unemployment and Underemployment

The problems of inferior housing and education are compounded by the shortage of job opportunities and by the low levels of compensation received by the working population. There are no reliable unemployment and underemployment statistics in Mexico. Population census does not permit accurate quantification of open unemployment, and census data generally are looked upon as underestimating the unemployment problem. Keeping this in mind, it might be pointed out that the 1970 census records 28,600 unemployed workers in the border municipalities, which represents an increase from 2.4 percent in 1960 to 4.1 percent in 1970. The highest percent of unemployment along the border is found in the larger municipalities, such as Juárez, Mexicali, and Tijuana that report 53.6 percent of the unemployed

(Table 10). These figures are, however, lower than they should be, since to them should be added the number of those seeking work for the first time. Thus, unemployment in the border municipalities in 1970 was probably no less than 7 percent of the PEA.

TABLE 10
Unemployment in Border Municipalities
(1970)

Municipalities	Unemployment	%
Total	28,600	100.0
Juárez	6,046	21.1
Mexicali	5,294	18.5
Tijuana	4,013	14.0
Matamoros	2,617	9.2
Laredo	1,454	5.1
Reynosa	1,368	4.8
Ensenada	1,222	4.3
Other	6,586	23.0

Source: *Censo General de Población, 1970*. Dirección General de Estadística, SIC.

More important perhaps than the problem of clear unemployment is that of underemployment. It is evident both in lack of work continuity throughout the year and in the extremely low levels of compensation received by the workers. There are no accurate estimates of underemployment in the border municipalities. The Second Study Commission of the National Tripartite Commission worked out an estimate of the border region at the state level which provides some underemployment data. The 1970 population census contains information from which underemployment figures may be gathered according to the following perceptions: time worked during period in question, income of PEA, and the number of employed people looking for work.

With the census information as a basis, and employing a method that included the use of other data (such as current minimum wage and average family income provided by the family income and expense poll of 1963 compiled by the Bank of Mexico), the Second Study Commission worked out two estimates of underemployment in the border states. According to the first estimate, 9.2 percent of the PEA is underemployed, and according to the stricter second estimate, the percentage of PEA underemployed rises to 16.1 percent (see Table 11). Additional research carried out by the Secretary of Industry and Commerce has determined that, if all workers receiving compensation lower than the minimum wage are considered underemployed, then manufacturing underemployment in the border region in 1970 amounted to 34.3 percent of the regional industrial PEA while construction underemployment reached 38.5 percent.

TABLE 11
Underemployment in Border States
(1970)

State	Underemployment		% PEA	
	Estimate I	*Estimate II*	*Estimate I*	*Estimate II*
Mexican Nation	2,162,635	3,292,635	16.6	25.3
Border States	193,764	339,435	9.2	16.1
Baja California	27,254	36,894	12.3	16.6
Sonora	13,657	37,548	4.8	13.2
Chihuahua	51,219	88,761	12.3	21.3
Coahuila	24,711	45,624	8.5	15.8
Nuevo León	34,892	56,585	7.1	11.5
Tamaulipas	40,198	70,335	10.5	18.4

Source: I Comisión Nacional Tripartita. II Segunda Comisión de Estudios, 1970.

Border Imports

From an economic point of view, the main problems of the border communities stem, on the one hand, from the lack of a sufficiently stable and competitive production structure and, on the other, from their weak ties with the rest of the country. The two problems are interrelated. The lack of national integration (or coordination) of the border region is in large measure a consequence of its meager production structure and of the scarcity of communications, even among the border cities themselves. Completion of the northern border highway extending over 1,865 miles is urgently needed. Communication among the other border towns is usually accomplished by means of American highways.

The poor production structure, the scarcity of industrial products, and the lack of competition among the local industries inevitably have led to the need for increased imports. This is made still worse by a poor organization in business operations and a scarcity of sufficiently diversified domestic products at competitive prices.

A study made by the Committee for the Economic Development of the Peninsula of Baja California[10] shows that, in 1968, 84 percent of Mexicali families did their routine shopping in the United States. Half of these families went shopping once a week and a third of them every day. The study shows that shopper motivations for purchasing consumer goods outside the country were as follows: 1) almost 90 percent of the routine shoppers believed that *prices were lower* than in Mexico; 2) 75 percent of those shoppers believed that foreign products were of *higher quality;* 3) 50 percent of the shoppers believed that the shopping centers were better on the American side and that the merchandise had a more hygienic appearance; and 4) among other motivations cited were polite behavior, credit opportunities, greater variety of goods, and the mere habit of shopping on the American side.

Not only does the border region's lack of economic integration (or coordination) with the rest of the country result in a tendency for the demand for routine consumer goods to be directed toward the outside, it has also led to a great dependence upon other foreign supplies and, of course, to the importation of machinery and equipment.

Energy Sources

The border region is supplied with energy sources (fuels), such as natural gas, almost entirely from the United States. Gas production by Petróleos Mexicanos is insufficient to supply the total national demand and there is not an adequate pipeline network along most of the border. Liquid propane imported by the border states in 1972 amounted to 418,374 tons, or 38 percent of the national import during the same year. Municipalities with the greatest demand were Cananea (25 percent), Nueva Rosita (22 percent), and Piedras Negras and Nuevo Laredo (19 percent jointly).

Local electric plant capacity supplying the border municipalities reached 466,000 kilowatts (kws) in 1972 (93 percent thermoelectric and 7 percent hydroelectric). The great concentration of electric power output along the border is noteworthy. Tijuana has a central thermoelectric plant whose capacity is 307,000 kws, almost 66 percent of the total power available along the border. The output of this plant is distributed to Tecate, Ensenada, and Mexicali. The Baja California municipalities are perhaps the only ones supplied with sufficient electric power.

In 1972, the border plants' power output was 1,863.9 million kilowatt hours (kw hrs.). Another 310.3 million kw hrs. had to be imported, primarily for Juárez (65 percent), Nogales (18 percent), and Acuña (9 percent). Most of the electric power imported is for Juárez, the largest municipality, whose population of close to half a million is in dire need of an adequate urban infrastructure. Insufficient electric power also has been a deterrent to industrial expansion, which might increase the supply of consumer goods and alleviate the serious problem of unemployment and underemployment.

Tourist Trade

Another factor contributing perhaps to the low retention coefficient of gross receipts from border trade is the lack of an adequate policy toward tourist promotion. Most foreign visitors remain in Mexico for a very short time, though they return rather frequently. Eight of every ten visitors spend less than twenty-four hours on the Mexican side. Their visits have a variety of purposes, the principal ones being shopping, making use of personal services, and enjoying entertainment and sports events. A smaller number of tourists come with the purpose of visiting relatives or performing business transactions.

It would seem that there are real possibilities of attaining more effective economic relations with American visitors, but there is no definite national policy for attracting the tourist trade to the border cities. It is not merely a question of advertising and promotion. There are presently many handicaps owing to the lack of urban facilities and the meager supply of consumer goods and services, as well as their questionable quality.

Furthermore, given the range and diversity of obstacles faced by socioeconomic development along the border, the intervention of several government agencies has been required. Because of a lack of coordination of promotional efforts, one cannot really speak of an existing national policy for the development of the border region.

Preliminary Evaluation of Current Economic Policies

As a means of helping to solve the complex problem of developing the border region, the federal government has taken several legal and administrative steps to try to bring the border region economically closer to the rest of the country, alleviate the unemployment situation, and encourage the Mexican consumer to shop at home.

Beginning in 1971 diverse measures have been taken to promote and support economic activity along the border. Among these are:

1) permission temporarily to import certain supplies and the extension of such permission to businesses supplying duty-free zones;

2) reimbursement of import duty on sales to duty-free zones and all along the border;

3) subsidies equal to the net federal income tax derived from the sale of new products;

4) subsidies equal to 25 percent of rail, air, or maritime freight required by

domestic products shipped to the border. This kind of subsidy might eventually be raised to 50 percent of the freight cost;

5) a decree issued March 1974, declaring all small and medium industries established along the border and in the free zones to be in the national interest;

6) permission to import certain agricultural and industrial commodities, such as machinery and other equipment, duty free;

7) creation of trusts for the construction of industrial cities, parks, and centers;

8) promotion of the building of new shopping centers along the border;

9) introduction of the *"artículo gancho"* ("hook or lure items");

10) promotion of the establishment of *maquiladora* plants.

The main coordinating agency for the various promotional measures cited is the Intersecretarial Commission for the Development of Northern Frontier and Free Zones and Perimeters, which was appointed in May 1971, and has been responsible for their management. Following are comments on some of the results obtained thus far by the three programs most heavily promoted by the Intersecretarial Commission, namely the *"artículos gancho,"* the new shopping centers, and the establishment of *maquiladora* plants. The emphasis given to these programs has been officially justified by the contention that their success will help solve two important problems in the region: the drop in the dollar retention coefficient from border trade, and the lack of sufficient job opportunities in the region.

Artículos gancho ("hook or lure items")

The idea behind making these items available is to encourage routine shopping in local shopping centers among border residents. To this end a program was established in 1970 for the duty-free importation of various commodities usually purchased from the American side of the border by Mexican citizens. The only condition placed by the Mexican government on border merchants is that these *"artículos gancho"* be sold at the same price or less than they bring on the American side. For this purpose, the Intersecretarial Commission has set quotas on commercial establishments and products, which are authorized and exercised through the Committees for Economic Promotion of the border cities.

Between December 1971 and April 1974, the program had sponsored the importation of *"artículos gancho"* in the amount of 906.8 million pesos, of which 82.5 percent were consumer goods and 17.5 percent were industrial equipment. Juárez imported the greatest percentage (53.1 percent), followed by Nuevo Laredo (10 percent), Reynosa (7.7 percent), Matamoros (7.6 percent), Piedras Negras (6.8 percent), and Nogales (3.8 percent).

Among the program's drawbacks is a corruptive tendency toward encouraging smuggling (contraband) with a ready market. It is not even certain that it results in conserving payments, since the border residents continue to buy imported products that have to be paid for whether obtained in Mexico or in the United States. Another drawback is that it tends to form import-oriented consumer patterns, a trend all too real and difficult to stop but which at least should not be further encouraged. Furthermore, since the so-called lure items are for the most part consumer goods, if traded freely in the border communities they will quite probably discourage the local producers of comparable items. Unfortunately, domestic products are not in sure demand basically because they need not be bought when purchasing the lure items. It appears that such a requirement existed at the planning stage, but was removed when the program was put in operation.

Shopping Centers

An extensive program was begun in 1972 to promote and facilitate the construction of shopping centers along the border in the free zones. Among the conditions that must be fulfilled by businessmen receiving permits for the establishment of shopping centers are the following: 1) the company's capital must be underwritten by Mexicans or, in exceptional instances, by a Mexican majority through the issue of registered stock; 2) the imported products must be sold at prices comparable to those charged for the same items in the United States; and 3) at least 50 percent of sales must be of domestic products.

Among the concessions granted to businessmen establishing shopping centers are: 1) subsidy of up to ten years of 100 percent of the import duty on consumer goods listed periodically by the Intersecretarial Commission; 2) subsidy of up to ten years of 100 percent of import duty on machinery and equipment required for the operation of shopping centers, so long as there is no domestic supply; and 3) rapid depreciation.

By May 1974, six shopping centers were completed at a cost of 66.4 million pesos, occupying a space equivalent to 95,680 square yards. The most important of these shopping centers are located in Mexicali, Tijuana, and San Luis Río Colorado. It will be remembered that these cities are not the main importers of lure items, demonstrating a lack of coordination between the two programs—the lure items and the shopping centers. Two other shopping centers are in the planning stage, one in Río Grande and another in Juárez, the latter so huge that it was estimated to cost 113.0 million pesos prior to devaluation and will occupy a space of 156,676 square yards.

The *Maquiladora* Plants

The mushrooming of *maquiladora* plants (see note 4) has helped to alleviate the unemployment problem in the border towns. It has already been pointed out that at present these plants very likely provide over 30 percent of the border region's employment in manufacturing, which is a positive accomplishment of no small importance.

However, the Mexican government is running a great risk in depending on this type of manufacturing for the industrial development of the border region and its employment policy toward it. The opposition from American labor unions in this regard is well known. They look upon the *maquiladora* industry as competitive with American production and labor. Hence it is not unlikely that the United States government will eventually take heed of complaints from American labor and curtail the expansion of the *maquiladora* industry across the border. Obviously, Mexico cannot afford to let its industrial and employment policies along the border remain subject to such a contingency. Furthermore, other nations are competing for the establishment of *maquiladora* plants on the basis of the availability of cheap labor.

The economic policies followed up to the present time to stimulate the development of the border region have been limited. They have largely emphasized the final stages of industrial activity, namely, assemblage or product-finishing *(maquila)* and trade. Special emphasis on such activities results in merely apparent or at best partial solutions to the economic and social problems of the region.

These problems, in fact, are so varied and complex that they clamor for the adoption of a coherent policy scheme which will simultaneously apply to such important sectors as agriculture, manufacturing, trade, and services. And such a policy plan must not exclude health conditions, housing, and education as well.

Along the border these socioeconomic problems are quite similar to those besetting large segments of the population in other parts of the country. What makes the border situation so special is the huge competition presented by American products. When combined with the handicaps of weak productive structure and weak ties with the rest of the nation, the availability of American products greatly hinders the development of a successful demand for domestic agricultural and manufactured products.

In general terms it can be said that border area consumer patterns are definitely import oriented. And yet one must admit that the limited domestic supply of consumer goods and other products needed in industry has contributed to form this tendency. As previously indicated, agriculture has had a constant downward trend, and no measures have been taken to stop it.

A long-range policy should be adopted whose ultimate objective is the strengthening of the ties between the border region's economy and that of the country as a whole. Certainly the chances of such an achievement in the near or not-so-distant future are slim. The most immediately viable plan is to set up pivotal points for development along the border. Apart from strengthening the productive structure, a greater integration within the border region itself naturally would be attained by means of this scheme. It is the only way to remedy the region's excessive dependence on foreign imports as well as occasionally on labor and raw materials originating far inland.

The strengthening of the productive structure would increase job opportunities and domestic product supplies. For this reason it is of the utmost importance that action be initiated toward the eventual consolidation of an agricultural, livestock, and manufacturing production and distribution complex in the border region. This does not mean that in the short run the many relative benefits inherent in the present abundance of service population should be discarded. But even for the development of this work force further steps should be taken, such as the building of recreation centers all along the border. The formulation of new programs for the promotion of the border tourist trade is perhaps the most promising short-run plan to raise the balance of foreign trade receipts and the border population's income. Such a plan should be based on the closely coordinated efforts of government and private enterprise alike.

Last, it should perhaps be stated that the data that we in Mexico possess of the border region's economy are inaccurate and inadequate. Although the 2.7 million Mexicans who live in the border municipalities seem to have a higher average income than most of their compatriots, save those of the Federal District, judging by various indicators used in this report, the inequality in distribution of income is probably no less than the national average. Large investment industries are not attracted to the border region because of the disadvantageous socioeconomic conditions prevailing. The lack of a firmer direction in economic policy and the absence of an infrastructure add to the unattractiveness. But above all, it is the negative effect of an easy access to imported supplies that takes away the incentive from local producers and distributors of domestic goods.

We recommend that further socioeconomic research be made on the northern border region and that firmer and better-formulated policies be adopted for the future development of this region in keeping with other aspects of national development.

NOTES

1. Statistical data used in this report for the most part are found in the valuable records prepared by the Secretaría de Industria y Comercio listed in the bibliography. In all other cases the source is noted.

2. Including the independent community of Colombia, in Nuevo León.

3. Mexicali, Tijuana, Tecate and Ensenada are considered to be border municipalities. Although the last does not touch the United States frontier, it is so considered because its socioeconomic activities are closely related with the border.

4. According to the Reglamento (definition) issued on October 31, 1972, to Article 321 of the Código Aduanero (Customs Law), *"maquiladora"* is any manufacturing plant that 1) with temporarily imported machinery, regardless of cost, exports its total production, or 2) with machinery already set up to supply the domestic market turns to either partial or total export production, so long as the direct manufacturing cost of the product to be exported is below 40 percent.

5. In March 1975, an estimate put the number at "approximately 500" employing a personnel of "nearly 80,000 Mexicans and indirectly creating jobs for another 160,000." See statement by Alfredo Santos quoted in *Excelsior,* 8 March 1975. However, it has been admitted that recently 22,000 workers have been fired.

6. Banco de México, "Informe anual preliminar" 1974 (preliminary annual report), in *Excelsior,* 27 February 1975.

7. Banco de México lumps all trade dealing with either merchandise or service made on the border, and representing the exchange of Mexican for American money and vice versa. This is determined by the trading done by means of checks under $100 and cash.

8. Banco de México, "Informe anual preliminar," 1974.

9. This coefficient indicates the percentage retained by Mexico of every dollar that comes into the Mexican border areas. It is arrived at by dividing the balance into the total income produced by border trade.

10. Cited in Francisco Alcalá Quintero, "Desarrollo regional fronterizo," *Comercio Exterior* 12 (1969): 962.

11. Ibid., p. 963.

8

Economic Factors
Influencing the International
Migration of Workers

F. Ray Marshall

The international migration of workers has become an important labor market phenomenon in Europe and the Western Hemisphere. The emigration of workers from Mexico to the United States is quantitatively one of the most important international migrations in the world. Labor groups in the United States have long been concerned about the economic consequences of the flow of Mexican nationals across the two-thousand-mile border separating the United States and Mexico. This concern was intensified during the 1970s by the growing size of the flow of alien workers and rising unemployment in the United States. There consequently have been growing demands for policies to halt or moderate this flow.

However, demands for tighter immigration controls often are based on very little analysis of the causes and consequences of these flows. Unfortunately, moreover, neither the data nor the conceptual framework to form the basis for sound public policy on this question have been generated. Most public policy proposals are based on presumed effects of particular interest groups rather than on a comprehensive analysis of all of the factors involved in the international migration of workers. Advocates usually base their policies on the presumed "national interest." However, the national interest in this matter is difficult to specify because international migrations have different effects on different groups within the countries involved. Moreover, the relationships are complex and dynamic, making it necessary to attempt to trace out causal relations through time.

This essay attempts to provide the beginnings of a conceptual framework for analyzing the international migration of workers. My main concern is with the migration of workers between the United States and Mexico, but I think much can be learned about the general principles involved in these movements by looking at experiences in other parts of the world. In reviewing the migration of Mexicans to the United States and then attempting to relate this experience to that of Western Europe, the main questions to be examined are:

1. What are the major economic and social causes of international labor migration?

2. Are these causes really basic, in the sense of being deeply rooted in economic and social relations, or can they be easily modified by government regulations?

3. What, if any, are the general patterns of international labor migration that transcend particular institutions or regulations in particular countries?

4. What are the effects of international migrations on different groups and general economic development in the sending and receiving countries?

5. Based on these considerations, what should United States policy be with respect to the employment of immigrants?

I do not know enough to answer all of these questions, so my remarks are not to be considered hard conclusions based on the kind of detailed research and analysis required to provide more definitive answers.

Brief Overview of Mexican Immigration to the United States

As can be seen from Tables 1 and 2, there has been a steady increase in the number of Mexican nationals in the United States in the last decade. While legal immigration increased from 18,000 in 1953 to 70,141 by 1973, the number of illegal aliens from Mexico probably was well over two million in 1974. During the latest ten-year period for which data are available (1963-73), illegal aliens probably constituted 20 percent of the growth in the United States work force. (The 20-percent figure is a rough estimate, assuming that for every alien apprehended and/or deported, two entered successfully, and of these persons successfully entering the United States, 75 percent entered the work force. The inaccuracy of the information on illegal aliens results also from the fact that the figures on apprehension and deportation involve some double counting because some individuals were deported more than once. It is felt, however, that in view of the empirical evidence, the estimates of the presence of illegal Mexican aliens in the country and the work force are conservative.)

Although there is a rising number of illegal aliens in the United States from throughout the world, Mexicans constitute an overwhelming proportion of the illegal aliens in the United States. In 1973, for example, 88 percent of all illegal aliens apprehended were Mexican nationals. Moreover, between 1939 and 1973, about nine million legal immigrants entered the United States from all countries of the world; about the same number of illegal Mexican aliens were deported during that period.[1]

The number of illegal aliens in the United States from Mexico and other countries attracted increasing national attention during the 1970s. With rising unemployment in the United States, there were growing demands for halting the flow of illegal aliens and deporting those already here.[2] It was argued that aliens depressed wages and working conditions and contributed to rising unemployment, especially for Mexican Americans in the Southwest. Leonard F. Chapman, Jr., director of the Immigration and Naturalization Service, an organization historically regarded as not overly concerned about the illegal alien problem, said in 1975 that an estimated million illegal aliens were displacing American workers, and were costing American taxpayers millions of dollars each year. Terming the alien problem a ''national crisis,'' he urged Congress to pass legislation already adopted by the House of Representatives to make it unlawful for employers to hire illegal aliens.[3] Prior to 1970, illegal aliens worked primarily in agriculture in the Southwest; during the 1970s their employment had spread to every occupational level and to the urban areas of the North and West.[4]

This essay will seek to clarify some of the economic issues involved in the employment of Mexican workers in the United States. The basic approach used is to discuss the facts of Mexican-United States immigration against the background of European experience. While conditions differ in different countries, the migration of workers across national boundaries is an ancient and worldwide phenomenon. It therefore should be possible, through comparative analysis, to isolate some of the general principles at work in the international migration of workers.

Although there has been some debate in Europe over whether the international migration of workers has been due to conditions pushing workers out of their native lands or pulling them into countries with better opportunities, both push and pull factors clearly are always at work. Moreover, throughout the world the main factors causing workers to move between countries have been associated with relative international disparities in economic conditions and job opportunities. In the Western Hemisphere, the main factors causing movement to the United States are related to much greater economic opportunities in the United States for unskilled and relatively uneducated workers. This is especially true of the movement into the United States from Mexico. In spite of the fact that Mexico's economic

TABLE 1
Legal Immigration from Mexico to the United States, 1869-1973

Year	Total Immigrants	Year	Total Immigrants	Year	Total Immigrants
1869	320	1909	16,251	1949	7,977
1870	463	1910	17,760	1950	6,841
1871	402	1911	18,784	1951	6,372
1872	569	1912	22,001	1952	9,600
1873	606	1913	10,954	1953	18,454
1874	386	1914	13,089	1954	37,456
1875	610	1915	10,993	1955	50,772
1876	631	1916	17,198	1956	65,047
1877	445	1917	16,438	1957	49,154
1878	465	1918	17,602	1958	26,712
1879	556	1919	28,844	1959	23,061
1880	492	1920	51,042	1960	32,084
1881	325	1921	29,603	1961	41,632
1882	366	1922	18,246	1962	55,291
1883	469	1923	62,709	1963	55,253
1884	430	1924	87,648	1964	32,967
1885	323	1925	32,378	1965	37,969
1886	N.A.	1926	42,638	1966	45,163
1887	N.A.	1927	66,766	1967	42,371
1888	N.A.	1928	57,765	1968	43,563
1889	N.A.	1929	38,980	1969	44,623
1890	N.A.	1930	11,915	1970	44,469
1891	N.A.	1931	2,627	1971	50,103
1892	N.A.	1932	1,674	1972	64,040
1893	N.A.	1933	1,514	1973	70,141
1894	109	1934	1,470		
1895	116	1935	1,232	Total	1,736,576
1896	150	1936	1,308		
1897	91	1937	1,918		
1898	107	1938	2,014	N.A. = Date Not Available	
1899	163	1939	2,265		
1900	237	1940	1,914		
1901	347	1941	2,068		
1902	700	1942	2,182		
1903	528	1943	3,985		
1904	1,009	1944	6,399		
1905	2,637	1945	6,455		
1906	1,997	1946	6,805		
1907	1,406	1947	7,775		
1908	6,067	1948	8,730		

Sources: For years 1869-1969, the data are taken from Julian Samora, "Mexican Immigration," in Gus Tyler, ed., *Mexican-Americans Tomorrow: Educational and Economic Perspectives* (Albuquerque: University of New Mexico Press, 1975), p. 68; the figures for 1970-73 are from Annual Reports of U.S. Immigration and Naturalization Service.

TABLE 2
Illegal Mexican Aliens Apprehended and/or Deported, 1924-73

Year	Number of People	Year	Number of People
1924	4,614	1950	469,581
1925	2,961	1951	510,355
1926	4,047	1952	531,719
1927	4,495	1953	839,149
1928	5,529	1954	1,035,282
1929	8,538	1955	165,186
1930	18,319	1956	58,792
1931	8,409	1957	45,640
1932	7,116	1958	45,164
1933	15,875	1959	42,732
1934	8,910	1960	39,750
1935	9,139	1961	39,860
1936	9,534	1962	41,200
1937	9,535	1963	51,230
1938	8,684	1964	41,589
1939	9,376	1965	48,948
1940	8,051	1966	89,638
1941	6,082	1967	107,695
1942	10,603	1968	142,520
1943	16,154	1969	189,572
1944	39,449	1970	265,539
1945	80,760	1971	348,178
1946	116,320	1972	430,213
1947	214,543	1973	655,968
1948	193,852		
1949	289,400	Total	7,345,795

Note: There is a considerable problem with the exact figures used to report illegal aliens. The official definitions have changed over time. Nevertheless, these figures do reflect correctly the orders of magnitude.

Sources: For the years 1924-41, see Samora, "Mexican Immigration," p.70; for 1942-73, see Vernon M. Briggs, Jr., *The Mexico-United States Border: Public Policy and Chicano Economic Welfare* (Austin: Center for the Study of Human Resources, 1974), p.9.

development in the 1960s and 1970s was the highest of any country in Latin America, conditions for most workers remain much lower than those of workers in the United States. Per capita income in the United States in 1970 was over $5,000 as compared with about $700 in Mexico. The birth rate in Mexico, 3.5 percent, is also one of the highest in the world.* There has been a movement of people from urban areas into Mexico City and towns on the

---

*By the last third of the Echeverríea administration (1970-76) it was reported that the Mexican birth rate had declined to 3.4 or 3.3. Early in 1977 a study at El Colegio de México reported a continuing decline to 3.2 [Editor's Note].

United States border. Conditions in these border towns, particularly relevant to the immigration problem, are relatively bad; unemployment is in the 30-to 40-percent range and minimum wages, while varying from place to place, are never more than one-third of the minimum in the United States.[5]

The demand for Mexican nationals has been relatively strong in the United States, especially during periods of generalized labor shortage in this country. Before the First World War the Mexican-United States border was open and workers were allowed freely to immigrate. Between 1910 and 1930, 750,000 Mexicans immigrated to this country. The first significant wave of immigrants was pushed out of Mexico largely as a result of the violence accompanying the internal conflict of the Mexican Revolution beginning in 1910; this apparently was the main instance where migration was caused primarily by noneconomic factors. The second major wave of Mexican immigrants came in response to the labor shortages around the time of World War I, especially in agriculture.

The depression of the 1930s interrupted the flow of Mexican workers into the United States. In 1924, for the first time the movement of people across the United States-Mexican border was regulated. The Immigration Act of that year made it a felony for people to enter this country illegally. The Act established quotas for immigrants from various countries, but did not cover Mexico. With rising unemployment during the 1930s, approximately two hundred thousand Mexicans who allegedly had entered the country illegally were deported. The ruthless nature of these arrests and deportations, together with the history of discrimination against Mexican Americans in this country, strained relations between the United States and Mexico and caused Mexican officials to balk at the request by the United States in 1941 to supply Mexican workers to meet labor shortages in American agriculture resulting from the outbreak of World War II.

However, the Mexican government relented and agreed to the Mexican Labor Program (the *Bracero* Program), which went into effect in August 1942.[7] This program provided for the importation of Mexican workers under conditions agreed to between the United States and Mexico. The Mexican workers were restricted to agricultural work and were promptly deported if they took jobs in other industries. This wartime program expired officially at the end of 1947, but continued unofficially until 1951, when a new program was adopted. Since this program, which expired in 1964, offered a measure of official protection for Mexican workers, the Mexican government has suggested that it be renewed,[8] but the United States has refused to agree to the continuation of such a program.

Support in the United States for a renewed *Bracero* Program is reduced by the widespread use of illegal aliens and commuters. Commuters are permitted to work in the United States with entry permits indicating their desire to become residents of the United States.[9] There were about 48,000 commuters in the United States in 1972, 39,500 of whom were from Mexico.[10] Although they technically are residents of the United States, many commuters actually live in Mexico and work in the United States, a condition characterized by Federal District Court Judge Youngdahl as an "amiable fiction."

Commuter permits are not provided for by law but rather by administrative interpretation, and the issuance of new permits apparently has been limited by more rigid enforcement of the requirement that commuters not be permitted to come into the United States to work in occupations where native workers are available. There have been demands from American unions and Mexican-American organizations to halt the use of permits by aliens who do not in fact intend to live in the United States.

The major reason commuters and alien workers can find jobs in the United States is that there is a strong demand for them. American employers often prefer Mexican workers to natives.[11] Illegal aliens are preferred by some employers because they tend to work "scared and hard." Although wages and working conditions in many secondary labor markets do not appear very attractive by United States standards, many Mexican workers are willing to endure considerable hardship and risk in order to acquire these jobs, which clearly are much superior to the opportunities available to them in Mexico.

But United States employers do not prefer alien workers merely because they are easily exploited. Indeed, in spite of considerable expense and personal risk in coming to the United States illegally, many Mexican workers return to the United States repeatedly after being deported; many illegal aliens were formerly *braceros*. Because even low-wage, low-status, marginal jobs appear good by Mexican standards, the alien workers are likely to be more satisfied with wages and working conditions than their native competitors. Moreover, as compared with natives, aliens are more likely to be younger unmarried males whereas native workers tend to work as families, placing heavier demands on housing and social services.

Employers also prefer aliens for some occupations because they form a more dependable supply of labor than natives who have more employment options and therefore leave undesirable jobs when they have the opportunity to do so. Discrimination against them, low skills, limited knowledge of English, a need to live with people who share their language and culture, and relative job satisfaction combine to restrict most aliens to certain low-wage jobs, at least when they first come to this country. However, as in other countries, the employment patterns of legal and illegal aliens seem to spread first from agriculture to unskilled and semiskilled jobs in other industries and then into skilled trades.

As alien workers become accustomed to conditions in the United States, their aspirations change and at least the more aggressive of them are motivated to improve their job skills. When alien workers first enter a receiving country, they ordinarily do so with limited objectives and intend to return home after earning money for particular purposes. Many workers return home, but many do not. Those who stay gradually adopt the host country's attitudes about job status and conditions. Indeed, there is some evidence that foreign workers who have become committed to the work routine in industrialized countries are more highly motivated in low-status jobs than their native counterparts. Moreover, the employer's familiarity with immigration from a particular country facilitates the spread of alien workers to new occupations and industries. Although it has not been studied systematically, this process apparently is at work in the United States, both for Blacks and Mexican Americans who have been displaced from agriculture and for foreign workers. However, relative to natives, most alien workers tend to be restricted mainly to lower-paying jobs which also are low status and, therefore, not considered very attractive to native workers.

Another factor in the demand for aliens is the employer's realization that few risks and very limited costs are involved in hiring these workers.[12] This is largely because of the difficulties involved in enforcing the law against illegal aliens. A number of factors make it difficult to bar Mexican aliens, including: (1) the physical problems associated with policing the long border between the United States and Mexico; (2) the fact that powerful economic interests in the United States profit from illegal aliens and therefore are not interested either in adopting restrictive measures or providing sufficient funds to the Immigration and Naturalization Service to enforce existing laws; (3) the size and heterogeneity of the population in the United States makes it relatively easy for aliens to hide themselves in populations with their language and culture; and (4) the fact that the law has no penalties against employers, and weak penalties for the aliens themselves, means that there are no effective legal deterrents to illegal aliens.

The European Experience

The use of alien workers has had a long history in Europe. In 1974 it was estimated that there were about 6.2 million immigrant workers in the

European Common Market countries, constituting approximately 6 to 8 percent of the work forces of most countries except Switzerland, where the proportion was nearly 40 percent.[13] (It is interesting to note that there probably were more illegal alien workers in the United States than immigrant workers in all nine Common Market countries.) During the 1950s and 1960s there was a trend toward general freedom of movement of workers within the Common Market and Nordic countries. There was, moreover, increasing migration of wǒrkers from the less-developed countries of southern Europe and the Mediterranean into the more-industrialized north European countries. Despite the freedom of movement, no country grants complete political freedom to immigrants, and provisions usually are made that immigrants cannot be hired unless domestic workers are not available. These European experiences permit a number of general conclusions about the international movement of workers:

1. The main initial movements of migration are for economic reasons; workers move mainly from countries with relatively low standards of living into countries with higher standards.

2. There are some general patterns of movement of workers and their families through time and into every country. In phase one, young unmarried adults predominate among the migrants. These workers usually move from rural areas of the less-developed countries and therefore often are employed initially in agriculture in the host countries. The migrants almost always consider the move to be temporary; they intend to remain in the host country for relatively short periods in order to earn enough money and then to return home for some particular purpose. Similarly, the host country almost invariably considers the immigrants to be temporary workers. Although most migrant workers tend to come from the working classes, they are likely to be the more highly educated and mobile of these classes.

In phase two, the younger unmarried who predominate in phase one are joined by larger numbers of married men without their families. There is considerable movement back and forth between receiving and sending countries at all times but especially during phase one. In phase two additional workers are attracted to the host country by stories told by returning workers about the benefits of employment there. These stories often exaggerate the benefits in order to rationalize the move by the original immigrants. During phase two the rate of return to the sending country declines.

In phase three the married men send for their families, causing an increase in the size of the economically inactive population. This phase is brought on by the fact that many married immigrants have increasing difficulty returning home because their original objectives are not attained or because aspirations charge; conditions in the host country are likely to be bad for immigrants relative to those of native host-country workers, but at first those conditions are likely to appear favorable to the immigrants. As immigrant children come into the host countries, the length of stay increases and conditions are set in motion that could cause the immigrants to become permanent residents of the host country. The higher the immigrants' levels of education and skills, the stronger the tendency to become permanent residents. In particular, immigrants see greater opportunities for themselves and especially for their children. Their aspirations often become incompatible with realities in their native countries. During this state the employment of immigrants spreads from the initial penetration sectors to other industries and occupations in the host country. Moreover, the consumer demand created by the immigrants and favorable experience by host-country employers with immigrants create additional demands for more immigrant workers, causing the migrant process to become self-sustaining.

The fourth stage in the immigration process is characterized by the immigration of a ''supporting'' population from the sending countries. These supporting people are ethnic employers, religious leaders, and others who cater to the immigrant population, which has now grown large enough to sustain these supporting populations.

3. Host countries tend initially to adopt measures to restrict the employment of immigrants and limit the immigration patterns to phase two. The host country also will attempt to restrict the employment of immigrants to those occupations for which it is difficult to attract native workers. Indeed, a strong motive for hiring immigrants is the apparent tendency for native workers to move out of low-status jobs as economies mature. Host-country employers are faced with the alternatives of raising wages to attract native workers into these occupations, exporting capital to the developing countries, mechanizing these jobs, or importing foreign workers. The importation of foreign workers appears to be the most attractive alternative because it poses minimum threats to both the loss of capital and the job conditions of native workers who are not likely to take these jobs; in any event, those native workers threatened by competition from foreigners are not likely initially to have much political and economic power. Skilled and more highly educated workers are likely to feel that they benefit from the employment of foreign workers because the lower wages paid these workers (relative to wages that natives of comparable productivity would have required for the same jobs) promotes faster economic growth and occupational upgrading of native workers. Profits are particularly likely to be higher as a result of the use of immigrants than would have been true under any of the alternatives. Moreover, the employment of immigrants who are more productive than

native competitors and the greater economic efficiency made possible by the use of immigrants tends to moderate inflationary pressures in the host countries, especially during phases one and two.

The leaders of host-country governments attempt to minimize political opposition to immigrant workers from native populations by initially restricting the employment opportunities of the immigrants and stimulating return migration to the sending countries after a few years. Political leaders are not likely to welcome permanent settlements of foreign workers because the latter often create social friction and increase social-welfare costs. If the immigrants can be limited to younger, unmarried workers, the taxes collected from them are likely to exceed the cost of social services provided to them. However, as families join the migrants, the ratio of taxes to costs declines. Host countries attempt to limit the stay of immigrants, and screen those most desired, by issuing permits limiting the duration of stay and the occupations in which the immigrants can work. Policies also are adopted to make it difficult for the immigrants to bring their families to the host countries.

4. Despite attempts by host countries to limit the use of immigrants to prescribed occupations for certain lengths of time, these restrictions are rarely successful in either halting the spread of immigrant workers from the initial penetration points or in preventing permanent settlements. We have already described the process whereby many immigrants become increasingly attached to the host countries. Strong demand factors also cause the spread of foreign workers into new industries and occupations. The immigrants might initially be brought into a country to fill jobs being vacated by natives. But once the use of immigrants starts, a number of factors motivate employers to expand their use in competition with native workers. For one thing, the immigrants are apt to be more docile and satisfied with low-wage jobs, which nevertheless look favorable to them when compared with conditions in their native lands. Moreover, the renewable permit requirement during the immigrants' early stay in the host country makes it possible to screen out the least desirable immigrant workers. Those workers retained by host-country employers are likely to be very highly motivated to advance economically when the attractions of occupational mobility in an industrial society become better known to them.[14]

The establishment of immigrants in certain occupations and industries is caused by the host-country employers' growing familiarity with workers from different countries. This information is exchanged among employers, who learn how to recruit and manage immigrants and who acquire preferences and stereotypes about workers from different countries. Some German employers, for example, apparently consider Turkish immigrants to be particularly good workers.[15] As a consequence, the employment of immigrants often will spread to other industries and occupations, although immigrants are likely to be disproportionately concentrated in the low-status jobs.

These demand factors, encouraging the expansion of immigrant employment, are apt to be reinforced by supply factors related to the attitudes of native workers toward immigrants. Native workers in industrialized countries are often strongly influenced by status considerations. A number of factors may cause immigrants to be regarded as low-status people. For one thing, relative to natives of the industrialized countries, foreign workers usually come from less-developed countries with different life-styles and lower levels of formal education. Moreover, status-conscious people are apt to associate status and jobs. Therefore, native workers will try to take measures to restrict the status jobs to themselves and to vacate lower-status jobs as they are filled by larger numbers of immigrants. In addition, wherever aliens have limited power to protect their wages and working conditions, their presence tends to depress job conditions, causing native workers to refuse to work in the same jobs with aliens. In order to minimize friction with more highly skilled native workers, employers often discriminate against immigrants in filling higher status jobs. Many native workers, therefore, benefit from the employment of immigrants by being upgraded faster than they otherwise would have been. However, as it becomes possible and profitable to substitute immigrants for natives, employers will do so. Friction between native and immigrant workers may be minimized as the economy grows, but it is likely to intensify during periods of rising unemployment.

5. Increasing competition for jobs is apt to exacerbate social relationships between immigrant and native workers. Conflict usually becomes particularly intense during the third phase of immigration as immigrant families settle into the country. Despite the employers' preferences for immigrant workers in low-level jobs, discrimination against the immigrants is likely to intensify as immigrants compete for housing and increase their participation in public programs. Conflict may be particularly intense where there are marked racial and ethnic differences between the immigrant groups and natives of the host country. Conflict between immigrants and natives tends to be more intense where host-country natives are relatively homogeneous racially, the government has made no plans to ease racial tensions, and the immigrant population rises relative to the native population. Under these conditions, racist and fascist political movements sometimes emerge among native populations, putting considerable stress on democratic processes.

During later phases of immigration, there also are movements among immigrants that intensify their dissatisfaction and produce growing political and social as well as economic unrest. The longer immigrants stay in the host country, the more their aspirations shift from those of industrializing to those of industrialized economies. As this happens, the initial satisfaction with jobs shifts to increasing dissatisfaction with discrimination against immigrants in the economic, political, and social life of the host countries. The children of immigrants growing up in host countries are particularly likely to resent discrimination and to organize to acquire equal rights.

6. The European experience also provides some insight into the economic effects of using foreign workers in the host country. However, the Mexican-United States and European experiences make it clear that the effects of immigrant workers cannot be specified apart from the effects on different interest groups, economic and labor market conditions, and stages of migration.

a. Initially at least, the immigrant workers themselves improve their material welfare. If they return home, they probably also experience permanent improvements in status. However, if they stay in the host country they will have higher material conditions than they would in their native countries, but lower status and economic welfare in comparison with host-country native workers. The immigrants' long-run welfare will depend upon the extent to which they can achieve political, economic, and social mobility in the host country.

b. The sending country may or may not gain from out-migration. There are negative and positive factors to be considered. If migration is permanent, the sending country loses some of its most productive workers who have been educated at the expense of the developing country but make their productive contributions elsewhere. Moreover, some employers in the developing countries might suffer from rising wages occasioned by declining labor supplies, although this is a minor matter in labor-surplus areas.

On the positive side, the sending countries might benefit because of the relief from population pressures on resources made possible by out-migration, the favorable effects on the international balance of payments from remittances by immigrants to their families during phases one and two, and the favorable effects on economic development from the skills acquired by returning migrants.[17]

Results for various host-country groups depend on economic and labor-market conditions and the phase of the immigration process. Employers clearly gain from higher profits caused by lower labor and/or capital costs and greater labor-force adaptability. The extent to which workers in the host country gain depends heavily on labor demand. If immigrants were only brought in to fill jobs vacated by natives, native workers would gain from immigration because they would have greater occupational mobility and would benefit from higher rates of economic growth made possible by the use of foreign workers.[18]

The workers who lose by the employment of immigrants are those who compete directly with them for jobs, housing, social services, and other amenities. European economists seem generally to have concluded that immigration has largely positive results for workers in the host countries, but this conclusion has to be modified when applied to conditions in the United States. American employers clearly gain and higher-paid workers move up faster in the short run but might face increasing competition in the long run as competition from immigrants increases. Moreover, the employment of illegal immigrant workers has a more depressing effect on wages than the use of legal aliens whose *initial* employment is ostensibly controlled in such a way as to prevent direct competition between immigrant and native workers. There have been such regulations in the United States but they have not been adequately enforced.[19]

Other factors in the United States intensify competition between United States citizens and immigrants. Unlike most European countries, the United States has had large racial and cultural minorities whose members have been restricted by institutional discrimination to low-wage jobs into which immigrants are initially hired. Moreover, the unemployment rate in the United States consistently has been higher than it has been in Europe. Perhaps the most important difference between the American and European experiences is the sheer size of the immigrant population. In absolute numbers, at least in this century, no other country in the world has experienced the influx of alien workers that the United States has.

We also have had a relatively large pool of unskilled workers who have been displaced rather rapidly from American agriculture. These workers often are forced to support their families and compete all of their lives with unmarried illegal aliens who work scared and hard for limited economic objectives. It is easy to see why employers prefer aliens, but it is not, as in Europe, because native workers are unavailable. It also would be hard to argue that economic growth in the United States is limited by the unavailability of workers to do menial work. Finally, the long history of the migration of people and the size of the interacting waves of migration back and forth between Mexico and the United States make it more difficult for Mexican-American workers to go through the process of assimilation observable in European countries.[20] Many Mexican immigrants have gone through the phases described above, but the assimilation of the Mexican-American population is made difficult by successive waves of immigrants from Mexico.

Domestic workers also are damaged because illegal aliens impede the formation of labor organizations to improve wages and working conditions. Unions in all countries have taken ambiguous positions with respect to immigrants. Although they generally oppose immigration on economic and sometimes racial grounds, unions usually attempt to organize workers once they enter a country and insist that they receive wages equal to those paid natives for the same work. Of course, the dilemma for unions is that their opposition to immigration often makes it difficult for them to organize the immigrant workers, especially where the opposition has had racial overtones.[21]

In the United States, unions are increasingly concerned about the immigration of Mexican nationals, legal and illegal, because Mexican workers allegedly are used as strikebreakers, making it difficult for unions to get organized. Unions also are concerned about the effect of competition from Mexican nationals on wages and working conditions. They particularly object to competition from commuters who live in Mexico, with Mexican costs of living, while competing with American workers for jobs.

Mexican-American workers have had ambivalent attitudes about Mexican immigrants. Their kinship with and sympathies for the immigrants have been tempered by the belief that Mexican Americans are the chief losers from the employment of Mexican aliens. For example, César Chávez, leader of the United Farm Workers Union, has complained about the use of Mexican strikebreakers to weaken his union and depress wages for farm workers, but pressure from urban Mexican-American leaders caused him to reverse his opposition to the immigration of Mexicans to the United States. The position he took in 1975 was that Mexicans should be allowed to settle in the United States, but they should come here legally, bring their families, and become citizens.

Policy Implications

Any policy recommendations for dealing with the Mexican alien question must be based on several realities exemplified by international labor migrations. The first reality is that there is no simple solution to the problem because of the numerous conflicting interests involved. The second reality concerns the difficulties involved in regulating these human flows when there are powerful economic forces perpetuating them and powerful social forces causing them to go through the various settlement phases. These phases and patterns are remarkably similar from country to country despite a variety of regulations attempting to restrict the employment of aliens. In the United States those who gain from the employment of alien workers have been much stronger politically and economically than those workers in low-status jobs who lose. The losers have been primarily low-income Mexican-American workers in the Southwest (who have had very little political or economic power), though the growing numbers of illegal aliens throughout the United States is causing workers in other areas to become alarmed. Skilled trade unions became more concerned about this problem in 1974 and 1975. The opponents of immigration also were strengthened by rising unemployment during the 1970s.

A final point to be considered is that the adoption of policies to deal with short-term and long-run problems associated with immigration clearly makes it possible to deal with the problem in a more orderly fashion. This is not possible with the present disjointed approach, mainly based on policies reflecting a combination of strong economic interests and neglect by most political leaders. The social and political problems attending immigration could be minimized by careful programs to lessen racial conflict, provide for the orderly assimilation of immigrants as full citizens, and measures to reduce the adverse effects on natives. The Dutch apparently have done a good job with assimilating immigrants of diverse racial and ethnic backgrounds. The United States, on the other hand, has done a very poor job, especially by refusing to take action to halt the flow of illegal aliens. Realizing the impossibility of neat solutions to their problem, I nevertheless think the following deserve careful consideration:

1. Immediate measures should be taken to halt the flow of illegal aliens by:

    a. Making it unlawful for employers to hire illegal aliens.

    b. More vigorous enforcement of the penalties for entering the country illegally. Identification papers that are difficult to counterfeit could be developed. Aliens deported the second time should suffer increasingly harsh penalties and should never be eligible for legal entry into the United States.

    c. An effort must be made to identify illegal aliens currently working in the United States. An amnesty program should be considered for those who already have been partially assimilated into the economy and society and who are not considered to be undesirable because of serious criminal activities.

2. The number of legal aliens permitted to enter the United States should be more nearly geared to labor market realities. The present quotas probably are too low, but new quotas and procedures should protect the interests of American workers, particularly Mexican Americans in the Southwest. Foreign workers should not be allowed to come into the United States where American citizens are available and willing and able to work. The fact that

foreign workers are *more productive* than citizens should *not* be used as a reason for their importation. Enforcement of this restriction will require much better labor market information and analysis than are currently available to the United States government.

A program also should be adopted for the full participation of selected aliens into the American economy and society over a period of years. This would include measures to minimize opposition from American citizens based on ignorance and prejudice. A careful study of Dutch policies might be instructive.

Finally, the United States and Mexico should cooperate in a joint program to promote economic development in northern Mexico, preferably in places more than fifty miles from the border. The present twin-plants program is not a good one because it probably attracts more people to border towns than can find jobs there, generating high levels of unemployment and encouraging workers to enter the United States illegally. There is a special need for measures to take the profit out of the present system of smuggling illegal aliens into the United States at considerable personal risk to the aliens. Indeed, the illegal alien system permits far too many abuses by crew chiefs, smugglers, and other labor brokers who control jobs and labor supplies. Ultimately, the problem of Mexican immigration to the United States will be solved by equalizing economic conditions on both sides of the border. Until that can be accomplished, policies should be adopted to minimize conflicting interests and their detrimental effects on both citizens of Mexico and the United States while maximizing the mutual benefits from migration through negotiated settlements and compromises.

NOTES

1. Vernon M. Briggs, Jr., "The Immigration of Mexican Nationals into the United States" (Paper presented at the International Conference on Migrant Workers, International Institute for Comparative Social Studies, Berlin, December 12-14, 1974).

2. See *U.S. News and World Report,* 3 February 1975.

3. *New York Times,* 30 December 1974.

4. M. A. Farber, "Battle Expected on Tighter Laws to Control Illegal Aliens," *New York Times,* 31 December 1974.

5. Inter-American Development Bank, *Economic and Social Progress in Latin America, Annual Report* (Washington, D.C., 1973).

6. Carey McWilliams, *North from Mexico* (New York: Greenwood Press, 1968); Julian Samora, *Los Mojados: The Wetback Story* (Notre Dame, Ind.: University of Notre Dame Press, 1971).

7. Ernesto Galarza, *Merchants of Labor: The Mexican Bracero Story* (Charlotte, N.C.: McNally and Loflin, 1964).

8. *New York Times,* 17 June 1973.

9. David S. North and William G. Weissert, *Immigrants and the American Labor Market*. A report to the U.S. Department of Labor (Washington, D.C., Trans-Century Corporation, 1973).

10. U.S. House of Representatives, Committee on the Judiciary, Subcommittee on Western Hemisphere Migration, *Hearings, March 29, 1973* (Washington, D.C.: Government Printing Office, 1973), p. 60.

11. Information on employer preferences is derived from interviews with employers in connection with the South Texas Labor Market Project at the Center for the Study of Human Resources, The University of Texas at Austin,1974-75.

12. Vernon M. Briggs, Jr., *The Mexican-United States Border: Public Policy and Chicano Economic Welfare*, Studies in Human Resources Development, no. 2 (Austin, Texas: Center for the Study of Human Resources, The University of Texas at Austin, 1974).

13. *New York Times*, 22 December 1974.

14. Giert H. Hofstede, "Work Goals of Migrant Workers" and Christine Laborte, "Einige Bemerkungen zum Arbeitsverhalten und zur Arbeitsmotivation in Die Bundesrepublik Deutschland" (Papers presented at The International Conference on Migrant Workers, Berlin, December 12–14, 1975).

15. Henry Kamm, "Turkish Workers in Germany Uneasy About Future," *New York Times*, 23 January 1974.

16. Hans-Joachin Hoffman-Nowotny, "Ethnic, Race, and Minority Relations" (Paper presented at the International Conference on Migrant Workers, Berlin, December 12–14, 1975).

17. W. H. Bohning, "Return Migrants' Contribution to the Development Process—The Issues Involved" (Paper presented at the International Conference on Migrant Workers, Berlin, December 12–14, 1975).

18. For a development of this theme see, W. R. Bohning, *The Migration of Workers in the United Kingdom and the European Community* (London: Oxford University Press, 1972); and Iden and D. Maillot, *The Effects of the Employment of Foreign Workers* (Paris: Organization for Economic Cooperation and Development, 1974).

19. David S. North, *Alien Workers: A Study of the Labor Certification Programs* (Washington, D.C.: Trans-Century Corporation, 1971).

20. George I. Sánchez, "History, Culture and Education" in *La Raza: The Forgotten Americans* (Notre Dame, Ind.: University of Notre Dame Press, 1966).

21. Stephen Castles and Godula Kosack, *Immigrant Workers and Class Structure in Western Europe* (London: Oxford University Press, 1973).

PART IV

The Migrants of the Border

9

Commodity-Migrants: Structural Analysis of Mexican Immigration to the United States

Jorge A. Bustamante

Introduction

The approach followed in this essay derives from two basic assumptions. One is of a theoretical nature and the other, methodological. In theory the set of economic conditions as well as social and political relations that characterize the system of production of the United States are the factors that have shaped the phenomenon of undocumented immigration from Mexico. In this context that phenomenon is conceived as a part of what Mauss and Fauconnet or Georges Gurvitch have called a total social phenomenon,[1] that is, the social structure of American society.

This is not to say that Mexican undocumented immigration is caused solely by pull factors from the United States. To be sure out-migration from the rural sectors in Mexico is *an alternative* to situations of unemployment and low living conditions. However, such an alternative should not be considered as *natural,* nor is it the only one conceivable. At the end of the Bracero Program (December 1964), conditions of unemployment in Mexico were high.[2] The previous trend of expansion of arable land had reached a point of no progress.[3] By the end of the last decade (1960-70) immigration to Mexican border cities was at lower rates than in previous decades when the Bracero Program was in operation.[4] These factors seem to indicate that conditions for immigration were drastically reduced in the United States with the termination of the Bracero Program, and out-migration in Mexico found other avenues, namely, urban centers within the country.[5] The point here is that the alternative to migration to the United States from Mexico is concomitant to conditions

183

existing in the United States that should be studied by focusing on its economic and social structure as a whole.

The understanding of the structural factors that shape the phenomenon of undocumented immigration from Mexico is conditioned by an understanding of its historical background. This is the assumption of a methodological nature that also guides the approach followed here. Based on both assumptions, the purpose of this essay will be to expand the understanding of the structural conditions under which the undocumented immigration from Mexico takes place. This will be done by focusing on the historical context of relations of production within which the Mexican immigrant is found working in the United States.

Given the limits of its purpose, the criterion to judge the validity of this paper's assertions should be one at a level of plausibility, that level which Weber defined for methodological purposes with the term *"Sinhaft adaquat."* [6] This term refers to a level which assumes the assessment of conditions and patterns of repetition aimed, not at the establishment of relationships of strict causality, but rather to achieve understanding of the historical context of meaning of those social relations that shape a social phenomenon.

The Conceptual Elements of Commodity-Migration

When immigration is defined as social behavior, we can conceive of it as an alternative to situational conditions. This alternative has a social character to the extent that is culturally given to the would-be migrant in a context of a social structure. Among the variety of factors that make migration factual, focus will be placed on what is viewed as a sufficient although not necessary condition for Mexican immigration to the United States, namely, a demand for cheap labor in the context of capitalist relations of production. Evidence from Hourwich[7] and Thomas,[8] supports the plausibility of focusing on the factors of the labor demand in the United States. This is based on the assertion that *on the whole* ''pull factors'' have had more weight than ''push factors'' in determining the conditions for immigration to the United States. It is assumed here that such a demand for cheap labor has to be known by the would-be immigrant in order to come to the United States as opposed to some other destination. The assumption implies that such a demand becomes part of the social relations of capitalism in which placing one's own labor on sale makes sense only because there are known labor buyers.

Using our interpretation of Weber's concepts of social action discussed elsewhere,[9] we could define the social nature of immigration as behavior made in reference to other peoples' behavior. In this context, the meaning of that "reference" is derived from the superstructure of "culture" corresponding to capitalist relations of production. The source from which the would-be immigrant "knows" the meaning of selling his labor in exchange for money is the superstructure or culture within which he has been socialized. It is from superstructural definitions that the worker has learned to accept as legitimate not being paid in full for the value of his labor's input into the product's exchange value. Briefly, it is from the "culture" of capitalist relations of production that the immigrant has learned to behave as if he were a commodity for the labor-force market.

The process of socialization in which the individual learns to conceive his labor force as a commodity is the same in which the worker learns about a labor-force market and about labor-force buyers. Migration in this context is nothing else but the self transportation of labor as a commodity to where the capital owner demands it. Social behavior corresponding to these conditions outlined above could be called commodity-migration. In terms of definition of immigration as social behavior, commodity-migration could be defined as migration (behavior) that is referred to other peoples' behavior (i.e., labor demands typified by the cultural definition of *"el patrón"*—the employer), to which a cultural meaning (commodity exchange) is imputed, and according to which both the migrant (commodity carrier) and the employer (commodity buyer) will orient reciprocally the future course of their actions.

The conceptualization of commodity-migration is by no means all-inclusive of possible kinds of migration. There are other migrant behaviors that would not correspond directly to the commodity relationship of a capitalist system of production. Our purpose here is to conceptualize the kind of social relations that involve the behavior of the Mexican immigrant as well as the behavior of all those who make the behavior of that immigrant "make sense." Thus, commodity-migration as a concept can only be applied to capitalist relations of production characterized by an inherent contradiction between labor and capital. In this context commodity-migration is understood as involving the following aspects:

1. Commodity-migrants enter into the relationships of production of a capitalist society occupying the lowest paid positions of that society's occupational structure, thereby becoming a source for capital expansion by providing additional sources of surplus value to capital investors.

2. Commodity-migrants are socially defined as deviants and sanctioned through prejudice and discrimination. Thus, the presence of commodity-

migrants is used as a factor reinforcing dominant values in accordance with which discriminatory practices are justified and social privileges are maintained. This in turn reinforces the superstructure and legitimizes the prevailing relations of production.

3. Commodity-migrants are cast into conflict with the lowest paid native workers with whom commodity-migrants compete for the lowest paid jobs. Thus, commodity-migrants operate as a means for preventing solidarity among workers.

4. In times of crisis, the powerlessness of commodity-migrants (which makes possible the aspects outlined above) makes them a favorite target to be blamed for the crisis. Commodity-migrants are being used as scapegoats for social, economic, or political problems, displacing the responsibility of dominant groups in society. This rationalization is used to prevent structural changes from taking place.

Mexican Immigration and Capital Expansion

It did not take long for mining, agriculture, industry, or railroad interests, or business and commercial enterprises in the United States, to see the advantages of "importing" labor from Mexico.

As early as 1910, social scientists responsible for assessing immigration conditions were suggesting an immigration policy that would encourage the importation of labor power from Mexico without the burden of increasing immigration. The following excerpts from the Dillingham Commission's report illustrate in what terms this contradiction might become possible.

> Because of their strong attachment to their native land, low intelligence, illiteracy, migratory life, and the possibility of their residence here being discontinued, few become citizens of the United States.
>
> Insofar as Mexican laborers come into contact with natives or with European immigrants they are looked upon as inferiors.
>
> The Mexican immigrants are providing a fairly acceptable supply of labor in a limited territory in which it is difficult to secure others, and their competitive ability is limited because of their more or less temporary residence and their personal qualities, so that their incoming does not involve the same detriment to labor conditions as is involved in the immigration of other races who also work at comparatively low wages. While the Mexicans are not easily assimilated, this is not of very

great importance as long as most of them return to their native land after a short time. They give rise to little race friction, but do impose upon the community a large number of dependents, misdemeanants, and petty criminals where they settle in any considerable number.

Thus it is evident that in the case of the Mexican he is less desirable as a citizen than as a laborer. The permanent additions to the population, however, are much smaller than the number who immigrate for work.[10]

These remarks of a congressional policy-advising committee seem to fit the previously stated propositions (1) and (2) of the conceptualization of a commodity-migration. It is of particular importance to realize that this view in the United States Senate anticipated the beginning of any massive immigration from Mexico. In the period 1900-1904 there were 2,259 immigrants from Mexico. In the following period, from 1905 to 1909, there were 21,732. From 1910 to 1914 the number of immigrants from Mexico increased to 82,588.[11] It is our contention that "push factors" like the Mexican Revolution have been overemphasized while, on the other hand, too little emphasis has been given to the effect of "pull factors" on Mexican immigration.

For example, the Corpus Christi *Herald* in 1910 advertised and invited investment in the Lower Río Grande Valley, offering as the region's principal attraction "the cheapest Mexican labor that you can find."[12] Parenthetically, we find the same type of propaganda being offered by the Chambers of Commerce of American border cities and their development commissions as late as 1975. This time it is the twin-city concept, but it has the same meaning—namely, cheap labor is available for American industry.

As a result of the efforts to obtain cheap labor early in the century, we also find a reaction of domestic laborers who felt affected by such competition. This situation, accompanied by lower wages and high unemployment rates of domestic employees in the border area, had as a consequence the displacement of domestic employees, particularly workers of Mexican descent. Samuel Gompers, president of the American Federation of Labor at the beginning of this century, illustrated the problem in this way: "When confronted by demands of high wages, shorter hours, and better conditions in New Mexico, the mine operators called across the border line and Mexican miners came to take the place of the Americans."[13] Since the owners of the mines of New Mexico and Colorado also owned the mines of Mexico, the experience and ability of Mexican miners was well known in the United States.

The "importation" of Mexican workers has had a negative impact on the "native" labor force. Very early in the development of mining, agriculture, and industry in the Southwest, Mexican workers were brought to the United States to act as strikebreakers, to hamper the union movement, and to lower the wages and working conditions of the American laborer. We quote Samuel Gompers again to illustrate this point:

> Distance was no barrier to the coal and gold mine operators of Colorado who wished to use unsuspecting Mexican miners in Colorado . . . [where] conditions had stultified Mexican-American laborers. They were not fully conscious of the wrongs done to themselves or the injury that they did to American workers by undermining existing standards and conditions.[14]

By 1924, the number of Mexican immigrants to the United States is estimated by Gamio at 890,746,[15] although Gamio himself questions the reliability of this figure which refers to immigrants who were admitted legally. No one knows how many Mexican immigrants entered the United States without visas at the beginning and during the massive population movement which took place between the first and second decades of this century. If we take into account certain factors that favored immigration without visa, we can estimate that the number without visa was greater than the lawful immigration. These factors were observed by Gamio in his investigations made in 1926:

1. the difficulties presented by the American immigration laws to illiterates who could not pass the literacy test;

2. the loss of time and money that was caused by waiting on the Mexican side while the legal requisites were taken care of before admission to the United States;

3. the amount of money paid to a smuggler or *"pasador"* in order to get into the United States was generally less than the $18 which the immigrant visa cost.[16]

At the turn of the century the Mexican peasant was by definition illiterate. Not only was education beyond his reach, but education was often prohibited to him. Thus his very ignorance kept him a peasant. His life was conditioned by the prevailing social structure. This was a peasant who had no alternative but to follow the route north, a route which did not really take him away from the cultural influence that he had known.[17] McWilliams says, "Migration from Mexico is deeply rooted in the past. It follows trails which are among the most ancient of the North American continent. Psychologically and culturally, Mexicans have never immigrated to the Southwest: They have returned."[18]

On the one hand, legal admission to the United States was too complicated and quite often beyond the peasant's reach; on the other hand, with the exception of five or six points of entry, there was little vigilance on the border which is about two thousand miles long. Thus, it seems logical that, for the most part, Mexican immigration to the United States would be illegal.

The creation of the Border Patrol in 1924 made necessary a greater distinction between those who crossed the border legally and those who violated the immigration laws. The mission of the Border Patrol is enforcement of these immigration laws. The laws up to this date are not well understood and are ignored by the immigrant who, in the absence of an official who might sanction him upon his illegal entry, does not really identify himself as a lawbreaker. The Border Patrol became this official who served as a reference point to the illegal immigrant with regard to the legal consequences of the violation of the immigration laws. Before the Border Patrol, the illegal immigrant only had to stay out of trouble and not implicate himself with the police or the judicial authorities. In doing this the immigrant could consider himself completely safe in the streets and roads, and fairly free to choose the most convenient work.[19] Only the courts could decree his deportation. Generally speaking, deportation came as a consequence of having become involved in some criminal offense, rather than of having entered illegally.

The creation of the Border Patrol was accompanied by a new administrative procedure that accelerated the expulsion of the illegal immigrant, which previously was accomplished through deportation. This new administrative procedure is called "voluntary departure." An illegal immigrant who has been apprehended is required to demonstrate his legal status in the country. If he cannot demonstrate this status, he is subject to deportation. If the illegal immigrant, however, wishes to avoid being deported, he is invited to leave the country voluntarily. If he refuses this invitation, theoretically he should be taken before a judge in order to prove his legal entry. If he cannot prove legal entry, he is then subject to deportation. Table 1 illustrates the effects on illegal immigration after the creation of both the Border Patrol and the administrative procedure of voluntary departure.

The very obvious increase that appears in the decade 1921-30 marks an important change in the history of the Mexican illegal immigrant. In 1924, his status was changed from being one of many migratory workers whose illegal entry would most probably remain unsanctioned, to that of the fugitive—a fugitive from the law, constantly hiding in order not to be apprehended and expelled from the country. The immigrant became known as the "wetback."

The establishment of the Border Patrol in 1924 not only modified the interaction between the illegal entrant and the employer, but it brought a new factor into being, namely the danger of being apprehended and returned to Mexico. Thus, the threat of being turned in presented a new dimension to the

TABLE 1
Numbers of Mexican Immigrant Workers Detained Without Visas

Year	Total	Year	Total	Year	Total
1924	4,614	1941	6,082	1958	37,242
1925	2,961	1942	DNA	1959	30,196
1926	4,047	1943	8,189	1960	29,651
1927	4,495	1944	26,689	1961	29,817
1928	5,529	1945	63,602	1962	30,272
1929	8,538	1946	91,456	1963	39,124
1930	18,319	1947	182,986	1964	43,844
1931	8,409	1948	179,385	1965	55,349
1932	7,116	1949	278,538	1966	89,751
1933	15,875	1950	485,215	1967	108,327
1934	8,910	1951	500,000	1968	151,000
1935	9,139	1952	543,538	1969	201,636
1936	9,534	1953	865,318	1970	277,377
1937	9,535	1954	1,075,168	1971	348,178
1938	8,684	1955	242,608	1972	430,213
1939	9,376	1956	72,442	1973	609,673
1940	8,051	1957	44,451		

Sources: From 1924 to 1941: Annual Report of the Secretary of Labor. From 1942 to 1960:
Special compilation of the Immigration and Naturalization Service reported to us.
From 1961 to 1973: Annual Report of the Immigration and Naturalization Service.

disadvantage of the undocumented immigrant. Since anyone can turn in an "illegal," such a threat began to narrow the social contacts that the undocumented immigrant might establish, with the exception of some form of relationship to the employer. In our estimation the implicit or explicit threat of being turned in, even by the employer, adds a new element to the situation with regard to wages and working conditions. In a real sense the immigrant worker without visa is at the mercy of the employer. The alternatives of accepting or not accepting a job are not necessarily open to the worker. An employer can in fact insist that the worker without visa accept the wages and working conditions or face the possibility of being turned in to the Border Patrol. How common this is we do not really know, but such instances have been reported by Saunders and Leonard,[20] Hadley,[21] and Jones.[22] Seventeen out of the 493 Mexican workers without visa interviewed by the author complained of the employer having turned them in to the Border Patrol without having paid their salaries. Fourteen were working in Texas, two in California, and one in Arizona.

The Depression of the 1930s prompted a number of measures that affected immigration from Mexico. Perhaps the most serious of these, although no statistics were kept, was what has been called "operation deportation" realized in 1930.[23] The general procedure was to require all those suspected of being aliens to prove that they were born in the United States. The person who could not satisfy this requirement was expelled by the country under the administrative procedure of "voluntary departure." This was done to reduce the number of unemployed during the Depression as well as the large number of people who were on welfare. This procedure also proved to be a hardship for many Mexicans who had in fact left Mexico as emigrants as many as twenty years before, and now found themselves expelled from their adopted country.

Many inhabitants of the urban areas along the border blamed the immigrant worker without visa for all their problems without giving much thought to the attitude of the growers. That viewpoint was summarized succinctly by U.S. Vice-President John Nance Garner, "In order to make profit out of this [agribusiness] you have to have cheap labor."

As the problem grew more serious it also began to get national attention. *The New York Times* said:

It is remarkable how some of the same Senators and Representatives who are all for enacting the most rigid barriers against immigration from Southern Europe suffer from a sudden blindness when it comes to protecting the Southern Border of the U. S. This peculiar weakness is most noticeable among members from Texas and the Southwest where the wetbacks happen to be principally employed.[24]

President Eisenhower asked Attorney General Brownell, who had visited the region, to propose a plan. The plan turned out to be the designation of General Joseph May Swing[25] as Commissioner of the Immigration and Naturalization Service, in charge of "Operation Wetback."

In July of 1954, General Swing described his assignment to a group of employers in South Texas and said: "When President Eisenhower appointed me for this job, his orders were to clean up the border. I intend to do just that."[26] "Operation Wetback" was pursued with military efficiency and the result was that over a million Mexican workers without visa were expelled from the country in 1954.

At the end of 1956, some people considered the problem of the Mexican worker without visa an episode of history. But as we move through the years we find that while there was a great decrease in the number of Mexican workers without visa from 1954 to 1959, once again in the 1960s and up till the present there has been an increase of Mexican immigrants.

One might in fact suggest that if agricultural production were so dependent on Mexican workers then presumably "Operation Wetback" would have brought about an economic catastrophe to the border region. Other elements intervened and economic catastrophe did not occur. The process of legalizing workers without visa and converting them into *braceros* (which we will discuss in the following section) was one thing. Many of the workers without visa who were expelled as "illegals" came back legally as *braceros*. "Operation Wetback" may have dried out a pool of cheap labor within the United States, but it certainly contributed to increased unemployment across the border in Mexico.

Law, Power, and Discrimination

The decade between 1930 and 1940 was a period in which it became obvious that the labor supply for the Southwest, whether legal or illegal, was obviously based in Mexico. It was also during this period that prejudice and discrimination toward this labor element was in a sense institutionalized. A deputy sheriff appearing before the LaFollette Committee hearings illustrates the point: "We protect our farmers here in Hern County. . . . They are our best people; they keep the county going. . . . But the Mexicans are trash. They have no standard for living. We herd them like pigs."[27]

In these remarks we find implicit those structural factors that are related to the position of power from which both the Mexican immigrant and the immigrant's employer interact socially. These factors are: (1) group interest of the undocumented immigrant's employer; (2) the value judgments that justify the protection of these interests; (3) the power of the immigrant's employer as his interests are "protected"; (4) the justification for treating Mexican immigrants in whatever manner is necessary; (5) the powerlessness of the Mexican immigrant; and (6) the prejudicial attitudes and the discriminatory behavior directed toward the Mexican immigrant. Other writers previously quoted (Saunders and Leonard, Hadley, and Galarza) have noted the same prejudicial attitudes and discriminatory behavior in a context that can be described as one of structural conditions for the exploitation of cheap labor.

The point here is that the exploitation of the Mexican immigrant was institutionalized during this period. However, this institutionalization derived from the openly expressed and widely disseminated views of prominent people in earlier years. Note for example:

Mr. Chairman, here is the whole problem in a nutshell. Farming is not a profitable industry in this country, and, in order to make money out of this, you have to have cheap labor . . . in order to allow land owners now to make a profit on their farms; they want to get the

cheapest labor they can find, and if they can get the Mexican labor, it
enables them to make a profit. That is the way it is along the border, and
I imagine that is the way it is anywhere else.[28]

The quotation expressed the views of John Nance Garner before he became
vice-president of the United States during the administration of Franklin D.
Roosevelt. The statement from such a high official in the United States
government suggests, if not the direct power, certainly the influence of
Mexican immigrant employers. Senator McCarran, many years later declared:

> Senator [Ellender], I think you will agree with me that on this side of
> the border there is a desire for these wetbacks. . . . Last year when we
> had the Appropriations Bill up, the item that might have prevented them
> from coming over to some extent was stricken from the bill. . . . We
> might just as well face this thing realistically. The agricultural people,
> the farmer along the Mexican side of the border in California, in
> Arizona, in Texas . . . want this help. They want this farm labor. They
> just cannot get along without it.[29]

This again illustrates the institutionalization of the exploitation of cheap
Mexican labor. There seems to be little regard in these statements for the
morality of the action and certainly not much regard for its legality. Thus,
undocumented immigration and the hiring of undocumented immigrants from
Mexico seems to be taken for granted in certain levels of the power structure.

In the meantime, Mexican immigrant employers defined the situation of
low wages as a question of interplay of "natural laws" of supply and demand.
Expressed in these terms they presumably did not view the reduction of wages
over time as anything bad. Gamio found that in 1926[30] the average wage for
the Mexican immigrant in Texas was $1.50 to $2.00 for an eight-hour day.
Saunders and Leonard found in 1950 that the average wage of the wetback in
the Lower Río Grande Valley was $2.50 for a twelve-hour day.[31] This then
means that twenty-four years later the South Texas grower had not increased
wages, whereas the profits for agribusiness in the same region of the Lower
Río Grande Valley had increased 1000 percent between 1920 and 1950.[32]

The Bracero Program

The Bracero Program was created by an agreement between the United
States and Mexican governments on July 23, 1942. The rationale for the
program was to overcome manpower shortages arising from the involvement

of the United States in World War II. Agricultural production was viewed as vital to winning the war. Thus, the lack of agricultural labor was considered a concern of the War Food Administration. This agency, in cooperation with the Department of Labor and the Immigration and Naturalization Service, established a labor recruitment program as an emergency war measure,[33] based upon the United States-Mexican agreement.

The main provisions of the United States-Mexican agreement for the Bracero Program were:

> Mexican workers were not to be used to displace domestic workers but only fill proven shortages. Recruits were to be exempted from military service, and discrimination against them was not to be permitted. The round-trip transportation expenses of the worker were guaranteed, as well as living expenses en route. Hiring was to be done on the basis of a written contract between the worker and his employer, and the work was to be exclusively in agriculture.
>
> *Braceros* were to be free to buy merchandise in places of their own choice. Housing and sanitary conditions were to be adequate. Deductions amounting to 10% of their earnings were authorized for deposit in a savings fund payable to the worker on his return to Mexico. Work was guaranteed for three-quarters of the duration of the contract. Wages were to be equal to those prevailing in the area of employment, but in any case not less than 30 cents per hour.[34]

These provisions as they related to adequate transportation, housing, wages, food, medical care, and guaranteed length of work, seldom were carried out and, more often than not, the agreements were violated by the American employers.[35]

Several factors facilitated the constant violation of the provisions of the agreement by the farmers: (1) they were able to hire Mexican workers as *braceros,* bypassing the recruitment centers run by the Mexican government, and without regard for the provisions of the agreement. This made it impossible for the Mexican government to enforce the guarantees established for the protection of the *bracero*[36]; (2) the overt cooperation of the Border Patrol in admitting workers as *braceros* regardless of Mexican government consent[37]; (3) the Border Patrol's practice of "drying out" wetbacks. This consisted of taking large groups of "wetbacks" to the border, after their apprehension for illegal entrance, making them place the tip of a toe on the Mexican side in order to make lawful their readmittance as *braceros*[38]; and (4) the powerlessness of the Mexican government to enforce the provisions of the agreement against American farmers, and the indifference of the United States government, which tended to encourage violations.

World War II ended, but the emergency wartime measure, the Bracero Program, remained. By several extensions the war measure lasted twenty-two years, ending finally on December 31, 1964. Table 2 shows the magnitude of the *bracero* movement involving more than four and one-half million workers.

The history of the Bracero Program did not accomplish one of the goals as conceived by the Mexican government, namely, eliminating discrimination and exploitation of the Mexican worker.

The Commuter

It is necessary to distinguish between the official definition of commuter and the commuter phenomenon. The former has been expressed in the following terms:

> The aliens referred to as commuters are those aliens who have been lawfully accorded the privilege of residing permanently in the United States, but who choose to reside in foreign contiguous territory and commute to their place of employment in the United States.[39]

In the legal sense, a commuter is the one who bears Form I-151, known as a "green card," issued to a person upon the rationale of the official definition.

The commuter history (as far as Mexicans are concerned) might be traced back to the second decade of the century, when the 1921, 1924, and 1927 Immigration Acts made reference to this category. But it was not until the Registration Act of 1940 that the category of commuter was sanctioned by Congress in its present form.

The commuter phenomenon acquired numerical importance beginning in 1954, the year of "Operation Wetback."[40] We must point out that available figures do not reflect the true dimensions of this category, as we learn from the "Report of the Select Commission on Western Hemisphere Immigration":

> Many thousands of Mexican citizens are permitted to enter this country for business or pleasure with entry documents that do not permit them to work. Undoubtedly some of these visitors do work, despite the best efforts of U. S. authorities. Such illegal, wetback, workers would be regarded in the popular mind as commuters but would not appear in any official or semi-official estimate of the volume of alien commuters.[41]

TABLE 2
**Braceros Admitted and Undocumented Immigrants from Mexico
Expelled from the United States, 1942-73**

Year	Braceros	Undocumented Mexican Immigrants Returned to Mexico
1942	4,203	10,603
1943	52,098	16,154
1944	62,170	39,449
1945	120,000	80,760
1946	82,000	116,320
1947	55,000	814,543
1948	35,345	193,852
1949	107,000	289,400
1950	67,500	469,581
1951	192,000	510,355
1952	197,100	531,719
1953	201,380	839,149
1954	309,033	1,035,282
1955	398,650	165,186
1956	445,197	58,792
1957	436,049	45,640
1958	432,857	45,164
1959	437,643	42,732
1960	315,846	39,750
1961	291,420	39,860
1962	194,978	41,200
1963	186,865	51,230
1964	177,736	41,589
1965	20,286	48,948
1966	8,647	89,683
1967	7,703	107,695
1968	0	142,520
1969	0	189,572
1970	0	265,539
1971	0	348,178
1972	0	430,213
1973	0	609,673

Source: Vernon Briggs, Jr., "The Mexico-United States Border: Public Policy and Chicano Economic Welfare," *Studies in Human Resource Development,* paper No. 2, Center for the Study of Human Resources, University of Texas at Austin, Texas, 1974, p. 9.

With reference to those who enter the United States but are not permitted to work, the American consul general at Tijuana, Mexico, stated, "Considerably in excess of 150,000 are estimated to be holding border crossing cards issued by I.N.S. at San Isidro."[42]

This means that the volume of the commuter phenomenon comprises: (1) the "green card" (Form I-151) holder; (2) the crossing card (Form I-186) holder who crosses legally but may work illegally in the United States; and (3) the Mexican worker without visa who lives on the border side of Mexico and crosses back and forth illegally.

I shall draw a picture of the commuter phenomenon by inferring from available scattered information. The first dimension is shown in Table 3, although it must be pointed out that at least the figure for 1967 appears to be incongruent with a statement made by George K. Rosenberg, Los Angeles district director of the Immigration and Naturalization Service, who said: "From time to time a sample count is taken and the last such sampling was taken between November 1, 1967, and December 31, 1967; the total number of commuters crossing the border between Mexico and California during this period was 15,284."[43]

This figure, however, and those in Table 3 are generally considered conservative, because regular statistics are not kept on other than "green card" commuters. The Form I-186 (crossing card or shopping card or seventy-two-hour card) is valid for four years.[44] Most of the aliens working illegally in the border area have entered legally by using the crossing card.[45]

No one knows how many persons cross legally, using the crossing and shopping card, and then work illegally in the United States. The number, however, must be in the thousands. In Tijuana it is estimated that 150,000 persons have cards, while the estimate is 75,000 in Juárez. El Paso issues between 2,500 and 3,000 of these cards monthly. Brownsville issues 1,500 to 2,000 monthly. Also, hundreds of these cards are revoked monthly at the check points, because the violators have been caught working.[46]

Some Changes in the Undocumented Immigration from Mexico

Social and economic implications arising from the illegal status of those who have entered the United States to work without a visa make it particularly

TABLE 3
Mexican Immigrants Admitted as Commuters to the United States

Year	Number	Year	Number	Year	Number
1952	9,079	1958	26,791	1964	34,448
1953	17,183	1959	22,909	1965	40,686
1954	30,645	1960	32,708	1966	47,217
1955	43,702	1961	41,476	1967	43,034
1956	61,320	1962	55,805	1968	44,000
1957	49,321	1963	55,986		

Source: Select Commission on Western Hemisphere Immigration, pp. 40-56.

important to distinguish between the undocumented immigrant and other types of Mexican immigrants previously discussed.

Table 2 illustrates a pattern of a sequential relationship between the Bracero Program and the number of undocumented immigrants apprehended during the years 1943-54. This pattern was broken by "Operation Wetback" on the one hand, and the drying out practice, on the other.[47] The latter created in reality the effect of an amnesty, since thousands of previously undocumented immigrants saw their migratory status being legalized by such a practice. That pattern of a sequential relationship suggests that the Bracero Program appears to be a magnet for undocumented immigration. The people involved as *braceros* and undocumented immigrants did not differ as to background, and whether they became one or the other apparently was just a matter of chance. Furthermore, the number of applicants for a *bracero* slot surpassed overwhelmingly the limits of the yearly established quotas, and every slot of the Bracero Program was a source of expectations. Thus, the higher the quotas, the greater the number of *bracero* candidates. This was particularly the case after 1951 when the recruiting process was conducted at Mexican border cities rather than in the interior as had been done before. The yearly pattern shown in Table 2 indicates that those who had migrated to the United States-Mexican border and failed to be recruited as bona fide *braceros* entered the United States anyway as *mojados* or *alambristas*. Statistics of Table 2 up to the year of "Operation Wetback," plus a comparison of census data on rates of immigration to Mexican border cities in the decades prior to and after the termination of the Bracero Program, indicate that a new program would increase rather than limit or decrease the immigration of undocumented Mexican workers.

It should be pointed out that Mexican undocumented immigration does not come from the less-developed areas of Mexico or involve the lowest income per capita sectors of the population. We can infer these characteristics from Figure 1 which shows the state of origin of Mexican undocumented immigration on a comparative basis for the following years: 1926-27, 1970, and 1973. In this graph we can see that out-migration to the United States from the southeast of Mexico, the less-developed region, has been minor. This region has the greatest rates of illiteracy, the lowest income per capita, and the greatest proportion of Indian population.[48] On the other hand, Figure 1 shows that the origin of undocumented immigration seems to be shifting toward the northern region of Mexico. Whereas in the 1920s Gamio found the majority of Mexican immigration coming from the states of the central plateau (Michoacán, Guanajuato, and Jalisco), in 1970 we found the border state of Chihuahua moving up to first place. This shift can be seen more precisely in Table 4 where we find that out-migration to the United States has increased in all but one border state (the exception being the state of Nuevo León where Monterrey, the second most important industrial center of the country, is located). Figure 1 and Table 4 indicate that factors such as communications, population growth, and proximity to the United States seem to be at variance with other economic conditions in determining which states will have greater out-migration to the United States.

In regard to Mexico's structural economic conditions affecting the undocumented immigration from Mexico, the most important one is unemployment. Data on unemployment in Mexico are nonexistent for scientific purposes. However, the findings of the Center of Agrarian Research on factors associated with unemployment in the rural sector are revealing. Day-laboring *jornaleros* (agricultural wage earners) have seen their number of work days per year reduced from 194 to 100, as an average, during the decade 1950-60.[49] In addition to this phenomenon, the proportion of production costs in agricultural enterprises attributable to labor have diminished from 22 percent to 7 percent between 1940 and 1960, whereas the proportion of costs related to machinery and use of technology has increased from 6 percent to 11 percent in the same period.[50] In spite of very high rates of industrial growth maintained for the last thirty years in Mexico, industry has not contributed to

TABLE 4
Percentage of Immigrants Born in the Border States of Mexico

	Investigation by Gamio 1926-28	Investigation by Samora 1968-70	Investigation by the Inter-secretarial Commission of the Mexican Government
	(a)	(b)	(c)
	%	%	%
Baja California	0.5	1.63	2.94
Chihuahua	4.4	18.46	12.70
Sonora	1.2	2.43	4.31
Coahuila	3.8	4.87	3.66
Nuevo León	8.0	6.09	2.75
Tamaulipas	2.1	5.07	1.79
All Frontier States	19.55	38.55	25.15
Rest of Country	80.45	61.45	74.85
	100.00%	100.00%	100.00%

(a) Manuel Gamio, *Mexican Immigration to the United States*, p. 13.
(b) Julian Samora, *Los Mojados: The Wetback Story*, p. 92.
(c) Comisión Intersecretarial Para el Estudio del Problema de la Emigración Subrepticia de Trabajadores Mexicanos a los Estados Unidos de América (mimeograph copy).

FIGURE 1

State of Origin of Mexican Undocumented Immigration to the United States

States That Averaged Below 0.80%

Baja California Sur	Colima
Campeche	Chiapas
Quintana Roo	Tabasco
Hidalgo	Oaxaca
Morelos	Tlaxcala
Puebla	Veracruz
Estado de Mexico	

.... Comisión Intersecretarial para el Estudio de la Migración Subrepticia de Trabajadores Mexicanos a los Estados Unidos, 1973.

– – – – – Samora, *Los Mojados, The Wetback Story.*

——— Gamio, *Mexican Immigration.*

the creation of new jobs proportionally to its capital expansion.[51] Adding to this picture it has been found that the input in the Gross National Product of the lowest 50 percent of the income scale has diminished from 19.9 percent to 15.4 percent from 1950 to 1963.[52]

If the present trend of unemployment conditions continues, out-migration from rural to urban areas, whether within Mexico or the United States, will be inevitable. The question is, who is going to pay, and when, the social costs of maintaining the current rates of growth of an army of unemployed people?

A Final Comment

In 1954 President Eisenhower placed General Swing in charge of the famous "Operation Wetback," which at its peak deported more than one million Mexicans in a single year. The importance of this historical fact is that once more the United States is confronting an economic depression coupled with a high rate of unemployment. Once again we begin to see a rise in the number of Mexican deportations. Under these conditions one could anticipate that the United States government might resort in the near future to another massive Mexican deportation program. This would be done with the hope of convincing the unemployed workers that it will correct the problem of unemployment without more drastic measures. Under these circumstances the Mexican unemployment problem would without doubt be aggravated by the explosive number of unemployed who probably would concentrate themselves in the Mexican border cities. If confronted by this possibility, Mexicans could expect neither help nor understanding from anyone.

House Bill H. R. 982, pet project of Congressman Peter Rodino (D-N.J.), which has been passed by the House of Representatives and is pending in the Senate, could be converted into a legal support to justify massive deportation of Mexicans. Campaigns have been organized to influence public opinion in case of such measures. Threatening remarks have been made that the Mexican immigrants represent a "silent invasion," an alien threat to United States employment.[53]

NOTES

1. Paul Fauconnet and Marcel Mauss, "La Sociologie, Objet et Methode," in M. Mauss, ed., *Essais de Sociologie* (Paris: Editions de Minuit, 1968). See also Georges Curvitch, *La Vocation Actuelle de la Sociologie*, 2 vols. (Paris: Presses Universitaires de France, 1950).

2. Teresa Rendón, "Estructura Económica y Empleo," in Sergio Alcántara and Teresa Rendón, *Empleo Rural en México* (Mexico City: El Colegio de México, forthcoming).

3. Ibid.

4. Jorge A. Bustamante, "El programa fronterizo de maquiladoras: observaciones para una evaluación," *Foro Internacional* 62 (1975): 183-204.

5. Rendón, "Estructura Económica."

6. Max Weber, *Wirtsehaft und Gesellschaft* (Tubingen: Verlag ron J. C. B. Mohr, 1925), p. 5.

7. Isaac Hourwich, *Immigration and Labor* (New York: E. P. Putnam's Sons, 1912).

8. Brindley Thomas, *Migration and Economic Growth* (Cambridge: Cambridge University Press, 1954).

9. Jorge A. Bustamante, "The Parsonization of Weber in American Sociology" (Paper presented in the American Sociological Association Annual Meeting, New Orleans, 1972).

10. U.S. Congress, Senate, Immigration Commission (Dillingham Commission), *Reports of the Immigration Commission,* 41 vol.: (Washington, D.C.: Government Printing Office, 1911), vol. 1, pp. 690-91.

11. Leo Grebler, et al., *The Mexican American People* (New York: The Free Press, 1970), p. 64.

12. Paul S. Taylor, *An American-Mexican Frontier: Nueces County Texas* (Chapel Hill: University of North Carolina Press, 1934), p. 105.

13. As quoted by Lamar B. Jones, "Mexican American Labor Problems in Texas" (Ph.D. diss., University of Texas, Austin, 1965), p. 15.

14. Ibid., p. 16.

15. Manuel Gamio, *Mexican Immigration to the United States* (New York: Dover Publications, 1971), p. 2.

16. Ibid., p. 10.

17. Arthur J. Rubel, *Across the Tracks, Mexican Americans in a Texas City* (Austin: University of Texas Press, 1966), pp. 41-45.

18. Carey McWilliams, *North from Mexico, The Spanish Speaking People of the United States* (New York: Greenwood Press, 1968), p. 58.

19. Jones, "Mexican American Labor Problems," p. 16.

20. Lyle Saunders and Olen F. Leonard, *The Wetback in the Lower Rio Grande Valley of Texas,* Inter-American Education Occasional Papers, no. 7 (Austin: University of Texas Press, 1951).

21. Eleanor M. Hadley, "A Critical Analysis of the Wetback Problem," in *Law and Contemporary Problems* 21 (1956): 334-57.

22. Jones, "Mexican American Labor Problems," pp. 18-21.

23. Abraham Hoffman, *Unwanted Mexican Americans in the Great Depression* (Tucson: University of Arizona Press, 1974). See also Mercedes Carreras de Velasco, *Los Mexicanos que devolvió la crisis 1929-1932* (Mexico City: Secretaría de Relaciones Exteriores, 1974).

24. *New York Times,* 28 November 1952; see also, Otey M. Scruggs, "Texas and the Bracero Program," *Pacific Historical Review* 32 (1963): 251-64.

25. General Swing's service record includes his participation in the "Pershing Expedition" that invaded Mexico in 1916.

26. John G. McBride, *Vanishing Bracero* (San Antonio, Texas: The Naylor Co., 1963), p. 5.

27. McWilliams, *North from Mexico,* p. 191.

28. U.S. Congress, House, *Hearings Before the Committee on Immigration and Naturalization, 1926,* (Washington, D.C.: Government Printing Office, 1926), pp. 20-24.

29. U.S. Senate, Subcommittee of the Senate Committee on the Judiciary S. 1917, Appropriation Hearings, 1953, p. 123 (Senator McCarran).

30. Gamio, *Mexican Immigration;* see Table XVI, figures for agriculture.

31. Saunders and Leonard, *The Wetback,* pp. 16-17.

32. Ibid.

33. *Report of the Select Commission on Western Hemisphere Immigration* (Washington, D.C.: Government Printing Office, 1968), p. 92.

34. Ernesto Galarza, *Merchants of Labor, The Mexican Bracero History* (Santa Barbara, Calif.: McNally and Loftin, 1964), pp. 47-48.

35. Ibid., pp. 251-54.

36. Ibid., p. 2.

37. Ibid., p. 3.

38. Ibid., p. 4.

39. *Report of the Select Commission on Western Hemisphere Immigration,* p. 101.

40. Julian Samora, *Los Mojados: The Wetback Story* (Notre Dame, Ind.: University of Notre Dame Press, 1971), pp. 51-55.

41. *Report of the Select Commission on Western Hemisphere Immigration,* p. 114.

42. Ibid., p. 16.

43. Ibid., p. 6.

44. Ibid., p. 9.

45. Ibid., p. 13.

46. Ibid., p. 12.

47. Galarza, *Merchants of Labor,* p. 4.

48. Luis Unikel, et al., *El Desarrollo urbano de México* (Mexico City: El Colegio de México, Centro de Estudios Económicos y Demográficos, 1974).

49. Centro de Investigaciones Agrarias, *Estructura agraria y desarrollo agrícola en México* (Mexico City: Fondo de Cultura Económica, 1974).

50. Ibid., p. 182.

51. David Ibarra, "Mercados, Desarrollo y Política Eonómica; Perspectivas de la Economía de México," in idem, et al., *El Perfil de México en 1980,* 2 vols. (Mexico City: Siglo XXI Editores, 1974), vol. 1, p. 118.

52. Ibid.

53. *New York Times,* 29 December 1974. See also *New York Times,* 24 December 1974.

10

Labor Market Aspects of Mexican Migration to the United States in the 1970s

Vernon M. Briggs, Jr.

Introduction

The migration of Mexican citizens to the United States has been a fact of life for as long as there has been a political border separating the two nations. During the latter half of the nineteenth century, the movement was only a trickle. But the magnitude increased significantly during most of the twentieth century. In fact, by the 1970s the migration has reached such magnitude that a congressional inquiry of economic conditions along the southern border of the nation succinctly characterized the situation as being ''a massive hemorrhage.''[1]

In 1973, there were 70,141 Mexicans admitted as legal immigrants to the United States. In that year, as has been the case in most years since 1960, the number of legal Mexican immigrants surpassed the total of any other single country in the world. The primary characteristic of the Mexican movement, however, is *not* legal migration but rather its overwhelming illegal aspect. During 1973, for example, there were 609,673 illegal aliens apprehended in the southwestern quadrant of the United States by the Immigration and Naturalization Service (INS) of the United States Department of Justice. Most of these apprehended individuals were Mexican. In fact, 88 percent of all illegal aliens apprehended in the United States in 1973 were of Mexican origin. To be sure, the apprehension figures are somewhat misleading in that there is doublecounting (i.e., the same individuals were arrested more than once during the year). But, when it is realized that those who are actually apprehended represent only a small fraction of the real flow, the essential thrust of the argument is not dulled. The INS has officially estimated that three million illegal aliens entered the United States undetected in 1973.[2] In addition, the INS estimates that there are between seven and twelve million illegal aliens currently residing in the United States.[3] Without fear of contradiction, it can be said that Mexicans are the majority of each category of illegal aliens—those apprehended each year; those not apprehended each year; and those who compose the accumulated number over the years who have gone undetected. As for labor market consequences, most illegal Mexicans enter the United States economy as adult workers whereas almost half of the legal Mexican immigrants come as dependents.

Brief Historical Overview

The vast land area that presently composes the American Southwest was acquired by conquest. This territory—approximately the size of India—was ceded to the United States under the terms of the Treaty of Guadalupe Hidalgo in 1848 which formally ended the Mexican-American War of 1846-48. An additional strip of land was bought from Mexico in 1853 (the Gadsden Purchase) after American railroad interests realized that the most practical route to California was in the Gila Valley (mostly in the present-day state of Arizona), which had not been included in the ceded territory.

The Mexican-American War was fought over land, not people. But as a result of the provisions of the treaty and the Gadsden Purchase, approximately seventy-five thousand people of Mexican citizenry were given the choice of becoming citizens of the United States or returning to Mexico.[4] Most elected to remain in the territory of their ancestors. Many believed that their land was only temporarily "occupied."[5] During the balance of the nineteenth century, fewer than thirty thousand Mexicans immigrated into this region.

It was not until the twentieth century that the number of migrating Mexicans became numerically significant. Between 1910 and 1930, an estimated 750,000 Mexicans legally migrated into the United States.[6] The short-run "push" force was the extreme violence that accompanied the civil war in Mexico that raged between 1910 and 1919. The immediate "pull" forces were the establishment and expansion of agricultural development throughout the American Southwest and the domestic labor shortage that occurred during World War I. Immigrants from Mexico were *excluded* from the National Origins Act of 1924, which set numerical quotas by nationality for immigrants from all non-Western Hemisphere nations.

During the 1930s the process was reversed. The mass unemployment in the

United States set forth a movement in the Southwest to "repatriate" Mexicans residing in the United States. The fact that many of these people had married American citizens or were eligible for citizenship but had not formally completed the immigration process was no barrier to those who believed it was necessary to reduce the regional labor pool. As it was, numerous destitute farmers from the "dust bowl" areas of Texas and Oklahoma were pouring into the agricultural labor market in California so that a new source of cheap labor was available and willing to work if jobs could be found. It was also during the 1930s that the first large-scale efforts to apprehend illegal aliens were launched. Over two hundred thousand such aliens (mostly Mexicans) were deported between 1930 and 1940.[7] These deportations were *in addition* to the several hundred thousand more who were forcibly "repatriated" during the same decade. Legal immigration from Mexico during the decade fell to about twenty-seven thousand.[8]

By the 1940s the situation had reversed itself. Economic conditions had changed markedly. The military requirements associated with World War II and its related manufacturing manpower needs led to a labor shortage in the agricultural sector. The agricultural interests of the Southwest had foreseen these developments prior to the Pearl Harbor attack in 1941. They made two fateful decisions: first, the pool of cheap labor in Mexico was to be tapped to fill the manpower deficit; second, the federal government was to be the vehicle of deliverance.[9]

The initial request of American growers for the establishment of a contract labor program was denied by the federal government in 1941. By mid 1942, however, the United States government favored the program but Mexico balked. The Mexican economy was flourishing; Mexican workers feared they might be drafted; there were bitter memories of the "repatriation drive" of the 1930s; and there was knowledge of the discriminatory treatment accorded people of Mexican ancestry throughout the Southwest. In addition, the unregulated hiring of Mexican citizens by foreign employers for work outside of Mexico is prohibited by Paragraph XXVI of Article 123 of the Mexican Constitution of 1917.

Negotiations between the two governments, however, resulted in a formal agreement being achieved in August 1942. The Mexican Labor Program, better known as the Bracero Program, was launched. Mexican workers were to be afforded numerous safeguards with respect to housing, transportation, food, medical needs, and wage rates. Initiated through appropriations for Public Law 45, the program was extended by subsequent enactment until 1947. For the growers the Bracero Program proved to be a bonanza.[10] *Braceros* were limited exclusively to agricultural work. Any *bracero* who was found holding a job in any other industry was subject to immediate deportation. When the agreement ended on December 31, 1947, the program was continued informally and was unregulated until 1951. In that year, under the guise of another war-related labor shortage, the Bracero Program was once again formalized by Public Law 78. This program continued until it was unilaterally terminated by the United States on December 31, 1964. Since then, the government of Mexico has made numerous proposals for its resumption but, to date, the United States has not acceded.[11] Several bills have been regularly introduced in the United States Congress by representatives of southwestern agricultural districts to revive the program, but they have yet to clear a congressional committee.

Paralleling the *bracero* years during the 1950s and early 1960s and following them since 1964 has been the mammoth flow of illegal Mexicans. Undoubtedly, many of these illegal aliens were former *braceros*. They had been attracted to the Mexican border towns from the rural interior of central and northern Mexico by the existence of the former contract labor program. To this degree, there is some truth to the proposition that the United States itself has created the illegal alien problem. By the same token, however, it is simplistic to conclude that the problem would not eventually have surfaced in the absence of the Bracero Program.

The Magnitude and Character of the Immigrant Flow

To gain perspective, it is useful to examine the statistics that indicate the magnitude of Mexican immigration over time. Table 1 in Chapter 8 shows the annual number of legal immigrants from Mexico to the United States since 1869. Table 2 in that same chapter presents the data on illegal entry from Mexico since 1924. Although Table 2 covers a much shorter time period, a comparison of the totals shows that the aggregate number of apprehended illegal Mexicans exceeds the aggregate number of legal immigrants by a ratio of better than 4 to 1. Indeed, the number of apprehended Mexican aliens has been in excess of the number of legal Mexican immigrants every year since 1930. But the gap has been widening perceptively in recent years with the ratio being larger than 8 to 1 in 1973.

In addition to the sheer numbers of people involved, it is necessary to note that the characteristics of the two groups of Mexican immigrants are quite different. The features of each category of migrants tells much about the consequence of the immigration process to the United States labor market. Looking first at the legal immigrants, it is necessary to place these Mexicans in the context of all legal immigrants. The immigration system of the United States since 1965 is designed to accomplish three goals: (1) to unify families; (2) to admit workers with skills that are in short supply; and (3) to permit entry to a small number of political refugees.[12] Since the end of World War II and with the enactment of major immigration statutes in 1952 and 1965, the characteristics of legal immigrants to the United States have tended to resemble the overall characteristics of the United States population.[13]

In many ways the legal immigrants from Mexico during the past twenty-five years have resembled the patterns for *all* legal immigrants to the United States. That is to say, the number of females slightly exceeds the number of males; the average age is somewhat younger; the marital status distribution is about the same; there is a strong preference for urban areas; and they have approximately the same labor force participation rate as is the United States average. There are, however, several important variations between legal Mexican immigrants and those from other countries. The foremost difference is their overwhelming preference to reside in one of the five southwestern states. Another factor is that legal Mexican immigrants have friends and relatives who are already citizens of the United States. But perhaps most important is the fact that legal Mexican immigrants tend to have a significantly different occupational distribution from that of legal entrants from other nations. While Mexican immigrants have backgrounds in most occupations, including skilled workers and professionals, a disproportionately high number are in blue-collar categories. Legal Mexican immigrants tend to have higher concentrations in craftsmen, household service workers, and both nonfarm and farm laborer categories.[14] The explanation for this occupational difference from other groups is likely to be due to the fact that a significant number of legal immigrants were once illegal aliens.

Turning to illegal Mexican immigrants, the statistical profile is, of course, more difficult to specify since the full dimensions and definitive characteristics of the movement are unknown. Even those apprehended often are reluctant to answer questions honestly. Nevertheless, from the limited available research, it is obvious that the illegal aliens have a distinctly different set of characteristics. Typically, the illegal alien from Mexico is male, usually unmarried, younger than thirty years of age, unskilled, from a rural area, poorly educated, speaks little if any English, is likely to be employed at least some time in the rural economy of the United States, and is most likely to be employed in an unskilled occupation as either a farm or nonfarm laborer.[15] The Immigration and Naturalization Service estimates that one-third of the illegal aliens from Mexico are employed in agriculture; another one-third in other goods-producing industries (especially meatpacking, auto-making, and construction); and one-third in service jobs.[16] These industrial employment patterns are quite distinct from the patterns for the American labor force.

As indicated earlier, there is a degree of interrelationship between the legal and illegal flows. Many illegal Mexican aliens later become legal immigrants through marriage to an American citizen; or by having a child born in the United States who is eligible for citizenship; or because the alien is able to make political connections with a sympathetic community organization or an influential employer who is willing to plead the alien's case. Should one of these circumstances occur, it is likely that the one-time illegal alien will qualify as a legal immigrant who can gain admission outside the established immigrant quota system.

The Causes of Mexican Migration

Most sizable migrations of human beings are the combined result of both "pull" and "push" forces. This has certainly been true of the movement of Mexicans. An analysis of the issue as well as the prescription of remedial policy measures should be cognizant of both.

The primary long-run "pull" force is the obvious difference between the economies of the United States and Mexico, which share a common border. Nowhere does a political border separate two nations with a greater economic disparity. In 1972, the Gross National Product of the United States was over $1.1 trillion; for Mexico it was $37 billion. The per capita income of the United States was $5,288 while in Mexico it was slightly above $707.[17] The vast economic disparity between the nations acts as a human magnet for both legal and illegal migrants. For most Mexican migrants, life in the United States by any barometer of human treatment will represent a considerable improvement over the life left behind.

A second factor is the immigration policy of the United States toward Mexico. With the brief exception of the Depression decade of the 1930s, it has been the demand for a cheap source of unskilled labor that has determined the policy of the United States. Mexicans have been welcomed as workers but not as settlers. The migration over the years has been geared to domestic labor policy (especially in agriculture) and not to a settlement process. The fact that United States policy in the 1970s is so tolerant of the wave of illegal entrants, so timid in the enforcement of its existing laws that prohibit illegal entry, and so hesitant to assume a posture of deterrence can lead only to the conclusion that the labor policy continues to dominate.[18]

A third factor is the cultural affinity that exists between Mexicans and Mexican Americans (called hereafter "Chicanos").[19] As indicated earlier there have been people of Hispanic ancestry living in what is now the southwestern United States long before there ever was a United States. Over the years, many others have come. In fact, the boundary between the United States and Mexico was an "open border" until 1924 when the Border Patrol was established and immigration restrictions were imposed for the first time. Even though Mexico was not included in the immigration quotas established by the Immigration Act of 1924, restrictions were imposed on the ease of entry of Mexicans and all other immigrants into the United States. It became for the first time a felony offense to enter the United States illegally. The flow of legal immigrants from Mexico has—with the exception of the 1930s—generally increased each year.

The Immigration Act of 1965 (which did not become effective until mid 1968) for the first time set a quota on the number of legal immigrants to be allowed from all Western Hemisphere nations. The figure was set at 120,000 with no more than 40,000 to be admitted from any single country. The actual number of immigrants each year from Western Hemisphere nations regularly exceeds these fixed maxima. This occurs because parents, spouses, and underage children of United States citizens are not counted in the quotas. Hence, for 1973, there was a total of 173,123 legal immigrants from the Western Hemisphere of whom 70,141 were legal immigrants from Mexico. Mexican immigration's share of the total from Western Hemisphere nations has increased each year since the imposition of the quota. In 1969, legal Mexican immigrants accounted for 29 percent of the total; by 1973, they were 40 percent of the total. Thus, the illegal Mexican aliens of the 1970s enter into a nation that already has a population in excess of 6.5 million Chicanos. Over 80 percent of these Chicanos reside in five states: California, Texas, New Mexico, Arizona, and Colorado. Most of the major cities in these five states already have sizable Chicano communities in which an immigrant or alien can find familiar food, language, cultural traditions, and, maybe, even friends or relatives.

A fourth "pull" factor is the anomaly of the current state of the law in the United States involving employment of illegal aliens.[20] It is against the law for an illegal alien to seek employment, but it is *not* against the law for an employer to hire an illegal alien. The Immigration and Nationality Act of 1952 made the importation and harboring of illegal aliens a felony. As a concession to Texas agricultural interests, however, the Act contains a section stating that employment and the related services provided by employers to employees (i.e., transportation, housing, or feeding) do not constitute an illegal act of harboring. The effect of this proviso is to make employers largely immune from prosecution if they hire alien workers. Thus, one of the most important barriers to effective control of illegal entrants is the fact that the act of employment of an illegal alien is not itself illegal. Since an employer incurs no risk, he is free to hire illegal aliens, which encourages a continuation of the human flow across the border. Because of the burgeoning dimensions of the issue, extensive public hearings were held by a sub-committee of the Committee on the Judiciary of the U.S. House of Representatives during 1971 and 1972. A bill that would require employers to make a "bona fide" effort to determine whether their employees are legal citizens of this country was passed by the House in 1972 (during the 92nd Congress) and again in 1973 (during the 93rd Congress) by overwhelming vote margins. The proposals (known popularly as the "Rodino bill" after the Chairman of the Subcommittee of the Committee of the Judiciary, Representative Peter W. Rodino [D-N.J.]) imposed sanctions against employers who "knowingly" hire illegal aliens. The penalties ranged from warnings to first-time offenders to fines and jail terms for repeat offenders. During both congressional sessions, the proposals died in the Senate. The chairman of the appropriate Senate committee, Senator James Eastland (D-Miss.) refused even to convene a subcommittee meeting to discuss the House bill. An explanation for this intransigence has been offered by Representative Leo J. Ryan (D-Calif.), who observed: "Members of the Senate represent a constituency which has a vested interest in no changes. The agriculture economy is based on the use of illegal aliens at a fairly low wage."[21]

As for the illegal aliens themselves, it is only an unimportant technicality that the law makes it a punishable offense for them to seek employment in the United States. Over 95 percent of those aliens who are apprehended by the INS are simply returned to Mexico by the most expedient form of transportation. Less than 5 percent of the illegal Mexicans are subjected by the INS to formal deportation proceedings that would render any subsequent entry a felony.[22] More frequent prosecution could serve as a deterrent. Neither Congress nor the president has believed to date that the issue warrants a sufficient increase in the number of hearing officers to raise the level of prosecutions significantly. As a result, those aliens allowed to leave through the voluntary departure system are in no way deterred from returning at will.

Thus, a realistic appraisal of the current situation is that if an illegal alien is caught, he is simply returned to his native land; if he is not apprehended, he works at a job that affords him an income higher than his alternatives in Mexico. For the businessman there is no risk of loss; there are only gains from tapping a cheap source of labor completely bound to his arbitrary terms of employment.

The Immigration and Nationality Act of 1952 expressly states that it is national policy to reserve available jobs for the domestic labor force. Referring to this Act, the California Court of Appeals ruled in 1970 that the number of illegal aliens in the Southwest "represent an abject failure of national policy." Moreover, the court observed that the lack of meaningful corrective action "must be ascribed to self-imposed impotence of our national government."[23]

The prevailing legal charade took an even more incredible twist in 1974. The Commissioner of Immigration, Leonard F. Chapman, issued an order that illegal aliens apprehended outside of the actual border area itself would no longer be detained or returned to their homelands.[24] The only exception would be those situations in which an alien was apprehended in connection with the commission of a crime. Furthermore, investigations of charges of the presence of illegal aliens would not be made unless the individual case involved at least fifty aliens. The commissioner cited the reasons for this action to be both a chronic shortage of funds and manpower. Of the scant 1,600 persons in the Border Patrol in late 1974, 1,350 were assigned to the entire length of the Mexican border.[25] The result of this action was twofold. First, it manifested a policy that if a Mexican alien could successfully pass through the border region he was essentially "home free." Second, it meant that border areas in other geographic regions were only minimally monitored if at all. Thus, the concentration on the Mexican border essentially left wide open the opportunities for non-Mexican illegal aliens to enter the United States in other regions with relative ease.[26] In March 1975, however, Congress passed an emergency appropriation to provide funds so that apprehension activities could be resumed.[27]

There is a fifth "pull" factor that is of minor significance in comparison with the aforementioned forces, yet it is of some consequence: namely, the lure of what is perceived to be "a promised land."[28] There are "word-of-mouth" accounts of better job opportunities, high wages, and improved living conditions that circulate from returnees and from letters containing remittances to family members who remain behind. These tales are often exaggerated or, at least, tend to minimize negative aspects. Nonetheless, it remains true that in purely economic terms, life in the United States is likely to offer far more options than the arduous and stifling prospects of perpetual poverty for most who choose to remain in northern and central Mexico.

When we turn to the long-run "push" factors, there are some surprises in store for us. Contrary to what one might expect, the impetus for outward migration from Mexico in the 1970s is not because the Mexican economy is stagnant. In fact, for the past decade Mexico has had the fastest rate of economic growth of any country in all of Latin America. The Gross National Product since the late 1960s has been increasing annually at a rate of 6 percent or more, with per capita income increasing annually at about 3 percent a year.[29] Yet, the Mexican economy is organized on a basis of state-regulated capitalism whereby most of the benefits of industrialization accrue disproportionately to the small upper-income sector. Pitifully little filters down to the vast lower-income group.[30] Thus, the massive migration of Mexicans (who are mostly from this lower-income strata) represents a safety valve for the Mexican government which reduces the potential for internal problems that could arise from its maldistribution of income and its surplus labor force. The Mexican economy is moving from an agricultural and handicraft phase into an industrial and technological stage. The political regime in Mexico feels it needs time to complete this transition. Moreover, the illegal aliens frequently bring back or send portions of their earnings which, in the aggregate, amount to a substantial sum of American dollars. As a result, illegal entry is one important way to gain desperately needed foreign exchange and to help Mexico's external balance of trade.

But despite the fact that the Mexican economy is growing, it remains a semideveloped country. For many, extreme poverty is the way of life.[31] Unemployment rates in Mexican cities that border the United States consistently hover in the 30 to 40 percent range. For many farmers and agricultural workers in Mexico's central and northern states, a hundred days of employment a year is the most that can be expected. When work is available, it is often of a hard physical nature for which the monetary reward is but a pittance. The minimum wage in Mexico's border cities—although varying from locality to locality—is seldom more than one-third of the *minimum* wage across the border in the United States.

Even at this low level, violations of the minimum wage law by Mexican employers is reported to be widespread.[32] Mexico's birth rate is among the highest in the world (about 3.6 percent a year). The available adult work force in Mexico will almost double between 1970 and 1980. Over 23 percent of the population is estimated to be illiterate. Droughts, pestilence, and diseases are common throughout the rural states. Housing is poor and frequently of a makeshift variety. Inadequate diets and malnutrition cause pervasive health problems. Unfortunately, many influential Mexican citizens and officials manifest little concern toward the plight of most of the poor. As one observer recently succinctly wrote:

Mexico is changing rapidly but too much of her past remains to haunt her. Quite aside from the population growth rate, there is another dimension: Too many upper and middle-class Mexicans lack a sense of national responsibility; too many adhere to the tradition of caring only for themselves and their immediate families and not about where their country is going; too many continue through tax loopholes and flagrant violations of Mexican law, to live with privilege that undercuts any destiny of equalitarianism, a notion as alien to many rich Mexicans as it was a century ago to the robber barons of the United States.[33]

This attitude is clearly seen by the refusal of the government of Mexico to consider the idea of accepting direct foreign aid to reduce the level of human cruelty within the nation. The ''national pride'' of the small affluent class that tightly controls the political system of Mexico is largely oblivious to internal pleas for reform and contemptuous of external offers of direct assistance. All things considered, therefore, it is understandable why many rural peasants and urban slum dwellers would seek to flee from the grinding poverty that is to many their destiny for as long as they remain in their homeland. The migration process is not seen by the participants as anything illegal or immoral. To the contrary, the topic is discussed openly and the procedures have been both regularized and ritualized. The process is often viewed as an accepted part of the fate of poor people.[34]

Closely associated with the pace of industrialization and incidence of poverty factors is the existence of a strong trend throughout Mexico of rural to urban migration. In 1970, 41.3 percent of Mexico's population resided in rural areas. The internal migrations have been toward two destinations: Mexico City and the northern cities located along the border with the United States. The aggregate population of the eight largest border towns of Mexico has increased by 44 percent in the decade between 1960 and 1970. The growth rate of parallel United States border cities during this same interval has also been very high (21 percent), and their growth is *not* unrelated to Mexican migration. The Mexican border towns, however, were mostly poverty stricken to begin with. The stacking-up of the poor rural migrants who have piled into these border cities has completely overriden the ability of these municipalities to provide a semblance of community services.[35] It is not surprising then that there is literally no interest in these cities for the Mexican government to undertake to stop the outflow. From the public services standpoint, any slowdown in the rate of migrants who settle in their cities is viewed as being beneficial. By the same token, there is a substantial amount of private sector business activity in these Mexican cities that thrives on the alien traffic. Numerous individuals and groups are involved in the smuggling of human beings into the United States: the forgery of identification papers (Social Security cards, resident alien cards, drivers' licenses, passports); loan-sharking (the practice of charging exorbitant interest rates on loans or credit extensions given to cover the charges by smugglers and document forgers); the recruitment of women for prostitution activities in the United States; the trafficking in drugs; and the arrangement of ''phony'' marriages with American citizens.[36]

Thus, when the ''pull'' and ''push'' forces are combined, the accumulated momentum for illegal entry is so strong that it may already be impossible for public policy to control even if an effort were to be made. The dire warning of the INS Commissioner, Raymond F. Farrell, in 1971 that the problem of illegal entry into the United States ''has grown progressively worse'' and his woeful prediction for the future that ''border violations will continue to mount'' has proven to be the voice of Cassandra.[37] In fact, by 1971 the successor to Farrell, Commissioner Leonard Chapman, publicly exclaimed that the United States is ''being overrun by illegal aliens'' and, as bad as the prevailing situation is, he warned that ''we are seeing just the beginning of the problem.''[38]

The Consequences of Mexican Migration

In general, the impact of immigration from all nations of the world upon the labor market of the United States in the 1970s has *not* been well understood. Since the Immigration Act of 1965 became effective in 1968, there have been about four hundred thousand legal immigrants admitted to the country annually. Of these it is estimated that approximately two hundred thousand legal immigrants enter the United States labor market each year.[39] In the early 1970s they accounted for about 12 percent of the annual increase in the labor force. These legal immigrants exert a ''substantial impact'' because their presence is unevenly felt: affecting cities more than suburbs and rural areas; some states more than others; and some occupations more than others.[40]

Legal Mexican immigrants have exerted significant influence upon the labor markets of the major cities of the southwestern United States, the states of California and Texas, and the blue-collar and service occupations. Except for several specific border communities, the impact of the legal immigrants from Mexico, however, has yet to become an unmanageable problem.

The consequences of the migration of the illegal Mexicans, however, is an entirely different story. The massive flow of illegal immigrants has had, is having, and will continue to cause a serious disruption in the normal labor force adjustment processes throughout the Southwest and, increasingly, in a number of northern cities. The illegal Mexican aliens constitute a body of workers who are typically dependent upon the terms of employment dictated by an employer. The aliens, usually grateful for what they receive, are willing to work long, hard, and for low pay. They have become a "shadow labor force"—especially in the Southwest—whose presence is often felt but seldom seen. In the industries in which they congregate, they depress wages and working conditions to such a degree that citizen workers cannot compete with them. The citizen worker must either choose to work and live as the illegal alien; or move to another region; or seek—if he can—another occupation.[41]

Historically, the impact of the illegal Mexican immigrant has been felt in the rural economy of the Southwest. Having typically come from a rural background with little knowledge of either urban work skills or of the English language, it was easier for the illegal alien to find employment in the rural areas. Moreover, the rural southwestern United States is a vast land area composed of small population clusters. The climate is dry and water is scarce. The population pattern has been referred to as being "an oasis society."[42] Hence, the large agricultural growers and ranchers have usually not been able to draw upon a labor supply in their local areas. Their needs are especially acute during planting and harvesting seasons when there is a requirement for large numbers of workers. The growers and ranchers have been more than willing to employ the cheap and totally dependent illegal aliens to meet their manpower needs. Sad to say, there are numerous accounts of illegal aliens being paid wages below prescribed minimum wage levels; of employers who deduct but do not transmit social security taxes; and of employers who report their alien workers to immigration authorities prior to the time they would collect their pay. In this way the aliens, who themselves deprive citizen workers of jobs at decent pay levels, are often victimized by unscrupulous employers who know that the aliens have no recourse to justice. As one government official, who has decried the widespread abuses and exploitation of the aliens, has stated: "Nobody gives a damn since aliens are nobody's constituents."[43]

Another serious impact of the illegal Mexican nationals upon the rural economy of the Southwest is that, since the 1940s, they have been a factor in the pressure for Chicanos to move from rural to urban areas.[44] In the 1950 and 1960 censuses, the Chicano population was the least urbanized of the major racial groups who populate the Southwest. The census of 1970, however, shows Chicanos to be the most urbanized group. Often these Chicanos who have been displaced from the rural economy have been totally unprepared for their new life in an urban labor market. In this way, the illegal Mexican aliens have caused serious economic hardship and geographic dislocation to the Chicano labor force of the rural Southwest.

The illegal Mexican aliens have had another adverse effect upon the citizen Chicanos. It is no accident that about half of the remaining seasonal migratory agricultural workers in the United States are Chicanos who come from the south Texas-Mexican border region. Many Chicanos of this region are literally *forced* to join the migratory labor force because the local labor market is overrun by illegal Mexican aliens and border commuters (i.e., people who live in Mexico with its lower cost of living but, because of ambiguities in the immigration statutes, are able to work legally in the United States).[45] Although public policy in the United States has tried repeatedly to improve the economic plight of these citizen migrant workers by trying to prepare them for nonmigrant vocations, all attempts have failed. The reason is that the programs have never been able to handle the basic problem that causes internal migrancy, namely, there are too few job opportunities available in their home base communities that offer wages at a level that will permit a decent standard of life. The depressing forces caused by the influx of illegal Mexican immigrants and by the border commuters have set in motion a process whereby poor Mexicans make poor Chicanos poorer.[46]

The illegal Mexican aliens have been a continuing force to forestall efforts of workers in low-wage industries of the Southwest to become unionized. Often their presence so depresses wages and working conditions that citizen workers who might otherwise seek to establish a trade union are forced to look elsewhere for employment. In the event that the citizen workers remain in the industry and attempt to form a union, the illegal Mexican aliens are frequently used as strikebreakers. Although numerous instances could be cited, the most prominent contemporary example is the on-going saga of the United Farm Workers (UFW) to establish a union for agricultural workers throughout the Southwest. César Chávez, the leader of the UFW, has repeatedly charged that employers are using illegal Mexican aliens as strikebreakers.[47] Chávez has stated that it is primarily because of the inability to keep Mexican aliens out of the fields that his union has had to appeal for a nationwide boycott as the only effective method to exert pressure on employers for bargaining recognition.[48]

Since the mid 1960s, however, a growing number of illegal Mexican immigrants have gone directly to urban areas to find low-skilled jobs. The more experienced illegal aliens have found that the urban areas often pay more, the work is less arduous, and, especially in the Southwest, it is just as easy to get ''lost'' in the urban barrio as it is in the open spaces of the rural areas. Also, agriculture is becoming more and more mechanized, which means that the labor requirements have been diminishing in rural areas.

In the urban areas, the illegal aliens typically move into the low-wage sector of the economy, which makes an already desperate situation even worse for the citizen workers with whom they compete. The illegal aliens, however, do not restrict themselves just to menial jobs. Increasingly, craftsmen and other skilled and semiskilled positions are being taken. Craft unions in the Southwest, especially in the building trades, have begun to campaign actively for tighter restrictions. The competition in the urban areas is not only for jobs but it is also for limited amounts of low-income housing, welfare funds, classroom space, public health facilities, and community services.

The group that directly suffers the most is the citizen Chicano of the Southwest. For decades this racial and ethnic minority group has been struggling against pervasive discrimination and seeking economic assimilation into American life. Now, in the aftermath of the civil rights revolution of the 1960s, they have come closer than ever before to the attainment of this elusive goal only to see their gains eroded by the unfair competition of alien workers from Mexico.[49]

Indirectly, of course, the United States itself suffers from the existence of an increasing number of illegal Mexicans in its midst. There may be some short-run private sector gains that are realized by the selfish exploitation of this helpless group. But in the long run, the presence of a growing number of workers who are denied political rights as well as minimum legal and job protection is a sure prescription for eventual trouble. It is easy to foresee a situation that will not only be out of control but that soon will be uncontrollable when a large number of workers are living under the constant fear of being detected, working in the most competitive and least unionized sectors of the economy, and often being victimized by criminal elements.

Over the two centuries of its existence, the United States has developed numerous laws, programs, and institutions that have sought to reduce the magnitude of human cruelty and the incidence of economic uncertainty for the majority of its citizens. For the illegal alien workers, however, these benefits are virtually nonexistent. It would be an exercise in self-deception to believe that this situation can continue at this current growth rate without eventual dire consequences to all concerned.

Conclusions and Policy Recommendations

The current migration of Mexicans into the United States represents one of the major population inflows in the nation's history. The most prominent characteristic of this mass migration is its illegal and unregulated character.

Furthermore, it is clear that neither the Mexican or United States governments are willing to acknowledge the importance of the problem. Mexico has been content merely to complain about alleged abuses of some illegal aliens who have been arrested and detained by American authorities and to propose that a contract labor program similar to the old Bracero Program be reformalized. The United States government has, tragically, shown no inclination to recognize the ramifications of the issue. Unfortunately, illegal entry from Mexico is still considered to be only ''a regional problem'' of the Southwest. Hence, the topic has not been very high on the list of national priorities.

The immigration policy of the United States with respect to legal and illegal Mexicans has never functioned in a vacuum. The policy has been related to domestic economic policy (more concern during periods of high unemployment, less during times of low unemployment), labor policy (a strong interest in Mexicans as temporary and seasonal workers for low-wage industries, less concern for them as permanent settlers), and racial policy (Mexicans are a racial and ethnic minority group who over the years have been treated in a discriminatory manner). For these reasons it is not easy to untangle the current problem from its historical evolution.

It is argued by some that the focus of attention should be upon workers as workers and not as workers of one nation versus workers of another nation. In the 1970s when multinational corporations move their products and funds with relative ease across international borders and when financiers speculate daily over anticipated changes in foreign currency rates, workers should not be divided by artificial political boundaries. There is, of course, some abstract support for this position in standard free-trade economic theory. The unimpeded movement of the world's economic resources supposedly assures that they will find their most rewarding and productive use and, thereby, maximize world output. But standard economic theory is essentially a form of social engineering in which individual differences of people and nations are minimized in the pursuit of aggregate social maximization. In the real world, political boundaries shape the conditions of life within the various nation states of the world community. It is largely within the confines of these boundaries that most of the crucial governmental policies that affect the quality of life for the citizens of each nation are made. Nominally there may be a world community, but the welfare of most people is dependent upon the decisions of their own government. They expect their government to safeguard and to further their interests as best as it can. Consequently, the study of political economy—as has always been the case—begins with the existence of political borders.

There are a number of policy measures that are urgently needed. With respect to legal Mexican immigrants, one problem is that their impact is unevenly felt. Specific cities and states have been hard hit. To assist in the absorption of these new citizens, the federal government should provide "special impact" funds to school districts and community organizations that assist these immigrants in the settlement process. Ample precedent for such funding exists in the form of similar programs to help those areas in which large military bases or related defense organizations are located. In addition, special programs should be initiated in these high-impact areas to assist immigrants to learn of existing legal protections for them; to make available information about training facilities and job placement centers; and to offer special classes in English with ample financial stipends for attendance.

Another needed reform relates to the labor certification procedures associated with new immigrants. Since the Immigration and Nationality Act of 1952, the Secretary of Labor has had the authority to block entry of immigrants if their presence endangers prevailing American labor standards. The Immigration Act of 1965 expanded this authority. It requires that a shortage of workers exist in the applicant's particular occupation and that his or her presence will not adversely affect prevailing wages and working conditions. Aside from the fact that the entire procedure is fraught with loopholes, the problem is that the certification is made only *once*—when the initial application for immigration is made. It has been suggested that a negative certification be adopted to assure that in actuality the legal immigrant workers do not seek employment in overcrowded occupations, or economically depressed areas, or serve as strikebreakers, or become employees of certain employers with histories of illegal activities.[50] The system would set up a probationary period of, say a year, during which time it could be ascertained whether the certification system has too many loopholes to be meaningful. In a 1971 study of the topic, it was found that only one of every thirteen immigrants to the United States was subject to the certification system.[51]

In the 1970s it is, of course, the illegal Mexican aliens that constitute the major labor migration flow into the United States. The problem is already of such a magnitude that it may not even be possible to reduce it to manageable proportions. But the effort *must* be made. The presence of "a shadow labor force" of rightless individuals who are easy prey for the most exploitative elements of American society is bad for both the aliens and the nation. But of even greater consequence than the victimization of these illegal aliens is that, collectively, they constitute a clear and present danger to the standard of living of all with whom they compete for jobs, housing, and community services. In particular, the Chicano citizens of the Southwest have borne disproportionately the weight of this burden. If left unchecked, other groups and other geographic areas will increasingly feel this pressure.

For these reasons, a number of policy changes are required. It is, for example, absurd that employers are virtually immune from prosecution when they employ illegal aliens. Legislation making it a criminal act to employ these aliens should be adopted at once. This can only be done at the federal level since immigration policy is considered to be solely the province of the federal government. Two states—California and Connecticut—passed laws making it unlawful for an employer to hire illegal aliens, only to have them declared unconstitutional. The Rodino bill, mentioned earlier, does impose sanctions and criminal penalties for repeat offenders among employers who "knowingly" hire illegal aliens. Although "knowingly" would undoubtedly be hard to prove, this legislation is an essential first step if any serious effort is to be made to address this issue. Such a sanction would at least place the moral weight of the government and of society against those employers who would violate its provisions. The situation would be analogous to Title VII of the Civil Rights Act of 1964 which bans employment discrimination. As important as that statute is, it has not made it any easier to prove an act of discrimination in an individual circumstance. But the Act does put the moral weight of the government on the side of antidiscrimination and, although extensive attention has been given to the Act's shortcomings, it remains true that there has been an amazing degree of voluntary compliance. Likewise, a Rodino-type statute can only strengthen efforts to assure that immigration policy is not used as a source of cheap workers lacking the most basic rights and who threaten the welfare of citizen workers or retard attempts to do away with low-paying and exploitive jobs by supplying additional workers for these positions. There are legitimate fears by some minority groups—especially some militant Chicano organizations—concerning the possibility of abuse of such legislation.[52] But, having noted these areas of potential trouble, it should be possible to exercise sufficient vigilance to assure that such distortions of legislative purpose do not occur.

There has been an alternative legislative proposal that has been offered to the Rodino bill. This proposal, submitted by Senator Edward Kennedy (D-Mass.) in 1974, has more severe civil penalties, in the form of fines against employers who hire illegal aliens, than those included in the Rodino bill, but it contains no criminal penalties or jail terms as does the Rodino proposal. Moreover, the Kennedy bill would extend a virtual amnesty to all illegal aliens currently in the country who have been here for at least three years. The latter aspect of the proposed legislation has gained much support from religious and community organizations. It has been strongly opposed, however, by the INS, which feels that the offer of one amnesty could only lead to additional offers in the future. Hence, they believe that the legislation would backfire by actually promoting alien migration over the long run. To date, the Kennedy bill has been bottled up in a Senate subcommittee.

In addition to sanctions against employers, there is a vital need to increase the manpower and the budget of the INS to a level commensurate with the scale of its responsibilities. The increase not only should be to hire additional staff for patrolling and apprehension duties but also for hearing officers and qualified prosecutors. The use of "the voluntary departure system" by INS should be actively discouraged. Records and identification of all arrestees should be made. Jail terms should be imposed on repeat offenders. In these ways, a posture of deterrence rather than acquiescence could be assumed. At the same time a concerted drive should be initiated by INS in the cities in which illegal aliens are known to reside to apprehend and to return them to their native land. All appropriate civil liberty protections should be applied to be sure that no false arrest or mistaken deportations occur. But the message should be made clear: illegal alien workers from any country are unwanted guests. Concurrently with these efforts, other loopholes in the existing immigration policies which tolerate daily and seasonal commuter workers from Mexico should also be corrected.[53]

Last, but of extreme importance, the United States should make overtures to Mexico concerning how efforts could be made to develop the economy of Mexico's northern states. Financial and technical aid should be made available. Mexico, however, should design the regional plan and set its own priorities. If the government of Mexico decides that it wants no part of such aid, then so be it. But it should be made apparent that a continuation of the existing unregulated exodus of its citizens is out of the question.

By this time, it should be obvious that this issue does not lend itself to any "nice" solution. In fact, illegal immigration into the United States is not a problem but a dilemma for policymakers. There is absolutely no answer that will make everyone better off. For, in addition to the economic factors involved, there are also complex moral, political, social, and diplomatic considerations. But no matter how many variables are placed in the final equation, the stark reality of the situation remains: unless coupled with a massive foreign aid program by the United States to develop jointly the economy of northern Mexico, hundreds of thousands of human beings are going to suffer no matter what is done or not done. Without such assistance, the steps proposed that call for more restrictive border policies mean that many of the would-be illegal Mexican aliens are condemned to lives of squalor. On the other hand, if the prevailing situation is allowed to continue, thousands of citizen workers (mostly Chicanos at present) will continue to work under deteriorating conditions in a generally surplus labor market. There are numerous human policy alternatives available to assist migrant workers when the problem is excess demand for labor that causes the migrant flow. There are literally none when the problem is one of labor surplus. The sooner the nation recognizes the policies that are needed, the easier will be the eventual adjustment. The fundamental question is not *whether* the government of the United States should act, but rather *when* it will and in *what* manner.

NOTES

1. Senator Walter F. Mondale, Chairman of the Subcommittee on Migratory Labor of the U.S. Senate Committee on Labor and Public Welfare, "Manpower and Economic Problems," in *Hearings on Migrant and Seasonal Farmworker Powerlessness,* pt. 7-B (Washington, D.C.: Government Printing Office, 1970), p. 4548.

2. "Illegal Aliens Put at 3 Million," *New York Times,* 27 January 1974.

3. "Statement by Leonard F. Chapman, Commissioner, Immigration and Naturalization Service," mimeographed (Chicago, 1974), p. 2. See also, "Address by the Honorable William B. Saxbe, Attorney General of the United States, before the Cameron County and Hidalgo County Bar Associations," mimeographed (Brownsville, Texas, 1974), p. 2.

4. Carey McWilliams, *North From Mexico* (New York: Greenwood Press, Inc., 1968), p. 52.

5. Rodolfo Acuña, *Occupied America* (San Francisco: Canfield Press, 1972), pp. 29ff.

6. Julian Samora, "Mexican Immigration" in Gus Tyler, ed., *Mexican-Americans Tomorrow: Educational and Economic Perspectives* (Albuquerque: University of New Mexico Press, 1975), p. 68 (Table 2).

7. Ibid., p. 69 (Table 3).

8. Ibid.

9. Ernesto Galarza, *Merchants of Labor: The Mexican Bracero Story* (Charlotte, N.C.: McNally and Loftin Publishers, 1964).

10. McWilliams, *North From Mexico,* p. 267.

11. See "Mexico to Seek Farm Labor Pact," *New York Times,* 12 June 1973.

12. David S. North and William G. Weissert, *Immigrants and the American Labor Market* (Washington, D.C.: Trans-Century Corporation, 1973), pp.7-8. See also Elliott Abrams, and Franklin S. Abrams, "Immigration Policy—Who Gets In and Why?" *The Public Interest* 38 (1975): 3-29.

13. Abrams and Abrams. "Immigration Policy," pp.24-25.

14. North and Weissert, *Immigrants and the American Labor Market,* pp. 47-48.

15. Julian Samora, *Los Mojados: The Wetback Story* (Notre Dame, Ind.: University of Notre Dame Press, 1971), ch. 2.

16. Robert F. Mathieson, "Influx of Illegal Aliens and the Unemployment Rate," *Houston Chronicle,* 3 January 1975.

17. The figures cited for the economy of the United States and Mexico are taken, respectively, from the *Economic Report of the President: 1973* (Washington, D.C.: Government Printing Office, 1973) and *Economic and Social Progress in Latin America: Annual Report 1973* (Washington, D.C.: Inter-American Development Loan Bank, 1973).

18. Vernon M. Briggs, Jr., *The Mexican-United States Border: Public Policy and Chicano Economic Welfare,* Studies in Human Resources Development, no. 2 (Austin, Texas: Center for Studies in Human Resources, 1974), pp. 10-11.

224 *Vernon M. Briggs, Jr.*

19. The word "Chicano" is increasingly being used in the United States to refer to the group of citizens generally called "Mexican Americans" in the literature. Militant Chicanos prefer the term because it accentuates the fact that many of them feel they are treated as Mexicans in the United States but as Americans in Mexico. Most young Chicanos believe that the word "chicano" derived from the Indian pronunciation of the word "Mexicano," "Meh-shee-cano," which, over the years, came to be shortened to "Chicano." Américo Paredes believes, on the basis of his study of the matter, that "chicano" is a shortened and affectionate version of "mexicano."

20. Briggs, *The Mexican-United States Border,* pp. 10-15.

21. "Illegal Aliens Earn $10 Billion a Year, Investigator Says," *New York Times,* 11 December 1974.

22. U. S. Congress, House, Committee on the Judiciary, Subcommittee No. 1, *Hearings on Illegal Aliens,* pt. 5 (Washington, D.C.: Government Printing Office, 1972), p. 1315.

23. Diaz v. Kay-Dix Ranch (1970), as reprinted in House of Representatives, *Hearings on Illegal Aliens,* pt. 1 (Washington, D.C.: Government Printing Office, 1971), p. 179.

24. Margaret Gentry, "U.S. Curbs Pursuit of Illegal Aliens," *Washington Post,* 24 October 1974.; see also "Statement by Leonard F. Chapman," p. 3.

25. "Statement by the Honorable William B. Saxbe," p. 8.

26. M. A. Farber, "Million Illegal Aliens in Metropolitan Area," *New York Times,* 29 December 1974.

27. "Funds Restored in Alien Searches," *New York Times,* 16 March 1975.

28. Samora, *Los Mojados,* p. 10.

29. Alejandro Portes, "Return of the Wetback," *Society* 11 (1974): 44.

30. Ibid.

31. For a good discussion of these economic conditions in the Mexican border cities, see Liborio V. Caldron, "Foreign Assembly Industries in Mexico: A Necessary Evil of an Underdeveloped Society," mimeographed; Giorgio Berni, "Border Industry: The Case of Ciudad Juárez, Chihuahua," mimeographed; and David Barkin, "Mexico's Albatross: The United States Economy," mimeographed (Papers presented at the Conference on Economic Relations Between Mexico and the United States, sponsored by the U.S. Department of State and the Institute of Latin American Studies of the University of Texas at Austin, Austin, Texas, April 16-20, 1973).

32. Richard Severo, "The Flight of the Wetbacks," *New York Times Magazine,* 10 March 1974.

33. Ibid.

34. Samora, *Los Mojados,* chs. 3 and 4.

35. Ibid., pp. 9-10.

36. Jack Webb, "People-Smuggling Racket is $125 Million Business," *Austin Statesman,* 29 May 1972,; idem, " 'Hide-and-Seek' Keeps Border Patrol on Guard," *Austin Statesman,* 30 May 1973; "Sometimes Death Waits Along Live Cargo Route," *Austin Statesman,* 31 May 1973; "Judge Sees Wire Fence as Way to Stop Racket," *Austin Statesman,* 1 June 1973. See also "Aliens Pay for Spouses," *The Austin American-Statesman,* 16 March 1975; M. A. Farber, "Unlawful Aliens Use Costly City Services" *New York Times,* 30 December 1974; and Evan Maxwell, "U.S.-Mexico Smuggling: The Buying and Selling of Humans," *Los Angeles Times,* 22 February 1977.

37. Michael Mallory, "Human Wave of Mexicans Splashes Across Border," *National Observer,* 16 October 1971.

38. "Can't Stop Alien Flood, Official Says," *San Antonio Express,* 23 October 1974.

39. North and Weissert, *Immigrants,* p. 2.

40. Ibid., p. x.

41. Samora, *Los Mojados,* p. 56.

42. Fred H. Schmidt, *Spanish Surnamed American Employment in the Southwest* (Washington, D.C.: Government Printing Office, 1970), p. 50.

43. E.g., see Laura A. Kierman, "5 Deported Aliens Sue for Md. Wages," *Washington Post,* 23 September 1974.

44. Vernon M. Briggs, Jr., *Chicanos and Rural Poverty* (Baltimore: The Johns Hopkins University Press, 1973), ch. 4.

45. Ibid., pp. 42-44.

46. Briggs, *The Mexican-United States Border,* pp. 10-21.

47. See "Chávez Charges Scheme," *Washington Post,* 23 September 1974.

48. Severo, "The Flight of the Wetbacks," p. 81.

49. George I. Sánchez, "History, Culture, and Education," in *La Raza: The Forgotten Americans* (Notre Dame, Ind.: University of Notre Dame Press, 1966).

50. North and Weissert, *Immigrants,* pp. 178-80.

51. David S. North, *Alien Workers: A Study of the Labor Certification Programs* (Washington, D.C.: Trans-Century Corporation, 1971), pp. 95-96.

52. E.g., see Briggs, *The Mexican-United States Border,* pp. 11-12.

53. Ibid., pp. 15-21.

11

Foreign Policy Aspects of the Border

Tad Szulc

Even as you read this, seven or eight thousand Mexican nationals are illegally entering the United States each day in search of work and, hopeful but uncertain, of a better life. And, for all we know, the daily illegal crossings may even run as high as ten thousand. The best estimate, vague as it remains, is that *three million* Mexicans surreptitiously entered the United States in 1974—the total was even higher in 1975 as Mexico's economic situation, affected by the American recession, tended to worsen.

Let us ponder for a moment the meaning of these staggering figures. Three million represents *5 percent* of Mexico's total population. It is nearly one-half the population of New York City. It is equivalent to the entire population of the Greater Washington Metropolitan Area. If one cares for military comparisons, it is the equivalent of 150 army divisions. Unquestionably, the illegal Mexican migrations to the United States are the greatest *peacetime* population dislocations in contemporary history. If one is to search for wartime analogies, only the movement of displaced persons at the end of the Second World War and the flight of refugees in South Vietnam are numerically comparable to what is happening on the American-Mexican border. And, in a sense, the Mexican situation is even worse: refugee movements tend to run their course in a fairly limited time period. The Mexican phenomenon is permanent—no end is in sight.

A few more statistics to spotlight the magnitude of the problem: federal calculations are that there are some seven million illegal aliens in the United States—the Immigration and Naturalization Service believes that the total of illegal aliens is somewhere between four and twelve million, which shows that nobody really knows the truth. The seven million figure is simply an acceptable extrapolation. In the same way, it is estimated that around 85 percent of it are illegal Mexican migrants: something on the order of *six million*. In addition, close to one million Mexicans live and work legally in the United States.

The assumption that three million or so Mexicans may enter the United States illegally this year is based on the Immigration Service's rule-of-thumb count that for each illegal immigrant apprehended in this country and returned to Mexico, two immigrants or more manage to escape repatriation. The returns in 1974 were nearly six hundred thousand, which would suggest that there were around 1.8 million illegal entries. But immigration specialists say that more than one million must be added to this number—to arrive at the three million count—because in the last two years the Immigration and Naturalization Service has virtually given up its efforts to find and round up illegal aliens in inland urban areas. It has no manpower and no money to enforce the law; in numerous instances, Immigration district offices have quietly asked local police departments to refrain from informing them about the presence of illegal aliens. The main effort is now centered on apprehensions in border areas—and the bulk of repatriations are Mexicans caught within twenty-four hours of crossing the frontier. Once the illegal migrant has moved up north, his chances of being left alone are extremely good.

One final statistical observation: the number of apprehensions, reflecting to some degree the rate of illegal crossings, rose *tenfold* between 1964, when the Bracero Program between the United States and Mexico was terminated by Congress, and 1974. Despite sophisticated sensor devices recently installed along the border and the increase in the Border Patrol's strength, there is little hope that even a dent can be made in the numbers of illegal immigrants from Mexico. New economic pressures in Mexico, providing the incentive for emigration to the United States, are likely to make up for the relatively improved border-control measures applied by the Immigration and Naturalization Service.

In brief, then, the problem of illegal Mexican immigration is wholly beyond control—and federal authorities in Washington are painfully aware of it. The best that can be done is to stabilize the rate of migration around the three million level, perhaps to reduce it somewhat, but the problem simply cannot be solved until such time as the Mexican economy is capable of providing for the country's citizens. Given the high birth rate in Mexico and the latest economic slump—ironically we export our recession and inflation to Mexico, receiving, in turn, the Mexican human exportation that swells our own unemployment rolls—there is no likelihood that the wave of Mexican labor invasions can be halted in this century.

This state of affairs poses at least two immensely serious problems:

1. The vast human tragedy affecting the millions of illegal Mexican immigrants—with vast ramifications among American Chicanos and our other minorities; and

2. A major foreign policy problem involving the governments of the United States and Mexico.

Let us, in reverse order, discuss these problems, starting with the foreign policy implications.

As a general rule, American-Mexican relations are surprisingly good. There exists, in fact, something of a "special relationship" between the two countries; Presidents Kennedy, Johnson, Nixon, and Ford made a point of holding periodic meetings on the border and in Washington with their Mexican presidential counterparts; Jimmy Carter continued the tradition by receiving newly installed José López Portillo in February 1977, the first head of state to visit him. These meetings have been extremely useful in finding solutions for a host of bilateral problems. In the broader foreign policy sense, the United States has long ago "agreed to disagree" with the Mexicans on such questions as hemispheric relations with Cuba, and those disagreements have not affected our basic friendship with Mexico. In fact, the Mexicans may derive some satisfaction that after fifteen years, the United States is now coming around to their view that nothing is to be gained from a hemispheric isolation of Cuba.

Bilaterally, there was a major breakthrough when President Kennedy returned the Chamizal area to Mexico, a piece of American territory created by a change in the course of the Río Grande, and claimed by the Mexicans.

In 1973, the United States and Mexico signed an agreement, replacing a 1944 pact and a 1965 accord, to deal with the problem of salinity in the waters of the Colorado River allotted annually to Mexico for irrigation and other purposes. This was the result of an immensely complicated negotiation conducted by the State Department and involving, among others, the Interior Department, the Congress, and state authorities along the border.

The American commitment was that 1,360,000 acre-feet of Colorado River waters delivered annually to Mexico above its Morelos Diversion Dam would have a tolerable salinity content though somewhat higher than that delivered to United States users at Imperial Dam.

The point, of course, was that water with excessive salinity would kill rather than help agriculture on the Mexican side of the border. The highly saline Colorado River drain waters made available to Mexico resulted from discharges from the Wellton-Mohawk Irrigation and Drainage project in Arizona. The United States agreed to construct a desalting plant, estimated at the time to cost $121 million (though it obviously will run higher when it is completed in 1979, given the intervening inflationary factors), to treat a major portion of the Wellton-Mohawk drain water. Before the plant becomes operational, the United States is committed to provide Mexico with desalinized water from storage reservoirs and later from the Coachella Canal in southern California. Finally, the United States pledged its support for Mexico in international financial institutions to obtain funds for the rehabilitation of the Mexicali Valley, where the Mexicans use the water from the Colorado River.

The two governments agreed in 1973 that the new accord constituted a permanent and definitive solution of the salinity problem. A special report by the Senate Foreign Relations Committee observed in 1974 that ''in respect to our international relations, the agreement removes a problem which has plagued our relations with Mexico for more than a decade . . . [;] it demonstrates once again the willingness of the United States to resolve its differences with other countries, as well as our will and ability to find constructive ways to do so.''

Another important United States contribution to the solution of the border problem was its support for the Mexican program of ''border industries'' that assemble appliances and a variety of other products from component parts obtained from American sources. The products are then exported to the United States under a highly preferential tariff treatment.

The philosophy behind both the desalinization agreement and the ''border industries'' program was a desire to strengthen the Mexican economy in areas adjoining the United States border so that, at least in part, there would be an incentive for unemployed or subemployed Mexicans to stay home rather than engage in illegal emigration to American labor markets. It is obviously impossible to quantify the results of these policies in terms of illegal emigration, but, American officials say, it has to help, if only a little bit.

The only bilateral American-Mexican problems that remain unsolved are illegal immigration and, to a lesser extent, the heavy traffic of narcotics and dangerous drugs from Mexico to the United States. Often, the two problems blend inasmuch as there are illegal immigrants who are drug carriers, infiltrated in the mass of work-starved *mojados,* ''wetbacks,'' as they are still called along the border. The expression comes, of course, from the days when Mexicans crossed to the United States by swimming or fording the Río Grande, emerging wet on the American side.

In the most immediate sense, the *mojados* are a United States domestic problem. The illegal crossings transcend by far the violation of immigration laws—such crossings are only considered as misdemeanors under the law—and represents an intractable social situation.

It is an objective fact that Mexican illegals—because they are willing to work harder and longer for lower wages without any legal protection of their rights—are displacing American workers, particularly Chicanos, blacks, and Indians, in every category of unskilled jobs, ranging from farm work to restaurant dishwashing and gas pumping.

With large-scale unemployment in the United States because of the present recession, the presence of some six million illegal Mexicans in the United States is a contributory cause to labor distortions. This is particularly true in border areas where unemployment currently runs as high as 20 percent of the labor force, more than twice the national unemployment figure of 8.7 percent.

The mechanization of farm work, particularly in cotton fields, has had the effect in recent years, even before the recession's advent, of reducing employment availability in the Southwest. This has affected American migrant workers as it has Mexican illegal immigrants. The combination of recession and shrinking job opportunities in agriculture in the Southwest has markedly changed the immigration patterns. Now the Mexicans stream to the big cities—Los Angeles, Chicago, and Dallas are the principal magnets for Mexican illegal aliens, New York and northern New Jersey for those of other nationalities (Dominicans, Colombians, and others)—creating new problems for themselves as well as for the local economies. Again, the displacement of American minority workers—the Chicanos, Blacks, and Indians as well as Puerto Ricans on the eastern seaboard—is a disturbing reality.

From the viewpoint of Mexican migrants, their tragedy is that they find fewer and fewer stable jobs in the big cities, now that the recession has hit hard, and they find themselves abandoned and exploited—or added to welfare rolls through the presentation of forged identity papers. The overwhelming reality is that nobody—not the federal government, not the states, and not the cities—is even remotely equipped to cope with the human magnitude of the Mexican problem. Since nobody is prepared or equipped to expel six million human beings from the United States—it is physically unfeasible and, besides, public opinion would never accept such wholesale deportations no matter what the American employment picture is—we simply have to live with this situation. And this situation is that we have in our midst millions of men, women, and children who are not even second-class citizens: they are in the most literal sense the flotsam and jetsam of the American society.

Because they fear discovery—and possible expulsion—they live the lives of the hunted. Unscrupulous employers, on farms as well as in the cities, pay them salaries below the official minimum wage, and often make them work long hours and weekends. A Mexican "illegal" knows that if he protests, the employer may report him to the Immigration and Naturalization Service, the dreaded *"Migra."* Forced kickbacks are not unusual.

Needless to say, they receive no fringe benefits. They cannot be covered by Social Security or union contracts. They must live as invisible people, unprotected by any United States laws. To put it simply, they are humans deprived of any shred of dignity.

It is this matter of human dignity that causes the concern of the Mexican government and creates the foreign policy problem with the United States. Mexico, not surprisingly, resents the treatment accorded its nationals in the United States: the problem has acquired such proportions that it is no longer relevant whether they came to America legally or illegally. Privately, many United States officials agree with this judgment—on humanitarian grounds—but the government cannot offer a legal remedy lest it undermine the immigration laws passed by the Congress—inhuman as these laws may appear to many.

Equally troublesome to Mexico City is the method of handling apprehended "illegals" who are subject to "voluntary departure." Mexico, obviously, does not question the sovereign right of the United States to expel migrants who violate the law. But it takes a dim view of the fact that captured "illegals," mostly those apprehended on or near the border, are massed in three major detention camps—the main one is in El Paso—before being placed on buses for the trip home to Mexico.

Mexicans have charged that the relocation centers are "concentration camps," a view that the Immigration and Naturalization Service rejects indignantly. It points out that Mexican consular representatives now are allowed to work out of the detention centers to be as helpful as possible to their apprehended fellow citizens.

But, inevitably, there are excesses—even possibly occasional brutalities—in a situation in which six hundred thousand human beings are processed annually for deportation. Arithmetically, this works out to nearly two thousand persons a day, virtually an assembly-line operation where harried immigration agents have no time for human niceties.

The erection of an electronic fence along parts of the two-thousand-mile border—it is modeled after the ill-fated "McNamara Line" in Vietnam—is likewise offensive to Mexicans. It has become something of a political problem in Mexico City: the charge is that illegal migrants are treated as subhumans or animals—or enemies of the United States—when wartime electronic devices are used to hunt down the *mojados.* Again, the relevancy of the Mexican sentiment on the subject is not important. What matters in terms of United States-Mexican relations is that this sentiment exists and brings forth new doses of bitterness.

The foreign policy problem was taken into account in the report of the Special Study Group on Illegal Immigrants from Mexico, headed by an assistant attorney general, Roger C. Cramton, and submitted to President Nixon on January 15, 1973. The Cramton Report, the most comprehensive United States government study on the subject, notes that

> . . . the large and rapidly rising numbers of illegal immigrants from Mexico constitute a serious problem for the United States and a source of tension with the Government of Mexico. . . . [this influx] creates a wide variety of social, economic, legal, diplomatic, political, and human difficulties in both countries. . . . [It urges measures to protect] illegal Mexicans against possible mistreatment in the United States and thereby reduce a source of friction with our great neighbor south of the border. . . . the exodus of large numbers of Mexican citizens, their illegal status in this country, and highly publicized accounts of alleged mistreatment and economic exploitation of Mexicans in the United States, are deeply offensive to Mexico's sense of national pride and dignity. . . . the effort to cope with the problems of illegal immigration must reflect a sensitivity to these interests of the Government of Mexico. . . . In the long run, a successful resolution of the problem will not be found solely, or even primarily, on this side of the border. . . . It should be the policy of our Government to seek increased mutual understanding and cooperation with respect to the problems caused by illegal immigration in the full range of contacts between the governments of the two countries.

The Cramton Report, trying to look at the problem from the viewpoint of the Mexican government as well as ours, takes the position that a secure border is the major answer in the foreseeable future to the problem of the treatment of illegal migrants. It states:

> Preventing Mexican nationals from crossing the border illegally is one of the few alternatives which holds forth any significant hope of preventing abuses against them. Once a Mexican alien manages to enter this country illegally, he becomes an invisible person by necessity, and one who may be especially vulnerable to exploitation by virtue of his status. . . . while increased border enforcement may not be directly

responsive to the expressed concerns of the Mexican Government it would reflect the deep concern of this Government for preventing possible exploitation of Mexican citizens. . . . If an overworked and inadequately supported staff is forced to process ever larger numbers of detainees, it becomes increasingly difficult to assure that the aliens will be treated with the dignity and humanity to which they are entitled. . . . Finally, a breakdown in control over the border fosters disrespect for the law in both countries, and creates a climate in which increased violations may arise.

Discussing electronic devices, the Cramton Report stresses that "a possible difficulty" in their use "is the concern of some representatives of the Mexican Government . . . that use of such equipment might be viewed as an act of hostility toward a friendly country and an affront to human dignity." But, it adds, the Study Group did not believe that use of modern detection devices "poses any threat to individual rights and liberties; indeed, this kind of equipment may well be less menacing to the individual than alternative security measures such as greatly increasing the force of uniformed officers patrolling in border regions or fencing off large sectors of the border." Still, as the report notes, "Mexican concern about this approach has been officially expressed."

The lengthy Cramton Report also addressed itself to the enormous difficulties involved in obtaining the Mexican government's cooperation in stemming the flow of illegal migrations. It says that while increased law enforcement on the Mexican side would "help to remove the grounds for complaints that Government officials or private interests were abusing Mexicans who entered this country," this could be "unattractive" to the Mexican government.

For one thing, the report acknowledges, the Mexican government might well find itself in the position of making a "police crack-down on their own citizens who are, after all, only trying to find employment." The Cramton Report finally concluded that "direct efforts to enhance Mexican enforcement capability appear infeasible."

The Cramton Report was submitted almost five years ago. Since then, virtually nothing has happened in terms of United States-Mexican relations to alleviate the problem, although the numbers of illegal migrants have been rising along a virtually vertical curve. In three years, there were two meetings of United States and Mexican commissions created in 1972 and charged with the question of illegal immigration; a third meeting, proposed by the American side, could not be held because of Mexican reluctance—according to American officials.

Presidents Ford and Echeverría discussed the problem when they met at the border in the fall of 1974, but no solutions were found. In January 1975, a special commission on Mexican immigration was formed under the White House's Domestic Council under the chairmanship of the attorney general. A subcommittee is directed by the State Department. But the basic deadlock has not been broken—and there is nothing to suggest that it will be broken in the foreseeable future.* The crux of this international stalemate is that Mexico insists on the return to the Bracero Program and the United States opposes it.

The Bracero Program grew out of United States manpower needs in the Second World War. Under a 1942 law, the Labor and Agriculture Departments were empowered to bring to the United States especially recruited Mexican contract workers for "temporary employment" in American agriculture. Four million Mexican workers were thus admitted during the twenty-two years the Bracero Program was in effect. At its peak, in 1956, over 445,000 were employed in this manner in the United States, enjoying the protection of the law.

In 1964, the year the Congress terminated the program, 177,000 Mexicans were legally employed in this country as "temporary workers." But such were Mexican population pressures that even during the Bracero Program other millions of Mexicans entered the United States illegally. In 1954, the year when 309,000 Mexicans were contracted as legal "temporary workers," the Immigration Service deported 1,075,168 illegal Mexican immigrants. This was an all-time record, not matched even in the 1970s.

The Bracero Program died because organized labor in the United States was opposed to it on the grounds that the "temporary" Mexicans took jobs away from Americans and tended to depress wages. The year 1967 was the last one when any "temporary" Mexican workers—just over six thousand of them

---

*President José López Portillo's visit in February 1977 to President Carter afforded the Mexican chief executive an opportunity to warn both the United States president in private meetings and the United States Congress in a public address that unless the current economic crisis is resolved, untoward social and political consequences might well result. The two executives reviewed the elements contributing to the situation as well as the problems affecting the relations between the two nations. It should be noted that the two executives agreed that high priority should be given to the study of the problems arising out of the border area. While the joint communiqué, as might have been anticipated at this stage, lacked specificity, the two executives indicated that they had considered carefully a number of important themes, including economic and monetary questions, investments, trade, immigration, drugs, contraband and other illegal activities, agriculture exchange, the nonproliferation of nuclear arms, the desire of Mexico for greater and better access to international financial institutions and capital markets, and the need to search for a better equilibrium of the commercial balance between the two countries. [Editor's Note].

—were permitted in the country. Since then, the legal flow of Mexicans to the United States has been a tiny trickle.

In theory, the Department of Labor may issue certificates authorizing employers to bring Mexican workers to the United States if an applicant can prove that there is no American labor available to fill available jobs. Then there are "green cards" (although they are actually blue in color), allowing some workers to commute daily to jobs in the United States. They are so precious to Mexican workers that there is a thriving industry to forge them. As the Cramton Report notes, "few Mexican workers have been employed" under the labor certification program in recent years. The only way Mexicans can legally enter the United States, other than with "green cards," is through grant of immigration visas; but under new restrictions placed on immigration from the Western Hemisphere in the 1966 immigration law, only sixty-seven thousand Mexicans were eligible in 1974. The figure for 1973 was sixty-six thousand.

The American immigration policy, described as "the Great Wall of China" in a recent Labor Department study, is thus encouraging illegal immigration from Mexico on a scale that, according to another estimate, will reach "epic" proportions by the year 2000. If we are concerned, as we should be, with the three million Mexicans entering the United States illegally this year, we should brace ourselves for what is to come in the years ahead. Here I would like to quote from a letter from the Office of Population of the Agency for International Development to the Commissioner of the Immigration and Naturalization Service:

> Once one fully comprehends the magnitude of the demographic problem in Mexico and its concomitant consequences, our immigration problem may be treated with the respect it deserves. Mexico had a population of about 50 million in 1970. At current growth rates, the population will reach about 85 million by 1985 and about 120 million by 1995. Not only has the rate of growth of the total population reached a crisis nature, but the labor force explosion in Mexico is even more horrendous. In 1970, there were about 16 million persons in the Mexican labor force. By 1985, this figure will be about 28 million and by 1995 about 50 million. It is, of course, the Mexican labor force (and wives and children) which make up the bulk of the illegal entrants into the United States. And even if the Mexican family planning program, which Mexico has just begun to develop, is eminently successful, it will have no impact on the size of the labor force for some fifteen or twenty years as all the labor force potentials for this period are already born. It is this population and labor force explosion exerting tremendous pressure on the land and the job

market in Mexico which contributes heavily to the "push" to enter the U. S. As serious as the Mexican immigration problem is today, this almost tripling of the labor force in 20 years, indicates that the problem will inevitably reach epic proportions during the next two decades.

This brings us back to the question whether—and how—the illegal Mexican immigration can be handled, if at all. We have seen that even by deporting around seven hundred thousand Mexicans a year, federal authorities are unable to stem the flow. At this point, we are acquiring possibly as many as two million new illegal Mexican migrants every year; those repatriated tend to return at the first opportunity, and they are followed by masses of "first-timers."

Palliatives are possible. The Cramton task force and others have proposed such steps as an adjustment of the status of "illegals" who have lived in this country for seven or ten years. This, at least, will grant a human status to hundreds of thousands of "illegals." Stricter border enforcement, already being applied with additional funds, personnel, and electronic devices, may result in more apprehensions. The so-called Rodino bill, penalizing employers for knowingly employing "illegals," may help a little bit—if it ever becomes law. But, passed three times by the House, it has been stuck for years in the Senate Judiciary Committee headed by Senator Eastland (D-Miss.)—who happens to own a large plantation. The Rodino bill, in fact, is opposed by border farmers who claim that if they are prevented from employing "illegals" at minimal wages (which is illegal), the cost of food will rise alarmingly.

As noted earlier, the Mexican government's answer to the problem is the revival of the Bracero Program on the theory that it would cut down on illegal migrations. This judgment is questioned by the United States government, pointing out that it was during the life of the Bracero Program that illegal immigration began to get seriously out of hand. The assumption in Washington is that even if a new program would let, say, a half-million Mexicans enter the United States as "temporary workers," we would still have to cope with two and a half million illegals a year. It would help, to be sure, but the Carter administration is aware, as was Ford's before it, that at this time of recession the Congress, responsive to labor unions' pressures, would never approve a *bracero* arrangement. This state of affairs has resulted in increasing tensions between the two governments. It is now the main dispute between the United States and Mexico, as recent diplomatic history has made clear.

In October 1973, during the session of the United Nations General Assembly, the former Mexican foreign secretary, Emilio Rabasa, informed

Secretary of State Kissinger of Mexico's desire for a new Bracero Program. For two months the State Department reviewed the whole situation, and, in December, Secretary Kissinger advised Rabasa in a private letter that a *bracero* agreement was out of the question. Instead, Kissinger told Rabasa, the United States would support the Rodino bill and try to make more Mexicans eligible for the Labor Department certification program.

On June 19, 1974, Rabasa handed the United States Embassy in Mexico City a note, described by American officials as "candid and harsh," urging again a new *bracero* agreement and protesting against the treatment by United States officials of Mexican illegal immigrants.

On June 26, the State Department formally replied in an equally candid tone. It stressed the "serious concern" of the United States government "over the huge number of Mexican workers who enter the United States illegally each year in search of employment," and emphasized that "the unemployment situation among American farm workers and the use of increased mechanical and chemical technology result in only a very small demand for imported temporary seasonal workers and that, as a consequence, a renewed *bracero* type program is not a feasible solution to the problem of Mexican workers illegally in the United States."

The American note also reminded Foreign Secretary Rabasa that:

> . . . the question of illegal immigration into the United States, as distinct from the issue of a *bracero* program, relates to the sovereign authority of the United States or any other state to regulate and control the admission of foreigners into its territory. . . . Facilities established to process in an orderly manner the repatriation of foreigners who have illegally entered the United States are an instrument of the sovereign authority. . . .

Finally, the note pointedly invited the foreign secretary to offer suggestions for cooperative actions "which the Government of Mexico might take to prevent the illegal entry into the United States of Mexican citizens."[1]

In August 1974, Kissinger and Rabasa again discussed the situation, and the latter proposed a quota system for legal Mexican emigration. When Presidents Ford and Echeverría met on the border on October 21, 1974, Ford indicated that the United States might consider a quota arrangement—no numbers were mentioned and Ford made it clear that no *bracero* pact was being contemplated—if Mexico would hold emigration at an agreed level. This, of course, would have required a major law-enforcement effort by the Mexicans, something that may have been politically impossible for President Echeverría, and may prove as difficult for his successor, López Portillo. A new White House committee, organized in January 1975, was reviewing the entire problem of Mexican immigration to the United States, and the Carter administration before long may be making proposals to Mexico in an effort to break the foreign policy deadlock over this question. Meanwhile, Americans may wish to ponder the moral implications of the situation as it now exists. Some serious effort is required to protect the illegal immigrants already in this country. Not long ago, an editorial in a New York newspaper quoted from the inscription on the Statue of Liberty, proclaiming that foreign nations send to us the "wretched refuse of your teeming shore." Then, referring to the Mexican problem, it observed that "it is hard to get the message back to the 'teeming shore' that those who were once welcome are now an intolerable burden."

NOTE

1. *New York Times*, 8 August 1974.

PART V

Health Along the Border

12

Considerations on the Health Status Along Mexico's Northern Border*

Ricardo Loewe Reiss

Introduction

It is not easy to study the health situation along the border, since the first thing you have to do is to delimit and define what is meant by the border. Delimitations and definitions vary with the point of view. For a specialist in international law, for example, the border is necessarily something different than for a social anthropologist. And when it comes to considering the border as a demarcation, not even a geographer can do it by merely drawing a line.

We health workers also do not have a sure delimitation and definition of what we mean by the border. Our field depends on the methodological points of view of several sciences. Thus a health worker will have to reckon with the laws and politics that support the health programs in order to delimit and define the border territorially. And yet these programs derive from an intricate juridical system, from international agreements between governments, from decisions at the national and state levels, and even from those at the local level. The problem becomes even more complex from the epidemiological point of view, since ecosystems set up their borders more in keeping with natural laws than with social laws. From the point of view of public health, the border will be subject to various definitions, depending on the problems studied at a given moment, and to various delimitations, depending on the distribution of those problems.

---

*Translated from the Spanish by Miguel González-Gerth [Editor's Note].

With respect to Mexico's border with the United States, the methodology for a study of health problems could depend on what the interest in the border happened to be. In the light of a rich existing bibliography, it would seem that such a starting point is too obvious. Then why so much concern for the northern Mexican border—and here I refer specifically to health problems—and not for the southern border? It would seem that there is a greater concern for preventing the smuggling of disease, so to speak, along the northern border than along the southern border. What diseases can the people of the United States "smuggle" into Mexico that the people of Guatemala cannot? And what diseases can we Mexicans illegally export to the United States without doing the same to Guatemala?

These questions simply reveal the fact that all of Mexico borders the United States or, put another way, that the Río Grande (Río Bravo del Norte) is the border between the United States and a large, an enormous "country," namely, Latin America. We Latin Americans are united not only by a common history but by a whole epidemiological panorama in which communicable and preventable diseases outnumber those which are not communicable. In the United States the degenerative and neoplastic diseases prevail, basically because up to now science has not been able to raise life expectancy to immortality. It is well known that the kind of disease that comes from poor health environment, malnutrition, and lack of information accounts for the high mortality among infants and preschool children in Latin America, whereas such factors have been spectacularly reduced through technological development north of our borders.

The concern for Latin America's border is therefore—and I will come back to this—first, that of creating mechanisms that will prevent the exportation of communicable diseases; second, that of preventing the reproduction of environmental and social conditions brought about by diseases such as drug dependence north of the border; and last, that of setting up barriers against the migration of certain diseases and carriers (vectors) from north to south, for ultimately they would return in greater strength if such barriers did not exist. Again, why is Mexico's southern border of little concern? Because the chance of exchanging health injuries is very small, since the ecological conditions of southern Mexico and Guatemala are basically the same.

The study of Mexico as a border with respect to the health problems of a subcontinent is, however, too vast to be practical. Most Mexican studies of border health problems employ two different and sometimes related limits: the aggregate of border municipalities and the aggregate of border states. This is due to the delimitation and subordination of the health programs, as well as to the nature of available information. Even binational (joint) epidemic prevention programs are set up according to political rather than ecological criteria regarding health injuries, a fact which hinders data gathering and processing. For the most part, specific health studies deal with conditions in municipalities, states, and countries, without giving a total picture of such problems, perhaps because total diagnoses would call for often impossible total solutions.

This essay does not go beyond the methodological limitations stated above. Its sole purpose is to give an undetailed picture of the health problems, the methods currently used to solve them, and some of the factors which condition and determine health. For this I will use three comparative sets of data: those relating to Mexico, to the six Mexican border states, and to the thirty-six border municipalities. The data are often incomplete. Thus the validity of such data is only incompletely representative of the whole, especially at the municipal level.

Health Injuries

The mortality rate along the border is remarkably lower than the national average (Table 1), though in the border municipalities it is higher than in the border states. This means that social conditions along the border as a whole are less aggressive than in the rest of the country, though at the same time there are more acute problems in the area closer to the border; probably because of migrants with low standards of living coming from the poorest parts of the country.

TABLE 1
General, Infant, and Preschool Mortality in Muncipalities and States
Along the Northern Border and in Mexico
(1971)

Area	General Mortality (a)	Infant Mortality (b)	Preschool Mortality (c)
Border Municipalities	7.6	64.9	8.4
Border States	7.3	74.3	4.6
Mexico	9.0	63.3	8.6

(a) Rate per 1,000 population

(b) Rate per 1,000 registered births

(c) Rate per 1,000 population ages 1 to 4

Source: Dirección General de Bioestadística, SSA, México.

Infant mortality (Table 1), a fairly reliable index of economic and social development, is very high in the country as a whole as well as in the border states. It appears lower in the municipalities adjacent to the border, probably because of better medical attention (at the time of delivery) than it does in the border states as a whole. Preschool mortality (Table 1) is high, throughout the country and in the border municipalities, but not in the border states as a whole. If we compare infant with preschool mortality, we get the impression that the chance of survival is better at the infant stage than at age four, while in the border states children die more quietly, without giving too much trouble.

The causes of death (Table 2) are comparable in the six border states and in the country as a whole. Predominant are contagious and avoidable diseases, such as influenza and pneumonia, enteritis and other diarrhetic diseases, and tuberculosis; so are conditions owing to nutritional factors, such as cirrhosis of the liver, diabetes mellitus, and vitamin deficiency; as well as violent deaths. The high rate of heart disease in the state of Nuevo León, where it occupies first place, is unusual. Together with the high mortality rate due to avoidable causes, it indicates something wrong with the distribution of health conditioning factors, for the children there who die from enteritis would never have grown up to die from the "disease of executives."

Influenza and pneumonia are less frequent in the border states presumably because of better environment. The same is true of enteritis, except in Coahuila, the state which, of all those along the border, has the worst health conditions. It is noteworthy that the geriatric diseases, such as cancer and cerebrovascular diseases, have a higher incidence in the border states than in the country as a whole. The same occurs with infant diseases. This indicates better general living conditions, despite poor medical services, especially at the time of delivery. In the final analysis, the principal health problem along the border is tuberculosis, and it is worse in the United States than in Mexico, a fact to be discussed later on, when dealing with socioeconomic health conditioning factors.

If we compare the causes of death in the municipalities with those in the country as a whole (Table 3), we notice that they are much lower, except in the case of tuberculosis and that of vitamin deficiency and malnutrition, which are concomitant phenomena. Medical attention at birth is poor in the border municipalities, a factor that increases the number of deaths caused by injuries at birth and other causes surrounding childbirth (excluding congenital disease). It should be pointed out also that mortality due to syphilis (as well as morbidity due to venereal disease) is the same or slightly lower than the national average.

Although available data are not very reliable, an examination of morbidity rates would show that the diseases preventable through vaccine, such as polio and measles, have diminished noticeably, which can be credited to relatively successful programs. On the other hand, diphtheria as a cause of death persists in Baja California, Coahuila, and Sonora.

Equine encephalitis from Venezuela has posed a health problem to humans

TABLE 2
Ten Principal Causes of Death in Mexico and in the Border States
(1971)

Cause of Death	All Mexico	Baja California	Coahuila	Chihuahua	Nuevo León	Sonora	Tamaulipas
All	9.0	7.2	9.2	8.0	6.7	8.3	6.6
Influenza and Pneumonia	138.1	88.8	116.3	108.8	79.7	110.4	62.7
Enteritis and Other Diarrhetic Diseases	126.5	61.1	137.1	97.5	63.0	102.3	77.5
Violent, Including Accidents	68.3	78.8	57.0	64.5	47.6	68.1	55.1
Heart Disease	62.1	74.6	72.0	81.7	84.5	72.4	61.3
Childbirth	48.7	65.4	54.6	37.9	45.9	53.2	40.7
Malignant Tumors	36.2	46.2	57.7	51.4	49.3	52.3	48.8
Cerebrovascular Diseases	24.8	33.4	34.5	25.6	26.4	29.6	30.6
Cirrhosis of the Liver	21.1	—	—	—	—	—	—
Tuberculosis, All Forms	17.9	26.4	32.4	25.9	21.0	26.5	28.6
Diabetes Mellitus	15.7	21.2	27.3	17.0	15.0	18.1	19.7
Nephritis and Nephrosis	—	15.7	—	—	—	—	—
Vitamin Deficiency and Other Forms of Malnutrition	—	—	19.5	16.7	13.9	—	11.9
Bronchitis, Emphysema, and Asthma	—	—	—	—	—	15.0	—

Note: Rates of general mortality per thousand and those of specific mortality per hundred thousand.

Source: Dirección General de Bioestadística. SSA, México.

during the last few years along the border, especially in Tamaulipas and somewhat less in Sonora, Coahuila, and Chihuahua. Leprosy is also a problem, although its morbidity rate is less than in the country as a whole, especially in Tamaulipas, and there it is higher in the border municipalities than in the rest of the state.

TABLE 3
Mortality Due To Selected Causes—Border
Municipalities* and National
(1971)

Cause	Border Municipalities (a)	National (a)
Influenza and Pneumonia	95.6	156.3
Enteritis and Other Diarrhetic Diseases	91.1	126.5
Violent, Including Accidents	45.2	68.3
Other Causes Surrounding Childbirth	43.4	46.1
Respiratory Tuberculosis	26.5	15.7
Vitamin Deficiency and General Malnutrition	13.5	12.4
Cirrhosis of the Liver	12.1	21.1
Lesions at Childbirth	11.1	2.7
Miscarriage	3.7	6.4
Measles	3.2	14.0
Typhoid Fever	1.5	4.9
Syphilis	0.4	0.5
Poliomyelitis	0.1	0.4
Ill-defined Symptoms	55.3	73.4
All Causes	760	900

*   Data given correspond to 14 of the 36 border municipalities, where 88.3% of the border municipalities' population and 28.5% of the border states' population lives.

(a)   Rate per hundred thousand.

Source: Dirección General de Bioestadística, SSA, México.

Health Resources and Services

The number of people per physician in the border states varies from 1,771 to 1,171, while in the country as a whole it is 1,500. Though not very reliable, these figures reveal a similarity between the border states and the national average. It should be pointed out, however, that they do not include the medical interns with the social services who are at present the backbone of rural medical help.

In the border states there is a capacity of 17,610 hospital beds (Table 4). This averages out to 447 people per bed. Even if the 671 beds in the rural health centers not subject to census are discounted, the result is better than the national average of approximately 550 people per bed.

TABLE 4
Synthesis of Resources for Medical
Attention in the Border States
(1973)

Agency	Number of Units	Number of Beds
Hospitals	*435*	*15,975*
DGSCSPET[1]	13	1,093
Other, SSA[2]	4	374
State	20	2,929
Municipal	6	528
IMSS[3]	67	5,019
ISSSTE[4]	10	492
Instituto Nacional Indigenista	12	39
Secretaría de la Defensa Nacional	6	237
Secretaría de Marina	3	50
Ferrocarriles Nacionales de México	6	248
Cruz Roja	1	12
Pemex	2	140
Private	285	4,814
Other Available Units	*445*	*1,635*
SSA[2]:		
Urban Health Centers	22	33
Suburban Health Centers	69	813
Rural Health Centers	269	671
Mobile Units	10	—
IMSS[3]:		
Clinics	69	118
Mobile Units	6	—
Total	880	17,610

[1]Dirección General de Servicios Coordinados de Salud Pública en Estados y Territorios.
[2]Secretaría de Salubridad y Asistencia.
[3]Instituto Mexicano del Seguro Social.
[4]Instituto de Seguridad y Servicios Sociales de los Trabajadores del Estado.

Source: Dirección General de Servicios Coordinados de Salud Pública en Estados y Territorios: Catálogo de Hospitales y otras unidades de atención médica en estados y territorios. México, 1973.

Both human and material resources are concentrated in the areas of greater population density. This does not affect their accessibility to the same extent as in the rest of the country, since this population is mostly urban and communications are good. Yet health resources are variously distributed among many agencies, each covering different population segments and offering different services (Table 5).

The Secretaría de Salubridad y Asistencia (Federal Department of Public Health) is supposed to reach 100 percent of the population with services that are primarily for the promotion of health and the prevention of specific diseases, and secondarily for medical assistance. The Instituto Mexicano del Seguro Social takes care of about 20 percent of the population through

Ricardo Loewe Reiss

TABLE 5
Agency Coverage in Nation and in Selected Border States and Municipalities
(1969 - 73)

Agency	Coahuila	Chihuahua	Sonora	Caborca, Sonora	Nuevo Laredo, Tamaulipas	Río Bravo, Tamaulipas	National
Secretaría de Salubridad y Asistencia	64.1*	64.8	68.3	44.1	54.0	—	56.3
Instituto Mexicano del Seguro Social	26.4	15.5	24.0	4.0	22.0	37.7	20.9
Instituto de Seguridad y Servicios Sociales de los Trabajadores del Estado	4.3	3.9	3.7	—	10.0	9.0	3.0
Other Government Agencies	0.5	3.0	2.4	—	—	—	2.7
Sundry Welfare Agencies	—	3.5	1.6	1.8	—	—	14.8
Private Organizations	4.7	9.3	—	—	—	7.0	2.3

* Percentage population of entity mentioned.

Sources: Dirección General de Servicios Coordinados de Salud Pública en Estados y Territorios; I Convención Nacional de Salud; Escuela de Salud Pública. México.

package social security services of which health is only a part. The Instituto de Seguridad y Servicios Sociales de los Trabajadores del Estado, also offers package social security services to the government workers who, with their families, account for approximately 4 percent of the population. Other government agencies, nongovernment health agencies, and the private sector operate at different levels of welfare, medical assistance and related federal programs. On the border (Table 5) the IMSS, ISSSTE, and other agency coverages are higher than the national average. The main reasons for this are the large number of border state services and the organized agricultural workers' access to social security.

The distribution of health resources according to agency reveals inequality of service to the population, since all agencies do not have the same ratio of resources to coverage. The Secretaría de Salubridad y Asistencia, for example, which is responsible for a greater coverage, has fewer resources than the social security agencies (Table 6). While these can count on 52.8 health personnel for every 10,000 assigned members, the former has only 6.9. The segment of population assigned to SSA benefits from 0.14 physicians per thousand. That covered by the social security agencies, on the other hand, benefits from 1.5. Reynosa, Tamaulipas, which serves as data basis for Table 6, has an overall ratio of 1.03 physicians per thousand. The agencies mentioned have different functions: the social security agencies are dedicated to fight actual disease; the Secretaría de Salubridad y Asistencia has less personnel because it is supposed to primarily promote health awareness and to prevent specific diseases; public welfare agencies offer free medical care; and private organizations are profit-oriented.

Regarding personnel for the health professions, the border states train 420 medical students, 194 dentistry students, and 786 nursing students annually. Upon graduation, these trainees represent an increase of approximately 4.5 percent, which is comparable to the growth in population. Schools in the border states currently train 9.3 percent of the physicians, 21.9 percent of the dentists, and 35.1 percent of the nurses in the country. It is curious that neither Baja California nor Sonora has a medical or dental school; Sonora does not even have a nursing school.

As already stated, the health programs fostered by the Secretaría de Salubridad y Asistencia (SSA) are geared toward the promotion of health awareness and the prevention of specific diseases. Among its programs, four stand out: (1) multiple vaccination against polio, measles, diphtheria, whooping cough, and tetanus, aimed at protecting all children; (2) rabies control along the border, by agreement between the Mexican government and the Pan American Health Office, which achieved a high degree of canine

TABLE 6

Health Resource Personnel: Number, Ratio Per 10,000 Population, and Contract Hours.

Reynosa, Tamps.

(1971)

Personnel	Social Security Agencies			SSA			Charity Hospitals			Private Clinics		
	Number	Ratio	Contract Hours (d)	Number	Ratio	Contract Hours	Number	Ratio (e)	Contract Hours	Number	Ratio (e)	Contract Hours
Physicians	118	11.5	837	10	1.4	40	7	—	84	20	—	101
Dentists	9	1.1	38	1	0.14	3	—	—	—	2	—	4
Registered Nurses	73	9.4	555	—	—	—	—	—	—	3	—	24
Other												
Professionals (a)	14	7.7	105	3	0.42	18	—	—	—	1	—	6
Technicians (b)	13	1.4	105	4	0.56	24	—	—	—	—	—	—
Practical Nurses	105	13.4	800	18	2.8	108	32	—	256	20	—	216
Other												
Auxiliaries (c)	26	3.1	190	8	1.58	66	—	—	—	1	—	12
Administration	53	6.8	408	3	0.44	18	9	—	74	8	—	82
Total	411	54.4	3038	47	7.34	277	48	—	414	55	—	445

(a) Includes chemists, nutritionists, social workers, and midwives.

(b) Includes radiologists, laboratory technicians, statisticians, etc.

(c) Includes laboratory assistants, statistical clerks, pharmaceutical assistants, nutritional assistants, and orderlies.

(d) Number of contract hours.

(e) Cannot be estimated because coverage is unknown.

Source: Pineda C., et al.; Escuela de Salud Pública, México.

vaccination and a lower incidence of the disease among dogs; (3) efforts toward timely detection and control of Venezuelan equine encephalitis; and (4) international germ control aimed at protecting the population against infection and the country against infestation.

Generally speaking, the SSA border programs are the same as those carried out throughout the nation and are adequate to the epidemiologic overview of the country, except for the antirabies program whose priority outstrips the danger, since hydrophobia occurs most frequently in the central and Gulf regions of Mexico. The protection levels reached through vaccination are satisfactory, especially in the case of vaccination against tuberculosis.

When considered in broad terms, neither the medical care provided by the SSA nor that provided by the other health agencies is dependent upon well-defined programs. Welfare and social security programs including medical care are too numerous to be considered here.

The public response to the health programs varies. The demand for medical help from dues-paying members of the social security programs is great, since they are forced to contribute, and because they do, they demand care. SSA hospital beds, on the other hand, are much less sought after, and when they are, it is by destitute emergency patients. Prevention programs find acceptance among the population whose passivity, however, requires its being sought out either at home or at work.

The year 1973 marked an effort toward better coordination among health agencies supported by both state and federal governments. The general policy includes: (1) dissemination of health education; (2) active public participation in health programs; (3) lowering the birth rate; (4) controlling factors conducive to communicable disease; (5) expanding prevention programs such as vaccination, better nutrition, environmental improvement; and (6) increasing resources and quality of health programs. This policy is intended for the entire nation by the SSA and is a matter that lies within the legal responsibility of the federal administration.

As part of a national health policy and program, binational agreements have been reached through the Pan American Health Office; the main purpose of these agreements is to stop infectious diseases from crossing to the United States. There is a Mexican-American Border Health Association that serves on an advisory basis for the solution of border health problems. There are two main reasons why the border population resorts to medical services on both sides, in an unplanned and unquantifiable way: on the one hand, diagnostic procedures and some special treatments are more advanced in the United States, and, on the other hand, medical attention is less expensive in Mexico.

Health Conditioning Factors

The physical environment along the Mexican side of the border is favorable to certain diseases, such as coccidiodmycoses, rabies, tick fever, and other types of rickettsiasis, brucellosis, Venezuelan equine encephalitis, tuberculosis, and poisoning due to the use of insecticides. Of all these, the last two are the most widespread and derive more from economic than from physical aspects of the environment: insecticides are employed in cotton growing and tuberculosis is partially enhanced by the cattle industry. Apart from the diseases mentioned above, an important health conditioning factor is the north-to-south migration of the *Aëdes aegypti,* the yellow-fever-carrying mosquito, especially around the state of Tamaulipas.

Demographic data worth mentioning are: population density of 9.8 per square kilometer in the border states compares with that of 13.4 in the border municipalities. The birth rate is high, as it also is across the country, while the mortality rate is lower and population increase from one census to the next is remarkably higher in the border states than the national average (Table 7).

People born in the border states represent 79.6 percent of their total population, while those born elsewhere in the country represent 19.5 percent and those born outside the country represent 0.9 percent. People born in the border municipalities represent 68.9 percent so that 31.1 percent of the population of these municipalities is immigrant.

The population of the border states is distributed among 22,844 localities. Of that population, 27.4 percent live in localities of less than 2,500 inhabitants and 40.8 percent in localities of less than 20,000. There is, then, a greater concentration of population in the border states than in the rest of the country (Table 8). The age distribution of this population is similar to that throughout the country. It is a young population, 46 percent of which is under fourteen and 85 percent under forty-four (Table 9).

Of the total population of the border states, 25.39 percent is employed. Of the population over twelve years of age, 41.05 percent is employed. Of those economically active 20.2 percent is unemployed part of the year. The economically active population, according to sectors, is distributed as follows: first, 30.1 percent—agriculture, cattle, mining, oil extraction, hunting, and fishing; second, 24 percent—manufacturing; third, 40 percent—services; and fourth, 5.9 percent—insufficiently defined employment.

The per capita annual income of the border states is $864 but in Chihuahua it is $514.82 and in Coahuila only $309.12. Of those employed, 78.5 percent earn less than two thousand pesos per month (or $1,920 a year) and 61.6 percent earn less than one thousand pesos per month (or $960 a year). If we take into account that for every one person employed there are three unemployed, we conclude that more than three-quarters of the population earn a per capita annual income of less than $480 (Table 10).

TABLE 7
Population, Birth Rate, General Mortality, and
Population Increase in Border States
(1971)

Area	Population (a)	Birth Rate (b)	General Mortality (c)	Population Increase (d)
Baja California	939,075	42.7	7.2	7.2
Coahuila	1,149,265	54.1	9.2	2.4
Chihuahua	1,678,774	41.2	8.0	3.4
Nuevo León	1,811,307	44.3	6.7	6.1
Sonora	1,154,911	45.1	8.3	4.3
Tamaulipas	1,534,517	38.5	6.6	4.5
Border States	8,267,849	38.9	7.2	4.4
Border Municipalities	2,347,838	41.2	7.4	—
National	50,829,000	43.9	9.0	3.5

(a) As of June 30, 1971.
(b) Births per thousand population.
(c) Deaths per thousand population.
(d) Percent yearly population increase.

Source: Dirección de Bioestadística, SSA, México.

A casual observer might think that unemployment, which increased from 70 percent to 75 percent in the last ten years, is due to the growing migration to the border states. And yet the scarcity of jobs is not a border problem but a national one. If there were no job opportunities on the border, there would be no migration. Clearly this migration has various points in the United States as its ultimate goal, but in the border states there are also numerous opportunities for temporary employment.

A careful analysis of the implications falls outside the scope of a study of health conditions. I should like to point out, however, that high job productivity, both in agriculture and industry, displaces labor at the same time that it creates certain privileges. High job productivity makes possible the kind of economy in which 40 percent of the wage-earning population is employed in the service sector. There is, of course, an underlying but clear, huge, and definite stratification among the population which, when it comes to health, allows to a small minority the luxury of dying of cancer or heart disease, while the majority are forced to die of cheaper diseases such as bronchopneumonia and enteritis.

In the border states the average size of the family is 5.4. About 90 percent of the population wears shoes; 87.4 percent of the population over twelve years of age is literate, though only 17.3 percent of those who can read and write have received any secondary education. One-third of the population lives in one-room dwellings: 71.9 percent of the housing is electrified; 61.4 percent has running water; 47.5 percent has indoor plumbing. Of that same housing 22.2 percent has dirt flooring, 67.6 percent has thatch, board, or comparable roofing, and 23.8 percent has board, mud, or comparable walls.

TABLE 8
Localities According to Size and
Population in Border States
(1970)

Size of Locality According to Population	Accumulated Population	%	Accumulated %
Less than 499	1,178,551	15.0	—
500 - 2,499	977,410	12.4	27.4
2,500 - 19,999	1,063,326	13.4	40.8
20,000 - 49,999	523,317	6.6	47.4
50,000 - 99,999	603,456	7.6	55.0
100,000 plus	3,502,112	45.0	100.0
Total	7,848,172	100.0	

Source: IX Censo General de Población. Dirección General de Estadística SIC, México, 1970.

These data show the standard of living in the border states to be higher than the national average, a fact which alters the epidemiological status of this area in quantity but not in quality with respect to that of the country as a whole.

TABLE 9
Population of Border States
According to Age Groups
(1970)

Age Group	Population	%
0-4	1,316,115	16.77
5-14	2,292,730	29.21
15-44	3,074,798	39.18
45 plus	1,164,526	14.84
Total	7,848,169	100.0

Source: IX Censo General de Población. Dirección General de Estadística, SIC, México, 1970.

Conclusion

The health status along Mexico's northern border, compared with that of the nation as a whole, is better with respect to disease and mortality, although it exhibits similar qualitative risks. The lessening of risks is due more to a higher standard of living than to specific health programs.

TABLE 10
Monthly Income Groups Among Border States Population
Declaring Income
(1970*)

Income Group**	%	Accumulated %
Less than $199	9.0	—
$200 - $499	20.2	29.2
$500 - $999	32.4	61.6
$1,000 - $1,999	16.9	78.5
$1,500 - $2,499	11.4	89.9
$2,500 - $4,999	6.8	96.7
$5,000 - $9,999	2.2	98.9
$10,000 - plus	1.1	100.0

*   Data for 1969.
**   One Mexican peso = 0.08 dollars.
Source: IX Censo General de Población, Dirección General de Estadística, SIC, México, 1970.

The border population suffers from lesser health injury than the national population; it does not demand greater health services, and the country's general policy for development gives little if any priority to health programs. The question of why and to whom public health along the Mexican-United States border is important was dealt with at the beginning of this study. If, as seems evident from the available data, the epidemiological status, the health services, and the socioeconomic conditioning factors regarding public health along the border are all similar to those in the rest of the country, then Mexico does not have any health problem peculiar to its northern border.

13

Physical Health Status
and Health Care Utilization
in the Texas Borderlands[1]

Charles H. Teller

Nature and Scope of the Dilemma

I have studied the health of Chicanos from the perspective of a Latin Americanist demographer-sociologist applying both disciplines' analytic techniques to contemporary cross-cultural social problems. The sociological and demographic literature on health along the United States-Mexican border is so dated or virtually nonexistent and the anthropological research so embedded in the "culture-and-personality-homogeneity" stereotypes, that it became necessary to search for raw data and gather other related information firsthand. What I learned in three years of observations, interviews, participation, questionnaires, and raw data searching is admittedly spotty, selective, and incomplete. The results, moreover, are influenced by my social change perspective. Scholars have not been asking many of the crucial questions that are important to Chicanos. Unfortunately, the multidisciplinary approach needed for effective investigation of most Borderlands contemporary dilemmas does not seem to attract either support or recognition.[2]

Even if there were an abundance of data and studies, it would be an enormous task to write an essay on the contemporary dilemmas of the health of the United States-Mexican border. The World Health Organization definition of health, "state of complete mental, physical and social well-being," is too formidable by itself. The border is about two thousand miles long, including countries, states, counties, and municipalities with diverse illness patterns and health care delivery systems. Nor is there anything approaching a homogeneity of peoples: rural peasants and urban Mexican nationals, first-generation immigrants and fourth-generation United States-born Chicanos, reservation and urban Native Americans, and rural and urban Anglo Americans. Finally, there is a large variety of social science perspectives that can be taken—historical, anthropological, biomedical, politicoeconomic, and sociological-demographic.

Thus, if one of the biggest obstacles is the lack of comprehensive research on this topic, where does one start? I have chosen to define some of the health needs of the major population group in the United States Borderlands and then to suggest what some of the barriers to satisfying these needs may be. Moreover, the discussion will be limited to the *physical* health needs of the *Texas* Borderlands population of Mexican origin or descent. While recognizing important political and economic differences within the region, this helps to reduce the complexity of cultural, socioeconomic, geographical, political, and institutional factors involved.

Having noted the lack of published health studies dealing with the Mexican-Texas Borderlands, I have selected five questions to guide this present exploratory attempt:

1. Is the Borderlands a unique health region?

2. What are the health status indicators?

3. To what degree are the medical services available in the Texas Borderlands able to meet the health needs?

4. Who benefits from the mutual border crossover for medical care?

5. Is what is being done about this gap adequate and likely to improve the situation?

A brief demographic introduction to the Texas Borderlands will set the stage for a listing of special factors that combine to make it a unique health region (Table 1). The thirteen-county, twelve-hundred-mile border strip has almost one million people who are predominantly of Mexican origin or descent. Six of the counties are essentially rural, the people of six others live mostly in small towns and cities, and one is a moderate-sized metropolitan area (El Paso). There are six important "twin-city" areas, and the fact that five of the six Mexican cities are larger than their Texas counterparts more than doubles the "effective" service area of the Texas Borderlands. All three demographic rates are high: four out of the five rural State Economic Areas (SEA) have the highest total fertility rates among the sixteen rural Texas SEA's and El Paso has the highest among the fifteen Standard Metropolitan Statistical Areas.[3] Age-specific death rates are higher than the state's average,[4] and out-migration rates (especially among young adults) were high enough to counterbalance high fertility and produce negative population growth rates in most border counties between 1960 and 1970.[5] The structural constraints on health status and medical care produced by the demography of

TABLE 1
Selected Demographic Information on the Border Counties
(1970)

County	Total Population (a)	Percent Spanish Language or Surname	Percent Rural Population	Percent Below Poverty Level		Percent Housing Units Lacking Plumbing Fixtures
				Total Population	Spanish Language or Surname	
Texas	11,195,416	18	20.3	18.8	35.9	6.5
Cameron	140,368	76	22.5	46.0	54.6	22.1
Hidalgo	181,535	79	25.9	49.8	57.1	25.7
Starr	17,707	98	67.9	54.9	56.9	47.7
Zapata	4,352	92	100.0	57.8	67.8	40.3
Webb	72,859	86	3.7	44.7	49.2	17.8
Maverick	18,093	90	15.1	50.8	56.5	25.7
Kinney	1,934	72	100.0	60.7	75.5	26.0
Val Verde	27,471	57	9.8	30.3	42.3	8.9
Terrell	1,940	44	100.0	23.9	37.4	6.0
Brewster	7,780	48	23.3	34.7	42.6	9.4
Presidio	4,842	75	45.3	50.3	59.2	25.2
Hudspeth	2,424	60	100.0	33.2	41.5	15.7
El Paso	359,291	57	4.0	21.4	28.7	8.5

(a) Underestimated but unadjusted due to the inability of the U.S. Bureau of the Census to perform a postenumeration survey of the suspected undercount.

Source: General Social and Economic Characteristics; Texas PC (1) C45; Bureau of the Census, April 1972.

the Texas Borderlands, other than the migration patterns, are a young age. structure with high labor force dependency ratios living in very poor and (at least in the Lower Valley) numerous, scattered communities and *colonias* (rural, unincorporated communities).

I have chosen not to speak about high fertility as a priority health dilemma. I feel that the main concerns of most borderland Chicano families in the health area are morbidity and access to acute health services. Their health problems do not stem primarily from large family sizes but from the economy and medical care delivery system of the region.

With this background, the Texas Borderlands can now be viewed as a unique area whose history and characteristics create health problems.

1. Colonialism: it can be considered a conquered or "occupied" geopolitical area (especially the Lower Río Grande Valley which was formally Nuevo Santander) manifesting dominant (Anglo)- subordinate (Chicano) socioeconomic and political relationships that are reflected in unbalanced provider-consumer interactions.

2. Poverty: the almost continuous stretch of border counties in the Middle and Lower Río Grande Valley constitutes the three poorest Standard Metropolitan Statistical Areas in the United States. Between one-half to three-fourths of the Spanish-language or surname persons living in these counties were below the poverty level in 1969, and from one-fifth to one-half of all families lived in housing units lacking plumbing facilities. The agribusiness interests are very strong and help maintain low wages.

3. Migration: international, seasonal, and daily (commuter) movement is relatively prodigious. Poor migrants from Mexico, old "snow bird" winter tourists from the North, and seasonal out-migrants from the Texas Border-lands carry their health problems with them, and the crunch on services is really felt in the winter. The large number of alien residents and undocumented workers means that many are not able to benefit from public medical care services and programs.

4. Geographic isolation: the Texas Borderlands are far removed from the major centers of health care services in San Antonio, Houston, Galveston, and Corpus Christi. A resident anthropologist recently described the Lower Valley as an "oasis in the middle of a physical, political, economic, and communications desert."

5. Tricultural environment: there are, broadly speaking, the southwestern Anglo, the northern Mexican, and the Chicano cultures, each with its respective language, music, foods, life-style, and historical background. Many Chicanos feel particularly trapped in the middle and not fully respected on either side, although one often hears the comment that they are treated with more dignity by Mexican doctors than by American ones.

6. International differences in health systems: the Mexican system is more of a public system with lower costs and less legal restrictions than the Texas system. The Texas medical and welfare establishment is particularly conservative, emphasizing the private, doctor-controlled fee-for-service curative medical care system.

7. Climate: the arid yet semitropical climate creates a special environment for certain endemic diseases and man-made contamination (for example, pesticides, crop dusting, lead poisoning, and waterborne diseases in irrigation canals).

None of these seven factors are unique in and of themselves; they can be found in other rural, urban slum, border, or multiethnic areas. But when they are all present at one time in one area, they create a unique health region where poor health status and a second-class medical care system are the result.

To my knowledge, nothing has been published that would approach a comprehensive treatment of physical health and health care in the United

States Borderlands.[6] Even more surprising is the relative poverty of research on the recognizably severe health problems of Chicanos. A good indication is the minimal attention given to health by the major compilation of the five-year Mexican-American Study Project at the University of California at Los Angeles. In all this encyclopedic 777-page inventory, *The Mexican-American People: The Nation's Second Largest Minority*,[7] there are all of three sentences dedicated to the topic of health.

Previously the main works on Chicano health were based on data gathered over ten years by anthropologists who took limited samples in small communities.[8] More recently there have been three comprehensive attempts to study Chicano health.[9] Much of the research cited concentrates on sociocultural and economic aspects of Chicano health care behavior, mainly because of the lack of data on health status and health services available to Chicanos. This is, undoubtedly, an important research area, but in order to address ourselves to contemporary dilemmas of health in the Borderlands, we also need to take a "crucial step in the process of creating a 'new' health system," as described by medical anthropologist Robert van Kemper: the "better understanding of the health care needs of [Chicanos], particularly with regard to the inter-relationship between their perceptions of the system, their utilization of the system, and the objective effectiveness of the system."[10]

Some efforts have been made by the federal government to respond to Chicanos' health needs, such as the Regional Medical Program, Areawide Comprehensive Health Planning Agencies, Area Health Education Centers, Migrant Health Programs, and Office of Economic Opportunity clinics. A number of special conferences have addressed themselves specifically to the mental, social, and physical health problems of the Spanish-speaking poor.[11] Most of the research priorities recommended by these conferences are concerned with the cultural differences in Chicano health care behavior (coping mechanisms, world view, and life-cycle periods) and few with the actual delivery of health care.

About the only concerted social science effort to study health care along several points in the Mexican-Texas border has been that by George Walker and his associates and students at the University of Texas Public Health School in Houston.[12] Research can find a gap in any region between the health needs of a subgroup of people, their demands for medical care, and their access to such care. Based on the social science and health literature on Chicanos, the Borderlands, and ethnic groups, the following six hypothesized factors could be cited as accounting for much of the gap between Chicano health needs and access to modern, "scientific" health care in the Texas Borderlands:

1. Geographic isolation: "In limited geographic areas, where the ethnic

population is characterized by a high degree of cultural homogeneity, attitudes and beliefs may influence behavior with respect to health practices and medical care. . . ."[13]

2. Mexican folk-health subculture—major values and beliefs that are dysfunctional to use of modern medical care: "A sense of fatalism and adherence to traditional ways, an acceptance of a mystical non-rational view of the world, an emphasis on form and *dignidad,* and a reluctance to accept personal responsibility. . . ."[14]

3. Poverty: "The direct consequences of poverty and a low educational level are reinforced by the culture of poverty including feelings of powerlessness, hopelessness, and social isolation. Both poverty and a minority ethnic identity relate to these feelings of alienation. . . ."[15]

4. Professionalism and the health-industrial complex: "The basic philosophy which governs the practice of medicine in Texas is that none other than physicians should have a role in making decisions which will affect the mode of delivering services or the means by which fees are established. . . ."[16]

5. Second-class health care delivery system: "How does one explain to a migrant family that a baby, if well, can receive immunizations at a well-baby clinic every Tuesday, but that if the baby becomes sick, he must be taken to the county hospital six miles away, and that older children and adults must come for immunizations at a different clinic on a different day at still different hours?"[17]

6. Institutional and personal racism: "A serious question may be raised as to whether it is these minority groups who are 'disinterested and uninformed' about health services, or whether it is the public health worker who is disinterested and uninformed about the needs and cultural patterns of these groups. . . ."[18]

Health Needs: Health Status Indicators

Mortality data provide the most fundamental indicators of the general level of health in a population. Social class, ethnic and racial, and geographic differentials in mortality can reveal how much improvement is needed until all segments of our society have equal health status. Unfortunately, an examination of the literature demonstrates that very little is known about the mortality structure and rates of the Chicano population, and even less for those living in the Borderlands.[19]

A recent report[20] reveals only six published mortality studies of the Texas-Mexican-American population. Of the six mortality studies, none provides the most basic age-standardized mortality rate for the state or a life table. Only the recent infant mortality study by Teller and Clyburn is of statewide scope, while the other five are of Mexican Americans in Houston and San Antonio. None analyze mortality in the Texas Borderlands. What data are available in this report show the following:

The Mexican-American population of Texas is generally in poorer health than the Anglo, but in better health than the Black. While mortality differentials between Anglos and Mexican-Americans seem to be declining, the latter still have higher age-standardized death rates, lower life expectancy, higher infant and maternal mortality, and higher percentages with peridontal and nutritional deficiencies. Although data on illness incidence and prevalence were inconclusive, Mexican-Americans were found to have higher mortality rates from tuberculosis, diabetes and other infectious diseases, from cardiovascular diseases, and higher morbidity rates from chronic conditions.[21]

Five types of indicators are available and convenient for analyses of health status in the Texas Borderlands: 1) disease-specific death rates; 2) infant mortality rates; 3) infectious disease rates; 4) medical histories; and 5) nutritional status.

Table 2 presents cause-specific death rates calculated for five Middle and Lower Río Grande border counties in 1969-71. Comparison groups are the Texas whites (which include Spanish surname) and Texas Blacks. The crude death rates for the five counties were lower than for the comparison groups, reflecting the border's younger age structure. What is striking, however, is that death rates from infectious and parasitic diseases for the combined counties were nearly twice that of Texas whites, and for dysentery and amebiasis, twice that of whites and nearly four times that of Blacks. On the other hand, the death rates from heart, cancer, and stroke are lower for the border counties.

It should not be overlooked that the death rate for symptoms of ill-defined causes for the border counties was nearly three times the white rate and substantially higher than the Black rate. This may reflect the differential quantity and quality of medical care received by the border residents. Such a poverty of care is further evidenced by the high rates of death from infective and parasitic diseases and deaths from such normally nonfatal diseases and causes as diabetes, anemias, and appendicitis.

The infant mortality rate has often been considered one of the most sensitive indicators of general levels of living. Defined as the number of deaths under one year of age per thousand live births in a given calendar year,

TABLE 2
Deaths From Selected Causes, Five Selected Border Counties
(1969-71)

Deaths/100,000 population

Cause	Cameron	Hidalgo	Maverick	Starr	Webb	5 Counties Combined	Texas White[1]	Texas Black
All Causes	751.36	689.30	585.86	617.46	697.46	703.65	822.50	998.74
Infective and Parasitic Diseases[2]	20.19	20.20	14.74	13.18	13.73	18.58	9.85	16.73
Dysentery and Amebiasis	0.47	0.18	1.84	0.00	0.92	0.54	0.21	0.14
Enteritis	4.99	8.63	0.00	1.88	2.75	4.34	1.94	3.42
TB, all forms	5.22	2.15	5.53	5.64	3.20	3.87	2.49	3.73
Septicemia	3.56	2.20	0.00	3.76	1.37	2.48	1.95	3.56
Malignant Neoplasms	125.86	106.70	70.01	97.89	119.87	113.26	141.19	145.14
Benign Neoplasms	2.85	1.84	1.84	5.64	1.83	2.32	1.83	2.53
Diabetes	22.56	18.73	16.58	26.35	28.37	21.83	15.38	23.72
Avitaminosis and Other Nutritional Deficiencies	0.71	1.10	0.00	0.00	0.92	0.85	1.04	2.08
Anemia	1.66	1.84	4.84	1.88	0.92	1.63	1.40	2.92
Diseases of the Heart	218.71	211.53	176.86	190.13	204.50	210.35	289.58	296.52
Hypertension	3.32	2.57	3.68	1.88	5.49	3.33	2.76	8.25
Cerebrovascular Diseases	63.39	66.10	53.43	56.47	64.97	64.73	90.52	120.28
Diseases of the Arteries	19.24	18.73	0.00	15.05	20.59	18.27	24.84	19.25
Influenza	2.14	1.84	9.21	3.76	0.42	2.09	4.78	2.03
Pneumonia	22.80	27.54	31.32	11.29	24.71	25.00	27.63	34.83
Bronchitis, Asthma, Emphysema	11.87	13.59	9.21	3.76	7.78	11.46	15.85	8.75
Appendicitis	0.71	1.10	0.00	1.88	0.00	0.77	0.63	1.00
Cirrhosis of the Liver	9.74	9.18	7.37	0.00	19.67	10.68	11.91	9.99
Kidney Infections	3.09	4.41	1.84	3.76	0.42	3.17	4.49	6.31
Congenital Anomalies	9.45	9.73	14.74	16.94	12.35	10.60	9.15	10.86
Symptoms of Ill-defined Causes	57.47	33.79	18.42	28.24	36.60	41.88	15.77	36.29
Accidents	60.08	57.66	58.66	47.06	44.68	55.82	64.34	71.24
Suicide	5.22	5.32	7.37	3.76	6.41	5.50	12.15	4.78
Homicide	4.27	2.75	5.53	1.88	5.49	3.79	7.81	49.51
Number of Deaths from all Causes	3164	3754	428	328	1525	9049	250,571	41,776

[1] Includes Spanish surname.

[2] Includes dysentery, amebiasis, enteritis, TB, and other infective or parasitic diseases.

Mortality data were drawn and combined for the years 1969, 1970, and 1971. The average of the three years was divided by the population data.

Source:　Causes: Texas Vital Statistics; Population: U.S. Census Reports, PC(1)-C45, Texas 1970.

the infant mortality rate directly measures the health of the infant population of an area. Indirectly, infant mortality measures the causal factors in maternal and infant health and illness, such as availability and quality of prenatal, postnatal, and delivery care, nutritional status and environmental conditions, each of which is in turn related to the socioeconomic status of the family. One of the very few health status indicators available for the Texas Borderlands is infant mortality, but unfortunately as we shall see, these data seem to be unreliable.

In an analysis of ethnic trends and differentials from special tabulations of vital statistics data of Texas, Teller and Clyburn[22] found, surprisingly, that two of the three border State Economic Areas (SEAs) had the lowest rates among the sixteen nonmetropolitan SEAs in the state in 1970-72. Moreover, the one border metropolitan SEA, El Paso, had the next-to-lowest of fourteen metropolitan SEAs. Table 3 shows the ethnic differentials by SEA.

These data seem to indicate a quite unexpected situation: lowest infant mortality in the poorest SEAs (border) in Texas, and within that region, lowest among the Spanish surnamed whose per capita income is one-third that of the Anglos. It is particularly unexpected that the component (postneonatal) most sensitive to income differential is not higher among Spanish surnamed in the two poorest border SEAs. Teller and Clyburn call into question the accuracy of these data by examining four indirect reliability checks.[23]

Are the infant mortality data underestimates or is this a unique health area where infant mortality is not a sensitive indicator of general levels of living? Both are probably true. Teller and Clyburn state: "The relatively low Spanish surname IMRs along the border seem to be related both to an artificial inflation of the denominator (live births) and an under-representation of the numerator (deaths)."[24]

A third source of data compares the infectious disease rates in the heavily Chicano South Texas Public Health Region 10 with that of the rest of the state and the nation. Table 4 indicates higher rates in Region 10 than Texas or the United States for tuberculosis, amebiasis, leprosy, polio, typhus, hepatitis, rubella, measles, and shingellosis. The reported incidence rate of TB was twice as high as the national rate and 61 percent higher than the Texas rate. The rates for communicable diseases easily controlled by immunization were much higher in Region 10 than in the rest of Texas: twelve times higher for polio, and six times for measles. Amebiasis, so common in most areas of Latin America, was fourteen times higher. The Texas Nutrition Survey of 1968[25] provides some interesting data on South Texas Public Health Region 10. The most important contribution of these data is that they illustrate the relatively poor situation of the Mexican-American female when compared

TABLE 3

Infant Mortality Rates of Border* State Economic Areas of Texas
(1970-72 Combined)

SEA	Neonatal Mortality Rate			Postneonatal Mortality Rate			Infant Mortality Rate			
	Anglo	Spanish Surname	Black	Anglo	Spanish Surname	Black	Anglo	Spanish Surname	Black	Total
Nonmetropolitan										
Trans-Pecos	22.1	13.0	**	3.3	8.4	**	25.4	21.4	**	23.6
Lower Río Grande Valley	16.7	12.4	**	7.1	7.1	**	23.8	19.4	**	19.9
Southwest Río Grande Plain	14.8	14.8	15.5	5.0	3.9	7.8	19.8	18.7	23.3	18.3
Total Texas Nonmetropolitan	15.6	14.4	21.6	4.3	7.5	11.5	20.1	21.9	33.1	22.2
Metropolitan										
San Antonio*	13.6	13.4	23.1	3.7	5.6	8.3	17.3	19.0	31.5	19.2
Corpus Christi*	13.0	13.7	15.4	3.7	6.5	5.9	16.8	20.2	21.3	19.0
El Paso	12.8	12.8	22.8	3.8	4.4	18.7	16.7	17.2	41.5	17.8
Total Texas Metropolitan	13.8	13.1	21.7	3.6	5.4	7.7	17.4	18.5	29.4	19.7
Total Texas	14.4	13.6	21.7	3.8	6.3	8.7	18.2	20.0	30.4	20.5

* Included are two close-to-border cities nearly half of whose population is Spanish surname.

** No rate computed because base is less than 100 live births.

Source: Unpublished data of Texas Department of Health.

to the Mexican-American male. While the ratio of male-to-female reported conditions is about the same (1.1) outside Region 10, females reported twice as many (0.5) conditions as males in Region 10. Anemia, tumors, kidney, and bladder trouble have notable sex ratio differentials.

Data on the health status of children in the Texas Borderlands are available from the results of the screening (medical history, physical examination, and certain laboratory tests) in 1973-74 of eligible welfare clients.[26] Screening areas of comparison include El Paso, Laredo, and the Lower Río Grande Valley. Higher percentages of El Paso children were found to have lead in the blood, abnormal hemoglobin, throat, and skin conditions relative to other nonborder Texas children. The Lower Río Grande Valley had relatively high incidences of heart, lung, scalp, and musculoskeletal disabilities. Laredo's only relatively high abnormality percentage was in the screening of hearing problems.

The Texas Nutrition Survey was conducted in 1968 on a sample of 1,810 families (8,005 individuals) living in census enumeration districts which had average income levels in the lower 25 percent of the state's economic scale.[27] To determine the nutritional adequacy of the sample population's diet, daily dietary data were recorded and biochemical analyses were made for six essential nutrients. Strong relationships were found between poverty status and unacceptable biochemical levels for the six nutrients: persons in the poorer income levels had two to three times higher rates of unacceptably low

TABLE 4
Comparison of Infectious Disease Rates Per 100,000 of
South Texas Health Region 10 with the
U.S.A. and Texas
(1972)

Disease	U.S.A. Cases	U.S.A. Rate	Texas Cases	Texas Rate	PH Region 10 Cases	PH Region 10 Rate	Texas Less PH Region 10 Cases	Texas Less PH Region 10 Rate
Amebiasis	2,199	1.1	180	1.5	91	10.4	89	.77
Brucellosis	196	0.09	5	0.04	0	—	5	0.047
Diphtheria	152	0.07	41	0.38	0	—	41	0.38
Leprosy	130	0.06	34	0.29	15	1.7	19	0.17
Polio	29	0.01	4	0.03	2	0.23	2	0.018
Typhoid	398	0.19	20	0.17	0	—	20	0.18
Typhus	18	0.008	13	0.11	11	1.3	2	0.018
Hepatitis A+B	63,476	31.2	4,216	36.5	411	47.1	3,805	35.6
Pertussis	3,287	1.6	185	1.6	20	2.3	165	1.5
Rubella	25,507	12.5	1,596	13.8	253	29	1,343	12.6
Measles	32,275	15.8	1,617	13.9	530	60.7	1,087	10.1
Tuberculosis	32,932	16.2	2,422	21	298	34.2	2,124	19.9
Shingellosis	20,207	9.9	1,015	8.7	108	12.3	907	8.5

Source: Personal Communication, Brooks Taylor, Region 10, Texas State Department of Health.

TABLE 5
Percent in "Unacceptable" Nutritional (Biochemical) Levels,
Low-Income Enumeration Districts in Texas and Three Border Counties
(1968)

Nutrition Status	Low-Income[1] Texas	Hidalgo	Cameron	El Paso
Low Hemoglobin (Anemia)	20	19	14	9
Low Serum Albumin	16	20	1	5
Low Vitamin A	41	82	76	35
Low Vitamin C	24	2	10	6
Low Thiamine	11	2	4	10
Low Riboflavin	21	27	22	17
% Underweight (male/female)	17/11	6/9	12/3	15/10
% Obese (male/female)	26/49	33/46	38/49	17/48
% Mexican American	45	98	90	90
% Spanish Used in Home	39	86	77	81
Number Individuals in Study	8005	708	470	767

[1]66% of the households had incomes below the poverty level.

Source: Personal communication, Dr. McGanity, U.T.M.B.G., Texas Nutrition Survey.

biochemical levels than the higher income levels of the Texas sample.[28]

Anemia was a problem at all income levels. However, Mexican Americans and blacks had a prevalence of unacceptable hemoglobin levels approximately twice that of the Anglo group. Table 5 shows the prevalence of unacceptable biochemical levels in the three-border-county enumeration districts sampled. Two South Texas counties had very low levels of vitamin A adequacy. These data give clear indication of the need for vitamin A fortification programs for the border counties.

In sum, this section on status indicators in the Texas Borderlands has singled out some of the most pressing health needs. The most puzzling finding of lower infant mortality rates in the border region, counties, and towns than in the rest of Texas points to the possibility that one of the greatest health problems of the Borderlands is the poor quality of health data. Without it, planning for improvements in health status cannot be done responsibly.

Medical Care: Parts of the System and Its Utilization

From the spotty data on health status indicators in the Texas Borderlands, it can be deduced that a balanced approach to the health problem is needed: one that includes environmental, preventive, curative, and rehabilitative health care and maintenance. A look at the health care delivery system is required, but in view of the lack of any comprehensive literature, data will be presented on selected components of the system. The question is: to what degree are the medical services available in the Texas Borderlands able to meet the health needs of the population they serve? Bruhn and Rowden provide[29] a useful descriptive analysis of current health manpower in thirteen Texas border counties and fifteen other nonborder counties that have fifty or more Chicanos. They found that while "there is a shortage and maldistribution of active 'patient care' physicians, dentists, pharmacists, registered nurses and occupational and physical therapists" in Texas compared to the national ratios, this shortage and maldistribution are most acute in these twenty-eight border and near-border counties (see Table 6). One-fourth (three) of the border counties have no patient care physicians, five have no dentists, three no pharmacists, and two no active registered nurses.

The authors also looked at the representation of Mexican Americans among health personnel in Texas. The following are the percentages in 1973 of

TABLE 6
Ratios of Selected Health Personnel Per 1,000 Population,
Texas Border Counties (a)
(1970)

Geographic Area	Patient Care Physicians	Dentists	Pharmacists	Active R.Ns	Total Population
United States	1.40	.55	.63	3.53	204,765,000
Texas	1.02	.41	.60	2.15	11,195,416
Border Counties:					
Cameron	.81	.19	.50	.96	140,368
Hidalgo	.59	.14	.48	.94	181,535
Starr	.23	.00	.40	.28	17,707
Zapata	.69	.00	.23	.46	4,352
Webb	.65	.01	.54	.91	72,859
Maverick	.50	.06	.39	.94	18,093
Kinney	.00	.00	.00	.00	1,934
Val Verde	.47	.18	.40	.80	27,471
Presidio	.62	.41	.41	.21	4,842
Hudspeth	.00	.00	.00	.84	2,424
El Paso	.93	.29	.44	1.96	359,291

(a) Terrill and Brewster were not included by the authors since they lack over 50% Spanish language or surname population.

Source: John G. Bruhn and David W. Rowden, "Health Manpower and Educational Needs Among Mexican Americans in Texas," in *Barriers to Medical Care Among Texas Chicanos,* Southwest Medical Sociology Ad Hoc Committee (Mimeo) December 1974, Tables 1 and 2; General Social and Economic Characteristics; Texas PC (1) C45; Bureau of the Census, April 1972.

Spanish surnamed among all those currently practicing in Texas: Texas Medical Association, 5 percent; Texas Dental Association, 2 percent; Texas State Board of Pharmacy, 7 percent; Texas Board of Nurse Examiners (registered nurses only), 4 percent; Texas Occupational Therapy Association, 6 percent; and Texas Physical Therapy Association, 5 percent. One of the key factors for this underrepresentation, it is said, is the shortage of educationally qualified manpower.[30]

The number of hospital beds per 1,000 population is another commonly used indicator of medical care availability. Table 7 presents the ratios for the Texas border counties, from southeast to northwest, for 1970. In only two of the thirteen counties does the ratio surpass the state average, and five have no hospitals at all. More striking are the utilization rates of the emergency rooms and outpatient departments; the rates in Cameron, Hidalgo, Starr, Maverick, and Brewster counties are far below the state average.

TABLE 7
General Hospital Facilities and Outpatient Utilization,
Texas Border Counties
(1971)

Border County	Number of Hospitals	Number of Beds per 1,000 population	Emergency Room	Outpatient Department	Outpatient Utilization per 1,000 population
Texas	505	4.6	480	113	70.0
Cameron	3	2.9	3	0	14.9
Hidalgo	4	2.2	4	0	10.2
Starr	1	1.2	1	1	6.6
Zapata	0	—	0	0	—
Webb	2	3.4	2	1	111.0
Maverick	1	3.6	1	1	12.2
Kinney	0	—	0	0	—
Val Verde	2	2.8	2	1	188.2
Terrell	0	—	0	0	—
Brewster	1	6.2	1	0	13.4
Presidio	0	—	0	0	—
Hudspeth	0	—	0	0	—
El Paso	10	6.2	8	5	72.4

Source: Health Care in the South: A Statistical Profile, Southern Regional Council, Inc., June 1974.

The percentage of Spanish surname births delivered by a midwife declined substantially between 1964 and 1971 (see Table 8), yet there was still much variation by city and county. Utilization of the midwife continued high in Brownsville (where there are forty-four of them) and where the lack of a municipal hospital is a major factor, whereas in Eagle Pass a vigorous campaign by the county hospital to attract parturients has been successful in reducing midwife utilization.

The percentage receiving prenatal care and the timing of this care is a good indicator of medical care utilization. In some border counties around 15 percent of the Spanish surnamed parturients had no prenatal care. If care received only during the third trimester were included with no care at all, then 26.4 percent of parturients in the counties of the Lower Río Grande Valley, 20 percent of Special Economic Area 3 (Middle Río Grande Valley), and 16.7 percent in El Paso had inadequate or no care in 1971. Anglo parturients had 4.1, 3.3, and 3.4 percent, respectively, with inadequate or no care in 1971.[31]

This type of data is hard to obtain from the Texas Department of Health, and when raw data are obtained they seem to be highly unreliable. Immunization status is reported at the end of each school year to the Texas Education Agency. Here is the percent of full protection levels by vaccine for two of the Middle Río Grande Valley border school districts, 1972:[32]

	DDT-TD	*Polio*	*Measles*	*Rubella*
Del Río	77	66	40	43
Eagle Pass	77	79	75	73
Texas	79	74	79	78

These data indicate that these two border districts are not much different from the state in their negligence in keeping up the immunization levels.

A health team performed histories and physical examinations on fourteen hundred patients in clinics and barrios of Hidalgo and Starr counties in 1972. A member of the group, Dr. Harry Lipscomb, testified before a Senate Committee about their survey:

> The people whom we examined represent an almost ''pure culture'' of a society totally peripheral to the influence of American health care. In a nation where levels of specialty care in medicine have achieved laudable height, this group has not yet found its way to our most rudimentary care facilities. Such simple necessities as glasses, false teeth, braces, hearing aids, dental repair, rehabilitation, plastic surgery, repair of congenital deformities, maintenance of simple hygiene, and repair of cervical lacerations following childbirth, this population uniquely seems to have never attained. The specialties of plastic surgery, obstetrics and gynecology, pediatrics, surgical ophthalmology, and otorhinolaryngology have no meaning to these people, for they have never had access to this high level of professional care.[33]

The household health survey is the most appropriate technique to measure the gap between perceived illness and demand for access to medical care. The Health Interview Survey of the National Center for Health Statistics has developed a sufficiently reliable and replicable methodology that can be used in surveys of the Chicano community. Key questions from the survey were included in household health surveys that the author conducted in two South Texas communities in 1973.[34] These surveys had dual purposes: one was to study Chicano health care behavior; the other, to evaluate the degree to which the available services were meeting the perceived health needs of the Chicano population in comparison with similar data for the Anglo residents.

TABLE 8
Percent of Spanish Surname Live Births Delivered by Midwives,
Selected Texas Border Cities and Counties
(1964, 1971)

City	Live Births		% Midwife Deliveries		Change in % of Midwife Deliveries, 1964-71
	1964	1971	1964	1971	
Brownsville	1546	2022	59.3	42.2	-28.9
McAllen	895	1113	12.4	9.6	-22.5
Mission	319	341	24.1	12.0	-50.2
Eagle Pass	580	396	55.7	17.7	-68.2
Laredo	1863	1966	12.3	13.0	+ 5.7
Del Río	492	508	19.9	8.1	-59.3
El Paso	4756	5354	3.0	0.8	-72.8
County					
Cameron	3612	3586	46.2	34.8	-24.8
Hidalgo	4885	5336	15.2		
Maverick	617	436	54.5	18.5	-62.4

Source: Texas State Health Department, unpublished data.

Data were gathered by a team of bilingual, bicultural interviewers on two hundred families representing randomly stratified samples of low-and middle-income Chicano and Anglo families in the two towns. In both samples about two-thirds of the Chicano families earned under $5,000 a year, while only 13 percent of the Anglos were so poor; about half the Anglo families could be considered "middle class" as compared with about 5 percent of the Chicano families. Underscored is the fact that the methodological problems of data collection and analysis of health interview surveys of ethnic groups are not insignificant. Differences in illness and health care observed between the ethnic groups can be due to such demographic characteristics as age, sex, socioeconomic status, family size, and distance from services, as well as to such culturally related interview situational factors as ethnicity of interviewers, definition of illness, male stoicism, and aversion to reporting subcultural self-treatment or empirical treatment practices.

There were not enough middle-class Chicanos to make statistically reliable class controls, but generally the few middle-class Chicanos received a level of care midway between middle-class Anglos and lower-class Chicanos. Chicanos in both towns came out relatively poorly when compared to Anglos in their dental care,[35] preschool child immunization levels, early prenatal care and sex constant. But in a key question on percent with an acute illness during the previous month, the results were favorable to the Chicanos. This is mostly accounted for by the much higher incidence of colds and flu reported by Anglo mothers for their children. It also has been suggested that lower-class Chicanos are likely to underreport their acute illnesses.[36]

Two-thirds of the Anglos and half of the Chicanos received medical care when ill. Among Chicanos, 35 percent of the lower class and 65 percent of the middle class received medical care when ill in the same month. Of these recipients, almost one-third of the Chicanos had to go out of town for treatment, as compared with 6 percent of the Anglos.

Anyone who has crossed the border into Mexico at one of the major bridges cannot help noticing the plethora of health care-related offices and stores on the Mexican side: dentists' offices, drug stores, homeopaths, herbalists, midwives, and general practitioners' clinics. In the Eagle Pass-Piedras Negras urbanized area, where the population ratio is about 1 to 3, the ratio of doctors who deliver babies is about 1 to 15. On the other hand, the Mexican twin cities are normally several times larger than the Texas cities, and Mexican nationals (including the daily commuters) utilize services on the United States side.

The only systematic and scientifically executed household health surveys of the twin cities along the Mexican-Texas border were done as part of a binational study of health resources and utilization patterns. The El Paso-Ciudad Juárez Project was conducted during the summer of 1970 and the Brownsville-Matamoros study the following summer.[37] These timely research efforts, initially stimulated by the United States-Mexico Border Public Health Association, have produced many useful data which have not yet been fully analyzed.

The El Paso-Juárez study obtained data on 312 El Paso and 426 Juárez families randomly selected.[38] It showed that 13.6 percent of all persons in the El Paso sample who had contact with private doctors during a two-week period went across to Juárez, while 8.6 percent from Juárez went to El Paso for the same purpose. El Pasoans crossed over more than their twin-city counterparts for private medical care and to use pharmacies, while those from Juárez did so more for private hospital care and, surprisingly, dental care.

The other border study results reported here are of the Brownsville side only—a representative sample of 1,902 individuals in 432 households. It showed that 7.8 percent of all persons in the Brownsville sample who had contact with a private physician during a two-week period went across to Matamoros, with the highest percentage (14.3 percent) among the next-to-lowest of the four income groups. Of those who visited a public health clinic during a two-week period, 5.3 percent (all in the lowest income groups) went to Matamoros. Of those who were confined to a hospital in the year prior to the study, only 2 percent (all in the lowest two income groups) were hospitalized in Matamoros. The picture given by this study is that use of the health services on the Mexican side of the border by United States border residents is not as high as expected and is restricted to the poorest segments of the population.

In sum, studies and raw data on the availability and utilization of health care services in the Texas Borderlands give reason for concern. On the supply side, the study of health personnel revealed significant shortages of patient care physicians, dentists,[39] pharmacists, and active registered nurses. On the utilization side, levels of dental and prenatal care and of child immunization were quite low and generally corresponded to the deficiencies in types of health personnel. To make up for some of these deficiencies, it does seem apparent that Texas border residents were crossing over to obtain needed primary care services, though not as frequently as expected. Although the percentages reported seem low, the crossover volume for private physicians, dentists, and pharmacists is not insignificant in terms of potential overloading of an already inadequate delivery system.

Health Care Behavior in the Borderlands: Culture, Poverty and the System

A relatively more demographic and health services approach has been taken here in order to provide some balance to the more suggestive ''attitudes and values'' approach more common in the study of health among Mexican Americans of the Southwest. A comparison of demographic data on mortality and morbidity (i.e., need) and institutional and survey data on health care utilization is intended to point out where the greatest health problems exist within a relatively limited socioethnic region of the Texas Borderlands. While the data are limited and the research uncomprehensive, they did provide a general picture of high mortality and morbidity rates and low curative and preventive care utilization. Let us now return briefly to the six key factors hypothesized earlier as accounting for much of this gap between need and utilization.

Factors one and two are related to what Weaver has cited as a central theme in the literature—''that the health care behavior of Mexican Americans is a consequence of (as well as a reinforcement for) a community-wide, designative culture.''[40] Beliefs in supernatural causation of illness and the use of a lay referral system have been cited as reasons why, in South Texas, ''many Mexican-American patients come under a physician's care only when the disease is far advanced [which] lowers the chances of a successful cure.'' And, ''the idea that one can prevent illness by certain health precautions is difficult to communicate to the many Mexican-Americans who still believe that any illness may have a direct supernatural origin.''[41] Yet the few recent health surveys in South Texas have revealed low prevalence in use of *curanderos, parteras, brujos, yerberos, espiritualistas,* and *hueseros,* but when used, it is in a complementary not competitive way. The myth that most Chicanos are peasant migrants rooted in a folk-medicine tradition which prevents their utilization of available medical care services is not tenable.

The other four factors cited earlier—poverty, professionalism and the health-industrial complex, two-class health care delivery system, and institutional and personal racism—certainly must interact to affect the health status and health care system in the Borderlands. Such conclusions must be viewed as tentative since definitive research on this subject has not been accomplished.

Is not something being done in this unique health region that has such obvious symptoms of a disaster area? The answer is yes, referring primarily to federal aid from Washington, but such assistance is unfortunately fragmented, uncoordinated, doctor-controlled, and a very small amount of money when compared with the need that exists. Various interesting programs have recently been tried in Laredo, Eagle Pass, Crystal City, and El Paso, but I would like to take the present situation in the three counties of the Lower Río Grande Valley as a case in point.

In the Magic Valley—or the Valle de las Lágrimas as some have called it—we saw earlier that the ratio of doctors and dentists to population is very low. The general hospitals have no resident staffs or outpatient clinics and demand that the prospective patient have a private admitting physician and pay a deposit which varies from $100 to $250 before being admitted. Federal money has come in recently to fund migrant and OEO-CAP clinics (most of the services involve ambulatory outpatient treatment), to provide food stamps, Medicaid, and Early Periodic Screening Detection Tests (EPSDT), and to provide, through the County Health Department clinics, a mother and infant nutrition program. Unfortunately, with the shortage of doctors, the eligibility requirements and the incredible bureaucratic entanglements, made worse by negative attitudes toward these federal programs by many of the providers, coverage has not even begun to approach the estimated need.[42]

The Senate subcommittee hearings on health care in the Lower Río Grande

Valley counties heard statements that express doubts about the effect of federal health care programs. One migrant health care director said:

> Until the people decide to take the initiative and start controlling some of the programs that are brought down from Washington, then it really is not a people movement, it is a Washington movement passed on to the people, and the reactions by some of the people in the community, the consumers, is one of distrust. I feel that if the people do control the program, that the services provided by the programs will be easier to receive and may be a little more humane in their presentation of services.[43]

A lawyer for the United Farm Workers stated:

> I have continually stressed what the Texas branch of the Union feels will contribute most to good health—fair wages. We do not want new programs which create complacent, tenure-oriented bureaucracies, and don't deliver. We want no new legislation, unless it is designed and is passed to support the farm worker in his struggle to gain a fair wage. We do not want legislation which purports to help, but really traps the workers in a maze of restrictions which would vitiate the farm movement.[44]

Most of these programs do not make much impact on sizable segments of the population, have not provided much-needed dental services, or recruited physicians to the Valley. The nonmigrant poor and the nonpoor but medically indigent remain in a precarious situation. Public ambulatory care is nonexistent for most and private care is too expensive. Some choose to cross the border into Mexico for care, others delay and wait until conditions get serious. Fees are driven up by the scarcity of doctors, by the seasonal infusion of the old, comfortable Northern "snowbirds," and by the seeking of specialty care by middle-and upper-class Mexican nationals.

The Future

One of the contemporary dilemmas that confronts the younger policy-oriented social scientist working in the Borderlands is the realization that his or her policy recommendations will probably do little to affect the four deeply set societal factors noted earlier: poverty, professionalism, dual health system, and racism. Yet the feeling is that analyses can be done that spawn recommendations which will make a dent in the system. I believe that one of the most necessary efforts, besides that of collecting basic descriptive data on health status indicators, is the initiation and evaluation of experimental Chicano-organized and administered consumer health corporations. The latter are designed to restructure the delivery of health service so that health care is made accessible to poor Chicanos in a personalized and culturally sensitive way. There are three basic components: economic, political, and cultural. It should be a prepayment or tax-supported plan in which the Chicano community determines for itself the direction and activities of environmental, preventive, curative, and mental health programs and projects that affect them. It is an approach contrary to that of assimilation or Anglicization as a prerequisite for improved utilization of the health care delivery system.

Such experiments should not be merely filling the Anglo shoes with Chicano providers. This might overcome the language or racial barriers (although not all educated Chicanos speak Spanish well), but it would not eliminate the economic, bureaucratic, and professionalism barriers. A very few similar efforts are now being attempted in San Antonio, the Lower Río Grande Valley, and in the Middle Río Grande Winter Garden area. An evaluation of such efforts should provide an opportunity for social scientists to test some of the subculture health behavior hypotheses and to measure whether the health status has improved. Moreover, the state health departments and National Center for Health Statistics must begin to provide health data on Chicanos, and binational Borderlands research should be financed by institutes and universities.

What does the near future hold in store in terms of attempts to raise physical health status? Health Maintenance Organizations (HMOs) seem unlikely to have much success in the Texas Borderlands where the essential conditions of ability to make monthly prepayments and the necessary critical mass of people are not likely to be present. Comprehensive health planning and regional medical programs are likely to be centralized in the new health systems agencies (HSAs) now being planned. These HSAs seem to have the potential of taking away much of whatever local autonomy and input consumer boards have had. Meanwhile, the present nationwide inflation seems to have had a serious dampening effect on the movement toward a national health insurance plan. Thus, in terms of Chicano-directed prepaid health care delivery programs, the near future is not promising. Medically indigent border Chicanos will continue to be forced to respond by delaying the seeking of care and by sporadic use of *curanderos* and of medical personnel and drugs on the Mexican side.

From my perspective both as a sociologist and advocate, vital changes are needed in the political economy of the Borderlands so that border Chicanos will cease to be used as pawns. Health care as well as agribusiness are high-profit areas that combine to help maintain the dependent and unhealthy socioeconomic environment of the Texas Borderlands. During the 1960s, most Chicanos were sold on the American Dream that the way to improve one's life was through formal education. Now, in the mid 1970s, many of those who followed this path and are involved in federally funded health care efforts are challenging the validity of this approach to social and economic mobility. Fair and decent jobs seem to be the necessary missing component preventing their people from obtaining a most basic human right—good physical health.

This is a unique health region, and it needs unique solutions!

NOTES

1. The author acknowledges the contributions of Steve Clyburn and Romeo Rodríguez, former research assistants at the University of Texas at Austin, the support of the Southwest Medical Sociology Committee, and the helpful insights of Robert Trotter and George Walker.

2. Ellwyn Stoddard, "The Current Status of U.S.-Mexico Borderlands Studies: Sociology and Cultural Anthropology," mimeographed (Paper presented at the Rocky Mountain Social Science Association, El Paso, Texas, April 1974), p. 25.

3. John Paul Marcum and Frank D. Bean, "Texas Population in 1970: Trends in Fertility, 1950-1970," *Texas Business Review* 47 (1973): 252-58.

4. Charles H. Teller and Steve Clyburn, "Mortality, Morbidity and Other Health Status Indicators of Chicanos in Texas," in "Barriers to Medical Care Among Texas Chicanos," mimeographed (Southwest Medical Sociology Ad Hoc Committee, Lubbock, Texas, 1974).

5. Benjamin S. Bradshaw and Dudley L. Poston, "Texas Population in 1970: Trends, 1950-1970," *Texas Business Review* 45 (1971): 1-13.

6. Ellwyn Stoddard, *U.S.-Mexico Borderlands Studies: An Inventory of Scholars, Appraisal of Funding Resources and Research Prospects* (El Paso: University of Texas at El Paso, Center for Inter-American Studies, 1974).

7. Leo Grebler, Joan W. Moore, and Ralph C. Guzmán, *The Mexican American People: The Nation's Second Largest Minority* (New York: The Free Press, 1970).

8. Lyle Saunders, *Cultural Differences and Medical Care* (New York: Russell Sage Foundation, 1966); Margaret Clark, *Health in the Mexican American Culture* (Berkeley: University of California Press, 1959); William Madsen, *Society and Health in the Lower Rio Grande Valley* (Austin: University of Texas, Hogg Foundation for Mental Health, 1961); Arthur J. Rubel, *Across the Tracks: Mexican-Americans in a Texas City* (Austin: University of Texas, Hogg Foundation for Mental Health, 1966).

9. See A. T. Moustafa and G. Weiss, "Health Status and Practices of Mexican Americans," Advance Report II (Los Angeles, University of California at Los Angeles, Graduate School of Business, 1968); Jerry L. Weaver, "Mexican American Health Care Behavior: A Critical Review of the Literature," *Social Science Quarterly* 54 (1973): 85-102; Southwest Medical Sociology Ad Hoc Committee, "Barriers to Medical Care Among Texas Chicanos," a project under a subgrant of the Carnegie Foundation Grant for Medical Sociologists to the American Sociological Association under the direction of Gustavo Quesada.

10. Robert Van Kemper, "Health Care Delivery System: Analysis and Evaluation for Mexican American Communities," mimeographed (Southern Methodist University, July 1973), p. 9.

11. Ibid.

12. George Walker, "Border Health Survey: Final Report on Phase Three of the El Paso-Ciudad Juárez Project," mimeographed (Paper presented at XXX Annual Meeting of United States-Mexico Border Public Health Association, Chihuahua, Chih., Mexico, April 18, 1972).

13. Moustafa and Weiss, "Health Status," p. 45.

14. Ari Kiev, *Curanderismo: Mexican-American Folk Psychiatry* (New York: The Free Press, 1968), p. 179.

15. Bonnie Bullough, "Poverty, Ethnic Identity and Preventive Health Care," *Journal of Health and Social Behavior* 13 (1972): 357-58. See also S. D. McLemore, "Ethnic Attitudes Toward Hospitalization: An Illustrative Comparison of Anglo and Mexican Americans," *Southwestern Social Science Quarterly* 43 (1963): 341-46.

16. Joe Bernal and Jackee Cox, "Political Barriers to Economical Health Care in Texas," in "Barriers to Medical Care Among Texas Chicanos," mimeographed (Southwestern Medical Sociology Ad Hoc Committee, Lubbock, Texas, 1974), p. 1.

17. W. Hoff, "Why Health Programs Are Not Reaching the Unresponsive in our Communities," *Public Health Reports* 81 (1966): 656. See also A. Gilbert and P. F. O'Rourke, "Effects of Rural Poverty on the Health of California's Farm Workers," *Public Health Reports* 83 (1968): 827-38.

18. Edward A. Suchman, *Sociology and the Field of Public Health* (New York: Russell Sage Foundation, 1964), p. 183.

19. Robert E. Roberts, "A Study of Mortality in the Mexican American Population," in Charles H. Teller, et al., *Cuántos Somos: The Impoverished Demography on Chicanos* (Austin, Texas: The Mexican American Studies Program, 1975); C. H. Teller and R. Rodríguez, "Annotated Bibliography on the Demography of the Mexican American Population, With Commentary," in Teller, et al., *Cuántos Somos;* Teller and Clyburn, "Mortality"; Moustafa and Weiss, "Health Status." In a recent paper Roberts and Askew suggest some possible explanations for the lack of data: 1) many areas nationally do not have a significant Mexican-American population; 2) even in the Southwest the vital statistics often are not identified as to race or ethnic background; 3) prior to 1950 even basic population data were lacking or, where they existed, were unreliable; 4) more recent ethnic studies have tended to emphasize the Black and the Indian; see, Robert E. Roberts and Cornelius Askew, Jr., "A Consideration of Mortality in Three Subcultures," *Health Services Report* 87 (1972): 262-70.

20. Charles H. Teller and Steve Clyburn, "Texas Population in 1970: Trends and Ethnic Differentials in Infant Mortality," *Texas Business Review* 48 (1974): 240-46. The authors place responsibility for the absence of available data on the National Center of Health Statistics for not facilitating data-gathering in the area and on the Texas Department of Health for not making their Spanish surname data available.

21. Ibid., p. 17.

22. Charles H. Teller and Steve Clyburn, "Illness and Access to Medical Care in a Tri-ethnic Texas Community," mimeographed (Austin, Texas: Department of Research and Transportation, Department of Transportation, 1974).

23. Ibid.

24. Ibid., p. 245. Authors speak of Mexican mothers crossing so that the newborn child might have dual nationality. If, upon return, the child should die, its death would not be reported to and recorded by U.S. authorities. Texas hospitals and midwives tend to report Mexican nationals as residents of Texas. Finally, it is suggested that the unique birth care system of the border may well be saving some of the babies who might otherwise be lost.

25. William McGanity, "Nutrition Survey in Texas," *Texas Medicine* 65 (1969): 40-49.

26. Data provided by Dr. William Brumage, Director of Screening Services, Texas State Department of Health.

27. McGanity, "Nutrition Survey in Texas."

28. "Health Factors Related to Low Income," in *Poverty in Texas* (Austin: Texas Department of Community Affairs, 1972), p. 11.

29. John G. Bruhn and David W. Rowden, "Health Manpower and Educational Needs Among Mexican Americans in Texas," in "Barriers to Medical Care Among Texas Chicanos," mimeographed (Southwest Medical Sociology Ad Hoc Committee, Lubbock, Texas, 1974).

30. Bruhn and Rowden, "Health Manpower," p. 6.

31. Special tabulations from the Texas Department of Health.

32. Ibid.

33. U.S. Congress, Senate, Joint Hearing before the Subcommittee on Health and the Subcommittee on Migratory Labor, *Health Services for Domestic Agricultural Workers* (Washington, D.C.: Government Printing Office, 1972), pp. 163-64.

34. Fred Sowers, "Ethnic Differences in Health Status: A Household Survey of Anglos and Chicanos in South Texas," mimeographed (Austin: University of Texas, 1973); Romeo Rodríguez, "A Comparison of Illness and Medical Care Among Chicanos and Anglos in South Texas," mimeographed (Austin: University of Texas, 1973).

35. Nearly 60 percent of the Chicanos had never been to a dentist, as compared to about 13 percent of the Anglos, and only 14 percent of the Chicanos had visited a dentist within the past year, while half of the Anglos had done so.

36. Moustafa and Weiss, "Health Status"; and Teller and Clyburn, "Mortality."

37. The third phase of this multipurpose study was carried out by students from the University of Texas Public Health School in Houston and the Department of Medicine of the University of Chihuahua Medical School, and presented in George Walker, "Border Health Survey."

38. It turned out not to be representative of either city, oversampling the middle income families in El Paso and the lower-middle-class families in Juárez.

39. In Webb County 71.8 percent of the preschool age children have never visited a dentist, and decayed teeth are a severe problem (personal communication from Dr. Claude Haisley, Laredo, Texas).

40. Weaver, "Mexican American Health Care," p. 85.

41. Madsen, *Society and Health,* pp. 334, 338.

42. See the "Annual Reports of the Hidalgo County and Cameron-Willacy County Migrant Health Projects." Brownsville, a town in desperate need of a Migrant Clinic, recently rejected an offer to open one there (personal communication to author from Leo Garza).

43. U.S. Senate, *Health Services,* p. 51.

44. Ibid., p. 325.

PART VI

The Individual and Social Psychology
of the Borderland Population

14

Mexicans and Americans:
Two Worlds, One Border
. . . and One Observer

Rogelio Díaz-Guerrero

Introduction

In a conference held in La Paz, Baja California, between October 31 and November 3, 1970, and entitled "Round Table on Problems of Transculturation in the Frontier Zone between Mexico and the United States of North America,"* I was invited to present a paper called: "Características y Valores de las Culturas Mexicana y Estadounidense." I proceeded to present some of the results of various cross-cultural studies in order to illustrate several differences between the values and characteristics of the Mexican and American cultures. There was an immediate and intensely emotional reaction from one of the Tijuana correspondents. He was in extreme disagreement with my assertion that Mexicans were passive or passive-affiliative.

After the smoke of the battle that followed had settled, it became clear that this gentleman was one of the most active political leaders in his area. His attitude, however, was not very atypical. Miguel León-Portilla points to the fact that of the various movements preceding the Mexican Revolution, many occurred in the Northwest. This is one demonstration of the ability of the northerner to fight for his own rights. León-Portilla underlines the fact

---

*Organized by the Seminario de Cultura Mexicana, with the help of its members in Baja California and the financial backing of the government of the then Territory of Baja California Sur.

that Francisco Madero, the Mexican apostle for democracy, was born in Coahuila, as were several of the best-known leaders of the Revolution: Francisco Villa, Álvaro Obregón, Plutarco Elías Calles, Abelardo Rodríguez, Adolfo de la Huerta, Joaquín Amaro, Felipe Ángeles, and Venustiano Carranza. In addition, there is the long history of determination to fight a hostile environment, that makes the *norteños* not only active but activists with greater frequency than other Mexicans. León-Portilla is also quick to point out that there is, undoubtedly, United States influence and, as he says, an ever-stronger consciousness in the *norteño* of his Mexicanism.[1]

There are some interesting data showing that not only psychological but, interestingly, socioeconomic indicators provide a basis for attributing a sociocultural influence to the United States of America in northern Mexico. Contrariwise, there is also evidence that the Southwest of the United States, including Texas, is being influenced by Mexican culture.

The question, however, is no longer whether or not such a reciprocal influence is taking place. We shall try to systematize a few of the questions that psychology, in its individual and social variants, may ask about the border and its people. All of these questions are important and for some we have answers based on varying amounts of research:

1. Is there any factual evidence that the American and the Mexican sociocultures, and the individuals and groups that compose them, are different in any respect?

2. What evidence is there of a diffusion of values and other characteristics across the border?

3. Are there any research data bearing directly on actual, interpersonal, and intergroup interactions of Mexicans and Americans in the towns on either side of the Río Grande?

The answers to these three questions are fundamentally independent from value judgments. Is there a place in this essay for statements such as positive and negative traits in either culture or beneficial versus negative influences of one culture over the other? With due recognition of the great difficulty that any individual, and even any scientific discipline, has regarding statements of what is good and what is bad for people, this is an important area of inquiry.

I conceive of each of the existing sociocultures as a historico-sociocultural experiment, emerging from the efforts of the human beings caught in each of the historical events. The highest in positive evaluation should be assigned a socioculture that would permit the optimal development of the human potentiality in its individual, group, societal, national, and international expressions. Probably no one knows what the range of characteristics is for each national example of such sociocultures. Even with the best of intentions, what I will consider positive or negative will remain a personal opinion, albeit an opinion based on my professional experience and research.

Let me hasten to indicate that we have: 1) a large amount of interesting data regarding specific results from psychological tests on urban Mexican and American children and adolescents with ages ranging from 6.7 years through 17.7 years; 2) interviews with their mothers and responses to questionnaires about parental attitudes; 3) some data regarding the sociocultural premises of both the Mexican and the American sociocultures; and 4) some unsystematic data regarding the diffusion of values and other characteristics across the Mexican-American border. All of these data are, of course, limited in scope but they are also the best data available regarding psychological and personality development in these two cultures which have faced each other for 150 years along a two-thousand-mile border and have clashed in war. These data, which are the principal basis for my paper, are fundamentally the result of cooperation between American behavioral scientists of the University of Texas in Austin and Mexican behavioral scientists of the Universidad Nacional Autónoma de México, a cooperation that has lasted for years and in which, easily, more than one hundred professors, instructors, research assistants, and students from both countries have collaborated.

The Historico-Sociocultural Background of Mexicans and Americans

For the Western world, one could hardly find a pair of nations that would be more intensely different in historico-sociocultural background than the United States of America and the Republic of Mexico. I shall not repeat here the innumerable differences between the Anglo-Saxon cultural background of the American people and the Hispanic of the Mexican. To make the difference even more interesting, the Mexican is not completely Western. The mestizo population of Mexico has an Eastern component from its pre-Hispanic heritage, stemming from the Asiatic origins of all Amerindian peoples.

Through cross-cultural studies and results obtained from psychological tests, it has been possible to reach back selectively into the two societies' histories for evidence regarding their general behavior toward religious and/or state authority.[2]

Lesley Byrd Simpson stresses Spain's efforts, particularly through its friars, to establish the City of God in Mexico.[3] Saint Augustine's *City of God* constituted a utopian vision of government where "The princes and the subjects served one another in love, the latter obeying while the former take thought for all.''[4] In Mexico the early friars were for the most part warm and understanding individuals who tended to the needs of the Indians and in turn exacted work from them. There are numerous historical testimonies of the friars speaking out for the interests of the Indians against the semifeudal government of colonial Mexico. In this Spanish colonial City of God, the kings were the friars and the subjects were the Indians. The vast accomplishment of the Indians in the building of churches and convents often was a labor of love.

The other selected historical event, which deserves to be investigated further, is the formation in Mexico, far more commonly than elsewhere in Spanish America, of the mestizo family. The relationship was between the Spaniard (the conqueror, the white, the civilized, the Christian) and the Indian woman (the defeated, the dark, the pagan, the savage, who was stolen from her family or bought at auction and frequently more than one per soldier, as Bernal Díaz del Castillo testifies). If we add the belief that the Indian women did not even possess souls, this male-to-female relationship probably illustrates an extreme example of discrimination against women. It is, at any rate, a likely historical antecedent of the traditional Mexican sociocultural premise that males are naturally superior to women.

With an ingredient of love under the auspices of the friars, Spain established and maintained in Mexico a hierarchy of absolute power. Vicente Riva Palacio expresses his amazement in *México a través de los siglos* at the tranquillity of the three centuries of the Mexican colonial period: ''It will be in vain to try to find there those passionate struggles between political or religious parties, that effervescence of the spirit so fecund in dazzling traits of virtue or of courage that characterize the critical epochs of the nations, the great convulsions of maturity and virility.''

It seems clear that during these three hundred years the City of God took deep roots in the Mexican people. Contrariwise, the history of Mexico ever since is one that was poetically anticipated by Vicente Riva Palacio: ''Great convulsions of maturity and virility.''[5] In his ''Background of Tyranny,'' Cosío Villegas conscientiously struggles in search of an explanation for the history, not only of Mexico, but of all Hispanic America ever since its independence.[6] The most important aspect of Cosío Villegas's argument, together with insights that nicely tie his thinking in with what has been said before, is evident in the following quotation from Leopoldo Zea:

All of Spanish America will divide itself in two groups: The group of those who aspire to convert their countries into modern nations and the group of those who will oppose all transformation, considering that the best form of government is the one they have inherited from Spain; the latter aspire to an order similar to that of Spain, but without Spain.

In their intentions, those in the second group have the greatest advantages. The first group, the revolutionaries, have no other advantage but their audacity and their persistence. The conservative groups count with the sturdy allies of habit and custom imposed by Spain during three centuries. The liberators are soon aware of this fact; to counteract it they do not find any other solution than a species of enlightened despotism; dictatorships for freedom. It was necessary to force the Spanish Americans into entering a new world of freedom, denying them the right of selecting any other road. This was particularly necessary, since the freedom for choice would have no other source of information than the same assemblage of habits and customs which had been originally imposed by force. Only when Spanish Americans should become aware and know their freedom, only then could they be abandoned to their destiny. Meanwhile, the liberators will assume responsibility for these nations; Bolívar made his powers felt to the people, to the nations that he liberated. The same was done by O'Higgins in Chile, Rivadavia in Argentina, and Dr. Francia in Paraguay. But before the dictatorships for freedom, there will rise the forces committed to the restoration of the old order. Liberal dictatorships or conservative dictatorships?[7]

It can be sobering for those who champion violent revolutions that, after 165 years of struggles and bloodshed, so much of the City of God's thinking is still functional, as we shall see later, in the organization of today's Mexican family.

An important dimension is the one underlying the sixty bipolar items comprising the "Views of Life" questionnaire.[8] In 1970, this questionnaire was applied to four hundred fourteen-year-old children paired socio-economically across eight nations. The primary dimension was tentatively labeled "Affiliative-Obedience *vs.* Active Self-Assertion." This general dimension sharply discriminates among the four pertinent different groups of fourteen-year-old populations as illustrated in Table 1.

Several of the pairs of statements, making up the subdimension of authority under this general dimension within the Views of Life questionnaire, are also given in Table 2. Here the results are broken down further to indicate social class as well as cross-cultural differences. The individuals who filled out questionnaires were asked to choose which of the alternative beliefs in each item were closer to their own personal beliefs.

288 Rogelio Díaz-Guerrero

TABLE 1
Differences Among Fourteen-Year-Old Boys from Four Cities in
Affiliative-Obedience vs. Active Self-Assertion

	Mexico City %	Austin %	Chicago %	London %
Affiliative-Obedience	60	38	26	15
Active Self-Assertion	40	62	74	85

Source: Taken from data collected in the Cross-National Study of Coping Styles and Achievement in 1968-69 by K. Miller (London), R. Havighurst (Chicago), R. Peck (Austin), and R. Díaz-Guerrero (Mexico City), using the Views of Life questionnaire. (See Peck and associates, forthcoming).

Note: N = 200 for each percentage.

Table from W. H. Holtzman, et al., *Personality Development in Two Cultures* (Austin: University of Texas Press, 1975), p. 332.

It can be seen that among the three English-speaking groups, most of the fourteen-year-old boys subscribe to active self-assertion as a sociocultural premise. Contrariwise, their Mexican counterparts preferred affiliative-obedience. Further, it can be noticed that the four populations are distributed on a continuum ranging from London, whose children appear as highly active, through Chicago and Austin with children moderately active, to Mexico City with the least active self-assertive children. The differences among all four groups are statistically significant. Let us notice that the most striking differences among cultures also appear for the lower working class rather than the upper middle class. The lower working class, particularly in a more traditional society, tends to be the primary carrier of traditional sociocultural premises which, we believe, are inherited from the past.

In the light of these results, which are illustrative of others, we can search back in history for several of the critical historical incidents in the overthrow of absolute religious or state authority for each of the cities in which the comparison has been made. London, as the seat of power for British kings over the centuries, laid the groundwork for the development of individual freedoms as well as the overthrow of absolute authority with the Magna Carta in 1215, the English Reformation in the sixteenth century, and the execution of Charles I by Parliament in 1649. In contrast, the first major reformation in Mexico occurred in 1860 and the Mexican Revolution took place in 1910, only sixty-seven years ago. It is interesting to point out that, although Austin and Chicago are both cities in the same nation, Austin shares a cultural heritage with Mexico. But in addition to their common Anglo-Saxon heritage, the American Revolution of 1776 predated the establishment of both Chicago and Austin as cities. On the other hand, Mexico City and London have existed as metropolises for many centuries. At any rate, the cultural antecedents of all four cities, with regard to the handling of authority and related sociocultural premises, are different.

TABLE 2
Cross-Cultural and Social-Class Differences in the Authority Factor

Item Number	Mexico City Lower (%)	Middle (%)	Austin Lower (%)	Middle (%)	Chicago Lower (%)	Middle (%)	London Lower (%)	Middle (%)
22a	18	41	52	67	60	72	81	89
22b	82	59	48	33	40	28	19	11
40a	61	40	43	37	29	24	17	17
40b	39	60	57	63	71	76	83	83
57a	65	51	32	34	23	14	11	12
57b	35	49	68	66	77	86	89	88

Source: From the Cross-National Study of Coping Styles and Achievement.

Note: Table gives percentages of fourteen-year-old boys from each city and social class who selected each statement in the forced-choice bipolar statement pairs constituting the Authority Factor in the Views of Life questionnaire. $N = 100$ for each percentage.

Item Statement Pairs from Authority Factor

22a When a person thinks his or her father's orders are unreasonable, he or she should feel free to question them.

22b A father's order should always be obeyed.

40a A teacher's order should always be obeyed.

40b When a person thinks his or her teacher's orders are unreasonable, he or she should feel free to question them.

57a A person should not question his or her mother's word.

57b Any mother can make mistakes, and one should feel free to question her word when it seems wrong.

Table from W. H. Holtzman, *Personality Development in Two Cultures*, p. 332.

Individual and Family Differences Between Mexicans and North Americans

Holtzman, Díaz-Guerrero, Swartz, et al., reported hundreds of significant differences in variables from the battery of tests that was applied to Mexican and American children and adolescents. Of these, thirty were uniformly significant differences regardless of the sex, social class, or age of the child. For a good number of other scores in their battery, they found interactions of culture by age, culture by sex, and culture by class. In addition, there were complex interactions of several of these variables at a time.[9]

A frequent finding for a number of variables was that the lower and the upper classes in Mexico differed more than did Mexicans and Americans. In other instances, Mexican males differed more from Mexican females than Mexicans from Americans.

In the mother's interview and the study of parental attitudes toward the children, as well as in the study of values preferred by the parents for their children, thirty-five significant differences regardless of age, sex or social class were reported. Again, a number of items from the mother's interview yielded significant interactions between culture and sex and culture and social class. If one considers that: (1) the tests used in the battery were carefully selected for their applicability to the two societies; (2) the study of children and adolescents implied as many as six replications one year apart; (3) many of the variables utilized derived from tests showing good test-retest reliability with spans ranging from one to five years between testings; (4) special care was taken in the training of the assistants in both countries; (5) repeated checks were made to determine scorer reliability cross-culturally; and (6) a number of methodological studies were carried out to determine the equivalence of the dimensions that were utilized to compare the individuals in the two cultures, it is a conservative conclusion to say that there are indeed differences between Mexicans and Americans in a number of psychological dimensions and that the extent of these differences varies from one measure to another. There is, of course, from the psychological point of view, considerable overlap in the distributions of the two populations which does not contradict at all the fact that there are indeed significant differences between them.

Among the uniform differences, we find that American children and adolescents possess greater word knowledge, less restrictiveness in classifying concepts, and greater field independency; that they perceive time as passing faster than the Mexicans do; that they show lower ability to differentiate between male and female traits; faster response time to inkblots; more pathology in fantasy, more movement in fantasy, more hostility in fantasy, more anxiety in fantasy; lesser *need* for neatness and order; greater *need* to do things just for fun; more concern of what others think of them; more *need* to seek out others; lesser *need* for independence than Mexican children; and that they tend to be more impulsive and have less specific anxiety about taking tests.

For the parents, Mexican mothers are less educated than the Americans. Only 9 percent of the Mexican mothers as compared with 41 percent of the American mothers work outside the home, far fewer Mexican homes than American have magazines, a dictionary, or an encyclopedia. Half as many Mexican mothers compared with the Americans have had teaching experience. From the parental attitude survey it was found, among other things, that Mexican mothers are less accepting of their children's behavior and more controlling; give their children less freedom to express themselves or to take part in family discussion; are less tolerant of children's rights to engage in activities of their own without including their parents; tend to be more authoritarian and, particularly from the lower classes, place higher value on strict obedience in their children. Finally, Mexican mothers value independence in their children less than American mothers, and curiosity, which implies looking into things on one's own, is less valued in their children by Mexican mothers.

In many of the tests that were utilized in the study, it also was found that there was less stability in the scores of Mexican children and adolescents across time than for the Americans. It appears that situational factors, the personality of the test giver, the nature of the interpersonal relation, perhaps even the setting, produced a less stable result in the tests for Mexicans than for Americans. It is not impossible to think that this ability to change behavior in accordance with the circumstances, the sensitivity to the entire situation, is similar to the facility with which Mexicans think of themselves as different from what they are in reality, the gesticulator of Rodolfo Usigli or the masks of Octavio Paz.

Some General Dimensions

The results just reported, the interactions mentioned but not described in detail, and the recent findings of other investigators working in Mexico and in the United States point to a number of personality differences closely related to contrasting aspects of the two cultures. Instead of continuing with further enumerations—since the reader is probably satisfied that the question about differences has been adequately answered—let us try to put together the knowledge derived from these and other cross-cultural studies in a series of statements that will refer to major personality dimensions which appear to be related to contrasts in the Mexican and American cultures. Each one will be stated as a hypothesis followed by a summary of the evidence bearing upon it.

Americans tend to be more active than Mexicans in their style of coping with life's problems and challenges.

An active style of coping, with all of its cognitive and behavioral implications, involves perceiving the problems set by life as existing in the environment. The best way to resolve such problems is to modify this environment, whether it is physical, interpersonal, or social. In the passive pattern of coping, it is assumed that, while problems are posed by the environment, the best way to cope with them is by changing oneself to adapt to the circumstances.

Most of the differences that have been found for the Holtzman Inkblot Test in the major developmental study between Mexican and American children can be understood in terms of coping style better than any other concept. In general, the American child tries to deal with the testing situation in a much more active fashion, even unsuccessfully, than the Mexican. Thus, the American child produced faster reaction time, used larger portions of the inkblot in giving his responses, gave more definite form to them, and was still able to integrate more parts of the inkblot while doing so. In addition, he incorporated other stimulus properties of the inkblot, such as color and shading, into his responses more often than did the Mexican child and elaborated his responses by ascribing more movement to his percepts. In attempting to deal with all aspects of these inkblots in such an active fashion, however, he failed more often than the Mexican child did; that is, the Mexican child gave responses with better form and less often produced responses that showed deviant thinking and anxious or hostile content.

On the cognitive style test, the Mexicans showed more restrictiveness in classifying concepts; that is, when presented with the object sorting test—which consists of seventy-five object-toys that are known to the subjects and must be classified in accordance with some categorical plan—the Mexican children produced a larger number of groupings, showing less ability to generalize, restricting the composition of their numerous groupings. In dealing with the Embedded Figures Test which consists of a series of plates where the subject is to find a hidden figure, that he has seen beforehand, within a complex figure, the Mexican child failed more often and took a longer time to find the hidden figure. In the Time Estimation Test, where he would have to indicate when a minute had passed, it was found consistently that he perceived time as passing more slowly. In scales of a personality test it is clear that Mexicans generally have a greater need for neatness and order and a lesser need to be spontaneously impulsive or to do things just for the fun of it. The Mexican adolescents also showed less concern for what others think of them and less need to seek out others for companionship than was the case for the American teenagers. At the same time, the Mexican adolescent has a greater need for independence, a need apparently growing out of his increasing awareness that he is indeed highly dependent upon others within his extended family and affiliative network.

Given a coping style based more upon passive obedience and a desire to please rather than active independence and struggle for mastery, specific anxiety and defensiveness concerning test-taking are more acute for the Mexican child than for the American. Exams are a necessary hurdle repeatedly demanded of children by society. An active coping style provides a self-directed means of reducing such anxiety. A passive-obedient coping style leads only to conformist behavior in the face of threatening tests, a form of inactivity that seems only to heighten specific anxieties. On the other hand, passive obedience and a desire to please have certain advantages. In tests where the instructions are specific and/or the task is one of memorization, the Mexican children did better than the Americans.

The sociocultural premises presented in Table 2 dealing with affiliative obedience versus active self-assertion are closely related to the active versus passive coping style. It should be pointed out that obedience, as portrayed in these statements, is in clear reference to defined types of authority figures. The parents and teachers of the child are not only highly respected but play a major role in providing the interdependent affiliation that is a major feature of the Mexican culture.

It is not surprising that in the Díaz-Guerrero Factorial Scale of Historico-Sociocultural Premises for the Mexican Family, among the items loading highest are: a person (son or daughter) ''should always obey his parents'' and ''a son should never question the orders from his father.'' Again, any fear or anxiety concerning the taking of examinations in school on the part of the Mexican child is not so much a fear of individual failure as it is a fear of failing to support the interdependent system in which the family plays a central role.[10] Octavio Paz captured the essence of this cultural characteristic in a somewhat extreme form when he said: ''There is nothing simpler, therefore, than to reduce the whole complex group of attitudes that characterize us—especially the problem that we constitute for our own selves—to what may be called the 'servant mentality' in opposition to the 'psychology of the master' and also to that of modern man, whether proletarian or bourgeois.''[11]

In unpublished studies of Mexican and American high school boys who were given the Semantic Differential, Charles E. Osgood and Díaz-Guerrero computed for each culture indigenous distance matrices that contain indexes of the distance between concepts in semantic space, that is, distance in subjective or affective meaning.[12] Of special interest are the distances measured between ratings of: I MYSELF, MOST PEOPLE, and each of twenty-seven occupations. For Mexicans the concept of: I MYSELF was closest in affective meaning to MOST PEOPLE (0.6), STOREKEEPER

(0.9), PEASANT (1.0), SERVANT (1.0), TEACHER (1.0), and ARTIST (1.0), and it was most unlike BEGGAR (3.9) and STUDENT (2.4). By contrast, for the Americans, the concept of I MYSELF was closest in affective meaning to SOLDIER (0.4), WORKER (0.6), STUDENT (0.7), and POLICEMAN (1.0), and was most unlike BEGGAR (5.6)—significantly farther than for the Mexicans—and ARTIST (3.4). These results are clearly consistent with the active versus passive coping style found in the present study.

Americans tend to be more complex and differentiated in cognitive structure than Mexicans.

The Mexican children, in the Holtzman, Díaz-Guerrero, Swartz, et al., study, tended to develop more slowly, on the average, in terms of their cognitive skills and mental abilities than was generally true for their American counterparts.[13] The American six-year-olds also showed a greater degree of complexity in their cognitive functioning, as evidenced by the fact that more factors were necessary to explain the intercorrelations among the cognitive tests for the Americans than for the Mexicans. In some test variables like arithmetic and block design, Mexican children in the first grade scored higher than their American counterparts. This trend reversed itself for the fourth graders and the difference widened still further for the seventh graders.

It is, however, important to point out that there is an exception to the above generalization. Tamm replicated a part of the Holtzman, Díaz-Guerrero, and Swartz study with bilingual children in the American School in Mexico City.[14] She found that bilingual children from upper-class Mexican families do not differ in cognitive development from closely matched American children. Significantly, these Mexican children came from families where there was both upper-class style of intellectual stimulation and encouragement to the children, and the strong desire of the parents to have the children study under American programs of education.

While there is no way one can separate the biological from the social factors in cognitive development across the two cultures, the evidence thus far strongly suggests that differences in level and pattern of cognitive development among Mexican and American children are due primarily to differences in the sociocultural premises, value orientation, and environmental milieu—within the family and the school—in the two societies.

Mexicans tend to be more family-centered, while Americans are more individual-centered.

Families in Mexico, as well as other Latin American countries, tend to stretch out in a network of relatives that often runs into scores of individuals. In the developmental study, it was found that the number of siblings in the Mexican family was 3.7 while it was only 2.0 for the American. In 18 percent of the Mexican families, there were other relatives present in the home while this happened in only 3 percent of the American families.[15]

In 1966, an early version of the Views of Life questionnaire was given to college students in Mexico and in the United States. One of the bipolar items consisted of the following pair of statements: a) one must fight when the rights of the family are threatened; or b) one must fight when the rights of the individual are threatened.

Only 22 percent of American college students selected the family-centered alternative, the remaining 78 percent selected the individual-centered alternative. Just the reverse occurred for the Mexicans, 68 percent selected the family version while only 32 percent preferred the individual one.

Mexicans tend to be more cooperative in interpersonal activities, while Americans are more competitive.

The data from the developmental study do not bear directly upon such a hypothesis, but there are a series of studies by S. Kagan and M. C. Madsen that have provided clear evidence that Mexican children tend to be highly cooperative in experimental games, while Anglo Americans are highly competitive.[16] Holtzman's paper in this book explains further this difference.

Mexicans tend to be more pessimistic in outlook on life than Americans.

The primary scale, designated internal determinism, from the parent attitudes survey, is relevant to this hypothesis. A number of the items in this factorially derived scale reflect either a pessimistic or an optimistic outlook on life, depending upon the answer given by the mother. In general, the Mexican mothers tended to appear more pessimistic, while the Americans were more optimistic in their general outlook on life.

American society has always been full of hope for the future and optimistic about its destiny, at least until very recently. By contrast, the history of Mexico has been one of losing an external war and suffering from devastating internal turmoil, until well into the twentieth century; it has been unable to provide opportunities for personal, economic, and worldly success for most of its people, at least until recently. It is quite understandable that such a milieu would induce a pessimistic, fatalistic outlook on life, especially, as we found, among the lower classes. Daniel Cosío Villegas describes the plight of the Mexican as contrasted with the American:

> The North American, fabulously rich, is accustomed to count up what he has, what he makes and what he loses; hence his tendency to base many of his value judgments on magnitude, on quantity. The Mexican, thoroughly poor as he usually is, has very little or absolutely nothing to total up, and consequently the notion of magnitude or quantity is somewhat strange to him; for this reason he bases, or endeavors to base, his judgments on the notion of quality. The North American, who in his country has natural resources that no country has known until now (perhaps Russia may have them), has found through experience that he can do things, and that their accomplishment requires only determination and effort. This makes him naturally active and confident. Mexico is poor in physical resources; for that reason the Mexican believes that his determination and his effort are not enough, that before and above man there are given conditions—providential, he would call them— which are very difficult or impossible to set aside. This makes him a skeptic, distrustful of action, a believer in forces superior to himself, more likely to cavil than to act. He leaves for tomorrow many of his enterprises, not from laziness or mere indecision, but because the insufficiency of his resources has taught him over and over again that you can't make the day dawn any sooner no matter how early you get up in the morning.[17]

While a certain Pollyanna character has prevailed until recently in American culture, the Mexican has more often than not perceived life as something to be endured rather than enjoyed. College students, reacting to the 1966 version of the Views of Life questionnaire, responded to a bipolar item consisting of the following alternatives: a) life is to be enjoyed; and b) life is to be endured. Only 13 percent of the Americans selected the "to be endured" alternative while fully 62 percent of the Mexicans selected it. To the Mexican, the optimism of the American may even seem to be out of touch with reality. Although carried to excesses in his poetic license, Octavio Paz has the following to say:

The North American system only wants to consider the positive aspects of reality. Men and women are subjected from childhood to an inexorable process of adaptation; certain principles, contained in brief formulas, are endlessly repeated by the press, the radio, the churches and the schools, and by those kindly, sinister beings, the North American mothers and wives. A person imprisoned by these schemes is like a plant in a flowerpot too small for it: he cannot grow or mature. This sort of conspiracy cannot help but provoke violent individual rebellions.[18]

Differences between the sexes, in cognitive and cognitive-perceptual abilities will be significantly greater between Mexicans than between Americans.

The developmental study shows a number of culture by sex interactions in the cognitive perceptual and cognitive ability results. While commonly there are no differences between males and females in the United States for these abilities, such differences are often significant between Mexican males and females, favoring the males. In some cases a higher order interaction indicates that it is the low-class female who is at the greatest disadvantage. M. M. Cáceres Rivas, in a cross-sectional study of 660 cases, fifty-five males and fifty-five females each in the second, third, fifth, sixth, seventh, and eighth grades, found that the males in every single grade obtained higher scores than the females in all of the subtests of the Wechsler Intelligence Scale for Children (WISC) with the exception, for some ages, of digit span and for all of them in digit symbol.[19] R. Ahumada obtained fundamentally the same results for the complete Mexican sample of approximately 450 cases in the developmental study.[20]

The Diffusion of Values and Other Characteristics Across the Border.

Peck and Díaz-Guerrero studied the meaning of respect and its diffusion across the Mexican-American border.[21] A simple and straightforward checklist was utilized. The subjects, all beginning college students, were told that the word "respect" had several important meanings and that not everybody used the word in the same way. They were provided with a list of twenty different ways in which the word "respect" might conceivably be used. Examples of these ways of using the word are: to look up to somebody with admiration, to love somebody, to fear somebody, to feel it is your duty to obey someone, and to anticipate the possibility of punishment from the respected person. A total of 1,814 students, five samples of at least two hundred students each, answered the questionnaire: Anglo-American students at the University of Texas; Anglo-American and Mexican-American students in Edinburg, Texas; Mexican students in Monterrey, Mexico; and Mexican students in Mexico City. Approximately half of these subjects were females. An analysis of variance was applied to each one of the items in the test across the groups. In order to establish what we called the core-culture pattern of meaning for Mexico and Texas, we looked for the items in which the Texas students differed significantly from the Mexicans and vice versa. It was found that the Texas-Anglo core-culture pattern of respect was to look up to with admiration, to treat like an equal, to give the other a chance, to consider the other's feelings, and to consider the other's ideas. The core-culture pattern of central Mexico was to love, to feel affection toward, to expect protection from, to feel protective toward, not to trespass on the other's rights, to have to obey (like it or not), duty to obey, and not to interfere with the other's life. I would call these findings an equality-efficiency meaning for the Texas Anglos and an affiliative hierarchy for the Mexicans.

From the complete analysis of all the groups' responses, several different item patterns appeared, indicating a cultural diffusion of values. The results are summarized in Table 3.

In Group I, we see the Mexican values that remained constant all the way from Mexico City through Monterrey to the Mexican American in Edinburg. In Group II we see those values that are held not only by the Anglos in Austin and Edinburg but also by the Mexican Americans in Edinburg. Group III shows that the diffused Mexican values—to love, to feel protective toward, and to avoid interference in the life of the respected person—are held just as much by Mexicans in Mexico City and Monterrey as by Mexican Americans and Anglo Americans in Edinburg. To look up to with admiration is an Anglo value, which is, however, shared by Mexican Americans in Edinburg and also by students in Monterrey. Finally, Group IV shows a border effect—namely, the two sets of items portrayed are chosen much more often by people in one of the border samples than by the samples in either Mexico City or Austin. They are indeed border-specific. In Monterrey, particularly, the women look up to the respected person with awe and fear. In both Edinburg and Monterrey, and apparently for Anglos as well as for Mexican Americans, the items of anticipating the possibility of being punished by the respected person and the desire to obey are chosen significantly more often than either in Mexico City or in Austin.

TABLE 3
The Cultural Diffusion of Values: Provisional Evidence

I.   "Culture-typed" meanings
      7.   Affection
      9.   Expect protection from
    13.   Avoid trespassing on rights   Mexican, in Mexico and U.S.
    15.   Have to obey, like it or not
    16.   Duty to obey

II. "National" meanings
      5.   Treat as equal
      6.   Give someone a chance   U.S., including Mexican Americans
      8.   Feel admiration   in Edinburg, who are perhaps
    12.   (Not) dislike   acculturated to U.S.
    17.   Consider feelings   pattern on these points.
    18.   Consider ideas

III. "Diffused" meanings
      4.   To love   Mexican, but also shared by
    11.   Protective toward   Edinburg "Anglos," who are
    20.   Avoid interfering in their life   perhaps acculturated to the
                         Mexican pattern on these points.

                         U.S., but shared by Monterrey
      1.   Look up with admiration   people, who are possibly accultur-
                         ated to the U.S. view on this point.

IV. "Border" effect
      2.   Look up with awe   Monterrey (especially women),
      3.   Fear   but not U.S. or Mexico City.

    10.   Expect punishment from   Edinburg and Monterrey, but
    14.   Like to obey   not U.S. or Mexico City.

Table from R.J. Peck and R. Díaz-Guerrero, "Two Core-Culture Patterns and the Diffusion of Values Across Their Border," *International Journal of Psychology* 2 (1967):275-82.

Restricted as they are, these data certainly permit some speculations. In the first place, there is some evidence here of diffusion of the meaning of respect across the border. In the second place, it can be seen that at least regarding the meaning of respect, three items diffused from Mexico to the United States while only one diffused from the United States to Mexico. Finally, looking at the items typical of the border, one could speculate that, compared with the rest of the items, they refer to the more negative meaning of the word "respect." If we consider that the core meaning pattern for Mexico is one of an affiliative hierarchy with its clear authoritarian counterparts, one might say that the students in Monterrey are trying to be more Mexican than the Mexicans, perhaps as a result of the fact that they are to some extent Americanized in their meaning of respect. It can be seen that Monterrey shows all four effects while Edinburg has only two. Here one can understand the Mexican Americans trying to be Mexicans since they are far more Americanized than the students in Monterrey. But this same explanation could not apply to the Anglos of Edinburg.

Calatayud, Reyes, Ávila, and Díaz-Guerrero carried out a study of the social, economic, and demographic characteristics of the middle and lower classes in six Mexican cities distributed from the north to the south of the Republic.[22] In Table 4 they are arranged from the northernmost to the southernmost as far as geographic and other contacts with the United States are concerned.

From sociological studies in the United States, and partially from the cross-cultural developmental study, we know that the correlations between mother's education and father's education, as well as the correlations between father's education and father's occupation, are much higher in the United States than in Mexico. Table 4 shows that the closest correlations between mother's education and father's education to those in the United States are in Monterrey. Although significant because of the sample of more than 500, they are exceedingly low in Mexico City and become insignificant in Mérida.

TABLE 4
Intercorrelation of Selected Social Indicators
Across Mexican Cities

	r_{1-2}	r_{2-3}
Monterrey	.54	.79
Saltillo	.37	.54
Guadalajara	.41	.49
Mexico City	.18	.31
Mérida	.08	.05

1 = mother's education,   2 = father's education,   3 = father's occupation.
Modified table from A. Calatayud, et al., *El perfil de teleaudiencia de "Plaza Sésamo"* (Mexico City: Ediciones INCCAPAC, 1974).

Still more dramatic are the differences from north to south regarding the amount of correlation between father's education and father's occupation: Monterrey comes closest to the United States pattern, Saltillo and Guadalajara fall significantly below Monterrey, Mexico City shows a significant but low correlation, and Mérida shows no correlation at all between these two variables. These striking findings cannot be the result of urbanization, since Mexico City is more urbanized than Monterrey and Guadalajara, and cannot be attributed exclusively to a northerner spirit, since Guadalajara belongs to central Mexico. They probably indicate a defined sociocultural influence from the United States upon Mexico. Males in northern Mexico are more careful regarding the educational credentials of their wives than males from Mexico

City or Mérida. Also, northern employers are far more concerned in matching occupation and education of job applicants than are those in Mexico City or Mérida.

Interactions at the Border: A Clinical Speculation

It is one thing to be able to make a good sketch of the individuals and families in the two dominant sociocultures and quite another to know what happens in the interpersonal and group relations at the Mexican-American border. Never has a research project been undertaken to explore systematically the type of interpersonal and social interactions that obtain between Mexicans and Americans in towns on both sides of the Río Grande. E. H. Spicer defines "ethnic boundaries" as those situations in which "the sense of identity receives some kind of expression and where individuals align themselves in some manner as members of one ethnic group or another."[23] He points out that ethnic boundaries, like fences, must be maintained and gives a number of examples of where and how the processes of maintenance take place. I was immediately reminded of José Vasconcelos's lively descriptions of his attendance at an American school in Eagle Pass during his childhood. To paraphrase Vasconcelos: Jim would say in class, "Mexicans are a semi-civilized people," and José would stand and state, "We had the printing press before you did." The teacher would bring peace by saying, "But look at Joe, he is a Mexican, isn't he a gentleman?" During the recreation period after the class was over, as Vasconcelos recounts in his *Ulises criollo,* he would reflect upon the many fights and the occasional appearance of a knife that would underscore the disagreements in the interpretations of the history and ways of life of the two countries. He says, "The daily sentimental shock in the school on the other side would provoke in me martial and patriotic fevers. I spent hours before the map looking through my mind's eyes at the roads through which a Mexican army, led by me, would arrive sometime in Washington to take revenge for the affront of '47 and reconquer what was lost."[24]

From this reaction of a passionate Mexican, but one with great intellectual resources, anyone can easily understand the search for identity of the Mexican American. E. Galarza makes good sense when he says, "For this reason I am continually unsure when I imagine I am dealing with an aspect of the Mexican culture, whether it is an *action* of that culture or a reaction to its containment."[25]

Thus, even when I like to associate myself with the optimistic feeling of Ithiel de Sola Pool about the benefits of pluralism in the Southwest, as well as with the happy ceremonial interactions—fiestas, fairs, and rodeos—that Spicer reports on both sides of the border, I also can sympathize with Galarza's statements and feelings about the progressive and apparently irreversible destruction of the subordinate culture by the dominant. There is a place for the cautious thinking of León-Portilla to the effect that the pluricultural reality of the Southwest can give rise to positive influences, but that if there are feelings of superiority by one group with respect to the others, much the contrary will occur.

This information leads me, as a clinical psychiatrist-psychologist, to feel that there is a great fear of loss of identity in both Americans and Mexicans if they dare to imitate or assimilate characteristics of the other group. I get the feeling that much could be accomplished if one could dispel this fear of the loss of national identity and replace it by the realization that probably no one can really lose his original cultural identity even if he tries. Selective assimilation of the positive aspects of the other culture can only produce better Mexicans, better Americans, and better international relations. The rather meager evidence about the diffusion of values across the border suggests that people are already selectively assimilating some positive functional aspects of the two cultures. At the same time, they are reacting to the realization that they may be becoming Mexicanized or Americanized by strengthening, or carrying to extreme, aspects of the authoritarian pattern—all in an effort, apparently, to be able to say, "I am more Mexican than thou" or "I am more American than thou."

The Mexicanism of the *norteños* will be fine if they stress positive aspects of the Mexican culture, but if they retreat into a tougher hierarchical family structure, they can only increase family tensions and might even lead their children to assimilate the negative rather than the positive aspects of the other culture. I am quite sure that the people of the middle and even the lower classes in Monterrey are not conscious of how "Americanized" they have become in their life-styles and socioeconomic characteristics and all that this means concerning interpersonal, romantic, and business relationships. But who is going to say that to marry a woman whose education is more in line with your position in the social hierarchy is bad? Who will dare to say that to fill a job on the basis of educational level instead of *compadrismo* is bad for the future of Mexico?

R. Peck in his unpublished study to test the hypothesis of an acculturation gradient in three culture triads from different parts of the world, one of which consists of Mexicans, Mexican Americans, and Anglo Americans, points out that the migrants in each culture triad are fundamentally different from the others in a test of occupational values, although they do portray some characteristics of both their original and their adopted culture. He also points out that the pattern of opportunities present in the new environment is quite influential regarding the occupational values of the fourteen-year-old subjects. In certain respects, the border will have its own culture somewhat different from the two dominant cultures.[26]

In the absence of a truly systematic study of border cultures, there is little more than newspaper information, anecdotes, hearsay, and speculation on which to develop a psychology of the border. One reads in newspapers that the amount of local economic exchange across the border is extensive. A psychologist born in Nuevo Laredo informed me that, for this town alone, tens of thousands of Americans come over to the Mexican side on weekends and tens of thousands of Mexicans go over to the American side during the week. The Americans apparently come over to enjoy the warm leisure of Mexico, drink its liquors, beers, and wines, buy its folk-art specimens, and enjoy the Mexican way of interpersonal interactions. The Mexicans during the week go to the American side to buy its industrially produced goods, to work on the other side, and—as many as can functionally do it—to take their children to the school on the other side. From this, it appears that people are smarter than demagoguery often makes them appear.

Vasconcelos's father, while living in Piedras Negras, sent him to school at the little town of Eagle Pass across the border. In spite of the conflicts at school, when Vasconcelos was sent to study in Mexico City, he was disillusioned:

> The current educational technology ran parallel to the furniture, some textbooks had only questions and answers and the things we had to memorize were not few. . . . Could it be possible that a school of a North American hamlet was better than one that was a part of an institute proud of having fathered Ignacio Ramírez and Ignacio Altamirano?[27]

The data from our developmental study fully justify Vasconcelos's opinion. True, it does not seem to be exclusively the United States educational technology that makes the difference, for there are sufficient data to indicate that the Mexican family, although providing opportunities for interpersonal emotional development, is certainly low in intellectual stimulation of the child. I do not know how, but, in my opinion, both the Spanish and the Mexican sociocultures tend in general to an antiintellectualism. Even Cervantes has Don Quixote losing his mind because of reading too many books. Parents of children of my generation were persistently concerned, when they had studious children, about the fact that this could hurt their brains. At the time, medical products containing phosphorus and other substances, assumed to be good for replacing the energies of the brain, enjoyed great popularity. I must have been given pounds of granulated substances and not a few pills of this sort.

In the 1966 version of the Views of Life questionnaire, Mexican and American college students responded to the following bipolar item: (a) it is not good to accelerate the intellectual development of children; (b) it is good to accelerate the intellectual development of children. While only 11 percent of the Americans subscribed to the first of these two statements, 44 percent of the Mexican students did. In view of the results of the developmental study, the basic philosophy, the "active school," of the recent educational reform under former president Echeverría appears to be valid. However, the success of its implementation can only be determined by rigorous evaluation of the results. It should also be taken into account that to confront passive-affiliative-obedient children and teachers, raised in the Mexican culture, suddenly with an "active school" is probably going to produce much confusion and difficulty. Actually, children should be exposed at an early age to a personalized educational approach and slowly helped to become self-confident first and active later. It also is quite unfortunate that the educational reform did not reach below the primary school and that, in accordance with the view that it is not good to accelerate the intellectual development of children, teaching children letters and numbers is still prohibited at the preschool level. The kindergarten curriculum is almost completely devoid of cognitive stimulation. Thus, any American influence that can come across the border for the early intellectual stimulation of Mexican children can only be positive.

With regard to early stimulation within the family, the only hope on the horizon comes from programs like "Plaza Sésamo" (Sesame Street). In a recent study, Díaz-Guerrero and Holtzman found significant gains in lowest-class children of Mexico City who were exposed to "Plaza Sésamo," as compared with those who were exposed only to noneducational programs.[28]

One of the most important personal dispositions of the Mexicans is to want to please others. The American, on the other hand, as indicated by our research results and the ideas of Riesman about the other-directed character of contemporary Americans, wants to be liked as an individual. A person who wants to be liked and one who likes to please others should get along famously. If this kind of relationship does not lead to socioeconomic exploitation of the one who likes to please, as may be often the case, the permanent relationship of Mexicans and Americans could be just as good as the first meeting. The data permit one to surmise that, as the meetings repeat themselves, the American may find discomfort in the apparent modifiability of the Mexican to situational aspects of the relationship. This can easily be misinterpreted by the American in the way Octavio Paz has misinterpreted the Mexicans, as though they carry a mask and are hypocrites. In actuality Mexicans are probably more flexible in playing roles and in being sensitive to emotional variations in the relationship, while Americans are more rigid and follow certain consistent patterns in their interactions. These consistent patterns, regardless of the nuances of the interpersonal situation, can easily lead the Mexican to feel that the American is cold, impersonal, and distant.

Talking distances, as observed by E. T. Hall, are much closer for the Mexican than for the American.[29] As Hall points out, the American may interpret the desire of the Mexican to get closer, as well as his affiliative embrace, as immoral sexual advances. The Mexican will likely interpret the American's withdrawal as one more sign of coldness and even distrust, if not rejection. It is not impossible that the stereotypes finally formed in each culture regarding the other will come from misinterpretations of the behavior of the people in the other culture in terms of the sociocultural premises of the onlooker's culture. Thus, from the point of view of Mexicans, the Americans' high activity may be interpreted as neurotic behavior, their straight-forwardness and impulsivity as rudeness and aggressiveness, their individual freedom as sexual looseness, their independence as coldness, their lack of expressiveness as stupidity, their physical bigness as awkwardness, and their self-assertion and search for individual success as egoism. On the other hand, from the sociocultural premises of the Americans, slowness is probably interpreted as laziness, overfriendliness as sexual advances, unpunctuality as irresponsibility, politeness and refinement as hypocrisy, free expressiveness as vulgarity, and intense family concern as pathological dependence.

The quest of Mexico ever since its independence has been to become a democracy. In my opinion, Mexico's inability to reach its goals arises from one of the main sources of its strength, the Mexican family. The idealized City of God has taken refuge within the Mexican family and, while its affiliative network is very positive, its power structure is negative.[30] Americans can learn a great deal from the strengths of the affiliative network that is the Mexican family. The power organization of this network, however, tends to destroy the individuality and the initiative of the male and to subordinate the female. Whoever finds a practical way of eliminating the negative aspects of the power structure within the Mexican family without destroying its affiliative strengths will have accomplished a major and peaceful cultural revolution. Irrational nepotism, *compadrismo, amiguismo,*

and corruption—all of which appear to start through affiliative channels—constitute another handicap for the Mexican democracy. There is much
inefficient love in these processes.

We have concentrated on what Mexicans can learn from Americans. What
is it that Americans can learn from Mexicans? There are many things. The
diffusion of the meaning of love for respect is a typical example. Most of the
things that Americans can learn from Mexicans have to do with the business
of how to live life better. The attribution of greater dynamism to foodstuffs by
the Mexican is a case in point. There are a great many foodstuffs that the
Mexicans perceive as containing the same excitement that Americans find
only in whiskey, beer, and apple pie. Even though Americans are more
optimistic than Mexicans about life in general, and while high school and
college students in Mexico say overwhelmingly that life is to be endured and
their counterparts in the United States say that life is to be enjoyed, in reality
Mexicans certainly look as though they are enjoying life far more than
Americans. Americans indeed look as though they are just enduring it.
Americans should think this over many times.

What are the negative aspects of American culture that should be avoided?
There are many but here we can enumerate only a few examples. Some of the
side effects of the affluent society in the United States are sickening: drugs,
waste of resources, and "growing up absurd."

But the only way to go beyond speculation in regard to what happens in the
interactions between Mexicans and Americans at the border is to develop an
ambitious program of interdisciplinary research in such a way that, at the end,
one could correlate interview and test results with specific interpersonal and
group interactions between Mexicans and Americans, within and across social
classes, ages and sexes, in social as well as in business situations. Such a
study would go a long way toward helping us understand patterns of
acculturation and interaction across cultures.

NOTES

1. Miguel León-Portilla, "The Norteño Variety of Mexican Culture: An Ethnohistorical
Approach," in E. H. Spicer and R. H. Thompson, eds., *Plural Society in the Southwest*
(Albuquerque: University of New Mexico Press, 1975), pp. 77–114.

2. W. H. Holtzman, et al., *Personality Development in Two Cultures* (Austin: University of
Texas Press, 1975).

3. Lesley Byrd Simpson, *Many Mexicos* (Berkeley: University of California Press, 1962).

4. Saint Augustine, *The City of God,* trans. Marcus Dodds (New York: Random House,
1950), p. 477.

5. Vicente Riva Palacio, ed., *México a través de los siglos,* trans. R. Díaz-Guerrero, 5 vols.
(Mexico City, 1888-89), 2:16.

6. Daniel Cosío Villegas, *American Extremes* (Austin: University of Texas Press, 1971).

7. Leopoldo Zea, *Esquema para una historia de las ideas en Iberoamérica,* trans. R. Díaz-Guerrero (Mexico City: Universidad Nacional Autónoma de México, 1956), pp. 26-27.

8. R. Díaz-Guerrero, "Interpreting Coping Styles Across Nations from Sex and Social Class Differences," *International Journal of Psychology* 8 (1973): 193-203.

9. Holtzman, *Personality Development.*

10. R. Díaz-Guerrero, "Una escala factorial de premisas histórico-socioculturales de la familia mexicana," *Revista Interamericana de Psicología* 6 (1972): 235-44.

11. Octavio Paz, *The Labyrinth of Solitude,* trans. Leander Kemp (New York: Grove Press, 1961), p. 70.

12. See C. E. Osgood, G. J. Suci, and P. H. Tannenbaum, *The Measurement of Meaning* (Urbana: University of Illinois Press, 1957); and R. Díaz-Guerrero and M. Salas, *El diferencial semántico del idioma español,* (Mexico City: Editorial F. Trillas, 1975).

13. Holtzman, *Personality Development.*

14. M. Tamm, "El Holtzman Inkblot Test, el Wechsler Intelligence Scale for Children y otros tests en el estudio psicológico transcultural de niños de habla española e inglesa residentes en México" (Ph.D. diss., Universidad Nacional Autónoma de México, Mexico City, 1967).

15. Holtzman, *Personality Development.*

16. S. Kagan and M. C. Madsen "Experimental Analyses of Cooperation and Competition of Anglo-American and Mexican Children," *Developmental Psychology* 6 (1972): 49-59.

17. Cosío Villegas, *American Extremes.*

18. Paz, *Labyrinth of Solitude,* p. 25.

19. M. M. Cáceres Rivas, "La variable sexual en relación al rendimiento intelectual en el WISC" (Tésis de Licenciatura, Universidad Nacional Autónoma de México, Mexico City, 1968).

20. R. Ahumada, "Desarrollo intelectual del escolar mexicano" (Ph.D. diss., Universidad Nacional Autónoma de México, Mexico City, 1969).

21. R. F. Peck and R. Díaz-Guerrero, "Two Core-Culture Patterns and the Diffusion of Values Across Their Border," *International Journal of Psychology* 2 (1967): 275-82.

22. A. Calatayud, et al., *El perfil de teleaudiencia de "Plaza Sésamo"* (Mexico City: Ediciones INCCAPAC, 1974).

23. E. H. Spicer, "Plural Society in the Southwest," in idem and Thompson, *Plural Society,* p. 55.

24. José Vasconcelos, *Ulises criollo* (Mexico City: Libreros Mexicanos Unidos, 1957), p. 319.

25. E. Galarza, "Mexicanos in the Southwest: A Culture in Process," in Spicer and Thompson, *Plural Society,* p. 261.

26. R. F. Peck, "A Test of the Universality of an 'Acculturation Gradient' in Three Culture-Triads," unpublished study.

27. Vasconcelos, *Ulises criollo,* pp. 354-55.

28. R. Díaz-Guerrero and W. H. Holtzman, "Learning by Televised 'Plaza Sésamo' in Mexico," *Journal of Educational Psychology* 66 (1974): 632-43.

29. E. T. Hall, *The Silent Language* (Greenwich, Conn.: Fawcet Publications, Inc. 1959).

30. R. Díaz-Guerrero, *Psychology of the Mexican: Culture and Personality* (Austin: University of Texas Press, 1975).

15

Personality Development and Mental Health of People in the Border States

Wayne H. Holtzman

Sociocultural factors that influence the individual's personality development, the realization of his human potentialities, and the nature of his social behavior in large and small groups have caught the attention of many behavioral scientists in recent years. The cultural anthropologist has concentrated on intensive case studies of families, kinship patterns, and value systems in their natural settings, using unobtrusive methods of participant-observer. The sociologist, demographer, or economist has focused upon social indicators, statistical surveys, and qualitative information that apply to whole societies. The psychologist falls between these two approaches in his search for a better understanding of individual human behavior. While recognizing the almost infinite variety of personal characteristics within different individuals, he abstracts and measures only a small number of attributes of particular interest. In this way, the psychologist may be able to say some fairly definite things about an individual or group, but only at the risk of overlooking even more important attributes.

The study of culture and personality in modern society requires the combined approaches of all the behavioral sciences, making the undertaking of definitive studies exceedingly difficult and expensive. For this reason, even the greatly stepped-up pace of research in this field has not yet produced many significant new insights concerning the border populations in Mexico and the United States. Nevertheless, from the numerous small studies that have been undertaken on well-defined samples drawn from different ethnic populations in border states ranging from California to Texas, one can at least formulate some tentative hypotheses that bear upon program and policy decisions. Unfortunately, similar studies in northern Mexico are almost nonexistent. One must look primarily to Mexico City for extensive work on the psychology of the Mexican.

One major cross-cultural longitudinal study involving a large number of Anglo-American children from a border state and Mexican children from Mexico City has been completed and provides a wealth of information bearing upon personality, cognitive, and perceptual development in these two major populations.[1] Rogelio Díaz-Guerrero has already touched upon the highlights of this research in his discussion of sociocultural premises and major personality differences that characterize the dominant cultures in Mexico and the United States. A closer look at some of the more specific results of this psychological research will provide a good basis for examining independent studies dealing with border populations.

More than four hundred Anglo-American children in Austin, Texas, and a similar number of Mexican children in Mexico City were given an extensive battery of psychological tests over a six-year period of annual testing. By restricting the Austin sample to English-speaking, white families who are broadly representative of "Middle America," the dominant Anglo-American value system characteristic of the American majority is well represented. For the Mexicans, as in the case of the American families, only children with native-born parents were selected for the developmental study, thereby narrowing the definition of culture to the dominant, emerging upper-middle and working classes in highly urbanized Mexico City. Within both groups considerable subcultural variation is present, making it possible to draw rather broad generalizations from the results. The extensive variety of tests repeatedly used for psychological assessment of the children provided measures of cognitive or mental abilities, perceptual or cognitive style, and personality characteristics, values, and attitudes. Midway in the study, intensive interviews were conducted with the mothers in their homes in order to obtain information about the family life-style, home environment, parental aspirations for the child, and other sociocultural variables believed to be important influences upon the child's development. Only the cross-cultural results are of special concern here.

Clear and uniform differences were found across the two cultures for many psychological dimensions and test scores, regardless of the sex, age, or socioeconomic status of the child. In other instances, the significant differences between Mexicans and Anglo Americans must be qualified since they are not uniformly present for both boys and girls, for all ages, or for both upper and lower social classes. Some of these interactions are particularly interesting. Only the highlights of these results can be presented here, particularly those findings that bear upon psychological interpretations of populations at the Mexican-American border.

Development of Mental Abilities

A major question of great interest in all modern societies concerns the extent to which aspects of a child's environment within the home, the school, the neighborhood, and the larger cultural milieu facilitate or impede the development of cognitive or mental abilities. When rigorously controlled for socioeconomic status, Mexican first graders performed slightly better than their American cohorts on arithmetic and block design, two important measures of mental ability. After several years of schooling, the initial advantage enjoyed by the Mexicans disappeared. By early adolescence, the Anglo-American children performed significantly better on all the cognitive tests with one exception, associative learning. When considered together with the greater number of analytic responses by Mexican children, this more rapid associative learning suggests a higher motivation to do well and a stronger wish to avoid error on the part of the Mexican children. It is also worth noting that the patterns of relationships among the various mental tests differ appreciably across the different age groups, indicating that the concept of "general intelligence" is probably not a useful construct for describing the mental abilities of children in the two cultures.

The cross-cultural differences for seven items from the mother's interview that are most directly related to intellectual development are indeed striking. The Mexican family is less likely to have intellectually stimulating reading material or study aids for the child in the home. Only rarely did the Mexican parent read regularly to the child before the child entered school, while the majority of Anglo-American parents read to their children on a regular basis. Most of the Mexican children were unable to read, count, or write before they entered school while most of the American parents took pride in the fact that their children had made significant progress in these cognitive skills prior to school entrance. Nearly all American mothers reported that their children regularly read unassigned books, while only two-thirds of the Mexican mothers reported such unassigned reading.

When it comes to spoken languages, however, the Mexican family shows decided advantages over the Anglo-American. Foreign languages (usually English in Mexico City) are spoken in half the Mexican homes, encouraging large numbers of Mexican children to broaden their horizons beyond their native language. In addition, it should be pointed out that Mexican families have a custom of regular storytelling to young children rather than reading to them from books. Consequently, one would expect the oral language facility and associated interpersonal relations to be more highly developed among Mexican children, other things being equal, than they would be for their Anglo-American counterparts.

Certain other differences in family characteristics, parental attitudes, and life-style may also enter into the picture as influencing the degree of cognitive development of children in the two cultures. Of greatest importance is the fact that the level of mothers' education in Mexico is markedly lower, on the average, than the level of education for the Anglo-American mothers, even when the education of fathers is held constant by cross-cultural matching. The number of children in the typical Mexican family is almost twice that of the Anglo-American family, creating a situation in the lower-class Mexican family where the mother must devote most of her energies simply to managing the household. In the upper-class Mexican family, an uneducated maid often enters the picture as an important caretaker of young children. In both instances, sibling pressures and influences are probably greater in the Mexican family than in the American, where frequently only one or two children are present. Other relatives are also much more likely to be living in the same home with the Mexican child, providing an immediate extended family that increases the degree of affiliative activity while deemphasizing solitary intellectual pursuits. A greater value is placed by American mothers on the development of independence and a high degree of intellectual curiosity than is typical of the Mexican mother.

All of these cross-cultural differences in family life-style and home environment point toward the greater opportunity, on the average, for the Anglo-American child, regardless of social class, to be encouraged toward independent thinking and intellectual activities where individual achievement is stressed rather than interpersonal fulfillment. The gulf between the social classes in the rapidly changing society of Mexico sharply distinguishes the working-class Mexican family, and its traditional orientation, from the professional and upper-class Mexican family, which looks increasingly like the American middle-class family with its high achievement values.

While the youngest children in both cultures have similar patterns and levels of most cognitive abilities when socioeconomic factors are held constant, after several years of schooling the two cultures diverge considerably. The Mexican children generally fall behind the American. Within the Mexican system of education, great stress is placed upon rote learning and homework. This type of passive learning does not encourage independent divergent thinking to the extent that the more active learning characteristic of American schools may do. Failure is more common in the Mexican school and children are often forced to go back and do a grade level over once again if they are unable to master the curriculum satisfactorily. In some cases, the Mexican child falls hopelessly behind and drops out of school at an early age. For the Anglo-American child, such failure is rather rare.

Active versus Passive Coping Style

Many of the differences between the Mexican and Anglo-American children can be understood better in terms of coping style than any other concept. On the Holtzman Inkblot Technique, the American child produced faster reaction time, used larger portions of the inkblot in reporting his percepts, gave more definite form to his responses, and was still able to integrate more parts of the inkblots while doing so. In addition he incorporated other stimulus properties of the inkblots, such as color and shading, into his responses by ascribing more movement to his percepts. In attempting to deal with all aspects of the inkblots in such an active fashion, however, he failed more often than the Mexican child. The Mexican child gave responses with better form and less often produced responses that showed deviant thinking and anxious and hostile content. In general, the Anglo-American child tried to deal with the testing situation in much more active fashion than did the Mexican child, even when he was unable to do so successfully.

On the cognitive style tests, the Mexicans showed more restrictiveness in classifying concepts, evidenced greater field dependency, and perceived time as passing more slowly. From scales on the personality tests, it is apparent that Mexicans generally have a greater need for neatness and order and a lesser need to be spontaneously impulsive or to do things just for the fun of it. Mexican adolescents also show less concern for what others think of them and less need to seek out others for companionship than is the case for the American teenagers. At the same time, however, the Mexican adolescent has a greater need for independence, a need growing out of his increasing awareness that he is indeed highly dependent upon others within his extended family and affiliative network.

Given a coping style based more upon passive obedience and desire to please, rather than active independence and struggle for mastery, specific anxieties and defensiveness concerning test-taking are more acute for the

Mexican child than for the Anglo American. Tests are a necessary hurdle repeatedly demanded of children by modern society. An active coping style provides a self-directed means of reducing such anxiety. A passive-obedient coping style leads only to conforming behavior in the face of threatening tests, a form of inactivity that seems only to heighten specific anxieties. When faced with a testing situation, the Mexican child is willing to cooperate, although he will seldom take the initiative. By contrast, the Anglo-American child will see the testing situation as a challenge to be mastered, an opportunity to show how much he can do.

Field Dependency and Socialization of the Child

The concept of field dependence and its converse, field independence, grew out of the early studies by Herman Witkin and his associates[2] as a way of explaining consistent perception patterns. This concept applies in a variety of situations where conflicting perceptual cues make it difficult for some people to extract the embedded figure from its surrounding ground. People differ considerably in their ability to extract an embedded figure from its context. Later studies by Witkin broadened the concept of field dependence to embrace the concept of differentiation. Psychological differentiation is closely tied to developmental change from undifferentiated early states to more highly differentiated adult states. High or low differentiation, or field dependence, has no relationship to general intelligence, personal maladjustment, or other aspects of the individual often judged to be good or bad within the value system of the culture. Women tend to be more field dependent than men; younger children tend to be more field dependent than older ones; and nurturant, affiliative, socially sensitive, intuitive individuals tend to be field dependent, while analytical, scientific individuals tend to be field independent. In a recent international study, Witkin and his colleagues[3] discovered that greater field independence is likely to be found in cultures that place great emphasis on autonomy in child rearing and that are loosely structured. Greater field dependence is likely to be found in cultures that emphasize conformance with adult authority and that have a strict hierarchical social organization.

In the cross-cultural study by Holtzman, Díaz-Guerrero, and Swartz, Mexican children were generally found to be more field dependent than their Anglo-American peers. A number of findings in the current investigation would tend to foster greater field dependence among Mexican children and greater field independence among Anglo Americans, following Witkin's reasoning. These differences are summarized as follows:

1. Mexicans, particularly women, tend to be passive obedient.

2. Fewer Mexican fathers, particularly from the lower-class group, share activities with their sons. (Previous studies have shown that children, especially sons, of families where the father is absent or distant tend to be relatively field dependent.)

3. Mexican children are given less responsibility in the home.

4. Mexican children are more likely to have their friends chosen by their parents.

5. Mexican mothers are more likely to admit to problems in child rearing and to express the attitude that child rearing is difficult.

6. Mexican mothers are less accepting and more controlling of their children.

7. Mexican mothers give their children less freedom to express themselves or to take part in family discussions.

8. Mexican mothers are less tolerant of children's right to engage in activities on their own without including their parents.

9. Mexican mothers tend to be more authoritarian.

10. Mexican mothers are more likely to press their children toward socially favored goals, such as getting good grades in school or making a name for themselves.

11. Mexican mothers, particularly from the lower classes, place higher value on strict obedience in their children.

12. Mexican mothers value independence in their children less than American mothers.

13. Curiosity, which implies looking into things on one's own, is less valued in children by Mexican mothers.

14. The high predominance of Catholicism, frequency of church attendance, and other signs of adherence to traditional values constitute greater social conformity pressures for the Mexican child.

While all of the above observations concerning differences in the family life-styles and socialization practices of Mexicans and Americans lead to the same general conclusion that Mexicans should be more field dependent and Americans more field independent, it should be noted that the actual differences cross-culturally, though highly significant in a statistical sense, are not large. The amount of overlap in the distributions for Mexican and American children on the scores from Witkin's Embedded Figures Test is very great in spite of the fact that the means themselves are different.

Social Class and Sex Differences in the Two Cultures

Social class differences in test performance are much more marked for the Mexican children than for the Anglo American. With increasing age, the upper-middle-class Mexican children tended to look more and more like their Anglo-American counterparts of either middle or working class. The lower-class Mexican children, on the other hand, continued to fall behind in cognitive skills and showed greater persistence in maintaining traditional attitudes, values, and life-styles. At the same time, it should be pointed out that the lower-class Mexicans have a strong desire to improve themselves.

For the Mexicans, but not the Anglo Americans, both sex and social class proved to be highly significant factors influencing the development of verbal ability as measured by a vocabulary test. Among the Mexican girls in particular, as age increases, the gulf between the upper- and lower-class girls widens markedly, placing the lower-class Mexican girl at a noticeable disadvantage. Few sex differences were found among the Anglo-American children, while a number of differences between boys and girls proved highly significant in Mexico. The most significant interaction of all involving culture and sex occurred for the masculinity-femininity ratings of the male and female drawings from the Human Figure Drawing Test. American girls drew more feminine male figures while American boys tended to draw more masculine female figures than was the case for Mexican girls and boys. While the Mexican children tended to accentuate the differences between male and female, the American children tended to minimize such differences in their human figure drawings. These findings are completely consistent with the general belief that male-female differences are much more important in Mexico than in the United States, particularly in recent years with the development of freer life-styles by American youth and the women's liberation movement.

As Díaz-Guerrero has noted in his analysis of the many differences found in this large-scale, cross-cultural study of the two cultures, one would expect that there would be more value placed on affective rather than cognitive aspects of life in Mexico, coupled with a preference for a static rather than a dynamic approach to the environment. The Mexican should be more family-centered, prefer leisure to work, and external to internal controls. In addition, he should be somewhat more pessimistic about life and passive-obedient in style of coping with his environment. For the Anglo American, on the other hand, the opposite of each of these statements should tend to be true.

This cross-cultural longitudinal study of personality development in Mexico and the United States deals only with the dominant subcultures in these two countries—the broad working and professional classes of white English-speaking, predominantly Protestant individuals in the urban centers of the United States and Spanish-speaking Catholic populations from central Mexico. While these two groups constitute the dominant populations in their respective nations, it is hardly possible at this time to speak of one "national character" that would be appropriate in either country. The amount of diversity even within these two well-defined dominant subcultures is so great that considerable overlap exists in the distribution of scores on all variables that have been studied. A more appropriate concept than national character is the idea of modal personality as proposed by Ralph Linton.[4] The modal personality is an abstraction that consists of the commonly shared values, attitudes, and traits—just a touch of stereotyping—while recognizing the great range and variety of individual personality configurations found in any culture.

Mexican Americans in the Borderlands

English-speaking white Middle America and Spanish-speaking central Mexico may represent the dominant subcultures in the United States and Mexico, but they are clearly not alone among the people who reside in the Borderlands. As McLemore[5] has pointed out, the historical presence of strong ethnocentrism, competition, and differential power among the Spanish, the Mexican Indians, the Plains Indians, and the Anglo Americans has led to the subordination of Mexican Americans throughout the border area. This subordination of the Mexican to the Anglo American was largely achieved in the United States Borderlands over a century ago. The Anglos tended to be middle-class Protestants who believed in manifest destiny and who were generally proslavery. The Mexicans were mostly lower-class Catholic mestizos who were proud of their traditions and opposed to slavery. These two opposing cultures might have achieved some shared values and interethnic solidarity if they had been left to their own devices, since substantial numbers of both Spanish- and English-speaking citizens of early Texas lived harmoniously together. Unfortunately the major world clashes among the European powers, and the strong surge of population pressure from the North and East, quickly polarized the competition and conflict.

In 1835, Texas consisted of about twenty-thousand Indians, six thousand Spanish-speaking Mexicans, and thirty thousand English-speaking Americans and their slaves.[6] By 1970, the Indians had all but disappeared, but the proportion of English- and Spanish-speaking citizins had not changed drastically. The number of Mexican Americans in the border states is estimated to be about six million, most of whom have Spanish as a mother tongue.[7] Almost without exception, border counties in all four border states have large majorities of Mexican-American citizens.

To what extent can one generalize from studies dealing with the psychology of the Mexican or the psychology of the Anglo American to the psychology of the Mexican American? Granting that there is considerable heterogeneity among Mexican Americans, just as there is among Anglo Americans and Mexicans, the majority of Spanish-speaking people in the border areas have a common culture that is remarkably similar on both sides of the border. Indeed, the area of northeastern Mexico and South Texas is generally referred to as *la patria chica* inhabited by *La Raza*. Extended families and patterns of work and play stretch several hundred miles on both sides of the border as they have, intermittently, for centuries. The great amount of cultural diffusion and assimilation at the border would lead one to predict that the Mexican-American modal personality would fall somewhere between the traditional Mexican and traditional Anglo-American patterns, some characteristics being identical to the Mexican while others being more like the Anglo-American.

In recent years, a number of studies have been conducted on the Mexican-American population in the Southwest. Until the late 1950s, most of this work was confined to descriptive, historical, educational, and sociological studies. Anthropologists began to turn their attention to the distinctive characteristics of Mexican Americans in South Texas and California in the late 1950s. During the past ten years with the increased awareness by the general public of Mexican Americans as a distinct ethnic group and the rise of the Chicano movement, the number of empirical studies of the Mexican-American people conducted by behavioral scientists has rapidly increased.

Four historical periods leading up to contemporary Mexican-American society have been identified by Alvarez.[8] The "Creative Generation" over a century ago was abruptly confronted by a new set of circumstances following the Mexican-American War and had to evolve new modes of thought and action in order to survive. The "Migrant Generation" after the turn of the century spread northward through Texas where racial attitudes were imposed and roles were predefined by the well-established subordination of the earlier Mexican Americans. Another state of collective consciousness rapidly emerged around the time of the Second World War. Called the "Mexican-American Generation" by Alvarez, these individuals reached out to participate fully in society as Americans with a strong sense of cultural loyalty to the United States. As Alvarez describes members of the Mexican-American Generation:

> Because of his psychic identification with the superordinate Anglo, he abandoned his own language and culture and considered himself personally superior to the economically subordinate Migrant Generation. The fact that he could see that he was somewhat better off educationally and economically than the Migrant Generation led the Mexican American of this period to believe himself assimilated and accepted into the larger society. He did not fully realize that his self-perceived affluence and privileges existed only in comparison to the vast majority of Mexican Americans. He did not realize that for the same amount of native ability, education, personal motivation and actual performance, his Anglo counterpart was much more highly rewarded than he.[9]

By the late 1960s, the Chicano Generation emerged along with the youth counter-culture movement and the demands for full citizenship for all minority groups in a pluralistic society.

These different generations are important to keep in mind when examining theories and empirical studies concerning the personality characteristics and social behavior of Mexican Americans. Many of the oldest citizens and some of the younger Mexican Americans differ little from Mexicans in their value orientation, traditional ways of life, and personalities. Members of the more assimilated, urbanized Mexican-American Generation have taken on Anglo values and have been absorbed into the same stream of Middle America. The Chicano Generation has moved out aggressively in search of its own identity. Consciously rejecting selected aspects of both Mexican- and Anglo-American value systems, many young Mexican Americans have found a new identity with the Chicano activist movement, which has been romanticized by journalists and writers.

With these considerations in mind, let us examine in more detail some of the recent studies dealing with the personality development of Mexican Americans.

Cognitive Development, Motivation, and School Adjustment

The educational gap between the Mexican American and the Anglo American in the Southwest is well known and hardly needs further documentation. Until ten years ago, most public school districts in the border states used only English as the language of discourse for teaching in the classroom. Some school administrators even pointed with pride to the fact that conversational Spanish was not permitted on the school grounds. The great majority of children whose native language was Spanish did very poorly in the early elementary grades, frequently dropping several years behind their Anglo-American classmates. Seasonal migratory patterns of farmworkers disrupted still further the early schooling for many Mexican-American children. Consequently, it is not at all surprising that one out of four Mexican Americans was found to have four years of schooling or less as recently as 1960.[10]

By the mid 1960s, sufficient popular support for bilingual education and new methods of teaching English as a second language to young children produced major changes in school policy throughout the Southwest. Large-scale programs of bilingual curriculum development have been vigorously pursued during the past five years and have resulted in the production of preschool and early childhood materials for the predominantly Spanish-speaking child. As a result of this major shift in educational policies and practices, studies comparing Mexican-American and Anglo-American school achievement ten years ago are more of historical interest than contemporary relevance. While the well-known educational gap does indeed still exist, it is now clearly evident that past school practices and marked social-class differences between Mexican-American and Anglo-American children account, rather than any innate inferiority of intellectual capacity, for the inferior school performance, on the average, of the Mexican American.

A recent study by Bernal[11] demonstrates that Mexican-American children can do as well in concept learning tasks as Anglo-American children, provided they are given equal facilitative conditions prior to testing. Bernal divided 192 eighth-grade children, selected from Anglos, Blacks, monolingual English-speaking Mexican Americans, and bilingual Mexican Americans into experimental and control groups. The control groups were given concept-learning tasks with a standard administration. The experimental cases were given feedback as to their accuracy after every problem attempted and the task was explained in some detail. Children were also encouraged to explain their reasoning when making correct choices as part of the facilitative conditioning in the experimental group. In each case, the research assistants serving as teacher-examiners were ethnically matched to the children. Colloquial Spanish terms were used frequently in the facilitative task for the bilingual children. Under the controlled conditions involving the standard administration, the Anglo Americans did much better than the other three ethnic groups while the Spanish-speaking Mexican Americans did very poorly. Under the facilitative conditions, however, there were no significant differences among any of the four ethnic groups, regardless of the child's social-class background.

As Hernández[12] points out in her comprehensive review of variables affecting school achievement of Mexican Americans, many factors have been found related to the generally poorer educational performance of Mexican-American children. In those studies where there is rigorous control for such confounding variables as socioeconomic status, home environment, teacher attitudes, and language differences, the gap between Mexican-American and Anglo-American school performance disappears. A more meaningful comparison in most instances is the examination of the educational differences between generations of Mexican Americans. In a comparative study, it was shown that Mexican-American children of illiterate parents can do well in school under proper circumstances.[13] Although the fathers from Cotulla were actually better educated than those in Racine, only 7 percent of the Mexican-American children in Wisconsin showed any severe age-grade retardation as contrasted to 42 percent of the children in Cotulla. It should be pointed out that the great majority of the four thousand people in Cotulla are Mexican American, currently there are relatively lax rules against speaking Spanish, and there is now an expanded bilingual education program. The general lack of resources and cultural milieu of Cotulla is a major difference in the two communities that accounts, in large part, for the poorer school performance of the Cotulla children.

One of the most interesting border towns with respect to Mexican Americans is Crystal City, Texas. Until the late 1960s, Crystal City schools were dominated by Anglo Americans in spite of the fact that nearly 90 percent of the population was Mexican American, most of them Spanish-speaking. Marked political changes have occurred in Crystal City during the past ten years, resulting in the complete shift of power from Anglo Americans to Chicanos. The militant challenge to the American ethos represented by the political shift has been well documented elsewhere.[14] In 1970, profound changes occurred in the public schools. Anglo teachers and students withdrew from Crystal City, a bilingual education program was instituted, and classes were conducted largely in Spanish. Whether self-identifying as "Mexican American" or "Chicano," four out of five students in Crystal City now firmly believe that they will at least graduate from high school. Out of a graduating class of 118 high school seniors in 1974, 47 immediately entered college. Although it is still too early to judge the eventual outcome of this educational and political revolution in Crystal City, it is already clear that the achievement motivation of the school children is very high in spite of the fact that the average educational level of their parents is lower than the fourth grade.

A more psychological approach to the study of Mexican-American personality and adjustment to school has been taken by Ramírez, Taylor, and Petersen.[15] Working only with lower-class children, three hundred Mexican-American and three hundred Anglo-American high school students in Sacramento, California, were given a scale for assessing attitudes toward teachers in education. A smaller sample of children was also given a projective technique consisting of ten pictures depicting students, teachers, and parents interacting in settings related to education. The smaller sample receiving the projective technique was selected to represent an equal number of children with very favorable views toward education, very unfavorable attitudes toward education, and neutral attitudes. The projective technique stories were scored for content indicative of power needs, achievement, affiliation, rejection, succorance, aggression, and autonomy.

The Mexican-American students were more negative toward education and scored lower on need for achievement, a finding consistent with the deemphasis of competition and individual achievement within the Mexican culture. The Mexican-American children also scored lower on *n* Affiliation and higher on *n* Rejection, a finding consistent with the culture's emphasis on suspiciousness of strangers and feelings of alienation engendered by school activities. Higher scores on *n* Power by the Mexican Americans were interpreted as indicating their stronger desires to control the means of influence over others because interpersonal relationships in the Mexican-American culture are based on roles of dominance and submission. Although Mexican-American males expressed more succorance toward females than did the Anglo-American males, they also expressed more aggression toward domineering females than did the Anglos. And finally, the Mexican-American females expressed more need for independence than did the Anglo-American females.

Awareness on the part of school personnel of the particular needs, perceptions, and attitudes of Mexican-American students can be used effectively to adapt the classroom atmosphere to the cultural characteristics of the students, thereby enhancing school adjustment and improving the achievement motivation of the children.

An opportunity arose in Austin, Texas, to compare the adjustment of Anglo-American and Mexican-American children in self-contained and team-teaching classrooms because of a large-scale program of research on teacher education.[16] Among Mexican-American sixth graders, the anxiety level in self-contained traditional classrooms was significantly higher than the level reported for the more experimental team-taught sixth-grade classrooms. No differences were found, however, between the two types of classrooms in the anxiety levels experienced by Anglo-American children. Team-teaching settings offered greater flexibility for individualizing instruction and attending to the emotional needs and interpersonal relations between teacher and pupil. For the Mexican child such personalized teaching is more important than for the Anglo.

Personality Differences at the Border

One of the major differences between Mexicans and Anglo Americans noted earlier is the tendency for the latter to be actively competitive and to perceive their own achievements in terms of individual independent efforts rather than to use the more passive and affiliative coping styles of the Mexican. A series of studies by Madsen, Kagan, and their associates has been addressed to the question of how competitive or cooperative young children of different ethnic backgrounds in the borderlands of southern California and northern Mexico are. Using simple but ingenious gamelike devices, they have found, in general, that rural Mexican children just south of the border are far more cooperative than Anglo-American children in Los Angeles, who tend to be very competitive even when such behavior is maladaptive. Generally speaking, Mexican-American children tend to fall in between these two extremes. Typical of their studies is one in which pairs of children within these three ethnic subcultures participate in a game where cooperative play allows both pair members to receive awards, while competitive play is irrational, allowing no one to reach his goal.[17] While the Mexican children were completely cooperative 63 percent of the time, the Anglo Americans were cooperative only 10 percent of the time. The Mexican-American children were more like the Anglos than the Mexicans, cooperating only 29 percent of the time. The Mexican-American children showed a more marked tendency to avoid direct conflict in initial moves while at the same time being like the Anglo Americans in refusing complete cooperation.

Direct rivalry in Anglo-American and Mexican children was also studied by Kagan and Madsen.[18] In this case the apparatus used in the experiments involved choice situations where behavior intended to lower the outcomes of a peer could be measured. Anglo-American children exhibited significantly more rivalry than Mexican children, a cultural difference that tended to increase with age, especially among Anglo-American boys. By eight years of age, the Anglo-American boys are apparently more willing than girls to take a loss in absolute gains in order to lower the outcomes of their peers. Kagan and Madsen conclude that Mexican children avoid conflict while Anglo-American children enter conflict even when to do so is irrational in terms of their own goals. These results are consistent with an earlier anthropological study of mothers' child-rearing patterns in six widely different cultures where it was found that Mexican and Anglo-American mothers are at opposite ends of aggression and obedience scales.[19]

Even among four-year-old nursery school children, ethnicity is related to cooperation and competition value preferences. Wasserman[20] studied expressions of humanitarian and success value preferences in 180 nursery school children drawn equally from Mexican-American, Black, and Anglo cultures in the Los Angeles area. Using a number of pictures with value-conflict situations, she found that Anglo Americans valued competition, expertise-seeking, and completion of task more highly than did either Mexican-American or Black children. It is interesting to note that no differences were found in the valuing of helpfulness, cooperation, concern for others, and sharing, as far as the comparison between four-year-old Anglo and Mexican-American children was concerned. Four-year-old Anglo children appeared to have internalized success values to a greater degree than other ethnic groups even before they enter kindergarten.

Another major personality difference between Mexicans and Anglo Americans is the tendency of Mexicans to be field dependent while the Anglo Americans tend more toward field independence. Ramírez[21] reports two studies that confirm these findings with Mexican Americans and Anglos—one in Houston, Texas, involving 124 fourth graders, and a second study in Riverside, California, using a large number of Mexican-American and Anglo children in the elementary grades. While these results are similar to those obtained by Holtzman, Díaz-Guerrero, Swartz, et al.,[22] in their longitudinal studies of Mexican and Anglo-American children, comparable studies of Mexicans south of the border and Mexican Americans north of the border must be undertaken before the relative position of the Mexican American on this personality dimension can be determined.

Interethnic conflict and prejudice are more likely to occur when there is perceived dissimilarity of beliefs about important issues. Perceived belief similarity and the accuracy of social perception among Black, Mexican-American, and Anglo-American high school students have been studied recently by Kaplan and Goldman.[23] One-third of the students within each ethnic group responded to an attitude inventory as they thought a typical Black student would respond. A second third in each ethnic group answered the inventory as they thought a Mexican American would. And a final third responded as they believed a typical Anglo American would respond. While all three ethnic groups were fairly accurate in perceiving how Black and Mexican-American students would respond to the inventory, the Black and Mexican-American students were substantially inaccurate in their perception of Anglos. Of particular interest is the fact that the Chicano subjects saw only very slight differences between themselves and either Blacks or Anglos with respect to how they would answer the items dealing with values and attitudes. One item in the inventory read, "It's good to mix only with people of your own kind." Each ethnic group when playing its own role tended strongly to disagree with this statement. But when they were role-playing the other ethnic groups, they tended to agree with the item. Each ethnic group sees the others as preferring to be by themselves when in fact they want to mix with others as well!

New methods of human relations training and techniques for making students of different ethnic background depend on each other for learning required material in school, such as those successfully developed by Aronson,[24] need to be widely adopted before interracial tensions will be reduced significantly.

Mental Health and Social Change

Competition, ethnocentrism, and conflict among the ethnic populations in the Borderlands have taken their toll on the Mexican American, in particular, for over a century. One would expect that as a result of the stresses and frustrations suffered by the Mexican American, a greater incidence of mental illness and severe emotional disturbances would be present among the Mexican Americans than among the Anglos. The first systematic data collected on this important question were gathered twenty years ago by Jaco in a major survey of all inhabitants of the state of Texas who sought psychiatric treatment for a psychosis for the first time in their lives during the two-year period of 1951-52.[25] Information was collected from every psychiatrist in private practice as well as from all the hospitals and clinics in Texas and surrounding states.

Only 6 percent of the new psychotic cases during this two-year period were Mexican Americans, 85 percent were Anglo Americans, and the remainder were primarily Black. When the data were standardized for age and sex composition, the average annual incidence rate per 100,000 population was only 42 for the Mexicans. The same incidence rate for Anglos was 80 while that for Blacks was 56. Additional checking by Jaco convinced him that the markedly lower incidence rate for psychosis among Mexican Americans was not a function of accessibility of treatment.

Could the lower incidence rate for Mexican Americans result from different ways of coping with stress? Could it be due to more cohesive family patterns and different life-styles? Or is it, at least in part, only illusory because the Mexican American seeks out *curanderos* rather than psychiatrists when mental illness is present? In 1957, Madsen, Espejo, Romano, and Rubel embarked upon a major anthropological project dealing with differential culture change and mental health in South Texas.[26] After intensive ethnographic studies of three variations of Mexican-American folk culture in which the referral networks for curing illness were carefully traced, Madsen and his colleagues concluded that the different world views and ways of coping with illness that characterized the Mexican folk culture and urban Anglo society are sufficient to account for a large part of Jaco's findings. Madsen goes on to propose that stress situations among Mexican Americans are less likely to produce mental illness because they are shared by the family group.[27] He hypothesizes that anxiety-producing stress seldom precipitates mental illness when the anxiety is shared and relieved by a tightly knit, primary group like the Mexican family.

More recent studies by Edgerton[28] and Karno[29] indicate that mental illness is also greatly underrepresented among the Mexican Americans of Los Angeles, a large metropolitan population rather far removed from the folk culture of rural South Texas. Edgerton also found that folk-psychiatry had greatly diminished in influence among Los Angeles Mexican Americans and that the great majority of them would not hesitate to seek help from a psychiatrist or mental health clinic.[30] Martínez and Martin[31] point out that the use of folk healers continues among Mexican Americans in Texas but that this in no way precludes reliance upon physicians and use of medical services for health problems not defined by folk concepts.

Whatever the reasons for the lower incidence of mental illness among Mexican Americans, it is clear that the recognition of mental illness is a social process. Rather than a problem in medical diagnosis, the recognition of mental illness is a social transaction that often takes the form of a negotiation.[32] The symptomatic content and prevalence of mental illness in various populations is dependent to a large extent upon how this negotiable social transaction is carried out.

Severe mental illnesses such as schizophrenia or depressive psychoses are only one aspect of mental health problems in the Borderlands. Chronic alcoholism, drug addiction, social alienation, child abuse, crime and delinquency, some forms of interpersonal aggression, dehumanizing and degrading social practices, family disintegration, neurotic behavior, and a host of other common psychological and social problems are of even greater importance in a society that is searching for better ways to promote mental and emotional health for all of its people. Absence of mental illness is not synonymous with the presence of mental health. All of us are faced at some time in life with identity crises, severe emotional stress, frustration, and failure. At one time or another each of us desperately needs help. A mentally healthy person is not only one who has learned to cope with most life stresses, but also one who understands when help is needed.

While every culture has some way of coping with psychological and social problems, complex industrialized societies create for their members unusual stresses that require professionally trained persons to provide a wide range of services to people in need of help. For each highly trained professional in the mental health field, a number of paraprofessionals, technicians, and volunteer workers are needed for services to be effective. A major problem for the disadvantaged and culturally different has been the severe lack of adequately trained personnel indigenous to the people served to provide services that can be effective. Most professionals come from middle-class Anglo-American backgrounds, creating particularly acute shortages of services for the large number of relatively uneducated, lower-class families who desperately need help.

In the past several years, there has been a great increase in the quality and kind of mental health services available to people in the border states. California took the lead in the nation in establishing community mental health clinics and outreach programs for the general public in the early 1960s. The other border states lagged considerably behind in the development of services, only recently accelerating their development. Until several years ago, no substantial mental health services were provided for the people throughout the Texas-Mexican Borderland. Individuals in search of help had to travel several hundred miles to San Antonio, Austin, or Big Spring. A reorganization of state services in the mid 1960s under a new Department of Mental Health-Mental Retardation was the first step in expanding services to communities throughout the state. The Río Grande Center was established in South Texas as an extension of the San Antonio State Hospital. The number of new patients from South Texas admitted to the San Antonio State Hospital rapidly dropped as a result. The Río Grande Center was staffed largely with indigenous mental health workers, with specialized psychiatric services on a consulting basis. Delivering a variety of mental health services to the people in their own community proved so successful that scores of outreach centers were quickly established in the regions surrounding every state hospital.

At the same time that these major changes were taking place in the state system for hospitals and special schools, community mental health centers under local citizens' boards sprang up throughout the state in both urban and rural areas. Isolated geographically, El Paso is one of the last metropolitan areas in the United States to develop comprehensive mental health services for the general public.

While the resident state hospital population continues to drop due to better treatment programs, the community mental health centers and outreach programs are rapidly expanding. Within anticipated budget increases of 50 percent for the next biennium, the Texas Department of Mental Health-Mental Retardation is planning to more than double the amount of funds available for services for those parts of the state with large Mexican-American populations.

Other state and federal programs have also been launched in the past five years in a vigorous attempt to provide better human services for the people of the Borderlands. While these belated efforts are indeed hopeful, there is still much that needs to be done before the conditions of life and potentials for human development in the border region are raised to a level commensurate with the rest of the country.

Contemporary American society is probably going through yet another major change as an aftermath to the convulsive period of the 1960s. A new generation arose in the mid sixties—a generation defiant of contemporary American values and determined to launch a counterculture to compensate for the perceived excesses of their predecessors. Recent studies on the attitudes of American youth by Daniel Yankelovich[33] point to major changes in the complexion and outlook of an entire generation of young Americans. The new values have spread from the minority of college students identified as forerunners to the majority of youth. Two motivations are implied by the new set of values: desire for personal self-fulfillment and a new vision of what a just and harmonious society might be. Determined to avoid the excesses of their forefathers, this new generation places a high value upon the pluralistic society in which neighboring peoples of different cultures are encouraged to maintain their own cultural identity while joining together for common purposes in the larger society.

Similar changes are occurring in Mexico although they have not been studied extensively. There is every indication that Mexicans and North Americans are becoming more alike. People of the Borderlands where the two nations continuously interact at a personal level may well be in the vanguard of cultural diffusion. While it is doubtful that such social change can be deliberately shaped even if consensus were reached as to what would be most desirable, there is one goal toward which all of us can aspire—the development of closer ties based upon common needs and mutual respect for the differences in value orientation, language, personality traits, and life-styles that characterize the rich diversity of the border peoples.

NOTES

1. W. H. Holtzman, et al., *Personality Development in Two Cultures* (Austin: University of Texas Press, 1975).

2. H. A. Witkin, et al., *Personality Through Perception* (New York: Harper & Row, Publishers, 1954).

3. H. A. Witkin, et al., "Social Conformity and Psychological Differentiation," *International Journal of Psychology* 9 (1974):11-19.

4. R. Linton, *The Cultural Background of Personality* (New York: Appleton-Century-Crofts, 1954).

5. S. D. McLemore, "The Origins of Mexican American Subordination in Texas," *Social Science Quarterly* 53 (1973):656-70.

6. J. N. Almonte, "Statistical Report on Texas, 1835," trans. Carlos E. Casteñeda, *Southwestern Historical Quarterly* 28 (1925):229.

7. J. Hernández, L. Estrada, and D. Alvírez, "Census Data and the Problem of Conceptually Defining the Mexican American Population," *Social Science Quarterly* 53 (1973):671-87.

8. R. Alvarez, "The Psycho-Historical and Socioeconomic Development of the Chicano Community in the United States," *Social Science Quarterly* 53 (1973):920-42.

9. Ibid., p. 936.

10. L. Grebler, J. W. Moore, and R. Guzman, *The Mexican-American People* (New York: The Free Press, 1970).

11. E. M. Bernal, "Concept Learning Among Anglo, Black, and Mexican-American Children Using Facilitation Strategies and Bilingual Techniques" (Ph.D. diss., The University of Texas, Austin, 1971).

12. N. G. Hernández, "Variables Affecting Achievement of Middle School Mexican-American Students," *Review of Educational Research* 43 (1973):1-40.

13. M. R. Brawner, "Migration and Educational Achievement of Mexican Americans," *Social Science Quarterly* 53 (1973):727-37.

14. A. Gutiérrez and H. Hirsch, "The Militant Challenge to the American Ethos: 'Chicanos' and 'Mexican Americans,' " *Social Science Quarterly* 53 (1973):830-45.

15. M. Ramírez, C. Taylor, and B. Petersen, "Mexican-American Cultural Membership and Adjustment to School," *Developmental Psychology* 4 (1971):141-48.

16. L. Schmidt and J. Gallesich, "Adjustment of Anglo-American and Mexican-American Pupils in Self-Contained and Team-Teaching Classrooms," *Journal of Educational Psychology* 62 (1971):328-32.

17. S. Kagan and M. C. Madsen, "Cooperation and Competition of Mexican, Mexican-American, and Anglo-American Children of Two Ages Under Four Instructional Sets," *Developmental Psychology* 5 (1971):32-39.

18. S. Kagan and M. C. Madsen, "Rivalry in Anglo-American and Mexican Children of Two Ages," *Journal of Personality and Social Psychology* 28 (1973):383-89.

19. L. Minturn and W. W. Lambert, *Mothers of Six Cultures–Antecedents of Child Rearing* (New York: John Wiley & Sons, 1964).

20. S. A. Wasserman, "Values of Mexican-American, Negro and Anglo Blue-Collar and White-Collar Children," *Child Development* 42 (1971):1624-28.

21. M. Ramírez, "Cognitive Styles and Cultural Democracy in Education," *Social Science Quarterly* 53 (1973):895-904.

22. Holtzman, et al., *Personality Development.*

23. R. M. Kaplan and R. D. Goldman, "Interracial Perception Among Black, White, and Mexican-American High School Students," *Journal of Personality and Social Psychology* 28 (1973):383-89.

24. E. Aronson, "The Jigsaw Route to Learning and Liking," *Psychology Today,* February 1975, pp.43-50.

25. E. G. Jaco, "Mental Health of the Spanish-American in Texas," in M. K. Opler, ed., *Culture and Mental Health* (New York: Macmillan Co., 1959), pp.467-85.

26. A. Rubel, *Across the Tracks: Mexican-Americans in a Texas City* (Austin: The University of Texas, 1966).

27. W. Madsen, "Mexican-Americans and Anglo-Americans: A Comparative Study of Mental Health in Texas," in S. C. Plog and R. B. Edgerton, eds., *Changing Perspectives in Mental Illness* (New York: Holt, Rinehart, & Winston, 1969), pp. 217-41.

28. R. B. Edgerton, "On the 'Recognition' of Mental Illness," in Plog and Edgerton, eds., *Changing Perspectives,* pp. 49-72.

29. M. Karno and R. B. Edgerton, "Perception of Mental Illness in a Mexican-American Community," *Archives of General Psychiatry* 20 (1969):223-38.

30. R. B. Edgerton, M. Karno, and I. Fernández, "Curanderismo in the Metropolis: The Diminishing Role of Folk-Psychiatry Among Los Angeles Mexican-Americans," *American Journal of Psychotherapy* 24 (1970):124-34.

31. C. Martínez and H. Martin, "Folk Diseases Among Urban Mexican-Americans," *Journal of the American Medical Association* 196 (1966):161-64.

32. R. B. Edgerton, "On the 'Recognition' of Mental Illness."

33. Daniel Yankelovich, *The New Morality: A Profile of American Youth in the 70's* (New York: McGraw-Hill Book Company, 1974).

PART VII

The Ecology of the Border Region

16

Ecology of the Border Region

J. Alberto Villasana Lyon *

Biologically speaking, man is imperfect, with no special physical capabilities. But he compensates for it by being able to plan, which permits him to change his environment, adapting it to his needs. He emerged from prehistory when he discovered that he could turn natural resources to his advantage, develop tools and techniques with which to master his surroundings, create a habitat, and impose a social order. And yet in times past, the low degree to which technology had developed, as well as a small world population, allowed the environment to remain a natural system, its components scarcely altered. Today it would be hard to find a place on earth where man has not left his footprints.

The first warnings of danger to the ecosystem came from the developed countries, a danger posed by the industrial sector of society. Even in these countries it was the people with the least resources who had to bear the abuse directed against the environment, such as large-scale mining and industrial waste. In the underdeveloped countries, except for very particular areas, there were no such problems. Thus it is understandable that when discussing the ecological problems along the United States-Mexican border, agreement on the objectives sought is not easy to reach. We Mexicans cannot get excited over ecological problems which are the by-products of industrial development. We tend to look upon such questions as the most recent fad in a rich country seeking distraction from the real problems, such as nutrition,

---

*Translated from the Spanish by Miguel González-Gerth [Editor's Note].

housing, and public health. Moreover, the limited resources at the command of the less developed country prevent it from dealing with ecological problems in any form.

In the neighboring country to the north, environmental pollution, tampering with hydrological systems, and dumping waste on the continental shelf are destroying the ecosystem. Thus far the result is a sense of alarm among the leaders of a population which, given its economic possibilities and its huge technological development, can call for means for reversing the ecological indices. The Mexicans—as those in other developing and less developed countries—are less alarmed. For the United States, the goal is to pursue the most convenient way of life, with high priorities directed toward national fulfillment, beyond economic development and high per capita income. For Mexico the issue is not a question of convenience, but is much more basic: it is a question of development and of life itself. Only recently has economic development been perceived as a complex problem, with the conservation of natural resources a vital component. And we are aware that it is imperative for Mexico to combine both interests in any program undertaken, if it is to be truly successful.

The solution to ecological problems obviously is not easy to find. Scientific interaction is required and, after specialists have given their various points of view, such analyses must provide a synthesis. Thus the "integral survey" has developed primarily in response to the need for data from specialists who can pool their expertise and prepare reports and maps which provide planners and decision makers with the necessary technical information. Doing integral surveys should not be regarded as academic or pro forma. It should be aimed at solving specific problems. Soil erosion, improper use of the land, salinity, inadequate agricultural methods, water and food pollution, substandard housing, and urban decay, all are ecological problems which only development can prevent and are different from those found north of the Río Grande. Pollution due to the dumping of industrial waste into rivers and streams hardly exists in Mexico. On the contrary, our pollution comes from poverty.

The principal indices of modern civilization, such as per capita income, education, nutrition, and economic possibilities, break sharply at the international boundary. It is as if someone had tried to cut vertically through dry sand, with grains that were on the top surface naturally sliding to the bottom of the cut. Undoubtedly, many people who have traveled the new highways that connect some of the larger cities, will consider my assertion an exaggeration. To demonstrate my point, I would urge them to accompany me in an examination of an area of about a thousand square kilometers not far from the national border.

The area in question has a population of approximately twenty-five hundred, living in thirty-two settlements and depending on rudimentary agriculture. Such activity is restricted to a spread of about 6,000 hectares (14,826 acres), of which less than 1 percent is irrigated, 40 percent used for dry farming (growing corn), and 59 percent worked only on a seasonal basis. The last instance is not the result of migratory habits but of the extremely poor condition of the soil, which cannot yield more than one harvest per year. The average harvest throughout consists of not more than 400 kilograms per hectare (356 lbs. per acre). In such circumstances, the consumption of grain for food precludes seed selection for improved planting. Furthermore, fertilization techniques are unknown. Occasionally, the people of the area, including children, resort to gathering wild plants or weeds of meager value (such as those known locally as *candelilla* and *gobernadora*). Even this practice, however, is diminishing gradually because large tracts of land are undergoing an intense process of erosion.

The villages themselves reflect the country. Palo Alto has a population of about a hundred and is typical of the area. It has nothing to offer its inhabitants. Their water comes from small pools that trap the surface flow during the rainy season. By the end of the summer there is more mud than water in the puddles. And, as if that were not bad enough, the people must carry the water for a third of a mile on their backs. There is no sewer system, no slaughter house, no hospital, no cemetery. The children go to school in a one-room building; fourteen of them, irrespective of age, are taught something resembling the first three grades by a single teacher. There is no electric power, no telephone, no mail service.

Several factors have determined such an environment; among those predominating are weather, geology, and culture.

To the south there is a series of synclinal and anticlinal strata of limestone (lutite) and sandstone whose axes form the system of filtration. In turn, the high rate of drainage has produced later sediments: small travertine formations, some conglomerates, and, primarily to the north, alluvial soil. There is no mineral exploitation in depth, and the use of rock for building is extremely limited. With some expense, two or three low mountain springs could be tapped. As an aquifer, the alluvial soil is of low potential, since we are talking about a desert area with an average annual rainfall of two hundred millimeters (less than eight inches). The constant changes of weather, with extreme variability in temperature and precipitation, cause weathering, erosion, and soil transportation. On the other hand, in flat areas where evaporation exceeds water supply, salts and carbonates are deposited which, in time, form hardened layers from twenty to forty inches in thickness.

From an agricultural point of view, the soil in the area is mostly what we call *lithosol,* the scientific term that applies to all soils of less than four inches' thickness. The rest is a combination of xerosols and regosols in hard beds, normally at a depth of less than a yard, and occasionally with a gravelly or rocky content. And all of them have a high sodium content. In general, they are difficult soils to work even with modern implements—one can only imagine how difficult it is without them.

The agricultural potential here depends on the possibility of irrigating about 20 percent of the land with underground water and that of the two or three little springs, thereby increasing production ten or twelve times. Small mountain valleys could pasture over a thousand head of cattle.

Despite this agricultural potential, there is no doubt that the scarcity of natural resources, especially the lack of water, and the low level of education will stand in the way of industrial development. Furthermore, the widely scattered population accounts for the deficiency in urban utilities. A population redistribution is necessary, concentrating it in two or three settlements of a thousand people each, and locating the settlements near their place of work. Thus it would be economically feasible to supply each one with water, a sewer system, electric power, medical services, and a complete school program. A reasonable network of roads is also necessary, so that the inhabitants can go to and from their farmlands.

The kind of superficial analysis I have made of this particular region will soon be available for any part of the country, since integral surveys are included in a federal government program. Its purpose is to gather basic information aimed at programming the socioeconomic development of many areas which up to now remain neglected. Of course, the natural resources are to be considered in regard to each area, but even more important is a consideration of the human resources.

The president's office, through the Comisión de Estudios del Territorio Nacional (CETENAL), now studying the national territory, began this work program in 1968 and has completed about 40 percent of it. This achievement is taken as an average because the various activities needed to bring together the data follow a sequence in which the initial phases, such as aerial photography, progress faster, and the later phases, such as the printing of maps for potential use, progress more slowly.

CETENAL has published a progress report of the work done to date throughout the national territory. It is appropriate, however, to emphasize here what concerns the Mexican-United States border. Aerial photographs of the whole border region are now available. Geodesic studies are 70 percent complete; only the stretch bordering the state of Coahuila is missing. Topographical maps are available for the southern parts of the states of California, Arizona and, partially, Texas. And geological exploration of both Californias has begun. Having this basic data will obviously expedite detailed study of many ecological problems that concern us.

Before concluding, I should mention two facts, which, if disregarded, might make the search for solutions to these ecological problems more difficult. I refer to: 1) the international nature of the general problem; and 2) the lack of common objectives.

I am acquainted with the legislation in both countries and I know there are laws that guard against harmful changes in the ecology. In certain aspects, such as air and water pollution, they are rather explicit. The mere act of polluting a river, for example, elicits government response to correct the misdeed. But in international relations there are no obligations, no means of protecting the environment, and all claims from either side of the border according to accepted precedents, are based on situations where harm, whether real or potential, has already been done and which call for definition and quantification of the problem before taking action toward its solution.

This kind of work is not easy to accomplish when dealing with ecology. A case in point is the dumping of industrial waste and untreated sewage into the Río Grande. Such a practice does not constitute "harm," as it is defined here, since it is done in areas where no further use of the river is made, but it does have ecological consequences. If we stop to consider how long it takes to gather and quantify data on the possible utilization of aquifers in the border region, we are talking about periods of five to ten years. The approved plan and its execution have in some cases taken as long as twenty, without figuring in the average those that have not been resolved.

Obviously, experience shows that the time elapsing between detection of a problem and finding its solution is often considerable. Many of us feel that it is out of line with our technological society. But this would not discourage us; rather it should goad us to search for new forms of understanding.

The second factor, which of course influences the first, is the lack of common objectives. It is the main reason for the example given. In the United States, ecology means the improvement of the standard of living. South of the border, as stated earlier, it means life itself.

When ecological problems are evident, they should be studied in relation to other problems, especially those involving development. If Mexico and the United States were to agree on a community of purpose, solutions beneficial to both countries could be promptly and effectively provided.

17

Environmental Management:
A Basis for Equitable Resource Allocation

Arthur W. Busch

This study of the ecology of the border is based on two premises: first, that human ecology is basically a problem of environmental management, and second, that most of the border problems of Mexico and the United States involve equitable resource allocation. For the nontechnical reader, this essay will begin with a general introduction to ecology.

Ecology, Natural Resources and Pollution

Ecology is the science dealing with organisms and their environment; it provides a basic approach to conservation of natural resources. Cutting across the other natural sciences, ecology is based on empirical observations of varying characteristics of species of organisms living in different environments. This initial empiricism has led to recognition of the inseparability of plants, animals, and mankind. Thus, "synecology" is used to describe the study of progressively complex interrelationships of natural assemblages of organisms, such as populations and communities.

What most people mean when they use the word ecology to describe current critical environmental situations is the visible impact of man's activities on the natural environment or what is perceived as natural environment. Of equal import should be the not-so-visible impact of man's activities, for there are many ecological aspects of industrial and agricultural production. These include relations of plants to soil types, diets of farm and range animals, pollution, overlumbering, overcultivation, overgrazing, abuse of herbicides and pesticides, dust storms, floods, forest fires, and game conservation. Often a man-made catastrophe has its origin in the unconscious application of ecologically unsound practices or the implementation of short-sighted expedient legislation and regulations.

The importance of general conservation, whether of oil, coal or timber, soils, migratory birds, or whales, cannot be emphasized too much with reference to mankind's welfare. Plants and animals are interrelated in highly complex natural communities, and they must be manipulated or replaced with scientific care. However, I am one who believes that man's impact or manipulations can be beneficial. Many of our activities result in greater productivity and, indeed, they must unless we limit our population by other than natural ecological controls of starvation and disease.

As information from the various branches of learning accumulates on the requirements of species populations and communities, such data are available to animal husbandry, agriculture, conservation, and public health. The question is whether the information becomes available in integrated perspective quickly enough for our pressing needs.

Solution of many problems in public health and medicine involve ecology. For example, effective control of numerous animal-borne diseases is achieved by control of the carrier, or vector, rather than by control of the agent or pathogen. Such programs are basically environmental-change-oriented and, of course, represent one of the man-induced beneficial changes noted earlier.

Because each species is hereditarily capable of tolerating only certain environmental conditions, these capabilities define the normal environment of a community. This environment is complex and consists of physical and biological factors. Physical factors include light intensity and quality, temperature, precipitation, evaporation, salinity, air quality, pressure, and many more. Some of the biological factors are food, population pressure or density, predation (crime), parasitism (unemployed), and disease.

The living community is considered the most perfect expression of integration of the *physical* environment. This has led to use of communities and/or individual species as indicative of conditions not conveniently measured directly, such as depth of ground water.

The biological factors in ecology are dynamic; there is no equilibrium in nature or the real world. The best we can do is achieve a limited steady state which is still a dynamic and transitory condition.

Human ecology, the specific subject of the essay, is the study of the structure, development, and change of human communities and societies in terms of the processes by which human populations adapt to their environments. Critical account must be taken of the technological systems and patterns of social organizations (including government) through which adaptation is effected.

Man's environment is enlarged as technology creates new resources and magnifies the efficiency with which old resources were exploited.

Human ecology has, as its most important asset, analysis of the ecosystem. Diagnosis of soil erosion problems, for example, requires consideration of human land-use impact on physical and other biotic components of the system. The consequence of technological progress is man's growing capacity to modify his ecosystem with an increasing probability that human welfare will be affected in complicated, difficult to anticipate, ways. Man has the opportunity to use ecological study to make the most of his actions in full cognizance of cause and effect trade-offs by applying the concept of relative risk.

Population growth is the key issue, providing the impetus for cultural and industrial development. Heretofore, population growth has involved primarily change in death rate; now birth rate becomes the issue. The doubling time of world human population has decreased from about sixteen hundred years at the time of Christ to thirty years today. As an example Mexico, second most populous nation in Latin America, has raised life expectancy from thirty-nine years in 1940 to sixty-seven years in 1968.

Population density is, of course, a major factor in environmental pollution. An area must be considered overpopulated for the extant mode of life if it requires a rapid net consumption of nonrenewable resources and it results in a continued deterioration of environmental quality. Determination of optimum population based on available resources can be quite straightforward, but this is just part of the issue. Politics, religion, and desired life-style all are factors that must be considered. Furthermore, as before, life and knowledge are dynamic in nature and optimum population size, therefore, must be evaluated in rate terms. However, a political structure capable of realistically setting optimum population standards must influence birth trends as governments attempt to produce desired economic conditions.

Continuing our emphasis on the dynamic nature of environmental issues, the concept of limiting factors must be foremost in our minds. This powerful concept was first recognized by Baron Justus von Liebig with his "law of the minimum" applied to soil fertility. For example, the rate of photosynthesis was shown by F. F. Blockman, in 1905, to be dependent on the least favorable of the environmental factors involved.

This elegantly simple fact of a limiting element (biological, chemical, physical, or subentity) was useful to me in the real world problem of how much pollution (in terms of oxygen demand) the Houston Ship Channel could assimilate continuously. The issue was the protection of recreation and fishing in Galveston Bay. My projection on the somewhat celebrated back of an old envelope in early 1970 has now, five years later, been borne out by several million dollars of public tax funds spent (by others) on computer studies. My appreciation for the concept of Baron von Liebig is, as you may guess, unbounded. In an area of study where precision is indeterminate, accuracy is unknown, and the consequences of poor decisions potentially catastrophic, the principle of limiting factors is of paramount value. A well-known Asian political figure observed that computers serve only to magnify man's ignorance. We in the ecological world will do well to keep this Confucius-like observation before us.

The materials of the environment useful to man are natural resources; any substance of the earth, oceans, or air may become invested with economic value and thereby become a resource. This includes, to my mind, the earth, oceans, and air; in themselves, they visibly have come to have value to man as source, as assimilators of waste, and as environmental entities.

A resource must meet a need of man, either naturally or by alternation, with an acceptable expenditure of energy. Isn't this a good simple definition of economic value?

Natural resources are animal, vegetable, or mineral, plus sunlight, the atmosphere, water, and soils of the earth. A critical classification is nonrenewable (as minerals) or renewable (as vegetation and water). Strictly speaking, water, as a renewable resource, is recycled and so can be many minerals, if we insist. The exceptions are the fuel minerals. Forests are perhaps the best example of management of a renewable resource for sustained production on a predictable dynamic, rate of yield, basis.

People would be without hope if they did not believe in the ability of man to meet his resource needs for an indefinite future. So-called shortages of water are simply excessive rates of demand in particular locations. The amount of water on Earth is not only as great as it ever was, but is projected to be increasing at a rate of 1.3×10^{12} gallons yearly from the combustion of fossil fuels alone. Technologically speaking, water of any quality in almost any quantity can be produced anywhere—at some cost. Water is the most used and most underpriced commodity of man. Lead times and capital funds for large-scale water supply development and pollution abatement are often problems and are aggravated where two nations are involved.

As population density increases, man-made pollution is a concomitant problem, and a greater one. Environmental contaminants include combustion products, agricultural fertilizers and pesticides, ionizing and nonionizing radiation, noise, heat, solids, and industrial residues.

The ecological impact of environmental contaminants is generally time-concentration sensitive; i.e., low concentrations may require long exposure for measurable effects to develop. Thus duration and frequency of exposure and recovery time are important. Pollutants showing ecological effects, including human health, present an increasingly significant problem only after years of exposure. While I believe zero concentration of any harmful substance is a worthwhile and justifiable *goal,* I cannot agree to banning such substances arbitrarily. Here the concept of relative risk is important. Recent controversy over use of chlorine for disinfection of water supplies is an example. Now chlorine is *suspected* of reacting with organic compounds to form *possibly* carcinogenic substances. Study is needed, I grant, but if a decision must be made today, I will stay with the use of chlorine. Prior to widespread implementation of chlorination many people did die from typhoid and other waterborne disease. That some few may possibly have adverse effects (not necessarily mortal) from drinking chlorinated water is not, in my opinion, a sound basis for elimination of chlorination or for the creation of a new federal bureaucracy such as we have created.

Air pollution is directly related to fuel usage, increased industrialization, and growing urban congestion (population). There seems to be a longer recorded history of sufficient human concern over air pollution than can be established for water pollution. Many writers have commented on the noxious quality of air in historical briefs, novels, and poems. A smoke abatement law was passed in England in 1273 during the reign of Edward I, and in 1306, public concern led to a royal proclamation prohibiting the burning of coal in London. Those who today call for stringent enforcement as the only means for effecting environmental management may take comfort from knowing that a manufacturer who was tried for disobeying that proclamation was found guilty and beheaded.

Air pollutants are commonly defined to include those substances present in sufficient concentration to produce a discernible or measurable effect on man, animals, vegetation, or inanimate materials (corrosion, primarily). Pollutants may include almost any natural or artificial composition of matter subject to being airborne. This means gases, aerosols (liquid droplets), and solid particles.

In December 1970, the United States Congress passed legislation requiring the establishment of standards that provide zero risk, plus a factor of safety, for human health and welfare, with reference to critical air pollutants. In addition, the law stipulates deadlines for attainment of these unprecedented requirements. Unfortunately for our discussion of the border, Congress did not address the issue of pollutants crossing international boundaries.

The stimulus for the United States Clean Air Act of 1970 was that emotion-charged year beginning with the first Earth Day in April 1970. There are numerous instances of nuisance and irritating levels of chronic air pollution such as in Los Angeles, Mexico City, and El Paso-Ciudad Juárez but only four major disasters are recorded, one of which occurred in Mexico and one in the United States. A brief presentation of the four is of interest to our discussion of a growing problem on the border.

In December 1930, a large number of persons in the Meuse Valley in Belgium became ill and sixty died. Sulfur compounds were concluded to have been the cause.

A similar case occurred at Donora, Pennsylvania, in October 1948, when twenty persons died and six thousand were made ill. Again, sulfur compounds, their oxidation products and particulates, were blamed.

At Poza Rica, Mexico, in November 1950, 22 persons died and 320 were hospitalized. In this case a specific source and compound, hydrogen sulfide, were responsible.

The worst air pollution disaster took place in London in December 1952. During a thirty-day period, deaths were thirty-five hundred more than normal. Autopsies showed only evidence of respiratory tract irritation. Highest mortality rates were for persons in their sixties and seventies, with more than 80 percent of deaths occurring among persons having known heart and respiratory disease.

To repeat a point: contaminants or pollutants are usually natural or useful substances that have many beneficial applications; only when they are so used, misused, or congregated as to cause excessive residual concentrations in the environment do they become pollutants. Basically, control of environmental pollution requires efficient manufacturing and energy conversion processes, conscientious efforts to eliminate waste at the source, the measurements of effects on humans, plants, animals and structures, economic (value) analysis, integrity in political decisions, and realistic presentation of facts to the public. Panic peddling is not a proper professional stance and cannot sustain continued support any more than Chicken Little was able to sway his audience.

There are two ways in which man depletes his natural resources: by consumptive use, without conscious efforts at recycle, and by pollution. Both consumption and pollution properly fall under environmental management. With full recognition of limiting rates of recycle and of natural process renewal of our waters and our air, we can manage by relative risk, allocating resources to each of the border nations on regional and area bases. We need an enlightened public with confidence in the integrity of competent leaders.

Political institutions must strive for problem solving, not perpetuation and growth of themselves. This human problem is not the least, but rather the precedent ecological issue on the border.

Border Characteristics

From the Pacific Ocean to the Gulf of Mexico the United States-Mexican border stretches for nearly two thousand miles. Four American and six Mexican states comprise the border: Texas, New Mexico, Arizona, and California on the north and Tamaulipas, Nuevo León, Coahuila, Chihuahua, Sonora, and Baja California on the south. About 3.5 million people live in the border area, most of them in the fourteen pairs of twin cities. San Diego-Tijuana contains nearly one million; El Paso-Ciudad Juárez, 850,000; Calexico-Mexicali, 320,000; and Brownsville-Matamoros, 240,000. These are by far the largest metropolitan complexes. El Paso is the largest American border city, with a population of almost one-half million. Ciudad Juárez is slightly larger than El Paso, while Tijuana and Mexicali each exceed 200,000 and Matamoros and Nuevo Laredo have more than 100,000 inhabitants each.

The six Mexican states totaled nearly 6 million people in 1960 with most of them along the border and representing some 12 percent of the total national population. The 1980 population projection is near 14 million. As noted earlier, Mexico is now the second most populous nation in Latin America and third in the hemisphere behind the United States and Brazil. Its gross national product growth rate in recent years is over 7 percent. Post-World War II growth has been especially significant, with electrical output, petroleum refining, construction, and manufacturing all increasing severalfold.

Major environmental problems along the border are water (quantity and quality) and air pollution. Water issues involve two rivers, the Río Grande and the Colorado. Air pollution problems are concentrated in urban areas. Most industrial air pollution is from sources on the American side of the border. Much of the air quality problem in Mexico stems from garbage burning and cooking fires. However, there are two major industrial sources of air pollution within about one hundred miles of the border. These are the iron and steel producers in Monterrey, Nuevo León, and the copper smelter in Cananea, Sonora.

Mexico is rich in minerals and timber. Farming, ranching, and fishing are important industries. Its land is rich but rugged in topography, and lack of sufficient rainfall is a major problem. Tourism is an important revenue source with gross earnings exceeding $1 billion by the middle 1960s. The demands of tourism on transportation systems and border crossings is a significant environmental factor and serves to show the nature of international problems of human ecology and/or environmental management. The following remarks of Mayor Fred Hervey of El Paso, presented in testimony before the Texas Senate Subcommittee on Mass Transit and the Texas House Committee on Transportation in October 1974, merit consideration:

> The cities of El Paso and Ciudad Juárez jointly constitute a contiguous urbanized metropolitan area of nearly one million people. This urbanization is bisected by a thin Rio Grande River which marks the international boundary between Mexico and the United States. Culturally, socially, and economically, there is a complete fusion between both cities today.
>
> We have 82 million crossings both ways between El Paso and Ciudad Juárez each year. Although the physical division is relatively insignificant, there is a vast difference in the governmental systems of both cities and both countries. This difference creates one of the most significant problems faced by border cities along the United States-Mexico international border.
>
> Simply stated, we have two national states with two governmental systems in which the local, state, and federal jurisdictions have different roles, authority, and responsibility.
>
> On the Mexican side, cities lack certain local autonomy and must rely on their state and national governments to bring about changes in major decision making.
>
> The role of the local government of the United States side has more [*sic*] authority to administer and regulate certain aspects of its own affairs.
>
> To a large extent our federal government contends that the international transportation problem now facing El Paso is a local matter. On the Mexican side, their federal government has jurisdiction and control over the planning and administration of international transportation. Consequently in El Paso and Ciudad Juárez, it is difficult to undertake any transportation planning and program implementation.
>
> Due to the lack of a federal international transportation agency to develop and implement international treaties, our efforts to establish and improve binational mass transit operations has become a hit and miss, crisis oriented procedure.
>
> At this time there is virtually no mass transportation system between

the cities of El Paso and Ciudad Juárez. This condition has existed since the streetcar service was discontinued through a federal decree in Mexico cancelling the franchise of the international streetcar system. We have now little else besides taxicabs and private vehicles to move people from one side of the border to the other. This condition simply creates congestion, friction, and inconvenience to people who must cross the border to visit, shop, and work.

Project Intercept, a program instituted in 1969 by the United States Federal Government to curb the increasing amount of drugs and narcotics coming into the United States from Mexico, has hindered the international relations between the United States and Mexico. Since its inception, this program has had a detrimental effect between our border cities. The program has created long lines of vehicles especially at peak hours attempting to cross into the United States from Mexico. Programs and changes such as Project Intercept have a direct bearing on the international transportation system of United States-Mexico border cities which must rely on one or two ports of entry to satisfy the daily commuting needs of hundreds of thousands of people.

There is a need for a new procedure by which the two national governments will assume the responsibility of assisting local governments in the matters of international transportation planning and implementation of projects beneficial to both sides of the border.

The Río Grande (Río Bravo del Norte)

The fifth longest North American river flows from the alpine meadows of the San Juan mountains of southwestern Colorado southeast and south 175 miles to the New Mexico border. Four hundred and seventy miles to the south the river turns southeast between Texas and the Mexican states of Chihuahua, Coahuila, Nuevo León, and Tamaulipas for about 1,250 miles to the Gulf of Mexico. Thus of its total length of approximately 1,900 miles, the Río Grande constitutes the Mexican-United States border, along the entire southwest boundary of Texas, for 1,250 miles. From a clear mountain stream the river changes character drastically before entering the Gulf of Mexico: declining elevation, decreasing latitude, and increasing temperatures and aridity change climate and vegetative conditions from cold to hot and from piñon, juniper, and sagebrush to desert plants such as yucca, cactus, creosote bushes, and mesquite. In far west Texas, the Río Grande cuts through the 1,500- to 1,700-foot deep canyons of the Big Bend area. Leaving this territory of rushing rapids with intermittent deep pools, the river wanders sluggishly to its great delta.

Tributaries and springs greatly influence river flow characteristics. The Pecos and Devils rivers enter from the left bank on the United States side. The Chama, Puerco, Salado, Conchos, and San Juan rivers enter the right bank, the first two in the United States and the last three in Mexico. In the very large drainage basin of 172,000 square miles, peak flow varies from April to October. Melting snow and mountain thunderstorms bring peak flows to the upper reaches in May or June while the lower portion usually peaks in June or September because of summer rainfall patterns. This highly variable flow is estimated to yield an annual average of more than nine million acre-feet of water, a third of which went unused to the Gulf before large-scale dam construction in the lower reaches after 1950. Agricultural requirements provided the stimulus for water treaties between the United States and Mexico in 1905 and 1944. These were complemented by the Río Grande compact between the American states of Texas, New Mexico, and Colorado in 1939 and the Pecos River compact between Texas and New Mexico in 1948. Total storage capacity of existing reservoirs is more than 13 million acre-feet. Some 3 million acres are irrigated within the Río Grande basin, about two-thirds in the United States.

The diversified and highly developed commerce of Texas is important to the border ecology. Texas normally produces one-third of the total United States petroleum output. It also is the largest United States producer of asphalt, graphite, natural gas liquid, and magnesium chloride, and it is second in the American states in output of sulfur, salt, helium, and bromine, and third in cement and clays. Despite Texas's huge mineral production and manufacturing output, agriculture, forest products, and commercial fishing are significant to its economy and to its environmental quality. Texas ranked third among the fifty states in 1972 cash receipts for crops, second for livestock products, and third in total farm receipts. It led all states in number of cattle and of sheep, ranked sixth in turkeys and ninth in chickens. (Whimsically, Texas has more cattle [15,350,000] than people. With a pollution population equivalent of sixty people per head of cattle, Texas's reputation for a manure problem is easily documentable!) Crops grown by Texas farmers include rice, pecans, sorghum, cotton, peanuts, vegetables, melons, fruit, and roses. Irrigation plays a vital role in these agricultural efforts even in the humid Gulf Coast plains of east and south Texas.

From El Paso to the Gulf of Mexico there are five discernible ecological areas along the Río Grande or its major tributaries:

1. The Upper Río Grande Valley is a narrow strip of irrigated land paralleling the river for some seventy-five miles. Cotton is the chief product of the valley which is also characterized by a dense urban and rural population. The surrounding area is desolate desert with few inhabitants.

2. The Big Bend is a loop of the Río Grande, a mountainous area of scant rainfall, sparse population and great beauty.

3. The Pecos Valley-Stockton Plateau is rolling-to-rough terrain with only ten to twelve inches of rainfall annually. In the 1950s large underground aquifers were discovered and now provide for irrigation of cotton, alfalfa, and other crops to join large-scale ranching.

4. The Río Grande Plain lies south of San Antonio between the Río Grande and the Gulf Coast, above the Lower Río Grande Valley. Its topography, climate, and plant life are similar to those of an area from the Balcones Escarpment of Texas to the Sierra Madre Oriental in Mexico past Monterrey, Nuevo León, some 160 miles south of Laredo. Much of the Río Grande Plain is covered densely with prickly pear, mesquite, dwarf oak, catclaw, huajillo, huisache, blackbrush, cenizo, and other wild shrubs. Yet this almost impenetrable country raises cattle, sheep, and goats. There is some prairie and some dryland farming. Irrigation produces late winter and early spring vegetables in Dummit and Zavala counties north of Laredo. Rainfall is between twenty and twenty-five inches annually.

5. The Lower Río Grande Valley has deep alluvial soils and a distinctive economy based on citrus and winter vegetable raising. Most of the acreage is irrigated with Río Grande water.

Water is of concern from four standpoints: proper quality, in the proper quantity, and physical structures necessary for both development of assured supplies and for protection from floods. The first issue is usually the too-much-too-little problem to be solved by smoothing river flow rates with dams and reservoirs. This effort began on the Río Grande with construction of Elephant Butte Dam, 135 miles upstream from El Paso, in 1915. With one exception, in 1942, this reservoir has contained all flood runoff from above the dam since its completion. Caballo Dam, built 28 miles below Elephant Butte in 1938, contains rainfall runoff from an area of 1,300 square miles. The first major water treaty between the United States and Mexico was signed in 1944 and assigned responsibility for managing water along the full 1,250-mile Texas-Mexican boundary to the International Boundary and Water Commission. This Commission, while unable to resolve all international problems since its inception, gets high marks for the quality of its operations from all knowledgeable persons.

As a result of Caballo and Elephant Butte reservoirs the Río Grande is almost completely regulated at El Paso. Essentially all of the average annual runoff of more than three million acre-feet is diverted for use. By treaty sixty thousand acre feet are allotted to Mexico. Irrigated land on the United States side between the beginning of the international boundary and Fort Quitman at the lower end of the Upper Río Grande Valley averages about sixty thousand acres.

Some of this irrigation water not evaporating or seeping into the soil drains back into the river. However, from Fort Quitman to Presidio, river flow has often been nil, except for runoff contributed by rainfall in that stretch. Because of this scarcity only some one thousand acres of irrigated land are in service between Fort Quitman and Presidio.

Below Presidio the Río Grande is replenished, beginning with the Conchos from Mexico. By treaty, the United States receives one-third of Río Conchos water. This, plus flows from springs and other tributaries, yields usually sufficient water between Presidio and the Lower Rio Grande Valley. With water available, almost all feasible agricultural land is developed on the United States side. The major area is some fifty thousand acres in the Maverick District.

Water management problems in the Lower Río Grande Valley, in terms of dependable supply, contributed impetus to the 1944 Water Treaty. This treaty authorized international dams and reservoirs and provided for regulation and diversion of river flow for optimum use of the water. Two major dams on the Río Grande have been completed: Falcon Dam, seventy-five miles below Laredo-Nuevo Laredo and Amistad, twelve miles upstream from Del Río. These two reservoirs provide sufficient storage to practically eliminate floods from waters falling above Falcon Dam. Falcon, Amistad, Elephant Butte, and Caballo plus Las Boquilla on the Conchos, El Azucar on the San Juan, and Don Martín on the Salado provide, as noted earlier, more than thirteen million acre-feet of total water storage capacity on the Río Grande Basin. This means that regulation and utilization of the United States share of Río Grande water has been virtually accomplished. The principal user of Falcon-Amistad water in the United States is the Lower Río Grande Valley.

One result of full regulation and utilization of river waters is that quality begins to diminish and quantity shortages occur if growth and demand along the river continue without regard for the limiting factors involved. Baron von Liebig's law of ecology remains in force and becomes increasingly discernible as human congestion builds. This is well illustrated in the Upper Río Grande Valley where the earliest full regulation was achieved. Water supply has been short several times since Elephant Butte Dam was completed. Between 1950 and 1967, water available averaged about 40 percent of the demand for thirteen of the seventeen years. When this occurs, underground water is pumped to supplement river water. Projections are for continuing depletion of ground water; that is, pumpage exceeds the rate of replenishment by rainfall and percolation into underground aquifers. The City of El Paso uses ground water almost exclusively; as early as 1967, 94 percent of city water was pumped with only 6 percent coming from the Río Grande. Projections are for a quadrupling to a daily demand of 185 million gallons by 2020. Quite obviously, conservation measures and direct water recycle must be implemented to supplement the estimated 7.4 million acre-feet of ground water available in the El Paso area; a large but finite quantity.

Already Ciudad Juárez municipal waste water is used for irrigation as is part of El Paso's effluent that is discharged to the Río Grande and diverted downstream for agricultural use.

Limited agricultural operations and relatively small cities enable the middle reaches of the Río Grande to have adequate volume of good quality water. However, any significant growth in demand even in these areas will encounter limits on available water.

The Lower Río Grande Valley, with its 750,000 to 1 million irrigated acres, places the greatest demand on Río Grande waters. Even with both Amistad and Falcon dams in operation a repetition of flow patterns for the first half of the twentieth century with present demand rates would bring twelve years with an average shortage of 6 percent of demand. During one consecutive four-year period shortages would have ranged from 26 percent to 73 percent of demand. Even if irrigation does not expand, urban demands will continue to grow as population increases.

In addition to inadequately treated municipal and industrial waste waters, the major water quality problem in irrigated areas is the increase in salts. This is due to evaporation and return of concentrated drainage waters and to leaching of salts from the soil. Water from Falcon and Amistad dams is pumped from the river at diversion points for Lower Río Grande Valley use. A fortunate characteristic is that the delta has built to a higher level along the river, causing drainage waters after irrigation application to flow away from the river, to the Gulf of Mexico. In this way salt buildup is reduced in the lower reaches of the Rio Grande. However, several drains of high salt content enter the Río San Juan in Mexico and the Río Grande below their confluence. A major source of salt was the Morillo Drain which joins the Rio Grande just above the Anzalduas Diversion Dam. During one four-year period the average annual Morillo Drain flow was twenty-eight thousand acre feet with an average salt content of over ten thousand milligrams per liter. This is a salt content of one percent; sea water is 3.5 percent; good fresh water is well below 0.1 of 1 percent. This flow carried an average of forty-five thousand tons of salt annually into the Río Grande during the four-year period.

To alleviate this specific problem, a bypass was constructed to carry the Morillo Drain flow directly to the Gulf of Mexico. One-half of the cost of this channel was borne jointly by the United States federal government and the Lower Río Grande Valley water users. The other half of the cost was paid by Mexico.

The importance of flood control, in addition to resource development, in this semiarid region of the border can be illustrated by reviewing briefly three great floods occurring in the past twenty years. In June 1954, a large storm, principally over the Devils and Lower Pecos river watersheds, produced the greatest peak discharge ever recorded on the Río Grande: 1,158,000 cubic feet per second near Del Río. Nature, on this occasion, equaled the maximum possible precipitation projections of the United States Weather Bureau. Amistad Dam was designed to regulate such a storm flow even if the conservation pool were filled prior to the storm.

A flood in September 1958, caused the Falcon Reservoir to fill and spill a fifty-thousand-cubic-feet-per-second peak which, combined with flood flows below Falcon and from the Río San Juan, produced a peak flow of 104,000 cubic feet per second at Río Grande City. Since the completion of Amistad Dam, a similar storm would not cause a significant spill from Falcon Dam.

In September 1967, Hurricane Beulah entered Texas north of Brownsville and dropped twenty inches and more of rain below Falcon Dam, principally in the Río Alamo and Río San Juan basins in Mexico. A flow of 220,000 cubic feet per second was recorded at Río Grande City. Total damage estimates in both countries were over $1 billion for buildings, trees, crops, livestock, roads, and canals. Current work is aimed at handling a possible repetition of such a storm.

Air Pollution along the Río Grande Border

Four major sources of air pollution exist along the United States-Mexican border. My discussion will center on the Texas-Mexican portion and will focus on the Texas problems. However, the problems are common to both sides of the entire international boundary.

Agriculture obviously involves a disturbance of a natural ecosystem; "balance" is shifted. Components considered "pests" are dealt with to protect crops and to ensure a higher level of production. Each of the several forms of control methods has a potential for causing other problems. Agriculture operations in the fourteen counties of Texas which form the Texas-Mexican border include orchards, field crops, and limited grazing. Percentage of each county in agricultural use ranges from 57 percent to 99 percent. Six of the fourteen counties are more than 90 percent agricultural, two between 80 percent and 90 percent, three between 70 percent and 80 percent, and three between 50 percent and 70 percent. Table 1 shows the acreage in harvested cropland and in rangeland for each county in 1969. Note that of a total fourteen-county area of 3,585,000 acres (8,859,258 hectares), 135,914 (335,231) are in harvested cropland and 2,639,500 (6,525,006) in rangeland.

TABLE 1
Agricultural Land Use

County	Harvested Cropland		Rangeland	
	Acres	*Hectares*	*Acres*	*Hectares*
El Paso	9,050	22,374	52,000	128,447
Hudspeth	4,420	10,931	275,000	684,547
Jeff Davis	280	694	223,000	550,077
Presidio	1,190	2,939	324,000	801,778
Brewster	4	9	420,200	1,045,190
Terrell	152	377	237,000	585,373
Val Verde	146	360	331,000	817,462
Kinney	815	2,017	114,500	283,402
Maverick	3,880	9,598	127,500	315,518
Webb	1,410	3,474	312,000	769,140
Zapata	767	1,897	84,000	207,878
Starr	6,100	15,046	80,500	190,839
Hidalgo	66,500	163,901	38,000	93,819
Cameron	41,200	101,612	20,800	51,535
Total	135,914	335,229	2,639,500	6,525,005

The ecosystem manipulation characteristic of agriculture usually tends to simplification and generally to reduce problems. Past misuse of rangelands has allowed undesirable plants to spread. Control of these plants (brush) is needed so that grass may compete, grow, and provide forage for livestock grazing. Typically 35 percent to 70 percent of land in the fourteen counties needs brush control. Measures available for controlling brush include manual and mechanical cleaning, and the use of herbicides—the least expensive of the three. However, because most herbicide application is by aerial spraying or dusting, dangerous residues may reach livestock and humans. Herbicides are also used to control weeds or grass in cultivated fields and orchards.

Pesticides are important in controlling insects in fields and orchards. A new hazard was brought about by the substitution of organophosphorus compounds for chlorinated hydrocarbons such as DDT. In banning DDT as unsafe for animal life, we endangered the human applicators of the highly toxic organophosphorus compounds which were substituted. During my tenure as Regional Administrator of the United States Environmental Protection Agency, a very successful bilingual program of applicator education was initiated. This was a joint project between EPA, the United States Department of Agriculture, and the state of Texas.

Other significant sources of air pollution from agricultural operations include burning of agricultural wastes, use of burners in orchards for heating, and wind erosion. Irrigation ditches are burned to clear them of vegetation; cotton gin wastes are often burned both to eliminate trash and to control pest larvae. A recent air pollution case in Texas involved burning of sugar cane fields as part of the harvesting operations.

Burners using unpressurized diesel fuel are a source of nuisance and health effects and can affect pollination of the orchard fruit crops. All of these latter problems, including wind erosion, are subject to abatement through the use of alternate or improved operational methods.

Industrial activities contribute to air pollution through fuel combustion or manufacturing process losses or residues. The Clean Air Act of 1970, mentioned earlier, required standards to be set and emission inventories to be made for six major air pollutants: particulates, sulfur oxides, nitrogen oxides, total hydrocarbons, photochemical oxidants (reactive hydrocarbons), and carbon monoxide. Table 2 shows data for point source emissions, by states, in the counties or air quality control regions along the United States-Mexican border, for five of the six pollutants.

TABLE 2
1973 Summary of Estimated Point Source Emissions of Air Pollution
Along the United States-Mexican Border—Metric Tons Per Year

State	Particulates	Sulfur Oxides	Nitrogen Oxides	Hydrocarbons	Carbon Monoxide
Texas	38,300	256,200	34,100	23,600	112,200
New Mexico	37,600	224,600	8,100	2,400	3,900
Arizona	35,300	525,300	6,200	600	4,000
California	59,600	7,600	19,500	5,800	3,000
Total	170,800	1,013,700	67,900	32,400	123,100

The largest tonnage is sulfur oxides, most of which are emitted within a 360-mile distance of the border and between El Paso and Ajo, Arizona. Smelters are the major contributor to this pollution which represents almost 19 percent of the estimated total sulfur oxides emitted in the United States. Progress is being made toward reducing these emissions by conversion of sulfur oxides to sulfuric acid.

The second greatest problem in United States industrial point source air pollution along the border is particulates. Quarrying of rock, sand and gravel, cement making, and concrete batching plants are major contributors.

Petroleum refining and chemical and petrochemical processing are the major sources of carbon monoxide and hydrocarbons shown in Table 2. Nitrogen oxides are primarily from the combustion of fuel in industrial and power generating operations. Other air pollutants not shown in Table 2 but of major significance, particularly in the El Paso-Ciudad Juárez area, are heavy metals such as lead and cadmium.

The relatively low level of industrialization along the border, as yet, is a favorable aspect of air quality management. Air pollution from old industrial plants is often difficult and disproportionately expensive to abate but there is no reason not to provide complete controls on new plants. Thus we may expect industrial discharges to decrease proportionately as a factor in air pollution along the border.

Two major factors, characteristic of border automotive traffic, greatly influence the problem of vehicle air pollutant emissions: the average age of the motor vehicles and the stop-and-go traffic at the ports of entry.

Transportation in general is a major source of carbon monoxide, hydrocarbons, and nitrogen dioxide. Particulates in auto exhaust are a lesser problem although substantial amounts of lead can be detected. An important factor in exhaust emission is vehicle speed because both hydrocarbons and carbon monoxide are highest when the engine is idling and both decrease with increasing vehicle speed.

Vehicle registrations in the border counties of California, Arizona, New Mexico, and Texas total over 1,400,000, with 256,000 of these in the fourteen Texas border counties. Mexican figures show a minimum of 200,000 registered vehicles in the "frontier" zone with many others registered in the United States but presumably included in the numbers mentioned previously.

The average age of vehicles in Mexico is considerably higher than that in the United States, and many of these do not have air pollution control devices on the engines. The Clean Air Act of 1970 required an increasingly greater reduction in air pollutants for automobiles manufactured after 1970.

When entering either nation, a vehicle must pass through a port of entry. This causes vehicular traffic to slow to a stop-and-go action and this, as mentioned, increases air pollution. Available data, for only a portion of the Texas-Mexican ports of entry, show an approximate total of 30 million vehicle crossings annually. California and Arizona data show an additional 20 million vehicle crossings per year.

Although data are limited, some appreciation for the relative magnitude of vehicular air pollution compared with industry can be obtained. In El Paso County alone, carbon monoxide emitted from vehicles is estimated as 122,000 metric tons annually compared to a total United States border industrial discharge of 123,100 metric tons. Hydrocarbons from vehicles in El Paso County approximate 16,000 metric tons per year. Total border industrial discharge of hydrocarbons is 32,400 metric tons per year. We can conclude that industry contributes most of the sulfur oxides and particulates, but the automobile is the greatest contributor of hydrocarbons and carbon monoxide (by a factor of seven) and is equal to industry in nitrogen oxides discharged.

A final source of air pollution along the United States-Mexican border is open burning which has been mentioned briefly (under "Border Characteristics" and in the discussion of agriculture). Open, or outdoor burning, is any burning in the open which emits visible smoke into the atmosphere and includes combustion of municipal garbage and refuse, agricultural burning of fields and irrigation ditch vegetation or from cleaning of land, and industrial burning either to salvage a product (such as steel drums) or for disposal of solid wastes.

Many of the towns and unincorporated rural villages are so small that burning is a more attractive alternative to more expensive landfill operations for garbage and refuse disposal. In fact, most rural communities feel they cannot afford a regular collection service and citizens individually either make trips to the dump site or burn their own solid wastes at home. Most open burning on the United States side of the border is in small and rural communities and in agricultural operations; burning by industry is not significant at present.

Institutions of the Border Ecosystems

The key to effective implementation of environmental management is the institutional arrangement which, of course, is set up by people who are part of the ecosystem. Mutual good faith and equity are essential in resolving environmental problems where our ignorance is so manifest. Our existing institutions must and can adapt to our new perceptions based on a broader perspective. In some cases, new entities or associations must be developed, for clearly, environmental issues will be resolved by political decisions as well as by scientific and technical discoveries. Obviously, each side of the border must support and cooperate with the other for progress to be achieved.

A brief review of the pluralistic United States political system and its capacity to apply an ecosystem approach is pertinent. A pluralistic political system is one in which multiple political entities provide ready access to interest groups. This multiple input through various access routes and single-interest perspectives results in a public policy representing compromise and sometimes piecemeal progress toward a final objective. The major deficiency then is common awareness of factual information; the extent to which we can and cannot quantify and the relative risk involved in a decision because of lack of knowledge. In fact, conflict is avoided in the United States Congress by not discussing broad questions of priorities and national goals other than in the separate committees which generate the fragmented approach to any major public policy issue.

Demands on our pluralist political system generally come from interest groups rather than the public en masse. For example, during the litigation over air pollution in El Paso, 86 percent of the national public was at least somewhat concerned over the environment with 51 percent expressing deep concern (subject to individual subjectiveness of definition). El Paso citizen polls showed 86 percent concerned with the city's air problems, 78 percent thought ''the government'' should ''do something'' and 63 percent were willing to pay higher taxes to abate pollution. In all likelihood, a poll focusing on those areas downwind of the offending smelter stacks would show different values. Ideally, the political activist group should do more than simply make judgments; it should construct support for its position. For example, water has a basic emotional appeal which can be powerfully developed at the local level. Water is seen as wealth; a resource which, with development, guarantees prosperity. In arid and semiarid areas the water right is a vital institutional arrangement. Even in areas with more water than can be used, ''inter-basin diversion'' is a fighting phrase, a frightening concept.

Interest groups are becoming activists with regard to an environmental issue; they perceive the stakes from their individual viewpoints. For water development projects, local support is usually dominant, as is often the case for air pollution. However, broader activity is attracted to national environmental legislation, and here quantification is much more difficult. The cost-benefit approach, frail as it is even for specific project justification, has been used by interest groups for and against national legislation, as well as by the National Academies of Science and Engineering and the federal agencies charged with the implementation of various acts. The subjective nature of the less tangible benefits (and possibly the most important part) of environmental management makes cost-benefit analysis a weak reed, highly susceptible to parochial bias and self-interest.

Industrial groups such as the Manufacturing Chemists Association, the National Coal Association, the American Mining Congress, the Edison Electric Institute, the American Petroleum Institute, the United States Chamber of Commerce, and the National Association of Manufacturers are aligned against the Isaak Walton League, Friends of the Earth, Audubon Society, the Sierra Club, and others strongly supporting pollution regulation. The industrial groups work with Congress in phrasing legislation. Environmental groups are tending to use the courts even after legislation is enacted to obtain judgments favoring their view of proper regulation-writing and implementation by the executive branch agencies. Here the pluralistic nature of our political system is lost in judicial determination of Congressional intent defining policy and of the adequacy of agency response to laws such as the National Environmental Policy Act. One can hope that the concept of relative risk will gradually supplant benefit-cost as a basis for priority-setting in a broader perspective. This concept, augmented by appreciation of the rate aspects of society and economic dynamics, offers the powerful factor of common sense to mitigate unquantified emotion and/or narrow self-interest. Basically, I believe that our economic and political system can assimilate any desired change at some rate to be set commensurate with urgency and criticality defined by relative risk.

Two examples of institutional entities showing progress on the United States-Mexican border support the premise that when the United States political system is presented with a unique problem it can respond promptly in the broad public interest. In fact, it is often easier for the United States to respond to an international problem than to a strictly domestic or internal issue.

The oldest example is water management along the Río Grande, where the International Boundary Commission was created in 1894, forty-six years after the Río Grande was set as part of the border. This was changed to the International Boundary and Water Commission (IBWC) in 1945. The IBWC is composed of Mexican and United States sections, each headed by an engineer-commissioner. Charged with safeguarding the rights of each nation and enabling each to obtain the benefits of mutual action, the Commission's jurisdiction is restricted to the boundary and to coordination of the two governments' plans for border works: construction, operation, and maintenance. Contracts with public or private agencies are authorized with both countries awarding large projects to private construction firms. The United States section has a construction division for small building tasks which handles maintenance work as well. The Mexican section deals only with management; planning, design, construction and maintenance responsibility is assigned to the Ministry of Hydraulic Resources. As a result, personnel and direct budget figures are much greater for the United States section than for the Mexican section. As noted earlier, these and other boundary programs are among the most successful international water management efforts anywhere. However, even with imaginative flexible cost-sharing arrangements, only part of the anticipated accomplishments has been achieved, primarily because of fragmented institutional entities whose cooperation is needed but is often subjugated to local self-interests. The IBWC experience points to the need for society to set goals and priorities for water use. Here again, the concept of relative risk and relative benefit can be used.

The second example of institutional progress along the United States-Mexican border is a joint air quality monitoring activity begun in 1972. Health authorities of Ciudad Juárez, El Paso, and Las Cruces, with the collaboration of the border field office of the Pan-American Health Organization, set up a program covering a fifty-mile radius centering in El Paso-Ciudad Juárez. This airshed covers more than 2 million persons in an interdependent economic activity reflected by an average of 1 million vehicle crossings and 3.3 million people crossings each month.

At the outset, program planners recognized that the border itself offered legal, judicial, economic, scientific, and urban planning barriers to effective cooperation. The purpose, objectives, a plan of action, and definition of responsibilities were outlined. In a document forming a basis for collaboration, this informal agreement simply set forth a goodwill understanding of the project for the health officials in developing joint activity. Program objectives have been met for the almost two years of its operation. Benefits include the establishment of working relationships between participating agencies and an increased awareness and appreciation for air pollution problems in the study area and the activities of each agency under its legislative authority. Laboratory facilities and services are being shared. Improved interchange of information and joint preparation of training activities have been achieved. Program directors have recommended expansion of the monitoring system beyond the present study of particulates and sulfur dioxide, and preparation of an emissions inventory to provide a basis for establishment of action priorities.

The newly opened international port of entry at Anapra is typical of the need for continuing emphasis on appropriate institutions for environmental management so that economic growth can be accommodated without penalizing the border ecosystem.

This new port of entry, within the Ciudad Juárez-El Paso airshed now under cooperative study, is located seven miles northwest of the border cities and thirty-eight miles south of Las Cruces. The port is initially serving as an industrial and agricultural crossing and later will be used by residents and tourists. New industries will be attracted to the area. Thirteen firms have expressed interest in locating twin plants at Anapra. The twin-plant program is based on customs regulations which allow a United States manufacturer to send component parts into Mexico for assembly and, when the finished goods are returned to the United States, he pays duty only on "value added" in Mexico. Equipment necessary for assembly operations may also be shipped into Mexico under bond, duty free. In effect, these regulations allow a United States manufacturer to use lower-cost Mexican labor for the labor intensive portion of his operation.

The New Mexico State Planning Office projects new jobs to add almost $3 million in yearly wages. Multiplier effects are projected to bring total new wages to some $4.5 million. Such new economic stimulus provides an opportunity for enlightened environmental management for broad public benefit.

In conclusion, it is my judgment that the ecology of the United States-Mexican border is in an active and good condition. Numerous problems with their attendant opportunities are apparent. But the IBWC and the joint air pollution study, which is apparently precedent-setting worldwide, show what can be done by competent public officials given proper taxpayer support.

APPENDIX I

Commentaries

A. Introduction
by Stanley R. Ross

The purpose of this Appendix is to give the reader some indication of the discussion arising from the presentation of the essays at the San Antonio conference. On occasion the editor will set the scene for a particular discussion with some additional material.

Culture

While the Mexican-United States boundary is an official dividing line, there is no insurmountable barrier. Rather there are important frontiers, including a cultural one. In this sense the border separates two different cultural worlds—not only that between Mexico and the United States, but also between Latin America and Anglo America. Despite the natural tendency to emphasize what is different, there is a unique mixture of Mexican and American heritages and cultures along the border.

The discussion session on culture got off to a good start when Ignacio Bernal argued that the consciousness of a distinctive Mexican culture was to be found clearly in the late eighteenth century in the heart of Mexico and, in a different way, probably goes back to the end of the seventeenth century. Therefore, he questioned the concept that such consciousness developed first at the border.

Américo Paredes responded that he "was referring not to the culture itself . . . but to a consciousness of ethnic identity . . . among the general populace." He explained that his thesis refers to "a feeling of strong ethnic identity . . . [since] a group under assault by an outgroup becomes much more conscious of its identity." Paredes agreed that culture developed in the central part of the country and that very early there were thinkers and writers who were aware of their *mexicanidad* ("Mexicanness"). However, he reiterated that what he was talking about was the particular feeling of identity on the popular level.

Rogelio Díaz-Guerrero, tying his comments to his own essay, suggested that there is less likelihood of an identity problem in central Mexico because one is part of a tremendously interdependent, protective family. On the frontier it's another matter. "Before being someone, we have to have the feeling of being something," he said. "One cannot have a political [or economic] point of view if one does not have an individual, personal identity."

Miguel González-Gerth cautioned that the search for cultural identity is a matter of degree depending on the border elements being discussed. Nettie Lee Benson expressed concern that the entire discussion of identity had been focused on the Mexican side. It is her view that there is fear of loss of identity by the other ethnic groups. "Not only does it apply to the language of the border—of these other ethnic groups—but also it applies to their life, their traditions."

Complaining of the lack of definition of culture, the late Daniel Cosío Villegas jocularly underscored the problem by noting that "some of these haughty men of the center of the country have considered those of the north as barbarians and would affirm that there is no sense in discussing culture in regard to a region visibly uncultured." Cosío explained that "this problem is not divided by the frontier. One cannot speak of the Mexican side or the North American side of the problem, therefore, but rather one must consider it all together as a totality."

Carlos Monsiváis said that he is aware of a Mexican frontier culture that is dissimilar from that on the American side. He identified this culture with the numerous migrants who have not been able to cross the border and who "have integrated a culture of poverty that is very Mexican." Turning to nationalism, the Mexican writer stated that nationalism, "as a strategy for recuperation and confrontation with an imperial power," continues to be important. But he felt that "cultural nationalism as such and as it has been manipulated in recent years does not contribute to that nationalism, but rather weakens it and gives it an appearance of existence that in reality it does not have."

Víctor Urquidi interjected that he thought that comparative data would be useful from other frontiers where cultures clashed or mixed. He anticipated that many of the problems of the Mexican-United States frontier would be similar to other such areas, especially where there is a strong economic interdependence. However, he also felt that there are special characteristics about the frontier of Mexico and the United States.

He spoke of the tremendous differential in income levels on the two sides of the border. Such elements—as well as the rural origin of much of the recent migration to the frontier zone—have to affect cultural relations and the cultural situation, he said. Finally, Urquidi affirmed his conviction that the lack of economic bases for the economic development of the Mexican frontier zone is a fact and an important influence on culture.

Felisa Kazen noted that the contemporary problems of culture in the border area is a complex issue not only of culture conflict, culture borrowing, and cultural identity, but also a manifestation of the existence of twin communities on the border. She contended that the symbiotic relationship between the twin cities is a crucial question. ''For example, when I think of contemporary cultural issues of the border, I think of the development of a unique language, which can be considered inferior English or inferior Spanish, but that also can be called a new, emergent dialect.''

Clearly defining his bias in favor of emphasizing aspects of conflict and for social change, Jorge Bustamante agreed that the development of language is the most important cultural phenomenon on the frontier—but viewed it as a social phenomenon rather than a grammatical one. He then proceeded to differentiate skill levels, income, and occupational distribution along ethnic and class lines, suggesting that in these categories similarities and differences may be found that are independent of the formal division of the border. While conceding differences of time and place, Bustamante suggested that there is a reality—social, economic, and political—that permeates the frontier and does not begin or end with the juridical boundary.

Peter Canga suggested that border culture might be viewed in terms of two diverse subcultures, one urban and the other rural. With increasing urbanization and the development of mass transportation, he thought it conceivable that the two subcultures might tend to merge. Similarly, David Garza thought it preferable to concentrate on those sociological aspects of border culture that tend to unite the experience of people on both sides. As an example, he added that the mass culture—or the popular industrial culture of Monsiváis

might represent the attempt by the *Chicano* and by the *Mexicano* of the same socioeconomic level to construct a reality that defines them in opposition to both of the national cultures in which they live and which gives meaning to their lives as opposed to the dominant myths of culture in both societies.

Clearly the participants tended to view border culture as a contrast and a conflict, while national culture along the border too often was endowed with a unity which it does not have.

Earlier volumes sponsored by the Weatherhead Foundation underscored the plural nature of society in the Southwest and examined the educational perspectives of the Mexican Americans.[1] It is interesting that at the San Antonio conference education entered the discussion more implicitly than directly. This is not to say that the educational factor does not loom large. It was just five years ago that a student of social problems in the area wrote:

> Not only has the American school system failed to educate Mexican-American children, but likewise has closed the door of social and economic opportunity in their faces. The school system has hampered the adjustment to Anglo-American society. It has damaged their identity, created feelings of inferiority, inadequacy, self-rejection, and group rejection, and it's now partially responsible for the constantly increasing unrest and tension among the Mexican-American student population.[2]

This commentary appeared when the new effort in bilingual educational research and practice had hardly gotten started. While it is much too early to judge the educational results, there seems to be general agreement that psychological benefits already are apparent.

The ideal would be mutual interpenetration of the two cultures at the border regions, with each culture complementing and enriching the other. However, what tends to occur is cultural penetration. For a cultural frontier to function meaningfully, it must neither be slammed shut with dogmatic and provincial hostility nor must it be abandoned to systematic alienation. Rather it must serve as a sifter and balance for values, as a field for experimentation for understanding.[3]

Individual and Social Psychology

Since there had been strong psychological overtones in parts of the cultural discussion, the group came quite logically to the topics of mental and physical characteristics and well-being in the border regions. In such discussions there is a natural tendency to focus on the negative as more provocative, but this is rarely appreciated by those being analyzed. However, it is essential if there is to be improvement of the human condition.

Several speakers raised questions about the validity of using data from Mexico City and Austin for an understanding of the border population. Others questioned the value judgments that, they felt, characterized the essays by Wayne Holtzman and Díaz-Guerrero. The commentator, Manuel Ramírez III, went much further and questioned the validity of western-style tests for *mestizos*.

Richard Santos argued that the locales of the study are outside the *provincias internas* historically, geographically, culturally, and linguistically. After all, he observed, the *mestizaje* of Mexico is not a genealogical or physicoanthropological *mestizaje*, but rather a cultural-linguistic *mestizaje*. Perhaps, with due regard for the dangers of stereotyping, the *mestizaje* of the Chicano is a third and different type, he suggested. "Bolton called the borderlands the tail of the Spanish cat. . . . I prefer to think about it more as the belly-button of the push-pull animal of Dr. Doolittle since we are caught between that which is truly Mexico and that which is truly the United States."

Rudolph Gomez, Arthur Rubel, David Garza, Armando Gutiérrez, and Alberto Villasana all questioned the value judgments they felt that the two psychologists had made in their study. Gomez felt that implicitly, but unconsciously perhaps, they viewed one style of coping as superior to another. Garza suggested that sociological studies indicating that minority children "in certain kinds of classroom settings in fact repress their adaptation to a certain kind of reality that in many ways is a very rational way to cope with a kind of prejudicial authoritative behavior from the teacher" weaken, if not vitiate, the kind of conclusion represented by the studies being discussed. Based on studies he had participated in at Crystal City, Gutiérrez suggested that perhaps "the perceived chance of success is the critical variable in terms of determining how one responds to his environment rather than some kind of cultural characteristic." Both Villasana and Arthur Rubel called attention to their feeling that underlying this study were some strong assumptions of what is good for people.

Américo Paredes observed that the group was struggling with the dilemmas of the social sciences, if not specifically those of the border. "We are not dealing with things we can discuss in a rarefied atmosphere that might be called objective. These are things that inevitably will be put into action, and if we make mistakes, they might become self-fulfilling mistakes." Referring to the value judgment problem, Paredes declared that he was no champion of jargon, but "we are always faced with the problem of trying to get value-free categories, and common ordinary words unfortunately are very value-laden."

William Madsen sought to identify an even larger problem—namely, how the human condition can be improved. Or, alternatively, what kind of a society are we heading for and how do we want that society to relate to others? If we aim for a multiethnic society—perhaps thereby to best meet the community and family need so abused in our mass society—a core of common values will be needed that override the secondary values that give identification. At least that has been so in the few areas where multiethnic societies have been involved. Arthur Corwin earlier had expressed doubts about the desirability of the dual or multiple society. For him the critical problem was one of acculturation to make people functional within society, both local and national. With that as his premise, Corwin questioned to what extent "you can preserve or attempt to preserve so-called native or *mestizaje* values."

Speaking of prescriptions for a better life, Rudolph Gomez observed that Wayne Holtzman's policy prescriptions are almost verbatim what George Sánchez wrote years ago relative to what needed to be done to improve the conditions of the Mexican Americans in Texas. While Holtzman infers his policy recommendations from his research and Sánchez operated more intuitively, Gomez rhetorically questioned the value of generating studies "if we are going to ask the same questions thirty years from now."

Holtzman conceded that it was legitimate to question the validity of western-style tests for the *mestizo* or for any culture in which they are not indigenous. This is the dilemma in any cross-cultural research. Therefore, they had been very careful in not generalizing beyond those they had studied. Díaz-Guerrero argued that 90 percent of the present-day influence in both Mexico and the United States is Western European. Mexico's heritage is Hispanic and to some degree indigenous. The Mexican American has the Anglo-Saxon heritage on one side and the Mexican, with all its complications, on the other.

The Mexican psychologist emphasized that the research produced data which need to be used properly and professionally. While the Mexican data are less reliable than that from the United States, "that doesn't mean they are invalid. . . . They are still highly reliable as measures taken psychologically go." Holtzman emphasized that theirs was not a bipolar theory of psychodynamics—which is far oversimplified—but rather a multidimensional one. While value-laden words are a dilemma whenever one seeks to communicate, the available data from a variety of sources—sociological, anthropological, and psychological—tend to converge and without major inconsistencies.

Holtzman agreed that his policy prescriptions—which he believes are broad and general enough to apply to other ethnic groups as well—paralleled those of George Sánchez, but he believes that there has been progress. ''At least now there is institutionalized acceptance of these in the form of laws and the form of administrative fiats, if not practices.'' Admitting that he and his colleagues are not value-free, but that what is good—in coping behavior—''in some ways is decided for us by society at large and the general direction in which mankind is going in a modern industrialized urban society'' which requires a different kind of coping than that required by an agrarian peasant society. Thus good and bad are defined at least in the sense of survival.

Noting some evidence of greater aggression and activity on the part of Chicanas, Holtzman suggested that it may be a reaction phenomenon whereby the individual overcompensates. Something like this is occurring in Mexican society. Remarking that their study is based on data collected in the Mexican capital eight to ten years ago, Holtzman stated that there have been changes in Mexican society which need to be measured. Indeed he called attention to the fact that one can observe a lot of compensatory trends occurring among the adolescents in Mexican society right now in Mexico City.

In conclusion, Holtzman expressed his pleasure that Madsen had brought out the importance of any society that is cohesive enough to identify itself as a society having to have shared values:

> I see a number of shared core values that extend to Mexico as well as the United States, if we think of a North American culture in a large context, while also allowing for subcultural variations, whether you are speaking of subculture in the sense of the differences between Mexico City and Chicago, between Monterrey and San Antonio, or between Laredo and Nuevo Laredo. These are all varying degrees of subcultures within the larger cultures. Mexicans and North Americans are far more alike than they are different if you look over the diversity of mankind across the globe. We're all more western than we would admit, and, I would dare say, there are few *mestizos* that are not highly westernized.

Health

A number of conference participants—Gustavo Quesada, Felisa Kazen, and Arthur Rubel—called for study in the health area of the whole region on both sides of the border without regard for the boundary line. At the very least, they argued that it should be viewed as a unique area and that comparable statistics should be gathered wherever possible. It is fascinating that the Mexican border area has comparatively high health and health service standards compared with the rest of Mexico, excepting the Federal District, while the Texas border is low when compared with general United States standards.

However, Ricardo Loewe reiterated his pessimism about the prospects for binational studies and efforts in the health area. For example, he noted that the Mexican-North American Society for Public Health is moribund. More important, any binational programs would necessarily have to be asymmetrical. First is the question of priorities, he said. Mexican political leaders are unlikely to give high priority to problems for which they do not have resources. Furthermore, the country is unlikely to give priority in the health area to the frontier when that region has the best health conditions of any Mexican section. Differing health problems inevitably would result in different political priorities resulting in the aforementioned asymmetrical assignment of resources. In addition, there are differences in the types of services on both sides of the border and technical and administrative obstacles. Finally, some health problems are better handled by an international agency than by binational arrangements.

Health conditions and services may be better in the north of Mexico, excepting Coahuila, as a developed region than in much of the rest of the country. However, Loewe added that the health conditions on the Mexican side are poorer than those on the United States side. And health services are more limited and health conditions poorer in the border region north of the boundary than in the rest of the United States. South Texas has fewer physicians, pediatricians, dentists, registered nurses, and physical therapists in proportion to population than the state as a whole or when compared to national averages.[4] Not surprisingly, statistics for the south Texas region show a higher incidence of certain diseases compared to the rest of the state: dysentery-type disease, leprosy, polio, and typhoid.[5] Gustavo Quesada, drawing on experience at Lubbock, suggested that the problem might be ethnic rather than regional. There is little doubt that minority groups in the border region (Mexican Americans and American Indians) do have a much inferior health status compared with Anglo Americans. Most observers agree that the explanation lies both in the paucity of health services available and the constraints on access to health services due to economic and cultural factors.

Américo Paredes stressed that the group was talking about ''people for whom medical care gets scarcer and scarcer and more and more expensive.'' Much has been said and written about the importance of cultural factors as a constraint, including the question of values of medical personnel not being shared by Mexican Americans. However, Jerry L. Weaver, in a recent review of the literature, tracing the evolution of thought on this subject, questions some of the sweeping generalizations. In the late 1940s and early 1950s, an important trend began when Lyle Saunders began to place health care in a cultural perspective. Then came Rubel and Madsen describing Mexican folk-medical culture as a separate, but largely complementary, arrangement. By this time the prevalent culture-oriented view was that the "health care behavior of Mexican-Americans is a consequence of (as well as a reinforcement for) a community-wide designative culture."[6]

Weaver notes that more recently the "single most important scholarly treatment of the nation's second largest minority"[7] largely ignores health behavior. He contends that the sweeping generalizations about Mexican-American health behavior are being questioned and that the significance of traditional folk-health culture has been overdrawn, particularly with reference to educated, urban, middle-class populations.

Rubel expressed concern that we keep talking in stereotypes or caricatures of what is a large and very variable population. To talk about 5 to 7 million people as an undifferentiated population or to generalize from studies of lower-class, multiproblem Chicanos because funding is available for such studies is bound to have negative consequences. "I cannot believe that Santos Reyes doesn't have more similarity in the way he relates to health problems with me than he does with somebody who is a migratory laborer with a first-grade education."

In the session wrapup Charles Teller gave equal emphasis to curative services, preventive medicine, and economic development. Robert Oseasohn began by responding to several questions or comments about more extensive use of midwives and of paramedical personnel. He pointed out that midwifery had been introduced in the United States in general about 1925 and "has been a notorious failure. It gets revived from time to time in academic medical centers, where it seems to flourish in a limited, protective environment." Oseasohn recalled several successful programs—one in Madera County, California—but such efforts tend not to be long-lived without the continuing support of the medical profession and the local or state political structure.

For Oseasohn the first obligation is to promote health. Second, there is great need for individuals trained in social welfare techniques. Third, rather than first-aid apparatus at the village level or trying to put doctors and hospitals at every crossroad, attention should be focused on making available—actually and financially—the means of transportation to get people to centers where proper care can be given. Oseasohn lamented the lack of innovation in health promotion and the nonassiduous effort devoted to environmental control.

Ecology

Pollution, whether of water or of air, is no respecter of international boundaries. Water quality is inextricably related to land use, and air quality is related to both. One Borderlands observer has warned that:

> As the Borderlands are confronted with expanding population and industrialization not only will water quality be affected but air quality will be an increasing concern—a growing irritant to the lungs of the area's inhabitants and a festering obstacle to continuing friendly relations between Mexico and the United States.[8]

Unless there are some strenuous, anticipatory efforts the situation promises inevitable deterioration. Clearly there is environmental interdependence.

Individual scholars as well as a United Nations Conference have noted the divergence of views on environmental development as perceived by developed and developing countries. The divergence clearly results from a different perception of national interests and national problems. The United Nations Conference noted that the environmental problems of developed countries are "very largely the outcome of a high level of economic development," while the environmental problems of developing countries are "predominantly problems that reflect poverty and the very lack of development of their society."[9]

While one can easily predict that delicate problems will arise between Mexico and the United States relative to environmental pollution, the record of cooperation and adoption of national legislation for the protection of the environment affords some basis for hope. The two nations have cooperated over the years in terms of flood control, sanitation, and the protection of wildlife. A 1936 Convention for the Protection of Migratory Birds and Game Mammals was supplemented by a 1972 agreement. That same year there was initiated in the Ciudad Juárez-El Paso area a Joint Air Pollution Sampling Program in an effort to gather more information on air pollution in the region. That pair of twin cities was the site of the first binational symposium on air pollution control in September 1973. Then, of course, there is the accord to resolve Mexico's just complaint about the salinity of the waters of the Colorado River delivered to it.

Through the Environmental Protection Agency, the United States has endeavored to identify and control sources of environmental pollution and contamination. Similarly, through its Law of March 23, 1971, a Constitutional Amendment of July 6, 1971, and Smoke and Dust Regulations issued September 17, 1971, Mexico has an environmental legislative package that could be described as "comprehensive, stringent, and responsive to Mexico's needs. In short, if these measures are taken at face value, one can conclude that Mexico can now boast of one of the world's most impressive legal regimes for environmental protection and control for virtually every aspect of the environmental crisis."[10]

During the discussion of environmental problems Carlos Nagel stressed the need for expanded educational programs on the environment, Armando Gutiérrez expressed concern about contaminated water in the barrios, and Arthur Corwin called attention to the very real problem of erosion along virtually the entire length of the border. David Alvírez warned of disaster ahead if the focus is on ecological and technological problems without "due attention to fertility problems and increased demand on resources resulting from demographic growth." Américo Paredes added that the demographic problem is "very, very sensitive. There is also the matter of what one might call philosophy or life-style. Perhaps it may be time for us to become very, very conscious of the concept of limited goods in the world as a whole and somehow figure a way of existing without unlimited growth."

Nettie Lee Benson expressed concern whether projected plans to move and concentrate people—which historically has not worked—would in effect substitute ecological concerns for human ones; Villasana clarified that what was involved was relocation in the same region and forming villages to which it would be viable to deliver public services and where there are resources which might enable them to achieve a better life. "What we are setting up is not a mobilization from region to region which we have had in the past and which was a bad experience, but rather a relocation of the people in the same area where they have more possibilities to advance their well-being."

Villasana cited the example of Ocampo, not far from the border,

> where there isn't any possibility for these people. . . . There's no water, there's no soil, there's no transportation; their natural vegetation doesn't offer any possibility of a decent way of living. So we are trying to move them, and if we can move them ten kilometers that would be something good and if they can be moved a hundred that would be even better.

Arthur Busch reported that there has been substantial progress in protecting fisheries and stopping ocean dumping, particularly in the Gulf of Mexico. He stressed the importance of avoiding the wasteful use of water to carry off wastes. He estimated that about 90 to 95 percent of the water that goes into

American homes is used simply to carry off other water. Noting that the nonwater fraction is less than .1 of 1 percent, Busch said:

> It's like combing through the haystack for the proverbial needle to get out that little bit of non-water which has such a magnified effect on public health. . . . So it's strictly poor management of water to insist on pumping water, treating it very expensively, putting it through a home, putting less than .1 of 1 percent non-water in it, and then taking it down and expensively treating it again, generally inadequately, and polluting our rivers with it. It's nonsensical, absolutely nonsensical. The emperor is marching up and down the street in his underwear all the time.

Finally Humberto Bravo explained that the Mexican Section for Environmental Improvement (Subsecretario de Mejoramiento Ambiental) within the Department of Public Health has an educational program to promote public awareness of environmental problems through television and other media. While these steps and those by Mexico's northern neighbor are desirable and necessary, clearly there is need to be prepared to cope with environmental problems of an instructional nature and most specifically those which will be occurring in the binational border area.

Politics

The session on politics strained to some degree against the constraints of the very specialized—both topically and geographically—studies presented. Clearly one must keep in mind not only provincial differences in the range of state and local governments involved on both sides of the border, but also the degree to which national politics and political instrumentalities effect and affect politicial decisions.

The highly centralized structure of the Mexican government—with both policymaking authority and fiscal resources concentrated in the Federal District and specifically in the executive branch of government—inevitably affects the priority given to problems and the assignment of resources for their solution. Similarly, what looms very large regionally on the United States side may have little weight as national political parties put together platforms and programs.

Considerable discussion and criticism at the conference session focused on the current and prospective role of the Raza Unida Party and the Chicano movement in general. David Garza began by questioning that the Mexican-American population is "up for grabs," politically speaking. He questioned it in terms of what he referred to as the "nature of false consciousness" among oppressed minority groups like the Mexican Americans. He explained that:

It is not just a question of thinking of their apathy with respect to the political situation that explains their nonparticipation or their failure to respond to third-party movements, but rather a question of the successful internalization of self-derogatory values and differential attitudes toward the political system whereby they accept a kind of role of nonparticipation in the political system and that it's legitimate that they not participate.

Garza went on to say that it is the Democratic Party that is much more likely to recruit and mobilize the Mexican-American minority than any third party. After all, the Democratic Party controls "the means of communication, the rewards system and the avenues of upward social mobility."

Rudolph Gomez challenged the view that Chicanos had to be told of their ethnicity or that this is part of the function of Raza Unida:

Chicanos don't have to be told or don't have to tell themselves of their ethnicity because this has been told them all of their lives in the United States from a variety of sources. Indeed, one of the developments that has come to light from the Chicano movement is the uniformity of the experiences Chicanos have had regardless of where they live.

The success the movement has had or promises to have, he continued, derives directly from this commonality of experience, from the association of the consciousness of being Chicano.

The Chicano movement has been, in Gomez's view, hampered by the absence of a Chicano community. He referred to the analytical self-differentiation between Mexican Americans and Chicanos, not to mention those in New Mexico and bordering regions who regard themselves as "Hispanos." You cannot assume the presence of a homogeneous community, he said.

Manuel Ramírez observed that the political development of the Chicano community in California, Arizona, and New Mexico is following very different lines than in Texas. In California for example, he said, the Chicanos have been having an impact on the Democratic Party and have changed its direction significantly.

Arthur Rubel expressed concern that, although different things appear to be occurring in places like Arizona and California than are occurring in Texas, the discussion at the conference was focused primarily on Texas. Among the southwestern states the Arizona border area is most like that of Texas, yet, he noted, the Raza Unida Party is very active in Texas and not very active in Arizona.[11]

Vernon Briggs called attention to the importance of the primary elections in a state where one party has been largely dominant. Under these circumstances the activity of the third party may well preclude the minority having its greatest impact at the time of the primary, which often is more important than the election itself. Felisa Kazen warned that there is no guarantee that, simply because you get people of one ethnic group voting together, their interests necessarily will be protected. As proof she called attention to Mexican-American party bosses and Mexican-American political machinery in predominantly Mexican-American communities in the border area, which never have consistently represented their own people.[12]

As for the Chicano movement as a whole, both Américo Paredes and Carlos Monsiváis tended to minimize its impact to date either on border communities or in Mexico. Paredes—in a sense identifying the same phenomenon as Kazen—pointed out that in places like Brownsville and Laredo when Mexican Americans obtained power they tended to make common cause with the power structure. Monsiváis noted that the Chicano movement had had little echo or influence in Mexico. In part he attributed this to the continued currency of the stereotyped *pocho* as a common denominator for the Mexican Americans. Furthermore, in his view it would be difficult if not impossible for the Chicano movement to be assimilated or even to be influential granted the largely closed Mexican political system.

Turning to the Mexican political environment, Rogelio Díaz-Guerrero suggested that there were many negative aspects to United States influence in Mexico, but that a most positive aspect was the tendency toward democratization and equality. Armando Gutiérrez interjected that if the Mexicans were looking for democracy on the north side of the border, they are "barking up the wrong tree." Díaz-Guerrero offered the hypothesis—not unrelated to some of the concepts offered in his own paper—that governmental development may well be connected with the rather hierarchical authoritarian situation within the Mexican family. "I would like to think that the lack of interest in the great outside and in the political situation of the whole community is partially, at least, due to the fact that we have such strong family patterns."

Mario Ojeda criticized the latter part of the Ugalde paper quite sharply. He complained of the scarcity of Mexican sources and the heavy concentration of North American sources, noting the increasing tendency of North American authors to quote each other. He felt that the explanation of Mexican political and economic policy was only partial and oversimplified.

Ugalde agreed that the latter half of his essay was incomplete, lacking full documentation and definitive supporting evidence. He observed that obviously it is very difficult to understand the decision-making process of the Mexican government when we do not even understand how the president is chosen. He agreed that his sources were heavily North American and that American researchers do have a tendency to cite one another. However, he did point out that "the majority of the works which have been written on Mexican frontier communities have been written by North Americans."

Responding to Ugalde's expressed view that in Mexico's case what is understood as political stability is simply the maintenance of the status quo, Sofía Méndez Villarreal argued that to attribute Mexico's political stability simply to the cooptation of professional and middle-class groups— and one might add cooptation of the workers as Ugalde did in response—is to ignore Mexico's development over the past twenty-five or thirty years. One cannot simply push aside economic conditions and factors. The very machinery of the PRI has played an important part in political stability for "indubitably the system itself has been sufficiently dynamic to create opportunities for employment, investment, and expansion of economic forces without which it would be very difficult for us to be able to understand the political and economic stability of Mexico." However, Ugalde argued that the political stability has been achieved at a very high economic cost, and the burden of that cost is borne along the frontier as well as elsewhere in Mexico.

Economics

During the discussion of the border region's economic development, the late Daniel Cosío Villegas noted that no government had tried to revitalize the north as President Luis Echeverría had done. Cosío then asked Eliseo Mendoza to discuss the economic progress that has been achieved in this region.

Mendoza interpreted the question to ask to what extent the government can serve as an inspirer of frontier economic development and to what extent this process can be accelerated. He said:

> I think that in recent years we definitely have achieved on the northern frontier an accelerated economic development, granted the economic, political and social problems that had existed there for many years. . . .
> I conclude that by more or less indirect indicators such as the increases in commercial activity, employment, economic diversification and the higher levels of productivity in agriculture or industry or in commerce itself. I am convinced that the bases for a more consistent, more accelerated development of the frontier are being established.

Mendoza concluded by calling attention to two other factors he regards as key elements: first, the important infrastructure projects in the frontier zone;

second, the effort to raise the frontier Mexican's conscious awareness of development.

Various seminar participants took issue with specific aspects of the border economic policy or practice. Sofía Méndez Villarreal noted that the "lure" article program was intended to save foreign exchange and stimulate both demand for and production of nationally produced articles. However, these are imported articles that have to be paid for, representing charges against foreign exchange. The introduction of such items tends to orient consumption abroad, something the quality of the foreign products also contributes to. Since the overwhelming proportion (some 82 percent) of the items are consumption goods, facilitating their importation tends to discourage the development of light industry which the government is endeavoring to promote in the border area.

Mendoza Berrueto argued in his response that while the "lure" articles program was aimed at saving international exchange, it also was linked with other programs seeking to achieve additional benefits. It is his contention that the items involved were being imported anyway through purchases by "commuters" and through smuggling. By redirecting such importation into legal channels, he argued, there is better control of such commercial activity, a reduction of contraband traffic, and employment in commerce resulting in profits, wages, and taxes.

The assembly plant program received critical attention from Cosío, Mario Ojeda, and Urquidi. Cosío, noting that the assembly plants—like the rest of the economy—had been adversely affected by the economic recession in the United States, raised the possibility that government-directed increases in the minimum wage to reflect increases in the cost of living may have made the assembly plants uneconomical. Ojeda complained that the assembly plants were forging just one more link of dependency for Mexico with the United States. He noted, further, the paradox of the assembly worker becoming motivated to cross the frontier to buy the article which he had helped to assemble. Urquidi seriously questioned the heavy reliance on "assembly plants" as the base for industrialization in view of the notorious and obvious instability of this type of industrialization.

As the conferees looked at the economic problems of the border region, there were many comments on interdependency and dependency, on the lack of solid bases for economic development, and on the contribution of migrants and commuters to the poverty of one of the poorest regions of the United States. There was general agreement that the dual goals had to be both the sound economic development of the entire region and the equalization of economic conditions on both sides of the border. Whether cause or consequence, the massive human migration is one of the most pressing complications in seeking solutions to the betterment of border life as well as affecting the relations of the two nations.

Migrants

No other problem looms as large as that of migration—and particularly illegal migration—for the border region and beyond. Impressive too is the all-pervasive character of the problem. No matter what theme the conference participants turned their attention to, the question of the migrants inevitably came up and loomed large. Indeed it is a problem of critical importance and overwhelming dimensions, the most significant problem affecting the relations of the two countries.

The undesirable consequences vary according to one's views and interests, but it would appear unquestioned that the presence of the migrants, particularly the illegals, causes disruption of the normal labor market in the Southwest and increasingly in some northern cities. While not causally responsible, the migrants clearly have added to the dimensions of the border region's problems.

Worse yet is the fact that the smuggling of aliens, particularly since the end of the Bracero Program, has become an organized and profitable business. *Coyotes* specialize in smuggling hungry people to the promised land— *mojados* (wetbacks) across the river and *alambristas* (wire jumpers) across the land boundary west of El Paso for $200 to $700. The Border Patrol, organized in 1924 for the specific purpose of combating the smuggling of illegal aliens, is inadequate in numbers to cope with the magnitude of the problem. It is estimated that only about one in three or four of the illegal entrants is caught and returned to Mexico. In fact, little effort is made to apprehend illegals outside of the area immediately adjacent to the international boundary. However, the problem is difficult not simply from a legal or enforcement point of view, but from the human vantage point as well.

During the Conference the problem of the migrants came up in virtually every session. In the session specifically devoted to this key question many participants took issue with the views of the essayists. Felisa Kazen noted that one could view the flow into the United States as one more step in the internal migration patterns within Mexico itself—from the less developed states into the Federal District and the northern states where industry is concentrated.

David Alvírez challenged Bustamante's argument that immigration does not affect wages or the Mexican Americans. Clearly he was unconvinced by militant Chicanos, who argue this way and advocate legalizing all illegal Mexican immigrants. Alvírez also felt that Bustamante had neglected the "safety-valve" function that migration has performed for Mexico. Víctor Urquidi took issue with both essayists. Bustamante, he said,

> definitely underestimates the demographic variables in Mexico, the impact of very high rates of population growth based on high birth rates and declining mortality, which increases the proportion of young people in the population and makes . . . the potential labor force increase even more rapidly than the general rate of population growth. In fact, because of the high proportion of young people in the Mexican population—46 percent are under the age of 15—the impact will be felt for the next 30 to 40 years. The major problem of Mexican development over the next 30 to 40 years will be to focus on employment in every fashion.

For Urquidi, Briggs simplifies on the other side. The Mexican economist remarked that Briggs's "easy solution in terms of massive foreign aid programs . . . seems utterly unrealistic." Urquidi argued that this would not solve any problems of a structural nature. In fact, the evidence suggests that "aid programs do not solve the development problem or speed up the development process very much." Far better, he argued, would be a change in United States trade policies. The United States market might become less restrictive in the future for Mexican exports—not only manufactured but also agricultural products.

Sofía Méndez, while agreeing that the push factors probably would strengthen in the coming years—due in part to the failure of policies to attain the desired result—challenged the view that technology is the principal cause of unemployment. Rather it is the rate of growth of investment which determines the proportions of the capital-labor mix, she said.

Humanitarian concerns preoccupied Gilbert Denman. He expressed regret for the discontinuation of the Bracero Program, which he said was due to false nationalism on the Mexican side and to United States labor's misconception about displacement of the American worker on the American side. *Braceros* could do things that the sophisticatedly trained Texas cowboys could not—such as how "to head cattle in the right direction, how to castrate them, how to dehorn them without hurting them." Denman argued that something must be done so these people can be protected.

In response, Bustamante stated that his preference is to look at the problems in terms of conflict rather than harmony because "the system is not fair . . . and ought to be changed." His expressed viewpoint "is not a scientific statement; it is an ethical statement." Briggs insisted that the illegal aliens do keep wages down: ". . . it has to have an impact, and it has to be detrimental, extremely detrimental." He strenuously objected to any suggestion that the Bracero Program be renewed under the guise of humanitarianism. While urging United States aid for development, Briggs is pessimistic that the United States would offer it or that Mexico would accept. As for the suggestion that the United States adjust its trade policy, Briggs felt certain that organized labor would oppose strongly any such effort, but "we can adjust to free trade a lot easier than we can to illegal entry."

A wide range of solutions was discussed by conference participants. Most of them are aimed at the immediate situation or represent endeavors intended to prevent it from worsening. In terms of longer-range goals there was general agreement on the desirability, but less unanimity on the attainability, of equalizing conditions on both sides of the border.

Drugs

Another problem of binational concern is that posed by drug traffic. The traffic includes amphetamines, marijuana, and the hard drugs, heroin and cocaine. In late 1974, authorities arrested more than a hundred persons in Mexico and the United States in connection with the production and distribution of billions of illegal amphetamines ("mini-bennies"). John R. Bartels, Jr., head of the Federal Drug Enforcement Agency, charged that "a group of interlocking conspiracies" formed a network that annually produced and distributed five billion amphetamines with a street value in excess of $1.6 billion.[13]

A Drug Enforcement Administration (DEA) study published in the fall of 1975 confirmed the virtual severing of the French connection attributable to police work on two continents and the Turkish government's crackdown, at United States insistence, on poppy growers. In 1974, 40 percent of confiscated street heroin came from Europe or the Near East; for the first six months of 1975, the figure had declined to only 25 percent. We have noted earlier the resultant sharp increase in the share of the market enjoyed by "Mexican brown" heroin.

Granted the length of the border, the estimated thirty-thousand illegal flights back and forth per year, and the limited number of investigators, it is small wonder that the agent in charge of the El Paso office of DEA described the enforcement effort as being "like trying to catch a snowstorm with a teacup."[14] It is estimated that only 10 percent of the shipments are intercepted.[15] Obviously any effective program to control and eradicate this traffic will have to be a binational effort.

In Mexico, there is growing concern about increased drug use and the potential rise in addiction among Mexico's youth. Marijuana long has been consumed in rural Mexico, but expert observers link the dramatic increase in marijuana use among youths of all classes in urban Mexico to the American "drug culture" of the 1960s. With the involvement of the same traffickers in heroin as in marijuana, Mexican experts fear an increase in addiction among the young people of the country.[16] These concerns resulted in the Mexican government's campaign against narcotics referred to in the introduction to this volume.

Summing Up

At the San Antonio Conference it became clear that while binational, the border region is a unique, specific area definable in historic, sociopolitical, psychological-cultural, ecological, and other terms. The reality involved does not begin or end at the juridical line of demarcation. The border zone has a life—an existence—of its own. Consequently, when considering the problems it is essential that, whenever possible, they should be viewed as a totality rather than be studied in splendid isolation on the Mexican side or the North American side.

It becomes important to find a framework within which a given problem may be dealt with in terms of both sides, of both nations. When that proves difficult or even impossible, then at least the whole problem should be viewed from two perspectives—the Mexican and the American—and dealt with in a detailed and objective fashion, avoiding one-sided approaches.

The problems are not only binational; they are also complex, interdisciplinary in character, and cannot be treated in isolation from one another. Just as the region repeatedly reveals its fundamental unity, so its problems are so intertwined that the researcher and policymaker must be aware of them even when considering only one problematic area. Furthermore, there must be an awareness of the international implications of whatever happens at the border region.

There is a very real need for research tools, statistical data, and research itself on almost every facet of life in the border area. While there is much more interest and considerably more being done recently than heretofore, one only has to take note that there is neither a definitive published bibliography nor a major historical study on Mexican migration to the United States.[17]

There was a time that Borderland studies were largely the province of historians. More recently the area has drawn the attention of a diversified group of social scientists, specialists in mental and physical well-being, and experts in pollution control, land and water utilization, and the generation and utilization of energy. Clearly there will be an increasing need for specialists in a wide range of disciplines who will also have Borderland expertise.[18] The Mexican-United States border region has more than once been described as a remarkable research laboratory.

First and foremost, it is an area for research aimed at the understanding of fundamental problems. It is to be hoped that both nations increasingly will recognize that the problems of the border region are national problems deserving of national attention.

As Jorge Bustamante suggested during the Conference:

> . . . the border provides to social scientists, to people interested in analyzing the problems of the border, a natural laboratory to understand those international implications of the relations between the two countries being manifested in the day-to-day interactions between peoples and institutions of the border area.

NOTES

1. See, Edward H. Spicer and Raymond H. Thompson, eds., *Plural Society in the Southwest* (Albuquerque: University of New Mexico Press, 1975) and Gus Tyler, ed., *Mexican-Americans Tomorrow, Educational and Economic Perspectives* (Albuquerque: University of New Mexico Press, 1975).

2. Clark S. Knowlton, "The Special Education Problems of the Mexican Americans," in Sterling M. McMurrin, ed., *The Conditions for Educational Equality* (New York: Committee for Economic Development, 1971), p. 142.

3. Jorge Mañach, *Frontiers in the Americas: A Global Perspective,* trans. Philip H. Phenix (New York: Teachers College Press, 1975), pp. 76-77.

4. Robert H. Waldron, "Current Status of Health Manpower in South Texas," mimeographed (Paper prepared for the Conference on Health Care for Children at Laredo, Texas, December 6-7, 1974).

5. Southwest Project of the ACLU Foundation as submitted to the Weatherhead Foundation, p. 2.

6. Jerry L. Weaver, "Mexican American Health Care Behavior: A Critical Review of the Literature," *Social Science Quarterly* 54 (1973): 35, 90-91.

7. Leo Grebler, Joan W. Moore, and Ralph C. Guzmán, *The Mexican-American People, The Nation's Second Largest Minority* (New York: The Free Press, 1970).

8. Albert E. Utton, *Pollution and International Boundaries: United States-Mexican Environmental Problems* (Albuquerque: University of New Mexico Press, 1973), Preface.

9. Allen Lowell Doud "International Environmental Development: Perception of Developing and Developed Countries," in Utton, *Pollution and International Boundaries,* pp. 41-50.

10. Julian Juergensmeyer and Earle Blizzard, "Legal Aspects of Environmental Control in Mexico: An Analysis of Mexico's New Environmental Law," in Utton, *Pollution and International Boundaries,* p. 115.

11. Clark Knowlton has written on the resort to violence in New Mexico. He attributes it to the presence of leaders like Reies López Tijerina and to the existence of the land issue as a "focusing point for Spanish American resentment, frustrations, and aspirations." "Violence in New Mexico: A Sociological Perspective," *California Law Review* 58 (1970): 41.

12. Knowlton has described how in New Mexico's Spanish-American areas, the political patron is the *jefe político,* who interacts with city and regional bosses. "The authority and the power of the political boss is enhanced by the voting habits of the Spanish-American voter." "Patron-Peon Pattern Among the Spanish-Americans of New Mexico," *Social Forces* 40 (1962): 12-17.

13. *New York Times,* 12 September 1974. Many of the illegal pills were smuggled across at San Ysidro, California, generally packed in plastic bags called "pillows," containing 25,000 tablets each.

14. Dan Rosen, "High in the Sky," *New York Times Magazine,* 15 June 1975.

15. Martin Kasindorf, "By the Time It Gets to Phoenix," *New York Times Magazine,* 26 October 1975.

16. *New York Times,* 25 January 1976.

17. Arthur F. Corwin, "Mexican Emigration History, 1900-1970: Literature and Research," *Latin American Research Review* 8 (1973):3-24.

18. Ellwyn R. Stoddard, *United States-Mexico Borderlands Studies. An Inventory of Scholars, Appraisal of Funding Resources, and Research Prospects* (El Paso: University of Texas, Center for Inter-American Studies, 1974).

B. Culture of the Frontier*
by Josefina Zoraida Vázquez

The essays on border culture offer a contrast in point of view, perhaps indicative of the authors' dissimilar backgrounds. Américo Paredes, a product of the border and, thus, part of his own subject of study, is intimately committed to it and considers it in the context of the identity problem experienced by a people torn between two cultures. Carlos Monsiváis, with his usual perspicacity, lays bare the contradictions and absurdities of "the dubious mixture of two national life-styles, each at its worst," which border culture represents to the Mexicans living in the national capital. Paredes looks at the border as a large area between the two countries, an area in which Mexicans of both nationalities come and go, encountering similar problems. Monsiváis limits himself to the border strip along the Mexican side, which may exert an influence on Mexican Americans but which, for all practical purposes, does not include them.

Paredes analyzes a social process that has been going on for 200 years.

*Translated from the Spanish by Miguel González-Gerth. The commentator noted that Carlos Monsiváis had departed from and differed with his written text. This commentary was written on the basis of the prepared paper [Editor's Note].

Monsiváis focuses his interest on the recent development in the border cities, stimulated by tourism and other trade, American-motivated employment (assembly plants or *maquiládoras*) and the *bracero* boom—or in other words, migrant towns without native hold or tradition, "whose principal function is to produce income." The two authors also focus on different geographical areas. Paredes deals primarily with the Mexican northeastern area, taken historically to comprise both sides of the national frontier. Carlos Monsiváis seems to focus his attention on the northwest area, from Juárez to Tijuana, with the latter being the object of most of his observations. Paredes presents a finished, polished, scholarly paper, while Monsiváis presents one that is highly suggestive and full of stimulating ideas but lacking a conclusion.

Of course, Paredes is a pioneer in this field of study. He made it his own long before it became fashionable. He is acquainted with the whole bibliography and continues to regard the subject as something more than a topic for research. His paper gives me the impression of having been invested in large measure with the author's search for self-definition, a difficult experience that sooner or later everyone must have. Now and then I find in the paper a sort of reproach directed at Mexicans for having somehow left to their fate their countless fellows who had to go on living in the long border strip, caught between two cultures and in a constant state of crisis.

Paredes skillfully takes his readers step by step from the geography of the Mexican northeast, the border area of the lower Río Grande, to the unsure identity of its inhabitants, in a hostile environment, who can be defined only in the context of a physical, economic, and cultural conflict experienced for almost two centuries. He describes the development of a range culture combining northern Mexican ranching activities with certain elements introduced from the United States, such as the hand gun, barbed wire, and legal hair-splitting over property rights. That new culture, which owes so much to that of old northern Mexico, gradually produced the image of the tough cowboy, an image that would later come home to roost among the Mexicans.

Paredes describes the difficult problems posed by such a culture for the Mexican border dweller, who early on became aware of his nationality while always facing hostile neighbors and who was suddenly cut off from relatives and friends by a line arbitrarily drawn according to the peace treaty of 1848. From then on the problem produced by the culture clash was aggravated by the pressure of living between two juridical systems and under norms set by two different governments. Thus the drama of constant migration begins: from south to north in search of employment, from north to south to escape "the law." Consequently a difficult challenge develops for the Mexican: that of being constantly exposed to "the other" without losing his cultural heritage; and the need to defend it day in, day out, against the constant aggression inherent in his contact with a people who feel sure of themselves because they are backed by a powerful political and social structure. Stereotypes, derogatory words, nicknames, and jokes make their appearance, manifesting the tension felt by two ethnic groups that need to coexist and even mingle but yet cannot avoid the conflict produced by an unresolved set of circumstances.

Perhaps the most original aspect of Paredes's essay is found in the insights dealing with social psychology, which explain some psychological reactions to historical events. Paredes indeed shows a fine sensitivity for the true significance behind a popular proverb or poem, a stereotype, or a certain incident. Therein lies what is most interesting to the student of social history, reminded of the usefulness offered by philology and folklore in social studies. The implications found in popular sayings and in the origin of names by this scholar are fascinating. When describing the formation of sterotypes, he invites the reader to think about the many details necessary for the understanding of any stage in the social development of a group. Considered in this way, the paper is a good example of how folklore can be used for reconstructing the past of social groups whose imprint is faint in more conventional historical records.

In the last pages of the essay one perceives a deep reproach toward Mexicans who lack sympathy for the problems of the Mexican American, the *pocho-pachuco,* that poor soul, according to Paredes, suspended between the pyramid and the skyscraper, scorned both north and south. Paredes is correct when he says that the newer generations seem more receptive to the problem of the *pocho-chicano,* whether because of a sharper social consciousness or, and this is his view, because massive means of communication have broadened our intercultural areas, since geographical-political boundaries no longer serve as cultural borders. Even Mexico City is actually so vulnerable to the cultural influence of the United States that soon we may no longer know ourselves. Such contention is perhaps extreme, and yet it bears some truth. Paredes's swift reflection on the waning of national frontiers as a result of changes in human life during the last twenty years will be borne out by anyone who has traveled across the Atlantic and Pacific oceans during that period of time. Day after day there seem to be fewer differences between one country and another. Only poverty continues to appear indigenous.

To my mind, the most stimulating part of Monsiváis's highly polemic paper is the first, which treats general topics of interest to students of our paradoxical nationalism. In it he asks questions regarding the commonplaces found in national rhetoric. The terms *mexicanidad* (Mexicanism), *idio-*

sincracia (temperament), and *raices* (roots) are all heard both along the border and in the metropolitan area, and they also are applicable to both, except that along the border they are on testing grounds. Everything is in flux there, and any attempt to set up dikes to preserve what is culturally Mexican might seem ridiculous.

What is the stuff that *mexicanidad* is made of? Monsiváis shrewdly points out that while officialdom might use the term merely as defiant rhetoric, certain population segments consider it specifically to be an "economic, political, and social defense system," aimed, not so much at the Americanization of mores, as at imperialism. When examining Mexican *idiosincracia, esenciás* (spiritual values), and *raíces,* he finds that though they should refer to "timeless precepts," in actual practice they are reduced to "the traditional cult of the hero, the 'Ballet Folklórico,' the trappings which identify a type found in the movies and popular songs, the mythical and magical conception of history, and the insistence on the impossible 'purity of language.' " Thus our cultural nationalism, the consequence of an overwhelming defeat as well as of the daily confrontation with a powerful neighbor, has become a handful of feeble myths mouthed by official propaganda exulting "a glamorous image of nationality" instead of being the result of a continuous democratic process set against the authoritarianism of the Mexican government. Monsiváis accurately observes that the flimsy rhetoric claiming either to reject or ignore everything foreign backfires as it betrays its worship of what it disclaims through the "inevitable paradox embodied in a fervently nationalistic cultural policy of a dependent society."

The solution submitted by Monsiváis seems to be the right one: "No amount of independence can be gained by any political system through self-praise but by the action that follows imperative self-analysis and self-criticism." I also agree with Monsiváis's idea that a culture must receive a constant stimulus from outside to survive. And yet, as a researcher on the subject of nationalism, I have certain doubts. What was it that held together the territory left to us by the peace treaty of 1848? At that time a high degree of national awareness existed only in the sparsely populated north (as Paredes points out) and in a few men scattered through the country. That is why only seven states came to the nation's defense when it was invaded by the United States. I have always thought that the mosaic which was Mexico in 1821 eventually became a nation—in whatever measure it has succeeded—thanks to the deliberate effort on the part of Mexican governments to survive by finding and making known some historical common denominators. Had it not been for such determination, Mexico would have disappeared from the map before the basic myths of nationality had a chance to take shape. It is for this reason that even now I find it partly justifiable that an official [history] textbook is required in the primary schools. The subject is undoubtedly profound and merits a great deal of thought.

The remainder of Monsiváis's paper is informative for those who are not acquainted with the border cities. The lively style piques our curiosity about those "sinful" cities, American in structure and imprisoned by a mass culture that makes their rich semiconscious residents wish for an international status.

As Paredes points out the slight attention paid in the interior, until recently, to the problems of the border Mexican, so Monsiváis notes the superficial impact made by border culture on the metropolitan area—a few films, a couple of actors, and a handful of expressions incorporated into juvenile slang. Of special interest is his account of how the motion picture industry changed the imported *pachuco* that was Tin Tan in the 1940s into the ordinary Mexican slum character he became in the 1950s—a change that implies a rejection of border cultural phenomena on the part of metropolitan culture. The paper draws the conclusion that border culture is "in very general terms the stage for a loss of identity."

It is quite clear that both authors contribute information that will help gradually to make comprehensible the illusive and multifaceted phenomenon taking place along thousands of miles of a border that probably is, above all, economic and political in nature.

C. The Politics of the Mexican-United States Border
by Rudolph Gomez

The complexity of the politics of the Mexican-United States border is revealed by Professors Armando Gutiérrez and Antonio Ugalde. Professor Ugalde concerns himself with the border and its influence upon the culture, economy, and politics of the Mexican states bordering the United States. He lists as factors influencing the economy and culture of the Mexican states the following: the large number of Mexicans entering the United States in search of work; the increasingly large numbers of Mexicans, particularly women, who work for American firms of the twin-city variety along the border; the stream of communications stemming from television, radio, and, to a lesser extent, from newspapers, and which are a part of the daily life of residents on both sides of the border; the existence of family ties between citizens of both countries living on the border; the business relationships that serve to bring the elites of both countries, residing on both sides of the border, into contact with each other; and, finally, the access to both countries enjoyed by tourists from each.

Dr. Ugalde's analyis of these factors suggests to him that there is a "border influence" that has an impact upon the culture and economy on the Mexican side of the border. He suggests, for example, that the employment of large numbers of Mexican women in the twin plants along the border may, in the long run, serve to modify the structure of Mexican family life, which traditionally has been dominated by the Mexican male head of the family. He also suggests that Mexican business elites believe they can learn much from their counterparts across the border, but that the reverse apparently does not obtain. These examples, and others of a similar vein, lead Ugalde to conclude that there is a substantial amount of influence crossing the border from the United States, which affects the *culture* and *economy* on the Mexican side of the border.

Politically, however, he finds that the presence of American influence on Mexican *electoral politics*—local, state, and national—is, at best, minimal. He acknowledges the paucity of empirical evidence on the subject but finds that which does exist supports his conclusion.

That Professor Ugalde finds little empirical evidence to support a hypothesis of American influence on *electoral politics* does not lead him to conclude an absence of such influence upon serious problems affecting both countries. What he does do, which I find extremely useful, is to suggest that problems such as that of Mexican migrant labor are national in scope for both countries. He implies that the border is incidental to the problem of unemployment for Mexico as a nation and incidental to the demand for cheap labor from Mexico across the width and breadth of the United States. This is a powerful insight, for it suggests that attempts to solve such problems properly rest with the national governments of both countries and not necessarily upon the governments of the localities, where the national problem can be seen in its human form of able-bodied persons seeking work from other persons who have it to offer.

Professor Gutiérrez's concern is with the *Texas border*. He is concerned with describing the economic, educational, health, and political conditions of Chicanos living in the Texas counties that border on Mexico. His analysis reveals that despite the numerical majority of Chicanos residing along the Texas-Mexican border, Chicanos are paid less, less educated, less healthy, less represented politically and governmentally than their Anglo counterparts. His data support his analysis.

Dr. Gutiérrez finds that, historically, state and local governments in Texas have suppressed Mexican-American attempts at improvement directly and indirectly—even by resorting to violence. He describes how the Democratic Party, which has depended upon Mexican Americans for electoral support,

388   Appendix I*Appendix I*

has used government office to create political machines that are interested primarily in their own well-being, and not with the well-being of Chicanos.

Only recently, coincident with the emergence of the Chicano movement, has the Democratic Party become marginally responsive to the Mexican American's demands for political, economic, and social reforms. Dr. Gutiérrez does not state, but rather implies, that whatever successes Chicanos in Texas have attained are the result of their own efforts, and also of the changing attitudes in American public life stemming from the ''Civil Rights Decade of the 1960s.''

Professor Gutiérrez examined the votes cast in the last three gubernatorial elections in order to detect the influence of Chicano voting behavior. He concludes that Chicanos along the Texas border still tend to vote for the Democratic Party, with some inroads made on that support by more Chicanos voting for La Raza Unida Party, but, perhaps most important, he reports that large numbers of Chicanos still do not vote. The greatest unresolved task confronting Chicanos desirous of using political and governmental means to improve their condition is that of mobilizing the Mexican-American population living along the Texas-Mexican border into an election-influencing voting bloc.

Both essays reveal the complexity of the political problems lying on both sides of the Mexican-United States border. And both intimate that the problems are soluble for both countries if the respective governments inform themselves of such complexities and will themselves to act upon them. These are certainly reasonable, and laudable, hopes. But are they realistic?

I do not wish to insinuate that the authors are not realists and that I am. All I wish to suggest is that the history of these political problems does not support the notion that either government sees these problems as high-priority items. Mexico, at least during this century, has had her attention riveted, first, on the Revolution; second, on the creation of a government that would gain legitimacy from its recognition by a majority of her population; third, on the problem of social and economic reforms for all Mexicans which has occupied a high priority; and fourth, on the problem of regulating foreign interests in Mexico which has been a critical one for the government. And finally, Mexico has tried to occupy a position in world affairs, not only commensurate with her capacities, but also commensurate with her aspirations. There are, doubtless, other problems with higher priority than the ones along the border with the United States. All this suggests that while Mexico would like to resolve her border problems, there are others of greater urgency that occupy more of her time, her resources, and her energies.

The same argument can be made for the United States in the twentieth century. Its concerns have been occupied with two world wars, a cold war, Korea, Southeast Asia, the United Nations, and domestically, with a depression, the "Red" menaces of the 1920s and 1950s, with civil rights in the 1960s, the war on poverty, Watergate, and the constitutional crises of the presidency, the Congress, and the Supreme Court. All these are in addition to the normal partisan politics that are part and parcel of self-government.

My observations about the higher priorities given problems other than those associated with the border by both Mexico and the United States are not meant to exculpate either nation. They are intended, solely, to remind us that nations, like men, are constantly confronted by a bewildering array of complex problems, and like most men, respond to those which, at the time, are most critical. The inevitable result is that other problems, very serious ones, are neglected and human misery accumulates.

What do these observations suggest to us about the probable future of Mexican-United States political border problems? I believe the problems will continue to be addressed incrementally by each of the respective governments—national, state, and local. These increments will help keep the problems from becoming so acute that international and domestic stability is threatened. But these incremental approaches also, inherently, place boundaries upon problem solving because they are addressed to the prevention of threats to stability and not to the problems themselves.

I find both solace and discontent from my observations. Solace because I remain hopeful that border problems will continue to be addressed, albeit incrementally, and therefore not build up to a point where relations between Mexico and the United States are threatened. But I also am discontented because I ask myself "Is this the best we can do?" And I respond by saying "We can do better, but we just won't let ourselves."

Politics will continue to limit our finest aspirations but, paradoxically, politics provides the best hope we have by which we can try to address, successfully, these problems. For, as Bernard Crick has written:

Political rule should be praised for doing what it can do, but also for not attempting what it cannot do. Politics can provide the conditions under which many non-political activities may flourish, but it cannot guarantee that they will flourish. "One cannot make men good," said Walter Bagehot, "by Act of Parliament."*

---

*Bernard Crick, *In Defense of Politics* (Baltimore: Penguin Books Limited, 1964), p. 151.

D. The Problems of Migration: A North American View
by Arthur J. Rubel

In their essays Briggs and Bustamante discuss a dilemma that requires binational consideration and multilateral resolution. At the risk of seeming dreadfully simple, let me sum up the issue by stating that immigration to the United States represents emigration from Mexico.

Both authors are in agreement that legal immigration to the United States from Mexico is not a matter that provokes a lot of their interest, or that of most scholars or government bureaucrats. Illegal movement across the border is what *really* concerns us here, and illegal immigration is what makes this particular border so very interesting as a social phenomenon. Having noted that, I want to draw our attention back again to some little-noted implications of the figures cited by Briggs on legal immigrants prior to 1924.

What I find noteworthy about the immigration statistics he provides for the period before enforcement of immigration laws on the Mexican-United States border is that during the three-quarters of a century that elapsed between the establishment of the new boundary and efforts to enforce rules governing its crossing, hundreds of thousands of Mexicans thought it important to obtain legal documentation before entering the United States. Looking only at the fifteen-year period between 1909 and 1923 (the last year of a truly open border), almost 352,000 Mexicans legally—that is, with proper documents—entered the United States. Those immigrants—inspected, examined, and duly certified—arrived during a period when there was no more indication to a traveler that he or she was entering the territory of another nation than if one were to walk from Monterrey, Nuevo León, to Saltillo, Coahuila. In his brilliant and delightful autobiography, *Barrio Boy,* Ernesto Galarza describes the difficulties he faced as a youngster on a railroad flatcar arriving in Nogales, Arizona, when he sought clear indications that he had indeed arrived in the new land. Finally, as the train stopped at its final destination in Arizona and at the urging of his mother, he simply rolled off his perch "into the arms of the American soldier, who looped one arm around me, pulled the slicker over my shoulders so that only my head showed, and with the other hand gripped one of our bundles."[1] And that was that!

In the absence of pertinent research data on the characteristics of those early, *legal,* immigrants, one may speculate that they were of higher levels of formal education, more wealthy, more urban than most of the immigrants of that period. That they did bear appropriate credentials suggests that archival research on demographic characteristics, such as those by which Briggs is enabled to distinguish contemporary legal from illegal immigrants, would give us a better idea than we now possess of one discrete segment of the early Mexican immigrant population to this country, a population about which we presently know precious little.

In thinking of these earlier legal immigrants, it seems one might speculate that they were less influenced by the ''push'' than the ''pull'' factors that both Briggs and Bustamante bring to our attention. I agree with the understandings of both these scholars that "*on the whole* 'pull factors' have had more weight than 'push factors.' " But my own experience in the lower Río Grande Valley, my conversations with peasants in southern Mexico, and my reading of the literature relevant to the issue,[2] compel me to insist that both Briggs and Bustamante underestimate the social and economic conditions in the ''giver'' nation that contribute to the massive flow of immigrants across the border. Moreover, far too little attention is paid to rural conditions that lead to the ''piling-up'' of immigrants and potential immigrants in the regions immediately south of the international boundary. Indeed, as Wiest[3] indicates, ''green-carders'' may strongly affect the economy of the southwestern United States, but the conditions that make them so important a factor are to be found in Michoacán as well as in the Mexican border towns.

Granted, the same rural conditions—underemployment, poor working conditions, a relatively very low wage scale (measured either against industrial wages in Mexico, or agricultural wages in this country); a population growing at an approximate rate of 3.6 percent yearly; and a relatively inelastic land base—contribute to a decision to emigrate from villages *either* to Mexican cities *or* to the United States. After deciding to leave home, *where* a villager chooses to go has very different consequences for him and his family—economic as well as cultural and social. Wiest's study of a Michoacán village, in which a major part of the income of 17 percent of the households is remitted by migrant laborer members, is pertinent here. Of the seventy households dependent on such remittances, one-quarter have ''green-carders'' who work regularly in the United States, and almost half of the migrants work in Mexico City.[4] However, in those households in which a wage earner is a ''green-carder'' in the United States the members tend to be dependent solely on the emigrant's remittances, whereas those with workers in Mexico City or other Mexican localities are dependent upon multiple contributors to the viability of the household.[5]

The residents of Acuitzeo, Michoacán, recognize some or all of the consequences of: 1) leaving their homes; and 2) deciding whether to go to Mexico City, to Morelia, or to the United States in search of work. These micro-studies of immigration decisions and the consequences attributed to them result in more holistic views of the multiplicity of factors that are weighed by households, families, and individuals. Such studies on a small scale do not deny the potency of economic factors during such decisions. Rather, they place the economic factors in more proper perspective.

Family decisions to support a worker, making it possible for him or her to leave for the United States, and the helpful acceptance of such emigrants by relatives and other residents of the *barrios* in the United States, cause me to wonder whether the process of ''labeling'' to which Bustamante has made reference is not most usefully confined to North American law enforcement agencies who do, in fact, consider the illegal immigrants as deviants and deal with them accordingly.[6]

I agree to some extent with Briggs when he states that ''Many Chicanos of [South Texas] are literally *forced* to join the migratory labor force because the local labor market is overrun by illegal Mexican aliens and border commuters. . . .'' However, before indicating my profound disagreement with his recommendations for resolving the problem, I find it useful to look at some anomalies in the relations of the immigrants to the Spanish-surname population already resident in the southwestern states.

I find a division of the Spanish-speaking work force in the Southwest into two discrete, competing groups—Mexican nationals and Chicano citizens—to be as artificial as it would be to request me to understand the contemporary border as anything but a political line of demarcation, imposed on a social and cultural unitary area, with no relationship to the realities other than military power. Again, I believe that the difference in *overall* understanding that I have, and that of the authors of these two essays, is a function of the nature of our source materials: micro-studies or macro-studies. My own information derives from micro-studies of Spanish-surname citizens in the work force of the Lower Río Grande Valley, San Antonio, and Chicago, and my view tends to resemble theirs closely.

In the volume *Across the Tracks,* I reported the extent to which Spanish-surname people[7] of Mexiquito were aware of the competition between themselves and Mexican nationals for the few available opportunities to work. But, then as now, I did not find the ''man in the street'' thinking in terms of discrete social groups—Mexican nationals and Chicanos—competing for employment, despite the continued use of the former by employers to break the strikes of citizen laborers.

Let me, for the moment, accept Dr. Bustamante's concept that the ''commodity-migrants are cast into conflict with the lowest-paid native workers, with whom commodity-migrants compete for the lowest paid jobs. . .'' The demographic and social research data speak in support of Bustamante's contention, but I am not persuaded that the newly arrived commodity-migrants have been diabolically placed by employers in such a way as to be concentrated and to compete for scarce work in the very regions of the country in which 85 percent of the population of Mexican origin is and has always been concentrated.[8] Nevertheless, there must be some forces that contribute to so economically unwise and dysfunctional a placement of these two groups of undereducated, underemployed, unskilled, season workers so that both must compete for too few and too low paying jobs in a too capricious employment market.

This situation is the more anomalous in view of the complementary residential distribution of rural blacks and rural Chicanos in Texas, the only one of the southwestern states in which both groups were represented as important components earlier than 1942. As Browning and McLemore noted a decade ago, ". . . of those Texas counties in which minority groups represent an important part of the population (i.e., 25 percent or more), the nonwhite population is concentrated to the east and the Spanish-surname population to the south and west along the border. In no county of Texas is there a situation in which both minorities each have 25 percent or more of the total population."[9] I find it not a coincidence that until the 1960s even the three major migratory agricultural streams were composed of discrete ethnic or racial components: the East Coast stream composed of blacks;[10] the mid-continent stream composed overwhelmingly of Chicanos; and the West Coast stream also overwhelmingly of Chicanos, some Native Americans, and relatively few Filipinos.[11]

In the light of those findings, is there an alternative explanation to Bustamante's for the joining of two "discrete" social groups competing for too few job opportunities? I find that it can be answered. As both papers have impressed on us, most commodity-immigrants are illegals; they are of rural background, low levels of formal education, and they are non-English speaking. For them successfully to negotiate occupational and other dimensions of the social system in this English-speaking society, they must rely upon individuals and communities for assistance and instruction. Moreover, their very vulnerability as illegals requires assistance from trustworthy residents sympathetic to their needs. Most often those to whom they look for help are kinsmen, no matter how distant, or people known to be from the same area of Mexico.[12] The difficulties and very real bodily risks inherent in an illegal crossing of the border (and I refer you to Bustamante's own compelling account[13] of one such experience) so necessitate assistance as to attract illegal commodity-migrants to the very localities in which citizen Chicanos are already established as the agricultural and other, largely unskilled, work force.

Although I earlier indicated my agreement with Briggs that large numbers of illegal immigrants concentrated along the border have a detrimental economic effect on resident Chicanos, I must state that I find his recommendations for solution to that problem difficult to agree with. Briggs's complaint that previous efforts to provide training for Chicano migrants and then to secure them employment and settle them out of the migrant streams have failed because "there are too few job opportunities available in their home-base communities that offer wages at a level that will permit a decent standard of life." Efforts to provide such jobs at home-base have been carried out without real resolution, without the kind of federal or state government support which would make it feasible. To argue, then, that subsequent efforts should concentrate on the mounting of a "massive foreign aid program by the United States to develop jointly the economy of northern Mexico . . ." and to conclude by stating that the "fundamental question is not *whether* the government of the United States should act, but rather *when* it will and in *what manner*," is to disregard the necessity of meaningful binational cooperation in the search for resolution of border problems. A call for such unilateral decision making elicits again the old refrain: *"Pobre México, tan lejos de Dios, y tan cerca a los Estados Unidos."*

NOTES

1. Ernesto Galarza, *Barrio Boy* (New York: Ballantine Books, 1972), p. 178.

2. Laura H. Zarrugh, "Gente de mi Tierra: Mexican Village Migrants in a California Community" (Ph.D. diss., University of California at Berkeley, 1974); Raymond E. Wiest, "Wage Labor Migration and the Household in a Mexican Town," *Journal of Anthropological Research* 29 (1973):180-209; John J. Poggie, Jr., *Between Two Cultures* (Tucson: University of Arizona Press, 1973); and Galarza, *Barrio Boy,* p. 178.

3. Wiest, "Wage Labor Migration," p. 184.

4. Ibid.

5. Ibid., p. 194.

6. H. Becker, "Foreword," in Henry A. Selby, *Zapotec Deviance* (Austin: University of Texas Press, 1974), pp. viii-ix.

7. Arthur J. Rubel, *Across the Tracks: Mexican-Americans in a Texas City* (Austin: University of Texas Press, 1966), pp. 17-18.

8. U.S. Bureau of the Census, *Current Population Reports* (Washington, D.C.: Government Printing Office, July 1972).

9. Harley Browning and S. Dale McLemore, *A Statistical Profile of the Spanish-Surname Population of Texas* (Austin: University of Texas Press, 1964), pp. 11-12.

10. W. H. Friedland and Dorothy Nelkin, *Migrant: Agricultural Workers in America's Northeast* (New York: Holt, Rinehart and Winston, 1971).

11. Rev. William E. Scholes, "The Migrant Worker," in Julian Samora, ed., *La Raza: Forgotten Americans* (Notre Dame, Ind.: University of Notre Dame Press, 1966), p.74.

12. Zarrugh, "Gente de mi Tierra," p. 33; Wiest, "Wage Labor Migration"; Julian Samora, *Los Mojados* (Notre Dame, Ind.: University of Notre Dame Press, 1971), pp. 96-97; J. Poggie, *Between Two Cultures*.

13. Jorge A. Bustamante, "Espaldas Mojadas: Informe de un Observador Participante," *Revista de la Universidad de México* 27 (1973):26-45.

E. The Problems of Migration: A Mexican View*
by Mercedes Carreras de Velasco

During the 1950s, Mexican social scientists showed little interest in the emigration of Mexican nationals to the United States. In the last ten years because of the problems encountered by Mexican Americans endeavoring to become integrated in the American socioeconomic system and the impotence of the Mexican government to contain or at least protect migrant labor, social scientists—both Mexican and American—have felt called upon to analyze the causes and mechanics of this process.

The essays by Briggs and Bustamante are good examples of this new trend. The Briggs essay is a "conjunctural" analysis based on the study of the present political situation. Bustamante's is a "structural" analysis that puts aside nationalist feelings and attempts to approach the subject scientifically—not in terms of the relations between the two countries but rather in terms of the socioeconomic situation as it affects both countries.

Bustamante attempts to describe the mechanisms governing the behavior of the migrant workers. His purpose is to explain why they are victims. His thesis is that Mexican migrants are a commodity needed for the expansion of agricultural capital in the American Southwest.

To look upon the migrant labor force as a commodity is to deal with the mechanics of United States capitalism. Bustamante looks upon this migration as the self-transportation of the commodity-migrant, concluding that the migrant "has learned" to behave as a commodity as a result of the superstructure of capitalist relations.

The explanation for this conclusion is not entirely clear because he does not adequately explain the laborer's decision to migrate. Support for conceptualizing the migrant worker's behavior as a commodity from the outset is to be found in the relationship of production to capitalism and, in particular, the relationship between a developed country and an underdeveloped country. Under such a relationship, commodity follows an established course and, in the case of worker migration, it takes on the social manifestation of a commodity-migrant behavior. But never does Bustamante explain the "meaning" of that "behavior." It would be desirable for Bustamante to define, for example, the capitalist production superstructure to which he refers, since there is a difference between the superstructure of the capitalist

---

*Translated from the Spanish by Miguel González-Gerth. The commentary has been shortened in the process of preparing it for publication [Editor's Note].

production system in Mexico and that of agricultural production in the American Southwest.

After submitting his thesis and his supposition, Bustamante analyzes the problem on two levels: on the economic level he looks upon the migrant as a commodity; on the ideological level he looks upon him as an individual involved in self-transportation. He describes historically the part played by Mexican migrants in the capital expansion of the agricultural Southwest. He explains that the migratory influx of these workers has been in response to American migrant policy devised for maintaining a cheap labor pool or "reserve army" for the expansion of agriculture. But where does this leave the present migrant influx, which continues in spite of no great current demand for agricultural workers in the United States?

It is clear that, given the capitalist production relations, particularly in the case of two neighboring economies of such disparity, Mexican migrants in the United States are going to find employment at the lowest level. And, in keeping with the law of supply and demand governing the system (based on relative skill), the migrants are going to end up as underpaid victims. Such a situation is used to maintain a state of conflict or of competition among the workers themselves, benefiting no one but the capitalist employers.

This exploitation continues to exist, not due to an ideology but rather because in a free enterprise system both capital and labor flow in the direction of greater return, and their value fluctuates according to the law of supply and demand in those areas of capitalist economy where there is a free interplay of production factors. It would be helpful to determine to what extent this is the case for the agricultural economy of the American Southwest. It also would be helpful to know more fully the relationship of the American need for labor and the migratory flow if we are to understand the deportation operations of 1930 and 1954, the Bracero Program, and the commuters.

Bustamante's conclusions disprove the most common beliefs about the emigration to the United States, namely, that 1) Mexican emigration keeps salaries down; 2) restricting the emigration would reduce American unemployment; and 3) a Bracero Program would preclude the illegal entry of workers. He seeks to discredit the first by explaining that the migrant is in no condition to press for higher wages because of his "powerlessness." Bustamante does not convincingly establish why he believes migrants do not contribute to increased unemployment in the United States. In his third conclusion he states that a *bracero* agreement under the present power structure would, in effect, lower wages and perpetuate exploitation, apart from encouraging illegal immigration even further.

It seems to me that the real explanation of the exploitation of the migrant worker is not to be found in the American power structure, but rather in the migrant's commodity status within a society based on capitalist production relationships. It is for this last reason, and not for that submitted by Bustamante, that a Bracero Program would encourage emigration and lead to a lowering of wages in the United States. And yet a *bracero* agreement can provide the means for negotiating acceptable minimum wages and for controlling illegal immigration, as was actually beginning to occur during the last years of the Bracero Program. There is no doubt that an agreement which includes the fixing of a minimum wage by the Mexican government would frustrate American labor's struggle to control wages.

Bustamante is of the opinion that a *bracero* agreement, besides encouraging emigration, would function as a safety valve for Mexican unemployment. He assumes that, staying in Mexico, the would-be migrants would pressure the system for changes in the sociopolitical makeup of the rural establishment when actually the opposite will happen: by staying in Mexico they will swell its manpower reserves and bring about increased pressure on the job market, resulting in lower salaries. This is precisely the path Mexico has chosen: not to sign an agreement and control emigration, thereby increasing the manpower reserves in order to maintain the status quo. Mexico has opted to do this on the grounds that control of emigration will best be achieved by providing a better means of livelihood within the country. Let us suppose such a turnabout were accomplished creating jobs for all potential emigrants, they would then become the commodity for Mexican capital expansion, in the same way they have contributed to American capital expansion. If this is the change envisaged by Bustamante, I am in accord. When the Mexican stays home, he will help to improve the status quo by helping capital expansion, provided he is given the chance.

Although his is basically a structural study, Bustamante is tempted to essay a conjunctural analysis. It is there that his study can be compared with Briggs's position. Briggs refers to the historical course of Mexican emigration to the United States only to note what its effect has been on the American labor force. He touches upon the structure of emigration and concurs with Bustamante, since Briggs also looks upon Mexican labor as a force acting upon a specific labor market. Though Briggs does not put labor and commodity on a par, his description of the process could obviously apply to a commodity within the system of capitalist production relations.

His thesis is that both legal and illegal immigration quantitatively and qualitatively influence the American labor market. He concludes that today the large number of illegal laborers is not beneficial to the United States and, therefore, must be checked. In order to see how this may be done, he analyzes the causes that determine the immigration, separating them under the classic push and pull factors. Among the pull factors, those that require change include American immigration policy and legislation providing punishment for all who employ illegal aliens. If this were so, such employers would run a risk, thus diminishing the pull factor.

Briggs also recommends increasing the authority and the budget of the Immigration and Naturalization Service to enable it to take definitive measures to discourage illegal immigration. His final recommendation, which he considers of great importance, is that the United States help Mexico to develop the economy of its northern states, because the emigration is given impetus by the fact that the Mexican economy, though growing, is "semideveloped" and the unemployment rate is extremely high. Although Mexico can set the course of development by establishing priorities, he stresses that if foreign aid is not accepted, a warning should be issued about the undesirability of its illegal labor.

Briggs blames the Mexican government for doing nothing but protest against the unfair treatment of its citizens and propose new agreements. This is not altogether true, for actually the most recent decision of the Mexican government has been not to sign any *bracero* agreement and to affirm that means will be found to create jobs for potential emigrants.

In regard to American technical and financial aid, I would like to point out that it would have a positive result only if it is made to fit strictly within the plans and programs for development established by Mexico. Nevertheless, one must keep in mind that the total solution to the unemployment problem will not be found in that alone, as it would generate new and great political and economic complications.

Not being an economist, I would ask Dr. Briggs to explain how it happens that, if unemployment can be taken care of so easily by means of capital investment and technology, a country which possesses such riches as the United States can also have such an acute unemployment problem. Or is it that in spite of not having solved its own problem, the United States is willing to come to the aid of our underprivileged classes, since Mexico's privileged class is indifferent to them, as Briggs affirms?

F. Economic Factors and Considerations*
by Eliseo Mendoza Berrueto

The factors affecting social movement between Mexico and the United States are, I believe, related to the causes and effects pointed out by Dr. Ray Marshall. Some can be regarded as pull factors in themselves, others as push factors, and still others are practically indistinguishable in terms of these two categories.

Dr. Marshall's paper refers in general terms to migration phenomena in Europe, and between Mexico and the United States. When more complete data become available, undoubtedly more definite conclusions will be reached. Above all we need a comparative study, if such can be made, of the fundamental motivations behind the labor migration occurring in these countries.

In almost every case such migration represents a search for employment at a given income level as well as an opportunity provided by an employer in need of labor to carry on a particular economic activity. This is obviously the case with Mexico and the United States. But instead of the attempts by persons friendly to the migrant laborers to institutionalize or legalize such labor, as proposed by Dr. Marshall, the illegal status of migrants is officially condoned. In some parts of the United States opportunity is granted to the illegal migrant to continue entering the country illegally to work, sometimes three or four times during the same year. This occurs because the employers, who need the labor, manage to overcome all efforts to institutionalize or legalize the entry process.

I do not have many original comments to make on Dr. Marshall's essay, principally because I am not a demographer. I should note, however, that the Mexican and American governments have been trying to meet this problem of migration in a more effective manner. Former President Luis Echeverría pointed out that the migration of Mexican laborers is a national concern, making specific reference to the unfair, sometimes inhuman, treatment to which Mexican migrants are subjected in the United States. On several occasions he stressed the urgent need for an effective solution, a solution that basically must be sought through an economic and social development of our country.

The relative importance of the factors constituting the migrant problem change with the times; furthermore, the factors themselves sometimes are real

---

*Translated from the Spanish by Miguel González-Gerth. The text has been edited to approximate the authorized length and for a more tightly knit presentation [Editor's Note].

and sometimes imaginary. This is particularly true in the case of pull factors. It is imperative that this phenomenon be systematically analyzed to enable us to understand the dynamics of the various causes of the migration process.

Finally, in Dr. Marshall's paper there is, I believe, an implicit comparison between the migration process in Europe and in Mexico. Perhaps owing to some factors referred to in the essay and others not mentioned, one might get the impression that the two migration processes are comparable not so much basically but in secondary aspects. However, I feel the migrations tend to reflect different socioeconomic structures. Also, they occur in countries at different cultural levels and with totally different historical backgrounds. The magnitude of the migration and its effects also tend to be different.

I believe that the essay by Víctor Urquidi and Sofía Méndez is one of the most systematic and significant of those recently prepared on the economics of the Mexican-United States border. Urquidi mentions some of the efforts made to accelerate the economic process along the border, in particular the work of the Intersecretarial Commission for the Development of the Northern Frontier and of the Free Zones and Perimeters. It was formed in May 1971, at a meeting presided over by President Echeverría in Nogales, Sonora. Since then it has operated at the Assistant Secretary level, with the participation of three departments—namely, Agriculture, Treasury, and Commerce. The chairmanship of this commission rotates, which explains why I have twice had occasion to preside over the group.

The precedent for the commission, some eight or nine years ago, was the Committee for the Economic Promotion of the State of Baja California. This committee, based in Mexicali, has been composed of representatives of the federal government, the state government, and local private enterprise. Its purpose is to promote economic activities directly affecting the border region. President Echeverría originally ordered the creation of the Intersecretarial Commission so that committees similar to the Baja California unit would be established. There are now ten such committees functioning in the following locations: Mexicali, La Paz, Nogales, Juárez, Acuña, Piedras Negras, Nuevo Laredo, Reynosa, Matamoros, and Chetumal (Quintana Roo), and another one is being established without fanfare in Chiapas as the program continues to extend its work along the southern border.

The commission aspires to an interdisciplinary approach to problems in order to cover the various fields required for the economic development of the border. There are important references to these fields—agriculture, industry, the tourist trade—in the essay by Urquidi and Méndez. Urquidi himself concludes, and the statistics bear him out, that agriculture has suffered a crisis in the last few years. I see this as a consequence of various factors. First, we must remember that along the northern border, cotton is one of the most economically important crops. It is a highly unstable commodity on the world market, which affects the desirability of planting and picking it. The various resources, including the land, devoted to cotton production, increase or decrease depending on previous conditions set by the international market. There have been attempts to eliminate the economic instability inherent in a one-crop agriculture. In particular, irrigation programs have been developed around Mexicali, San Luis del Río Colorado, Matamoros, Reynosa, Valle Hermoso, and so forth, to make possible a greater variety of crops, mainly sorghum and saffron, but also wheat. This is not easy to achieve because the farmer naturally is going to use his resources in whatever he thinks will bring him the best return. Still, by manipulating the guaranteed price and other mechanisms, such economic diversification can be obtained, which can add to the stability of the general agricultural economy.

Several efforts have been made to increase farm mechanization, and to improve the techniques and the yield of border livestock production. We have granted many permits for the importation of agricultural machinery, even including machinery that can be manufactured in Mexico, when faster delivery from the United States or a better price proves to be more attractive to the border farmer or rancher. This is intended to be a permanent measure and one that has been liberalized recently. It applies to both new and used machinery. As a consequence, there should be considerable technical improvement in agriculture as well as greater diversification, so that in the near future the raising of livestock will become more stable, more productive, and more lucrative.

In manufacturing, as the Urquidi-Méndez essay notes, the assemblage or single-phase manufacturing process appears to be the only major development in border industry. Although such manufacturing plants are an important factor in the employment picture, it must be recognized that it is not on the basis of this kind of work that border industry and economy have developed. In part this is so because the border region depends directly upon the economic situation of the entire country.

Furthermore, assemblage or single-phase manufacturing is a highly unstable industry—an easy-come, easy-go type of investment. It makes a very limited technological contribution to the region where the plant is located. Indeed, as Urquidi points out, it seldom becomes an integral part of the national economy. Assemblage, to make things clear, is an enterprise engaged in carrying out an assembling or cutting process, or a process of similar nature, after which everything temporarily imported is returned to the country of origin. If such manufacturing plants become an integral part of our national economy, through the infusion of national investment capital, that is a completely different matter. We then would be talking about a national industry. Our industrial development must begin with Mexican enterprise, with a technology adequate to our resources, with national investments committed to national economic development objectives in an industry that eventually will compete in the export market both in the United States and in other countries.

How can these objectives be achieved? Border manufacturing in general is light manufacturing, representing small and medium industry. Neither on the Mexican side nor, I believe, on the American side of the border are there important centers of manufacture. The agricultural areas in the Imperial Valley, in the Mexicali Valley, and around Matamoros on the Texas border are important statistically and commercially. But there are no large industrial centers. In fact, it would seem that the Mexican border cities have a more diversified economy than do their American counterparts. To a great extent this is so because many American border cities depend on the trade specifically generated by the Mexicans in the border region. This trade is based on the influx of Mexican tourists, which originates not just in Nuevo Laredo but also in Monterrey, Saltillo, Torreón, and even farther south, crossing the border into the United States to buy a large amount of consumer goods.

It can readily be seen that the development of national industry along the border is of great importance. The development taking place in the region today suggests that it is along the lines of light and medium manufacturing (industry linked to the production of consumer goods, and mainly food, clothing, shoes, and so on) that an excellent opportunity lies for giving impetus to border industry development. Such development employs the available labor and, to lower production costs, imports equipment either on a temporary or permanent basis.

For various reasons the figures given for assemblage manufacturing are not always accurate. In the free zones, such as Baja California Norte, Baja California Sur, and Quintana Roo, many *maquiladora* plants are not registered in order to facilitate the importation of foreign products, equipment, or parts, something that can be accomplished much more readily under the free-zone system. Thus only about five hundred *maquiladora* plants are registered, but through efforts made during the last few months by both the office of the Director of Customs and the office of the Director of Trade, we can now come close to confirming the existence of around eight hundred *maquiladora* plants. Between September 1973 and March 1975, sixty-two such plants closed down and seventy-nine opened, making for a net gain of seventeen plants. However, the same gain is not true for the number of workers employed or for the wages and salaries paid. From the sixty-two plants closed down, 9,000 workers were laid off, while in the seventy-nine plants opened only 5,500 jobs became available, resulting in a decrease of 3,500 jobs.

The loss is also true of wages. The wages paid by the plants being closed were in the range of 20 million pesos per month, while the wages disbursed by the plants newly established during the eighteen months amount to 11.5 million pesos, resulting in a net loss of 8.5 million pesos per month.

There are many possible causes for these developments. We have recent data from our Committees for the Promotion of the Border. Some of the explanations offered are ridiculous: "We closed the plant because we discovered that it was involved in sugar contraband," or "because it caught fire." The most frequent accurate explanations are the lack of raw materials and the impact of the economic recession in the United States. The United States recession, I believe, is critically important to the slowing down of production and the disappearance of some of these plants. Beyond that, there also have been labor problems, strikes, and many other factors affecting the manner in which these plants have functioned recently.

A decree was issued at the presidential level for the development of light industry, making it easy to establish such manufacturing plants. Concessions are granted and even subsidies for the importation of machinery, equipment, and building materials. Additional assistance, such as financing, is available on a ten-year basis, so that small-scale industry can be built along the border with 100 percent Mexican capital whose net worth is up to 5 million pesos.

Under this decree there have been applications for the establishment of twenty-six small and medium industries, half of which have been approved. Seven more are under consideration, while the remainder have been turned down because they did not meet the economic development criteria for which this aid program was devised.

I now would like to say something about the problem of the "hook" or "lure items" *(artículos gancho)*. Professor Urquidi categorizes this type of sale merchandise as a failure. I believe there are many factors that have not been taken into account and others that cannot easily be called forth as evidence to prove the contrary.

When the border development program was established in 1971, the chambers of commerce of all the Mexican border cities advised the Department of Commerce that the border consumer was the most demanding in the whole country. He is used to the American shopping centers where he is given easy terms and prices lower than ours in modern, spacious, comfortable, hygienic, well-stocked centers. He is price-conscious, he is a smart shopper, and he is very difficult to keep at home. Therefore, they said, we need the federal government to make it possible for us to import from the United States all those products that, being less expensive and of better quality, have served as lure, an attraction for the Mexican to cross the border. While buying that particular item or two or three, he buys all the rest of his needs. Thus there emerged the concept of the mechanism known as the "hook" or "lure item." We proceeded to facilitate the importation of such products.

At first we allowed very large quotas, of which maybe 30 percent were used. Why? Because we did not have sufficient data on how the border trade functions. One of the by-products of this program has been the fact that we now know quite accurately the purchasing power involved, the demand that exists in different border cities for different products, even in terms of income brackets.

While it is true that the "hook" or "lure items" represent a mere transfer of the product previously bought by the Mexican consumer across the border, nevertheless the sale now takes place in Mexico and it means more trade, more employment, and more sales tax here. In the last few years the demand for Mexican products along the border has increased. This suggests, although there is no definite proof, that the "hook" or "lure item" is serving its purposes: to keep the Mexican consumer on the Mexican side and to increase the demand for Mexican products in border stores.

Regarding the coordination of shopping centers and "hook" or "lure items," Urquidi agrees that there is no such thing. He contends that precisely in the large shopping centers, like those in Mexicali and Tijuana, where there has been huge financial investment, the "hook" or "lure items" are least in evidence. We must remember that Mexicali and Tijuana are free zones with a very large volume of duty-free imports for local supply. Therefore, what is permitted as a "lure item" cannot be especially attractive since everything is available duty free in a free zone.

Federal and local authorities have begun to cooperate on plans for the possible building of the complete infrastructure required by modern shopping centers on the Mexican side of the border. Such centers would provide the facilities, now sought in the United States, so that Mexicans could do all their shopping locally.

Finally, I wish to refer to certain aspects of tourism. I believe that the statements made by Urquidi and Méndez are very important. While, for certain European countries, we are promoting special tours—so-called international weeks—we tend to forget that the United States is one of the nations with the greatest economic potential as well as the highest per capita income, and the source of a very important tourist trade. American tourists, however, normally visit for only a few hours and do not venture far inland. What we need are more tourists who are really tourists, who stay not a few hours but a few days. Then we can offer them hotel and restaurant facilities, national parks, and really attractive elements, including a variety of products. There is much to be done in this area.

Professor Urquidi is correct when he states that what is needed is a definite plan for the integral development of the northern border region. I believe that right now there are sufficient elements to formulate such a plan, to determine the pivotal points for development that we might build upon, concentrating our efforts toward the development of tourism, trade, agriculture, and industry and, in particular, toward the better utilization of agricultural and livestock capacities. There are in the Urquidi-Méndez paper many important observations, which should guide future efforts for accelerated economic promotion and development along the northern border and stimulate increased efficiency among the various institutions making those efforts. This must be done not only for reason of social justice, but also if we are to solve the many problems of a political and social nature facing us.

G. A Mestizo World View and the Psychodynamics of Mexican-American Border Populations
by Manuel Ramírez III

The research reported by Drs. Holtzman and Díaz-Guerrero is a valuable contribution to the developing field of inter-American psychology. Their research program resulted in cooperation, exchange of information, and lasting productive ties between psychologists in Mexico and in the United States. These investigations give encouragement to those doing research on the sociocultural systems and psychodynamics of Mexican Americans. The study also has stimulated others to question whether theories and methodologies of social science, as interpreted and used in the West, are particularly appropriate for assessing and understanding the psychodynamics of *mestizo* peoples. These questions become increasingly critical as social scientists take greater interest in Mexican Americans and other *mestizo* populations.

Data obtained with methodologies and instruments not originally designed for the sociocultural system and dynamics of *mestizo* people may not assess the characteristics one is attempting to measure. This is indicated by the work of Bernal,[1] showing the importance of the social atmosphere of testing situations to the performance of Mexican-American children on concept-learning tasks; Guttman's work in Mexico relating ecology and culture to performance on projective tests;[2] and research showing that the Children's Embedded Figures Test is not a valid measure of cognitive style for Mexican-American children.[3] For example, does taking a projective test indeed have the same meaning for a Mexican child that it does for an American child? If it does not, how does one compare the data on the two cultures?

Second, it is becoming apparent that data on *mestizo* peoples have been interpreted by some researchers on the basis of inappropriate models. It is possible that some data cannot be interpreted in any meaningful fashion on the basis of existing knowledge. For example, according to the research papers under discussion Mexicans tend to be active in changing themselves in the face of environmental pressures or demands (coping style) requiring great internal activity but at the same time are intellectually passive. Mexican children do better on arithmetic and block design (two measures that are correlated with field independence) than American children, yet Mexican mothers are using more field dependent socialization practices in child rearing than American mothers. It is difficult to resolve such questions or apparent contradictions without reevaluating the practice of using the same instruments, methodologies, and theoretical bases for studying two populations.

A major obstacle to answering any questions or interpreting data on *mestizo* populations is that scant information exists about the psychodynamics and world view of *mestizo* peoples that has not been collected and interpreted using North American-Western European methodologies and theories. Information available from life histories of "Latinos," from oral histories, folklore, legends, novels and other literary works, art and philosophical works, could and should be gathered and examined in an attempt to understand the psychodynamics and socioculture of these peoples as well as the historical antecedents of such works and the world views conveyed by them.

It may well be necessary to follow a complicated procedure for establishing even a foundation for collecting and interpreting experimental data on *mestizo* peoples:

1. Study of oral history and literary and nonliterary media.

2. Carry out extensive participant observations of families, individuals in schools, employment, recreation, and community institutions with ethnomethodology and/or naturalistic research techniques.

3. Do life histories on *mestizo* peoples of the United States Southwest and Latin America from rural and urban areas, of different socioeconomic classes,

ages, and regions within the countries, recognizing the diversity existing within a culture and between cultures studied comparatively.

4. Develop methodologies and instruments for data collection that are compatible with the information obtained in Steps 1-3.

5. Develop a conceptual framework consistent with the information gathered.

Perhaps the results from this procedure would eventually yield hypotheses concerning questions such as those raised by Drs. Díaz-Guerrero and Holtzman. For example, why do Mexican children fall behind American children on arithmetic and block design with increasing age? Why have certain Mexican values "diffused" to the United States and others moved in the opposite direction?

Furthermore, such a procedure might lead to a renewed investigation into the study of psychodynamics in a fashion that does not demand a highly fragmented view of personality, an artificial compartmentalization of psychodynamics, which may be even more misleading in the study of persons from cultures whose orientation to the world stresses unity and search for harmony with the environment. At the very least, it could bind together information to produce a more complete and natural picture of the psychodynamics under investigation. (This is the approach being advocated by Sarason[4] and other community psychologists.) Unfortunately most Western theories and conceptualizations encourage a fragmented view of psychodynamics, especially in the separation of "cognitive" and "affective" development. This is especially dangerous when it leads investigators to conclude that a certain culture is intellectually inferior without considering social factors such as the quality of the schools or racism and oppression to which many *mestizos* are subjected. Witness what such separation has done in bilingual education programs in the United States—some so-called bilingual education programs emphasize only the affective side of Mexican-American culture, ignoring the fact that research shows bilingual, bicultural children to have intellectual advantages over other children.[5]

This leads us to the important area of adoption and diffusion of culture and values—an area in which much research and thinking are needed. Drs. Holtzman and Díaz-Guerrero include discussion of some aspects of this process in their essays, and this, it is hoped, will help lead social scientists to see the importance of studying border populations and Mexican Americans. Much-needed attention could then be given to the diversity within cultures, the importance of values shared by cultures, and values unique to a *mestizo* culture.

The need to supplant the bipolar model, which places Anglos and Mexicans at opposite ends, should be clear. Not only does such a model reinforce the mistaken assumption that persons between these poles are in complete conflict and frustration, it also gives weight to those who would attempt to select "what is good" from each culture and put it together on a subjective basis. For example, by indicating that American children have superior cognitive development and Mexican children have an affective advantage, educators conclude that Mexican-American culture interferes with intellectual development.

The bipolar model is much too simple. Mexican Americans and border populations cannot be viewed as simply "somewhere between Mexicans and Anglos" in values or psychodynamics. Drs. Holtzman and Díaz-Guerrero indicate that they found many similarities between Mexican and American children in their data. This is an excellent example of why a bipolar model is unsuitable. While more complex, a model showing various dimensions and degrees of similarity and difference, shared characteristics, and unique values and attitudes, needs to be developed and utilized. Research on the cognitive styles of bicultural children shows that there are indeed different dimensions of biculturalism.[6] Mexican-American biculturals show different degrees of similarity to either the American or Mexican sociocultural system along several different dimensions such as interpersonal relationships, communication, incentive-motivation, communication, and learning and teaching styles. In addition, our observations show that the flexibility exhibited by bicultural children along each of these dimensions depends on their socialization experiences, such as the degree to which their families participate in American, Mexican, and Mexican-American cultures. It also depends on the particular characteristics of the specific situation in which the behavior is being observed. These observations suggest the need for a model that is much more complex than the bipolar view for conceptualizing the psychodynamics of biculturals.

Additional research can lead to a conceptual framework and a methodology that is not based solely on a North American-Western European world view. We must look to new perspectives and approaches, most especially now that psychology has reached a methodological dead end. As Sarason[7] has stated, and as Dr. Díaz-Guerrero has indicated in his paper, social scientists will have to take culture and history seriously if they hope to arrive at meaningful theories of behavior.

The psychodynamics of Borderland populations must be studied from a *mestizo* basis and viewpoint as well as from other perspectives before understanding of life-styles, problems, and aspirations of these people can be achieved. The work of Drs. Holtzman and Díaz-Guerrero has stimulated interest, reevaluation, and the beginnings of new approaches for attaining such understanding.

NOTES

1. E. M. Bernal, *Concept Learning Among Anglo, Black and Mexican-American Children Using Facilitation Strategies and Behavioral Techniques* (Ph.D. diss., University of Texas at Austin, 1971).

2. D. Guttman, "Psychological Naturalism in Cross-Cultural Studies," in E. P. Williams and H. L. Rausch, eds., *Naturalistic Viewpoints in Psychological Research* (New York: Holt, Rinehart & Winston, 1969).

3. M. Ramírez and A. Castañeda, *Cultural Democracy, Bicognitive Development and Education* (New York: Academic Press, 1974).

4. S. Sarason, *The Psychological Sense of Community* (San Francisco: Josey-Bass, 1974).

5. E. Peal and W. E. Lambert, "The Relation of Bilingualism to Intelligence," *Psychological Monographs: General and Applied* 76, no. 27, whole no. 546 (1962).

6. Ramírez and Castañeda, *Cultural Democracy.*

7. Sarason, *The Psychological Sense of Community.*

H.   Health Along the Border
by Robert Oseasohn

It is difficult to describe the health aspects along the border because it is not nearly circumscribed or homogeneous, and health is notoriously difficult to measure. Characteristically, when we "feel good" and are able to perform our usual functions, we usually don't think too much about them. However, when illness or accident occurs, particularly when disability or death ensues, we become acutely aware of disease or loss of health. Because it is difficult to measure health, facts about it are not only scanty for the border communities, but for most parts of the world as well. Accordingly, we rely on indices such as mortality rates. But even these are often imprecise and incomplete. Accurate mortality rates depend, for example, on careful recording of a series of events—the fact of death itself; the cause(s); and a population census. Not all deaths are reported; in some areas, reasons for death are only guessed at; and, it is said, some populations have not been enumerated accurately. However, the nature of border places, people, and agents of disease, accumulated experience in these communities, and what has been observed in other parts of the world, do permit us to outline in broad terms what many of the currently important health problems are likely to be and to suggest approaches toward their solutions.

Compared with certain European countries or parts of the United States and Canada, for example, the border communities would be expected to show higher maternal mortality and morbidity rates, higher infant death rates, and higher mortality rates associated with infectious diseases such as tuberculosis and enteritis. However, the border communities, like so many others, probably have a growing burden of death and disability associated with heart disease, stroke, cancer, violence, alcohol abuse, and mental upset.

Before we consider what specific actions might be taken to improve border health, it may be useful to ask how improved health conditions have come about in other parts of the world. Thomas McKeown has stated that:

> If health depended primarily on treatment of the sick, we could accept the popular view that "having an operation" is the essence of medical care and surgery the summit of medical achievement. The problems confronting medicine would then be essentially financial: how to pay for and extend the traditional services in developed countries and, more difficult, how to reproduce them in developing countries. But the facts are quite different. We owe the advance in health mainly, not to what happens when we are ill, but to the fact that we do not so often become ill. And we remain well, not because of specific preventive measures such as vaccination and immunization, but because we enjoy a higher standard of living and live in a healthier environment.
>
> If this interpretation is correct, the problems confronting the medical services everywhere are incomparably more complex. It becomes important to assess the contribution which various influences, some of them not of a medical character, are making to health. It is also necessary to re-examine the traditional services and to ask ourselves whether they are really well-suited to the work they have to do.[1]

The tuberculosis situation, still a border health problem, may be used to illustrate this point of view. Tuberculosis mortality began to decline in Europe during the nineteenth century, long before specific therapy was introduced. Present-day chemotherapy is a powerful tool with which to control further the disease, but the role of environmental determinants such as housing, nutrition, and working conditions should not be overlooked. Attention to these basic factors should promote health and prevent disease occurrence more efficiently than costly curative services, which often can do little more than patch up already established disease and disability. The course of most chronic diseases is influenced only slightly by currently available treatment.

David Morley recently wrote a book, *Paediatric Priorities in the Developing World,* which discusses the organization and delivery of health services in developing countries—those with young populations, heavy death and disability burdens, and limited resources. It suggests the following technique for setting priorities among health problems:

Four criteria are used: community concern, which includes knowledge, attitudes, feelings and the degree of urgency; prevalence, which refers to the frequency with which the problem occurs; seriousness, that is, its destructive effects on individuals and society; and susceptibility to management, which takes into account the availability of methods for management as well as the cost and difficulty of applying them.[2]

One relatively small Latin American country, operating on a limited budget, has made a remarkable effort to improve its national health by placing top priority on environmental conditions, and beginning at the village and neighborhood level, to develop community concern. This has been carried out by personal involvement of the federal health ministry staff, regional health workers, and by young people trained in social welfare and community organization who are assigned to small communities and work intensively in them. This philosophy fits with Morley's view: "Begin with what they know. . . . Build on what they have. . . ."[3]

Community organization leads to discussion groups and questions about needs. Villagers are helped to survey their needs and to sum up what was learned for general discussion and decision making. Incentives are offered to facilitate certain environmental measures—small, inexpensive, versatile tractors are made available to groups willing to cultivate community gardens; seed and technical advice on how best to use it has been offered as well as a few "starter" domestic animals. Assistance has been given with which to construct protected water supplies in which local residents furnish the needed manpower. Little or no new funds have been spent on enlarging hospital facilities or educating more physicians. Instead, a new abbreviated community nursing curriculum was devised and a new school started to provide a corps of community-oriented health workers prepared to manage the bulk of local problems themselves. The progress of this promising and innovative program should be watched closely.

In many parts of the United States, services necessary to meet community needs in health and disease have become seriously fragmented, and often important pieces of a balanced program are missing. The first aim of health services should be to promote health. But, traditionally, health promotion has been an area of little concern and even less talent. Our energies and dollars go instead into disease-oriented screening programs of dubious value. We should be concerned with safe water, disposal of waste, adequate nutrition, proper housing, and to equally vital safeguards to prevent family disruption, violence, and alcoholism.

Which individuals and agencies are responsible for setting health priorities in the border communities? What are the goals? Who is responsible for implementation? To whom are those entrusted with health services accountable? Who is in charge here?

NOTES

1. Thomas McKeown, *Medicine in Modern Society* (London: George Allen and Unwin, 1965), p. 9.
2. David Morley, *Paediatric Priorities in the Developing World* (London: Butterworth and Co., Ltd., 1973), p. 60.
3. Ibid., p. 50.

I. The Ecology of the Border*
by Humberto Bravo Alvarez

An analysis of the essays by Arthur W. Busch and J. A. Villasana Lyon brings out many points that should be taken into account in future international accords or treaties dealing with environmental pollution. To begin with, we must make a clear distinction between environmental pollution produced by human action and that which is not—despite an obvious interaction. The governments of nations south of the Río Grande already have registered a deep concern for environmental problems. They have become aware that the poor suffer most from pollution because they have to live where the environment is worst.

As Mr. Busch points out, the geographical border between Mexico and the United States stretches for some two thousand miles with a large population (approximately 3.5 million) living in cities located along both sides of the border. Because basic cultural, economic, and political differences are involved, it is reasonable to expect environmental pollution problems, usually requiring technical solutions attainable only at the highest levels of international relations. This is why technically simple solutions in this area cannot be quickly forthcoming nor be applicable in actual practice.

Environmental problems found along the border run the complete gamut: air pollution, water pollution, soil pollution, and solid waste disposal. Many of these problems conceivably could be solved—without appealing to

---

*Translated from the Spanish by Miguel González-Gerth [Editor's Note].

governmental agencies—by civic groups interested in good human relations (conservationists and service organizations, such as the Rotary Club), which could exert pressure, each in its own country, so that the sources of pollution affecting it can be controlled, thus diminishing the harm done to the environment along the whole border region.

In both countries and to varying degrees there are poor, even extremely poor people. The region of Appalachia in the United States is an example, and in Mexico such situations are numerous. This does not make it less imperative that we try to lower the rate of pollution now threatening our environment. The emerging nations must learn *not to repeat* the costly errors already made by the developed nations, often creating societies of disproportionate consumerism. Furthermore, the emerging nations should learn from research done by the developed nations how to precisely measure, prevent, and control environmental pollution. At the same time, the government *expenditures* relevant to this objective should reflect a specific social responsibility. Though admittedly it is difficult to measure the total benefits to mass population, such expenditures should be made according to the obligation our governments have to protect the lower as well as the upper levels of society.

Mr. Villasana points out the importance of one factor—public education. No doubt a society educated in its rights to an environment conducive to health development is likely to cooperate with beneficial government action. But as long as the education parameter is lacking, public awareness cannot be counted on, and here again it is the civic groups and the communications media that can render an invaluable aid.

Specific action in the area of development can be controlled on both sides of the border through the free distribution of environmental information to interested groups and individuals. Keeping the public informed should be an objective, since it is, in fact, the public who has most to lose. The corresponding services in both countries should maintain close relations on the same technical level in order to obviate problems due to a lack of understanding. One last recommendation is that help be sought by Mexico from international agencies set up for the purpose of aiding underdeveloped countries in the environmental area.

Their expertise could help determine the technical nature of existing and future problems as well as the options available for attaining solutions within the bounds of economic reality.

APPENDIX II

Identification of Participants

Essayists

IGNACIO BERNAL Y GARCÍA PIMENTAL is the Director of the Museo Nacional de Antropología, a post he held from 1962 through 1968 and again from 1970 to the present. Professor at the Universidad Nacional Autónoma de México, Bernal received his doctorate from that institution and honorary doctorates from the University of California at Berkeley, the University of tpe Americas, and St. Mary's University of San Antonio. He has represented his country at UNESCO and the Instituto Panamericano de Geografía e Historia, serving as president of the Commission on History. Decorated by half a dozen countries and recipient of Mexico's National Prize, Dr. Bernal's bibliography contains over two hundred items including books, chapters, articles, reports, and essays.

VERNON M. BRIGGS, JR., is professor of economics at the University of Texas at Austin. Trained at the University of Maryland and Michigan State University, where he received, respectively, the M.A. and Ph.D. degrees, Dr. Briggs has served as an associate member of the National Manpower Policy Task Force for the Department of Labor and as research director of the Public Advisory Committee on Administration of Training Programs under the Department of Health, Education, and Welfare. Honored for his teaching excellence, Professor Briggs has written extensively on minority labor problems, including books, monographs, chapters, and articles relating to the Black and Chicano and apprenticeship programs, rural poverty, and public policy.

ARTHUR W. BUSCH in 1972 was named regional administrator of the Environmental Protection Agency responsible for a five-state region.

Previously he had for many years served on the faculty of Rice University as professor of environmental engineering. Trained at Texas Technological University and MIT, Mr. Busch has served on the engineering staffs of industrial firms, as a member of the President's Air Quality Advisory Board, and as a consultant for industry, government, and engineering firms. His honors include the Harrison Prescott Eddy Medal for noteworthy research presented by the Water Pollution Control Federation and a Certificate of Merit awarded by the American Chemical Society. Author of a book entitled *Aerobic Biological Treatment of Waste Waters,* and more than sixty professional papers, Mr. Busch now is vice-president for environmental affairs for the Southwest Research Institute.

JORGE A. BUSTAMANTE, a native of Chihuahua, was trained in law at UNAM and in Sociology (M.A. and Ph.D.) at Notre Dame. He has been an attorney in private practice and a faculty member both at UNAM and at the University of Texas at Austin. Currently appointed at El Colegio de México, Dr. Bustamante is teaching and doing research in the Center for Sociological Studies. His research interest focuses on Mexican migration to the United States and the problems the immigrants face in the border regions. He is a consultant to Mexico's National Population Council. The author of a whole series of articles and chapters on Mexican immigration, Dr. Bustamante is under contract with the Fondo de Cultura Económica for a volume based on his dissertation entitled "Mexican Immigration and the Social Relations of Capitalism."

ROGELIO DÍAZ-GUERRERO was born in Guadalajara. Educated at the universities of Guadalajara, the National School of Medicine, UNAM, and the University of Iowa, Dr. Díaz-Guerrero currently is research professor of psychology at the National University. He has served as president of the Mexican Psychological Society, the Interamerican Psychological Society, and of the Monterrey Center for Social Research. Much of his study has been devoted to research on the personality development of children in Mexico and elsewhere. He is the author of more than one hundred articles and chapters. He has written half a dozen books, including most recently his *Psychology of the Mexican: Culture and Personality* (1975).

JOE B. FRANTZ is a Texan who has looked and gone beyond the state's horizons. Receiving all three degrees from the University of Texas, Dr. Frantz is professor of history at the University of Texas at Austin. He also has taught at the universities of Chicago, Northwestern, Colorado, and Chile. He went to

Peru and Ecuador to help establish American Studies programs. Active professionally, Professor Frantz has served as president of the Texas Institute of Letters and as a member of the National Historical Publications Commission. Past chairman of the department of history, he currently is director of research in Texas history and director of the Johnson Library's Oral History project. He is author or editor of eight books, including the coauthored *Turner, Bolton, and Webb: Three Historians of the American Frontier* (1965), as well as numerous chapters and articles.

ARMANDO GUTIÉRREZ is a native of Corpus Christi, Texas. Trained in political science at Texas A&I University and at the University of Texas at Austin, he is an assistant professor of government at the latter institution. His special interest is in Mexican-American politics and American government. He is the author or coauthor of articles which have appeared in the *Social Science Quarterly, The Journal of Politics,* and the *American Political Science Review* and has a book forthcoming on Chicano politics in Texas.

WAYNE H. HOLTZMAN, president of the Hogg Foundation for Mental Health, is professor of psychology and education at the University of Texas at Austin. Earlier he served as dean of the college of education at the University of Texas. He has served as consultant and member of many professional and public panels, committees, and commissions. He has been president of the Interamerican Society of Psychology, the Southwestern Psychological Association, and the Texas Psychological Association. He has been honored with fellowships or awards from the Social Science Research Council, the Menninger Foundation, and the Center for Advanced Study in the Behavioral Sciences. Internationally known for the Holtzman Inkblot Technique, which he developed, Professor Holtzman's bibliography contains almost a hundred items, including one on the Inkblot Technique (1961), *Computer-Assisted Instruction, Testing and Guidance* (1971), and the recent *Personality Development in Two Cultures,* coauthored with Rogelio Díaz-Guerrero.

RICARDO LOEWE REISS, a native of the Federal District, was educated at UNAM where he received his medical degree, with specialization in surgery and obstetrics, and at the Mexican School of Public Health where he received a master's degree in public health and medical administration. He has served as head of the Technical Department for Health Education at the Secretary of Health and Assistance and as a consultant to many other government agencies and institutions, including National Polytechnic Institute, Mexican Institute for Social Security, and Institute for the Protection of Children. In 1973, he participated in the elaboration of the section on health education in the National Health Plan. Dr. Loewe is the author of a number of scholarly articles in his field of special interest—public health and the development of public health services and facilities.

F. RAY MARSHALL is professor of economics at the University of Texas at Austin, where he directs the Center for the Study of Human Resources. He currently is serving as Secretary of Labor in the Carter administration. He also has served as chairman of the department of economics. Dr. Marshall received his advanced degrees from Louisiana State University (M.A.) and from the University of California at Berkeley (Ph.D.). He serves on numerous committees and panels relating to apprenticeship and manpower administration for governmental and professional groups. He has been a consultant to the Labor Department and to the Department of Health, Education and Welfare. He has been honored with fellowships by the Ford Foundation, Harvard University, and the Fulbright program. He has authored or coauthored more than a dozen books and monographs, not to mention chapters and articles. His books include *The Negro Worker* (1967), *Cooperatives and Rural Poverty in the Rural South* (1971), and *Human Resources and Labor Markets* (1972).

SOFÍA MÉNDEZ VILLARREAL is an economist, trained at UNAM. She also has received a diploma in economics and social planning at the Instituto Latinoamericano de Planificación Económica y Social (ILPES-CEPAL) in Santiago and the B.Phil. degree in economics from Oxford University. She has worked as a statistician and analyst of economic problems for the UN's Economic Commission for Latin America and the department of economic studies of the Banco Central de México. She is currently a full-time researcher at the Center for Economic and Demographic Studies of El Colegio de México.

CARLOS MONSIVÁIS, a thoughtful intellectual and provocative writer, was born and educated in the Federal District, emphasizing philosophy and economics in his studies. He is a member of the editorial staff of the magazine *Siempre,* coordinating that publication's supplement on Mexican culture *(La Cultura en México).* He also is a researcher for the department of historical investigations of the Instituto Nacional de Antropología e Historia. Lic. Monsiváis has taught at the University of Essex in England. Specializing on

Mexican culture in general and literature in particular, he has written more than half a dozen books. Included among Monsiváis's writings are: *Antología de la poesía mexicana del siglo XX* (1966), *Características de la cultura nacional* (1969), and *Pueblo en armas* (1973).

AMÉRICO PAREDES is professor of english and anthropology at the University of Texas at Austin. A product of the Valley, Dr. Paredes received all three degrees from the University of Texas, with a special interest in folklore. He has served as editor of the *Journal of American Folklore*, director of the Center for Mexican-American Studies, and director of the Center for International Studies in Folklore and Oral History, both of the last at the University of Texas. His honors include a Guggenheim Fellowship, membership on the National Humanities Faculty, and service as the United States Representative on the Committee on Folklore of the Pan American Institute of Geography and History. Especially interested in Mexican and Mexican-American folk culture, Dr. Paredes is the author of numerous books and articles, including *With His Pistol in His Hand: A Border Ballad and Its Hero* (1958) and *Folktales of Mexico* (1970).

TAD SZULC formerly was a UPI correspondent at the United Nations and then reported for the *New York Times* from forty-three countries. From 1969 to 1972, he was correspondent for the Washington Bureau of the *Times,* specializing in foreign affairs. He is the recipient of the María Moors Cabot Gold Medal from Columbia University, the Overseas Press Club Citation, and the Sigma Delta Chi Medal. His books include a number on Latin America, including *Twilight of the Tyrants* (1959), *Cuban Invasion* (1962), *Latin America* (1966), and *The United States and the Caribbean* (1971), edited for the American Assembly. A contributor to such leading publications as the *New York Times Sunday Magazine, Saturday Review, Harper's, The New Yorker, Saturday Evening Post, Look,* and *Esquire,* Mr. Szulc is a free-lance journalist.

CHARLES H. TELLER is a research sociologist and demographer with the Division of Human Development of the Instituto de Nutrición de Centro América y Panamá. He studied at Brandeis (B.A. in history), Clark (M.A. in geography), and Cornell (Ph.D. in sociology) universities and served with the Peace Corps. Prior to his present position, he was a member of the faculty of the University of Texas at Austin. With a primary interest in social demography and the sociology of health and medical care, Dr. Teller has done research on access to health facilities in Latin America and the United States. His studies reflect those interests.

ANTONIO UGALDE, after receiving his doctorate at Stanford University, taught a year at the University of New Mexico before joining the faculty of the department of sociology of the University of Texas at Austin. A consultant to the World Health Organization, he did research under the international agency's auspices. Dr. Ugalde also has served as acting director of the Center for Mexican-American Studies and Research at the University of Texas. His special interest is in the culture of urban life, and he is the author of *Power and Conflict in a Mexican Community* (1970) and coauthor of *The Urbanization Process of a Poor Mexican Neighborhood* (1974).

VÍCTOR L. URQUIDI, trained in economics at the London School of Economics, is president of El Colegio de México. He is a member of the executive committee of the Club of Rome and of the United Nations Advisory Committee on the Application of Science and Technology to Development. Earlier he served as a research economist for the Banco de México, the International Bank for Reconstruction and Development, and for the Mexican Ministry of Finance. He also was a principal economist for the United Nations Economic Commission for Latin America, directing that organization's regional office in Mexico. His special interest is economic development, and he has served as a consultant in this area for the principal Mexican governmental agencies. His extensive writings include coauthorship of the *Economic Development of Mexico* (1953) and authorship of *Free Trade and Economic Integration in Latin America* (1962) and *The Challenge of Development in Latin America* (1964).

J. ALBERTO VILLASANA LYON, trained in civil engineering at UNAM, currently is coordinator of CETENAL (Comisión de Estudios del Territorio Nacional) under the jurisdiction of the Secretary of the Presidency. His specialty has been the use of aerial photographic surveys in territorial and urban planning. He has served as director of Photogrammetry at Estudios y Proyectos, a consulting firm, as technical manager of Cía. Mexicana Aerofoto, and as general manager of Wild de México. A consultant for the cartographic section of the United Nations, Ing. Villasana represents his country at the Instituto Panamericano de Geografía e Historia and as an adviser for the International Water and Boundary Commission. He has taught as a member of the engineering faculty of the Universidad Nacional Autónoma de México.

Commentators

HUMBERTO BRAVO ÁLVAREZ is head of environmental research of the Instituto de Geofísica of the Univesidad Nacional Autónoma de México. He also is an adviser to the Subsecretary of the Ministry of Commerce and a member of the Advisory Committee on the Standardization of Environmental Regulations in the Ministry of Industry and Commerce. A native of Veracruz, Dr. Bravo was educated at UNAM and at West Virginia University where he received the doctorate in environmental engineering. He undertook advanced studies in air pollution instrumentation, sanitary engineering, and industrial hygiene at the Robert A. Taft Engineering Center, Kittering Laboratory, University of Cincinnati. The founder and first president of the Mexican Society For Air and Water Pollution Control, he participated in the development of the Ley Federal de la Prevención y Control de la Contaminación Ambiental (1971).

RUDOLPH GOMEZ is graduate dean and director of research at the University of Texas at El Paso. Prepared in political science at Utah State University, Stanford University, and the University of Colorado, Dr. Gomez also served as chairman of the department of political science at El Paso. He has been recognized by designations as a Woodrow Wilson Fellow and as a Fulbright-Hays Visiting Professor. Professor Gomez has written more than a dozen articles and books including volumes on Colorado government and politics (1964, 1967, and 1972), Peruvian public administration (1969), and two readers entitled, *The Changing Mexican Americans* (1972) and *The Social Reality of Ethnic America* (1974). Dr. Gomez's most recent effort, *Mexican Americans in American Bureaucracy,* is in press.

ELISEO MENDOZA BERRUETO was born in Coahuila where he trained to be a school teacher and did some teaching. His advanced education included study at the Escuela Nacional de Economía. During these years he was very active in student organizations. During the Echeverría administration, Lic. Mendoza served as Subsecretary of Commerce, responsible for both internal and external commerce, in the Secretaría de Industria y Comercio. As an economist, he has taught at UNAM, National Polytechnical Institute, University of Guadalajara, and El Colegio de México where he also directed the Center for Economic and Demographic Studies. He has worked for various governmental banks and agencies, including the Banco Nacional de Crédito Ejidal, Banco Agrario de la Laguna, and Industria Nacional Químico Farmacéutica. He served as director of economic and social planning of the Plan

Lerma. He has twice served as president of the Intersecretarial Commission for the Development of the Northern Frontier. He has written extensively on the problems of economic development in Mexico.

ROBERT OSEASOHN, after earning his B.S. degree at Tufts University, received his medical education at the Long Island College of Medicine. He is professor of medicine and chairman of the department of epidemiology and health at McGill University. Prior to joining the McGill faculty, Dr. Oseasohn taught at Western Reserve University, the University of New Mexico, and at the University of Texas Health Sciences Center at Houston where he was professor of epidemiology and associate dean. He has served as a consultant to the Department of Health, Education, and Welfare, the World Health Organization, and the National Aeronautics and Space Administration. Dr. Oseasohn is the author of more than three dozen articles on medical research and on the delivery of health care services in both urban and rural environments.

MANUEL RAMÍREZ, III was born in Río Grande City, Texas, and studied at the University of Texas at Austin where he received both the B.A. and Ph.D. degrees, the latter in clinical and developmental psychology with a minor in anthropology. He currently is a member of the faculty of the University of California at Santa Cruz where he also is director of the Follow Through Project. The author of a number of articles in such journals as the *Social Science Quarterly* and the *Interamerican Journal of Psychology*, Dr. Ramírez is the coauthor of two recent volumes: *Cultural Democracy, Bicognitive Development and Education* (1974) and *Mexican-Americans and Educational Change* (1974).

ARTHUR J. RUBEL is the author of a study, *Across the Tracks* (1966), which is regarded as one of the classics in the literature on the Mexican American. Professor of anthropology at Michigan State University, Dr. Rubel studied at the universities of Chicago (B.A.) and North Carolina (M.A. and Ph.D.). He minored in epidemiology in the School of Public Health at North Carolina and received a predoctoral research fellowship from the National Institute of Mental Health. Before joining the faculty at Michigan State, Professor Rubel taught at the University of Notre Dame, the University of North Carolina at Greensboro, and UNAM. He is the author of numerous articles and essays on anthropology and health care.

JOSEFINA ZORAIDA VÁZQUEZ holds two doctorates, one from the Universidad Central de Madrid and the other from UNAM. In addition, she has studied at Harvard University, Louisiana State University, and the Universidad de Cuyo in Mendoza, Argentina. She has held fellowships from the O.A.S., the Rockefeller Foundation, and the University of Texas at Austin (Farmer Fellow). She has taught at the Instituto Nacional Politécnico, the Universidad Feminina, Iberoamericana, UNAM, and El Colegio de México in Mexico and at Duke University and the University of Texas in the United States. She was in charge of the rewriting of the official social sciences school texts for the six elementary years and has written a number of books including *La imágen del indio en el español del siglo XVI* (1962), *Nacionalismo y educación en México* (1970), and *Historia de la historiografía* (1973). Professor Vázquez is director of the Centro de Estudios Históricas at El Colegio de México.

MERCEDES CARRERAS DE VELASCO is a researcher in the department of historical investigations of the Archive, Library, and Publications Section of the Secretaría de Relaciones Exteriores. She has been in charge of the research project on the Bracero Program (1942-64) and coordinator of the documentary project on the protection of Mexicans in the United States (1940-73). Ms. Velasco received her master's degree in history from Eg Colegio de México. She has published a study about returning migrants entitled *Los mexicanos que devolvió la crisis 1929-1932* (1974) and has in press a work entitled *La emigración de mexicanos a E.U.A.: Perspectiva Histórica* to appear in the Secretary of Public Education's Sep/Setentas series.

Discussants

DAVID ALVÍREZ, a sociologist, is head of the department of behavioral sciences at Pan American University at Edinburg, Texas. A product of Southern Methodist University and of the University of Texas at Austin, Dr. Alvírez has participated in or directed several field studies of Mexican migrants including one on demographic trends and another on assimilation.

NETTIE LEE BENSON has many claims to fame—as professor of history at the University of Texas, as a scholar in the Mexican history field, and as the director for many fruitful years of the Latin American Collection at Texas. Her special interest has been in Mexican history in the period of and immediately following independence. She has a long and knowledgeable association with the valley region of southern Texas.

ARTHUR F. CORWIN, a Latin American historian, has developed a strong interest in the border and in Mexican migration. Author of a book on the abolition of slavery in Cuba (1967), Dr. Corwin has taught at institutions of higher education both in Latin America and in the United States, most recently the University of Connecticut. He has worked with Project Hope's Program for Health Workers in Laredo and the border area and with the Border Study Project of the area's community colleges. Currently, he is director of a cooperative project for the study of Mexican migration.

DANIEL COSÍO VILLEGAS, economist, educator, diplomat, and political analyst, has a list of distinctions too long to enumerate. Regarded as the "dean" of Mexican historians, Lic. Cosío directed, coordinated, and wrote a significant portion of the ten-volume *Historia Moderna de México*. He founded leading journals in history, economics, and international studies and established (and for a quarter of a century directed) the Fondo de Cultura Económica. He served as president of El Colegio de México and was a member of the prestigious Colegio Nacional. At the time of his death in 1976, he was directing a project to prepare a multivolume history of the Mexican Revolution.

FELISA M. KAZEN, an anthropologist and a member of the faculty at Harvard University where she also earned her doctorate, knows the border region well both from a personal and professional point of view. She has been involved in border research projects related to the demographic and assimilative trends of Mexican migrants sponsored by the Population Research Center of the University of Texas at Austin and the Southwest Center for Urban Research in Houston. She has published a number of scholarly papers on these themes.

WILLIAM MADSEN is an anthropologist who has done extensive field work in the South Texas border region. Currently, he is professor of anthropology at the University of California at Santa Barbara. Professor Madsen is the author of many articles and books among which are: *Cristo-Paganism: A Study of Mexican Religious Syncretism* (1957), *The Virgin's Children: Life in an Aztec Village Today* (1960), *Society and Health in the Lower Rio Grande Valley* (1961), and *Mexican-Americans of South Texas* (1964). He has directed numerous research projects, including one for the Southwest Development Laboratory.

JACINTO QUIRARTE currently is dean of the college of fine and applied arts and professor of art history at the University of Texas at San Antonio. He received his doctorate from UNAM and taught at the University of the Americas, the Central University of Venezuela, Yale University, the University of New Mexico, and the University of Texas before assuming his present position. He has published a volume on *Mexican American Artists* (1973) and has in press a study of Maya vases.

SANTOS REYES, JR., a native of San Antonio, is a member of the faculty of the School of Social Work and former director of the Center for Mexican American studies at the University of Texas at Austin. He has had rich and varied educational and professional experience, including service with the Department of Public Health and Welfare. He has published a study of Chicano students in graduate schools of social work.

Institutional Representatives

Mr. Peter Canga, Texas Office of Economic Opportunity
Dr. David T. Garza, Institute of Urban Studies, University of Houston
Professor Mario Ojeda Gómez, El Colegio de México
Miss Martha T. Muse, President, The Tinker Foundation
Mr. Carlos Nagel, Arizona-Sonora Desert Museum
Dr. Alejandro Portes, Department of Sociology, University of Texas at Austin
Professor Gustavo M. Quesada, School of Medicine, Texas Tech University
Dr. Tomás Rivera, College of Multidisciplinary Studies, University of Texas
  at San Antonio
Dr. Richard G. Santos, Director, Ethnic Studies Program, Our Lady of the
  Lake College, San Antonio

Special Guests

Dr. Richard E. W. Adams, Dean, College of Humanities and Social Sciences,
  University of Texas at San Antonio
Dr. R. Keith Arnold, Director, Division of Natural Resources and Envir-
  onment, University of Texas at Austin
Sr. José Treviño Botti, Centro de Estudios Internacionales, El Colegio de
  México
Dr. Mauricio Charpenel, Faculty Consultant, Institute of Latin American
  Studies, University of Texas at Austin

Dr. Orlando de la Rosa, Director, Universidad Nacional Autónoma de México in San Antonio

Mr. Gilbert M. Denman, Jr., Chairman, Ewing Halsell Foundation, San Antonio

Dr. Peter T. Flawn, President, University of Texas at San Antonio

Dr. William P. Glade, Director, Institute of Latin American Studies, University of Texas at Austin

Lic. Roberto Heredia Correa, Archivo General de la Nación and UNAM.

Dr. Maria Luiza Marcílio, Visiting Professor of Historical Demography, University of Texas at Austin

Dr. Arnulfo Martínez, Vice President, Pan American University

Dr. Thomas G. McGann, Department of History, University of Texas at Austin

Dr. James W. McKie, Dean, College of Social and Behavioral Sciences, University of Texas at Austin

Dr. Henry M. Schmidt, Department of History, Texas A and M University

Dr. Karl M. Schmitt, Department of Government, University of Texas at Austin

Mr. and Mrs. William Sinkin, San Antonio

Dr. Oswaldo Sunkel, Tinker Visiting Professor of Latin American Studies, University of Texas at Austin, and Mrs. Sunkel

Mr. Hugh Treadwell, Director, University of New Mexico Press

Dr. Duncan Wimpress, President, Trinity University

Representatives of the Weatherhead Foundation

Dr. Richard W. Weatherhead, President
Ms. Muriel A. Golden, Administrative Director
Professor Richard Eells, Trustee
Professor John H. Parry, Consultant
Mr. Stanley Salmen, Trustee

Conference Chairman and Staff

Dr. Stanley R. Ross, Chairman of the Conference, Professor of History, and former Vice-President and Provost, University of Texas at Austin

Ms. Geraldine D. Gagliano, Executive Assistant

Professor Miguel González-Gerth, Translator, Department of Spanish-Portuguese, University of Texas at Austin

Mr. Martín Jankowski, Assistant to the Chairman

Bibliography

Bibliographical References

Almaráz, Félix D., Jr. "The Status of Borderlands Studies: History." *The Social Science Journal* 12 (1975): 9-18.

American Council of Race Relations. *Mexican Americans: A Selected Bibliography*. Chicago, 1949.

Barrios, Ernie, ed. *Bibliografía de Aztlán: An Annotated Chicano Bibliography*. San Diego, Calif., Centro de Estudios Chicanos, San Diego State College, 1971.

Bath, C. Richard. "The Status of Borderlands Studies: Political Sciences." *The Social Science Journal* 12 (1975): 55-67.

Bogardus, Emory S., comp. "The Mexican Immigrant: An Annotated Bibliography." In Carlos E. Cortés, ed., *Mexican American Bibliographies*. New York: Arno Press, 1974.

Caballero, César, and Hedman, Kenneth, eds. *Chicano Studies Bibliography*. El Paso: University of Texas at El Paso Library, 1973.

Cabinet Committee on Opportunities for Spanish Speaking People. *The Spanish Speaking in the United States: A Guide to Materials*. Detroit, Mich.: Blaine-Ethridge Books, 1975.

California State College at Long Beach Library. *Chicano Bibliography*. Long Beach, 1970.

Corwin, Arthur F. "Mexican Emigration History, 1900-1970: Literature and Research," *Latin American Research Review* 8 (1973): 3-24.

Cosío Villegas, Daniel. *Nueva historiografía política del México moderno*. Mexico City: Editorial de El Colegio Nacional, 1966.

Cotera, Martha P., comp. *Educator's Guide to Chicano Resources*. Crystal City, Texas: Crystal City Memorial Library, 1971.

Cumberland, Charles C. "United States-Mexican Border: A Selective Guide to the Literature of the Region." In Carlos E. Cortés, ed., *Mexican American Bibliographies*. New York: Arno Press, 1974.

Dobie, J. Frank. *Guide to Life and Literature of the Southwest*. Austin: University of Texas Press, 1943.

Gildersleeve, Charles R. "The Status of Borderlands Studies: Geography." *The Social Science Journal* 12 (1975): 19-28.

Gómez-Quiñones, Juan. comp., *Selected Materials for Chicano Studies*. Austin: Center for Mexican American Studies, University of Texas, 1973.

———— and Camarillo, Alberto, comps., *Selected Bibliography for Chicano Studies*. Los Angeles: Aztlán Publications, Chicano Studies Center, University of California, 1974.

González y González, Luis. *Fuentes de la historia contemporánea de México: libros y folletos*. 3 vols. Mexico City: El Colegio de México, 1961-62.

Griffin, Charles C., ed. *Latin America: A Guide to the Historical Literature*. Austin: University of Texas Press, 1971.

Hedman, Kenneth, and McNeil, Patsy, comps. *Mexican American Bibliography: A Guide to the Resources of the Library of the University of Texas at El Paso*. El Paso: University of Texas Library, 1970.

Hispanic Foundation, Library of Congress. *Handbook of Latin American Studies*. 36 vols. to date. Cambridge, Mass.: Harvard University Press and Gainsville, Fla.: University of Florida Press, 1936–.

Jenkins, John H. *Cracker Barrel Chronicles: A Bibliography of Texas Town and County Chronicles.* Austin, Texas: Pemberton Press, 1965.

Jones, Robert C. "Mexicans in the United States: A Bibliography." In Carlos E. Cortés, ed., *Mexican American Bibliographies.* New York: Arno Press, 1974.

Jordan, Lois B. *Mexican Americans: Resources to Build Cultural Understanding.* Littleton, Colo.: Libraries Unlimited, Inc., 1973.

Meier, Matt S., and Rivera, Feliciano, comps. *A Bibliography for Chicano History.* San Francisco: R & E Research Associates, 1972.

México: Dirección General de Geografía y Meteorología. *Bibliografía geográfica de México.* Mexico City, 1955.

Mickey, Barbara H., comp. *A Bibliography of Studies Concerning the Spanish Speaking Population of the American Southwest.* Greeley, Colo.: Colorado State College, 1969.

Navarro, Eliseo, comp. *Annotated Bibliography of Materials on the Mexican American.* Austin: University of Texas Graduate School of Social Work, 1969.

––––––. *The Chicano Community: A Selected Bibliography for Use in Social Work Education.* New York: Council of Social Work Education, 1971.

Newell, Charldean, ed. *Bibliography on Texas Government.* Austin: Institute of Public Affairs, University of Texas, 1951 (with supplement, 1956).

Nogales, Luis G., ed. *The Mexican American: A Selected and Annotated Bibliography.* 2d ed., revised and enlarged. Stanford, Calif.: Center for Latin American Studies, Stanford University, 1971.

Ortego, Philip D. *Selective Mexican American Bibliography.* El Paso, Texas: Border Region Library Association, 1972.

Pino, Frank, comp. *Mexican Americans: A Research Bibliography.* 2 vols. East Lansing: Latin American Studies Center, Michigan State University, 1974.

Quintana, Helena, comp. *A Current Bibliography on Chicanos.* Albuquerque: University of New Mexico College of Education, 1974.

Ross, Stanley R. "Bibliography of Sources for Contemporary Mexican History." *Hispanic American Historical Review* 39 (1959): 234-38.

––––––. *Fuentes de la historia contemporánea de México, periódicos y revistas.* 2 vols. Mexico City: El Colegio de México, 1965-67.

––––––. *Fuentes de la historia contemporánea de México, periódicos y revistas, 1959-68.* 3 vols. Mexico City: UNAM, Centro de Estudios Bibliográficos de la Biblioteca Nacional, 1976-77.

Sánchez, George I., and Putnam, Howard, comps. "Materials Relating to the Education of Spanish Speaking People in the United States: An Annotated Bibliography." In Carlos E. Cortés, ed., *Mexican American Bibliographies.* New York: Arno Press, 1974.

Saunders, Lyle. *A Guide to Materials Bearing on Cultural Relations in New Mexico.* Albuquerque: University of New Mexico Press, 1944.

––––––. "Spanish Speaking Americans and Mexican Americans in the United States: A Selected Bibliography." In Carlos E. Cortés, ed., *Mexican American Bibliographies.* New York: Arno Press, 1974.

Stoddard, Ellwyn R., ed. "Bibliographical References." *The Social Science Journal* 12 (1975): 77-112.

––––––. "The Status of Borderlands Studies: An Introduction." *The Social Science Journal* 12 (1975): 3-8.

––––––. "The Status of Borderlands Studies: Sociology and Anthropology." *The Social Science Journal* 12 (1975): 29-54.

Talbot, Jane Mitchell, and Cruz, Gilbert R., eds. *A Comprehensive Chicano Bibliography, 1960-1972.* Austin, Texas: Jenkins Publishing Co., 1973.

Taylor, James R. "The Status of Borderlands Studies: Economics." *The Social Science Journal* 12 (1975): 69-76.

Ulloa, Berta. *La Revolución Mexicana, 1910-1920.* Mexico City: Secretaría de Relaciones Exteriores, 1963.

————. *La Revolución Mexicana a través del Archivo de la Secretaría de Relaciones Exteriores*. Mexico City: Universidad Nacional Autónoma de México, 1963.

United States. Department of Housing and Urban Development. *Hispanic Americans in the United States: A Selective Bibliography, 1963-1974*. Washington, D.C.: Government Printing Office, 1974.

United States. Interagency Committee on Mexican American Affairs. *The Mexican American: A New Focus on Opportunity: A Guide to Materials Relating to Persons of Mexican American Heritage in the United States*. Washington, D.C.: Educational Resources Information Center, 1969.

University of Houston Libraries. *Mexican Americans: A Selected Bibliography*. Houston, Texas, 1972.

University of Utah Libraries. *Chicano Bibliography*. Salt Lake City, 1971.

University of Utah Marriott Library. *Chicano Bibliography*. Salt Lake City, 1973.

Wagner, Henry R. *The Spanish Southwest, 1542-1794: An Annotated Bibliography*. 1937. Reprint. New York: Arno Press, 1967.

Wolf, T. Philip. *A Bibliography of New Mexico State Politics*. Albuquerque: Division of Government Research, University of New Mexico, 1974.

Woods, Richard D., *Reference Materials on Mexican Americans: An Annotated Bibliography*. Metuchen, N.J.: The Scarecrow Press, Inc., 1976.

Historical References

Alba, Víctor. *The Mexicans: The Making of a Nation*. New York: Praeger Publishers, 1967.

Alessio Robles, Vito. *Coahuila y Texas desde la consumación de la independencia hasta el tratado de paz de Guadalupe Hidalgo*. 2 vols. Mexico City, 1945-46.

————. *Coahuila y Texas en la época colonial*. Mexico City: Editorial Cultura, 1938.

Archer, Christon I. *The Army in Bourbon Mexico, 1760-1810*. Albuquerque: University of New Mexico Press, 1977.

Bancroft, Hubert Howe. *The Works of Hubert Howe Bancroft*. 39 vols. San Francisco: A. L. Bancroft & Co., 1882-90.

Bannon, John F. *The Spanish Borderlands Frontier, 1513-1821*. Albuquerque: University of New Mexico Press, 1974.

Bauer, Karl J. *The Mexican War, 1846-1848*. New York: Macmillan Co., 1974.

Beck, Warren A. *New Mexico: A History of Four Centuries*. Norman: University of Oklahoma Press, 1962.

Beezley, William H. *Insurgent Governor: Abraham González and the Mexican Revolution in Chihuahua*. Lincoln: University of Nebraska Press, 1973.

Bender, Averam B. *The March of Empire: Frontier Defense in the Southwest, 1848-1860*. New York: Greenwood Press, 1968.

Blaisdell, Lowell L. *The Desert Revolution: Baja California, 1911*. Madison: University of Wisconsin Press, 1962.

————. "Harry Chandler and Mexican Border Intrigue, 1914-1917." *Pacific Historical Review* 35 (1966): 385-93.

Bosch García, Carlos. *Historia de las relaciones entre México y los Estados Unidos, 1819-1848*. Mexico City: Universidad Nacional Autónoma de México, 1961.

————. *Problemas diplomáticos del México independiente*. Mexico City: El Colegio de México, 1947.

Brack, Gene M. *Mexico Views Manifest Destiny, 1821-1846: An Essay on the Origins of the Mexican War*. Albuquerque: University of New Mexico Press, 1975.

Braeman, John, et al., eds. *Twentieth Century American Foreign Policy*. Columbus: Ohio State University Press, 1971.

Brandenburg, Frank R. *The Making of Modern Mexico*. Englewood Cliffs, N.J.: Prentice-Hall, Inc., 1964.

Brooks, Philip C. *Diplomacy and the Borderlands: The Adams-Onís Treaty of 1819*. Berkeley: University of California Press, 1939.

Callcott, Wilfrid H. *Santa Anna: The Story of an Enigma Who Once Was Mexico*. Norman: University of Oklahoma Press, 1936.

Calvert, Peter. *The Mexican Revolution, 1910-1914: The Diplomacy of Anglo-American Conflict*. Cambridge: Cambridge University Press, 1968.

Carreño, Alberto María. *La diplomacia extraordinaria entre México y los Estados Unidos, 1789-1947*. 2 vols. Mexico City: Editorial Jus, 1951.

————. *México y los Estados Unidos de América*. 1922. Reprint. Mexico City: Editorial Jus, 1962.

Carreras de Velasco, Mercedes. *Los mexicanos que devolvió la crisis, 1929-1932*. Mexico City: Secretaría de Relaciones Exteriores, 1974.

Chávez Orozco, Luis. *Historia económica y social de México*. Mexico City: Ediciones Botas, 1938.

Clendenen, Clarence C. *Blood on the Border: The United States Army and the Mexican Irregulars*. New York: Macmillan Co., 1969.

————. *The United States and Pancho Villa: A Study in Unconventional Diplomacy*. Ithaca, N.Y.: Cornell University Press, 1961.

Cline, Howard F., *The United States and Mexico*. Rev. ed. Cambridge, Mass.: Harvard University Press, 1963.

Connor, Seymour V. *Texas: A History*. New York: Thomas Y. Crowell Co., 1971.

Cook, Sherburne F. *Erosion Morphology and Occupation History in Western Mexico*. Berkeley: University of California Press, 1963.

Cosío Villegas, Daniel. *American Extremes*. Translated by Américo Paredes. Austin: University of Texas Press, 1964.

————. *Los Estados Unidos contra Porfirio Díaz*. Mexico City: Editorial Hermes, 1956.

————. *Historia moderna de México*. 9 vols. in 10. Mexico City: Editorial Hermes, 1955-72.

Cue Cánovas, Agustín. *Los Estados Unidos y el México olvidado*. Mexico City: B. Costa-Amic, 1970.

————. *Ricardo Flores Magón, la Baja California, y los Estados Unidos*. Mexico City: Libro-Mex, 1957.

Cumberland, Charles C. *Mexican Revolution: The Constitutionalist Years*. Austin: University of Texas Press, 1972.

————. *Mexican Revolution: Genesis Under Madero*. Austin: University of Texas Press, 1952.

————. *Mexico: The Struggle for Modernity*. New York: Oxford University Press, 1968.

Divine, Robert A. *American Immigration Policy, 1924-1952*. New Haven, Conn.: Yale University Press, 1957.

Dusenberry, William H. *The Mexican Mesta: The Administration of Ranching in Colonial Mexico*. Urbana: University of Illinois Press, 1963.

Fabela, Isidro. *Historia diplomática de la Revolución Mexicana*. 2 vols. Mexico City: Fondo de Cultura Económica, 1958-59.

Faulk, Odie B. *Arizona: A Short History*. Norman: University of Oklahoma Press, 1970.

————. *Land of Many Frontiers: A History of the American Southwest*. New York: Oxford University Press, 1968.

————. *Too Far North–Too Far South: The Controversial Boundary Survey and the Gadsden Purchase*. Los Angeles: The Westernlore Press, 1967.

————, and Stout, Joseph A. Jr., eds. *The Mexican War: Changing Interpretations*. Chicago: Sage Books, 1973.

Forbes, Jack D. *Apache, Navajo, and Spaniard*. Norman: University of Oklahoma Press, 1960.

Frantz, Joe B., ed. *Texas and Its History*. Austin, Texas: Graphic Ideas, 1972.

Fuentes Díaz, Vicente. *La intervención norteamericana en México, 1847*. Mexico City: Imprenta Nuevo Mundo, 1947.

Fuentes Mares, José. *Juárez y los Estados Unidos*. Mexico City: Libro-Mex, 1960.

Fuller, John D. P. *The Movement for the Acquisition of All Mexico, 1846-1848*. Baltimore: The Johns Hopkins University Press, 1936.

Geijerstam, Claes af. *Popular Music in Mexico*. Albuquerque: University of New Mexico Press, 1976.

Gerhard, Peter. *A Guide to the Historical Geography of New Spain*. Cambridge: Cambridge University Press, 1972.

González Flores, Enrique. *Chihuahua de la Independencia a la Revolución*. Mexico City: Ediciones Botas, 1949.

González Navarro, Moisés. *La colonización en México, 1877-1910*. Mexico City, 1960.

———. *Las huelgas textiles en el porfiriato*. Puebla, Mexico: J. M. Cajica, 1970.

———. *México: El capitalismo nacionalista*. Mexico City: B. Costa-Amic, 1970.

Grieb, Kenneth J. *The United States and Huerta*. Lincoln: University of Nebraska Press, 1969.

Haley, P. Edward. *Revolution and Intervention: The Diplomacy of Taft and Wilson with Mexico, 1910-1917*. Cambridge: MIT Press, 1970.

Handlin, Oscar. *Children of the Uprooted*. New York: George Braziller, 1966.

———. *Race and Nationality in American Life*. Boston: Little, Brown, & Co., 1957.

———. *The Uprooted: The Epic Story of the Great Migrations That Made the American People*. Boston: Little, Brown, & Co., 1951.

Harris, Charles H., III. *A Mexican Family Empire: The Latifundio of the Sánchez Navarro Family, 1765-1867*. Austin: University of Texas Press, 1975.

Haystead, Ladd, and Fite, Gilbert C. *The Agricultural Regions of the United States*. Norman: University of Oklahoma Press, 1955.

Heizer, Robert F., and Almquist, Alan J. *The Other Californians: Prejudice and Discrimination Under Spain, Mexico, and the United States to 1920*. Berkeley: University of California Press, 1971.

Henry, Robert S. *The Story of the Mexican War*. 1950. Reprint. New York: F. Ungar Publishers, 1961.

Higham, John. *Strangers in the Land*. New Brunswick, N.J.: Rutgers University Press, 1955.

Hill, James E. "El Chamizal: A Century-Old Boundary Dispute." *The Geographical Review* 55 (1965): 510-22.

Hoffman, Abraham. *Unwanted Mexican Americans in the Great Depression: Repatriation Pressures, 1929-1939*. Tucson: University of Arizona Press, 1974.

Horgan, Paul. *Great River: The Rio Grande in North American History*. Rev. ed. 2 vols. in 1. New York: Holt, Rinehart, & Winston, 1960.

Hundley, Norris. *Dividing the Waters: A Century of Controversy Between the United States and Mexico*. Berkeley: University of California Press, 1966.

Hutchinson, Cecil Alan. *Frontier Settlement in Mexican California: The Híjar-Padrés Colony and Its Origins, 1769-1835*. New Haven, Conn.: Yale University Press, 1969.

John, Elizabeth A. H. *Storms Brewed in Other Men's Worlds: The Confrontation of Indians, Spaniards, and French in the Southwest, 1540-1795*. College Station: Texas A & M University Press, 1975.

Johnson, William Weber. *Heroic Mexico: The Violent Emergence of a Modern Nation*. New York: Doubleday & Co., 1968.

Jones, Robert C. *Mexican War Workers in the United States: The Mexico-United States Manpower Recruiting Program, 1942-1944*. Washington, D.C.: Pan-American Union, 1945.

Katz, Friedrich. *Diaz und die mexikanische Revolution: die deutsche Politik in Mexiko, 1870-1920*. Berlin: Deutscher Verlag der Wissenschaften, 1964.

Knauth, Josefina Vázquez de. *Nacionalismo y educación en México*. 2d ed. Mexico City: El Colegio de México, 1975.

Knowlton, Clark S., ed. "Spanish and Mexican Land Grants in the Southwest." *Social Science Journal* 13 (1976): 3-64.

Larson, Robert W. *New Mexico's Quest for Statehood, 1846-1912*. Albuquerque: University of New Mexico Press, 1968.

Lathrop, Barnes F. *Migration into East Texas, 1835-1860*. Austin: Texas State Historical Association, 1949.

Lewis, Archibald R., and McGann, Thomas F. *The New World Looks at Its History: Proceedings of the Second International Congress of Historians of the United States and Mexico, Austin, Texas, 1958*. Austin: University of Texas Institute of Latin American Studies, 1963.

Liss, Peggy. *Mexico Under Spain: 1521-1556. Society and the Origins of Nationality*. Chicago: University of Chicago Press, 1975.

Liss, Sheldon B. *A Century of Disagreement: The Chamizal Affair, 1864-1964*. Washington, D.C.: University Press of Washington, D.C., 1965.

López Cámara, Francisco. *La estructura económica y social de México en la época de la Reforma*. Mexico City: Siglo Veintiuno, 1967.

————. *La génesis de la conciencia liberal en México*. Mexico City: El Colegio de México, 1954.

Manning, William R. *Early Diplomatic Relations Between the United States and Mexico*. Baltimore: The Johns Hopkins University Press, 1916.

Mañach, Jorge. *Frontiers in the Americas: A Global Perspective*. Translated by Philip H. Phenix. New York: Teachers College Press, 1975.

Martínez, Pablo L. *Historia de Baja California*. 2d ed. Mexico City: Editorial Baja California, 1961.

Mendívil, José Abraham. *Cuarenta años de política en Sonora*. Hermosillo, Sonora: Imprenta Económica, 1965.

Mendizábal, Miguel O. de. *La evolución del noroeste de México*. Mexico City: Imprenta Mundial, 1930.

Meyer, Jean. *La Cristiada*, 3 vols. Translated by Aurelio Garzón del Camino. 3d ed. Mexico City: Siglo Veintiuno, 1974.

Meyer, Lorenzo. *Los grupos de presión extranjeros en el México revolucionario, 1910-1940*. Mexico City: Secretaría de Relaciones Exteriores, 1973

————. *México y los Estados Unidos en el conflicto petrolero, 1917-1942*. Mexico City: El Colegio de México, 1968.

Meyer, Michael C. *Huerta: A Political Portrait*. Lincoln: University of Nebraska Press, 1972.

————. *Mexican Rebel: Pascual Orozco and the Mexican Revolution, 1910-1915*. Lincoln: University of Nebraska Press, 1967.

Mörner, Magnus. *Race Mixture in the History of Latin America*. Boston: Little, Brown, & Co., 1967.

Nance, Joseph M. *After San Jacinto: The Texas-Mexican Frontier, 1836-1841*. Austin: University of Texas Press, 1963.

Peña, José E. de la. *With Santa Anna in Texas*. College Station: Texas A & M University Press, 1975.

Pitt, Leonard. *The Decline of the Californios: A Social History of the Spanish Speaking Californians, 1846-1890*. Berkeley: University of California Press, 1966.

Pletcher, David M. *The Diplomacy of Annexation: Texas, Oregon, and the Mexican War*. Columbia: University of Missouri Press, 1973.

Powell, Philip Wayne. *Soldiers, Indians and Silver: North America's First Frontier War*. Tempe: Arizona State University Press, 1975.

Price, Glenn W. *Origins of the War with Mexico: The Polk-Stockton Intrigue*. Austin: University of Texas Press, 1967.

Quirk, Robert E. *An Affair of Honor: Woodrow Wilson and the Occupation of Veracruz*. New York: McGraw-Hill, 1964.

Ramírez, José Fernando. *Mexico During the War with the United States.* Edited by Walter V. Scholes. Translated by Elliott B. Scherr. Columbia: University of Missouri Press, 1950.

Rasmussen, Wayne D. *A History of the Emergency Farm Labor Supply Program, 1943-1947.* Washington, D.C.: U.S. Department of Agriculture, 1951.

Rice, Elizabeth Ann. *The Diplomatic Relations Between the United States and Mexico, as Affected by the Struggle for Religious Liberty in Mexico, 1925-1929.* Washington, D.C.: Catholic University of America Press, 1959.

Rippy, J. Fred. *The United States and Mexico.* Rev. ed. New York: Alfred A. Knopf, 1931.

Rives, George L. *The United States and Mexico: 1821-1848.* 2 vols. New York: Charles Scribner's Sons, 1913.

Romero Flores, Jesús. *Historia de los estados de la República Mexicana.* Mexico City: Ediciones Botas, 1964.

Ross, Stanley R. *Francisco I. Madero, Apostle of Mexican Democracy.* 1955. Reprint. New York: AMS Press, 1970.

———, ed. *Is the Mexican Revolution Dead?* New York: Alfred A. Knopf, 1966.

Sauer, Carl Ortwain. *Sixteenth Century North America.* Berkeley: University of California Press, 1975.

Schmitt, Karl M. *Mexico and the United States, 1821-1973.* New York: John Wiley & Sons, 1974.

Scholes, Walter V. *Mexican Politics During the Juárez Regime: 1855-1872.* Columbia: University of Missouri Press, 1969.

Schroeder, John H. *Mr. Polk's War: American Opposition and Dissent, 1846-1848.* Madison: University of Wisconsin Press, 1973.

Scott, Robert E. *Mexican Government in Transition.* Urbana: University of Illinois Press, 1964.

Scruggs, Otey M. "The United States, Mexico, and the Wetbacks, 1942-1947." *Pacific Historical Review* 30 (1961): 149-64.

Simmons, Marc. *Spanish Government in New Mexico.* Albuquerque: University of New Mexico Press, 1968.

Simmons, Merle E. *The Mexican Corrido: As a Source for Interpretive Study of Modern Mexico (1870-1950).* New York: Kraus Reprint Company, 1969.

Simpson, Lesley Byrd. *Many Mexicos.* Rev. ed. Berkeley: University of California Press, 1964.

Singletary, Otis A. *The Mexican War.* Chicago: University of Chicago Press, 1960.

Smith, Justin H. *The War with Mexico.* 2 vols. New York: Macmillan Co., 1919.

Smith, Robert F. *The United States and Revolutionary Nationalism in Mexico, 1916-1932.* Chicago: University of Chicago Press, 1972.

Spicer, Edward H. *Cycles of Conquest: The Impact of Spain, Mexico, and the United States on the Indians of the Southwest.* Tucson: University of Arizona Press, 1962.

Tannenbaum, Frank. *Mexico: The Struggle for Peace and Bread.* New York: Alfred A. Knopf, 1950.

Teitelbaum, Louis M. *Woodrow Wilson and the Mexican Revolution, 1913-1916.* New York: Exposition Press, 1967.

Terrazas Sánchez, Filiberto. *La guerra apache en México: viento de octubre.* Mexico City: B. Costa-Amic, 1974.

Tuchman, Barbara. *The Zimmerman Telegram.* New York: Macmillan Co., 1966.

Tyler, Ronnie C. *The Mexican War: A Lithographic Record.* Austin: Texas State Historical Association, 1973.

———. *The Big Bend. A History of the Last Texas Frontier.* Washington, D.C.: Government Printing Office, 1975.

Ulloa, Berta. *La revolución intervenida: relaciones diplomáticas entre México y los Estados Unidos, 1910-1914.* Mexico City: El Colegio de México, 1971.

Valadés, Adrián. *Historia de Baja California, 1850-1880.* Mexico City: UNAM, 1974.

Valadés, José C. *Breve historia de la guerra con los Estados Unidos*. Mexico City: Editorial Patria, 1947.

———. *México, Santa Anna y la guerra de Texas*. 3d ed. Mexico City: Editores Mexicanos Unidos, 1965.

———. *El porfirismo; historia de un régimen*. 2 vols. Mexico City: Editorial Patria, 1948.

Villa, Eduardo W. *Historia del estado de Sonora*. Hermosillo, Sonora: Editorial Sonora, 1951.

Wagoner, Jay J. *Arizona Territory, 1863-1912: Political History*. Tucson: University of Arizona Press, 1970.

———. *Early Arizona: Prehistory to Civil War*. Tucson: University of Arizona Press, 1975.

Weems, John Edward. *To Conquer A Peace: The War Between the United States and Mexico*. Garden City, N. Y.: Doubleday & Co., 1974.

Whitaker, Arthur P. *The Mississippi Question, 1795-1803*. New York: Appleton-Century, 1934.

———. *The Spanish-American Frontier, 1783-1795*. Lincoln: University of Nebraska Press, 1969.

Wilkie, James W. *The Mexican Revolution: Federal Expenditure and Social Change Since 1910*. Berkeley: University of California Press, 1967.

Zavala, Silvio. *Los esclavos indios en Nueva España*. Mexico City: El Colegio Nacional, 1968.

Zorrilla, Luis G. *Historia de las relaciones entre México y los Estados Unidos de América, 1800-1958*. 2 vols. Mexico City: Editorial Porrúa, 1965.

Other Published Books and Articles

Acosta, Adalberto Joel. *Chicanos Can Make It*. New York: Vantage Press, 1971.

Acosta, P. B.; Aranda, R. G.; Lewis, J. S.; and Read, M. "Nutritional Status of Mexican American Preschool Children in a Border Town." *American Journal of Clinical Nutrition* 27, (1974): 1359-68.

Acuña, Rodolfo (see also Acuña, Rudolph F.). *Occupied America: The Chicano's Struggle Toward Liberation*. San Francisco: Canfield Press, 1972.

Acuña, Rudolph F. *Cultures in Conflict: The Problems of the Mexican Americans*. New York: Charter Publishers, 1970.

———. *A Mexican American Chronicle*. New York: American Book Co., 1971.

———. *The Story of the Mexican Americans: The Men and the Land*. New York: American Book Co., 1969.

Aguirre, L. R., et al. "La causa chicana: una familia unida." *Social Casework* 52 (1971): 259-324.

Aguirre Beltrán, Gonzalo. *El proceso de aculturación*. Mexico City: Universidad Nacional Autónoma de México, 1957.

Alford, Harold J. *The Proud Peoples: The Heritage and Culture of Spanish-Speaking Peoples in the United States*. New York: David McKay Co., 1972.

Alinsky, Saul. *Rules for Radicals*. New York: Random House, 1972.

Alisky, Marvin. *Government of the Mexican State of Nuevo León*. Tempe: The Center for Latin American Studies, Arizona State University, 1971.

———. *Guide to the Government of the Mexican State of Sonora*. Tempe: The Center for Latin American Studies, Arizona State University, 1971.

Allen, Steve. *The Ground Is Our Table*. New York: Doubleday & Co., 1966.

Almaguer, Tomás. "Historical Notes on Chicano Oppression: The Dialectics of Racial and Class Domination in North America." *Aztlán* 5 (1974): 27-56.

Almond, Gabriel, and Sydney Verba. *The Civic Culture: Political Attitudes and Democracy in Five Nations*. Princeton, N. J.: Princeton University Press, 1963.

Alvarez, Rodolfo. "The Psycho-historical and Socioeconomic Development of the Chicano Community in the United States." *Social Science Quarterly* 53 (1973): 920-42.

————."The Unique Psycho-historical Experience of the Mexican-American People." *Social Science Quarterly* 52 (1971): 15-29.

American Ethnological Society. *Proceedings of the 1968 Annual Spring Meeting, Seattle, Washington*. Seattle: University of Washington Press, 1968.

————. *Spanish Speaking People in the United States*. Seattle: University of Washington Press, 1969.

Anderson, Henry. *Fields of Bondage*. Salinas, Calif.: H. Anderson, 1963.

Anderson, Henry P. *The Bracero Program in California, with Particular Reference to Health Status, Attitudes, and Practices*. Berkeley: University of California School of Public Health, 1961.

Anderson, James G., and Johnson, William M. *Socio-cultural Determinants of Achievement Among Mexican-American Students*. Las Cruces: New Mexico State University, 1968.

Applegate, Howard G., and Bath, C. Richard, eds. *Air Pollution Along the United States-Mexican Border*. El Paso: Texas Western Press, 1974.

Arbingast, Stanley A., ed. *Atlas of Texas*. Austin: University of Texas Bureau of Business Research, 1963.

Aronson, E. "The Jigsaw Route to Learning and Liking." *Psychology Today*, February (1975) pp. 43-50.

Aschmann, Homer. *The Central Desert of Baja California: Demography and Ecology*. Riverside, Calif.: Manessier Publishing Co., 1967.

Baerresen, Donald W. *The Border Industrialization Program of Mexico*. Lexington, Mass.: D.C. Heath & Co., 1971.

Baker, B. Lea. *Economic Aspects of Mexican and Mexican-American Urban Households*. San Jose, Calif.: San Jose State College Institute for Business and Economic Research, 1971.

Balan, Jorge; Browning, Harley L.; and Jelin, Elizabeth. *Men in a Developing Society: Geographic and Social Mobility in Monterrey, México*. Austin: University of Texas Press, 1973.

Ballis, George. *¡Basta! la historia de nuestra lucha*. Delano, Calif.: Farm Workers Press, 1966.

Banton, Michael, ed. *The Social Anthropology of Complex Societies*. New York: Frederick A. Praeger, 1966.

Barker, George C. *Pachuco: An American-Spanish Argot and Its Social Functions in Tucson, Arizona*. Tucson: University of Arizona Press, 1958.

Barona Lobato, Juan. "Legal Considerations, Interpretations and Projections of Minute 242." *Natural Resources Journal* 15 (1975): 35-42.

Barrera, Mario. "The Study of Politics and the Chicano." *Aztlán* 5 (1974): 9-26.

Bassols Batalla, Angel. *Los aspectos geoeconómicos y humanos de la explotación en el territorio de la Baja California*. Mexico City: Sociedad Mexicana de Geografía y Estadística, 1959.

Beals, Ralph, and Humphrey, Norman. *No Frontier to Learning: The Mexican American Student in the United States*. Minneapolis: University of Minnesota Press, 1957.

Bean, Frank. "Components of Income and Expected Family Size Among Mexican Americans." *Social Science Quarterly* 54 (1973): 103-16.

————, and Bradshaw, Benjamin S. "Intermarriage Between Persons of Spanish and Non-Spanish Surname: Changes From the Mid-Nineteenth to the Mid-Twentieth Centuries." *Social Science Quarterly* 51 (1970): 389-95.

Beck, J. M., and Saxe, R. W. *Teaching the Culturally Disadvantaged Pupil*. Springfield, Ill.: Charles C. Thomas, 1969.

Beegle, J. Allan, et al. "Demographic Characteristics of the United States-Mexico Border." *Rural Sociology* 25 (1960): 107-62.

Belshaw, Michael H. *A Village Economy: The Land and People of Huecorio*. New York: Columbia University Press, 1967.

Bigart, Robert J. "The Social Cost of Space." *Rocky Mountain Social Science Journal* 9 (1972): 111-15.

Bishop, Charles E. *Farm Labor in the United States.* New York: Columbia University Press, 1967.

Blalock, Hubert M. *Toward a Theory of Minority Group Relations.* New York: John Wiley & Sons, 1967.

Bonine, Michael F.; Holz, Robert K.; Gill, Clark C.; Weiler, James P.; and Arbingast, Stanley A., eds. *Atlas of Mexico.* Austin: University of Texas, Bureau of Business Research, 1970.

Borah, Woodrow, and Cook, Sherburne F. "Marriage and Legitimacy in Mexican Culture: Mexico and California." *California Law Review* 54 (1966): 946-1008.

Brace, Clayton, et al. *Federal Programs to Improve Mexican American Education.* Washington, D.C.: U.S. Office of Education, 1967.

Bradshaw, Benjamin S., and Bean, Frank D., "Trends in the Fertility of Mexican Americans, 1950-1970." *Social Science Quarterly* 53 (1973): 688-96.

Brawner, Marlyn R. "Migration and Educational Achievement of Mexican Americans." *Social Science Quarterly* 53 (1973): 727-37.

Briggs, Vernon M., Jr. *Chicanos and Rural Poverty.* Baltimore: The Johns Hopkins University Press, 1973.

———. "Chicanos and Rural Poverty: A Continuing Issue for the 1970's." *Poverty and Human Resources Abstracts* 7 (1972): 3-24.

———. *The Mexico-United States Border: Public Policy and Chicano Welfare.* Austin: University of Texas Center for the Study of Human Resources and Bureau of Business Research, 1974.

Brody, Eugene B., ed. *Minority Group Adolescents in the United States.* Baltimore: Williams and Wilkins, 1968.

Brooks, Melvin S. *The Social Problems of Migrant Farm Laborers: Effect of Migrant Farm Labor on the Education of Children.* Carbondale: Southern Illinois University Press, 1960.

Browning, Harley L., and McLemore, S. Dale. *A Statistical Profile of the Spanish-Surname Population of Texas.* Austin: University of Texas Bureau of Business Research, 1964.

Brussel, Charles B. *Disadvantaged Mexican American Children and Early Educational Experience.* Austin, Texas: Southwest Educational Development Corp., 1968.

Bullogh, Bonnie. "Poverty, Ethnic Identity and Preventive Health Care." *Journal of Health and Social Behavior* 13 (1972): 347-59.

Burma, John H., ed. *Mexican Americans in the United States: A Reader.* Cambridge, Mass.: Schenkman Publishing Co., 1970.

———. *Spanish Speaking Groups in the United States.* Durham, N.C.: Duke University Press, 1954. Reprint. Detroit, Mich.: Blaine Ethridge Books, 1974.

Busch, Arthur W. "Use and Abuse of Natural Water Systems." *Journal of the Water Pollution Control Federation* 43 (1971): 1480-83.

Bushnell, Eleanor, ed. *The Impact of Reapportionment on the Thirteen Western States.* Salt Lake City: University of Utah Press, 1970.

Bustamante, Jorge Agustín. "Don Chano: autobiografía de un emigrante mexicano." *Revista Mexicana de Sociología* 33 (1972): 333-74.

———. "El espalda mojada: informe de un observador participante." *Revista Mexicana de Ciencia Política* 71 (January-March 1973): 81-107.

———. "The Historical Context of the Undocumented Immigration From Mexico." *Aztlán* 3 (1972): 257-81.

———. "The Wetback as Deviant: An Application of Labeling Theory." *American Journal of Sociology* 77 (1972): 706-18.

Cabrera, Luis. "Use of the Waters of the Colorado River in Mexico: Pertinent Technical Commentaries." *Natural Resources Journal* 15 (1975): 27-34.

Cabrera, Ysidro Arturo. *Emerging Faces: The Mexican Americans*. Dubuque, Iowa: William C. Brown Co., 1971.

————. *A Study of American and Mexican American Culture Values and Their Significance in Education*. San Francisco: R & E Research Associates, 1972.

Cahiers des Ameriques Latines, no. 12 (1975). Special issue devoted to "Les Migrations Au Mexique." Paris: Institut des Hautes Etudes de l'Amérique Latine, Université de la Sorbonne Nouvelle, Actes du ler Colloque Franco-Mexicain, May 1975.

California. State Department of Education. Mexican American Research Project. *Report*. Sacramento, 1968.

California. State Department of Employment. *Report to the Legislature on Spanish Speaking Californians*. Sacramento, 1968.

California. Office of Economic Opportunity. *California Migrant Master Plan*. Sacramento, 1966-67.

Callahan, James M. *American Foreign Policy in Mexican Relations*. New York: Cooper Square, 1967.

Campa, Arthur L. *Treasure of the Sangre de Cristos: Tales and Traditions of the Spanish Southwest*. Norman: University of Oklahoma Press, 1963.

Candelas, J.P., "El Instituto de Seguridad y Servicios Sociales de los Trabajadores del Estado y la salud pública de la frontera mexicana-estadounidense." *Salud Pública de México* 13 (1971): 195-208.

Carranza, Eliu. *Pensamientos en los Chicanos: A Cultural Revolution*. Berkeley: California Book Co., 1969.

Carter, Thomas P. *Mexican Americans in School: A History of Educational Neglect*. Princeton, N.J.: College Entrance Examination Board, 1970.

Castañeda, Alfredo; Ramírez, III, Manuel; Cortés, Carlos E.; and Barrera, Mario, eds. *Mexican Americans and Educational Change*. New York: Arno Press, 1974

Castellanos, M. *Plan de salud del estado de Baja California*. Mexico City: Primera Convención Nacional de Salud, 1973.

Castro, Tony. *Chicano Power: The Emergence of Mexican America*. New York: Saturday Review Press, 1974.

Caughey, John W. "The Spanish Southwest: An Example of Subconscious Regionalism." In Merrill Jensen, ed., *Regionalism in America*. Madison: University of Wisconsin Press, 1952.

Clark, Margaret. *Health in the Mexican American Culture: A Community Study*. Berkeley: University of California Press, 1970.

Coles, Robert. *The Old Ones of New Mexico*. Albuquerque: University of New Mexico Press, 1973.

Coltharp, Lurline. *The Tongue of the Tirilones: A Linguistic Study of a Criminal Argot*. Alabama Linguistic and Philological Series no. 7. University: University of Alabama Press, 1965.

Cooney, Rosemary Santana. "Changing Labor Force Participation of Mexican American Wives: A Comparison With Anglos and Blacks." *Social Science Quarterly* 56 (1975): 262-73.

Corwin, Arthur F. "Causes of Mexican Emigration to the United States: A Summary View." *Perspectives in American History* 7 (1973): 557-635.

————. *Contemporary Mexican Attitudes Toward Population, Poverty, and Public Opinion*. Gainesville: University of Florida Press, 1963.

————. "Mexican American History: An Assessment." *Pacific Historical Review* 42 (1973): 269-308.

Craig, Richard B. *The Bracero Program: Interest Groups and Foreign Policy*. Austin: University of Texas Press, 1971.

D'Antonio, William V., and Form, William H. *Influentials in Two Border Cities: A Study in Community Decision-Making*. Notre Dame, Ind.: University of Notre Dame Press, 1965.

————, et al. "Institutional and Occupational Representations in Eleven Community Influence Systems." *American Sociological Review* 26 (1961): 440-45.

————, and Samora, Julian. "Occupational Stratification in Four Southwestern Communities." *Social Forces* 41 (1962): 14-25.

Davidson, Chandler, and Gaitz, Charles M. "Ethnic Attitudes as a Basis for Minority Cooperation in a Southwestern Metropolis." *Social Science Quarterly* 53 (1973): 738-48.

Davis, Richard H. *Health Services and the Mexican American Elderly.* Los Angeles: The Ethel Percy Andrews Gerontology Center and the University of Southern California Press, 1973.

Day, Mark. *Forty Acres: César Chávez and the Farm Workers.* New York: Frederick A. Praeger, 1971.

Díaz Gómez, Cutberto, ed. *México: sus necesidades, sus recursos.* Mexico City: Editora Técnica, 1970.

Díaz-Guerrero, Rogelio. *Estudios de psicología del mexicano.* 3d ed. Mexico City: F. Trillas, 1970.

————. "Neurosis and the Mexican Family Structure." *American Journal of Psychiatry* (1975): 411-17.

————. "Youth in Mexico." In J. H. Masserman, ed. *Current Psychiatric Therapies.* Vol. 14. New York: Grune and Stratton, 1969, pp. 121-35.

Dillman, C. Daniel. "Border Town Symbiosis Along the Lower Rio Grande as Exemplified by the Twin Cities, Brownsville, Texas, and Matamoros, Tamaulipas." *Revista Geográfica* 71 (1969): 93-113.

————. "Commuter Workers and Free Zone Industry Along the United States-Mexican Border." *Proceedings of the Association of American Geographers* 2 (1970): 48-51.

————. "Urban Growth Along Mexico's Northern Border and the Mexican National Border Program." *The Journal of Developing Areas* 4 (1970): 487-507.

Dolbeare, Kenneth, and Edelman, Murray, eds. *American Politics: Policies, Power, and Change.* Lexington, Mass.: D. C. Heath & Co., 1971.

Donnelly, Thomas C. *The Government of New Mexico.* Albuquerque: University of New Mexico Press, 1953.

Dregne, H. E. "Salinity Aspects of the Colorado River Agreement." *Natural Resources Journal* 15 (1975): 43-54.

Dunbier, Roger. *The Sonoran Desert: Its Geography, Economy, and People.* Tucson: University of Arizona Press, 1968.

Eaton, Joseph W. *Measuring Delinquency: A Study of Probation Department Referrals.* Pittsburgh: University of Pittsburgh Press, 1961.

Edgerton, Robert B., and Plog, Stanley C., eds. *Changing Perspectives in Mental Illness.* New York: Holt, Rinehart, & Winston, 1969.

————, Karno, Marvin and Fernández, Irma. "Curanderismo in the Metropolis: The Diminished Role of Folk Psychiatry Among Los Angeles Mexican Americans." *American Journal of Psychotherapy* 24 (1970): 124-34.

Edwards, Esther P. "Children of Migratory Agricultural Workers in the Public Elementary Schools in the United States: Needs and Proposals in the Area of Curriculum." *Harvard Educational Review* 30 (1966): 12-52.

Emerson, Thomas Irwin. *Political and Civil Rights in the United States: A Collection of Legal and Related Materials.* Boston: Little, Brown, & Co., 1967.

Escoto Ochoa, Humberto. *Integración y desintegración de nuestra frontera norte.* Mexico City: Editorial Stylo, 1949.

Espejo, José A. *Geografía de Chihuahua.* Mexico City: Editorial El Nacional, 1951.

Estrada, Leo, et al., eds. *Cuántos Somos: The Impoverished Demography on Chicanos.* Austin: University of Texas, Mexican American Studies Program, forthcoming.

Evans, Norman A. "The Salt Problem in the Colorado River." *Natural Resources Journal* 15 (1975): 55-62.

Fabila, Alfonso. *El problema de la emigración de obreros y campesinos mexicanos.* Mexico City: Talleres Gráficos de la Nación, 1928.

Fabrega, Horacio, Jr., and Roberts, Robert. "Ethnic Differences in the Outpatient Use of a Public Charity Hospital." *American Journal of Public Health* 62 (1972): 936-41.

Fagen, Richard R., and Touhy, William S. *Politics and Privilege in a Mexican City.* Stanford: Stanford University Press, 1972.

Farías, L. M. *Plan de salud del estado de Nuevo León.* Mexico City: Primera Convención Nacional de Salud, 1973.

Felice, Lawrence G. "Mexican American Self-concept and Educational Achievement: The Effects of Ethnic Isolation and Socioeconomic Deprivation." *Social Science Quarterly* 53 (1973): 716-26.

Ferman, Louis A. *Poverty in America.* Ann Arbor: University of Michigan Press, 1968.

Fernández, C. J., and Vides, M. T. "Situación epidemiológica en la frontera norte de México y programa de vigilancia." *Salud Pública de México* 12 (1970): 161-82.

Fisher, Lloyd H. *The Harvest Labor Market in California.* Cambridge, Mass.: Harvard University Press, 1953.

Flores, Edmundo. *Vieja revolución, nuevos problemas.* Mexico City: Joaquín Mortíz, 1970.

———. *Tratado de economía agrícola.* Mexico City: Fondo de Cultura Económica, 1961.

Fogel, Walter. *Education and Income of Mexican Americans in the Southwest.* University of California Mexican American Study Project, Advance Report no. 1. Los Angeles: Graduate School of Business Administration, University of California, 1965.

———. *Mexican Americans in Southwest Labor Markets.* University of California Mexican American Study Project, Advance Report no. 10. Los Angeles: Graduate School of Business Administration, University of California, 1967.

Forbes, Jack D. ed. *Aztecas del Norte: The Chicanos of Aztlán.* Greenwich, Conn.: Fawcett Publications, 1973.

———. "Black Pioneers: The Spanish Speaking Afroamericans of the Southwest." *Phylon* 27 (1966): 233-46.

Form, William H., and Rivera, Julius. "The Place of Returning Migrants in a Stratification System." *Rural Sociology* 23 (1958): 286-97.

Foster, George M. *Culture and Conquest: America's Spanish Heritage.* Chicago: Quadrangle Books, 1960.

———. *Problems in Intercultural Health Programs.* New York: Social Science Research Council, 1958.

———. *Traditional Societies and Technological Change.* New York: Harper & Row, 1973.

Freithaler, William O. *Mexico's Foreign Trade and Economic Development.* New York: Frederick A. Praeger, 1968.

Friedland, W. H., and Nelkin, Dorothy. *Migrant: Agricultural Workers in America's Northeast.* New York: Holt, Rinehart and Winston, 1971.

Friedrich, Paul. *Agrarian Revolt in a Mexican Village.* Englewood Cliffs, N.J.: Prentice-Hall, Inc., 1970.

Frisbie, Parker. "Militancy Among Mexican American High School Students." *Social Science Quarterly* 53 (1973): 865-83.

Fromm, Erich, and Maccoby, Michael. *Social Character in a Mexican Village.* Englewood Cliffs, N.J.: Prentice-Hall, Inc., 1970.

Fuller, Varden. *No Work Today! The Plight of America's Migrants.* Public Affairs Pamphlet no. 190, New York, n. d.

Furnish, Dale Beck, and Ladman, Jerry R. "The Colorado River Salinity Agreement of 1973 and the Mexicali Valley." *Natural Resources Journal* 15 (1975): 83-108.

Galbraith, John Kenneth. *American Capitalism: The Concept of Countervailing Power.* Rev. ed. Boston: Houghton Mifflin Co., 1956.

Galarza, Ernesto. *Barrio Boy.* Notre Dame, Ind.: University of Notre Dame Press, 1971.

————. *Merchants of Labor: The Mexican Bracero Story.* Charlotte, N.C., and Santa Barbara, Calif.: McNally & Loftin, 1964.

————. *Mexican Americans in the Southwest.* Santa Barbara, Calif.: McNally & Loftin, 1964.

————. *Spiders in the House and Workers in the Field.* Notre Dame, Ind.: University of Notre Dame Press, 1970.

Gallardo, Lloyd. *Mexican Green Carders: Preliminary Report.* Washington, D.C.: U.S. Department of Labor, Bureau of Employment Security, 1962.

Gamio, Manuel. *Forjando patria.* 2d ed. Mexico City: Editorial Porrúa, 1960.

————. *The Mexican Immigrant: His Life Story, with Autobiographical Documents.* 1931. Reprint. New York: Arno Press, 1969.

————. *Mexican Immigration to the United States.* 1930. Reprint. New York: Arno Press, 1969.

————. *Número, procedencia y distribución geográfica de los inmigrantes mexicanos en los Estados Unidos.* Mexico City: Talleres Gráficos Editorial y "Diario Oficial," 1930.

García, A. C. "Evaluación de los centros de salud de la frontera norte." *Salud Pública de México* 12 (1970): 140-59.

Garcia, F. Chris. *La Causa Politica: A Chicano Political Reader.* Notre Dame, Ind.: University of Notre Dame Press, 1974.

————. *Chicano Politics: Readings.* New York: MSS Information Corp., 1973.

————. "Manitos and Chicanos in Nuevo México Politics." *Aztlán* 5 (1974): 177-88.

————. "Orientations of Mexican American and Anglo Children Toward The United States Political Community." *Social Science Quarterly* 53 (1973): 814-29.

————. *The Political Socialization of Chicano Children: A Comparative Study with Anglos in California Schools.* New York: Frederick A. Praeger, 1973.

García Robles, Alfonso. *The Denuclearization of Latin America.* New York: Carnegie Endowment for International Peace, 1967.

Gardner, B. Delworth, and Stewart, Clyde E. "Agriculture and Salinity Control in the Colorado River Basin." *Natural Resources Journal* 15 (1975): 63-82.

Gardner, Richard. *Grito! Reies Tijerina and the New Mexico Land Grant War of 1967.* Indianapolis, Ind.: The Bobbs-Merrill Co., 1970.

Garza, Rudolph O. de la. "Voting Patterns in 'Bi-Cultural' El Paso: A Contextual Analysis of Chicano Voting Behavior." *Aztlán* 5 (1974): 235-60.

————, et al., eds. *Chicanos and Native Americans: The Territorial Minorities.* Englewood Cliffs, N.J.: Prentice-Hall, Inc., 1973.

Gecas, Viktor. "Self-conceptions of Migrant and Settled Mexican Americans." *Social Science Quarterly* 54, (1973): 579-95.

Gerson, Louis L. *The Hyphenate in Recent American Politics and Diplomacy.* Lawrence: University of Kansas Press, 1964.

Gilbert, A., and O'Rourke, P. F. "Effects of Rural Poverty on the Health of California's Farm Workers." *Public Health Reports* 83 (1968): 827-38.

Gilmore, N. Ray, and Gilmore, Gladys W. "The Bracero in California." *Pacific Historical Review* 32 (1963): 265-82.

Glade, William P., and Anderson, Charles W. *The Political Economy of Mexico.* Madison: University of Wisconsin Press, 1963.

Glenn, Norval. "Some Reflections on a Landmark Publication and the Literature on Mexican Americans." *Social Science Quarterly* 52 (1971): 8-10.

Gómez, David F. *Somos Chicanos: Strangers in Our Own Land.* Boston: Beacon Press, 1973.

Gomez, Rudolph, ed. *The Changing Mexican American.* Boulder, Colo.: Pruett Press, 1972.

————; Cottingham, Jr., Clement; Endo, Russell; and Jackson, Kathleen, eds. *The Social Reality of Ethnic America.* Lexington, Mass.: D. C. Heath & Co., 1974.

González, G. L., and Intriago, M. R. "Estudio sobre los recursos para la salud en Matamoros, Tamaulipas." *Salud Pública de México* 14 (1972): 697-706.

González, Nancie L. *The Spanish Americans of New Mexico: A Distinctive Heritage.* University of California Mexican American Study Project, Advance Report no. 9. Los Angeles: University of California, 1967.

———. *The Spanish Americans of New Mexico: A Heritage of Pride.* Albuquerque: University of New Mexico Press, 1969.

González, Simón. *Education for Minorities: The Mexican Americans.* New York: John Wiley & Sons, 1971.

González Casanova, Pablo. *La democracia en México.* Mexico City: Ediciones Era, 1965.

González de León, A. "The Mexican Position: National and International Considerations." *Natural Resources Journal* 15 (1975): 109-112.

González Piñeda, Francisco, and Humeau, Antonio del. *Los mexicanos frente al poder.* Mexico City: Instituto Mexicano de Estudios Politicos, 1973.

González Salazar, Gloria. *Subocupación y estructura de clases sociales en México.* Mexico City: Universidad Nacional Autónoma de México, 1972.

Gordon, Milton M. *Assimilation in American Life: The Role of Race, Religion and National Origins.* New York: Oxford University Press, 1964.

Graham, Lawrence. *Politics in a Mexican Community.* Gainesville: University of Florida Press, 1968.

Grebler, Leo. *Mexican Immigration to the United States: The Record and Its Implications.* University of California Mexican American Study Project, Advance Report no. 2. Los Angeles: University of California, 1966.

———. *The Schooling Gap: Signs of Progress.* University of California Mexican American Study Project, Advance Report no. 7. Los Angeles: University of California, 1967.

———. Moore, Joan W.; and Guzman, Ralph C. *The Mexican American People: The Nation's Second Largest Minority.* New York: The Free Press, 1970.

Greenburg, Martin H. *Bureaucracy and Development: A Mexican Case Study.* Lexington, Mass.: D. C. Heath & Co., 1970.

Griffith, Beatrice W. *American Me.* Boston: Houghton Mifflin, 1948.

Grimes, Allan Pendleton. *Equality in America: Religion, Race, and the Urban Majority.* New York: Oxford University Press, 1964.

Gutiérrez, Armando, and Hirsch, Herbert. "The Militant Challenge to the American Ethos: 'Chicanos' and 'Mexican Americans.' " *Social Science Quarterly* 53 (1973): 830-45.

———, and Hirsch, Herbert. "Political Maturation and Political Awareness: The Case of the Crystal City Chicano." *Aztlán* 5 (1974): 295-312.

Gutiérrez, T. E. *Plan de salud del estado de Coahuila.* Mexico City: Primera Convención Nacional de Salud, 1973.

Haddox, John. *Los Chicanos: An Awakening People.* El Paso: Texas Western Press, 1970.

Hancock, Richard H. *The Role of the Bracero in the Economic and Cultural Dynamics of Mexico: A Case Study of Chihuahua.* Stanford: Stanford University Press, 1959.

Hansen, Roger D. *The Politics of Mexican Development.* Baltimore: The Johns Hopkins University Press, 1971.

Harrington, Michael. *The Other America: Poverty in the United States.* New York: Macmillan Co., 1962.

Hedrick, Basil C. J.; Kelley, Charles; and Riley, Carroll J., eds. *The North Mexican Frontier: Readings in Archaeology, Ethnohistory and Ethnography.* Carbondale: Southern Illinois University Press, 1971.

Heffernan, Helen. *Reality, Responsibility and Respect in the Education of Children from Families Who Follow the Crops.* Sacramento, Calif.: State Department of Education, 1964.

Heins, Marjorie. *Strictly Ghetto Property: The Story of Los Siete de la Raza.* Berkeley: Ramparts Press, 1972.

Heist, Elizabeth H. "Border Music of the 1970s in the Southwestern United States." In Claes af Geijerstam, *Popular Music in Mexico.* Albuquerque: University of New Mexico Press, 1976.

Heller, Celia S. *Mexican American Youth: Forgotten Youth at the Crossroads*. New York: Random House, 1966.

———. *New Converts to the American Dream? The Mobility Aspirations of Young Mexican Americans*. New Haven, Conn.: College and University Press, 1971.

Henshel, Anne-Marie. *The Forgotten Ones: A Sociological Study of Anglo and Chicano Retardates*. Austin: University of Texas Press, 1972.

Hernández, John W. *The Rio Grande Environmental Project*. Las Cruces: New Mexico State University Water Resources Research Institute, 1973.

Hernández, José; Estrada, Leo; and Alvírez, David. "Census Data and the Problem of Conceptually Defining the Mexican American Population." *Social Science Quarterly* 53 (1973): 671-87.

Hernández, Norma G. "Variables Affecting Achievement of Middle School Mexican American Students." *Review of Educational Research* 43 (1973): 1-40.

Hernández Vela Salgado, Edmundo. "Principal Economic Aspects of the Problem of Salinity of the Colorado River." *Natural Resources Journal* 15 (1975): 129-34.

Hidalgo, Ernesto. *La protección de mexicanos en los Estados Unidos*. Mexico City: Secretaría de Relaciones Exteriores, 1940.

Hiestand, Dale L. *Economic Growth and Employment Opportunities for Minorities*. New York: Columbia University Press, 1964.

Hoff, W. "Why Health Programs Are Not Reaching the Unresponsive in Our Communities." *Public Health Reports* 81 (1966): 654-58.

Holburt, Myron B. "International Problems of the Colorado River." *Natural Resources Journal* 15 (1975): 11-26.

Holtzman, Wayne H. "Cross-Cultural Research on Personality." In N. S. Endler, et al., eds. *Contemporary Issues in Developmental Psychology*. New York: Holt, Rinehart, & Winston, 1968.

———. *Holtzman Inkblot Technique*. New York: Psychological Corporation, 1961.

———, et al. *Inkblot Perception and Personality*. Austin: University of Texas Press, 1961.

———, et al. *Personality Development in Two Cultures: A Cross-Cultural Longitudinal Study of School Children in Mexico and the United States*. Austin: University of Texas Press, 1975.

Hughes, Everett Cherrington. *Where People Meet: Racial and Ethnic Frontiers*. Glencoe, Ill.: The Free Press, 1952.

Hundley, Norris. "The Politics of Water and Geography: California and the Mexican-American Treaty of 1944." *Pacific Historical Review* 36 (1967): 209-26.

Institute for Personal Effectiveness in Children. *Mexican American Housing Patterns: The Relationship of Mexican American Living Patterns to Housing Design*. 10 vols. San Diego, Calif., 1971.

Inter-American Development Bank. *Economic and Social Progress in Latin America, Annual Report*. Washington, D.C., 1973.

Jaco, E. Gartly, ed. *Patients, Physicians and Illness*. Glencoe, Ill.: The Free Press, 1956.

———. *The Social Epidemiology of Mental Disorder: A Psychiatric Survey of Texas*. New York: Russell Sage Foundation, 1960.

Jenkinson, Michael. *Tijerina: The Land Grant Conflict in New Mexico*. Albuquerque, N.M.: Paisano Press, 1970.

Johnson, Henry S., and Hernández, William J., eds. *Educating the Mexican American*. Valley Forge, Pa.: Judson Press, 1970.

Juárez, Albert. "The Emergence of El Partido de la Raza Unida: California's New Chicano Party." *Aztlán* 3 (1972): 177-205.

Jurado, Miguel David. "Mexican American Community Political Organization: The Key to Chicano Political Power." *Aztlán* 1 (1970): 53-79.

Kagan, Spencer, and Madsen, Millard C. "Cooperation and Competition of Mexican, Mexican

American, and Anglo American Children of Two Ages Under Four Instructional Sets." *Developmental Psychology* 5 (1971): 32-39.

———. "Rivalry in Anglo American and Mexican Children of Two Ages." *Journal of Personality and Social Psychology* 24 (1972): 214-20.

Kaplan, Robert M., and Goldman, Roy D. "Interracial Perception Among Black, White, and Mexican American High School Students." *Journal of Personality and Social Psychology* 28 (1973): 383-89.

Karno, Marvin, and Edgerton, Robert B. "Perceptions of Mental Illness in a Mexican American Community." *Archives of General Psychiatry* 20 (1969): 233-38.

Kelly, Isabel. *Folk Practices in North Mexico: Birth Customs, Folk Medicine, and Spiritualism in the Laguna Zone.* Austin: University of Texas Press, 1965.

Kibbe, Pauline R. *Latin Americans in Texas.* Albuquerque: University of New Mexico Press, 1946.

Kidder, Alfred V. *An Introduction to the Study of Southwestern Archaeology.* New Haven, Conn.: Yale University Press, 1963.

Kiev, Ari. *Curanderismo: Mexican American Folk Psychiatry.* New York: The Free Press, 1968.

Klapp, Orin E., and Padgett, L. Vincent. "Power Structure and Decision Making in a Mexican Border City." *American Journal of Sociology* 65 (1960): 400-406.

Kling, Merle. *A Mexican Interest Group in Action.* Englewood Cliffs, N.J.: Prentice-Hall, Inc., 1961.

Kneese, Allen V. "A Theoretical Analysis of Minute 242." *Natural Resources Journal* 15 (1975): 135-40.

Knowlton, Clark S. "Cultural Factors in the Non-delivery of Medical Servies to Southwestern Mexican Americans." In M. L. Riedesec, ed., *Health Related Problems in Arid Lands.* Tempe: Arizona State University Press, 1971.

———, ed. *Indian and Spanish American Adjustments to Arid and Semiarid Environments: A Symposium Held During the Fortieth Annual Meeting of the Southwestern and Rocky Mountain Division of the American Association for the Advancement of Science, Lubbock, Texas, April 1964.* Lubbock: Texas Technological College, 1964.

———. "Patron-Peon Pattern Among the Spanish Americans of New Mexico." *Social Forces* 10 (1962): 12-17.

———. "The Special Education Problems of the Mexican Americans." In Sterling M. McMurrin, ed., *The Conditions for Educational Equality.* New York: Committee for Economic Development, 1971.

Kurtz, Donald V. *The Politics of a Poverty Habitat.* Cambridge, Mass.: Ballinger Publishing Co., 1973.

Kushner, Sam. *Long Road to Delano.* New York: International Publishers, 1975.

LaBrucherie, Roger A. "Aliens in the Fields: The Green Card Commuters Under the Immigration and Naturalization Laws." *Stanford Law Review* 21 (1969): 1750-76.

Ladman, Jerry R., and Poulson, Mark O. *Economic Impact of the Mexican Border Industrialization Program: Agua Prieta, Sonora, Special Study no. 12.* Tempe: State University Center for Latin American Studies, 1972.

Lamb, Ruth. *Mexican Americans: Sons of the Southwest.* Claremont, Calif.: Ocelot Press, 1970.

Lázaro Salinas, José. *La emigración de braceros.* Mexico City, 1955.

Leal Carrillo, Stella. *Importancia económica y social de la población mexicana en los Estados Unidos de Norteamérica.* Mexico City: Universidad Nacional Autónoma de México, 1963.

Leonard, Olen E., and Johnson, Helen W. *Low Income Families in the Spanish Surname Population of the Southwest.* Washington, D.C.: United States Department of Agriculture Economic Research Service, 1967.

Lesley, Lewis B. *Uncle Sam's Camels.* Cambridge, Mass.: Harvard University Press, 1929.

Lewels, Francisco J. *The Uses of the Media by the Chicano Movement: A Study in Minority Access.* New York: Praeger Publishers, 1974.

Lewis, Oscar, *The Children of Sánchez: Autobiography of a Mexican Family*. New York: Random House, 1969.

———. "The Culture of Poverty." *Scientific American* 215 (1966): 19-25.

———. *Five Families*. New York: Mentor Books, 1959.

———. *Life in a Mexican Village: Tepoztlán Revisited*. Urbana: University of Illinois Press, 1951.

———. *Pedro Martínez: A Mexican Peasant and His Family*. New York: Random House, 1964.

Limón, José E. "El Primer Congreso Mexicanista de 1911: A Precursor to Contemporary Chicanismo." *Aztlán* 5 (1974):85-118.

Linton, R. *The Cultural Background of Personality*. New York: Appleton-Century-Crofts, 1945.

Litsinger, Dolores Escobar. *The Challenge of Teaching Mexican American Students*. New York: American Book Co., 1973.

Loewe Reiss, Ricardo. *La macrópolis: problemas y perspectivas sociales y sanitarias de las grandes ciudades*. Mexico City: Escuela Nacional de Arquitectura, UNAM, 1971.

López y Rivas, Gilberto. *The Chicanos: Life and Struggles of the Mexican Minority in the United States*. New York: Monthly Review Press, 1973.

McCleskey, Clifton. *The Government and Politics of Texas*. 4th ed. Boston: Little, Brown, and Co., 1972.

———, and Merrill, Bruce. "Mexican American Political Behavior in Texas." *Social Science Quarterly* 53 (1973): 785-98.

Machado, Manuel. *An Industry in Crisis: Mexican-United States Cooperation in the Control of Foot-and-Mouth Disease*. Berkeley: University of California Press, 1968.

Macías, Ysidro Ramón. "Nuestros antepasados y el movimiento." *Aztlán* 5 (1974): 143-54.

McLemore, S. Dale. "The Origins of Mexican American Subordination in Texas." *Social Science Quarterly* 53 (1973): 656-70.

McWilliams, Carey. *The California Revolution*. New York: Grossman Publishers, 1968.

———. *Factories in the Field*. Boston: Little, Brown and Co., 1934.

———. *North From Mexico: The Spanish Speaking People of the United States*. 1949. Reprint. New York: Greenwood Press, 1968.

Madregal, Romeo. *Demografía en el noroeste de México*. Monterrey, Mexico: Centro de Investigaciones Económicas, Universidad de Nuevo León, 1965.

Madsen, Claudia. *A Study of Change in Mexican Folk Medicine*. New Orleans: Middle American Research Institute, Tulane University, 1968.

Madsen, William. "The Alcoholic Agringado." *American Anthropologist* 66 (1964): 355-61.

———. *Mexican Americans of South Texas*. New York: Holt, Rinehart, & Winston, 1964.

———. *Society and Health in the Lower Rio Grande Valley*. Austin: University of Texas Hogg Foundation for Mental Health, 1961.

———. *The Virgin's Children*. Austin: University of Texas Press, 1960.

Mann, Dean E. "Conflict and Coalition: Political Variables Underlying Water Resource Development in the Upper Colorado River Basin." *Natural Resources Journal* 15 (1975): 141-70.

———. "Politics in the United States and the Salinity Problem of the Colorado River." *Natural Resources Journal* 15 (1975): 113-28.

Manuel, Hershel T. *Spanish Speaking Children of the Southwest: Their Education and the Public Welfare*. Austin: University of Texas Press, 1970.

Marcum, John P., and Bean, Frank D. "Texas Population in 1970: Trends in Fertility, 1950-1970." *Texas Business Review* 47 (1973): 252-58.

Marden, Charles F. *Minorities in American Society*. New York: American Book Co., 1968.

Marshall, Ray, and Perlman, Richard. *An Anthology of Labor Economics*. New York: John Wiley & Sons, 1972.

————, et al. *Human Resource Development in Texas*. Austin: University of Texas, Center for the Study of Human Resources and Bureau of Business Research, 1974.

————, and Briggs, Jr., Vernon M. *The Negro and Apprenticeship*. Baltimore: The Johns Hopkins University Press, 1967.

Martin, William E. "Economic Magnitudes and Economic Alternatives in Lower Basin Use of Colorado River Water." *Natural Resources Journal* 15 (1975): 229-39.

Martínez, Elizabeth S., and Longeaux y Vázquez, Enriqueta. *Viva la Raza! The Struggle of the Mexican American People*. Garden City, N.Y.: Doubleday & Co., 1974.

Martínez, Oscar J. "Border Relations: A Brief Comment." *The El Paso Economic Review* 13 (1976).

Martínez, P. D. "Ambiente sociocultural en la fraja fronteriza mexicana." *Salud Pública de México* 12 (1970): 833-39.

Matthiesen, Peter. *Sal si Puedes: César Chávez and the New American Revolution*. New York: Random House, 1969.

Meier, Gerald M., ed. *Leading Issues in Development Economics*. New York: Oxford University Press, 1964.

Meier, Matt S., and Rivera, Feliciano. *The Chicanos: A History of Mexican Americans*. New York: Hill and Wang, 1972.

————, eds. *Readings on la Raza: The Twentieth Century*. New York: Hill and Wang, 1974.

Meining, Donald W. *Imperial Texas: An Interpretive Essay in Cultural Geography*. Austin: University of Texas Press, 1969.

————. *The Southwest: Three Peoples in Geographical Change, 1600-1970*. New York: Oxford University Press, 1971.

Mendoza Berrueto, Eliseo. *La descentralización del crédito ejidal: el caso de la comarca langunera*. Mexico City: Universidad Nacional Autónoma de México, 1961.

Menefee, Seldon C. *Mexican Migratory Workers of South Texas*. Washington, D.C.: Works Progress Administration, 1941.

Merrill, John H. *Gringo: The American as Seen by Mexican Journalists*. Gainesville: University of Florida Press, 1963.

Mexico. Secretaría de Industria y Comercio. *Antecedentes, objetivos, realizactiones de la Comisión Intersecretarial de Desarrollo Fronterizo*. Mexico City, 1973.

————. *Estudio del desarrollo comercial de la frontera norte*. Mexico City, 1972.

————. *Indicadores socioeconómicos de la zona fronteriza norte*. Mexico City, 1974.

————. *Zona fronteriza norte de México: diagnóstico agropecuario*. Mexico City, 1974.

————. *Zona fronteriza norte de México: viabilidad industrial*. Mexico City, 1974.

————. *Zonas fronterizas de México: perfil socioeconómico*. Mexico City, 1974.

Mexico. Secretería de Relaciones Exteriores. *La protección de mexicanos en los Estados Unidos*. Mexico City, 1940.

Mexico. Secretaría del Trabajo y Previsión Social. *Los braceros*. Mexico City, 1946.

Miller, Michael V., and Preston, James D. "Vertical Ties and the Redistribution of Power in Crystal City." *Social Science Quarterly* 53 (1973): 772-84.

Minturn, L., and Lambert, W. W. *Mothers of Six Cultures; Antecedents of Child Rearing*. New York: John Wiley & Sons, 1964.

Mittelbach, Frank G., and Marshall, Grace. *The Burden of Poverty*. University of California Mexican American Study Project, Advance Report no. 5. Los Angeles: University of California, 1966.

————, and Moore, Joan W. "Ethnic Endogamy; the Cast of Mexican Americans." *American Journal of Sociology* 74 (1968): 50-62.

————, et al. *Intermarriage of Mexican Americans*. University of California Mexican American Study Project, Advance Report no. 6. Los Angeles: University of California, 1966.

Montiel, Miguel. "The Social Science of the Mexican American Family." *El Grito* 3 (1970): 56-63.

Moore, Joan W. *Mexican Americans: Problems and Prospects*. Madison: University of Wisconsin Press, 1966.

———, and Cuéllar, Alfredo. *Mexican Americans*. Englewood Cliffs, N.J.: Prentice-Hall, Inc., 1970.

———, and Mittelbach, Frank G. *Residential Segregation in the Urban Southwest*. University of California Mexican American Study Project, Advance Report no. 4. Los Angeles: University of California, 1966.

Moore, Truman. *The Slaves We Rent*. New York: Random House, 1965.

Moquin, Wayne, and Van Doren, Charles, eds. *A Documentary History of the Mexican Americans*. New York: Praeger Publishers, 1971.

Morin, Alexander. *The Organizability of Farm Labor in the United States*. Cambridge, Mass.: Harvard University Press, 1952.

Morris, John W. *The Southwestern United States*. New York: D. Van Nostrand, 1970.

Moustafa, A. Taher, and Weiss, Gertrud. *Health Status and Practices of Mexican Americans*. University of California Mexican American Study Project, Advance Report no. 11. Los Angeles: University of California, 1968.

Muñoz, Carlos Jr. "Politics and the Chicano: On the Status of the Literature." *Aztlán* 5 (1974): 1-8.

———. "The Politics of Protest and Chicano Liberation: A Case Study of Repression and Cooptation." *Aztlán* 5, nos. 1 and 2 (Spring and Fall 1974): 119-42.

Nabokov, Peter. *Tijerina and the Courthouse Raid*. Albuquerque: University of New Mexico Press, 1969.

Nall, Frank C., and Speilberg, Joseph. "Social and Cultural Factors in the Responses of Mexican Americans to Medical Treatment." *Journal of Health and Human Behavior* 8 (1967): 299-308.

National Conference on Educational Opportunities for Mexican Americans, Austin, Texas, 1968. *Proceedings*. Austin, Texas: Southwest Educational Development Corp., 1968.

Nava, Julian, ed. *The Mexican American in American History*. New York: American Book Co., 1973.

———. *Mexican Americans, Past, Present, and Future*. New York: American Book Co., 1969.

———, ed. *Viva la Raza!* New York: D. Van Nostrand, 1973.

Navarro, Armando. "The Evolution of Chicano Politics." *Aztlán* 5 (1974): 57-84.

Needler, Martin. *Politics and Society in Mexico*. Albuquerque: University of New Mexico Press, 1971.

Nimmo, Dan D., and Oden, William. *The Texas Political System*. Englewood Cliffs, N.J.: Prentice-Hall, Inc., 1971.

North, David S. *Alien Workers: A Study of the Labor Certification Programs*. Washington, D.C.: Trans-Century Corp., 1971.

———, and Weissert, William G. *Immigrants and the American Labor Market*. Washington, D.C.: Trans-Century Corp., 1973.

Nostrand, Richard L. "Hispanic American Borderland: Delineation of an American Culture Region." *Annals of the Association of American Geographers* 60 (1970): 638-61.

Opler, Marvin K., ed. *Culture and Mental Health*. New York: Macmillan Co., 1959.

Ortiz, C. A. "Evaluación del programa de vacunación con BCG en Ciudad Juárez, Chihuahua, 1970." *Salud Pública de México* 13 (1971): 693-99.

Padgett, L. Vincent. *The Mexican Political System*. Boston: Houghton Mifflin Co., 1966.

Padilla, Fernando V., and Ramírez, Carlos B. "Patterns of Chicano Representation in California, Colorado, and Nuevo Mexico." *Aztlán* 5 (1974): 189-234.

———. "Socialization of Chicano Judges and Attorneys." *Aztlán,* 5 (1974): 261-94.

Palmore, Glenn, et al. *The Ciudad Juárez Plan for Comprehensive Socioeconomic Development: A Model for Northern Mexico Border Cities.* El Paso: University of Texas Bureau of Business and Economic Research, 1974.

Paredes, Américo. "Los Estados Unidos, México, y el machismo." *Journal of Inter-American Studies* 9 (1967): 65-84.

———. *Folktales of Mexico.* Chicago: University of Chicago Press, 1970.

———. *With His Pistol in His Hand: A Border Ballad and Its Hero.* Austin: University of Texas Press, 1971.

———, and Paredes, Raymund. *Mexican American Authors.* Boston: Houghton Mifflin Co., 1972.

Patella, Victoria, and Kuvlesky, William P. "Situational Variation in Language Patterns of Mexican American Boys and Girls." *Social Science Quarterly* 53 (1973): 855-64.

Paul, Benjamin D., ed. *Health, Culture, and Community: Case Studies of Public Reaction to Health Programs.* New York: Russell Sage Foundation, 1956.

Paz, Octavio. *The Labyrinth of Solitude: Life and Thought in Mexico.* Translated by Lysander Kemp. New York: Grove Press, 1961.

———. *The Other Mexico: Critique of the Pyramid.* Translated by Lysander Kemp. New York: Grove Press, 1972.

Peñalosa, Fernando, and McDonagh, Edward C. "Social Mobility in a Mexican American Community." *Social Forces* 44 (1966): 498-505.

Poniatowska, Elena. *Massacre in Mexico.* New York: Viking Press, 1975.

Poston, Jr., Dudley L. and Alvírez, David. "On the Cost of Being a Mexican American Worker." *Social Science Quarterly* 53 (1973): 697-709.

Pozas Arciniega, Ricardo. *Juan the Chamula: An Ethnological Re-creation of the Life of a Mexican Indian.* Berkeley: University of California Press, 1962.

Prago, Albert. *Strangers in Their Own Land: A History of Mexican Americans.* New York: Four Winds Press, 973.

Prescott, J. R. V. *The Geography of Frontiers and Boundaries.* Chicago: Aldine Publishing Co., 1965.

Price, John A. *Tijuana 68: Ethnographic Notes on a Mexican Border City.* San Diego, Calif.: San Diego State College, 1968.

———. *Tijuana: Urbanization in a Border Culture.* Notre Dame, Ind.: University of Notre Dame Press, 1973.

Ramírez, III, Manuel. "Cognitive Styles and Cultural Democracy in Education," *Social Science Quarterly* 53 (1973): 895-904.

———, and Castañeda, Alfredo. *Cultural Democracy, Bicognitive Development, and Education.* New York: Academic Press, 1974.

———, et al. "Mexican American Cultural Membership and Adjustment to School." *Developmental Psychology* 4 (1971): 141-48.

Ramos, Reyes. "A Case in Point: An Ethno-methodological Study of a Poor Mexican American Family." *Social Science Quarterly* 53 (1973): 905-19.

Ramos, Samuel. *Profile of Man and Culture in Mexico.* Translated by Peter G. Earle. Austin: University of Texas Press, 1968.

Rendon, Armando. *Chicano Manifesto.* New York: Macmillan Co., 1971.

Report of the President's Task Force on Higher Education. Washington, D.C.: Government Printing Office, 1970.

Report of the Select Commission on Western Hemisphere Immigration, January 1968. Washington, D.C.: Government Printing Office, 1968.

Reyes Nevares, Beatriz. *The Mexican Cinema: Interviews with Thirteen Directors.* Translated by Carl J. Mora and Elizabeth Gard. Albuquerque: University of New Mexico Press, 1976.

Roberts, Robert E., and Askew, Jr., Cornelius. "A Consideration of Mortality in Three Subcultures." *Health Services Report* 87 (1972): 262-70.

Rocco, Raymond A. "The Role of Power and Authenticity in the Chicano Movement: Some Reflections." *Aztlán* 5 (1974) 167-76.

Rochin, Refugio I. "The Short and Turbulent Life of Chicano Studies: A Preliminary Study of Emerging Programs and Problems." *Social Science Quarterly* 53 (1973): 884-94.

Roeder, Sandra. *A Study of the Situation of Mexican Americans in the Southwest*. Washington, D.C.: U.S. Department of Justice, Community Relations Service, 1967.

Romanell, Patrick. *The Making of the Mexican Mind: A Study in Recent Mexican Thought*. Notre Dame, Ind.: University of Notre Dame Press, 1967.

Romano V., Octavio. "The Anthropology and Sociology of the Mexican Americans: The Distortion of Mexican American History." *El Grito* 2 (1968): 13-26.

Ronfeldt, David. *Atencingo: The Politics of Agrarian Struggle in a Mexican Ejido*. Stanford: Stanford University Press, 1973.

Rosaldo, Renato; Calvert, Robert A.; and Seligmann, Gustav L., eds. *Chicano: The Evolution of a People*. Minneapolis, Minn.: Winston Press, 1973.

Rose, Peter Isaac. *They and We: Racial and Ethnic Relations in the United States*. New York: Random House, 1964.

Rubel, Arthur J. *Across the Tracks: Mexican Americans in a Texas City*. Austin: University of Texas Press, 1966.

———. "Concepts of Disease in a Mexican American Culture." *American Anthropologist* 62 (1960): 795-814.

———. "The Role of Social Science Research in Recent Health Programs in Latin America." *Latin American Research Review* 2 (1966): 37-56.

———, et al. "Working Class Mexican Psychiatric Outpatients." *Archives of General Psychiatry* 16 (1967): 704-12.

Ruiz, Ramón. *Mexico: The Challenge of Poverty and Illiteracy*. San Marino, Calif.: The Huntington Library, 1963.

Samora, Julian, et al. *Mexican Americans in the Southwest*. Chicago: McNally and Loftin, 1969.

———. *Los Mojados: The Wetback Story*. Notre Dame, Ind.: University of Notre Dame Press, 1971.

———. *La Raza: The Forgotten Americans*. Notre Dame, Ind.: University of Notre Dame Press, 1966.

Sánchez, George I. *The Forgotten People: A Study of New Mexicans*. Albuquerque: University of New Mexico Press, 1940.

Saunders, Lyle. *Cultural Differences and Medical Care: The Case of the Spanish Speaking People of the Southwest*. New York: Russell Sage Foundation, 1954.

———. *The Spanish Speaking Population of Texas*. Austin: University of Texas Press, 1949.

———, and Leonard, Olin E. *The Wetback in the Lower Rio Grande Valley of Texas*. Austin: University of Texas Press, 1951.

Schmidt, Fred H. *After the Braceros: An Inquiry into the Problem of Farm Labor Recruitment*. Los Angeles: University of California Institute of Industrial Relations, 1964.

———. *Spanish Surnamed American Employment in the Southwest*. Washington, D.C.: Government Printing Office, 1970.

Segalman, Ralph. *Army of Despair: The Migrant Worker Stream*. Washington, D.C.: Educational Systems Corp., 1968.

Segovia, Rafael. *La politización del niño mexicano*. Mexico City: El Colegio de México, 1975.

Sepúlveda, César. "Implications for the Future: Design of Viable International Institutions." *Natural Resources Journal* 15 (1975): 215-22.

Servín, Manuel P., ed. *The Mexican Americans: An Awakening Minority*. Los Angeles: Glencoe Press, 1970.

Shannon, Lyle W., and Shannon, Magdaline. *Minority Migrants in the Urban Community: Mexican American and Negro Adjustment to Industrial Society*. Los Angeles: Sage Publications, 1973.

————, and McKim, Judith L. "Mexican American, Negro, and Anglo Improvement in Labor Force Status Between 1960 and 1970 in a Midwestern Community." *Social Science Quarterly* 52 (1974): 91-111.

Shockley, John S. *Chicano Revolt in a Texas Town*. Notre Dame, Ind.: University of Notre Dame Press, 1973.

Silberman, Charles E. *Crisis in the Classroom*. New York: Random House, 1969.

Simmen, Edward, ed. *The Chicano: From Caricature to Self Portrait*. New York: New American Library, 1971.

————, ed. *Pain and Promise: The Chicano Today*. New York: New American Library, 1972.

Skinner, Charles M. *Myths and Legends Beyond Our Borders*. Philadelphia: J. B. Lippincott, 1899.

Smith, Bradley. *Mexico: A History in Art*. Garden City, N.Y.: Doubleday & Co., 1968.

Sociedad Mexicana de Antropología. *El norte de México y el sur de los Estados Unidos*. Mexico City, 1943.

Sosa Riddell, Adaljiza. "Chicanas and el Movimiento." *Aztlán* 5 (1974): 155-66.

Spicer, Edward H., ed. *Perspectives in American Indian Culture Change*. Chicago: University of Chicago Press, 1961.

————, and Thompson, Raymond H., eds. *Plural Society in the Southwest*. Albuquerque: University of New Mexico Press, 1975.

Spota, Luis. *Murieron a mitad del río*. Mexico City: B. Costa-Amic, 1969.

Stambaugh, J. L. *The Lower Rio Grande Valley of Texas*. San Antonio, Texas: Naylor Co., 1954.

Steiner, Stanley. *La Raza: The Mexican Americans*. New York: Harper & Row, 1970.

Stockton, John R., et al. *Water for the Future*. 4 vols in 5. Austin: University of Texas, Bureau of Business Research, 1959.

Stoddard, Ellwyn R. "The Adjustment of Mexican American Barrio Families to Forced Housing Relocation." *Social Science Quarterly* 53 (1973): 749-59.

————, ed. *Comparative U.S.-Mexico Border Studies*. Occasional Papers, no. 1. El Paso, Texas: Border State University Consortium for Latin America, 1970.

————. "Ethnic Identity of Urban Mexican American Youth." *Proceedings of the Southwest Sociological Association* 20 (1970): 131-35.

————. *Mexican Americans*. New York: Random House, 1973.

————. *Prostitution and Illicit Drug Traffic on the U.S.-Mexico Border*. Occasional Papers, no. 2. El Paso, Texas: Border State University Consortium for Latin America, 1971.

————. *The Role of Social Factors in the Successful Adjustment of Mexican American Families to Forced Housing Relocation*. El Paso, Texas: Community Renewal Program, Department of Planning, Research and Development, City of El Paso, 1970.

————. "The U.S.-Mexican Border: A Comparative Research Laboratory." *Journal of Inter-American Studies* 11 (1969): 477-88.

————. *U.S.-Mexico Borderland Studies: An Inventory of Scholars. Appraisal of Funding Resources, and Research Projects*. El Paso: University of Texas Center for Inter-American Studies, 1974.

————. "A Conceptual Analysis of the 'Alien Invasion': Institutionalized Support of Illegal Mexican Aliens in the U.S." *International Migration Review* 10 (1976): 157-89.

Swadesh, Frances L. *Los Primeros Pobladores: Hispanic Americans of the Ute Frontier*. Notre Dame, Ind.: University of Notre Dame Press, 1974.

Taft, Donald R., and Robbins, Richard. *International Migrations*. New York: Ronald Press, 1955.

Tamayo, Jorge. *Geografía general de México: geografía física*. Mexico City: Talleres Gráficos de la Nación, 1949.

Taylor, Paul S. *An American-Mexican Frontier: Nueces County, Texas*. Chapel Hill: University of North Carolina Press, 1934.

————. *Mexican Labor in the United States*. 2 vols. 1934. Reprint. New York: Arno Press, 1970.

Tebbel, John, and Ruiz, Ramón Eduardo. *South by Southwest: The Mexican American and His Heritage*. Garden City, N.Y.: Doubleday & Co., 1969.

Texas. Good Neighbor Commission. *Texas Migrant Labor: The 1967 Migration*. Austin, 1967.

Texas State Department of Community Affairs. *Poverty in Texas, 1973*. Austin, 1974.

Texas State Education Agency. *Report on the Educational Needs of Migrant Workers*. Austin, 1962.

Texas Health Data Institute. *Selected Demographic and Health Characteristics Based Upon County Summation of 1970 Census Data*. Austin, 1971.

Torres, L. E., et al. "Epidemiología de la lepra en Tamaulipas." *Salud Pública de México* 12 (1970): 183-93.

Trock, W. L. "Institutional Factors Affecting Land and Water Development of the Lower Rio Grande Valley, Texas." *Water Resources Research* 5 (1969): 1364-66.

Tuck, Ruth. *Not with the Fist: Mexican Americans in a Southwest City*. New York: Harcourt, Brace, 1946.

Turner, Frederick C. *The Dynamic of Mexican Nationalism*. Chapel Hill: University of North Carolina Press, 1968.

Tuohy, William S. "Psychology in Political Analysis: The Case of Mexico." *Western Political Quarterly* 27 (1974): 289-307.

Tyler, Gus, ed. *Mexican Americans Tomorrow: Educational and Economic Perspectives*. Albuquerque: University of New Mexico Press, 1975.

Ugalde, Antonio. *Power and Conflict in a Mexican Community: A Study of Political Integration*. Albuquerque: University of New Mexico Press, 1970.

————. *The Urbanization Process of a Poor Mexican Neighborhood*. Austin: University of Texas, Institute of Latin American Studies, 1974.

Urquides, María. *The Invisible Minority*. Washington, D.C.: Government Printing Office, 1966.

Urquidi, Víctor L. *The Challenge of Development in Latin America*. New York: Praeger Publishers, 1964.

United States Commission on Civil Rights. *Concentration of Spanish Surnames in the Five Southwestern States*. Washington, D.C.: Government Printing Office, 1962.

————. *Counting the Forgotten: The 1970 Census Count of Persons of Spanish Speaking Background in the United States*. Washington, D.C.: Government Printing Office, 1974.

————. *Mexican Americans and the Administration of Justice in the Southwest*. Washington, D.C.: Government Printing Office, 1970.

————. *Reports*. 6 vols. Washington, D.C.: Government Printing Office, 1971-74.

United States Congress, House. *Employment of "Green Card" Aliens During Labor Disputes: Hearings Before Special Subcommittee on Labor, on H. R. 12667*. House Reports, 91st Cong. 1st Sess. Washington, D.C.: Government Printing Office, 1969.

————. *Hearings Before Subcommittee Number 1 of the Committee on the Judiciary, House of Representatives, on Illegal Aliens*. 7 vols. House Reports, 92nd Cong. 1st and 2d Sess. Washington, D.C.: Government Printing Office, 1970-72.

————. *Hearings Before Subcommittee Number 1 of the Committee on the Judiciary, House of Representatives, on HR 9112, HR 15092, and HR 17370*. House Reports, 91st Cong. 2d Sess. Washington, D.C.: Government Printing Office, 1970.

————. *Mexican Farm Labor Program: Hearings Before Subcommittee on Equipment, Supplies, and Manpower, on HR 3822*. House Reports, 84th Cong. 1st Sess. Washington, D.C.: Government Printing Office, 1955.

————. *Mexican Farm Labor Program: Conference to Accompany HR 2010*. House Reports, 87th Cong. 1st Sess. Washington, D.C.: Government Printing Office, 1961.

United States Department of Commerce, Economic Development Administration. *Industrial and Employment Potential of the United States-Mexico Border*. Washington, D.C.: Government Printing Office, 1968.

United States Department of the Interior. *The Plan for the Rio Grande National Wild and Scenic River*. Washington, D.C.: Government Printing Office, 1969.

Utton, Albert E., ed. *Pollution and International Boundaries: United States-Mexican Environmental Problems*. Albuquerque: University of New Mexico Press, 1973.

Vaga, Nick. "The Mexican American in the Social Sciences, 1912-1970: Part I, 1912-1935." *El Grito* 3 (1970): 3-24.

―――. "The Mexican American in the Social Sciences, 1912-1970: Part II, 1935-1970." *El Grito* 4 (1970): 17-51.

Valdez, Luis, and Steiner, Stanley. eds. *Aztlán: An Anthology of Mexican American Literature*. New York: Alfred A. Knopf, 1972.

Vázquez de Knauth, Josefina. *Nacionalismo y educación en México*. Mexico City: El Colegio de México, 1970.

―――. *Mexicanos y norteamericanos ante la guerra del 47*. Mexico City: Secretaría de Educación Pública, 1971.

Vernon, Raymond. *The Dilemma of Mexico's Development: The Roles of the Private and Public Sectors*. Cambridge, Mass.: Harvard University Press, 1963.

Villareal, José Antonio. *Pocho*. Garden City, N.Y.: Doubleday & Co., 1959.

Vital, David. *The Inequality of States: A Study of the Small Power in International Relations*. New York: Oxford University Press, 1967.

Vivó Escoto, Jorge A. *Geografía de Mexico*. Mexico City: Fondo de Cultura Económica, 1948.

Wagner, Nathaniel, and Haug, Marsha J., eds. *Chicanos: Social and Psychological Perspectives*. St. Louis, Mo.: C. V. Mosby Co., 1971.

Wasserman, Susan A. "Values of Mexican American, Negro, and Anglo Blue Collar and White Collar Children." *Child Development* 42 (1971): 1624-28.

Weatherford, Gary D., and Jacoby, Gordon C. "Impact of Energy Development on the Law of the Colorado River." *Natural Resources Journal* 15 (1975): 171-214.

Weaver, Jerry L. "Health Care Costs as a Political Issue: Comparative Responses of Chicanos and Anglos." *Social Science Quarterly* 53 (1973): 846-54.

Weber, David J., ed. *Foreigners in Their Native Land: Historical Roots of the Mexican Americans*. Albuquerque: University of New Mexico Press, 1973.

Welch, Susan; Comer, John; and Steinman, Michael. "Political Participation Among Mexican Americans: An Exploratory Examination." *Social Science Quarterly* 53 (1973): 799-813.

Whitehead, Carlton J., and King, Albert S. "Differences in Managers' Attitudes Toward Mexican and Non-Mexican Americans in Organizational Authority Relations." *Social Science Quarterly* 53 (1973): 760-71.

Williams, C. L. "Realizaciones de la Asociacion Fronteriza Mexicana-Estadounidense de Salubridad." *Salud Pública de México* 14 (1972): 527-32.

Williams, J. Allen; Beeson, Peter G.; and Johnson, David R. "Some Factors Associated With Income Among Mexican Americans," *Social Science Quarterly* 53 (1973): 710-15.

Wingfield, Clyde, ed. *Urbanization in the Southwest*. El Paso: University of Texas, Texas Western Press, 1968.

Witkin, Herman A., et al. *Personality Through Perception*. New York: Harper & Row, 1954.

Wright, Harry K. *Foreign Enterprise in Mexico: Laws and Policies*. Chapel Hill: University of North Carolina Press, 1971.

Yankelovich, Daniel. *The New Morality: A Profile of American Youth in the Seventies*. New York: McGraw-Hill, 1974.

Yetman, Norman R., and Steele, C. Hoy, eds. *Majority and Minority: The Dynamics of Racial and Ethnic Relations*. Boston: Allyn & Bacon, 1971.

Index

active/passive characteristics, among Mexican and American children, 291–94, 312–13
aftosa, (hoof and mouth disease), 37
agriculture, 144–46, 401
air quality, joint monitoring of, 358
Alessio Robles, Vito, 46
aliens. *See* migrants
Anapra, port of, 358–59
arms traffic, 17
artículos gancho, 158–59, 376, 403–4
Azcárraga, Emilio, 52
Aztlán, 77

Ballet Folklórico, 52
Bancroft, Hubert Howe, 45
Bannon, John Francis, 48
Barela, Chico, 38
biculturalism, 408
Bolton, Herbert Eugene, 34–35, 45–46
border industrialization program: described, 10–11, 229; and employment, 11, 109–10; evaluation of, 160, 401–2; extent of, 147, 402–3; impact of, 148–49; and Mexican interest groups, 110–12; and United States influence, 99, 101, 376; and United States pressure groups, 110, 160; women in, 67, 110, 387
Borderlands: defined, 3–4, 35; first use of term, 34–35; historiography of, 45–48
border, Mexican–United States: dimensions of, 1; history of, 4–5, 7–8
Border Patrol, 189
borders: European, x, xi; history of, 2–3; in North America, ix, xi; pre-Hispanic, 25–27
boundary, defined, 2–3
Bracero Program, xii, 14–15; abuse of, 194–95; creation of, 193–94; history of, 168, 206–7, 234–35; proposed renewal of, 236–37, 378–79; provisions of, 194; and undocumented immigration, 198

Cárdenas, Lázaro, 58–59

Carrasco, Fred, 76
Casino de Agua Caliente, 57–58
"cattle culture," 69, 71–72
Chamizal Treaty, 8, 43–44, 228
Chapman, Leonard F., Jr., 12–13, 165, 212
Chávez, César, 177
"Chicano," origin of, 224 n 19
Chicano movement, impact of, 374
Chicanos: cognitive development of, 319–20; education of, 122, 318–19; ethnicity of, 373; failure to vote of 132–35; health of, 260–61; history of, 317–18; housing of, 122–23; income of, 120; Mexican view of, 63–65, 92–93; and migrants, 14, 177, 216–17, 218, 392–93; modal personality of, 317–18; school adjustment of, 321–22; in Texas border area, 118, 119
cognitive development: of Chicanos, 319–20; Mexican and American, compared, 310–12
cognitive structure, of Mexicans and Americans, 294
colonial period, 4–5, 29–30; social impact of, 285–86
Colorado River, 9–10, 228–29
Comisión de Estudios del Territorio Nacional, 336–37
commodity-migration, 185–86, 395
commuters, 168–69; defined, 195–97; numbers of, 197
conservation, 339
cooptation, 107
corridos, 75–78, 82, 83–84
Cortina uprising, 74, 77, 123–24
Cosío Villegas, Daniel, 43, 44–45, 46, 286, 296, 362
cowboy, 71–72
Cramton Report, 15, 232–33
Crystal City, 90, 320–21
cultural affinity, as cause of migration, 210
cultural penetration, 5–6, 297–301, 327–28, 364
culture: flow of, 86–87; indigenous, 31, 32